Cisco TelePresence Fundamentals

G000108672

Tim Szigeti, CCIE No. 9794
Kevin McMenamy
Roland Saville
Alan Glowacki

Cisco Press

800 East 96th Street

Indianapolis, IN 46240

Cisco TelePresence Fundamentals

Tim Szigeti, Kevin McMenamy, Roland Saville, Alan Glowacki

Copyright©2009 Cisco Systems, Inc.

Published by:
Cisco Press
800 East 96th Street
Indianapolis, IN 46240 USA

Printed in the United States of America
First Printing May 2009
Library of Congress Cataloging-in-Publication Data

Cisco TelePresence fundamentals / Tim Szigeti ... [et al.].
    p. cm.
 ISBN-13: 978-1-58705-593-5 (pbk.)
 ISBN-10: 1-58705-593-7 (pbk.)
 1. Multimedia communications. 2. Computer conferencing. I. Szigeti, Tim. II. Title.
 [DNLM: 1. Cisco Systems, Inc.]

 TK5105.15.C57 2009
 006.7--dc22

2009013062
ISBN-13: 978-1-58705-593-5
ISBN-10: 1-58705-593-7

Warning and Disclaimer

This book is designed to provide information about Cisco TelePresence. Every effort has been made to make this book as complete and as accurate as possible, but no warranty or fitness is implied.

The information is provided on an "as is" basis. The authors, Cisco Press, and Cisco Systems, Inc. shall have neither liability nor responsibility to any person or entity with respect to any loss or damages arising from the information contained in this book or from the use of the discs or programs that may accompany it.

The opinions expressed in this book belong to the author and are not necessarily those of Cisco Systems, Inc.

Trademark Acknowledgments

All terms mentioned in this book that are known to be trademarks or service marks have been appropriately capitalized. Cisco Press or Cisco Systems, Inc., cannot attest to the accuracy of this information. Use of a term in this book should not be regarded as affecting the validity of any trademark or service mark.

Corporate and Government Sales

The publisher offers excellent discounts on this book when ordered in quantity for bulk purchases or special sales, which may include electronic versions and/or custom covers and content particular to your business, training goals, marketing focus, and branding interests. For more information, please contact: **U.S. Corporate and Government Sales:** 1-800-382-3419, corpsales@pearsontechgroup.com

For sales outside the United States please contact: **International Sales:** international@pearsoned.com

Feedback Information

At Cisco Press, our goal is to create in-depth technical books of the highest quality and value. Each book is crafted with care and precision, undergoing rigorous development that involves the unique expertise of members from the professional technical community.

Readers' feedback is a natural continuation of this process. If you have any comments regarding how we could improve the quality of this book, or otherwise alter it to better suit your needs, you can contact us through email at feedback@ciscopress.com. Please make sure to include the book title and ISBN in your message.

We greatly appreciate your assistance.

Publisher: Paul Boger	**Cisco Representative:** Eric Ullanderson
Associate Publisher: Dave Dusthimer	**Cisco Press Program Manager:** Anand Sundaram
Executive Editor: Brett Bartow	**Copy Editor:** Apostrophe Editing Services
Managing Editor: Patrick Kanouse	**Technical Editors:** John Johnston, Mike Lee
Senior Development Editor: Christopher Cleveland	**Proofreader:** Language Logistics, LLC
Project Editor: Mandie Frank	
Editorial Assistant: Vanessa Evans	
Book Designer: Louisa Adair	
Composition: Mark Shirar	
Indexer: Ken Johnson	

Americas Headquarters	Asia Pacific Headquarters	Europe Headquarters
Cisco Systems, Inc.	Cisco Systems (USA) Pte. Ltd.	Cisco Systems International BV
San Jose, CA	Singapore	Amsterdam, The Netherlands

Cisco has more than 200 offices worldwide. Addresses, phone numbers, and fax numbers are listed on the Cisco Website at **www.cisco.com/go/offices.**

CCDE, CCENT, Cisco Eos, Cisco HealthPresence, the Cisco logo, Cisco Lumin, Cisco Nexus, Cisco StadiumVision, Cisco TelePresence, Cisco WebEx, DCE, and Welcome to the Human Network are trademarks; Changing the Way We Work, Live, Play, and Learn and Cisco Store are service marks; and Access Registrar, Aironet, AsyncOS, Bringing the Meeting To You, Catalyst, CCDA, CCDP, CCIE, CCIP, CCNA, CCNP, CCSP, CCVP, Cisco, the Cisco Certified Internetwork Expert logo, Cisco IOS, Cisco Press, Cisco Systems, Cisco Systems Capital, the Cisco Systems logo, Cisco Unity, Collaboration Without Limitation, EtherFast, EtherSwitch, Event Center, Fast Step, Follow Me Browsing, FormShare, GigaDrive, HomeLink, Internet Quotient, IOS, iPhone, iQuick Study, IronPort, the IronPort logo, LightStream, Linksys, MediaTone, MeetingPlace, MeetingPlace Chime Sound, MGX, Networkers, Networking Academy, Network Registrar, PCNow, PIX, PowerPanels, ProConnect, ScriptShare, SenderBase, SMARTnet, Spectrum Expert, StackWise, The Fastest Way to Increase Your Internet Quotient, TransPath, WebEx, and the WebEx logo are registered trademarks of Cisco Systems, Inc. and/or its affiliates in the United States and certain other countries.

All other trademarks mentioned in this document or website are the property of their respective owners. The use of the word partner does not imply a partnership relationship between Cisco and any other company. (0812R)

About the Authors

Tim Szigeti, CCIE No. 9794, is a technical leader at Cisco within the Enterprise Systems Engineering (ESE) team, where he has spent the last decade specializing in quality of service technologies. His current role is to design network architectures for the next wave of media applications, including TelePresence, IP video surveillance, digital media systems, and desktop video. He has coauthored many technical papers, including the *Cisco Enterprise QoS Design Guide* and the *Cisco TelePresence Network Systems Design Guide*, and the Cisco Press book *End-to-End QoS Network Design*. Tim holds a bachelor of Commerce degree in management information systems from the University of British Columbia.

Kevin McMenamy is senior manager of technical marketing in the Cisco TelePresence Systems Business Unit (TSBU). Kevin has been doing technical marketing at Cisco since February 2000, focused primarily on voice- and video-related technologies, including Cisco IP/TV, Cisco H.323 video conferencing, Cisco IP Telephony, and Unified Communications, and now Cisco TelePresence. Prior to Cisco, Kevin worked at FVC.COM, which manufactured H.321 video conferencing solutions, and at Winnov L.L.P, which manufactured the video capture cards used in the Cisco IP/TV streaming servers and in PCs for Microsoft's NetMeeting and WhitePine Software's CUCME applications. Kevin has filed several U.S. patents with Cisco on voice and video signaling and security concepts and has coauthored and contributed to numerous technical papers including the *Cisco IP Videoconferencing Design Guide*, the *Cisco IP Video Telephony Design Guide*, the *Cisco IP Telephony Design Guide*, the *Cisco Quality of Service Design Guide*, the *Cisco SAFE Blueprint*, *Cisco CallManager Fundamentals*, and most recently the *Cisco TelePresence Network Systems Design Guide*.

Roland Saville is a technical leader within the Cisco Enterprise Systems Engineering (ESE) team. For the past 13 years at Cisco, he has focused on a broad range of technology areas, including VoIP, security, wireless, RFID, and TelePresence as a systems engineer, consulting systems engineer, and technical marketing engineer. He has coauthored many technical papers including the *Cisco SAFE Blueprint* documents, *Cisco TelePresence Network Systems Design Guide*, and several U.S. patents relating to RFID technology. Roland holds a bachelor of science degree in electrical engineering from the University of Idaho and a master of business administration from Santa Clara University.

Alan Glowacki is a technical marketing engineer in the TelePresence Systems Business Unit (TSBU). Alan has been working on video communications since 1995 when he joined First Virtual Communications as employee number 20. After five years with First Virtual Communications, Alan joined Cisco, focusing on H.323 video conferencing. During his time with Cisco, he authored many technical papers including the first *H.323 Videoconferencing Solution Reference Design Guide*. After three and a half years with Cisco, he left to try another startup only to return to Cisco in 2006. Upon his return to Cisco, Alan returned his focus to video by joining the TSBU.

About the Technical Reviewers

John Johnston, CCIE No. 5232, is a network engineer in the Enterprise Systems Engineering (ESE) team at Cisco. He has worked at Cisco for 10 years with previous experience as a consulting engineer for MCI professional services. John has been working with TelePresence for the last two years and has been in the networking industry for more than 14 years. He holds a BSEE from the University of North Carolina at Charlotte and tinkers with electronic projects in his spare time. John enjoys spending his time with his wife Shelly and their daughter Sophie.

Mike Lee, CCIE No. 7148 and CISSP, is currently working as a network architect in the TelePresence Exchange Business Unit (TXBU) at Cisco. He has worked at Cisco for eight years with previous experience as a technical leader for Service Provider Solutions Engineering, focusing on Layer 2 and Layer 3 VPN, QoS, and MPLS. Mike currently holds numerous industry certifications and is a triple CCIE in Routing and Switching, Security, and Service Provider and also holds a CISSP. Mike has been working in the networking industry for more than 12 years, starting with his time in the U.S. Army. Mike enjoys spending his time with his wife Barbara and three children, Ashley, Jennifer, and Seth.

Dedications

Tim: I'd like to dedicate this book to my firstborn son, who's expected to come out the same month as this book. I find it very ironic that I can grind out hundreds of pages of techno-babble but am yet completely stonewalled when it comes to writing you a name. At least with this project off my plate, I can focus on that more important assignment. It also amuses me to think that by the time you can read and appreciate this dedication, that TelePresence will probably be considered by your generation to be dinosaur-technology, invented sometime after fire and the wheel, but before instant-telepathy or whatever the popular communication technology of your day will be. At any rate, I'm so glad this project is behind me because I'm finding it hard to concentrate on anything at all these days because I'm so excitedly waiting for you!

Kevin: I would like to dedicate this book to my wife Jennifer and my daughter Brooke Lynn. Jen, you are foundation on which this house is built. Brooke, you are the light of my life.

Roland: I would like to dedicate the book to my wife, Tania, and my three dogs, Vida, Barbie, and Ginni. They are the reason I get up in the morning and my inspiration for doing the best I can at everything I do.

Alan: I would like to dedicate this book to my wife, Lezlie, and two children, Taylor and Alec. They have been very understanding and supportive over the past 15 years considering the amount of travel and long hours required during this time. Without my family I would not be where I am today.

Acknowledgments

Tim: Any project of this magnitude can only be achieved by collaborative team effort. As such, there are many players to acknowledge and thank.

First, I'd like to thank my coauthors. Kevin, your limitlessness is truly amazing: Your limitless energy, limitless patience, and limitless knowledge make working with you on any project truly an honor and a pleasure. I'm always learning from you. Roland, your grasp of such a wide array of technologies is staggering, as is your ability to identify the key issues with any scenario and where the breaking points are. To me, you're an engineering philosopher: Someone who truly understands how the sum of the parts comprises the whole and the role of each and every cog within the machine. Alan, you bring a wealth of knowledge and experience with video to any project. Thank you for stepping in and helping us push through to the finish; without you, this project might have stalled out indefinitely.

Thanks also to our technical reviewers. John Johnston (JJ), not only did you do a highly thorough job technically reviewing this book, but you also spent countless hours designing and testing in our TelePresence network labs. I still can't believe that you voluntarily came in on your holidays to build the testing tools we needed at the circuit-board level from Radio Shack parts! Thanks also to Mike Lee, for allowing us to leverage your service provider technical expertise to ensure content accuracy. I'm sure we'll be coming to you many times yet.

Thanks, too, to the Cisco Press team. Brett Bartow, thank you for giving us the ball, when you had other authors lined up to produce a book on TelePresence. I know this project took longer than we hoped because of the workload we were all under at our "day-jobs," but you kept us focused and steadily moved us forward to completion. Thank you, too, Chris Cleveland; you managed our technical review rounds and editing and were very patient and flexible with us during the whole process, even while we essentially kept asking you to move furniture around the living room over-and-over until it looked just right! Thanks also to Mandie Frank for project editing and San Dee Phillips for copy editing. Also our appreciation extends to Louisa Adair for being accommodating with the cover design. Thank you, too, Vanessa Evans for keeping all our affairs relating to this book in order.

I'd also like to personally thank members of the Cisco Enterprise System Engineering (ESE) team, including Nimish Desai, Mike Herbert, and Aeisha Bright for guiding me and letting me leverage some of your designs. Thanks also to the ESE management team, including Aziz Abdul, Neil Anderson, and Brian Christensen for allocating us all the time, lab resources, gear, and expertise we asked for. We lacked for nothing and were free to explore and research wherever the interesting problems were found. Thanks to you, too, Paul McNab, for investing many years and many dollars into developing ESE into the visionary and elite team that it is.

Similarly, many thanks are owed to our colleagues within the Cisco TelePresence Business Unit (TSBU), including Nathan Shaw, Jonathan Liang, Mike Paget, and Shobana Shankar. You've been a pleasure to work with and have been generous in training and initiating us network-jockeys into the world of TelePresence. And ultimate thanks to TSBU engineering and management, including Chris Dunn, Randy

Harrell, Philip Graham, Marthin De Beer, and all your brilliant people, without whom TelePresence simply wouldn't exist! What an amazing technology you've developed and many humble thanks for allowing us to write about it.

Kevin: I would like to acknowledge the founders of TSBU, Marthin De Beer, Phil Graham, Randy Harrell, and their teams for having the vision and stamina to invent such a phenomenal product and for giving me the opportunity to come to TSBU early in the process to contribute to its success and to play a lead role in creating TSBU's technical marketing team. I would also like to acknowledge Shaik Kaleem, who has been my manager for the majority of my time at Cisco and is a good friend and mentor. I would also like to acknowledge the hundreds of friends at Cisco with whom I have worked for many years on other voice- and video-related products for coming together to help TSBU bring this product to market and to drive the network architecture design recommendations for it, specifically Tim Szigeti, Roland Saville, and John Johnston from the Enterprise Systems Engineering (ESE) team who collaborated with us so closely, produced the *Cisco TelePresence Network Systems Design Guide* and helped coauthor this book.

Roland: I would like to acknowledge John Johnston and Mike Lee for painstakingly taking the time to review the material we have written to ensure that not only does it read well and make sense, but that it is also technically accurate. I would also like to acknowledge Brett Bartow, Chris Cleveland, and Mandie Frank for their infinite patience with the authors as we wrote this book and for keeping us focused and moving forward when we really needed it.

Alan: I would like to thank my coauthors and reviewers John Johnston and Mike Lee for all their long hours authoring, reviewing, and re-reviewing this content. This project has been challenging for everyone due to the time lines and workload of everyone involved. I would also like to personally thank Tim Szigeti for taking the lead on this project and driving all authors to move ahead during the tough times.

Contents at a Glance

Contents

Icons Used in This Book

Command Syntax Conventions

The conventions used to present command syntax in this book are the same conventions used in the IOS Command Reference. The Command Reference describes these conventions as follows:

- **Boldface** indicates commands and keywords that are entered literally as shown. In actual configuration examples and output (not general command syntax), boldface indicates commands that are manually input by the user (such as a **show** command).

- *Italic* indicates arguments for which you supply actual values.

- Vertical bars (|) separate alternative, mutually exclusive elements.

- Square brackets ([ ]) indicate an optional element.

- Braces ({ }) indicate a required choice.

- Braces within brackets ([{ }]) indicate a required choice within an optional element.

Foreword

Back in 2004, Cisco decided to look into creating a new type of visual collaboration experience that would surpass the more traditional videoconferencing. After investigating different technologies, the decision was made to build this experience internally at Cisco. Thus, the TelePresence Systems Business Unit was formed and the ultimate outcome was the Cisco TelePresence System that has changed the way that enterprises communicate forever.

Cisco believes in internally trying their own products and, through its Cisco on Cisco organization and in the 3 years since shipping, has deployed more than 350 systems in 42 countries globally and enabled functions such as interoperability with traditional video-conferencing, multipoint, intercompany, and integrated scheduling. At this time, there have been more than 280,000 meetings scheduled and more than 51,000 meetings that have avoided travel, saving the company an estimate of $174 million dollars. TelePresence has become a way of life here at Cisco.

The TelePresence Systems Business Unit was founded on the principle of "It's all about the experience." And that experience shows up in the complete solution that was created. Cisco TelePresence is a solution that encompasses everything from the end user in the room to the administrator. It looks at the room environment and the network to create the best experience for the end users, and it looks at the management interfaces to make the administrator's job as easy as possible. Integration with the Cisco Unified Communications platform enables a seamless integration with your existing telephony network, both for internal and external (B2B) communications.

Tim, Kevin, Roland, and Alan have been part of TelePresence from the beginning. They were instrumental in the creation of the experience and the success that TelePresence has. They have created our deployment guides and successfully worked with our customers, including many of the Fortune 500, to deploy within their own global networks. It is through their dedication and knowledge that TelePresence has become a dominant player in the industry.

I have had the privilege of working with the authors for several years. Their understanding of the Cisco TelePresence Systems and the fundamentals around the solution is unsurpassed. Their book provides the reader with all the information necessary to create a successful deployment. Anyone involved in deploying, managing, or monitoring of TelePresence will greatly benefit from reading this book.

Chris Dunn

Director, Engineering

TelePresence Systems Business Unit

Introduction

I well remember my first Cisco TelePresence experience.

It was in the fall of 2006, and my manager had been urging me for several weeks to check out the first pair of production TelePresence rooms at the Executive Briefing Center at the Cisco headquarters in San Jose. However, I had kept putting it off because I was "too busy." Being familiar with many forms and flavors of video conferencing systems, I was a bit skeptical that there was really anything new or cool enough to merit my walking seven buildings over and seeing for myself. But eventually I relented and made the arduous ten-minute trek, and my life hasn't been the same since.

It's difficult to encapsulate in words how authentic TelePresence is; it just has to be experienced firsthand to really "get it." But I distinctly remember looking at a life-size image of a colleague on the high-definition screen and seeing the second hand on his watch tick in real time and thinking, "This can change everything." And indeed it has and is continuing to do so.

The Cisco company vision has been and continues to be, "changing the way we work, live, play, and learn," and never has a single technology (since perhaps IP itself) had such a cross-functional impact and potential as Cisco TelePresence.

TelePresence quite literally changes the way we work. I can personally attest to this because for the past decade, I had been traveling on average two to three times per month: wasting hundreds of hours in airport lines and lounges, spending tens of thousands of company dollars per year, and burning who knows how many tons of fossil fuels. Now, I walk to the nearest TelePresence room and conduct meetings with colleagues and customers alike and then walk home, simultaneously saving time, money, and the environment.

TelePresence is also changing the way we live. For instance, many Cisco employees usually have at least some members of their families living far away from them. In recent years, during holiday seasons, Cisco has invited employees and their families to book their respectively nearest TelePresence rooms (of which several hundred have been deployed globally) and "visit" with each other. Ongoing research and development is aimed at bringing TelePresence into the home, which would bring all of us closer to our distant friends and families, without having to even leave the couch.

Similarly, TelePresence is changing the way we play. Recent initiatives in the sports and entertainment fields have seen the introduction of TelePresence in various sports venues, allowing for distant friends to "trash talk" while watching a game or for fans to "visit" with their heroes, even though distances of thousands of miles might physically separate the parties.

And finally, TelePresence is changing the way we learn. Geographically disparate teachers and students are meeting and interacting with a degree of ease and effectiveness as never before. Classrooms on opposite ends of the planet are linked together through TelePresence, giving students a broader cultural exposure and a better global perspective.

And the list of ways TelePresence technologies can be applied goes on and on....

And so, in short, I was hooked. Soon after, I was honored and excited to join a cross-functional team of experts, including Kevin, Roland, Alan, and many others, who were tasked with researching and developing Cisco TelePresence solutions.

Shortly thereafter, a social incident further underscored to me the universal appeal of TelePresence. For years, my wife and I had an understanding that at dinner parties, if people asked me what I do, I was permitted to reply with "I'm in computers" and leave it at that. If I was pressed, I could expand with "I design networks for computers," but no further. Otherwise, according to her, if I launched into the technical details of my day-to-day work (which I always thought was interesting), people's eyes would glaze over with sheer boredom, and they would politely nod with feigned interest, and secretly wish they never asked, and made quick mental notes never to invite us again. However, one evening, after having been assigned to work on TelePresence designs for about a year, I found myself at a dinner party with an elderly gentleman next to me asking me what I did. I replied with the usual permitted one-liner, but as he pressed me for more, I quickly glanced at my wife, saw the shooting look of warning in her eye, gathered up some courage, and defiantly began launching into the detailed work we had been doing on TelePresence. To my amazement, he seemed not only interested, but also excited about some of the possibilities for TelePresence. And it wasn't long before the whole table of eight began joining in the animated conversation, talking about TelePresence solutions and potentials at length, at the end of which, I shot a triumphantly victorious look back at my wife, and the rules have been permanently relaxed since.

Back at work, our team immediately started doing research and testing to publish a series of technical papers on best practices for deploying TelePresence systems, and only then did we really begin to grasp how many layers of technology were actually involved in TelePresence solutions, from audio to video to codecs to networks to firewalls to border controllers and so on and so forth. The papers became longer and longer, and we then recognized that having a single depository of such technical information would require a book. And after nearly two more years of work, you hold the result in your hands.

Objectives and Approach

The objectives of this book are to introduce you to Cisco TelePresence technologies, both at a conceptual level and at a technical design and deployment level.

To realize this objective, this book is divided into three main parts:

- The first introduces and overviews Cisco TelePresence systems.

- The second delves into the concepts of the various technologies that comprise TelePresence systems and networks.

- The third details best practice design recommendations on how these technologies are integrated and optimally deployed as comprehensive Cisco TelePresence solutions.

Upon completion, you should have a solid working knowledge of Cisco TelePresence systems and technologies and thus can confidently design, deploy, operate, and manage Cisco TelePresence solutions.

Who Should Read This Book?

The primary group of readers for this book would be technical staff tasked with deploying Cisco TelePresence systems. These might include network administrators, systems administrators, audio/video specialists, VoIP specialists, and operations staff.

A secondary group of readers would be technical decision makers tasked with evaluating the business value and technical feasibility of deploying Cisco TelePresence systems.

A tertiary group of readers would be system engineers, partners, trainers, and other networking professionals who might need to ramp-up technically on Cisco TelePresence systems, with the objective of selling or educating others on these systems.

How This Book Is Organized

This book is organized in such a manner that it can be read cover-to-cover and be used as a quick reference guide to specific technical information and design recommendations.

The content is broken into three main sections: the first section introduces Cisco TelePresence; the second section expands on the various technologies that play a role in TelePresence systems and networks; and the third section describes the Cisco validated best practice recommendations to optimally deploy TelePresence solutions.

The two chapters comprising **Part 1, "Introducing Cisco TelePresence,"** cover the following topics:

- **Chapter 1, "What Is TelePresence":** This chapter introduces Cisco TelePresence, by tracing the evolution of video communications from the 1964 World's Fair to 2006, when Cisco released their first TelePresence system, which featured state-of-the-art technologies designed to transport high-definition audio and video, in realtime, over a converged IP network infrastructure.

- **Chapter 2, "Cisco TelePresence Solution Overview":** This chapter overviews the various components that comprise Cisco TelePresence systems and solutions, including the Cisco TelePresence codec (which is the heart of Cisco TelePresence systems), the Cisco 7975 Series IP Phone, the Cisco Unified Communications Manager, the Cisco TelePresence Manager, the Cisco TelePresence Multipoint Switch, and the Cisco TelePresence Intercompany Solution.

The five chapters comprising **Part II, "TelePresence Technologies,"** discuss the following topics:

- **Chapter 3, "TelePresence Audio and Video Technologies":** This chapter delves into more detail on how the Cisco TelePresence codec interacts with the high-definition displays and cameras, microphones and speakers, the IP Phones, auxiliary components, and, most importantly, the network. Audio/video encoding and packetization are extensively discussed, as are the effects of latency, jitter, and loss on TelePresence flows.

- **Chapter 4, "Connecting TelePresence Systems":** This chapter details how individual components interconnect and interrelate within Cisco TelePresence systems. Additionally, the three main TelePresence deployment models, intracampus, intra-enterprise and Intercompany, are described.

- **Chapter 5, "Network Availability Technologies":** This chapter presents a foundational context for the best practice designs detailed in Chapter 9, "TelePresence Network Design Part 1: Availability Design," by introducing concepts and metrics relating to network availability for TelePresence deployments. A broad spectrum of availability technologies are overviewed, including device, network, and operational availability technologies.

- **Chapter 6, "Network Quality of Service Technologies":** This chapter lays a base for the validated designs detailed in Chapter 10, "TelePresence Network Design Part 2: QoS Design," by introducing concepts and metrics relating to network quality of service for TelePresence deployments. Various quality of service tools are overviewed, including classification, marking, policing, shaping, queuing, and dropping tools.

- **Chapter 7, "TelePresence Control and Security Protocols":** This chapter provides background for the the designs detailed in Chapter 11, "TelePresence Firewall Design," and Chapter 12, "TelePresence Call-Signaling Design," by introducing concepts and technologies relating to signaling, control, and security design for TelePresence deployments.

The technical substance of this book is in the second half, specifically in the seven chapters comprising **Part III "TelePresence Solution Design,"** which detail the following topics:

- **Chapter 8, "TelePresence Room Design":** This chapter describes topics that are rarely covered in Cisco Press books and that many networking professionals might be unfamiliar with but nonetheless are critical to properly designing rooms to support Cisco TelePresence, including wall, floor, and ceiling surfaces; lighting and illumination; acoustics; and heating, ventilation, air-conditioning. and power.

- **Chapter 9, "TelePresence Network Design Part 1: Availability Design":** This chapter details network considerations, targets, and design recommendations for highly available TelePresence networks. Campus designs include virtual switch designs and both EIGRP- and OSPF-routed access designs; branch designs include both dual-tier and multitier branch profiles.

- **Chapter 10, "TelePresence Network Design Part 2: QoS Design":** This chapter details network considerations, targets, and design recommendations for QoS-enabled TelePresence networks. The service level requirements of TelePresence are specified in terms of bandwidth, burst, latency, jitter, and loss. QoS designs for campus networks are detailed, as are WAN/branch and MPLS VPN networks.

■ **Chapter 11, "TelePresence Firewall Design":** This chapter outlines firewall design options for TelePresence deployments. Protocol requirements are examined for TelePresence scheduling, signaling, media, and management flows.

■ **Chapter 12, "TelePresence Call-Signaling Design":** This chapter examines TelePresence call-signaling components, including the Cisco Unified Communications Manager, Cisco Unified Border Element and Cisco Session Border Controller, and TelePresence signaling operation and design.

■ **Chapter 13, "Multipoint TelePresence Design":** This chapter expands the complexity of TelePresence deployments by introducing the Cisco TelePresence Multipoint Switch, which enables up to 48 TelePresence segments to be joined together in a single conference. Additionally, this chapter examines the network design implications of TelePresence multipoint deployments.

■ **Chapter 14, "Inter-Company TelePresence Design":** This chapter applies Metcalfe's Law to TelePresence deployments by introducing a solution that enables one business to place TelePresence calls to another, namely the Cisco TelePresence Inter-Company Solution. The end-to-end requirements of this solution are specified, including quality, security, scalability, and reliability. The components of the Inter-Company solution are analyzed, with emphasis on the Cisco Session Border Controller and Cisco Unified Border Element. Additionally, the network architecture and security of the Inter-Company solution are examined in depth.

Finally, this book concludes with the **Appendix, "Protocols Used in Cisco TelePresence Solutions."** This appendix summarizes and details the many network protocols used by Cisco TelePresence Systems.

Tim Szigeti

March 2009

Part I: Introducing Cisco Telepresence

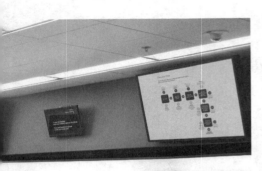

Telepresence as a concept has been around for many years and can be applied to a large number of applications. From virtual dining-room applications in which people are made to feel that they are sharing a meal at the same table together, to mystical "beam me up, Scotty" scenarios, such as projecting a presenter onto a stage using holographic projection technologies so the presenter appears to be standing on stage in front of the audience. Any immersive application that makes one person feel as though another person is physically present in their environment with them can be called telepresence. Wikipedia.org defines telepresence as "a set of technologies which allow a person to feel as if they were present, to give the appearance that they were present, or to have an effect, at a location other than their true location." Although these types of applications are "cool," their usefulness has so far been isolated to niche markets, one-off events, or to futuristic research studies.

However, there is one application in particular in which telepresence has found a viable market: the business meeting. In today's global economic climate, companies are hungry for technologies that enable them to communicate with their customers, partners, and employees more frequently and more effectively. They want to speed their decision-making processes, allowing geographically separated groups to collaborate more effectively together on projects, increasing intimacy with their customers, and lowering their costs of doing business. Business travel is at an all-time high, yet traveling is expensive, time-consuming, and takes a toll on people's bodies and personal lives.

However, the market is skeptical of video technologies that promise to deliver these benefits. For years the video conferencing industry has promised that it would replace the need for face-to-face meetings and lower travel costs, but for the vast majority of companies that have deployed it, video conferencing has for the most part failed to deliver

CHAPTER 1

What Is Telepresence?

on those promises. Video conferencing has struggled for years with complicated user interfaces, lack of integrated scheduling, and in many cases poor video quality. These issues have directly impacted overall utilization rates and caused major skepticism about the true value of video's use as a communications tool.

Many people refer to telepresence as high-end video conferencing, or the "next generation" of video conferencing. Many people categorize any video conferencing system that provides high-definition video and wideband audio as telepresence, but in reality telepresence is its own unique video technology. Telepresence is much more than just high-definition video and wideband audio. Providing a true telepresence experience requires attention to details overlooked in most video conferencing environments. Later in this chapter, video conferencing and telepresence will be compared highlighting the difference in the two technologies.

Note: It is important to point out the difference in the use of the terms "telepresence" and "TelePresence". Throughout this book the term "telepresence" will refer to telepresence as a technology where as, "TelePresence" is a direct reference to Cisco TelePresence.

Evolution of Video Communications

Video conferencing has been around for more than four decades. In 1964, at the World's Fair in New York, AT&T provided the world a preview of the first video conferencing endpoint, the AT&T Picturephone, illustrated in Figure 1-1. Six years later, AT&T released the Picturephone to consumers in downtown Pittsburgh, PA. Although the Picturephone ultimately failed to gain mass adoption because of its high price tag and the fact that users in 1970 weren't ready for video phones in their homes, it exposed the world to the possibility of video communications that ultimately sparked interest and development of private video conferencing systems that debuted throughout the 1970s.

In 1982, Compression Labs introduced the first commercial group video conferencing system, the CLI T1, enabling video communications over leased-line T1 circuits at 1.544 Mbps. Even with its high price of ~$250,000 and $1000 per hour line costs, the CLI T1 once again sparked the interest in video communications, bringing additional vendors into the market. In 1986, PictureTel introduced its first video conferencing system with a price of ~$80,000 and $100 per hour line cost, dramatically reducing the price of the system and its operational cost. The rapid cost reductions, market adoption, and overall visibility accelerated the development of video standards and new product development.

Figure 1-1   *AT&T Picturephone*

Throughout the late 1980s and early 1990s, work on new video standards continued. In 1990, two standards emerged that would provide a basis for interoperability between various vendors' video conferencing systems. H.320 provided a standard for running multimedia (audio/video/data) over ISDN networks, whereas H.261 provided a standard for video coding at low bit rates (40 kbps to 2 Mbps). With the release of these two standards, video conferencing as most of us know it today was born. Throughout the mid-1990s, H.320-based video conferencing systems were introduced to the market by a number of vendors. These standards enabled vendors to provide endpoints with lower cost of ownership, utilizing a public ISDN network, and providing interoperability with other vendors' H.320 systems. The fact that a public network was now available for video conferencing meant the sky was the limit. Users could dial one another over a public network for the first time, providing the first opportunity for mass adoption.

In the mid-1990s, new protocols were released for video conferencing over analog telephone lines (H.324) and data conferencing (T.120). Along with these new protocols came enhancements to video coding with the introduction of the H.263 standard, which provided more efficient video coding and higher resolutions. About the same time, Internet Protocol (IP) networks (and specifically, Ethernet LANs) were starting to take hold. In 1996, the H.323 standard was released, which defined protocols used for providing multimedia over packet-based networks. With the release of H.323, the market saw a slew of low cost, IP-based, desktop video conferencing endpoints, such as Microsoft NetMeeting, PictureTel LiveLan, Intel ProShare, and several others. At the same time, traditional video conferencing vendors started to introduce H.323 support into their room and group systems.

It wasn't until the late 1990s and early 2000s that H.323 video conferencing started to pick up steam. Low-cost desktop video conferencing endpoints never took off like everyone expected, but the mid- to low-end group systems started to take hold. In 1999, Polycom introduced the ViewStation, as shown in Figure 1-2, offering a "set top box" style video conferencing unit that revolutionized the video conferencing market. Unlike its large, complex, and expensive predecessors, the ViewStation was compact, simple to set up, much easier to use, and much less expensive. Immediately, a large portion of the market started to shift from large expensive systems to the smaller lower-cost systems in hopes of outfitting more rooms and expanding the reach of video conferencing.

Figure 1-2   *Polycom Viewstation*

During the early and mid-2000s, the video conferencing market moved ahead slowly, never really fulfilling the expectations of analysts or vendors. Even with the availability of lower-cost, easier-to-deploy endpoints, video conferencing couldn't break the trend. Every year seemed to be the year video would break out, but it never seemed to happen. Vendors made great strides in lowering the cost of systems and improving overall video quality, but the systems couldn't seem to gain mass adoption. Even in companies like Cisco that deployed hundreds of these lower-cost systems, utilization remained low, in many cases below 10 percent. Users seemed intimidated by the custom touch panels or the remote controls used to initiate calls and control the systems. Users often complained about wasting half the meeting trying to get the video call connected due to the complicated remote control or custom touch screen interfaces. In many cases, companies deployed video systems from different vendors, further complicating the life of users by introducing different remote controls for each vendor system. Custom touch panels are a great alternative to remote controls, allowing complete control of the entire video conferencing room including lighting, audio, and full control of the system. However, the more devices the touch panels controlled, the more complicated the interface became, making it difficult for the average user to navigate. Even when users could get calls connected, the overall experience often provided little value-add to the meeting. Poorly designed rooms and small images of multiple people around large tables made it difficult to read body language and facial expressions. These two factors played a large roll in the low utilization of most video conferencing deployments.

During this period, Cisco was heavily involved in pushing H.323 video conferencing. Cisco entered into an original equipment manufacturer (OEM) agreement with RADVision providing the first Cisco H.323 video conferencing solution. These products included H.323 Multipoint Control Units (MCU), H.320/H.323 gateways, with an H.323 Gatekeeper and Proxy that ran within the Cisco Internetwork Operating System (IOS) on various Cisco router platforms. Cisco produced H.323 video conferencing deployment guides and assisted numerous customers in building out large-scale H.323 video conferencing networks. Despite its efforts, video conferencing continued to experience low user adoption rates. Cisco had recently introduced IP Telephony to the market in 1999 and was enjoying excellent market penetration in that arena and believed that the answer to making video conferencing ubiquitous was to make it "as easy to use as a phone call." In 2004, Cisco introduced Video Telephony to the market, allowing customers to use their Cisco IP Phones as the user interface to make and receive video calls, simply by dialing the phone number of another user's IP Phone. Intuitive telephony-like features were also included, such as putting the call on hold, transferring the call, and conferencing in a third participant. Hundreds of thousands of Cisco Video Telephony endpoints were deployed in the market, but despite its extreme ease-of-use and telephony-like user experience, usage rates for Video Telephony were only slightly better than that of existing video conferencing systems.

Also in the mid-2000s, the H.264 standard was created that provided even more-efficient encoding, enabling higher quality video at low-bit rates, and support for high-definition video (720p and 1080p) at higher bit rates (~ 2 Mbps and above). At the time this book was written, video conferencing vendors such as Polycom, Tandberg, LifeSize, and others had begun offering high-definition-capable endpoints, hoping that the improved image quality would breathe life back into the video conferencing market. It's just now that high-definition video conferencing endpoints are deployed and used in good numbers, so only time will tell the fate of these next-generation video conferencing endpoints. At the same time, Microsoft, Cisco, and others began a renewed effort to push collaboration applications to the desktop, with applications such as Microsoft Office Communicator and Cisco Unified Personal Communicator.

As early as 2000, telepresence systems started to show up on the market, providing a more holistic approach to creating a virtual meeting experience than existing video conferencing systems. Rather than focus on providing a low-cost video conferencing experience, they focused on providing a high-quality, immersive experience, so people felt as if they were actually in the same room together. Using multiple screens and cameras, they divided the meeting room in half, positioning the screens, cameras, tables, and chairs in such a way as to mimic the feeling that everyone in the meeting was sitting at the same table. These early telepresence pioneers were small, privately owned companies serving a relatively small niche market.

In 2004, Hewlett-Packard was the first large, multinational vendor to bring an immersive telepresence system, immediate credibility, and increased focus to the telepresence market. The Halo Telepresence system offered a white glove service and targeted the executive meeting rooms. Rooms within a room were built to provide the proper environment, and a new dedicated Halo Exchange Video Network (HEVN) was introduced, providing a fully managed telepresence service. However, even with the backing of a major technology company, telepresence was still challenged with limited adoption and slow growth rates.

Early Telepresence systems were targeted at the executive ranks with an expensive high-touch model. Due to this executive level approach, vendors offered turnkey solutions and required a fully managed service over a dedicated network. This approach seemed like a good idea at the time because there were similar video conferencing solutions with the same model. However, the high system costs coupled with the high recurring fee for the managed service severely limited their deployment. Even though many customers' networks were not ready for telepresence at the time, customers realized that providing separate networks for specific applications was not the right path in the long term.

In late 2006, Cisco entered the market with its first telepresence system focused on providing a truly immersive experience, deployable over existing IP networks and used by anyone within a company. Cisco leveraged its vast networking knowledge to design their TelePresence system to run over converged IP networks. At the same time, a grass roots effort was underway that would provide design guidance for service providers looking to offer Cisco TelePresence as a hosted or managed service. Additionally, this design guidance allowed service providers to offer an Inter-Company solution for Cisco TelePresence. This work also allowed Cisco TelePresence to extend past companies' intranetwork boundaries for the first time, further broadening the power of Cisco TelePresence. Cisco TelePresence Inter-Company offerings continue to expand, providing even more momentum to Cisco TelePresence. As previously discussed, early telepresence systems were supported on overlay networks and managed by providers, which severely limited the proliferation of telepresence systems. Providing telepresence over converged IP networks requires systems that provide standard management tools, security, and a well-defined network architecture. Figure 1-3 shows the first Cisco TelePresence system: the CTS-3000.

Figure 1-3   *Cisco TelePresence CTS-3000*

It's All About the Experience!

Rather than starting off with a set of technologies and then figuring out what it could build, Cisco took the opposite approach. Cisco decided that the time was right for telepresence, but rather than integrating off-the-shelf components, Cisco decided to build the system from the ground up. Taking a blank sheet of paper, a small group of engineers and executives at Cisco with many years of experience in video conferencing, IP Telephony, video and audio codec technology, and networking gathered together to define a set of requirements that would become the tenets used to design and build the Cisco TelePresence solution.

The first guiding principle of Cisco TelePresence was that the experience was paramount. It demanded an experience that was so lifelike and realistic that users would literally forget that they weren't actually in the same room together. Cisco was so captivated by this idea, it created the mantra, "It's All About the Experience," and posted this mantra all over the hallways of the building it worked in. If the technology could not be made to deliver this level of quality at a reasonable price and bandwidth rate, then forget it, it wouldn't build it.

The second guiding principle was that the system had to be so incredibly easy to schedule and use that literally anyone could do it. It had to completely do away with all the complicated user interfaces, remote controls, and dialing schemes of traditional video conferencing and would not require a help desk technician or a technically savvy user to set up and create a meeting. In fact, it made a conscious effort to purposely avoid adding in a lot of features, buttons, and nerd-knobs that video conferencing systems have, and focused on simplicity so dramatically that it reduced the entire user experience of initiating a Cisco TelePresence meeting down to a single button, which it coined, "One Button to Push."

The third guiding principle was that the solution had to be utterly reliable. It had to work every single time, time after time after time. Only then would users trust it enough to actually use it; in fact, they would come to rely upon it, which in turn would drive high usage levels and deliver a true return on investment.

These three guiding principles, Quality, Simplicity, and Reliability, became the foundation from which all other design requirements would be based. From there, the team embarked on a journey to go and build, from the ground up, an experience that would deliver those attributes.

Although a great deal of the solution was designed and built from the ground up, including the 1080p multistream codec technology, audio subsystem, cameras, displays, and even the furniture. Cisco also had the benefit of leveraging much of the technology and standards it had used for IP Telephony, which at the time was redefined as Unified Communications. For example, Cisco TelePresence leveraged and reused the Cisco Session Initiation Protocol (SIP) stack and Cisco CallManager (now known as Unified Communications Manager) as its call control platform. It reused the 802.3af Power over Ethernet technology used by Cisco IP Phones to power its cameras. It reused the 802.1Q/p Automatic VLAN and quality of service (QoS) framework for attaching to the access layer of the LAN. It reused the same Cisco Media Convergence Server MCS-7800 series server platforms and Cisco Linux Voice Operating System used to run many of the voice server applications such as Cisco CallManager, Cisco Unity, and many others. It even reused the Cisco 7900 Series IP Phones, which serve as the user interface to the Cisco TelePresence system. By taking this approach, Cisco provided a solution that in many ways behaved just like an IP Phone on the network, allowing customers who had already invested in Cisco Unified Communications to see Cisco TelePresence as "just another type of endpoint" on that existing platform. Furthermore, by taking this approach, Cisco TelePresence was built upon an already proven platform, allowing Cisco TelePresence to achieve something that no other product in the history Cisco has ever done; release 1.0 was rock-solid stable, right out of the starting gate.

The other thing that differentiated Cisco TelePresence from other ventures in the history of Cisco was that with TelePresence, Cisco was not content to just offer the endpoints and let someone else provide the backend components, or just offer the network infrastructure and let other vendors provide the endpoints and backend components. Cisco decided that for Cisco TelePresence to be successful, it had to provide a complete, end-to-end solution: endpoints, multipoint, scheduling and management, call control, and network infrastructure. Furthermore, Cisco did not want to just sell the hardware and software and leave it up to the customers to figure out how to deploy it and manage it successfully. The product offering would need to be backed by a suite of Planning, Design, and Implementation (PDI) services, day-2 support and monitoring services.

Cisco also knew that the only way to prove to the market that telepresence was truly a new category of technology that could finally deliver on the promise of increasing productivity and reducing travel costs was to immediately deploy large numbers of TelePresence systems throughout Cisco, demonstrating that it could be done and that the Return on Investment (ROI) model was valid. Cisco took a bold step, slashing travel budgets globally and deploying more than 200 TelePresence systems in Cisco offices worldwide within the first 18 months of its first TelePresence shipment. This not only catapulted Cisco into the market leadership position in the number of TelePresence systems installed, but also made Cisco the largest user of telepresence in the world. At the time this book was written, Cisco had more than 350 production TelePresence systems installed internally, with more than 65,000 employees using them day in and day out. The average weekly utilization rate for these systems is more than 46 percent, with more than 4000 meetings conducted per month, an estimated savings of $174,000,000 in travel cost, and a total savings of 95,000 metric tons of carbon emissions to date. Furthermore, it is estimated that these numbers will dramatically increase with the deployment of personal TelePresence systems.

Cisco's aggressive launch into the telepresence market caused a huge ground swell around telepresence. Cisco had always been viewed as an infrastructure company, and for the first time, Cisco was viewed as a video company. Many people questioned whether Cisco could make this move into high-end video communications and compete with existing video vendors, but Cisco has proven it can make this transition with a market-leading telepresence solution. The Cisco entrance into the telepresence market has prompted existing video conferencing vendors to develop telepresence solutions instead of continuing to focus strictly on high-definition video conferencing. Only time will tell where telepresence leads us, but it is off to an interesting beginning.

How Is TelePresence Different Than Video Conferencing?

Both video conferencing and telepresence applications are designed to provide virtual meetings. However, there are fundamental differences in the overall technology and meeting experience delivered by each application. As mentioned in the preceding sections, the lines between video conferencing and telepresence have been blurred as the market focus on telepresence has intensified. Many vendors are now categorizing any video conferencing unit that supports high-definition video as a telepresence product.

Some argue that a high-definition video conferencing system can be made to produce a telepresence experience, and in fact some video conferencing vendors are utilizing existing high-definition codecs in their telepresence systems today. However, telepresence is a set of technologies, including video and audio, that provides an experience enabling all users to feel as if they are in the same room, an experience that not all high-definition video conferencing systems truly provide.

A number of distinctions are often made between the two technologies. The following three guiding principals for Cisco TelePresence are used to show the differences between the two technologies:

- Quality
- Simplicity
- Reliability

Quality

Few will debate the quality of experience found in Cisco TelePresence systems. Cisco TelePresence systems are designed with every detail in mind, from the video and audio quality, to the furniture included in some larger Telepresence systems. High-quality video is required to produce an "in-person" experience. Cisco TelePresence systems use specialized cameras that are strategically placed above system displays, providing optimal eye contact for all meeting participants. Cisco TelePresence cameras are also fixed focus and tuned for the room environment, allowing consistent images across all sites. Cisco TelePresence systems also provide large integrated displays providing vivid, lifelike images in high-definition quality. Audio systems provide crisp, lifelike audio, using wideband codecs. Audio systems are specially engineered for the TelePresence system, room dimensions, and table layouts, providing multichannel audio tuned for voice frequencies and eliminating off-screen audio sources. Microphones and speakers are strategically placed, providing immersive audio that emanates from the speakers location in the room. Cisco TelePresence systems also provide room requirements outlining lighting, acoustic requirements, and in some cases integrated furniture. All these factors contribute to the quality level that is required for any Cisco TelePresence system. Telepresence is the sum of all these attributes. If any one of these areas is overlooked, the result will not be a true telepresence experience.

Today's video conferencing systems have the capability to provide good audio and video quality with many systems supporting high-definition video and wide-band audio. However, video conferencing systems were built for flexibility and adaptability. Video conferencing systems are shipped with pan-tilt-zoom cameras that are designed to capture large rooms with long tables accommodating all participants on a single display. Most video conferencing systems ship with displays that range in size and can even be replaced with larger displays or projector systems for large rooms. Advanced audio codecs have been developed by a few of the video conferencing vendors that provide excellent audio quality.

Most video conferencing systems are shipped with tabletop microphones that are often deployed in smaller conference rooms and routinely replaced by in-house microphone systems for large meeting rooms. Video conferencing systems are deployed in many different room environments from the high-end executive board rooms to the small meeting room with a video conferencing system on a cart. Unfortunately, video conferencing units on carts far outnumber high-end video conferencing rooms, resulting in highly variable, inconsistent experiences from one room to the other.

Simplicity

The complexity and inconsistency of the various user interface provided by existing video conferencing systems is one of the biggest reasons for the low utilization rates found in most video conference deployments. Video conferencing systems ship with remote controls that are used to initiate meetings, focus cameras, share documents, and more. These remote controls have frustrated users for years and are often replaced with customized touch panels. However, customized touch panels are usually only deployed in high-end rooms, whereas smaller rooms use vendor-supplied remote controls, making it difficult for the average user to navigate different and complicated interfaces. Many companies find it necessary to employ a dedicated video conference staff tasked with scheduling, initiating, and managing meetings to address the complexity found in video conferencing systems.

Telepresence systems are designed with simplified user interfaces and in some cases, such as with the Cisco TelePresence system, a simple (IP Phone) interface that is used for all systems. As mentioned earlier, some vendors have developed new telepresence systems while at the same time branding existing high-definition video conferencing systems as telepresence systems. This will continue to provide challenges for users that experience the simplified user interface of a telepresence system one day and a complicated remote control found in smaller room the next. For telepresence to reach its full potential, the user interface must continue to be simplified and remain consistent, ensuring any user is comfortable running a telepresence meeting.

Telepresence systems are often described as inflexible and lacking many features found in video conferencing systems. This is by design, removing unnecessary features to simplify the overall user experience. The more features added into a system, the more complicated the system becomes. Early telepresence systems provided only the basic features required for business meetings, but as customer adoption grew, the demand for more features followed. This provides a challenge for all telepresence vendors; how to keep systems simple and intuitive while adding new and advanced feature sets. In reality, many features that are never used, or are only used by a small number of customers, are implemented across all technologies, ultimately complicating implementations and usability. The "less is more model" has proved successful for Cisco TelePresence to date, but time will tell how long this philosophy will last in the face of customer demand for more and more features.

Reliability

System reliability has been a perceived issue with video conferencing systems for years. In reality, the video conferencing systems themselves are fairly reliable. However, outside factors have plagued them for years. The complexity of the video conferencing user interface played a big part in the perceived reliability issue. Users often walked into rooms, misdialed or pressed the wrong button on the custom touch screen panel, the call failed to connect, and the user assumed there was an issue with the system. It was just as common for a user to walk into a room and try to use the system only to find out the display was powered off or had been disconnected from the video codec. This was often the case in the Cisco internal video conferencing deployment. Displays were often used for different purposes, or someone needed to use the network jack and reconnected the system to the wrong jack. Whatever the reason, users quickly abandon the use of video conferencing systems when they encounter issues initiating calls.

Cisco TelePresence systems have made it a priority to provide systems that work every time. As described previously, Cisco TelePresence systems have simplified the dialing interface to address issues with user error and integrated all components to eliminate these types of avoidable issues. System displays, and even lighting on some systems, are centrally controlled by the TelePresence system, ensuring that every time a user pushes the button to connect the TelePresence call, it works. Single screen TelePresence systems are often mounted to walls with network and power jacks located behind the system, so users don't have the ability to unplug power or network connections. The importance of integrated system displays is often overlooked for single screen systems. Something as small as an input setting being changed can cause a call to fail and the system to be deemed unreliable.

Integrating all system components also provides enhanced manageability, allowing systems to report issues for any system component that might cause call failures. Considering early Telepresence systems were primarily used by CXO-level executives, it was imperative that any system failure be identified as quickly as possible. As Telepresence systems have moved into the mainstream, this manageability has proven invaluable.

Bandwidth Requirements

Network requirements for video conferencing and Telepresence are often mis-stated. How many times have you heard, "Telepresence requires a lot more bandwidth than video conferencing"? A high-definition video conferencing system requires the same, or in some cases more, bandwidth than a Cisco TelePresence system, running the same video resolution, to provide a comparable image quality. Cisco TelePresence systems have implemented advanced standards-based compression algorithms, lowering overall bandwidth consumption. These advanced compression algorithms have allowed Cisco TelePresence systems to provide 1080p video resolution at, close to, the same bandwidth consumption of video conferencing systems running 720p video resolution.

Most video conferencing systems enable lower resolutions that require much less bandwidth; however, video conferencing systems running at 720p resolution consume between 2 Mbps to 4 Mbps, whereas single screen Cisco TelePresence systems running at the same resolution only require 1.5 Mbps to 3 Mbps. Remember that some TelePresence systems have three video displays. Comparing the network requirements of a single-screen video conferencing system to a multiscreen TelePresence system is not comparing apples-to-apples. Video conferencing systems should be compared to single screen TelePresence systems.

Summary

This chapter provided a high-level overview of telepresence as a technology and its use for virtual meetings. Telepresence enables video communications to take a big step forward, enhancing the overall experience found in virtual meetings. The lines between video conferencing and telepresence are blurred with traditional video conferencing endpoints, supporting high-definition video and wide-band audio, claiming to be telepresence systems. As outlined in this chapter, telepresence is more than video and audio quality. Telepresence must provide users with the feeling that everyone in the meeting is in the same room. Traditional video conferencing systems were not intended to provide this level of experience. Telepresence systems have been designed from the ground up to provide a vivid "in-room" experience by focusing on all aspects of a virtual meeting experience.

Cisco used its network expertise to develop a product that is deployed on existing IP networks, allowing customers to extend the reach of telepresence. In a relatively short time, Cisco has become the largest telepresence vendor and consumer, using its own converged IP network to deploy more than 350 Cisco TelePresence systems. However, with the uptake in telepresence, it won't be long before even larger telepresence deployments are commonplace.

The remaining chapters of the book focus on providing the fundamentals of Cisco TelePresence and its underlying technologies. You can expect to gain an understanding of the overall technology, protocols, and Cisco TelePresence system design. Additional detail is provided regarding security, network design, and best practice recommendations.

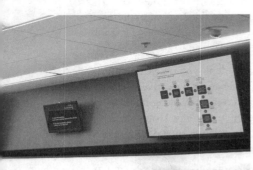

This chapter provides an overview of all Cisco TelePresence components:

- Cisco TelePresence Codec

- Cisco 7975 Series IP Phone

- Cisco TelePresence System 3000

- Cisco TelePresence System 3200

- Cisco TelePresence System 1000

- Cisco TelePresence System 500

- Cisco Unified Communication Manager

- Cisco TelePresence Manager

- Cisco TelePresence Multipoint Switch

- Cisco TelePresence Inter-Company

- Operation, Administration, and Management

- Related TelePresence Services

Cisco TelePresence Solution Overview

The Cisco TelePresence Solution

As detailed in Chapter 1, the Cisco TelePresence solution was officially released in December 2006, providing the first true replacement for face-to-face meetings. Prior to its release, a number of telepresence systems, from numerous vendors, were available on the market; however, their adoption was limited to a small number of customers, with just a few systems each. These systems required overlay networks and focused on white-glove service for executive users. Cisco focused on providing an exceptional experience but also realized that scheduling and ease of use was the key to providing a solution that would be deployed on existing IP networks and used by all employees. For years the video conferencing industry struggled to gain mass adoption and acceptable utilization rates, and in many cases the issue was related to ease of use and system reliability.

Early Telepresence vendors offered systems providing a good overall experience while addressing reliability issues found in existing video conferencing systems. Unfortunately, these offerings were based on managed service models requiring dedicated networks, and in many cases, custom rooms to house Telepresence endpoints. These systems were not only expensive but also carried a high monthly cost associated with the dedicated bandwidth and managed service fees. In some cases, solutions required an operator to do everything from starting the meeting to enabling data sharing. This model provided a high-end niche Telepresence market but did not allow Telepresence to reach its full potential. For Telepresence to realize its full potential, it needed to extend past the boardroom and into the mainstream.

Cisco focused on delivering a Telepresence solution that provided an immersive true in-person experience, used by all employees, scheduled by the employees, providing tools commonly used in face-to-face meetings, and, *most important*, run over existing IP networks. At the time of its release, Cisco TelePresence was the only Telepresence system on the market that did not require a dedicated network.

Instead of providing dedicated bandwidth that couldn't be used by other applications when TelePresence wasn't being used, Cisco focused on converged IP networks. This allowed enterprise customers to deploy Cisco TelePresence over their existing infrastructure, realizing the upside and long-term value of a converged IP network. However, in some cases customer networks were not ready for an application such as TelePresence. This required some enterprise customers to temporarily deploy Cisco TelePresence over a parallel network until changes were made enabling the TelePresence system to be moved to the customers' converged IP network.

The initial Cisco TelePresence product release consisted of two TelePresence systems:

- A conference room-based TelePresence system (CTS-3000) supporting up to six participants at each location

- A small meeting room system (CTS-1000) supporting up to two participants at each location

The solution also included a middleware scheduling platform—Cisco TelePresence Manager (CTS-Manager)—providing integration with Microsoft Exchange and a simple dialing interface known as One Button to Push. The initial launch of Cisco TelePresence was an immediate success, with most systems deployed for use by CXO level executives. However, it quickly became evident that additional products and functionality were required to meet customer needs.

Shortly after its initial release, additional products and functionality were introduced. Multipoint support was added, enabling meetings with three or more TelePresence systems. Additionally, two new TelePresence systems were announced in early 2008:

- The CTS-3200, supporting up to 18 participants for large meeting rooms, was delivered in mid-2008.

- The CTS-500, supporting a single user for the executive or home office, was delivered shortly after the CTS-3200.

With the addition of these two new systems, Cisco TelePresence broadened its market at the high end, with the CTS-3200, while allowing greater system access to the masses with the CTS-500. Figure 2-1 illustrates the components of the Cisco TelePresence solution.

Along with all product and feature enhancements, a Cisco TelePresence Inter-Company offering was announced in late 2007, expanding the reach and extending the relevance of Cisco TelePresence. The addition of Inter-Company allowed customers to extend the benefits of Cisco TelePresence beyond their own enterprises. Enterprises now have the capability to meet virtually with any partner or customer at any time, saving money and improving productivity.

With the expansion of the Cisco TelePresence portfolio and the addition of Inter-Company, Cisco TelePresence adoption continues to grow at an amazing rate.

Cisco TelePresence Codec

The Cisco TelePresence codec was developed from the ground up by Cisco in early 2004, providing native 1080p high definition video and wide-band spatial audio utilizing standard audio and video compression methods. This state of the art codec is now the basis for all Cisco TelePresence systems. Unlike many video conferencing products on the market today, the Cisco TelePresence codec provides integration and management for all in room components. Integrating system cameras, displays, projectors, and auxiliary documentation cameras provide a highly reliable system with a consistent user experience. The

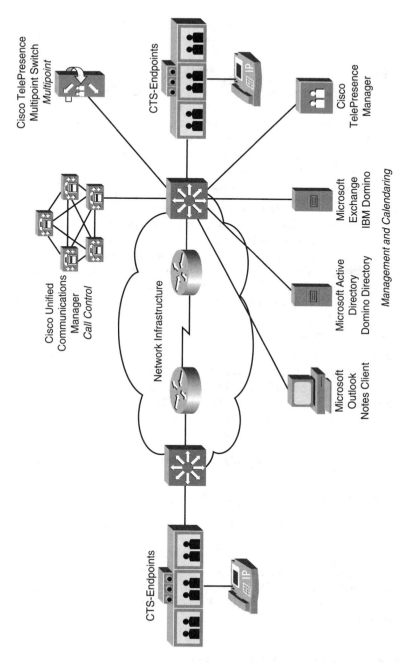

Figure 2-1 *Cisco TelePresence*

Cisco TelePresence codec also leverages the *Cisco Unified Communications Manager (CUCM)* and existing network technologies, providing a scaleable platform used in some of today's largest voice networks.

Current and past video conferencing systems often use off-the-shelf components, such as displays, auxiliary cameras, custom touch-screen user interfaces, and in-house audio systems, to build out rooms. Although providing great deployment flexibility, this approach also makes system use and management more difficult. Each Cisco TelePresence system is built as an integrated system including video, audio, and lighting, all managed by the Cisco TelePresence codec. The Cisco TelePresence codec also manages system software for all components, putting system displays in standby mode, or completely powering on and off system displays and integrated lighting, saving power and HVAC resources during off hours.

Integrating all in-room components with the Cisco TelePresence codec also provides a central management and configuration point for all components in a TelePresence room. Administrators can access the codec using Hypertext Transfer Protocol Secure (HTTPS) or Secure Shell (SSH) Common Line Interface (CLI) for system management. The secure web management interface provides a central view of all in-room component status, real-time call statistics, and access to system logs. Also, from the web interface, administrators can tune and verify cameras, displays, audio, and projection systems functionality. Providing this level of system integration enables administrators to quickly identify status and troubleshoot any component in the Cisco TelePresence system.

As previously mentioned, the Cisco TelePresence codec is fully integrated with the CUCM, making it a key component of the Cisco Unified Communications portfolio. As with Cisco IP Telephony, Cisco TelePresence relies on CUCM for its configurations, software upgrades, management and call processing. Utilizing CUCM allows centralized system management while allowing the system to leverage established techniques for network automation and Quality of Service (QoS), such as:

- Cisco Discovery Protocol (CDP) and 802.1Q for discovery and assignment to the appropriate VLAN

- 802.1p and Differentiated Services Code Point (DSCP) for QoS

- HTTP for automatic downloading of configuration and firmware updates

- Session Initiation Protocol (SIP) for all call signaling communications

From an administrator's perspective, the entire Cisco TelePresence virtual meeting room appears as a single SIP endpoint on CUCM. It is managed using tools and methodologies that are similar to those used with a Cisco Unified IP Phone. Figure 2-2 illustrates the Cisco TelePresence codec.

Industry-Leading Audio and Video

The Cisco TelePresence codec uses industry-leading 1080p and 720p high-definition video resolution and 48kHz wideband spatial audio. The codec also supports Common Intermediate Format (CIF) video resolution and G.722/G.711 audio for interoperability with non-TelePresence endpoints and audio-only participants.

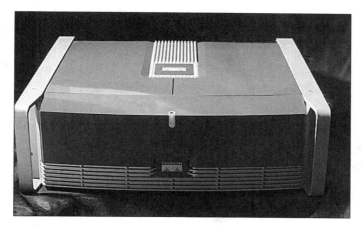

Figure 2-2   *Cisco TelePresence codec*

Video Resolution and Compression Formats

The Cisco TelePresence 65-inch displays and cameras natively support 1080p and 720p resolutions and use digital media interfaces to connect to the codecs. This ensures the integrity of the video signal from end to end, eliminating the need for any digital and analog conversion.

Inside the Cisco TelePresence codec, an onboard array of Digital Signal Processors (DSP) encode the digital video signal from the cameras into Real-Time Transport Protocol (RTP) packets using the H.264 encoding and compression standard.

The quality of the video enjoyed by the meeting participants is a function of three variables:

■ Resolution (the number of pixels within an image)

■ Frame rate (how often pixels are redrawn on the display)

■ Degree of compression applied to the original video signal

Video Resolution

The 1080p resolution provides the highest quality video image currently available on the market, supplying a resolution of 1920 x 1080 and 2,074,000 pixels per frame. The 720p resolution provides a resolution of 1280 x 720 and 922,000 pixels per frame. Compared with today's DVD standard video with a resolution of 720 x 480 and 346,000 pixels per frame, you can see the dramatic increase in resolution and pixel count. Figure 2-3 illustrates the difference between these three resolutions.

Frame Rate

The frame rate of the displayed video directly corresponds to how motion within the video is perceived by the participants. To maintain excellent motion handling, the Cisco TelePresence system encodes and displays video at 30 frames per second (30fps) at all times. In addition, the cameras and displays use progressive-scan technology to refresh

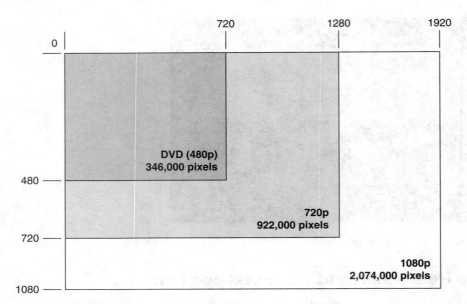

Figure 2-3   *Video resolution*

the pixels within the video signal faster than with traditional television and video conferencing equipment that use an interlaced refresh format.

Compression

Note that 1080p video uncompressed is delivered at approximately 1.5Gbps. The Cisco TelePresence codecs must take this native video received from the cameras and compress it to a more feasible amount of bandwidth in as little time as possible. As mentioned previously, the codec achieves this by using an array of Digital Signal Processors (DSP) to compress the original 1.5-Gbps video from each camera down to under 4Mbps (per camera), representing a compression ratio of over 99 percent, which is done in under 90ms. The customer is provided with some amount of control over how much compression is applied. However, For each of the two resolution formats supported (1080p and 720p), the Cisco TelePresence codec supports three quality levels. Each quality level is really a function of the degree of compression applied with each quality level requiring a different amount bandwidth. For simplicity, these three levels are referred to as good, better, and best. The best quality level has the least amount of compression applied and, therefore, requires the most bandwidth, while the good quality level has the most amount of compression applied and requires the least amount of bandwidth.

Providing two resolutions and three quality levels within each resolution provides flexibility when deploying Cisco TelePresence. More importantly, it allows the Cisco TelePresence codec to automatically adapt to adverse network conditions by lowering the quality level and resolution to deal with packet loss.

Considering the three variables of resolution, frame rate, and the degree of compression applied, Table 2-1 illustrates the different quality settings supported by the Cisco TelePresence codec and the requisite bandwidth required for each quality setting.

Table 2-1 *Resolution, Quality, and Bandwidth*

Resolution	1080p			720p		
Quality Level	Best	Better	Good	Best	Better	Good
Frame Rate	30	30	30	30	30	30
Bandwidth	4Mbps	3.5Mbps	3Mbps	2.25Mbps	1.5Mbps	1Mbps

These bandwidth values apply per camera. Therefore, a CTS-3000 or CTS-3200 that has three cameras and three displays, running at 1080p resolution at the best quality level, requires 12Mbps of video bandwidth, whereas a CTS-1000 or CTS-500 requires 4Mbps of video bandwidth.

Note The bandwidth numbers in Table 2-1 are for the TelePresence video only and do not include video for document sharing, audio, or any additional TelePresence features. Refer to Chapter 10, "TelePresence Network Design Part 2: QoS Design" for a more complete analysis of bandwidth requirements.

Audio Resolution and Compression Formats

The Cisco TelePresence system codec uses advanced microphone, speaker, and audio encoding technologies to preserve the quality and directionality of the audio so that it appears to emanate from the location of the person speaking at the same volume as it would if that person were actually sitting across the table from you.

The quality of the audio enjoyed by the meeting participants is a function of three variables:

- **Frequency spectrum captured by the microphones:** The Cisco TelePresence microphones are designed to capture a 48-kHz spectrum of audio frequencies. The Cisco TelePresence speakers are designed to reproduce that same rich frequency spectrum.

- **Spatiality (that is, directionality) of the audio:** To preserve the spatiality (that is, directional perception) of the audio, for larger Cisco TelePresence systems, individual microphones are placed at specific locations on the virtual table, along with speakers located under each display.

- **Degree of compression applied to the original audio signal:** Inside the Cisco TelePresence Codec an onboard array of DSPs encode the audio signal from the microphones into RTP packets using the Advanced Audio Coding-Low Delay (AAC-LD) encoding and compression standard. The resulting bandwidth required to transport the audio signals between the systems is 64kbps per microphone. Therefore, a CTS-3X00 requires 192kbps of audio bandwidth, whereas the CTS-1000 or CTS-500 requires 64kbps of audio bandwidth.

Note The Cisco TelePresence system also offers support for features such as audio add-in that requires additional bandwidth. The additional audio bandwidth is not included in the description here. See Chapter 3, "TelePresence Audio and Video Technologies," for additional applications and how each affects the overall bandwidth requirements of the system.

Collaboration Tools

Two common tools found in most conference rooms today are speaker phones and projectors. Most of today's meetings consist of one or more individuals sharing documents with a group of people, often located in multiple locations. Using a web/audio conferencing tool such as WebEx allows users to simultaneously share documents and bridge audio between multiple sites, while using a projector to locally display content for in-room participants.

The Cisco TelePresence codec provides these features, allowing non-TelePresence users to participate, through audio only, in a TelePresence meeting and share documents with all meeting participants.

Auto Collaborate is a feature that allows any user in a TelePresence room to easily share any application on a laptop PC or an item from an in-room document camera. As with any in-room projector, a user simply connects a laptop to the VGA cable on the TelePresence table to start sharing. With an optional ceiling mounted or desktop document camera, users also have the option of sharing additional items such as documents, fabric samples, and so on with TelePresence participants. Users simply select the document camera softkey on the 7975 Series IP Phone and use the simple touch-screen phone interface to power on and control the document camera. Users don't need to worry about granting control for sharing from one PC to another or a document camera. The last device to become active is the device that displays in all TelePresence rooms.

The VGA cable and document camera in the TelePresence room connect directly to the codec that automatically displays the image locally, using the system projector, while encoding the image and sending it to all TelePresence systems in the meeting. Application data is compressed using H.264 at 5 frames per second (fps), which is sufficient for sharing slides or items from a document camera but, in most cases, is not sufficient for full-motion video. If full-motion video is a requirement, a high-speed presentation codec can be added to the system providing 30fps for document and video sharing.

Most TelePresence meetings have attendees who don't have access to a TelePresence room. TelePresence meetings can easily connect to a web/audio conferencing application such as WebEx or Meeting Place to accommodate non-TelePresence participants.

When the TelePresence meeting is in progress, one TelePresence room connects to the audio bridge, essentially adding the audio bridge to the TelePresence meeting, using the audio add-in feature. At the same time, the presenters in the TelePresence rooms join the web conference, allowing shared content to be viewed by all TelePresence and audio/web participants.

After the TelePresence meeting is connected to the audio/web conference, non-TelePresence participants can participate in the meeting using audio and view or even present, shared content throughout the meeting. The overall experience is similar to today's meetings where a group of individuals meet in a conference room, dial into an audio bridge using a speaker phone, use a projector to locally display content, and share the local content with remote participants using web conferencing.

Audio add-in is a feature allowing audio-only participants to participate in a TelePresence meeting. From any TelePresence room a user simply selects the conference softkey on the 7975 Series IP Phone and dials the number of the audio participant or audio conferencing bridge. The audio add-in participants are connected through the initiating Telepresence system where audio is decoded, mixed, and played out all system speakers. The audio is then re-encoded in AAC-LD and sent to all Cisco TelePresence rooms in the same meeting.

Audio and Video Multiplexing

Each Cisco TelePresence system connects to the network using a single 100/1000 Ethernet connection. All TelePresence systems support multiple audio and video channels, allowing support for system video, audio, and shared data. Single-screen TelePresence systems support two audio channels and two video channels, whereas three screen TelePresence systems support four audio and four video channels. RTP multiplexing minimizes the number of video and audio connections across the network, providing a single video and single audio connection between any two Cisco TelePresence systems. Video and audio multiplexing is covered in detail in the following chapters.

Cisco 7975 Series IP Phone

One of the biggest issues with video conferencing is the ease of use especially around the user interface. As mentioned in the previous chapter, high-end video conferencing systems often use custom touch-screen panels while smaller conference room systems rely on hand-held remote controls. Users have not adapted well to either approach, rendering such systems difficult to use.

To further enhance the Cisco TelePresence meeting participants' experience, cumbersome hand-held remote controls and custom touch-screen panels are eliminated, the cameras are fixed in their positions (no panning, tilting, or zooming controls), and the microphones are fixed in their positions on the table. There are virtually no moving parts or user interfaces that users must master to use a Cisco TelePresence meeting room.

Rather, the Cisco TelePresence meeting room solutions use a Cisco Unified 7975 Series IP Phone, conveniently located on the table to launch, control, and conclude meetings. This makes Cisco TelePresence as easy to use as a telephone. Using the Cisco Unified 7975 Series IP Phone (see Figure 2-4), the user simply dials the telephone number of the Cisco TelePresence room with which they want to have a meeting, and the call is connected. Softkey menu buttons on the phone allow the user to place the call on hold or conference in an audio-only participant. The Cisco TelePresence solution takes simplicity one step further. When used in conjunction with Cisco TelePresence Manager, scheduled meetings display on the phone's color touch-screen display, allowing users to simply touch the appropriate meeting on the screen and launch their scheduled meeting.

Image Courtesy of Cisco Systems, Inc. Unauthorized use not permitted.

Figure 2-4   *Cisco 7975 Series IP Phone*

Cisco TelePresence System 3000

The CTS-3000 is the flagship product for Cisco TelePresence. Released during the initial Cisco TelePresence launch, the CTS-3000 is the first Cisco TelePresence room system and the basis for all TelePresence systems to follow.

The CTS-3000 is designed to seat six participants and provide an immersive, lifelike experience. The CTS-3000 also provides tools used in everyday meetings, such as sharing of documents and adding in audio-only participants. Figure 2-5 shows the Cisco TelePresence System 3000.

The CTS-3000 with its many new features provides an exceptional experience not found in other Telepresence offerings:

- Three native 1080p high-definition cameras

- Three 65-inch high-definition plasma displays

- Purpose-built meeting table with integrated lighting shroud

- Multichannel wide-band spatial audio

Image Courtesy of Cisco Systems, Inc. Unauthorized use not permitted.

Figure 2-5   *Cisco TelePresence System 3000*

Three Native 1080p High-Definition Cameras

The CTS-3000 provides native 1080p resolution at 30fps, providing the best video quality of any Telepresence system on the market today. Each CTS-3000 is fitted with three native 1080p cameras, in a cluster, above the center display. As mentioned previously, these cameras are fixed with no moving parts.

Each camera is tuned to capture a section (segment) of the CTS-3000 table, providing consistent color and depth for all images in the room. Each CTS-3000 contains three segments, where each segment is defined as one camera and one display. Using three fixed cameras enables the CTS-3000 to be viewed remotely as it is in real life. From the remote view, a CTS-3000 system provides a continuous view across all three table segments. For example, if a local participant extends an arm from one camera's focal range to another, remote participants see the arm across two displays as if they were in the same room. Each CTS-3000 supports four video channels, one for each of the three TelePresence segments and a fourth used for sharing presentations or an auxiliary video source between TelePresence systems. Figure 2-6 illustrates a top-down view of the focal range for all three cameras/segments.

Three 65-Inch High-Definition Plasma Displays

Maintaining life-size images is key to creating an immersive in-person experience. The CTS-3000 provides three 65-inch, 1080p, plasma displays, allowing all participants to be viewed in life size, each display accommodating two participants.

Cisco provides all system displays and includes enhancements and software to improve overall display performance not found in off-the-shelf displays. The TelePresence codec

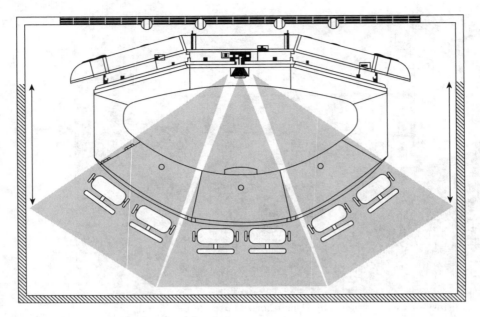

Figure 2-6   *CTS-3000 camera focal view*

manages displays, providing informational status and administrative control for each display. Additionally, system displays can be placed in standby mode when the system is not used or configured to turn off during nonbusiness hours to save power and minimize heat.

Purpose-Built Meeting Table, Integrated Projector, and Lighting Shroud

The CTS-3000 includes a purpose-built meeting table, integrated projector, and lighting shroud. Maintaining a consistent user experience is paramount to the success of any TelePresence deployment. Without this consistency, replicating a face-to-face meeting is nearly impossible.

The CTS-3000's arched table design, extending to both outer displays, is half of the virtual table. This design provides the illusion of a continuous table when two CTS-3000\3200 systems connect in a call, providing a feeling that all users are gathered around the same table in the same room. Strategically positioned table legs help keep meeting participants in their respective segment and within camera view. Table seams are also aligned with the camera field of view, providing a second reference point for meeting participants.

The CTS-3000 table legs not only provide users with a reference point for seating positions, but also supply power and Ethernet connections for participants in a TelePresence meeting. A total of six power connections and six Ethernet ports are available on each CTS-3000 table.

An integrated high-definition projection system is also included with the CTS-3000 for viewing shared presentations, videos, and so on. The projection system is mounted under the center table segment, projecting its image onto the white screen below the center display. Displaying the content under the center display enables meeting participants to easily view content without shifting seating positions or having to look up or off to one side of the room.

Integrated lighting eliminates shadows on the faces of meeting participants. An integrated lighting shroud above and around the sides of the system displays provides key (front) lighting, eliminating shadows caused by fill (overhead) lighting. Key lighting is crucial to a natural experience and is often overlooked in other telepresence systems and high-end video conferencing rooms. Without the lighting shroud, specialized fixtures would be required to provide consistent lighting and eliminate shadows on meeting participants. The design of the lighting shroud gives off the exact amount of light required to reduce shadows without over lighting the faces of participants. You can find more detailed information about room lighting in Chapter 8, "TelePresence Room Design."

Multichannel Wide-Band Audio

Wide-band, full-duplex, spatial audio provides a user experience not found in other telepresence systems. The CTS-3000 provides four separate audio channels:

- Three wide-band AAC-LD channels used for TelePresence participants
- One G.711/G.722 channel that adds in audio-only participants or provides audio associated with document sharing (auto-collaborate)

Each CTS-3000 has three microphones and three speakers, one for each table segment. Speakers are located directly under each display, allowing audio to emanate from the segment of the active speaker, naturally drawing the attention of participants to the person speaking. If the fourth audio channel is added to a call, its audio is mixed and played out all three speakers. This allows the audio add-in to be heard across all table segments without drawing attention to one segment of the system.

Cisco TelePresence System 3200

The CTS-3200 was released in mid-2008, providing a TelePresence system for up to 18 meeting participants. The CTS-3200 system is essentially a CTS-3000 with a second row of seating and additional components for additional meeting participants. This design provides consistency, giving users the same look and feel whether they are in a CTS-3000 room or a CTS-3200 room.

As Figure 2-7 shows, much of the CTS-3200 system is similar to the CTS-3000; however, the following changes have been made to accommodate the additional meeting participants:

- Extended camera focal view
- Second row seating
- Extension of each table segment
- Optional displays for shared content

Image Courtesy of Cisco Systems, Inc. Unauthorized use not permitted.

Figure 2-7   *CTS-3200*

Extended Camera Focal View

As mentioned previously, the CTS-3000 cameras are tuned to capture a segment of a CTS-3000; however, the lenses in the CTS-3000 system don't provide the focal depth needed for a CTS-3200 with its second row of participants. The CTS-3200 uses the same camera cluster as the CTS-3000, but the actual lenses in the camera are different. This allows the deeper focal depth required to capture the second row of participants.

Cameras for the CTS-3200 are still fixed with no moving parts but must maintain consistency of focus and color for two rows of participants without having noticeable parallax at the back of the room.

Second Row Seating

A second row of seating is added to the CTS-3200, providing seating for up to 12 additional meeting participants. The rear table for a CTS-3200 supports two different configurations depending on room size and customer requirements.

The CTS-3200 can be configured for a total of 12 seats in the second row for rooms with a minimum width of 31 feet or for 8 seats in rooms with a minimum width of 21 feet. The ability to configure the CTS-3200 for different size rooms helps customers address their specific needs for large TelePresence rooms. This flexibility also enables customers to easily convert a CTS-3000 to a CTS-3200, assuming the current room dimensions meet the minimum CTS-3200 requirements. Chapter 8, "TelePesence Room Design," covers room requirements in greater detail.

The second table row also contains additional microphones. Audio from the second row microphones is mixed with the front row microphones, preserving the spatial audio of the system. Audio bandwidth requirements for the CTS-3200 are the same for as the CTS-3000 with the six additional system microphones mixed into three existing audio channels.

It is also worth noting that the second row of seating added for the CTS-3200 is not elevated. This enables the CTS-3200 to be installed in a conference room with a standard 8-foot ceiling instead of requiring a 10-foot plus ceiling to accommodate a raised back row of seating. Having to raise ceilings in rooms makes consistent lighting across all participants a challenge and drives the cost of room remediation up substantially.

Extension of Each Table Segment

To maintain the natural feeling of being in the same room, table segments in the first row of the CTS-3200 extend to the back row. This extends the spatial audio to the second row seating, keeping interaction among all participants as natural as possible.

Depending on the configuration of the CTS-3200, the back table contains an additional 4 or 6 microphones covering all three segments. If the room is set up for 12 seats in the back row, 6 microphones cover the 12 participants. The directional microphones attached to the table are positioned to capture audio from 2 participants. Audio from all microphones in a segment is mixed by the CTS codec and sent out, allowing interaction from multiple participants, in the same segment, as if everyone were in the same room. Figure 2-8 illustrates the CTS-3200 table designs.

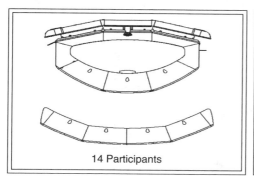
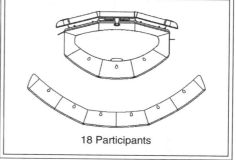

14 Participants   18 Participants

Figure 2-8   *CTS-3200 table layout*

When viewing a CTS-3200 from a remote TelePresence system, all participants in the front and back row of a segment will be viewed on a single display. Participants in the front row will be life-size, while the participants in the second row will be slightly smaller, as they would be in person, due to their distance from the cameras.

Optional Displays for Shared Content

As with the CTS-3000, the CTS-3200 comes with a high-definition projection system that mounts under the center segment of the front table. The projected image works well for participants seated at the front table. However, participants seated at the rear table cannot see the projected video from their seating positions.

The CTS-3200 allows for up to three additional auxiliary displays, supporting the fourth video channel, used for shared presentations. Many customers choose to mount one display directly above the center system display and one off to each side of the CTS-3200 for easy viewing for all participants. A list of the latest supported auxiliary displays can be found in the latest CTS-3200 documentation.

Cisco TelePresence System 1000

The CTS-1000 was released at the time of the initial TelePresence launch and focused on addressing small conference rooms. The CTS-1000 is designed to support two participants. The goal of the CTS-1000 is to provide the same audio and video quality found in the CTS-3000 for small conference rooms. The CTS-1000 consists of the following:

- One native 1080p high-definition camera
- One 65-inch high-definition plasma display
- Integrated lighting shroud
- One wideband audio microphone and speaker

Unlike the CTS-3000 and CTS-3200, the table for a CTS-1000 is not included with the system. The CTS-1000 is designed to fit in a multipurpose room, accommodating different customer table preferences. Figure 2-9 shows a CTS-1000 system.

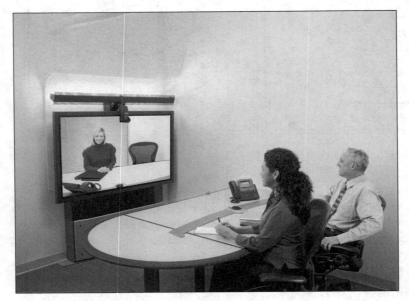

Image Courtesy of Cisco Systems, Inc. Unauthorized use not permitted.

Figure 2-9   *CTS-1000*

One Native 1080p High-Definition Camera

The CTS-1000 uses the same 1080p high-definition camera used in the CTS-3000, providing native 1080p video in a small form factor. The camera is mounted in the center of the plasma display, extending just below the bezel to provide optimal eye contact. As with the CTS-3000, the camera has no moving parts and is tuned to capture up to two meeting participants, the equivalent of a single table segment on a CTS-3000 or CTS-3200.

One 65-Inch High-Definition Plasma Display

The CTS-1000 uses a single 65-inch high-definition plasma, providing two life-size images at 1080p resolution. The CTS-1000 uses the same plasma display that is used for the CTS-3000 and CTS-3200. A CTS-1000 is capable of displaying video from a CTS-1000, CTS-500, or a single segment from a CTS-3000 or CTS-3200. If a CTS-1000 connects directly to a CTS-3000 or CTS-3200, CTS-1000 participants see the active segment of the remote system. Video from the CTS-3000 or CTS-3200 will be switched as participants in the different segments speak, allowing CTS-1000 participants to see the segment of the current speaker on the remote system. The participants on the CTS-3000 or CTS-3200 view the CTS-1000 on their center display, at all times, while the two outer displays remain inactive. If multiple CTS-1000 systems are in a multipoint meeting with a CTS-3000 or CTS-3200, the CTS-1000's will be distributed across the CTS-3000 segments.

The CTS-1000 does not include a projection system for displaying shared documents; however, the CTS-1000 supports either presentation-in-picture or an optional LCD display for viewing shared documents.

Presentation-in-picture provides the ability to view shared documents in the lower left, center, or right side of the display. Meeting participants can select the position of the presentation-in-picture using the 7975 Series IP Phone interface. When a CTS-1000 is not in a call, the primary display can be used for displaying content locally from any PC. A user simply connects a PC to the VGA cable, used for sharing documents, and the PC is displayed on the 65" plasma.

Viewing shared content on an auxiliary display is also supported, providing a larger viewing area for shared content. An auxiliary display connects to the CTS codec, and all shared content displays on the auxiliary display automatically disabling presentation-in-picture. A list of supported auxiliary displays can be found in the latest CTS-1000 documentation.

Integrated Lighting Shroud

As with the CTS-3000 and CTS-3200, the CTS-1000 provides an integrated lighting shroud. The lighting shroud attaches above the display, providing proper key lighting for meeting participants and eliminating shadows from fill lighting. As described previously, fill lighting is required to eliminate facial shadows and provide the consistent lighting found in the larger room systems.

One Wide-band Microphone and Speaker

The CTS-1000 has a single wideband microphone and speaker that provides the same high-quality audio found in the CTS-3000 and CTS-3200. The microphone is placed on the table used for the CTS-1000 while the speaker is integrated into the CTS-1000 system enclosure. Each CTS-1000 supports two audio channels. The primary audio channel is for meeting participants, while the second is used for adding audio-only participants or audio associated with shared documents. Both audio channels are mixed by the codec and sent to the remote TelePresence system over a single connection.

Cisco TelePresence System 500

At the time this book was written, the CTS-500 was the latest TelePresence system released targeting personal and shared space use. The CTS-500 is designed to support one participant in a home or executive office while providing the same high-quality video and audio experience in the larger Cisco TelePresence systems. The CTS-500 is also a perfect fit for shared locations, providing kiosk services or specialized agent support. The CTS-500 consists of the following items:

- One native 1080p high-definition camera

- One 37-inch high-definition LCD display

- Integrated lighting shroud

- Integrated wideband microphone and speaker

- Multiple configuration options

Similar to the CTS-1000, no furniture is supplied with the CTS-500. As mentioned, the CTS-500 is designed for an executive or home office, allowing customers to utilize existing office furniture. Figure 2-10 shows a CTS-500 system configured on a free-standing pedestal.

One Native 1080p High-Definition Camera

The CTS-500 uses the same camera technology as the larger Cisco TelePresence systems, providing the same high-quality 1080p video. The CTS-500 camera has no moving parts and is tuned for a small office environment. Providing a camera with no moving parts in a personal system ensures the same quality image and consistent experience as larger TelePresence systems.

One 37-Inch High-Definition LCD Display

The display provided with the CTS-500 is sized to fit a home or executive office. The 37-inch LCD display provides a high-quality 1080p image equivalent to video in the larger Cisco TelePresence systems. It isn't possible to provide life-size images on a 37-inch display, so remote participants are optimally sized for the CTS-500 display, providing the best possible user experience.

Image Courtesy of Cisco Systems, Inc. Unauthorized use not permitted.

Figure 2-10   *CTS-500*

The CTS-500 display provides the same presentation-in-picture feature or optional auxiliary display for viewing shared content as the CTS-1000, allowing users to view shared content in a window on the system display or full screen on an auxiliary display.

A new feature available with the CTS-500 is the capability to integrate Cisco Digital Media Signage (DMS). The CTS-500 display provides a second HDMI port that can be used to provide video to the display when the system is not in a TelePresence call. Integration with Cisco DMS makes the CTS-500 a perfect fit for a virtual agent and other shared-space applications. Full integration of the system display enables the CTS codec to switch display inputs based on the status of the system. If the system is not in a call, the system plays video from a Cisco DMS. When a TelePresence call is placed or received, the system automatically switches inputs and shows the TelePresence call.

As with the larger Cisco TelePresence systems, the CTS-500 display completely integrates with the TelePresence system, thus allowing the TelePresence system to manage video inputs, provide display firmware updates, and provide display status. The importance of integrating system displays into personal systems is often overlooked. The number one reason is reliability; something as simple as the display setting input can make the difference between a successful or failed call. If a user places a call and the display input is not properly set or powered off, the user will likely get frustrated and use a phone for a voice-only call. This sounds like a simple issue, but this type of issue has plagued video conferencing for years.

Integrated Lighting Shroud

As with all Cisco TelePresence Systems, an integrated lighting shroud is included with the CTS-500, providing the proper key lighting, eliminating facial shadows, and improving overall office lighting. Considering most CTS-500s go into personal offices with little or no change to room lighting, the integrated lighting becomes even a bigger factor to provide consistent lighting for meeting participants.

Integrated Wideband Microphone and Speaker

Unlike larger Cisco TelePresence systems that use table microphones, the CTS-500 has an integrated microphone. CTS-500 users sit within four to six feet of the system, enabling the use of an integrated microphone mounted at the bottom of the system display. Integrating the microphone also eliminates desktop microphones that might be covered by paperwork and cause clutter on the desk.

Speakers are also integrated into the CTS-500 system and mounted at the top of the system display on both sides of the native 1080p high-definition camera.

Multiple Configuration Options

Because the CTS-500 system is designed for a home or executive office, it is important that users have options when it comes to placement and configuration of the system. The following three configuration options enable the CTS-500 to fit into any office configuration while providing the immersive experience users have grown accustom to with Cisco TelePresence:

- **Freestanding pedestal:** Provides a standalone configuration allowing the CTS-500 to be placed against a wall without any furniture required to house the codec or wall mount for the system display. The pedestal mount is height-adjustable, providing flexibility for different room and individual requirements.

- **Desktop:** Provides a stand for the system display so that it can be placed on the desk with the codec housed under or behind the desk.

- **Wall mount:** Allows the system display to be mounted, on the wall, above the desk with the codec housed under or behind the desk.

Figure 2-11 shows the mounting options for a CTS-500.

> **Note**   At press time, Cisco TelePresence supported the three endpoints described above. However, Cisco has additional endpoints and new features planned to address customer needs.

Cisco Unified Communications Manager

Cisco Unified Communications Manager (CUCM) is the foundation of the Cisco TelePresence solution, providing centralized configuration, management, and call routing for all CTS endpoints. Cisco TelePresence is an integrated component of the Cisco Unified

Desktop

Pedestal

Wall Mount

Image Courtesy of Cisco Systems, Inc. Unauthorized use not permitted.

Figure 2-11 *CTS-500 mounting options*

Communications portfolio that continues to offer new and exciting communications applications. CUCM runs some of the largest IP telephony deployments in the world, supporting 99.999 percent availability and providing a stable and feature-rich platform to work from.

Configuration and management of CTS endpoints is made simple, leveraging existing methodologies and technologies used to deploy Cisco IP Telephony today. As far as CUCM is concerned, a CTS endpoint is just another SIP device. CTS endpoints are configured and upgraded no differently than a Cisco IP Phone, providing a consistent interface across Cisco communication devices. Using CUCM for Cisco TelePresence enables current Cisco IP Telephony customers to integrate Cisco TelePresence into their existing CUCM infrastructure while applying existing knowledge to a new technology.

CUCM also provides advanced call routing and *Call Admission Control (CAC)* for Cisco TelePresence. Unlike other telepresence systems that rely on gatekeepers for these features, Cisco TelePresence leverages a true IP PBX. This allows PBX features to be applied to TelePresence endpoints, providing advanced call processing features. Leveraging CUCM also allows Cisco TelePresence to use additional applications that are integrated with CUCM, such as Unity for busy/no answer call handling and Cisco Unified Contact Center. A good example of this integration is the Cisco Expert on Demand solution, which provides customers access to virtual experts through TelePresence systems. Users walk up to a CTS-1000 or CTS-500, use the 7975 Series IP Phone touch screen to dial, and CUCM routes the call to the Cisco Unified Contact Center that provides call center features for the TelePresence solution. This is the first of many solutions and features that will be implemented for Cisco TelePresence using the Cisco suite of integrated collaboration applications.

Using CUCM as the platform for Cisco TelePresence also provides a highly reliable platform. As mentioned previously, CUCM provides five 9s reliability and is currently running some of the largest IP telephony networks in the world. In fact, the base code for CUCM (Cisco Voice Operating System) is used for both the Cisco TelePresence Manager and Cisco TelePresence Multipoint Switch.

Cisco TelePresence Manager

Cisco TelePresence Manager (CTS-Manager) is the heart of the TelePresence solution, providing integration for all Cisco TelePresence components. CTS-Manager is a server-based platform with a web user interface providing the same look and feel as other TelePresence components. The CTS-Manager ties all TelePresence components together, providing the ease of use, scheduling, and management services that drive the entire solution. The CTS-Manager is not a mandatory component of Cisco TelePresence, but as you can see, deploying a TelePresence network without it provides substantial challenges. CTS-Manager provides the following features to the Cisco TelePresence Solution:

- Calendaring integration and management

- One-Button-to-Push meeting access

- Resource and location management for Cisco TelePresence Multipoint switch

- CTS system management and reporting

- Concierge services

Calendaring Integration and Management

CTS-Manager integrates with Microsoft Exchange and IBM Domino, providing scheduling for Cisco TelePresence systems. A simple scheduling interface is always a challenge for any shared resource. Cisco TelePresence addresses this issue by providing users with a familiar Outlook or Notes scheduling interface. TelePresence rooms are listed as resources and scheduled exactly the same as standard conference rooms, eliminating the learning curve for scheduling Cisco TelePresence rooms.

One-Button-to-Push Meeting Access

When the initial research was conducted for Cisco TelePresence, the biggest complaint with existing video systems was ease of use. Users complained about remote controls, complicated custom touchpad dialing interfaces, and the lack of consistency from system to system. Some customers employ large video scheduling groups to manage systems and automatically launch video calls to avoid any user confusion. Some customers even go as far as providing a meeting coordinator in the room just in case something goes wrong during the call setup. At that time it was decided that initiating a call from a Cisco TelePresence system would be *easier* than dialing a phone. Figure 2-12 show the 7975 Series IP Phone screen with One-Button-to-Push entries.

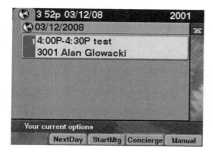

Figure 2-12   *7975 Series IP Phone One-Button-to-Push*

What's simpler than providing users with a touchscreen phone that allows them to touch the meeting instance on the phone screen to initiate their calls? This feature is referred to as One-Button-to-Push dialing. Users have the option to manually dial using the phone for last-minute ad-hoc meetings; however, prescheduled meetings present users with One-Button-to-Push dialing. This feature alone has allowed Cisco to deploy more than 350 TelePresence systems internally, providing more than 4000 meetings a week, with a scheduling support staff of only seven people. Figure 2-13 illustrates the process of scheduling a meeting that provides One-Button-to-Push dialing.

Resource and Location Management for Cisco TelePresence Multipoint Switch

As described previously, CTS-Manager provides the scheduling integration for a Cisco TelePresence deployment. Scheduled multipoint meetings require knowledge of available resources and the location of those resources. CTS-Manager maintains CTMS resource information in its internal database, enabling it to schedule multipoint meetings accurately. Each CTMS is configured to report its location and number of schedulable segments to the CTS-Manager, enabling it to schedule multipoint resources based on available segments and location. When the CTS-Manager receives a request for a scheduled meeting with more than two CTS systems, it first checks the location of each CTS system and determines the most appropriate CTMS. After a CTMS has been chosen, the CTS-Manager checks for available CTMS resources for the requested date and time; if there are resources available, CTS-Manager schedules the meeting and pushes the meeting information to the CTMS. If there are no available resources on the first CTMS, the CTS-Manger works its way through the list of CTMSs until it finds available resources for the meeting.

The CTS-Manager also provides administrators with the ability to centrally view the status of all deployed CTMSs through its web-based interface. You can also use the web interface to manage all scheduled multipoint meetings and move all scheduled meetings from a failed CTMS to a backup if a CTMS failure occurs.

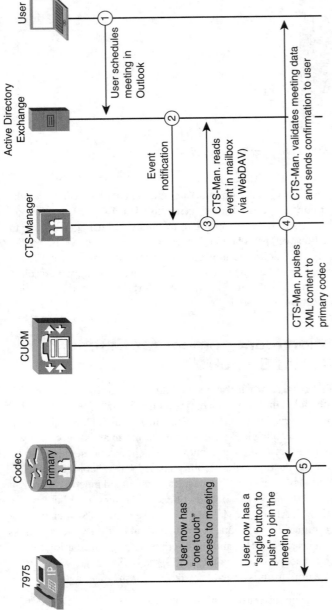

Figure 2-13 *Scheduling example for One-Button-to-Push*

CTS System Management and Reporting

CTS-Manager provides a central view of all CTS systems and CTMS devices. Administrators can quickly view the status of all CTS endpoints from a single web page and determine if a problem is on a CTS system itself or its communication with another solution component. The CTS-Manager provides a number of categories and error states that display for each CTS system. The categories are as follows:

- **Connectivity:** Provides CTS and phone registration status with CUCM and CTS-Manager to CTS communication

- **Cisco TelePresence System:** Provides CTS error status

- **Cisco Unified Communication Manager:** Verification of room profile and email address configuration in CUCM

- **Microsoft Exchange:** Verification of CTS-Manager mailbox subscription and calendar synchronization for each room

CTS-Manager also provides administrators a view of all scheduled meetings and the ability to export scheduled meeting data to a *.tsv* file that can be used for billing and usage reports.

Concierge Services

Concierge services are available with the Cisco TelePresence solution, allowing users to quickly connect, at any time, through audio or video, to a live person that can help with any question or issues the users might have. Providing one-button access to live assistance helps maintain system reliability by providing answers to users' questions and quickly addresses any system or network issue. Using the CTS-Manager web interface, concierges can be defined and assigned to each CTS system. The concierge configuration is then pushed to the CTS system providing a soft key on the 7975 Series IP Phone for direct concierge connection.

Concierge services are supported using video-only or audio-only connections. If video concierge is implemented, users can always connect to the concierge using video, even if a video call is in progress. For example, if a user is in a TelePresence call and experiences issues or has a question, he or she simply pushes the concierge softkey, the original TelePresence call is placed on hold, and a second TelePresence call is placed to the concierge. After the question has been answered, the call to the concierge is ended, and the original call is resumed.

If concierge services support audio-only and a user selects the concierge softkey during a video call, the video call is placed on hold while the concierge is connected. If the CTS dialing the concierge does not have an audio add-in connected to the active meeting, the user has the option to add the concierge into the meeting.

Cisco TelePresence Multipoint Switch

Today, multipoint capability is a required component for any collaborative application. More than 40 percent of today's meetings consist of individuals from three or more sites. The Cisco TelePresence Multipoint Switch provides this functionality, allowing TelePresence meetings to expand beyond two TelePresence systems. However, it is important that multipoint devices don't compromise the overall experience by adding excessive delay resulting in unnatural user interaction. Cisco developed the CTMS from the ground up to specifically address user experience while maintaining the overall ease of use. The CTMS is also a key component in providing interoperability with non-TelePresence video systems allowing non-TelePresence systems to participate in TelePresence meetings.

The Cisco TelePresence Multipoint Switch is a server-based platform with capacity for up to 48 segments in a single meeting or spread across multiple meetings. Unlike with traditional Multipoint Control Units (MCU), features such as transcoding have been avoided to minimize delay. With its software switching architecture, the CTMS introduces very little delay, ~10ms, into each TelePresence multipoint meeting helping maintain the natural experience found in point-to-point meetings. Voice-activated switching determines which site, or segment, displays on CTS systems in a multipoint meeting. Traditional video conferencing MCUs provide two display options for multipoint meetings; voice-activated switching, which displays the active site on all systems in a meeting; and continuous presence, which provides a continuous view of multiple sites on each system. To maintain the in-person experience, the CTMS does not provide a continuous presence option for multipoint meetings. However, with the addition of three-screen systems, two switching modes are available:

- Room-based switching, which displays the entire room on all remote systems

- Speaker switching, which allows each segment to be switched independently

Figure 2-14 shows a basic example of the two switching modes.

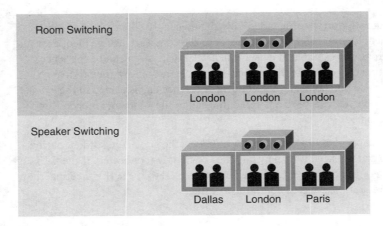

Figure 2-14 *CTMS switching modes*

Figure 2-14 provides a basic illustration of what is displayed in a CTS-3000 or CTS-3200 for both switching modes in a three-site multipoint call. As shown in the room switching example, participants always see a single room on their displays, while in speaker switching, it is possible for participants to see a segment from each site or any combination based on the active segments. Room and speaker switching are explained in greater detail in Chapter 13, "Multipoint TelePresence Design."

The CTMS is an integrated component of the overall Cisco TelePresence solution designed to provide multipoint telepresence meetings while maintaining a consistent user experience. Integration with the overall telepresence system enables users to book multipoint meetings, choose meeting preferences, and control meeting options during a call using the 7975 Series IP Phone in the telepresence room. This integration also allows the CTMS to communicate directly with the CTS system, providing end of meeting notifications and other relevant information to users during the meeting. The CTMS also communicates directly with CTS-Manager, providing its available resources, receiving scheduled meeting information, and providing system status.

As mentioned above, the CTMS is an integral part of the interoperability solution provided by Cisco TelePresence. Interoperability with existing video conferencing systems is an important feature allowing video conferencing systems to participate in Cisco TelePresence meetings. At press time, interoperability between telepresence vendors is limited because of the implementation of video standards and complexities with multiscreen Telepresence systems. The goal for Cisco TelePresence interoperability is to provide a solution that plugs into video conferencing deployments with as little change to the existing environment as possible while interoperating with >90 percent of the existing video systems on the market. For this reason, a simple solution providing a cascade link between the CTMS and the Cisco Unified Video Conferencing (CUVC) MCU is used. This model enables telepresence meetings to be scheduled using Outlook or Notes and initiated using One-Button-to-Push, whereas non-telepresence video systems use their current method of dialing to access the meeting. Figure 2-15 illustrates a view of interoperability.

Note At the time this book was written, additional interoperability solutions were being investigated, providing support for optional interoperability solutions.

Cisco TelePresence Inter-Company

Providing a true in-person virtual meeting experience within the enterprise enables customers to reduce travel and improve productivity. However, extending the virtual meeting experience beyond a local enterprise provides businesses additional benefits, enabling them to meet with partners and customers. For any collaboration tool to reach its full potential, it must extend beyond the boundaries of a single enterprise. However, there are always challenges providing collaboration tools that extend from one company's network to another. With today's focus on security, and the different security policies implemented by companies, the challenges continue to grow.

The Cisco TelePresence Inter-Company architecture provides a secure intercompany solution for Cisco TelePresence. Following this architecture, service providers are building out

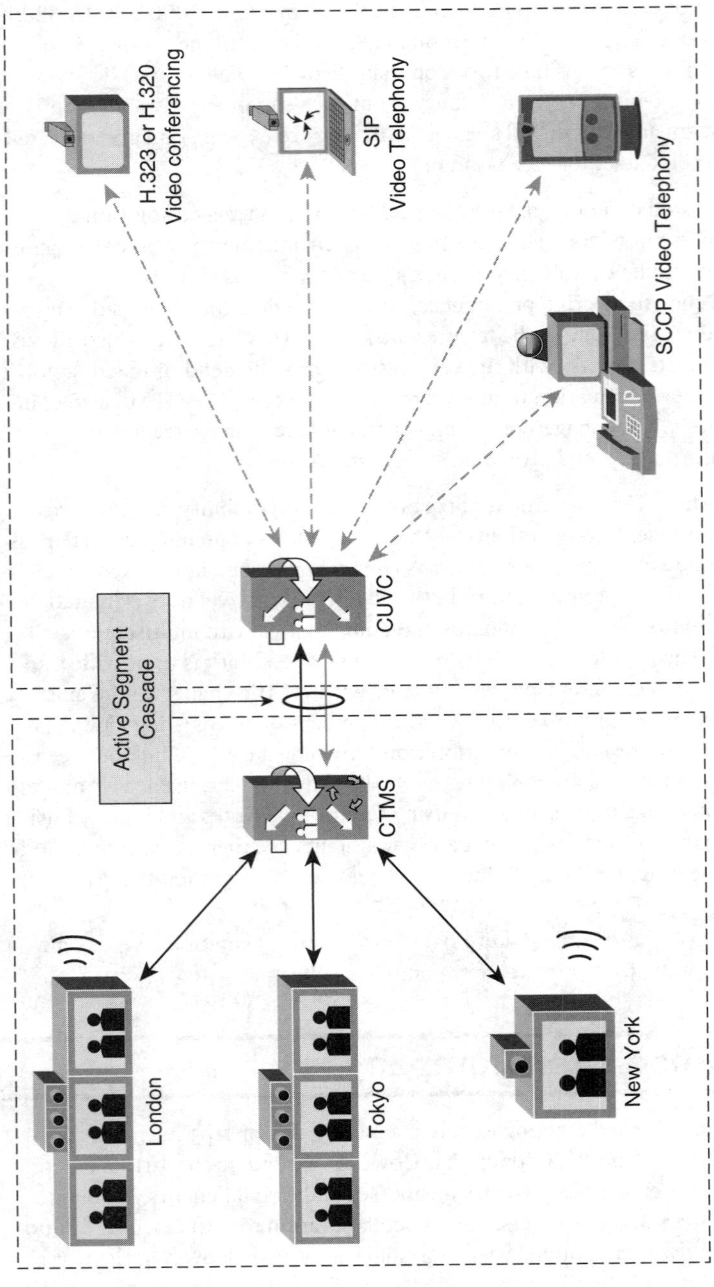

Figure 2-15 *CTMS interoperability*

and offering Cisco TelePresence solutions. These solutions also provide customers with options for different deployment scenarios depending on which provider is used. Some providers offer customers the option to connect their existing Cisco TelePresence deployment into their Cisco TelePresence Inter-Company network, whereas other carriers provide managed or hosted Cisco TelePresence deployments as well. Advanced services are available with these intercompany offerings providing concierge services, multipoint services for intercompany meetings, and scheduling for intercompany meetings, providing the simplicity of One-Button-to-Push dialing for end users.

Another area of growth is public Cisco TelePresence suites that provide added benefit to customers with intercompany connectivity. Public Cisco TelePresence suites allow customers to conduct TelePresence meetings with employees on the road, customers or partners without Cisco TelePresence deployments, or interviews with potential employees. These public suites are available to anyone and are usually rented by the hour, allowing connectivity to any TelePresence system on the Inter-Company network.

Cisco TelePresence Inter-Company will continue to expand offering new services and features, dramatically expanding the reach of TelePresence. The Cisco TelePresence offering continues to add features for providers, allowing them to expand their secure TelePresence Inter-Company network while continuing to offer additional advance services. Chapter 14, "Inter-Company TelePresence Design," provides an in-depth look at the overall secure Inter-Company architecture.

Operation, Administration, and Monitoring

Providing management and operational support for TelePresence deployments is a prime concern for every TelePresence customer. In most cases, CXO-level executives frequent TelePresence rooms, bringing a high-visibility level to the solution. As we know, executives at this level have high expectations and expect things to work. A number of tools are available for customers looking to manage a TelePresence deployment.

As discussed previously, Cisco TelePresence is composed of numerous components and layers, including endpoints, servers, network infrastructure, scheduling for rooms and how users interact with the scheduling tools. Inherent management capabilities are built into the products, and also a number of Cisco network management applications. Cisco network analysis modules and appliances can provide additional capabilities for monitoring and troubleshooting the overall network and the TelePresence solution.

The following TelePresence components provide management for the Cisco TelePresence Solution:

- **Cisco TelePresence System Administration:** Each Cisco TelePresence component provides an administrative interface that allows configuration, troubleshooting, and management.

- **Cisco Unified Communications Manager:** Provides endpoint configuration and firmware management along with dial plan and call routing management.

- **Cisco TelePresence Manager:** Allows monitoring and status of all CTS endpoints and a view of all past, present, and future scheduled TelePresence meetings.

CTS-Manager also provides a centralized view of all CTMS devices and global resource management of multipoint resources.

- **Cisco TelePresence Multipoint Switch:** Provides CTMS configuration, CTMS troubleshooting, and real-time statistics for multipoint meetings.

- **Microsoft Active Directory and Microsoft Exchange/IBM Domino:** Manages accounts, mailboxes, and permissions for CTS-Manager and the rooms in which the CTS endpoints reside.

- **Microsoft Outlook/Lotus Notes:** Where both users and administrators view the availability of the rooms and schedule meetings.

As you have seen throughout this chapter, different components of the Cisco TelePresence solution provide different levels of management for the overall system. The core management components for the solution are the CTS-Manager and CUCM.

CTS-Manager is the core management tool providing centralized management for all TelePresence components and scheduled meetings. The CTS-Manager provides management through CLI or web-based administration. Administrators use the web-based interface for viewing status of all CTS devices, CTMS devices, calendaring integration, and scheduled meetings. This centralized view enables administrators to quickly identify issues with any component of the Cisco TelePresence system. Utilizing the CTS-Manager administrators or concierges can manage all aspects of scheduled meetings, such as editing meeting options, monitoring the status of a scheduled meeting, or gathering call detail records (CDR) for billing purposes. CTS-Manager also supports Simple Network Management Protocol (SNMP), allowing traps to be sent to a management system and providing alerts for system administrators.

The Cisco TelePresence systems also provide a command-line interface (CLI) or web-based management interface that enables you to connect directly or link from the CTS-Manager, providing detailed information for the CTS device. As mentioned in previous chapters, the CTS management interface provides status for all system components including the codec, system displays, cameras, projector, speakers, and microphones. This enables administrators to quickly access system health and gather call statistics for troubleshooting potential network issues. SNMP is also supported, allowing traps to be sent to a management system providing system administrators with alerts regarding potential system or network issues.

The CTMS also provides a CLI and web-based administration that is similar to both the CTS-Manager and CTS. As with the CTS, the CTMS management page can be accessed directly or linked to from the CTS-Manager. The CTMS management interface provides administrators with the ability to manage all aspects of multipoint meetings. Meeting administrators have the ability launch and monitor multipoint meetings, providing in-meeting support for TelePresence users requesting changes during a multipoint meeting.

CUCM provides another level of management for the TelePresence components and CTS devices in particular. All configuration and firmware management for CTS devices is managed using CUCM. CTS devices are managed through CUCM using the same methodologies currently used for Cisco telephony devices. CUCM also provides CDRs for all calls placed to and from CTS endpoints.

Looking at the different components, you can see that each component provides a different level of management. However, a hierarchical management structure is in place for managing and troubleshooting TelePresence components using the CTS-Manager.

Related TelePresence Services

Before the public release of Cisco TelePresence, Cisco had already deployed ~20 systems internally and early field trials at multiple customers. During that time it was evident that a process needed to be put in place to ensure the success of every TelePresence deployment. From its early days in IP telephony, Cisco learned that deployment of new mission-critical applications could prove painful if not done correctly. For this reason, a set of processes were put in place to help ensure the success of every Cisco TelePresence deployment.

The last thing Cisco wanted was to ship TelePresence to customers and have the systems deployed in rooms with poor environmentals or on networks not capable of meeting the required Service-Level Agreements (SLA). This would guarantee poor satisfaction among new customers, ultimately following in the footsteps of past video conferencing solutions. A process outlining Planning, Design, and Implementation (PDI) was crafted, covering all aspects of room enviromentals and network readiness. This process starts before TelePresence units ship and is completed after the TelePresence rooms have been installed. To date, this process has proved invaluable, yielding some of the highest customer satisfaction levels for a new product ever seen at Cisco. With this satisfaction has come tremendous customer adoption, making Cisco TelePresence one of the fastest growing solutions in company history.

Along with the PDI process, Cisco introduced two TelePresence service offerings—Cisco TelePresence Essential Operate Service and Cisco TelePresence Select Operate and TelePresence Remote Assistance Service. These offerings provide customers with confidence that their TelePresence networks will provide the highest availability possible.

Cisco TelePresence Planning, Design, and Implementation

The PDI process provides a consistent method of deploying Cisco TelePresence that gets guaranteed results. Some view this process as rigid and unnecessary, but the results speak for themselves. As previously described, replicating a face-to-face meeting requires the proper room environment and a network designed to provide the appropriate service levels to ensure video and audio integrity. The PDI process consists of the following five steps:

Step 1.   Prequalification

Step 2.   Assessment

Step 3.   Product Shipment

Step 4.   Installation

Step 5.   Certification

Note The PDI process is designed for larger TelePresence systems, CTS-3200 and CTS-3000, but still is applied in part to CTS-1000 and CTS-500 systems. The CTS-1000 and CTS-500 are designed for shared conference room and office space, therefore, relaxing the overall room requirements. However, network requirements assessments remain the same for the CTS-1000 and CTS-500.

Step 1: Prequalification

Prequalification is required for all components of a Cisco TelePresence deployment, including the CTS-1000 and CTS-500. The Prequalification consists of a high-level checklist for the room, environment, and network. This process is often completed by interviewing the customer and helping identify any obvious issues with room size, location, or network deficiencies. One challenge that is often encountered is securing a dedicated room for a CTS-3000 or CTS-3200 with the proper size and or design. The prequalification helps ensure that the room is a good candidate before sending someone out to the location to perform a *Room Readiness Assessment (RRA)*.

Step 2: Assessment

The Assessment phase is critical, providing customers the assurance that they are ready for a TelePresence deployment. Any TelePresence system is a substantial investment. Deploying a TelePresence system without evaluating environmental and network readiness is a recipe for failure.

The assessment phase provides detailed information about room and network readiness for a Cisco TelePresence deployment. The first step in the assessment phase is to perform RRAs for each CTS-3000 and CTS-3200 room. The RRA provides details regarding existing size, lighting and acoustics for each room, and recommended remediation the rooms might require.

The second step is a *Network Path Assessment (NPA)*, which provides an end-to-end view of the network between Cisco TelePresence devices. During the process, service levels are gathered between each location, network QoS policy is evaluated, and network hardware is evaluated. This data allows recommendations regarding overall network and QoS policies to be made during the process.

Step 3: Product Shipment

When the assessment phase is complete and the customer agrees to any remediations required to meet room or network requirements, product is released for shipment. At this point, project planners work with customers to firm up dates for system installation and final deployment details.

Step 4: Installation

At the time of installation, it is recommended that all room and network remediation be complete. Cisco TelePresence installations are performed by a trained *Authorized*

Technology Partner (ATP), ensuring quality installation. CTS-3200 and CTS-3000 rooms require usually three days to four days to install, whereas a CTS-1000 or CTS-500 can be installed in less than one day.

Note   At the time of the writting of this book, the CTS-500 is the only Cisco TelePresence system that can be installed by the customer. Larger systems must be installed by an ATP.

Step 5: Certification

The last step in the PDI process is the *Cisco TelePresence certification (CTX)* for CTS-3000 and CTS-3200 rooms. A CTX is not performed on CTS-1000 or CTS-500 systems because specific room requirements do not exist for these systems. Instead, each CTS-1000 and CTS-500 is tested after installation to validate that the system is functional, cameras are properly tuned, and the SLAs for packet loss, jitter, and latency are met.

The CTX performed on a CTS-3200 or CTS-3000 room can be done locally or from a remote TelePresence system. The CTX process verifies all aspects of the room and system evaluating the workmanship of the system installation, room illumination, room acoustics, camera tuning, and network SLAs for packet loss, jitter, and latency.

When the CTX is complete, the PDI process is complete, and the system is ready to use. Again, this process has proved to be invaluable and continues to provide one happy customer after another.

Cisco TelePresence Essential Operate Service

The Cisco TelePresence Essential Operate Service was introduced to help maintain a reliable, high-quality Cisco TelePresence meeting experience and get the most from the technology investment. This service is provided by Cisco or a set of ATP partners with the expertise to support Cisco TelePresence networks, providing customers 24-hour-a-day, 365-day-a-year access to a highly trained support staff. This service provides all the required features to maintain a high-quality Cisco TelePresence deployment including minor software updates the next business day or within four hours on the same business day hardware replacement.

Cisco TelePresence Select Operate and TelePresence Remote Assistance Service

The Cisco TelePresence Select Operate Service and TelePresence Remote Assistance Service provides customers with the option of having their Cisco TelePresence deployment managed by Cisco. This allows customers to deploy Cisco TelePresence and provide the highest level of support to its customers without burdening IT groups with day-to-day management of the system. This service provides real-time monitoring and troubleshooting of all Cisco TelePresence devices and remote user assistance 24 hours a day, 365 days a year at the touch of a button. Along with monitoring and support, the service also provides Change Management and utilization and performance reporting for the Cisco TelePresence deployments.

Summary

This chapter provided an overview of the Cisco TelePresence solution components and related services. Cisco TelePresence takes a unique new approach at video communications, providing high-definition 1080p video with wide-band spatial audio. Combined with the high-quality video and audio, special attention to environmentals provides a true in-person user experience not found in other systems. Cisco also focused on providing a system that runs over existing IP networks, providing customers with deployment and management options and allowing TelePresence to reach its full potential.

All Cisco TelePresence systems are fully integrated with all system components, providing enhanced management and reliability. Everything from system displays, cameras, microphones, speakers, projectors, and lighting are managed by the Cisco TelePresence codec, enabling all components to be upgraded and managed from a single interface. Integrating components provides the assurance that simple configuration issues don't jeopardize system perception given that these simple issues plagued video conferencing systems in the past.

Along with the integration of system components, ease of use is addressed in the Cisco TelePresence solution, making the system easier to use than a phone. TelePresence users schedule meetings using existing calendaring systems and that information is used to provide One-Button-to-Push dialing for the end user. Users simply press their meeting instance on the touch screen of the 7975 Series IP Phone in the TelePresence room to initiate meetings. All system interaction is done through the touch screen on the 7975 Series IP Phone including meeting and document camera control.

The Cisco TelePresence solution includes features such as system management, meeting management, and multipoint. These integrated components provide enhanced meeting and management support not found in other systems on the market. Cisco Unified Communication Manager provides a proven platform for managing endpoint configuration and firmware while providing an integration point for other Cisco Communication platforms.

Finally, The Cisco TelePresence solution provides implementation and support packages that provide customers proven tools to make their deployments successful. At the time this book was written, Cisco had deployed over 350 rooms worldwide for its own use. Lessons learned throughout this deployment were gathered and are now used as the Planning, Design, and Implementation process for every Cisco TelePresence deployment.

Part II: Telepresence Technologies

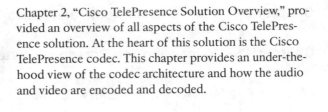

Chapter 2, "Cisco TelePresence Solution Overview," provided an overview of all aspects of the Cisco TelePresence solution. At the heart of this solution is the Cisco TelePresence codec. This chapter provides an under-the-hood view of the codec architecture and how the audio and video are encoded and decoded.

CHAPTER 3

TelePresence Audio and Video Technologies

Codec Design Requirements

When Cisco began its quest to design and build a true-to-life telepresence experience, it had a rather large obstacle to overcome. No other vendor at that time had anything that could deliver the level of video and audio quality and integrated systems approach that Cisco wanted to create. So Cisco decided to build the codec from the ground up, purpose-built to meet the following requirements:

- First, it had to deliver multiple channels of 1080p resolution video, at a consistent 30 frames per second, at extremely low encoding and decoding times and at a bandwidth utilization rate the average large enterprise customer could afford to deploy.

- Second, it had to provide multiple, full-duplex channels of wideband audio. Furthermore, those channels could not be mixed together, nor stereo (left/right), but had to be discrete, independent channels to preserve the spatiality and directionality of the audio.

- Third, to meet its ease-of-use and reliability ideals, it had to provide a fully integrated system that could be completely managed by a single interface. Therefore, it could not utilize off-the-shelf components, such as cameras and displays, but needed integrated components that were managed and controlled by the system.

- Fourth, it had to provide integrated, easy-to-use data collaboration and audio conferencing so that participants could easily share documents and presentations with each other and allow audio-only participants to join the meeting.

- Finally, it had to do all these things in a completely standards-based way, leveraging the existing converged IP network and Unified Communications platforms Cisco was famous for.

As luck would have it, the time was right for the development of such a product:

- Digital Signal Processor (DSP) technology was just beginning to be capable of 1080p resolution video at the latency targets required.

- Camera lens and sensor technology was getting small enough to deliver a 1080p camera that was small enough to be discretely mounted over the bezel of the display.

- Display technology in the size (65-inch) and resolution (1080p) required was becoming affordable.

- The networking technologies required to make a system like this manageable and deployable on a converged IP network were finally mature—IP Telephony being one of the driving forces in the decade prior to Cisco TelePresence to allow technologies such as quality of service (QoS), Power over Ethernet (PoE), high availability, and Session Initiation Protocol (SIP) to become mature, allowing the same techniques to be leveraged by Cisco TelePresence.

The word codec is used in two different ways:

- It is used as the name of the physical device containing a CPU, memory, an operating system, Digital Signal Processors (DSP), and audio, video, and network interfaces: the Cisco TelePresence codec.

- It is widely used throughout the industry to refer to various audio and video encoding and decoding algorithms, such as the H.264 and AAC-LD codecs.

Codec System Architecture

The Cisco TelePresence codec is a purpose-built, ultra-high performance encoding and decoding appliance. It runs the Linux operating system on an embedded Compact Flash module and contains an array of Digital Signal Processors (DSP) that perform all the encoding and decoding of the audio and video.

Codec Physical Design

The Cisco TelePresence codec was designed to operate in a hands-off environment where physical access to the device would be rare. It is rack-mounted to the assembly frame of the TelePresence system and then surrounded by the structural assembly and furniture of the system. All the cameras, displays, microphones, speakers, IP Phone, and other auxiliary components plug into it, and it, in turn, attaches to the network through a single 1000Base-T Gigabit Ethernet interface. There are no keyboard, monitor, or console ports on the system. It is managed entirely over IP through its network interface using protocols such as Secure Shell (SSH), Secure Hypertext Transfer Protocol (HTTP) and Simple Network Management Protocol (SNMP).

Figures 3-1 and 3-2 show the front and back views of the Cisco TelePresence codec.

Master and Slave Codec Architecture

On multiscreen systems such as the CTS-3000 and CTS-3200, the Cisco TelePresence codec uses a distributed architecture with multiple physical codecs participating together as a single, logical unit.

The codecs are rack-mounted to the assembly frame underneath each of the three displays:

- One under the center display (referred to as the primary codec)

- One under the left display (referred to as the secondary codec)

- One under the right display (referred to as the secondary codec)

Figure 3-1   *Cisco TelePresence codec – front view*

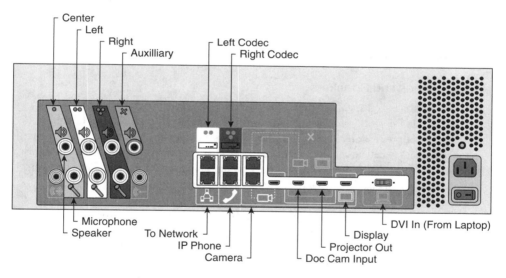

Figure 3-2   *Cisco TelePresence codec – back view*

The primary codec controls the entire system and is the sole interface to the network. The left and right secondary codecs are controlled by the primary codec.

Codec and Component Connectivity

The left and right (secondary) codecs attach to the center (primary) codec through 1000Base-T Gigabit Ethernet jumper cables, and the center (primary) codec attaches to the network through a 1000Base-T Gigabit Ethernet jumper cable.

Displays

The displays connect to their respective codecs through High Density Multimedia Interface (HDMI) cables. As mentioned previously, these are not off-the-shelf displays. They are custom designed by Cisco and engineered specifically for use in Cisco TelePresence systems. Features that are commonly found on off-the-shelf displays, such as multiple user-selectable video input ports, an infrared receiver port and associated remote control, and speakers are not present on these displays. They simply have a power receptacle jack, an on/off switch, and an HDMI port. The codec uses certain pins within the HDMI cable for control signaling messages that control the power state (on, standby, off) of the display, its color temperature (3500 k, 4100 k, 5000 k), and to upload new display firmware code.

Cameras

The cameras connect to their respective codecs through two different cables:

- **A 1000Base-T Gigabit Ethernet jumper cable:** Provides IEEE 802.af Power over Ethernet to the camera and is also used for control signaling messages, such as setting the gain and color settings, and to upload new camera firmware code.

- **A Digital Video Interface to High Density Multimedia Interface (DVI-HDMI) cable:** The DVI-HDMI cable is used for the video connection between the camera and the codec.

These cameras are custom designed by Cisco and engineered specifically for use in its TelePresence systems.

Microphones and Speakers

The microphones and speakers attach to the center (primary) codec only. The primary codec contains an audio processing board with DSP resources on it. The secondary codecs do not process any audio. The microphones are custom-designed boundary microphones with an excellent acoustic frequency range and are electronically shielded against cellular interface. They connect to the codec using 6-pin mini-XLR cables. The speakers are off-the-shelf speakers chosen for their excellent sound reproduction qualities and durability and connect to the codec using TRS cables. The speakers are nonamplified. (They do not require a power connection.) The codec contains an amplifier and outputs amplified, speaker-level audio signals to the speakers.

IP Phone

The Cisco Unified IP Phone 7975 Series provides the user interface to the system, allowing the user to make and receive TelePresence calls using a familiar telephony paradigm. The IP Phone attaches to the center (primary) codec using a 1000Base-T Gigabit Ethernet jumper cable. The primary codec provides IEEE 802.3af Power over Ethernet to the IP Phone and communicates using eXtensible Markup Language (XML) over Hypertext Transfer Protocol (HTTP) or Java over Transport Control Protocol (TCP) to create the user interface that displays on the IP Phone's touch-sensitive screen.

Auxiliary Components

Auxiliary components include PCs, document cameras, and auxiliary displays for viewing the associated video from these devices. The PC is provided by the user and is attached to the center (primary) codec through a Video Graphics Adapter to Digital Video Interface (VGA-DVI) cable and a 3.5mm mini-stereo audio cable. The document camera is an optional third-party component that can be purchased and installed by the customer and is attached to the center (primary) codec through a DVI-HDMI cable and through a 1000Base-T Gigabit Ethernet cable. The Gigabit Ethernet cable controls the document camera, such as power on/off, zoom in/out, and so on.

The video from the PC and the document camera can be displayed on the TelePresence system in one of three ways:

- Multiscreen systems such as the CTS-3000 and CTS-3200 come bundled with an off-the-shelf third-party projector, which is mounted underneath the center of the table and projects onto a white surface below the center display. This projector connects to the center (primary) codec through an HDMI cable.

- Single screen systems such as the CTS-1000 and CTS-500 do not include a projector but can display the auxiliary video as a Presentation-in-Picture (PIP) image within the primary display. In this case, the PIP video is passed over the same HDMI cable that the primary display is attached to.

- Optionally, on any model system, the customer can choose to purchase auxiliary displays, mounted either above the center display or off to the left or right sides of the system. In this case, the customer can use the Cisco TelePresence Auxiliary Expansion Box, which acts as a 1:3 HDMI splitter, with one HDMI connection from the center (primary) codec and three HDMI outputs to the projector and auxiliary displays.

Network Connectivity

For the system to be standards-compliant with current networking methodologies and protocols, Cisco needed to design a way to make this entire system, with its multiple codecs and attached components, to appear as a single IP address on the network. To achieve this, the system leverages private, nonroutable RFC 1918 IP addresses between the primary and secondary codecs, between the codecs and their cameras, between the primary codec and the document camera, and so on. The primary codec, in turn, attaches to the upstream Ethernet LAN through a 1000Base-T Gigabit Ethernet cable and can obtain an IP address dynamically through Dynamic Host Configuration Protocol (DHCP) or use a statically assigned IP address. Therefore, the entire system uses a single Gigabit Ethernet port with a single Media Access Control (MAC) address and a single IP address. You can find more details on the connectivity of the system to the LAN in Chapter 4, "Connecting TelePresence Systems."

Codec Operating System Software

As mentioned previously, the Cisco TelePresence codec runs the Linux operating system on an embedded Compact Flash module. The Linux OS is highly customized and secured including only those functions and modules necessary for it to operate.

Management Interfaces

A shell interface (accessible only through SSH on the primary codec) runs on top of the underlying OS to give administrators the command-line interface (CLI) necessary to administer the system. The primary codec also runs a highly customized version of Tomcat web server, which provides a web-based alternative to the CLI administration interface. The CLI and the web-based interface collectively are referred to as Cisco TelePresence System Administration.

Figures 3-3 and 3-4 illustrate the CLI and web-based administration interfaces.

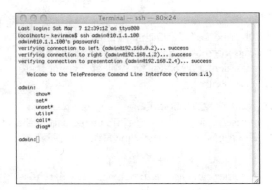

Figure 3-3   *Cisco TelePresence System Administration CLI*

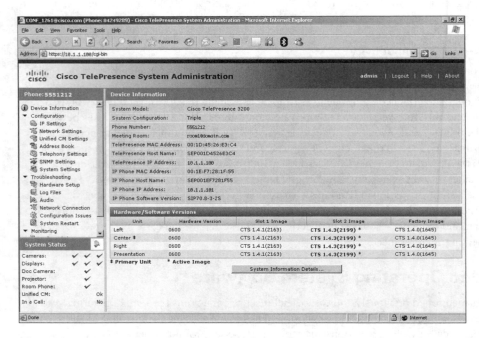

Figure 3-4   *Cisco TelePresence System Administration web interface*

Compact Flash and Component Firmware

The Cisco TelePresence System Administration software comes as a signed binary archive image (*.sbn* file) and contains the operating system and all other software modules, including the firmware to be loaded into all its peripherals, the video and audio subsystems, cameras, displays and other components. The *.sbn* file is preloaded in the factory on the Compact Flash module and can be upgraded or downgraded by obtaining the desired version from Cisco.com and then loading that file on the Cisco Unified Communications Manager (CUCM) server.

When the system is powered on, or anytime it receives a restart command from the CUCM to which it is registered, the primary codec downloads its configuration from the CUCM. The configuration file, in turn, contains the filename of the software load that the system should be running (for example, the filename *SIPTS.1-5-0-2000R.sbn*), and if the current version running on the Compact Flash does not match the filename contained in the configuration file, the codec downloads the new file from the CUCM. The Compact Flash on the codec is divided into three partitions: a factory slot, slot 1, and slot 2. The new file is downloaded to either slot 1 or slot 2. If slot 1 is currently the active slot, the codec downloads the new image to slot 2. If slot 2 is currently active, the codec downloads the new image to slot 1 and then reloads itself to install the new image.

Upon booting up, the codec checks the firmware of the secondary codecs and syncs its Compact Flash slots with those of the secondary's. The codec also checks the firmware of all the attached peripherals and compares their versions against the versions bundled within its running image. If any of them do not match, the codec pushes the new firmware to that peripheral.

Notice at the bottom of Figure 3-4 the Compact Flash contents of each of the three codecs is listed and which slot is currently the active slot on each codec. The System Details button on that page launches a new page that displays the firmware for every component attached to the system. This same information can be accessed through the CLI interface using the **show upgrade detail** command or by querying the correct SNMP MIB variables.

Component Status

The primary codec keeps track of all the components attached to it, including the secondary codecs, cameras, displays, document cameras, projectors, microphones, and so on. If any component is malfunctioning, an alarm status is displayed on the Administration web interface and can trigger SNMP trap notifications if configured with an SNMP trap destination. The state of the system and all its components can be viewed on-demand at any time through the web interface, CLI, or through SNMP MIB polling mechanisms.

Encoding and Packetization

Now that the physical connectivity of the codecs and all their components have been reviewed, the following sections walk through the end-to-end path of how video and audio are taken from the cameras, microphones, and auxiliary components, encoded, packetized, and multiplexed onto the IP network, received on the other end, buffered, decoded, and finally displayed.

Camera and Auxiliary Video Inputs

There are three types of video inputs on the codec, as shown previously in Figure 3-2:

- The connection from the Cisco TelePresence camera

- The connection from the user's PC

- The connection from the document camera

Although the PC and the document camera are two separate inputs, only one is active at any given time. (Either the PC is displayed, or the document camera video image is displayed.) These latter two inputs will be referred to collectively as the *auxiliary video inputs* throughout the remainder of this chapter.

Camera Resolution and Refresh Rate (Hz)

The Cisco TelePresence cameras operate at 1080p (1920x1080) resolution with a refresh rate of 30 Hz. The camera sensors encode the video into a digital format and send it down the DVI-HDMI cable to their respective codecs. The left camera is attached to the left secondary codec, the center camera to the center primary codec, and the right camera to right secondary codec.

Note On single-screen systems, such as the CTS-1000 and CTS-500, there is no left or right, only center.

Auxiliary Video Inputs Resolution and Refresh Rate (Hz)

At the time of writing, the PC video input (VGA-DVI) and the document camera (DVI-HDMI) on the Cisco TelePresence codec operate at 1024x768 resolution with a refresh rate of 60 Hz. The PC must be configured to output this resolution and refresh rate on its VGA output interface. Likewise, the document camera must be configured to output this resolution and refresh rate on its DVI output interface. The majority of PCs on the market at the time the product was designed use 1024x768 resolution and VGA interfaces, although an increasing number of models are beginning to support higher resolutions and are beginning to offer DVI and even HDMI interfaces instead of, or in addition to, VGA. Future versions of the Cisco TelePresence codec might support additional resolutions, refresh rates, and interface types for these connections.

Note VGA is an analog interface. DVI comes in three flavors: DVI-A that is analog, DVI-D that is digital, and DVI-I that can dynamically sense whether the connected device is using analog (DVI-A) or digital (DVI-D). It is worth mentioning that the first generation Cisco TelePresence codec offers a DVI-A connector for the PC connection. The other end of the cable that attaches to the PC is VGA. So the signal from the PC is a VGA analog to DVI-A analog connection.

Video Encoding

When the video coming from the cameras is presented at the HDMI inputs of the codecs, the video passes through the DSP array to be encoded and compressed using the H.264 encoding and compression algorithm. The encoding engine within the Cisco TelePresence codec derives its clock from the camera input, so the video is encoded at 30 frames per second (30 times a second, the camera passes a video frame to the codec to be encoded and compressed).

H.264 Compression Algorithm

H.264 is a video encoding and compression standard jointly developed by the Telecommunication Standardization Sector (ITU-T) Video Coding Experts Group (VCEG) and the International Organization for Standardization/International Electrotechnical Commission (ISO/IEC) Moving Picture Experts Group (MPEG). It was originally completed in 2003, with development of additional extensions continuing through 2007 and beyond.

H.264 is equivalent to, and also known as, MPEG-4 Part 10, or MPEG-4 AVC (Advanced Video Coding). These standards are jointly maintained so that they have identical technical content and are therefore synonymous. Generally speaking, PC-based applications such as Microsoft Windows Media Player and Apple Quicktime refer to it as MPEG-4, whereas real-time, bidirectional applications such as video conferencing and telepresence refer to it as H.264.

H.264 Profiles and Levels

The H.264 standard defines a series of profiles and levels, with corresponding target bandwidths and resolutions. Basing its development of the Cisco TelePresence codec upon the standard, while using the latest Digital Signal Processing hardware technology and advanced software techniques, Cisco developed a codec that could produce 1080p resolution (1920x1080) at a bit rate of under 4 Mbps. One of the key ingredients used to accomplish this level of performance was by implementing Context-Adaptive Binary Arithmetic Coding (CABAC).

CABAC

CABAC is a method of encoding that provides considerably better compression but is extremely computationally expensive and hence requires considerable processing power to encode and decode. CABAC is fully supported by the H.264 standard, but Cisco TelePresence, with its advanced array of Digital Signal Processing (DSP) resources was the first implementation on the market capable of performing this level of computational complexity while maintaining the extremely unforgiving encode and decode times (latency) needed for real-time, bidirectional human interaction.

Resolution

The resolution of an image is defined by the number of pixels contained within the image. It is expressed in the format of the number of pixels wide x number of pixels high (pronounced x-by-y). The H.264 standard supports myriad video resolutions ranging from Sub-Quarter Common Interchange Format (SQCIF) (128x96) all the way up to ultra-high definition resolutions such as Quad Full High Definition (QFHD) or 2160p (3840x2160). Table 3-1 lists the most common resolutions used by video conferencing and Telepresence devices. The resolutions supported by Cisco TelePresence are noted with an asterisk.

Table 3-1   *H.264 Common Resolutions*

Name	Width	Height	Aspect Ratio
QCIF	176	144	4:3
CIF*	352	288	4:3
4CIF	704	576	4:3
480p	854	480	16:9
XGA*	1024	768	4:3
720p*	1280	720	16:9
1080p*	1920	1080	16:9

Aspect Ratio

The aspect ratio of an image is its width divided by its height. Aspect ratios are typically expressed in the format of x:y (pronounced x-by-y, such as "16 by 9"). The two most common aspect ratios in use by video conferencing and telepresence devices are 4:3 and 16:9. Standard Definition displays are 4:3 in shape, whereas high-definition displays provide a widescreen format of 16:9. As shown in Table 3-1, Cisco TelePresence supports CIF and XGA that are designed to be displayed on standard-definition displays, along with 720p and 1080p that are designed to be displayed on high-definition displays. The Cisco TelePresence system uses high-definition format displays that are 16:9 in shape, so when a CIF or XGA resolution is displayed on the screen, it is surrounded by black borders, as illustrated in Figure 3-5.

Frame Rate and Motion Handling

The frame rate of the video image constitutes the number of video frames per second (fps) that is contained within the encoded video. Cisco TelePresence operates at 30 frames per second (30 fps). This means that 30 times per second (or every 33 milliseconds) a video frame is produced by the encoder. Each 33 ms period can be referred to as a *frame interval*.

Motion handling defines the degree of compression within the encoding algorithm to either enhance or suppress the clarity of the video when motion occurs within the image. High motion handling results in a smooth, clear image even when a lot of motion occurs within the video (people walking around, waving their hands, and so on). Low motion handling results in a noticeable choppy, blurry, grainy, or pixelized image when people or objects move around. These concepts have been around since the birth of video conferencing. Nearly all video conferencing and telepresence products on the market offer user-customizable settings to enhance or suppress the clarity of the video when motion

Figure 3-5   *16:9 and 4:3 images displayed on a Cisco TelePresence system*

occurs within the image. Figure 3-6 shows a historical reference that many people can relate to, which shows a screenshot of a Microsoft NetMeeting desktop video conferencing client from the 1990s that provided a slider bar to allow the users to choose whether they preferred higher quality (slower frame rate but clearer motion) or faster video (higher frame rate, but blurry motion).

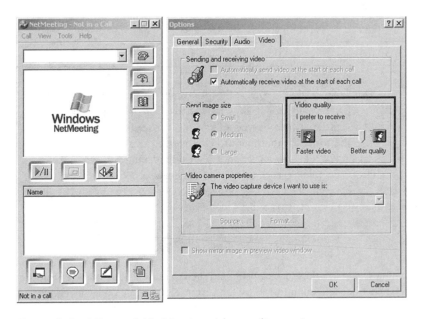

Figure 3-6   *Microsoft NetMeeting video quality setting*

Cisco TelePresence provides a similar concept. Although the Cisco TelePresence cameras operate at 1080p resolution 30 Hz (1080p / 30), the encoder within the Cisco TelePresence codec to which the camera attaches can encode and compress the video into either 1080p or 720p resolutions at three different motion-handling levels per resolution providing the customer with the flexibility of deciding how much bandwidth they want the system to consume. Instead of a sliding scale, Cisco uses the terms Good, Better, and Best. Best motion handling provides the clearest image (and hence uses the most bandwidth), whereas Good motion handling provides the least-clear image (and hence the least bandwidth). The Cisco TelePresence codec also supports the CIF resolution (352x288) for interoperability with traditional video conferencing devices, and the XGA resolution (1024x768) for the auxiliary video channels used for sharing a PC application or a document camera image. Table 3-2 summarizes the resolutions, frame rates, motion-handling levels, and bit rates supported by the Cisco TelePresence codec.

Table 3-2 *Cisco TelePresence Supported Resolutions, Motion Levels, and Bit Rates*

Resolution	Frame Rate	Motion Handling	Bit Rate
CIF	30 fps	Not configurable	768 kbps
XGA	5 fps	Not configurable	500 kbps
XGA	30 fps	Not configurable	4 Mbps
720p	30 fps	Good	1 Mbps
720p	30 fps	Better	1.5 Mbps
720p	30 fps	Best	2.25 Mbps
1080p	30 fps	Good	3 Mbps
1080	30 fps	Better	3.5 Mbps
1080p	30 fps	Best	4 Mbps

Tip Note that Cisco TelePresence always runs at 30 fps (except for the auxiliary PC and document camera inputs that normally run at 5 fps but can also run at 30 fps if the customer wants to enable that feature). Most video conferencing and telepresence providers implement variable frame-rate codecs that attempt to compensate for their lack of encoding horsepower by sacrificing frame rate to keep motion handling and resolution quality levels as high as possible. Cisco TelePresence codecs do not need to do this because they contain so much DSP horsepower. The Cisco TelePresence codec can comfortably produce 1080p resolution at a consistent 30 fps regardless of the amount of motion in the video. The only reason Cisco provides the motion handling (Good, Better, Best) setting is to give the customer the choice of sacrificing motion quality to fit over lower bandwidths.

The video from the Cisco TelePresence cameras and the auxiliary video inputs (PC or document camera) is encoded and compressed by the Cisco TelePresence codec using the H.264 standard. Each input is encoded independently and can be referred to as a *channel*. (This is discussed further in subsequent sections that details how these channels are packetized and multiplexed onto the network using the Real-Time Transport Protocol.) On multiscreen systems, such as the CTS-3000 and CTS-3200, each camera is connected to its respective codec, and that codec encodes the cameras video into an H.264 stream. Thus there are three independently encoded video streams. The primary (center) codec also encodes the auxiliary (PC or document camera) video into a fourth, separate H.264 stream.

Frame Intervals and Encoding Techniques

Each 33-ms frame interval contains encoded slices of the video image. A reference frame is the largest and least compressed and contains a complete picture of the image. After sending a reference frame, subsequent frames contain only the changes in the image since the most recent reference frame. For example, if a person is sitting in front of the camera, talking and gesturing naturally, the background (usually a wall) behind the person does not change. Therefore, the inter-reference frames need to encode only the pixels within the image that are changing. This allows for substantial compression of the amount of data needed to reconstruct the image. Reference frames are sent at the beginning of a call, or anytime the video is interrupted, such as when the call is placed on hold and the video suspended, and then the call is taken off of hold and the video resumed. An Instantaneous Decode Refresh (IDR) Frames   An IDR frame is a reference frame containing a complete picture of the image. When an IDR frame is received, the decode buffer is refreshed so that all previously received frames are marked as "unused for reference," and the IDR frame becomes the new reference picture. IDR frames are sent by the encoder at the beginning of the call and at periodic intervals to refresh all the receivers. They can also be requested at any time by any receiver. There are two pertinent examples of when IDRs are requested by receivers:

- In a multipoint meeting, as different sites speak, the Cisco TelePresence Multipoint Switch (CTMS) switches the video streams to display the active speaker. During this switch, the CTMS sends an IDR request to the speaking endpoint so that all receivers can receive a new IDR reference frame.

- Whenever packet loss occurs on the network and the packets lost are substantial enough to cause a receiver to lose sync on the encoded video image, the receiver can request a new IDR frame so that it can sync back up.

This concept of reference frames and inter-reference frames result in a highly variable bit rate. When the video traffic on the network is measured over time, peaks and valleys occur in the traffic pattern. (The peaks are the IDR frames, and the valleys are the inter-IDR frames). It is important to note that Cisco TelePresence does not use a variable frame rate (it is always 30 fps), but it is variable bit rate. (The amount of data sent per frame interval varies significantly depending upon the amount of motion within each frame interval.) Figure 3-7 illustrates what a single stream of Cisco TelePresence 1080p / 30 encoded video traffic looks like over a one second time interval.

Long-Term Reference Frames   A new technique, implemented at the time this book was authored, is Long-Term Reference (LTR) Frames. LTR allows for multiple frames to be marked for reference, providing the receiver with multiple points of reference to reconstruct the video image. This substantially reduces the need for periodic IDR frames, hence further reducing the amount of bandwidth needed to maintain picture quality and

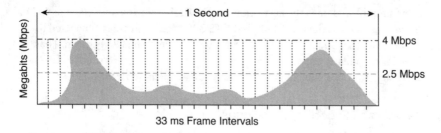

Figure 3-7   *1080p / 30 traffic pattern as viewed over one second*

increasing the efficiency of the encode and decode process. With LTR, the periodic spikes in the traffic pattern illustrated in Figure 3-7 would be substantially less frequent, resulting in overall efficiencies in bandwidth consumption. It would also enable the receiver to more efficiently handle missing frame data, resulting in substantially higher tolerance to network packet loss.

Audio Encoding

The microphones used in Cisco TelePresence are purposefully designed to capture the sounds emanating from a human subject sitting within a few feet of the microphone, along with the regular background noises that accompany that person within the room he or she sits in, while filtering out certain unwanted frequency ranges (such as the high-frequency whirrs of spinning fans in laptop computers or the low-frequency hums of heating and ventilation systems) and electrostatic interference (such as GSM/GPRS cellular signals).

The center (primary) Cisco TelePresence codec has four microphone input ports: three for the Cisco TelePresence microphones and one auxiliary audio input. The Cisco TelePresence microphones use a proprietary 6-pin Mini-XLR connector. The auxiliary audio input is a standard 3.5 mm (1/8-inch) mini-stereo connector, which enables the users to connect the audio sound card of their PC along with the VGA video input discussed in the previous sections.

On single-screen systems such as the CTS-1000 and CTS-500, only the center microphone input and the auxiliary audio input are used. On multiscreen systems, such as the CTS-3000 and CTS-3200, the left and right inputs are also used.

Each audio input is encoded autonomously, resulting in up to four discrete channels of audio. This is superior to most other systems on the market that mix all the microphone inputs into a single outgoing channel. By maintaining the channels separately, Cisco TelePresence can maintain the directionality and spatiality of the sound. If the sound emanates from the left, it will be captured by the left microphone and reproduced by the left speaker on the other end. If it emanates from the right, it will be captured by the right microphone and reproduced by the right speaker on the other end.

AAC-LD Compression Algorithm

Cisco TelePresence uses the latest audio encoding technology known as Advanced Audio Coding–Low Delay (AAC-LD). AAC is a wideband audio coding algorithm designed to be the successor of the MP3 format and is standardized by the International Organization for Standardization/International Electrotechnical Commission (ISO/IEC) Moving Picture Experts Group (MPEG). It is specified both as Part 7 of the MPEG-2 standard and Part 3 of the MPEG-4 standard. As such, it can be referred to as MPEG-2 Part 7 and MPEG-4 Part 3, depending on its implementation; however, it is most often referred to as MPEG-4 AAC, or AAC for short.

AAC-LD (Low Delay) bridges the gap between the AAC codec, which is designed for high-fidelity applications such as music, and International Telecommunication Union (ITU) speech encoders such as G.711 and G.722, which are designed for speech. AAC-LD combines the advantages of high-fidelity encoding with the low delay necessary for real-time, bidirectional communications.

Sampling Frequency and Compression Ratio

The AAC-LD standard allows for a wide range of sample frequencies (8 kHz to 96 kHz). Cisco TelePresence implements AAC-LD at 48 kHz sampling frequency. This means that the audio is sampled 48,000 times per second, per channel. These samples are then encoded and compressed to 64 kbps, per channel, resulting in a total bandwidth of 128 kbps for single-screen systems (two channels) and 256 kbps for multiscreen systems (four channels).

Automatic Gain Control and Microphone Calibration

Automatic Gain Control (AGC) is an adaptive algorithm to dynamically adjust the input gain of the microphones to adapt to varying input signal levels. Whether the people are sitting close to the microphones or far away, speaking in a soft voices or yelling, or any combination in between, the microphones have to continuously adapt to keep the audio sounding lifelike and at the correct decibel levels to reproduce the sense of distance and directionality at the far end.

Keeping multiple discrete microphones autonomous and yet collectively synchronized so that the entire room is calibrated is no small task. Cisco TelePresence uses advanced, proprietary techniques to dynamically calibrate the microphones to the room and relative to each other. It is more complex for Cisco TelePresence than other implementations because the microphones need to be kept discrete and autonomous from each other. This preserves the notion of location, which is critical to the proper operation of multipoint switching in which the active speaker switches in on the appropriate screen. For example, if a person is sitting in the center segment of the room but facing the left wall when she talks, the speech emanating from her hits both the left and center microphones. The system must be smart enough to detect which microphone is closest to the source and switch to the correct camera (in this case the center camera), while playing the sound out both speakers on the other end to retain the sense of distance and directionality of the audio. It does this by assigning a 0 to 100 scale for each channel. In this scenario, the speech emanating from the person might be ranked an 80 at the center microphone and a 45 at the left microphone. These two microphone inputs are independently encoded and transported to the other end where they are played out both the center and right speakers at the appropriate decibel levels so that the people on the other end get the sense of distance and directionality.

However, because the center microphone was a higher rank than the left microphone, the correct camera would be triggered (in this case, the center camera).

Real-Time Transport Protocol

The preceding content covered the basic concepts of video and audio inputs and encoding processes. The video is encoded using H.264, and the audio is encoded using AAC-LD. Now those video and audio samples must be turned into IP packets and sent onto the network to be transported to the other end. This is done using the Real-Time Transport Protocol (RTP).

RTP is a network protocol specifically designed to provide transport services for real-time applications such as interactive voice and video. The services it provides include identification of payload type, sequence numbering, timestamps, and monitoring of the delivery of RTP packets through the RTP control protocol (RTCP). RTP and RTCP are both specified in IETF RFC 3550.

RTP Packet Format

RTP defines a standard packet format for delivering the media, as shown in Figure 3-8.

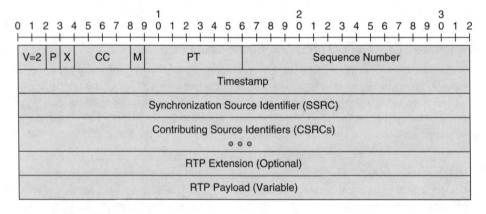

Figure 3-8 *RTP packet format*

The following are the fields within the RTP packet:

- **Version (V):** A 2-bit field indicating the protocol version. The current version is 2.

- **Padding (P):** A 1-bit field indicating padding at the end of the RTP packet.

- **Extension Header (X):** A 1-bit field indicating the presence of an optional extension header.

- **CRSC Count (CC):** A 4-bit field indicating the number of Contributing Source (CSRC) identifiers that follow the fixed header. It is presented only when inserted by an RTP mixer such as a conference bridge or transcoder.

- **Marker (M):** A 1-bit marker bit that identifies events such as frame boundaries.

- **Payload Type (PT):** A 7-bit field that identifies the format of the RTP payload.

- **Sequence Number:** A 16-bit field that increments by one for each RTP packet sent. The receiver uses this field to identify lost packets.

- **Timestamp:** A 32-bit timestamp field that reflects the sampling instant of the first octet of the RTP packet.

- **Synchronization Source Identifier (SSRC):** A 32-bit field that uniquely identifies the source of a stream of RTP packets.

- **Contributing Source Identifiers (CSRC):** Variable length field that contains a list of sources of streams of RTP packets that have contributed to a combined stream produced by an RTP mixer. You can use this to identify the individual speakers when a mixer combines streams in an audio or video conference.

- **RTP Extension (Optional):** Variable length field that contains a 16-bit profile specific identifier and a 16-bit length identifier, followed by variable length extension data. Intended for limited use.

- **RTP Payload:** Variable-length field that holds the real-time application data (voice, video, and so on.).

Frames Versus Packets

To understand the role of RTP within TelePresence, you need to understand the behavior of voice and video over a network infrastructure. Figure 3-9 shows a sample comparison of voice and video traffic as it appears on a network.

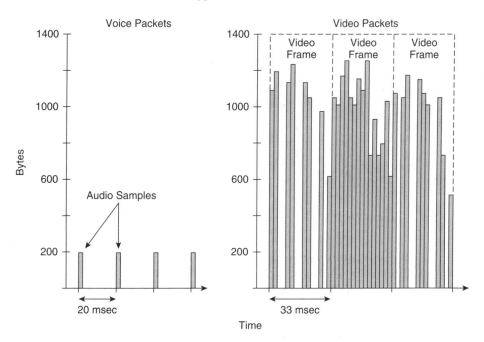

Figure 3-9   *Comparison of voice and video on the network*

As you can see in Figure 3-9, voice appears as a series of audio samples, spaced at regular intervals. In the case of Cisco TelePresence, voice packets are typically sent every 20 msec. Each packet contains one or more encoded samples of the audio, depending on the encoding algorithm used and how many samples per packet it is configured to use. G.711 and G.729, two of the most common VoIP encoding algorithms, typically include two voice samples per packet. The sizes of the voice packets are consistent, averaging slightly over 220 bytes for a 2-sample G.711 packet; therefore, the overall characteristic of voice is a constant bit-rate stream.

Video traffic appears as a series of video frames spaced at regular intervals. In the case of Cisco TelePresence, video frames are sent approximately every 33 msec. The size of each frame varies based on the amount of changes since the previous frame. Therefore, the overall characteristic of TelePresence video is a relatively bursty, variable bit-rate stream.

A video frame can also be referred to as an *Access Unit* in H.264 terminology. The H.264 standard defines two layers, a Video Coding Layer (VCL) and a Network Abstraction Layer (NAL). Figure 3-10 shows a simplified example.

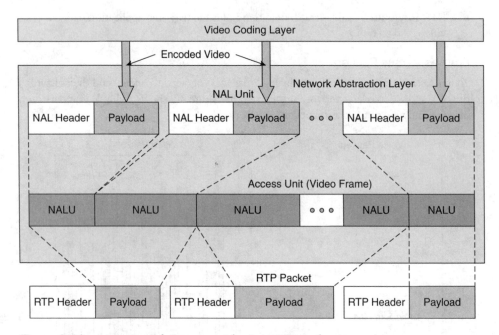

Figure 3-10   *Mapping TelePresence video into RTP packets*

The VCL is responsible for encoding the video. Its output is a string of bits representing the encoded video. The function of the NAL is to map the string of bits into units that can then be transported across a network infrastructure. IETF RFC 3984 defines the format for H.264 video carried within the payload of the RTP packets. Each video frame consists of multiple RTP packets spaced out over the frame interval. The boundary of each video frame is indicated through the use of the marker bit, as shown in Figure 3-8. Each RTP packet contains one or more NAL Units (NALU), depending upon the packet type: single

NAL unit packet, single-time or multi-time aggregation packet, or fragmentation unit (part of a NALU). Each NALU consists of an integer number of bytes of coded video.

Note RTP Packets within a single video frame and across multiple frames are not necessarily independent of each other. In other words, if one packet within a video frame is discarded, it affects the quality of the entire video frame and might possibly affect the quality of other video frames.

TelePresence Video Packet and Frame Sizes

The sizes of individual RTP packets within frames vary, depending upon the number of NALUs they carry and the sizes of the NALUs. Overall, packet sizes average 1100 bytes for Cisco TelePresence video. The number of packets per frame also varies considerably based upon how much information is contained within the video frame. This is partially determined by how the video is encoded; either reference frames or inter-reference frames.

Note Coding is actually done at the macroblock layer. An integer number of macroblocks then form a slice, and multiple slices form a frame. Therefore, technically slices are intrapredicted (I-slices) or interpredicted (P-slices). For simplicity of explanation within this chapter, these have been abstracted to reference frames and inter-reference frames. A thorough discussion of the H.264 Video Coding Layer is outside the scope of this book.

Compression of reference frames is typically only moderate because only spatial redundancy within the frame is eliminated. Therefore, reference frames tend to be much larger in size than inter-reference frames. Reference frame sizes up to 64 KB to 65 KB (and approximately 60 individual packets) have been observed with TelePresence endpoints. Inter-reference frames have much higher compression because only the difference between the frame and the reference frame is sent. This information is typically sent in the form of motion vectors indicating the relative motion of objects from the reference frame. The size of TelePresence inter-reference frames is dependent upon the amount of motion within the conference call. Under normal motion, TelePresence inter-reference frames tend to average 13 KB in size and typically consist of approximately 12 individual packets. Under high motion they can be approximately 19 KB in size and consist of approximately 17 individual packets. From a bandwidth utilization standpoint, much better performance can be achieved by sending reference frames infrequently. During normal operation, Cisco TelePresence codecs send reference frames (IDRs) only once every several minutes in point-to-point calls to reduce the burstiness of the video and lower the overall bit rate.

TelePresence Packet Rates

A single TelePresence camera configured for 1080p best resolution can send up to approximately 4 Mbps of video traffic at peak rate. With an average of 1100 bytes per packet, this yields approximately 455 packets per second. However, with normal motion, each camera typically generates somewhere between 3 Mbps to 3.5 Mbps of video; yielding a packet rate between 340 packets to 400 packets per second. Likewise a single TelePresence microphone generates a voice packet of roughly 220 bytes every 20 msec. This yields a voice packet rate of approximately 50 packets per second. The audio rate is fixed regardless of the amount of speaking going on within the meeting. Therefore under normal motion, a TelePresence endpoint with one cameras and one microphone (such as the CTS-1000 or CTS-500) typically generates approximately 390 packets to 450 packets per second. Likewise, under normal motion, a TelePresence endpoint with three cameras and three microphones (such as the CTS-3000) typically generates approximately 1170 packets to 1350 packets per second. Note that this does not include the use of the auxiliary video and audio inputs, voice and video interoperability with legacy systems, and any signaling and management traffic; all of which increase the packet rate.

Multiplexing

The underlying transport protocol for RTP is not specified within RFC 3550. However, RTP and RTCP are typically implemented over UDP. When implemented over UDP, the port range of 16384 to 32767 is often used. RTP streams often use the even-numbered ports, with their accompanying RTCP streams using the next higher odd-numbered port. In this case, RTP sessions are identified by a unique destination address pair that consists of a network address plus a pair of ports for RTP and RTCP. Cisco TelePresence endpoints are capable of both sending and receiving multiple audio and video streams. The primary codec multiplexes these streams together into a single audio RTP stream and a single video RTP stream. Multiplexing is accomplished through the use of different Synchronization Source Identifiers (SSRC), shown previously in Figure 3-8, for each video camera and each audio microphone, including the auxiliary inputs. In the case of Cisco TelePresence, SSRCs indicate not only the source position of the audio or video media, but also the destination position of the display or speaker to which the media is intended. Therefore, the receiving primary codec can demultiplex the RTP session and send the individual RTP streams to the appropriate display or speaker. This is how spatial audio is achieved with TelePresence and how video display positions are maintained throughout a TelePresence meeting.

When endpoints join a multipoint call, they first attempt to exchange RTCP packets. Successful exchange of these packets indicates the opposite endpoint is a Cisco TelePresence device, capable of supporting various Cisco extensions. Among other things, these extensions determine the number of audio and video channels each TelePresence endpoint can send and receive and their positions. Audio and video streams are sent and received based on their position within the CTS endpoint, which is then mapped to a corresponding SSRC. Figure 3-11 shows an example for a three-screen endpoint, such as a CTS-3000, communicating with a CTMS.

Each CTS-3000 or CTS-3200 can transmit (and receive) up to four audio streams and four video streams from the left, center, right, and auxiliary positions. These correspond to the left, center, and right cameras, microphones, and the auxiliary input. Therefore, in a point-to-point meeting between CTS-3000s or CTS-3200s, there can be as many as four audio SSRCs multiplexed together in a single audio RTP stream and four video SSRCs multiplexed together in a single video RTP stream sent from each endpoint.

As Figure 3-11 illustrates, the CTMS can transmit up to four video streams, corresponding to the left, center, and right displays of the CTS-3000 or CTS-3200, and either a projector or monitor connected to the auxiliary video output. However, the CTMS transmits

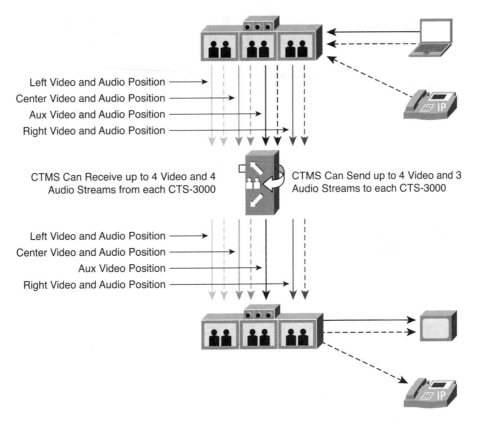

Left Video and Audio Position
Center Video and Audio Position
Aux Video and Audio Position
Right Video and Audio Position

CTMS Can Receive up to 4 Video and 4
Audio Streams from each CTS-3000

CTMS Can Send up to 4 Video and 3
Audio Streams to each CTS-3000

Left Video and Audio Position
Center Video and Audio Position
Aux Video Position
Right Video and Audio Position

Figure 3-11 *Audio and video positions for three-screen TelePresence endpoints*

only up to three audio streams, corresponding to the left, center, and right speaker positions of the CTS-3000 or CTS-3200. Audio sent by an originating CTS-3000 or CTS-3200 toward the auxiliary position is redirected to one of the three speaker positions of the destination CTS-3000 or CTS-3200 by the CTMS. The CTMS chooses the three loudest audio streams to send to the remote CTS-3000 or CTS-3200 when there are more than three streams with audio energy.

Figure 3-12 shows the audio and video positions for a multipoint call consisting of CTS-1000s or CTS-500s.

Each CTS-1000 or CTS-500 can transmit up to two audio streams and two video streams from the center and auxiliary positions. These correspond to the single camera and microphone of the CTS-1000 or CTS-500, and the auxiliary input. Therefore, in a point-to-point meeting between CTS-1000s or CTS-500s there can be as many as two audio SSRCs multiplexed together in a single audio RTP stream and two video SSRCs multiplexed together in a single video RTP stream sent from each endpoint.

As Figure 3-12 illustrates, the CTMS can still transmit up to three audio streams, corresponding to the left, center, and right microphone positions of the CTS-3000 or CTS-3200, even though the CTS-1000 or CTS-500 have only a single speaker. The CTS-1000 or CTS-500

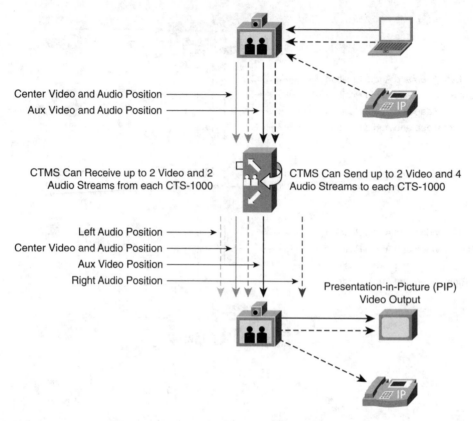

Center Video and Audio Position

Aux Video and Audio Position

CTMS Can Receive up to 2 Video and 2
Audio Streams from each CTS-1000

CTMS Can Send up to 2 Video and 4
Audio Streams to each CTS-1000

Left Audio Position

Center Video and Audio Position

Aux Video Position

Right Audio Position

Presentation-in-Picture (PIP)
Video Output

Figure 3-12 *Audio and video positions for single-screen TelePresence endpoints*

mixes the audio from each of the three positions to play out on its single speaker. The CTS-1000 or CTS-500 can receive only up to two video streams, corresponding to the center display and picture-in-picture auxiliary video output.

RTP Control Protocol

The RTP Control Protocol (RTCP) provides four main functions for RTP sessions:

- Provides feedback on the quality of the distribution of RTP packets from the source.

- Carries a persistent transport-level identifier called the canonical name (CNAME), which associates multiple data streams from a given participant in a set of RTP sessions.

- Provides a feedback mechanism to scale the actual use of RTCP itself. Because all participants send RTCP packets, the rate of arrival of RTCP packets can determine the number of participants and the rate at which RTCP packets should be sent so that the network is not overwhelmed by RTCP packets.

- Can be optionally used to convey minimal session control information between participants.

Several different RTCP packets packet types convey the preceding information. These include a Sender Report (SR), Receiver Report (RR), Session Descriptor (SDES), and Application Specific (APP) packets; among others. Typically RTCP sends compound packets containing combinations of these reports in a single packet.

As mentioned previously, each RTP stream has an accompanying RTCP stream. These RTCP streams can be sent using the next higher odd-numbered port or optionally multiplexed in with the RTP streams themselves. Initial TelePresence software versions multiplexed in the RTCP streams within the RTP streams. For interoperability, current TelePresence software versions support both options. RTCP signals packet loss within TelePresence deployments, causing the sender to send a new reference frame (IDR) to resynchronize the video transmission. Additionally, RTCP is used between TelePresence endpoints to inform each other of the number of audio and video channels they are capable of supporting. The number of channels corresponds to the number of displays, cameras, microphones, and speakers supported by the particular endpoint. Finally, the Cisco TelePresence Multipoint Switch (CTMS) uses RTCP packets to perform session control within multipoint calls. The CTMS informs TelePresence endpoints that do not have active speakers to stop transmitting video. When a particular table segment or room has an active speaker, the CTMS detects this through the audio energy and informs the table segment or room, through RTCP packets, to send video.

Depacketization and Decoding

So far this chapter has discussed how video and audio signals are encoded, packetized, and multiplexed onto the IP network. The following sections describe what happens when the packets reach the destination TelePresence endpoint and how the video and audio signals are decoded.

Managing Latency, Jitter, and Loss

The first step in decoding is to receive, buffer, and reassemble the packets to prepare them to be decoded. Recall that the encoder encodes and packetized the video and audio signals at a smooth, consistent rate. (A 30 Hz camera clock rate and 48 kHz audio sampling rate result in fixed, consistent, encoding intervals.) However, as the packets containing those video and audio samples traverse the IP network, there will inevitably be variation in their arrival times and possibly the order in which they arrive. Therefore, the receiving endpoint must buffer the packets, reordering them if necessary, until an adequate number of packets have arrived to begin decoding a given video frame or audio sample. Lost packets or packets that arrive too late to be decoded (late packets) must also be dealt with by the decoder.

The following sections detail how the Cisco TelePresence codec handles latency, jitter, and loss in the packets that it receives. For more details on proper network design to reduce the latency, jitter, and loss on the network, see Chapter 10, "TelePresence Network Design Part 2: QoS Design."

Latency

At the human experience level, latency is defined and measured as the time it takes for the speech or gestures of one individual (the speaker) to reach the ears and eyes of another (the listener), and for the audible or visual reaction of that listener to come all the way back to speaker so that they can hear and see the listener's reaction. Hence, the human experience is round-trip in nature. This is referred to as *conversational latency*, or *experience-level latency*; 250 ms to 350 ms is the threshold at which the human mind begins to perceive latency and be annoyed by it.

At the technical level however, the latency in Cisco TelePresence is defined and measured as the time it takes for an audio or video packet containing speech or motion to travel from the Ethernet network interface of the speaker's TelePresence system to the Ethernet network interface of the listener's TelePresence system in one direction. The listener's TelePresence system processes the incoming packets and computes a running average of the latency based on timestamps within the RTP packets and their associated RTCP sender reports. Therefore, latency is measured only at the network-level from one TelePresence system to another, not at the experience-level. It is measured unidirectionally by each TelePresence system, not measured round-trip, and does not take into account the processing time (encoding and decoding) of the packets.

Latency Target

To maintain acceptable experience-level latency, Cisco recommends that customers engineer their networks with a target of no more than 150 ms of network-level latency, in each direction, between any two TelePresence systems. Given the circumference of the earth, the speed of light, and the cabling paths that light travels on between cities, it is not always possible to achieve 150 ms between any two points on the globe. Therefore, Cisco TelePresence implements the following thresholds to alert the network administrator and the user when network-level latency exceeds acceptable levels.

Latency Thresholds

When network-level latency exceeds 250 ms averaged over any 10-second period, the Cisco TelePresence system receiving those packets generates an alarm, and an onscreen message displays to the user. The alarm is written to the syslog log file of that TelePresence system, and an SNMP trap message is generated. The onscreen message displays for 15 seconds, after which it is removed. The onscreen message does not display again for the duration of the meeting, unless the media is interrupted or restarted, such as when the user places the meeting on hold and then resumes it (using the Hold or Resume softkeys), or the user terminates the meeting and then reestablishes it (using the End Call or Redial softkeys).

Tip   Cisco TelePresence release 1.5 added support for satellite networks. This feature requires a software license to activate. When activated, the latency threshold is adjusted from 250 ms to 2 seconds.

Understanding Latency Measurements in Multipoint Meetings

As audio and video packets traverse, a Cisco TelePresence Multipoint Switch (CTMS), the RTP header containing the original timestamp information, is overwritten, and a new timestamp value is applied by the CTMS. Therefore the latency measured by each participating TelePresence system is only a measurement of the latency from the CTMS to that endpoint. It is possible for the end-to-end latency from one TelePresence system through the CTMS to another TelePresence System to exceed the 250 ms-latency threshold, without the TelePresence system realizing it.

For example, if the latency from one TelePresence system in Hong Kong to the CTMS in London is 125 ms, and the latency from the CTMS in London to the other TelePresence system in San Francisco is 125 ms, the end-to-end latency from the Ethernet network interface of the Hong Kong system to the Ethernet network interface of the San Francisco system is 250 ms, plus approximately 10 ms added by the CTMS, for a total of 260 ms. The TelePresence System in San Francisco will not realize this and will think that the latency for that meeting is only 125 ms. Therefore, care should be taken when designing the network and the location of the CTMS to reduce the probability of this situation occurring as much as possible. The CTMS is the only device in the network that is aware of the end-to-end latency between any two TelePresence systems in a multipoint meeting. Network administrators can view the end-to-end statistics (calculating the sum of any two legs in that meeting) through the CTMS Administration interface. More information on CTMS and network design best practices for multipoint appears in Chapter 13, "Multipoint TelePresence Design."

Jitter

Simply put, jitter is variation in network latency. In Cisco TelePresence, jitter is measured by comparing the arrival time of the current video frame to the expected arrival time of that frame based on a running clock of fixed 33 ms intervals. Unlike most other video conferencing and telepresence products on the market that use variable frame rate codecs, Cisco TelePresence operates at a consistent 30 frames per second (30 fps). Therefore, the sending codec generates a video frame every 33 ms, and the receiving codec expects those video frames to arrive every 33 ms.

Frame Jitter Versus Packet Jitter

Video frames vary in size based on how much motion is represented by a given video frame. When a low amount of motion occurs within the encoded video, the video frame is relatively small. When a large amount of motion occurs within the encoded video, the video frame is large. Cisco TelePresence 1080p video frames can be as large as 65,000 bytes (65 KB) and averages approximately 13 KB.

These video frames are then segmented into smaller chunks and placed within the payload of RTP packets. Cisco TelePresence video packets tend to be approximately 1100 bytes each, with relatively minor variation in size.

Given a constant end-to-end network latency and relatively constant packet sizes, you can expect to have low packet-level jitter. However, there will still inevitably be variation in the arrival times of video frames simply due to the variation in their size. This variation is primarily a function of the serialization rate (speed) of the network interfaces the packets constituting those video frames traverse but can also be affected by queuing and shaping algorithms within the network routers along the path that might need to queue (buffer) the packets to prioritize them relative to other traffic, shape them prior to transmission, and then transmit (serialize) them on their outgoing interface. On fast networks (45 Mbps DS-3 circuits or faster), the time required to serialize all the packets constituting a large 65 KB video frame versus the time required to serialize a small 13 KB video frame is inconsequential. On slower networks (10 Mbps or slower), the time difference between the serialization of these frame sizes can be significant.

Cisco TelePresence systems implement jitter buffers to manage these variations in video frame arrival times. Upon receipt at the destination, the packets are buffered until an adequate portion of the video frame has arrived, and then the packets are removed from the buffer and decoded. The size (depth) of the jitter buffer dictates how much jitter can be managed before it begins to be noticeable to the user. Packets exceeding the jitter buffer are dropped by the receiving codec because they arrived too late to be decoded. The depth of the jitter buffer has an important consequence to the experience-level latency; every millisecond spent waiting in the jitter buffer increases the end-to-end latency between the humans, so jitter buffers must be kept as small as reasonably possible to accommodate network-level jitter without adding an unacceptable amount of experience-level latency.

Jitter Target

To maintain acceptable experience-level latency, Cisco recommends that customers engineer their networks with a target of no more than 10 ms of packet-level jitter and no more than 50 ms of video frame jitter in each direction between any two TelePresence systems. Given the desire to deploy TelePresence over the smallest and, hence least expensive, amount of bandwidth possible and the need in some circumstances to implement shaping within the routers along the path to conform to a service providers contractual rates and policing enforcements, 50 ms of jitter at the video frame-level jitter is not always possible to accomplish. Therefore, Cisco TelePresence implements the following thresholds and jitter buffer behavior to alert the network administrator when video frame-level jitter exceeds acceptable levels.

Jitter Thresholds

Cisco TelePresence uses a quasi-adaptive jitter buffer. At the beginning of every new meeting, the jitter buffer starts out at 85 ms in depth. After monitoring the arrival time of the video frames for the first few seconds of the meeting, if the incoming jitter exceeds 85 ms average, the jitter buffer is dynamically adjusted to 125 ms. After that, if the jitter exceeds 125 ms averaged over any 10-second period, the Cisco TelePresence system receiving those video frames generates an alarm and dynamically adjusts the jitter buffer to 165 ms. The alarm is written to the syslog log file of that TelePresence system, and an SNMP trap message is generated. No onscreen message is displayed to the user.

Any packets exceeding the 165 ms jitter buffer depth are discarded by the receiving TelePresence system and logged as "late packets" in the call statistics. No alarms or onscreen messages are triggered by this threshold. However, late packets are just as bad as lost packets in that they can cause a noticeable effect on the video quality, so care should be taken to design the network so that video frame jitter never exceeds 165 ms.

Packet Loss

Loss is defined as packets that did not arrive (because they were dropped somewhere along the network path) are measured by each TelePresence system by comparing the sequence numbers of the RTP packets it receives versus the sequence numbers it expected to receive. Packet loss can occur anywhere along the path for a variety of reasons; the three most common follow:

- Layer-1 errors on the physical interfaces and cables along the path, such as a malfunctioning optical interface

- Misconfigured network interfaces along the path, such as Ethernet speed or duplex mismatches between two devices

- Bursts of packets exceeding the buffer (queue) limit or policer configurations on network interfaces along the path, such as Ethernet switches with insufficient queue depth or oversubscribed backplane architectures, or WAN router interfaces that police traffic to conform to a service provider's contractual rates

A closely related metric is *late packets*, which are packets that arrived but exceeded the jitter buffer (arrived too late to be decoded) and hence were discarded (dropped) by the receiving TelePresence system. Lost packets and late packets are tracked independently by Cisco TelePresence systems, but they both result in the same outcome, noticeable pixelization of the video.

Loss is by far the most stringent of the three metrics discussed here. Latency can be annoying to the users, but their meeting can still proceed, and jitter is invisible to the user, but loss (including packets that arrived but exceeded the 165 ms jitter buffer and manifest into late packets) is immediately apparent. Consider the following calculation:

1080p resolution uncompressed (per screen)

2,073,600 pixels per frame

```
× 3 colors per pixel
× 1 byte (8 bits) per color
× 30 frames per second
= 1.5 Gbps uncompressed
```

The Cisco TelePresence systems use the H.264 codec to compress this down to 4 Mbps (per screen). This represents a compression ratio of > 99 percent. Therefore, each packet is representative of a large amount of video data, and, hence, a small amount of packet loss can be extremely damaging to the video quality.

At the time this book was written, Cisco TelePresence was just beginning to implement a new technique known as Long-Term Reference Frames. This enables the system to recover from packet loss significantly faster by maintaining multiple reference frames and, therefore, reducing the number of IDR reference frames that need to be retransmitting when packet loss occurs.

Loss Target

To maintain acceptable experience-level video quality, Cisco recommends that customers engineer their networks with a target of no more than .05 percent packet loss in each direction between any two TelePresence systems. This is an incredibly small amount, and given the complexity of today's global networks, 0.05 percent loss is not always possible to accomplish. Therefore, Cisco TelePresence implements the following thresholds to alert the network administrator when packet loss (or late packets) exceeds acceptable levels.

Loss Thresholds

When packet loss (or late packets) exceeds 1 percent averaged over any 10-second period, the Cisco TelePresence system receiving those packets generates an alarm, and an onscreen message appears. The alarm is written to the syslog log file of that TelePresence system, and an SNMP trap message is generated. The onscreen message appears for 15 seconds, after which it is removed, and a 5-minute hold timer is started. During the 5-minute hold timer, syslog/SNMP alarms continue to be generated, but no onscreen message displays.

When packet loss (or late packets) exceeds 10 percent averaged over any 10-second period, the Cisco TelePresence system receiving those packets generates a second alarm, and a second on-screen message appears (unless the hold timer is already in affect). The alarm is written to the syslog log file of that TelePresence system, and an SNMP trap message is generated. The on-screen message displays for 15 seconds, after which it is removed, and a 5-minute hold timer starts (if it weren't already started by loss threshold #1). During the 5-minute hold timer, syslog/SNMP alarms continue to be generated, but no onscreen message appears.

If loss (or late packets) exceeds 10 percent averaged over any 60-second period, in addition to the actions described, the system downgrades the quality of its outgoing video. When the video downgrades, an alarm generates, and an onscreen icon and message display indicating that the quality has been reduced. The video quality is downgraded by reducing its motion handling (by applying a higher-compression factor to the motion) but the resolution is not affected. For example, if the meeting runs at 1080p-Best, it downgrades to 1080-Good. If the meeting runs at 720p-Best, it downgrades to 720p-Good.

Tip Ten percent packet loss can be measured as 1 out of every 10 packets lost, in which case every inter-reference frame would be impacted, causing the video to completely freeze; or it can be measured as 10 ten packets consecutively lost followed by 90 packets consecutively received, which would have a much less severe effect on the video quality. For example, ten-percent packet loss due to a duplex mismatch, in which packets are dropped consistently and evenly, would have a much more severe effect than ten-percent packet loss due to a queue in the network tail dropping several packets in a burst and then forwarding the remaining packets.

Finally, if loss equals 100 percent for greater than 30 seconds, the codec hangs up the call. If the packets begin flowing again anytime up to the 30-second timer, the codec immediately recovers.

Summary of Latency, Jitter, Loss Targets and Thresholds, and Actions

Table 3-3 summarizes the latency, jitter, and loss targets, and thresholds and threshold behaviors of Cisco TelePresence.

Table 3-3 *Latency, Jitter, and Loss Targets and Thresholds*

Metric	Target	Threshold #1	Threshold #2	Threshold #1 Action	Threshold #2 Action
Latency	150 ms	250 ms (2 sec for satellite mode)	None	Syslog/SNMP Alarm Onscreen Message	No action.
Jitter	10 ms of packet jitter 50 ms of video frame jitter	125 ms of video frame jitter	165 ms of video frame jitter	Syslog/SNMP Alarm	Packets are discarded.
Loss	%0.05	1%	10%	Syslog/SNMP Alarm Onscreen Message	Syslog/SNMP Alarm. Onscreen Message. Quality (motion) is reduced.

Demultiplexing and Decoding

As previously discussed, Cisco TelePresence uses a multiplexing technique, using the SSRC field of the RTP header, to transport multiple video and audio channels over RTP. Each call (session) consists of two RTP streams: one for video and one for audio. On single-screen systems, the video RTP stream consists of two video channels: one for the Cisco TelePresence camera and one for the auxiliary (PC or document camera) video inputs. Likewise, the audio RTP stream consists of two audio channels: one for the Cisco TelePresence microphone and one for the auxiliary (PC) audio input. On multiscreen systems, the video RTP stream consists of four video channels, and the audio RTP stream consists of four audio channels.

Video and Audio Output Mapping

These channels must be demultiplexed, decoded, and played out the corresponding output (to the appropriate screen for video and to the appropriate speaker for audio). Because the entire TelePresence system connects to the network using a single 1000Base-T Gigabit Ethernet interface, all the packets are received by the primary (center) codec. The primary codec analyzes the SSRC field of the RTP headers and sends the left video channel to the left secondary codec and the right video channel to the right secondary codec. The primary codec then proceeds to buffer and decode the center and auxiliary video packets and all audio packets, and the two secondary codecs buffer and decode their respective video packets.

Figure 3-13 illustrates how these channels are mapped from the transmitting TelePresence codec to the receiving TelePresence codec. Refer to Figure 3-2 at the beginning of this chapter for a view of the back of the Cisco TelePresence codec to understand what each connector in Figure 3-13 represents.

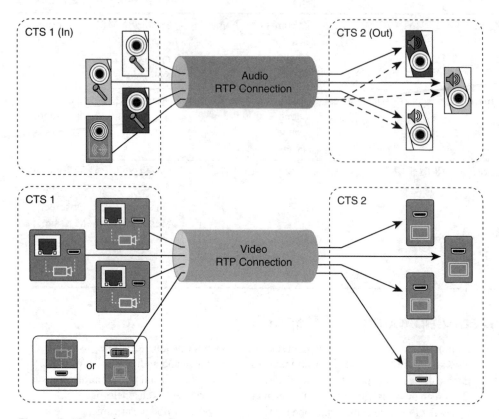

Figure 3-13   *Video and audio output mapping*

Note   Figure 3-13 illustrates a multiscreen system. Single-screen systems would behave exactly the same way, except that the left and right channels would not be present.

Display Outputs, Resolution, and Refresh Rate (Hz)

The left, center, and right video channels are decoded by each Cisco TelePresence codec and sent out the corresponding HDMI interface to the left, center, and right displays. At the time this book was written, the CTS-1000, CTS-3000, and CTS-3200 use 65-inch plasma displays, whereas the CTS-500 uses a 37-inch LCD display. In all cases, these displays run at 1080p resolution at 60 Hz refresh rate using progressive scan. Therefore, the Cisco TelePresence codec must decode the video (whether it was encoded at 1080p / 30 or 720p / 30) and send it to the display at 1080p / 60.

The auxiliary video channel is also decoded and sent out the auxiliary HDMI interface to either the projector or an auxiliary LCD display or displayed as Presentation-in-Picture

(PIP) on the center display. Depending on its destination, the Cisco TelePresence codec decodes the video (which was encoded at 1024x768 at either 5 fps or 30 fps) and sends it out at the correct refresh rate. When it is sent out the auxiliary HDMI interface to either the projector or an auxiliary LCD display, the Cisco TelePresence codec outputs it at 49.5 Hz using interlaced scanning. When it is sent as PIP to the primary HDMI display port, it overlays it on top of the center channels video and outputs it at 1080p / 60.

Frames per Second Versus Fields per Second Versus Refresh Rate (Hz)

It's worth inserting a quick word here on the difference between frames versus fields versus refresh or scan rates (Hz). These terms are frequently confused in the video conferencing and telepresence industries. (For example, a vendor might state that its system does 60 fields per second.)

In a Cisco TelePresence system, the camera operates at a scan rate (also known as *refresh rate* or *clock rate*) of 30 Hz. The codec encodes that video into H.264 video frames at a rate of 30 frames per second (30 fps). The plasma and LCD displays used in Cisco TelePresence operate at a scan rate of 60 Hz using progressive scan display technology. Because the displays are 60-Hz progressive scan, Cisco can claim 60 fields per second support as well. But what actually matters is that the source (the camera) is operating at 30 Hz, and the video is encoded at 30 fps. To truly claim 60 fps, the camera would need to run at 60 Hz, the encoder would need to pump out 60 video frames per second (every 16 ms or so), and the displays would need to run at 120 Hz. This would provide astounding video quality but would also result in double the DSP horsepower and bandwidth needed and quite frankly is unnecessary because the current 30-fps implementation is already the highest-quality solution on the planet and is absolutely adequate for reproducing a true-to-life visual experience.

Instead of getting caught up in a debate over Hz rates and progressive scan versus interlaced scan methods, the most accurate method for determining the true "frame rate" of any vendors' codec is to analyze their RTP packets. As described earlier in the Real-Time Transport Protocol section and illustrated in Figure 3-8, all vendors implementing RTP for video transport use the marker bit to indicate the end of a video frame. Using a packet sniffer, such as the open source program Wireshark (http://www.wireshark.org), and filtering on the RTP marker bit, a graph (similar to those illustrated in Figure 3-9) can be produced with the marker bits highlighted. The x-axis on the graph displays the time those packets arrived and, hence, the number of milliseconds between each marker bit. Dividing 1000 by the number of milliseconds between each marker bit reveals the number of frames per second. With Cisco TelePresence, the marker bits appear every 33 ms (30 fps). With other vendor implementations, which use variable frame-rate encoders, there are much larger and variable times between marker bits. For example, if the time between any two marker bits is 60 ms, the video is only approximately 15 fps for those two frame intervals. If it's 90 ms, the video is only approximately 11 fps. Because the time between marker bits often varies frame-by-frame in these implementations, you can compute the time between all marker bits to derive an average fps for the entire session.

Figure 3-14 shows a screenshot of a Wireshark IO Graph of a competitor's (who shall remain nameless) 720p implementation. In this screenshot, you can see that the RTP packets that have the marker bit set to 0 (false) are colored red (gray in this screen capture), whereas the RTP packets that have the marker bit set to 1 (true) are colored black so that they stand out. The time between the first marker bit on the left (99.839s) and the next marker bit after that (99.878s) is 39 ms (which is approximately 25 fps), whereas the difference between the 99.878s marker bit and the next marker bit after that (99.928s) is 50 ms (20 fps).

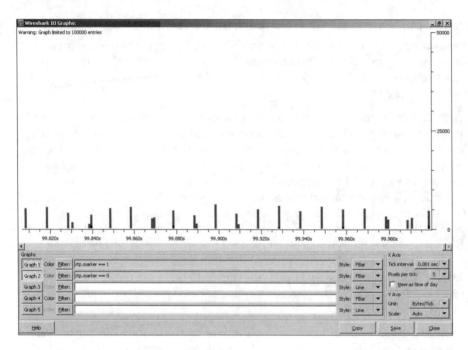

Figure 3-14   *Example Wireshark IO graph*

Audio Outputs

As discussed previously, the audio from the left, center, and right microphone channels is played out the corresponding left, center, and right speakers. The speakers are mounted underneath each display, except for on the CTS-500 in which case they are mounted above the display because the microphone array is mounted underneath the display. This preserves the directionality and spatiality of the sounds, giving the user the audible perception that the sound is emanating from the correct direction and distance. The auxiliary audio is blended across all the speakers because this source is not actually associated with the left, center, or right positions.

Amplification and Volume

The Cisco TelePresence codec contains an embedded amplifier, and the amplification levels and the wattage of the speakers are closely matched to reproduce human speech and other in-room sounds at the correct decibel levels to mimic, as closely as possible, the volume you would experience if the person were actually sitting that far away in person. This means that the users can speak at normal voice levels. (They never feel like they have to raise their voices unnaturally.)

Acoustic Echo Cancellation

As sound patterns are played out of the speakers, they naturally reflect off of surfaces within the environment (walls, ceilings, floors) and return back to enter the microphones. If these sounds were not removed, people would hear their own voices reflected back to them through the system. *Acoustic Echo Cancellation (AEC)* is a digital algorithm to sample the audio signal before it plays out of the speakers and creates a synthetic estimate of that sound pattern, then samples the audio coming into the microphones, and when the same pattern is recognized, digitally subtracts it from the incoming audio signal, thereby canceling out the acoustic echo. This sounds simple enough but is complicated by the naturally dynamic nature of sound in various environments. Depending on the structures and surfaces in the room such as tables, chairs, walls, doors, floors, and ceilings, the distance of those surfaces from the microphones, the materials from which those surfaces are constructed, the periodic movement of those surfaces, and the movement of human bodies within the room, and the number of milliseconds the algorithm must wait to determine whether the sound coming into the microphones is echo can vary significantly. Therefore, the algorithm must automatically and dynamically adapt to these changing conditions.

The Cisco TelePresence codec contains an embedded AEC that requires no human tuning or calibration. It is on by default and is fully automatic. In nonstandard environments, where the Cisco TelePresence codecs are used with third-party microphone mixers, you can disable the embedded AEC using the following CLI command:

```
CTS>set audio aec {enable ¦ disable}
```

Note For more information about the concepts of human speech and acoustic echo, see Chapter 8, "TelePresence Room Design."

Audio-Only Participants

It is common to have one or more participants who cannot attend the meeting in person but are available to dial in and attend through a phone. These callers need to join the TelePresence meeting through an audio-only call, which known as the Audio Add-In feature.

In addition to AAC-LD, Cisco TelePresence also supports the G.711 audio encoding standard. This makes it interoperable with virtually any telephone device or audio conferencing bridge whether that is a standard Plain Old Telephone Service (POTS) phone, a cellular phone, an IP Phone, or an audio-conferencing bridging service, such as Cisco Meetingplace, Cisco Webex, or the numerous other audio bridging services in the market.

The feature is invoked just like it is on regular telephones and cellular phones. The user simply presses the Conference softkey on the Cisco TelePresence IP Phone user interface and places a standard telephone call to the destination phone number. Alternatively, the remote person can dial the telephone number of the TelePresence room, and the user can answer the incoming call and then press the Conference/Join softkey to bridge the caller in.

Under the hood, the way this feature works is that the audio call is established as a completely separate session. (It is signaled using the Session Initiation Protocol [SIP], and a G.711 RTP stream is negotiated.) The RTP stream of audio coming into the TelePresence system from the remote party is decoded and blended out all of the speakers (just like the auxiliary audio is) and is simultaneously mixed in with the auxiliary audio stream going out to all the other participating TelePresence rooms, allowing all the TelePresence participants to hear the audio caller. In the opposite direction, sound coming from all three microphones within the room, with all three of the audio channels received from the other participating TelePresence rooms, is mixed and sent out over the G.711 RTP stream to the audio participant, allowing him to hear everything that's said by the TelePresence participants. Figure 3-15 illustrates how this is done.

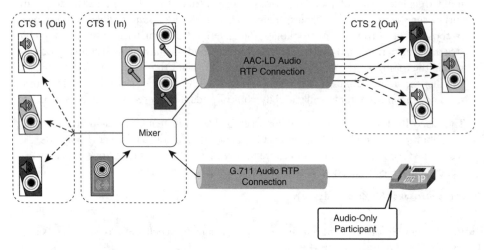

Figure 3-15   *Audio-only participants input and output mapping*

Note   Future versions of Cisco TelePresence might incorporate support for additional audio algorithms for the audio add-in stream, such as G.722, to increase the fidelity of the Audio Add-In participant.

If multiple audio-only participants are needed, the user can use an audio conferencing bridging service, such as Cisco Webex, as illustrated in Figure 3-16.

To successfully dial into a bridging service such as Cisco Webex, the TelePresence user initiating the Audio Add-In feature must navigate the Interactive Voice Response (IVR) menu of the bridging service and enter the correct conferencing ID number and password to join that audio meeting. This is a good segue into the next topic, DTMF.

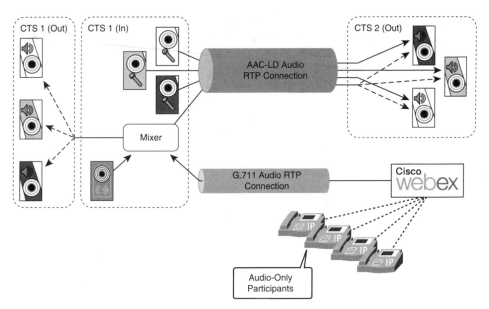

Figure 3-16   *Multiple audio-only participants using a conferencing bridging service*

Dual-Tone Multi-Frequency

Dual-Tone Multi-Frequency (DTMF) enables the user to interact with voice prompts using the touch-tone buttons on the telephone to enter digits, *, and # symbols. This enables the user to navigate IVR menus, enter conference numbers and passwords, check their voicemail, and so on. DTMF has been around throughout the history of telephony and has been adapted into the numerous protocols used in IP-based telephony. H.323, Media Gateway Control Protocol (MGCP), Session Initiation Protocol (SIP) and others all incorporate support for DTMF using one or more methods.

Depending on the protocol in use, there are fundamentally two forms of DTMF signaling:

- **In-band:** Puts the DTMF tones inside the audio stream

- **Out-of-band:** Interprets the DTMF tones and converts them into messages carried over the signaling protocol

In the case of SIP, there are two predominant methods for incorporating DTMF support:

- **RFC 2833:** Defines the RTP payload type used for carrying DTMF tones in-band within the RTP audio stream

- **Key-Pad Markup Language (KPML):** Defines a method relaying DTMF tones through the SIP signaling protocol

Which method is used for a given call is negotiated through SIP during the session establishment phase and can be RFC 2833, KPML, or none, depending on what type of audio device the TelePresence system connects to.

RFC 2833

RFC 2833 is maintained by the Internet Engineering Task Force (IETF) and was standardized in 2000. It defines a method for carrying DTMF signaling events and other tones and telephony events within RTP packets.

RTP defines a variety of payload types and contains a payload type field within the RTP header to indicate what payload type the packet contains (audio, video, DTMF, and so on). Refer back to Figure 3-8 for details of the RTP header contents. The payload type for DTMF is referred to as a *named event*. RFC 2833 defines several different named event types; one of those is DTMF events. When a DTMF tone is identified, the encoder translates it into an RTP packet, setting the payload type (PT) field to the numerical number associated with DTMF payload events, and inserting the actual DTMF event into the body of the RTP payload. The numerical identifier used for DTMF events can be negotiated ahead of time during the session establishment period. For example, Cisco devices generally use payload type 97 for DTMF events, but this can be negotiated on a call-by-call basis.

Key-Pad Markup Language

Key-Pad Markup Language (KPML) is also maintained by the IETF and was converted from an IETF Internet draft to a published RFC (RFC 4730) in November 2006. It defines a method for carrying DTMF signaling events with SIP event packages within the SIP signaling protocol.

SIP RFC 3265 defines a method within SIP by which an application can SUBSCRIBE to specific event packages and receive NOTIFY messages whenever such an event occurs. RFC 4730 leverages this SUBSCRIBE/NOTIFY architecture to define a DTMF event package. During the SIP session establishment phase (through the INVITE, 180 TRYING, 183 SESSION PROGRESS, and 200 OK messages), the SIP User Agents advertise support for KPML in the Allowed-Events and Supported headers. After being advertised, the User Agent who wants to receive DTMF events sends a SUBSCRIBE message to the other User Agent indicating that it wants to subscribe to the KMPL event package. The User Agent receiving the SUBSCRIBE request sends a 200 OK acknowledgment to the subscriber. Thereafter, any DTMF event initiated by the User Agent who received the SUBSCRIBE request is sent in a NOTIFY message to the subscriber, contained as an XML document within the body of that NOTIFY message.

Other Protocols

Other protocols have similar approaches for DTMF support. H.323, for example, commonly uses RFC 2833, or H.245 Alpha-Numeric notation, among others. Media Gateway Control Protocol (MGCP) commonly uses RFC 2833, or MGCP-DTMF relay. In the case of Cisco TelePresence, the CUCM handles all the call signaling and deals with converting between the various signaling protocols to enable end-to-end DTMF. For example, if a Cisco TelePresence system called a Cisco Webex audio conferencing bridging service, it would need to traverse an IP-PSTN gateway. For example, if that gateway were running MGCP, there are two ways that DTMF might be configured:

- **RFC 2833:** If the gateway advertises RFC 2833 support only, the Unified CM would advertise RFC 2833 to the Cisco TelePresence system.

- **DTMF-relay:** If the gateway advertised DTMF-relay, the CUCM would advertise KPML to the Cisco TelePresence system.

Note For more information about the SIP and other call signaling concepts, see Chapter 12, "TelePresence Call-Signaling Design."

How DTMF Tones Are Processed in Cisco TelePresence

In the case of Cisco TelePresence, the user presses the buttons on the Cisco TelePresence IP Phone, but the Cisco TelePresence Primary (center) codec is the one doing all the SIP signaling and handling all the media; the IP Phone is just the user interface instrument to the system.

The first generation of Cisco TelePresence used the eXtensible Markup Language (XML) programming language as an interface between the Cisco IP Phone and the primary codec. When a user wanted to enter DTMF tones, they pressed the Tones softkey, which would bring up a page where the user could enter the digits they wanted to send and then press the Send softkey. That XML content was then sent to the primary codec over an HTTP session. The codec would read the XML contents and convert them into SIP-KPML messages, or RFC 2833 payloads.

At the time this book was written, Cisco TelePresence was moving away from XML to a newer, more robust method using Java MIDlets. With this method, a small Java application (called a MIDlet) runs on the IP Phone and intercepts the button presses. These button presses are then communicated over a TCP session between the Java MIDlet running on the IP Phone and the primary codec. The codec reads the Java TCP messages and converts them into SIP-KPML messages, or RFC 2833 payloads.

In both cases, the button presses are sent by the IP Phone to the primary codec, and the codec converts them and plays them out onto the network. If RFC 2833 is in use, the primary codec converts the XML or Java MIDlet event into an RTP DTMF event and multiplexes it into the audio RTP stream. If KPML is in use during the SIP session establishment phase, the Unified CM would send a SUBSCRIBE request to the primary codec subscribing to the KPML event package. The primary codec, therefore, converts the XML or Java MIDlet event into an XML document and sends it in a NOTIFY message to the CUCM.

Interoperability with Out-of-Band Collaboration Applications

Another aspect of supporting audio-only participants is providing a method for all participants to collaborate on shared documents and presentations. As described previously in this chapter, Cisco TelePresence provides for auxiliary video inputs and outputs so that users can attach their PCs to the system, and how that signal is encoded and multiplexed over RTP so that all the other TelePresence participants can see it. But how do the audio-only participants get to view it, and can the audio-only participants share a document or presentation with the TelePresence participants?

At the time this book was written, the predominant method of sharing documents and presentations on an audio conference is through the use of web-based collaboration tools such as Cisco MeetingPlace or Cisco Webex. There have been other methods in the past, such as the infamous T.120 protocol, but those are pretty much defunct. Therefore, the way forward is to engineer a method whereby the auxiliary video channel can automatically convert into a format viewable by the web conference participants and vice versa. At the time this book was written, this functionality was in the process of being developed.

In the meantime, there is a method for achieving the desired results, but it requires steps on the part of the user to enable it. It's relatively simple but requires a three-step process:

Step 1.   The user attaches his or her PC to the auxiliary (VGA) video input of the TelePresence system. This allows whatever he or she is sharing to be instantly viewed by all the other TelePresence participants.

Step 2.   The user dials into the audio conferencing server and enters the appropriate DTMF tones to bridge the TelePresence meeting into the audio conference (as described in the previous sections).

Step 3.   The user also fires up the web browser on his or her PC and logs onto the web conferencing server for that audio conference and joins the meeting as a web-participant as well and then activates the sharing feature within that web conference.

Now whatever the user shares on her PC is sent simultaneously by his or her PC over VGA to the Cisco TelePresence Primary codec and over HTTP to the web conference. Although this adds a degree of complexity to the ease-of-use of TelePresence, the good news is that it works with virtually any audio and web conferencing product on the planet.

Interoperability with Video Conferencing

In addition to supporting audio-only participants, Cisco TelePresence also supports video conferencing participants. This is done by bridging together the TelePresence multipoint meeting (hosted on a Cisco TelePresence Multipoint Switch [CTMS] and a regular multipoint video conference [hosted on a Cisco Unified Video conferencing MCU]). Bridging multipoint meetings together has been around for years in the video conferencing industry and is referred to as *cascading*. The Cisco implementation of cascading between

TelePresence and video conferencing is similar to previous implementations in the market, except that Cisco had to create a way of mapping multiscreen TelePresence systems with standard single-screen video conferencing systems. Cisco calls this *Active Segment Cascading*.

Note At the time this book was written, a multipoint cascaded conference is the only method for interoperating between Cisco TelePresence and traditional video conferencing endpoints. Direct, point-to-point calls between a TelePresence system and a video conferencing endpoint are not allowed. This is highly likely to change in the future as Cisco continues to develop additional interoperability capabilities within the TelePresence solution.

Note Interoperability with video conferencing is also covered in Chapter 13. To reduce the need to repeat that discussion, it is recommended that you review Figure 13-10 and 13-11 in Chapter 13 before reading further. These figures provide a high-level understanding of the Active Segment Cascading methodology, giving context to the following details. Also, for the sake of brevity, the descriptions of how the encoding and decoding and multiplexing work are abbreviated in the following sections, as those have already been thoroughly covered in the preceding sections of this chapter.

Interoperability RTP Channels

When Cisco engineered its video conferencing interoperability solution, the vast majority of video conferencing equipment ran at CIF or 4 CIF resolutions (720p was just beginning to become widely deployed), and no video conferencing endpoints or MCUs (including the CUVC platform) were capable of receiving and decoding the Cisco 1080p resolution video and AAC-LD audio. Therefore, Cisco had two choices:

- Degrade the experience for the TelePresence participants by encoding the entire meeting at a much lower resolution and using inferior audio algorithms to accommodate the video conferencing participants

- Maintain the 1080p/AAC-LD experience for the TelePresence participants and send an additional video and audio stream for the video conferencing MCU to digest

For obvious reasons, Cisco chose the latter method.

Note The methods described herein are highly likely to change in the future as video conferencing equipment becoming increasingly capable of higher definition video resolutions (720p and 1080p) and AAC-LD audio becomes more commonplace within the installed base.

When a Cisco TelePresence system (single-screen or multiscreen model) dials into a CTMS meeting that is configured for interoperability, the CTMS requests the TelePresence endpoint to send a copy of its 1080p video in CIF resolution and a copy of its AAC-LD audio in G.711 format. These CIF and G.711 streams are then switched to the CUVC MCU, which, in turn, relays them to the video conferencing participants. In the reverse direction, the CUVC sends the CTMS its CIF resolution video and G.711 audio from the video conferencing participants, and the CTMS relays that down to the TelePresence participants.

CIF Resolution Video Channel

Multiscreen TelePresence systems, such as the CTS-3000 and CTS-3200, provide three channels of 1080p / 30 resolution video. However, only one can be sent to the CUVC at any given time, so the Cisco TelePresence codec uses a voice-activated switching methodology to choose which of the three streams it should send at any moment in time. If a user on the left screen starts talking, the left codec encodes that cameras video using H.264 at 1080p / 30 (or whatever resolution/motion-handling setting the system is set to use) and also at CIF / 30. If a user in the center starts talking, the left codec stops encoding the CIF video channel, and the center codec now begins encoding the center cameras video using H.264 at 1080p / 30 (or whatever resolution/motion-handling setting the system is set to use) and CIF / 30. This switching occurs dynamically throughout the life of the meeting between the left, center, and right codecs based on the microphone sensitivity (who is speaking the loudest) of each position.

Single-screen TelePresence systems such as the CTS-1000 and CTS-500 have only one screen (the center channel), so no switching is required.

When encoded, the CIF channel is multiplexed by the primary codec into the outgoing RTP video stream along with the other four video channels (left, center, right, and auxiliary). In the case of a single-screen system, the CIF channel is multiplexed in with the other two video channels (center and auxiliary).

G.711 Audio Channel

On multiscreen TelePresence systems, such as the CTS-3000 and CTS-3200, there are three channels of AAC-LD audio. Instead of sending one at a time, the primary (center) codec mixes all three channels together and encodes the mix in G.711 format. Therefore, all parties can be heard at any given time.

The G.711 channel is multiplexed into the outgoing RTP audio stream with the other four channels (left, center, and right AAC-LD audio channels, and the auxiliary audio channel).

Single-screen systems have only a single microphone channel (center), so there is no need to mix. The center channel is encoded in both AAC-LD and G.711 formats and multiplexed together into the outgoing RTP audio stream along with the auxiliary audio channel, for a total of three audio channels.

Additional Bandwidth Required

As a result of having to send these additional CIF resolution video and G.711 audio channels, additional bandwidth is consumed by each participating TelePresence System. The CIF resolution video is encoded at 704 kbps, and the G.711 audio is encoded at 64 kbps, for a total of 768 kbps additional bandwidth.

CTMS Switching of the Interop Channels

As previously discussed, the multiple channels of video and the multiple channels of audio are multiplexed using the SSRC field in the RTP header. Ordinarily, there are four video positions and four audio positions within the SSRC field (left, center, right, and auxiliary). A fifth SSRC position was defined to carry the CIF and G.711 interop channels within the video and audio RTP streams.

When the CTMS receives the video and audio streams from any TelePresence system, it reads the SSRC position of the RTP header and decides where to switch it. Left, center, right, and auxiliary positions are switched to the other TelePresence participants, and the interop position is switched to the CUVC MCU.

In the opposite direction, the CIF video and G.711 audio coming from the CUVC MCU to the CTMS is appended with the SSRC position of the interop channel and sent down to all the participating TelePresence rooms.

Decoding of the Interop Channels

When a Cisco TelePresence system receives RTP packets containing the SSRC value of the interop position, the primary (center) codec forwards the CIF video RTP packets to the left secondary codec to be decoded. The center codec decodes the G.711 audio, mixes it with the left channel of decoded AAC-LD audio, and plays the mix out the left speaker. This way, the video conferencing participants always appear on the left display and are heard coming out the left speaker, along with any TelePresence participants seated on that side of the system. On single-screen systems, it obviously appears on the single (center) display and speaker.

Because CIF video is 4:3 aspect ratio (352x288 resolution), and the TelePresence displays are 16:9 aspect ratio and run at 1080p / 60 resolution, the CIF video must be displayed in the best possible way. Stretching it to fit a 65-inch 1080p display would look terrible, so the left codec pixel doubles the decoded video to 4CIF resolution (704x576) and displays it on the 1080p display surrounded by black borders, as previously shown in Figure 3-5.

Summary

This chapter provided an under-the-hood look into the audio and video subsystems of the Cisco TelePresence system. The chapter covered the following topics:

- **Codec design requirements:** Discussed the thought process that went into designing the Cisco TelePresence codec

- **Codec system architecture:** Described the physical design, distributed master/slave codec architecture, and operating system software of the Cisco TelePresence codec

- **Codec and component connectivity:** Described the physical connectivity of the codecs, cameras, displays, microphones, speakers, and auxiliary components

- **Encoding and packetization:** Described how the audio and video is encoded, packetized, and multiplexed onto the network

- **De-packetization and decoding:** Described how the audio and video are received, demultiplexed, and decoded, and described how the system manages latency, jitter, and packet loss

- **Audio-only participants:** Described how the system enables audio-only partici-pants or audio conference bridges to be joined into the meeting

- **Dual-Tone Multi-Frequency (DTMF) Implementation:** Described how the system interacts with machines that require the user to enter DTMF tones, such as audio con-ference bridges and Interactive Voice Response (IVR) systems

- **Interoperability with out-of-band collaboration applications:** Described how the system interacts with web-based collaboration tools, such as Cisco Webex

- **Interoperability with legacy video conferencing:** Described how the system interacts with legacy video conferencing systems

Further Reading

IETF Standards:

Real-time Transport Protocol (RTP): http://www.ietf.org/rfc/rfc3550.

RTP Payload Format for H.264 Video: http://www.ietf.org/rfc/rfc3984.

RTP Payload for DTMF Digits, Telephony Tones and Telephony Signals: http://www.ietf.org/rfc/rfc2833.

A Session Initiation Protocol (SIP) Event Package for Key Press Stimulus (KPML): http://www.ietf.org/rfc/rfc4730.

ITU-T Standards:

Advanced Video Coding for Generic Audiovisual Services (H.264): http://www.itu.int/rec/T-REC-H.264.

ISO/IEC Motion Pictures Experts Group (MPEG) Standards:

Advanced Audio Coding-Low Delay (MPEG4-Part3): http://www.en.wikipedia.org/wiki/Advanced_Audio_Coding.

As discussed in previous chapters, TelePresence solutions are composed of many different hardware and software components, various technologies, and protocols. The goal of this chapter is to show how these individual elements interconnect and interrelate to each other.

This chapter begins with a microperspective and look at how internal TelePresence components—such as the codecs, cameras, displays, microphones, and speakers—connect to each other. Following this, the chapter zooms out to a macroperspective and looks at how TelePresence systems connect and interact with LAN access networks. The chapter concludes with a look at the bigger picture to consider the various deployment models that TelePresence solutions can take, both within the enterprise and connecting enterprises through a service provider network.

Understanding the basics of these interconnections—both internal and external—give you a foundational context for the design chapters that follow.

CHAPTER 4

Connecting TelePresence Systems

Internal TelePresence System Connections

TelePresence systems are composed of cameras, displays, microphones, speakers, codecs, auxiliary accessories, and an IP Phone. At the time of writing, four different TelePresence systems exist:

- CTS-500

- CTS-1000

- CTS-3000

- CTS-3200

The following sections take a look at how each of these systems internally connects its respective components.

> **Note** TelePresence systems will continue to evolve and expand over time; nonetheless, breaking down the internal connection schematics of current systems is a valuable exercise because it reveals a foundational pattern that is likely to continue within future TelePresence system designs.

Connecting a CTS-500 System

The CTS-500 is a personal TelePresence system intended to support single-user TelePresence conferencing. The CTS-500 system includes a 37-inch display with an integrated codec, camera, microphone, and speaker. Additionally, the CTS-500 has a connection for an optional Cisco Digital Media Player (DMP), which you can use to display live or streaming video content when you do not use the CTS-500 for TelePresence meetings. The minimum room dimensions to support a CTS-500 are 8 x 6 x 8 feet.

Specifically, the CTS-500 includes the following:

- One Cisco TelePresence codec (a primary codec)

- One Cisco Unified 7975G IP Phone

- One 37-inch LCD display

- One high-definition camera

- One microphone

- One speaker

- One input for auxiliary audio

- One input for auxiliary video that you can use for a document camera or PC

The Cisco TelePresence primary codec is the center of the CTS systems. Essentially, all internal TelePresence components connect to it, and it, in turn, provides the sole access point to the network infrastructure.

Explicitly, the Cisco Unified 7975G IP Phone connects to the TelePresence primary codec through an RJ-45 cable that provides it with network connectivity and 802.3af Power-over-Ethernet (PoE).

Another RJ-45 cable connects from the TelePresence primary codec to the camera, providing the camera with 802.3af PoE. A second cable from the primary codec to the camera provides video connectivity.

A *High Definition Multimedia Interface (HDMI)* video cable also connects the primary codec to the 37-inch LCD display. This cable has a proprietary element for carrying management information instead of audio signals because the audio signals are processed independently by the master codec.

Additionally, a speaker cable and a microphone cable connect the speaker and microphone to the primary codec, respectively.

The primary codec also has inputs for auxiliary audio and auxiliary video. Auxiliary video can come from a PC connection or from a document camera connection. An *IP power switch (IPS)* provides control for the on/off function of the document camera, attached projector, and lighting shroud of the CTS unit through an Ethernet connection.

Finally, an RJ-45 cable provides 10/100/1000 Ethernet connectivity from the primary codec to the network infrastructure. Figure 4-1 illustrates these interconnections for a CTS-500 system.

Connecting a CTS-1000 System

The CTS-1000 is a multi-user TelePresence system that can support one or two users at a given location. For purposes of this discussion, the CTS-1000 is virtually identical to the CTS-500 except for two main differences:

- The CTS-1000 includes a 65-inch plasma display (as compared to the 37-inch LCD display used by the CTS-500).

- The CTS-1000 does not support the optional DMP.

With the exception of these two components, the parts list and connection details of these systems are identical. Figure 4-2 shows the connectivity of the CTS-1000.

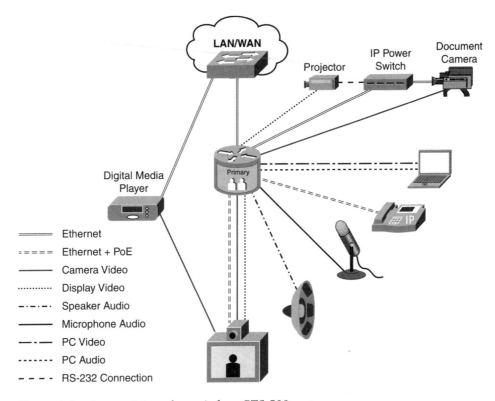

Figure 4-1 *Connectivity schematic for a CTS-500 system*

Connecting a CTS-3000 System

The CTS-3000 is a conference room TelePresence system that supports up to six users at a single location. The most obvious changes—aside from the expanded form-factor (with furniture to match)—are the two additional 65-inch displays. To support the additional processing required by the additional displays (and corresponding cameras), the primary codec distributes processing to secondary codecs. The minimum room dimensions to support a CTS-3000 are 8 x 15 x 19 feet.

Specifically, the CTS-3000 includes the following:

■ One Cisco TelePresence primary codec

■ Two Cisco TelePresence secondary codecs

■ One Cisco Unified 7975G IP Phone

■ Three 65-inch plasma displays

■ Three high-definition cameras

■ Three microphones

■ Three speakers

■ One input for auxiliary video that you can use for a document camera or PC

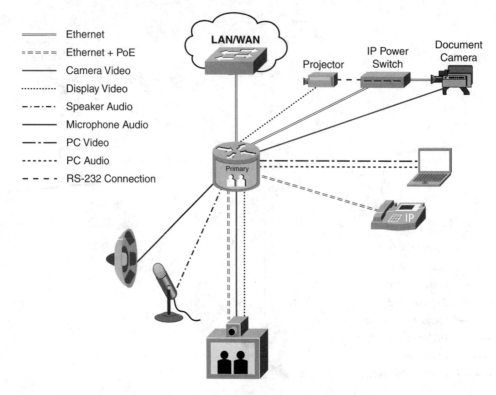

Figure 4-2 *Connectivity schematic for a CTS-1000 system*

As with the CTS-500 and CTS-1000 systems, the primary codec is the central part of the CTS-3000 system to which all other components interconnect. Explicitly, the Cisco Unified 7975G IP Phone connects to the TelePresence primary codec via an RJ-45 cable that provides it with network connectivity and 802.3af PoE.

A video cable connects the primary codec to the center 65-inch plasma display; another cable connects the right display to the (right) secondary codec; and a third connects the left display to the (left) secondary codec. As with the CTS-1000 system, this cable is essentially an HDMI cable but with a proprietary element for carrying management information instead of audio signals (because the master codec independently processes the audio signals). Each of these secondary codecs, in turn, connects to the primary codec via a RJ-45 cable; however, no 802.3af PoE is required over these Ethernet links because the secondary codecs have independent power supplies.

Three cameras are mounted on the central display, and each camera connects to its respective codec:

- The left camera connects to the (left) secondary codec.

- The center camera connects to the primary codec.

- The right camera connects to the (right) secondary codec.

Each camera connects to its respective codec via two cables: an RJ-45 cable, which provides 802.3af PoE and network connectivity to the camera, and a video cable to carry the video signals to the codec.

Additionally, three speaker cables and three microphone cables connect the (left, center, and right) speakers and (left, center, and right) microphones to the primary codec, respectively.

The primary codec also has inputs for auxiliary audio and auxiliary video. Auxiliary video can come from a PC connection or from a document camera connection (but not both at the same time). An IPS provides control for the on/off function of the document camera, attached projector, and lighting shroud of the CTS unit through an Ethernet connection.

Finally, an RJ-45 cable provides 10/100/1000 Ethernet connectivity from the primary codec to the network infrastructure. Figure 4-3 illustrates these interconnections for a CTS-3000 system.

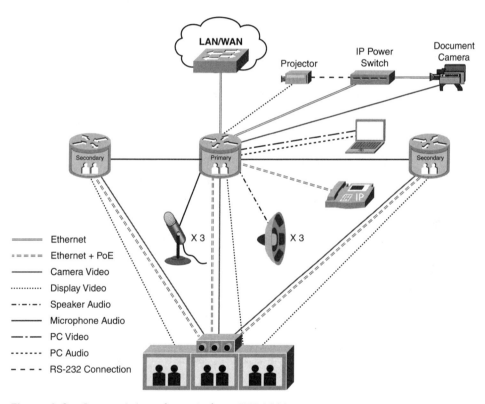

Figure 4-3   *Connectivity schematic for a CTS-3000 system*

Connecting a CTS-3200 System

The CTS-3200 is a large-scale conference room TelePresence system that enables TelePresence technology for large room venues, supporting up to 18 users at a single location. Although the number of displays and cameras are unchanged (as compared to the CTS-3000), you can add additional microphones to the CTS-3200 to support additional participants. The minimum room dimensions to support a CTS-3200 are 8 x 24 x 23 feet.

Specifically, the CTS-3000 includes the following:

■   One Cisco TelePresence primary codec

■   Two Cisco TelePresence secondary codecs

■   One Cisco Unified 7975G IP Phone

■   Three 65-inch plasma displays

■   Three high-definition cameras

■   Nine microphones

■   Three speakers

■   One input for auxiliary audio

■   One input for auxiliary video or another optional secondary codec for high-speed auxiliary video that you can use for a document camera or PC

As with the previously discussed CTS systems, the primary codec is the central part of the CTS-3200 system to which all other components interconnect.

Explicitly, the Cisco Unified 7975G IP Phone connects to the TelePresence primary codec via an RJ-45 cable that provides it with network connectivity and 802.3af PoE.

A video cable connects the primary codec to the center 65-inch plasma display, another cable connects the right display to the (right) secondary codec, and a third connects the left display to the (left) secondary codec. As with the CTS-3000 system, this cable is essentially an HDMI cable but with a proprietary element for carrying management information instead of audio signals (because the master codec independently processes the audio signals). Each of these secondary codecs, in turn, connects to the primary codec via an RJ-45 cable; however, no 802.3af PoE is required over these Ethernet links because the secondary codecs have independent power supplies.

Three cameras are mounted on the central display, and each camera connects to its respective codec:

■   The left camera connects to the (left) secondary codec.

■   The center camera connects to the primary codec.

■   The right camera connects to the (right) secondary codec.

Each camera connects to its respective codec through two cables:

■   An RJ-45 cable, which provides 802.3af PoE and network connectivity to the camera

■   A video cable to carry the video signals to the codec

Additionally, three speaker cables connect the (left, center, and right) speakers to the primary codec, respectively.

One microphone cable connects the center microphone to the primary codec. The remaining eight microphones connect to the audio extension box, which is, in turn, connected to the primary codec. The audio extension box also houses the HDMI splitter. The HDMI splitter connects to the auxiliary video output of the primary codec. You can connect up to four displays or a projector and three displays to the HDMI ports on the audio extension box.

The primary codec also has inputs for low-speed (5 frames per second) auxiliary audio and video inputs, such as for sharing documents or slide-based presentations. Video input can come from a PC or optional document camera. An IPS provides control for the on/off function of the document camera, attached projector, and lighting shroud of the CTS unit through an Ethernet connection.

Optionally, you can connect another secondary codec to the primary codec to provide high-speed (30 frames per second) auxiliary audio and video input, such as for sharing high-quality video presentations. The auxiliary codec connects to the primary codec via the RJ-45 cable from the Ethernet port normally used for the document camera. Auxiliary audio still connects to the primary codec.

The primary codec of the CTS-3200 provides a connection for an optional headset.

Finally, an RJ-45 cable provides 10/100/1000 Ethernet connectivity from the primary codec to the network infrastructure. Figure 4-4 illustrates the interconnections for a CTS-3200 system.

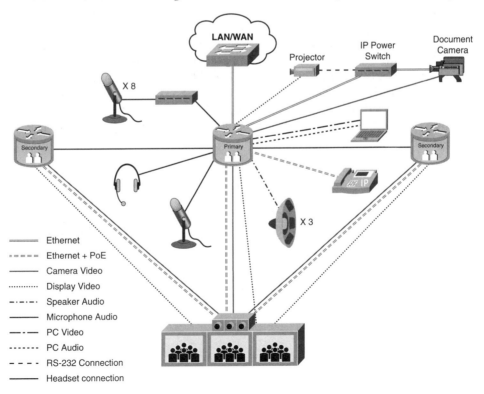

Figure 4-4 *Connectivity schematic for a CTS-3200 system*

In summary, a basic pattern of connectivity is in each of these TelePresence systems. Specifically, the primary codec is the heart of all TelePresence systems; all other components connect (directly or indirectly) to the primary codec, which provides power, connectivity, and control to all subcomponents. Larger systems, such as the CTS-3000/3200, leverage secondary codecs to distribute processing. And finally, all TelePresence systems connect to the network through a single RJ-45 cable from the primary codec (not including optional accessories, such as the DMP). In this manner, all TelePresence system subcomponents are abstracted from the network, and the system appears as a single unit from the network's perspective.

The following section takes a closer look at how to achieve this abstraction by examining the protocol interactions between TelePresence systems and the network.

TelePresence Network Interaction

As highlighted in each TelePresence system connectivity schematic, the primary codec is the interface between the CTS system and the network infrastructure. The primary codec connects to the network access-edge switch through an RJ-45 10/100/1000 port. The access-edge Catalyst switch that it connects to provides IP services, 802.1Q/p VLAN services, QoS services, and security services to the TelePresence system.

Additionally, the primary codec provides an RJ-45 connection to the Cisco Unified 7975G IP Phone, to which it supplies 802.3af PoE. When the IP Phone starts up, it sends a Cisco Discovery Protocol (CDP) message to the primary codec. The codec receives this CDP message and passes it on to the access-edge switch, supplementing it with its own CDP advertisement. The access-edge switch and codec exchange CDP messages, and the switch (if configured according to best practice recommendations for IP telephony deployments) places the primary codec and the 7975G IP Phone in an *802.1Q Voice VLAN (VVLAN)*, wherein 802.1Q/p *Class of Service (CoS)* markings are trusted. The primary codec passes 802.1Q tags between the 7975G IP Phone and the network access-edge switch, extending the VVLAN all the way to the IP Phone. Figure 4-5 illustrates this 802.1Q/p VVLAN assignment.

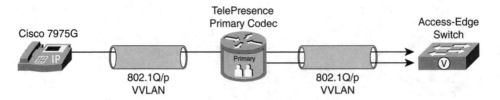

Figure 4-5   *Voice VLAN extension through Cisco TelePresence primary codec*

Note The network interaction previously described assumes that CDP is enabled and VVLANs are configured. If this is not the case, the network interaction begins with the DHCP requests described in the following paragraphs.

If configured for dynamic IP addressing, the Cisco 7975G IP Phone and the primary codec each generate a Dynamic Host Configuration Protocol (DHCP) request to the network and are supplied with IP addresses (one for the IP Phone and another for the primary codec). The DHCP server might also provide the IP Phone and primary codec the IP address of the download server, through DHCP option 150, from which they download their configuration files and firmware loads. This function is often provided by the Cisco Unified Communications Manager (CUCM) server. Alternatively, either or both of the devices can be configured with a static IP address and TFTP server address.

Additionally, the TelePresence systems use a private network for internal communications between the primary and secondary codecs and between codecs and cameras. By default, the internal address range is 192.168.0.0/24 through 192.168.4.0/24; however, if the TelePresence codec receives a 192.168.x.x address from the network, the internal private network switches to 10.0.0.0/24 through 10.0.4.0/24. Figure 4-6 illustrates a default internal network IP address assignment.

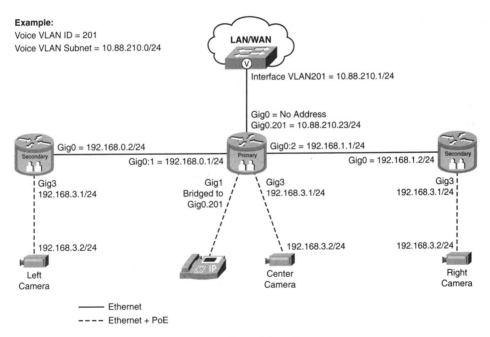

Figure 4-6 *Default TelePresence internal IP addressing scheme*

Note Even though only 192.168.0.0/24 through 192.168.3.0/24 are illustrated in Figure 4-6, 192.168.4.0/24 is reserved within the system for future (internal) use.

Similarly, if the TelePresence system uses 10.0.0.0/24 through 10.0.3.0/24 for its internal networking address range, 10.0.4.0/24 is reserved within the system for future (internal) use.

Following are three key points regarding the internal networking of TelePresence systems:

- From the network's perspective, the TelePresence primary codec appears as a single endpoint device with a single IP address. (Remember, the 7975G IP Phone also appears as a separate endpoint device with its own IP address).

- The internal components (such as secondary codecs and cameras) do not receive a default gateway; therefore, they cannot route beyond the primary codec.

- If the primary codec uses 192.168.0.0/24 through 192.168.4.0/24 as its internal networking addresses (which is the default), it cannot connect to external servers or endpoints that uses these same addresses (because it will attempt to reach such addresses via its internal network, not its external default gateway). Conversely, if the primary codec has been assigned an IP address from the network in the 192.168.x.x range, it uses internal networking addresses in the range of 10.0.0.0/24 through 10.0.4.0/24 and similarly cannot connect to external servers or endpoints that might use these same addresses. Table 4-1 summarizes the IP addressing best practices for networks supporting TelePresence.

Table 4-1   *TelePresence System IP Addressing Best Practices*

For Environments Where the CTS Uses 192.168.x.x for Its Internal Communications	For Environments Where the CTS Uses 10.x.x.x for Its Internal Communications
Avoid Using the Following Subnets:	**Avoid Using the Following Subnets:**
192.168.0.0/24	10.0.0.0/24
192.168.1.0.24	10.0.1.0/24
192.168.2.0.24	10.0.2.0/24
192.168.3.0.24	10.0.3.0/24
192.168.4.0.24	10.0.4.0/24

Provided no IP addressing issues exist, the IP Phone then initiates a Trivial File Transfer Protocol (TFTP) session with the CUCM to download its configuration and firmware files. The primary codec initiates an HTTP session over TCP port 6970 for its configuration and firmware files. Note that DNS might also be required to translate the CUCM hostname to an IP address.

The primary codec then communicates with CUCM through *Session Initiation Protocol (SIP)*. The Cisco 7975G IP Phone also communicates with CUCM through SIP, identifying itself as a shared line with the primary codec. Additional messaging occurs between the 7975G IP Phone, TelePresence primary codec, and Cisco TelePresence Manager through Extensible Markup Language (XML) and Simple Network Management Protocol (SNMP). Figure 4-7 illustrates these network protocol interactions.

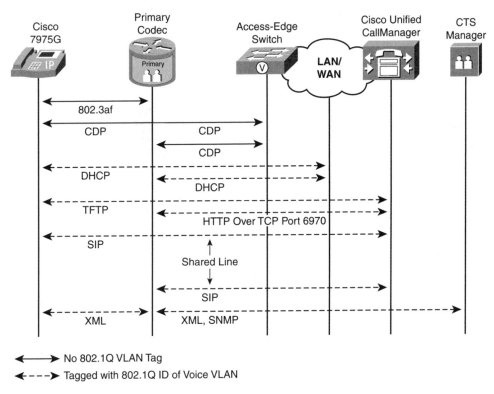

Figure 4-7 *Cisco TelePresence network control, management, and signaling protocols*

When the TelePresence system completes these protocol interactions, it is ready to place and receive calls. When a call initiates, the following steps occur:

1. The Cisco 7975G IP Phone sends an XML Dial message to its primary codec.

2. The initiating TelePresence primary codec forwards the request as a SIP Invite message to the CUCM.

3. The CUCM, in turn, forwards the SIP Invite message to the destination TelePresence primary codec (or Session Border Controller, in the case of business-to-business calls, which will be discussed in detail in Chapter 14, "Intercompany TelePresence Design").

4. The destination codec forwards the message as an XML Ring message to its associated 7975G IP Phone. (The TelePresence primary codec can optionally be set to automatically answer the incoming call, in which case the codec answers the call immediately and proceeds to Step 6, which is to send a SIP OK message to CUCM.)

5. If auto-answer is not enabled, when the user presses the Answer softkey on the 7975G IP Phone, the 7975G IP Phone replies with an XML Answer message to the destination codec.

6. The destination codec sends a SIP 200 OK message to the CUCM.

7. The CUCM relays this SIP 200 OK message to the initiating TelePresence primary codec, and the call is established.

8. Real-time media, both audio and video, passes between the TelePresence primary codecs over Real Time Protocol (RTP).

Figure 4-8 illustrates the signaling and media paths for Cisco TelePresence.

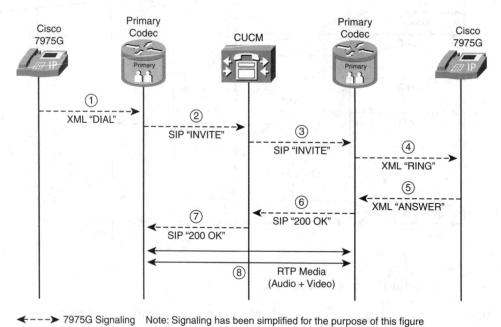

Figure 4-8 *Cisco TelePresence signaling and media paths*

CTS-1000 and CTS-500 systems send only one audio and one video stream (excluding auxiliary audio and video inputs for the moment). On the other hand, CTS-3000 and CTS-3200 primary codecs process three separate audio and three separate video streams. However, these codecs do not send three separate audio streams and three separate video streams over the network. Rather, CTS-3000 and CTS-3200 primary codecs multiplex the three audio streams into one RTP stream and three video streams into one RTP stream and, hence, send only a single audio and a single video stream over the network. These streams, in turn, are demultiplexed by the receiving codec. Figure 4-9 illustrates the multiplexing of audio and video streams performed by the CTS-3000 primary codecs.

Auxiliary audio and video inputs, both for single systems (such as the CTS-500/1000) and for triple systems (such as the CTS-3000/3200), also multiplex into the same audio and

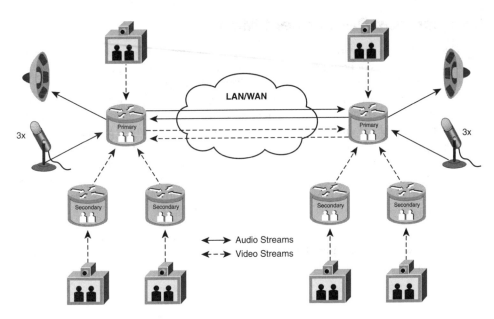

Figure 4-9 *CTS-3000/3200 multiplexing of audio and video streams*

video streams. Therefore, in the case of the CTS-1000 or CTS-500, the primary video and auxiliary video multiplex into one outgoing video stream; likewise the primary audio and auxiliary audio multiplex into one outgoing audio stream.

In the case of the CTS-3000 or CTS-3200, the auxiliary video is treated as the fourth video channel and multiplexed in with the rest of the video; likewise the auxiliary audio is treated as the fourth audio channel and multiplexed in with the rest of the audio.

A main advantage of multiplexing the audio and video streams is that this forces these streams to follow the same path over the network and, thus, ensures that they all play out together in sync. If these flows were separated into three (or more) streams, it would be much more difficult to ensure that all flows arrive within the same time window and all play out at the same time reference.

TelePresence Network Deployment Models

You can deploy TelePresence systems over enterprise networks in one of three principle deployment models:

- Intracampus deployment model

- Intra-enterprise deployment model

- Intercompany deployment model

The following sections provide an overview of these TelePresence network deployment models and logical phases of TelePresence deployments.

Intracampus Deployment Model

The intracampus network deployment model has TelePresence systems limited to a single enterprise campus or between sites interconnected through a high-speed (Gigabit or higher) *metropolitan-area network (MAN)*. This deployment model is applicable for enterprises that have a large number of buildings within a given campus and employees who are often required to drive to several different buildings during the course of the day to attend meetings. Deploying multiple TelePresence systems intracampus can reduce time lost by employees driving between buildings to attend meetings, without sacrificing meeting effectiveness, and thus improve overall productivity. The intracampus deployment model is also commonly used with the other deployment models—where customers deploy multiple CTS rooms within their headquarters campus to meet demand for room availability as part of a global intra-enterprise or intercompany deployment.

The network infrastructure of an intracampus deployment model is predominantly Cisco Catalyst switches connecting through GigE or 10GigE links. Figure 4-10 illustrates the intracampus TelePresence deployment model.

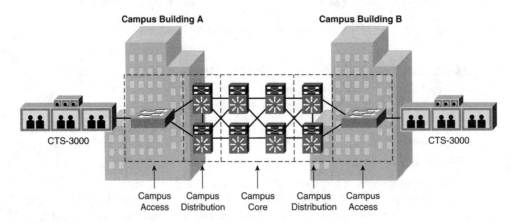

Figure 4-10   *TelePresence intracampus network deployment model*

Intra-Enterprise Deployment Model

The intra-enterprise network deployment model for TelePresence systems connects not only buildings within a campus, but also geographically separated campus sites and branch offices. The intra-enterprise model expands on the intracampus model to include sites connected through a WAN(< 1 Gigabit), whether private WAN or VPN.

The intra-enterprise deployment model is suitable for businesses that often require employees to travel extensively for internal meetings. Deploying TelePresence systems within the enterprise not only improves productivity—by saving travel time—but also reduces travel expenses. Furthermore, the overall quality of work/life is often improved when employees have to travel less.

The network infrastructure of an intra-enterprise deployment model is a combination of Cisco Catalyst switches within the campus and Cisco routers over the WAN, which can include private WANs, MPLS VPNs, or Metro Ethernet networks. WAN speeds can range from 34 Mbps E3 circuits to 10 Gbps OC-192 circuits. Figure 4-11 illustrates the intra-enterprise TelePresence deployment model.

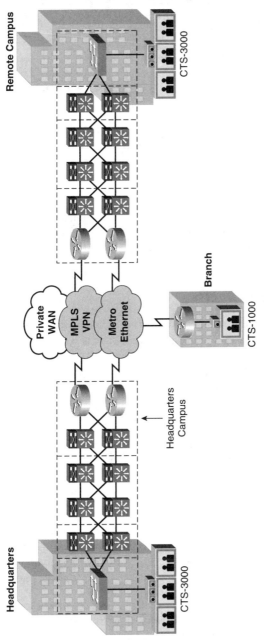

Figure 4-11 *TelePresence intra-enterprise network deployment model*

Note   A valuable consideration when selecting WAN/VPN service providers is to identify those that have achieved Cisco Powered Network designation. Furthermore, an increasing number of Cisco Powered providers have earned QoS Certification for WAN/VPN services. This means that they have been assessed by a third party for the capability of their *service level agreements (SLA)* to support real-time voice and video traffic and for their use of Cisco best practices for QoS. For a list of recommended service providers, see the following URL: http://www.cisco.com/cpn.

The use of Cisco Powered networks is recommended—but not mandatory—for Cisco TelePresence intra-enterprise deployments. The key is meeting the service levels required by TelePresence, as detailed in Chapter 10, "TelePresence Network Design Part 2: QoS Design."

In both the intracampus and intra-enterprise deployment models, customers can also deploy multipoint TelePresence resources to facilitate multisite meetings (meetings with three or more TelePresence rooms). These resources might be located at any one of the campus locations or might be located within the service provider cloud as either a colocated resource or a managed/hosted resource.

Multipoint platforms and network design recommendations, such as additional bandwidth and latency considerations, Cisco TelePresence Multipoint switch considerations, scaling considerations, and so on, are discussed in further detail in Chapter 13, "Multipoint TelePresence Design."

Intercompany Deployment Model

The intercompany deployment model connects not only TelePresence systems within an enterprise, but also allows for TelePresence systems within one enterprise to call systems within another enterprise. The intercompany model expands on the intracampus and intra-enterprise models to include connectivity between different enterprises, both in a point-to-point or in a multipoint manner. It offers a significant increase in value to the TelePresence deployment by greatly increasing the number of endpoints to which a unit can communicate. This model is also at times referred to as the *business-to-business (B2B)* TelePresence deployment model.

The intercompany model offers the most flexibility and is suitable for businesses that often require employees to travel extensively for both internal and external meetings. In addition to the business advantages of the intra-enterprise model, the intercompany deployment model lets employees maintain high-quality customer relations without the associated costs of travel time and expense.

The network infrastructure of the intercompany deployment model builds on the intra-enterprise model and requires the enterprises to share a common MPLS VPN service provider. Additionally, the MPLS VPN service provider must have a "shared services" Virtual Routing and Forwarding (VRF) instance provisioned with a Cisco IOS XR Session/Border Controller (SBC).

The Cisco SBC bridges a connection between two separate MPLS VPNs to perform secure inter-VPN communication between enterprises. Additionally, the SBC provides topology and address hiding services, NAT and firewall traversal, fraud and theft of service prevention, DDoS detection and prevention, call admission control policy enforcement, encrypted media pass-through, and guaranteed QoS.

Figure 4-12 illustrates the intercompany TelePresence deployment model.

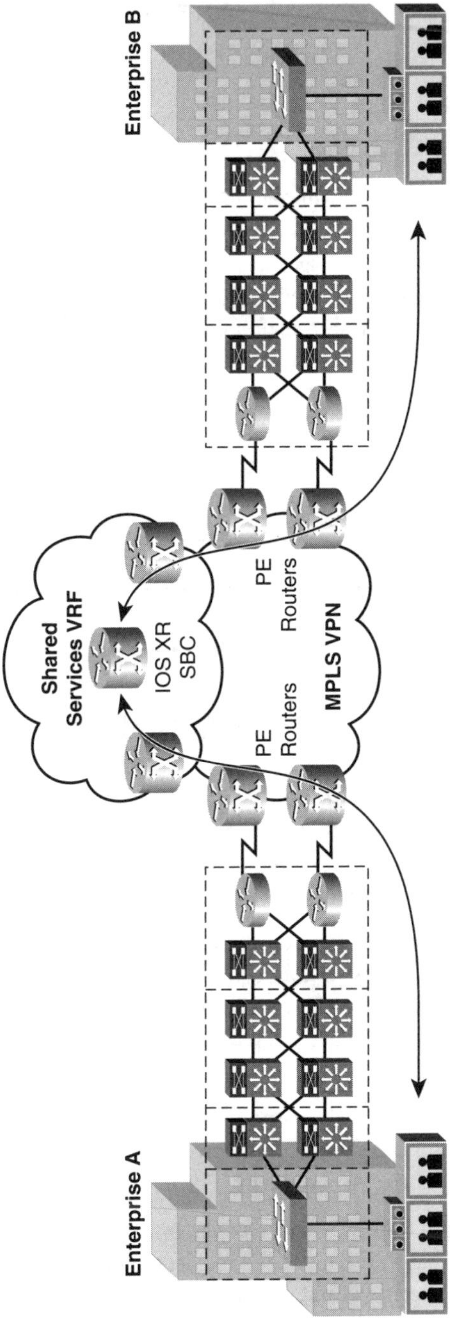

Figure 4-12 *Intercompany TelePresence deployment model*

Note   The initial release of the intercompany solution requires a single service provider to provide the shared services to enterprise customers, which includes the secure bridging of customer MPLS VPNs. However, as this solution evolves, multiple providers can peer and provide intercompany services between them, and as such, can remove the requirement that enterprise customers share the same SP.

Although the focus of this chapter is TelePresence deployments within the enterprise, several of these options can be hosted or managed by service providers. For example, the Cisco Unified Communications Manager and Cisco TelePresence Manager servers and multipoint resources can be located on-premise at one of the customer campus locations, colocated within the service provider network (managed by the enterprise), or hosted within the service provider network (managed by the service provider). However, with the exception of inter-VPN elements required by providers offering intercompany TelePresence services, the TelePresence solution components and network designs remain fundamentally the same whether the TelePresence systems are hosted/managed by the enterprise or by the service provider.

Chapter 14 provides additional details and considerations relating to the intercompany TelePresence deployment model.

TelePresence Phases of Deployment

As TelePresence technologies evolve, so too will the complexity of deployment solutions. Therefore, customers will likely approach their TelePresence deployments in phases, with the main phases of deployment as follows:

- **Phase 1. Intracampus/Intra-enterprise deployments:** Most enterprise customers will likely begin their TelePresence rollouts by provisioning (point-to-point) intra-enterprise TelePresence deployments. View this model as the basic TelePresence building block on which you can add more complex models.

- **Phase 2. Intra-enterprise multipoint deployments:** Because collaboration requirements might not always be facilitated with point-to-point models, the next logical phase of TelePresence deployment is to introduce multipoint resources to the intra-enterprise deployment model. Phases 1 and 2 might at times be undertaken simultaneously.

- **Phase 3. Intercompany deployments:** To expand the application and business benefits of TelePresence meetings to include external (customer- or partner-facing) meetings, an intercompany deployment model can be subsequently overlaid over either point-to-point or multipoint intra-enterprise deployments.

- **Phase 4. TelePresence to the executive home:** Because of the high executive-perk appeal of TelePresence and the availability of high-speed residential bandwidth options (such as fiber to the home), some executives might benefit greatly from deploying TelePresence units to their residences. Technically, this is simply an extension of the intra-enterprise model but might also be viewed as a separate phase because of the unique provisioning and security requirements posed by such residential TelePresence deployments, as illustrated in Figure 4-13.

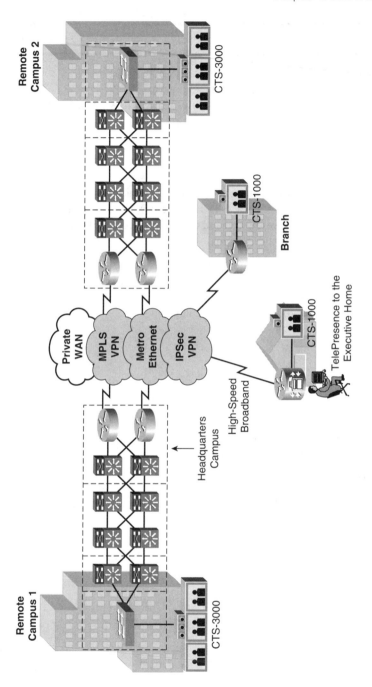

Figure 4-13   *TelePresence to the executive home (an extension of the intra-enterprise deployment model)*

Summary

This chapter examined how the internal components of CTS-500, CTS-1000, CTS-3000, and CTS-3200 interconnect. A dominant element of each internal TelePresence connection schematic is that the primary codec is at the heart of each system, with each subcomponent—including displays, cameras, microphones, speakers, auxiliary devices, and secondary codecs—connecting to it, directly or indirectly. Furthermore, each enclosed TelePresence system is abstracted from the network and connects to it by a single 10/100/1000 RJ-45 cable, sourced from the primary codec.

The chapter also examined the network protocol interactions that take place as a TelePresence system comes online, including CDP, DHCP, TFTP, SIP, and XML. Best practices for TelePresence network addressing were also presented to take into account the internal addressing schemes used within TelePresence systems.

Following this, the perspective shifted from a microperspective to a macroperspective to consider the main deployment models used for TelePresence systems. These include the intracampus model, intra-enterprise model, and interenterprise (B2B) model. The chapter concluded with a phased approach for TelePresence deployments.

Further Reading

Cisco CTS Documentation:

CTS-500 Data Sheet: http://tinyurl.com/by7gtc
Cisco CTS-1000 Documentation: http://tinyurl.com/84dkfs
Cisco CTS-3000 Documentation: http://tinyurl.com/7kx5pv
CTS-3200 Documentation: http://tinyurl.com/9afjel

Cisco IOS XR SBC Documentation:

Cisco IOS XR Session Border Controller Configuration Guide, Release 3.7: http://tinyurl.com/aao5or

Having discussed TelePresence technologies and how these interconnect and interoperate within a CTS system, attention can now expand to examining networking technologies that you need to deploy within a TelePresence-ready network infrastructure. Consider the first set of network technologies: availability technologies.

The goal of network availability technologies is to maximize network uptime and—conversely—to minimize network downtime so that the network is always ready to provide needed services to critical applications such as TelePresence.

TelePresence has extremely high requirements for network availability. Specifically, if just one TelePresence packet is lost in 10,000, this becomes noticeable to the end user, thus making TelePresence a hundred times more sensitive to packet loss than *voice over IP (VoIP)* alone. As such, networks supporting TelePresence need to have correspondingly higher degrees of availability built into their designs.

Because availability technologies play such a crucial role to network designs supporting TelePresence, a brief review of some of the key concepts and technologies relating to network availability can provide better context for Chapter 9, "TelePresence Network Design Part 1: Availability Design."

CHAPTER 5

Network Availability Technologies

Network Availability

Network availability is the foundational cornerstone of network design, upon which all other services depend.

The three primary causes of network downtime are as follows:

■ **Hardware failures:** Include system and subcomponent failures and power failures and network link failures

■ **Software failures:** Include incompatibility issues and bugs

■ **Operational processes:** Include human error; however, poorly defined management and upgrading processes can also contribute to operational downtime

To offset these three types of failures, the network administrator strives to provision the following:

■ **Device resiliency:** Achieved by deploying redundant hardware (including systems, supervisors, linecards, and power supplies) that can failover in any cases of hardware and software failure events

■ **Network resiliency:** Achieved by tuning network protocols to detect and react to failure events as quickly as possible

■ **Operational resiliency:** Achieved by examining and defining processes to maintain and manage the network, leveraging relevant technologies that can reduce downtime, including provisioning for hardware and software upgrades with minimal downtime (or optimally, with no downtime)

Note Because the purpose of this overview of availability technologies is to provide context for the design chapters that follow, emphasis for this discussion is on device and network resiliency, rather than operational resiliency.

You can quantitatively measure and justify the rationale for network availability by using the following formula, shown in Figure 5-1, which correlates the *Mean Time Between Failures (MTBF)* and the *Mean Time To Repair (MTTR)* such failures.

For example, if a network device has an MTBF of 10,000 hours and an MTTR of 4 hours, its availability can be expressed as 99.96 percent [(10,000) / (10,000 + 4), converted to a

$$\text{Availability} = \frac{\text{MTBF}}{\text{MTBF} + \text{MTTR}}$$

MTBF = Mean Time Between Failure
MTTR = Mean Time To Repair

Figure 5-1   *Availability Formula*

percentage]. Therefore, from this formula, you can see that you can improve availability by either increasing the MTBF of a device (or network) or by decreasing the MTTR of the same.

The most effective way to increase the MTBF of a device (or network) is to design with redundancy. This can be mathematically proven by comparing the availability formula of devices connected in serial (*without* redundancy) with the formula of devices connected in parallel (*with* redundancy).

Figure 5-2 shows the availability of devices connected in series. S_1 and S_2 represent two separate systems (which might be individual devices or even networks). A_1 and A_2 represent the availability of each of these systems, respectively. A_{series} represents the overall availability of these systems connected in serial (*without* redundancy).

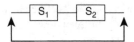

S_1, S_2 - Series Components

System is available when both components are available:

$$A_{series} = A_1 \times A_2$$

Figure 5-2   *Availability formula for devices connected in serial*

For example, if the availability of the first device (S_1) is 99.96 percent and the availability of the second device (S_2) is 99.98 percent, the overall system availability, with these devices connected serially, is 99.94 percent (99.96% × 99.98%). Therefore, you can see that connecting devices in serial actually *reduces* the overall availability of the network.

In contrast, Figure 5-3 shows the availability of devices connected in parallel. S_3 and S_4 represent two separate systems (devices or networks). A_3 and A_4 represent the availability of each of these systems, respectively. $A_{parallel}$ represents the overall availability of these systems connected in parallel (*with* redundancy).

Continuing the example, using the same availability numbers for each device as before, yields an overall system availability, with these devices connected in parallel, of 99.999992% [1 − (1 − 99.96%) × (1 − 99.98%)].

Therefore, you can see that connecting devices in parallel significantly increases the overall availability of the combined system. This is a foundational principle of available network design, where individual devices and networks are designed to be fully redundant

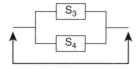

S₃, S₄ - Parallel Components

System is unavailable when both components are unavailable:

$$A_{parallel} = (1 - A_3) * (1 - A_4)$$

Figure 5-3 *Availability formula for devices connected in parallel*

whenever possible. Figure 5-4 illustrates applying redundancy to network design and its corresponding effect on overall network availability.

Availability = 99.938% with Four-Hour MTTR (Downtime is 325 Minutes/Year)

Availability = 99.961% with Four-Hour MTTR (Downtime is 204 Minutes/Year)

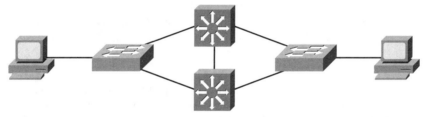

Availability = 99.9999% with Four-Hour MTTR (Downtime is 30 Seconds/Year)

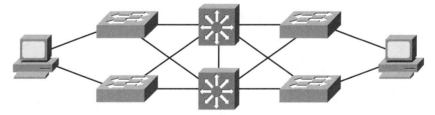

Figure 5-4 *Impact of redundant network design on network availability*

A *five nines* network (referring to a network with 99.999% availability) has been considered the hallmark of excellent enterprise network design for many years. Reaching such a level of availability is quite challenging; especially when considering that a five nines network allows for only five minutes of downtime per year for network events and upgrades.

Another commonly used metric for measuring availability is *Defects Per Million (DPM)*. While measuring the probability of failure of a network and establishing the service-level agreement (SLA) that a specific design can achieve is a useful tool, DPM takes a different approach. It measures the impact of defects on the service from the end user's perspective. It is often a better metric for determining the availability of the network because it better reflects the user experience relative to event effects. DPM is calculated based on taking the total *affected user minutes* for each event, total users affected, and the duration of the event, as compared to the total number of service minutes available during the period in question. The sum of service downtime minutes is divided by the total service minutes and multiplied by 1,000,000, as shown in Figure 5-5.

$$DPM = \frac{\text{Sum of (Number of Users Affected * Outage Minutes [for each outage])}}{\text{Total Number of Users * Total Service Minutes}}$$

Figure 5-5   *Defects Per Million calculation*

For example, if a company of 50 employees suffered two separate outages during the course of a year, with the first outage affecting 12 users for 4 hours and the second outage affecting 25 users for 2 hours, the total DPM would be 224 based on the following calculations:

```
[(12 users × 240 min) + (25 users × 120 min)]/(50 users × 525,960 min/year)] ×
1,000,000, rounded].
```

Note   The benefit of using a *per-million* scale in a defects calculation is that it allows the final ratio to be more readable because this ratio becomes extremely small as availability improves.

DPM is useful in that it is a measure of the observed availability and considers the impact to the end user and the network. Adding this user experience element to the question of network availability is important to understand and is becoming a more important part of the question of what makes a highly available network.

Table 5-1 summarizes availability targets, complete with their DPM and allowable downtime/year.

Table 5-1   *Availability, DPM, and Downtime*

Availability (Percent)	DPM	Downtime/Year		
99.000	10,000	3 Days	15 Hours	36 Minutes
99.500	5,000	1 Day	19 Hours	48 Minutes
99.900	1000	–	8 Hours	46 Minutes
99.950	500	–	4 Hours	23 Minutes
99.990	100	–	–	53 Minutes
99.999	10	–	–	5 Minutes
99.9999	1	–	–	0.5 Minutes

Having reviewed these availability principles, metrics, and targets, a discussion of some of the availability technologies most relevant for systems and networks supporting TelePresence systems follows.

Device Availability Technologies

Most network designs have single points of failure, and the overall availability of the network might be dependent on the availability of a single device. A prime example of this is the access layer of a campus network. Most endpoint devices connect to the access switch through a single *network interface card (NIC)*; this is referred to as being single-homed; therefore, access switches represent a single point of failure for all attached single-homed devices, including CTS codecs.

Note   Beginning with CTS 1.5 software, Cisco TelePresence Multipoint Switches can utilize a NIC teaming feature that can enable these to be multihomed devices, that is, devices that connect to multiple access switches. Multihoming eliminates the access switch from being a single-point of failure and thus improves overall availability.

Ensuring the availability of the network services is often dependent on the resiliency of the individual devices. Device resiliency, as with network resiliency, is achieved through a combination of the appropriate level of physical redundancy, device hardening, and supporting software features. Studies indicate that most common failures in campus networks are associated with Layer 1 failures, from components such as power supplies, fans, and fiber links. The use of diverse fiber paths with redundant links and linecards, combined with fully redundant power supplies and power circuits, are the most critical aspects of device resiliency. The use of redundant power supplies becomes even more critical in access switches with the introduction of *Power over Ethernet (PoE)* devices such as IP phones. Multiple devices are now dependent on the availability of the access switch and its capability to maintain the necessary level of power for all the attached end devices. After physical failures, the most common cause of device outage is often related to the failure of supervisor hardware or software. The network outages due to the loss or reset of a device due to supervisor failure can be addressed through the use of supervisor redundancy. Cisco Catalyst switches provides two mechanisms to achieve this additional level of redundancy:

■   Cisco StackWise/StackWise-Plus

■   Cisco Nonstop Forwarding (NSF) with Stateful Switchover (SSO)

Both of these mechanisms, discussed in the following sections, provide for a hot active backup for the switching fabric and control plane, thus ensuring that data forwarding and the network control plane seamlessly recover (with subsecond traffic loss, if any) during any form of software or supervisor hardware crash.

Stackwise/Stackwise Plus

Cisco StackWise and StackWise Plus technologies create a unified, logical switching architecture through the linkage of multiple, fixed configuration 3750G and 3750E switches.

Note   Cisco 3750G switches use StackWise technology, and Cisco 3750E switches can use either StackWise or StackWise Plus. (StackWise Plus is used only if all switches within the group are 3750E switches; whereas, if some switches are 3750E and others are 3750G, StackWise technology will be used.)

Also to prevent excessive wordiness, "StackWise" is used in this section to refer to both StackWise and StackWise Plus technologies, with the exception of explicitly pointing out the differences between the two at the end of this section.

Cisco StackWise technology intelligently joins individual switches to create a single switching unit with a 32-Gbps switching stack interconnect. Configuration and routing information is shared by every switch in the stack, creating a single switching unit. Switches can be added to and deleted from a working stack without affecting availability.

The switches unite into a single logical unit using special stack interconnect cables that create a bidirectional closed-loop path. This bidirectional path acts as a switch fabric for all the connected switches. Network topology and routing information is updated continuously through the stack interconnect. All stack members have full access to the stack interconnect bandwidth. The stack is managed as a single unit by a master switch, which is elected from one of the stack member switches.

Each switch in the stack has the capability to behave as a master in the hierarchy. The master switch is elected and serves as the control center for the stack. Each switch is assigned a number. Up to nine separate switches can be joined together.

Each stack of Cisco Catalyst 3750 Series switches has a single IP address and is managed as a single object. This single IP management applies to activities such as fault detection, VLAN creation and modification, security, and quality of service (QoS) controls. Each stack has only one configuration file, which is distributed to each member in the stack. This allows each switch in the stack to share the same network topology, MAC address, and routing information. In addition, it allows for any member to immediately take over as the master, if there is a master failure.

To efficiently load balance the traffic, packets are allocated between two logical counter-rotating paths. Each counter-rotating path supports 16 Gbps in both directions, yielding a traffic total of 32 Gbps bidirectionally. When a break is detected in a cable, the traffic is immediately wrapped back across the single remaining 16-Gbps path (within microseconds) to continue forwarding.

Switches can be added and deleted to a working stack without affecting stack availability. (However, adding additional switches to a stack might have QoS performance implications, as will be discussed in more detail in Chapter 10, "TelePresence Network Design Part 2: QoS Design.") Similarly, switches can be removed from a working stack without any operational effect on the remaining switches.

Stacks require no explicit configuration but are automatically created by StackWise when individual switches are joined together with stacking cables, as shown in Figure 5-6. When the stack ports detect electromechanical activity, each port starts to transmit information about its switch. When the complete set of switches is known, the stack elects one of the members to be the master switch, which will be responsible for maintaining and updating configuration files, routing information, and other stack information. This process is referred to as *hot stacking*.

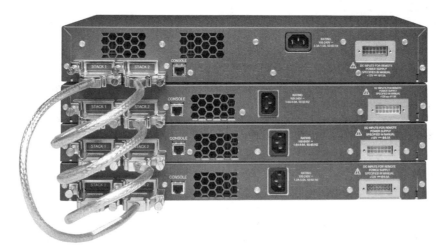

Figure 5-6   *Catalyst 3750G StackWise cabling*

Courtesy of Cisco Systems, Inc. Unauthorized use not permitted.

Note   Master switch election occurs only on stack initialization or if there is a master switch failure. If a new, more favorable switch is added to a stack, this will not trigger a master switch election, nor will any sort of preemption occur.

Each switch in the stack can serve as a master, creating a 1:N availability scheme for network control. In the unlikely event of a single unit failure, all other units continue to forward traffic and maintain operation. Furthermore, each switch is initialized for routing capability and is ready to be elected as master if the current master fails. Subordinate switches are not reset so that Layer 2 forwarding can continue uninterrupted.

The three main differences between StackWise and StackWise Plus are as follows:

■   StackWise uses source stripping, and StackWise Plus uses destination stripping (for unicast packets). Source stripping means that when a packet is sent on the ring, it is passed to the destination, which copies the packet and then lets it pass all the way around the ring. After the packet has traveled all the way around the ring and returns to the source, it is stripped off of the ring. This means bandwidth is used up all the way around the ring, even if the packet is destined for a directly attached neighbor. Destination stripping means that when the packet reaches its destination, it is re-moved from the ring and continues no further. This leaves the rest of the ring band-width free to be used. Thus, the throughput performance of the stack is multiplied to a minimum value of 64 Gbps bidirectionally. This capability to free up bandwidth is sometimes referred to as *spatial reuse*.

Note   Even in StackWise Plus, broadcast and multicast packets must use source stripping because the packet might have multiple targets on the stack.

■   StackWise Plus can locally switch; StackWise cannot. In StackWise Plus, packets originating and destined to ports on the same local switch will not have to traverse the Stack ring, which results in more efficient switching. In contrast, in StackWise, because there is no local switching and because there is source stripping, even locally destined packets must traverse the entire stack ring.

■   StackWise Plus can support up to two Ten Gigabit Ethernet ports per Cisco Cata-lyst 3750-E.

Finally, both StackWise and StackWise Plus can support Layer 3 NSF when two or more nodes are present in a stack. NSF is discussed in the following section, along with SSO.

Nonstop Forwarding with Stateful Switchover

SSO is a redundant route- and switch-processor availability feature that significantly re-duces MTTR by allowing extremely fast switching between the main and backup proces-sors. SSO is supported on routers (such as the Cisco 7600, 10000, and 12000 series families) and switches (such as the Catalyst 4500 and 6500 series families).

Prior to discussing the details of SSO, a few definitions might be helpful. For example, "state" in SSO refers to maintaining—among many other elements—the following be-tween the active and standby processors:

■   Layer 2 protocols configurations and current status

■   Layer 3 protocol configurations and current status

■   Multicast protocol configurations and current status

■   QoS policy configurations and current status

■ Access list policy configurations and current status

■ Interface configurations and current status

Also, the adjectives *cold*, *warm*, or *hot* denote the readiness of the system and its components to assume the network services functionality and the job of forwarding packets to their destination. These terms appear in conjunction with Cisco IOS verification command output relating to NSF/SSO and with many high availability feature descriptions:

■ **Cold:** Cold redundancy refers to the minimum degree of resiliency that has been traditionally provided by a redundant system. A redundant system is *cold* when no state information is maintained between the backup or standby system and the system it offers protection to. Typically a cold system would have to complete a boot process before it came online and would be ready to take over from a failed system.

■ **Warm:** Warm redundancy refers to a degree of resiliency beyond the cold standby system. In this case, the redundant system has been partially prepared but does not have all the state information known by the primary system, so it can take over immediately. Some additional information must be determined or gleaned from the traffic flow or the peer network devices to handle packet forwarding. A warm system would already be booted up and would need to learn or generate only state information prior to taking over from a failed system.

■ **Hot:** Hot redundancy refers to a degree of resiliency where the redundant system is fully capable of handling the traffic of the primary system. Substantial state information has been saved, so the network service is continuous, and the traffic flow is minimally or not affected.

To better understand SSO, it might be helpful to consider its operation in detail within a specific context, such as within a Cisco Catalyst 6500 with two supervisors per chassis.

The supervisor engine that boots first becomes the active supervisor engine. The active supervisor is responsible for control-plane and forwarding decisions. The second supervisor is the standby supervisor, which does not participate in the control- or data-plane decisions. The active supervisor synchronizes configuration and protocol state information to the standby supervisor, which is in a *hot-standby* mode. As a result, the standby supervisor is ready to take over the active supervisor responsibilities if the active supervisor fails. This "take-over" process from the active supervisor to the standby supervisor is referred to as *switchover*.

Only one supervisor is active at a time, and supervisor-engine redundancy does not provide supervisor-engine load balancing. However, the interfaces on a standby supervisor engine are active when the supervisor is up and, thus, can be used to forward traffic in a redundant configuration.

NSF/SSO evolved from a series of progressive enhancements to reduce the impact of MTTR relating to specific supervisor hardware/software network outages. NSF/SSO builds on the earlier work known as *Route Processor Redundancy (RPR)* and *RPR Plus*

(RPR+). Each of these redundancy modes of operation incrementally improves upon the functions of the previous mode:

- **RPR:** The first redundancy mode of operation introduced in Cisco IOS Software. In RPR mode, the startup configuration and boot registers are synchronized between the active and standby supervisors; the standby is not fully initialized; and images between the active and standby supervisors do not need to be the same. Upon switchover, the standby supervisor becomes active automatically, but it must complete the boot process. In addition, all line cards are reloaded, and the hardware is reprogrammed. Because the standby supervisor is "cold," the RPR switchover time is 2 or more minutes.

- **RPR+:** An enhancement to RPR in which the standby supervisor is completely booted, and line cards do not reload upon switchover. The running configuration is synchronized between the active and the standby supervisors, which run the same software versions. All synchronization activities inherited from RPR are also performed. The synchronization is done before the switchover, and the information synchronized to the standby is used when the standby becomes active to minimize the downtime. No link layer or control-plane information is synchronized between the active and the standby supervisors. Interfaces might bounce after switchover, and the hardware contents need to be reprogrammed. Because the standby supervisor is "warm," the RPR+ switchover time is 30 or more seconds.

- **NSF with SSO:** NSF works in conjunction with SSO to ensure Layer 3 integrity following a switchover. It allows a router experiencing the failure of an active supervisor to continue forwarding data packets along known routes while the routing protocol information is recovered and validated. This forwarding can continue to occur even though peering arrangements with neighbor routers have been lost on the restarting router. NSF relies on the separation of the control plane and the data plane during supervisor switchover. The data plane continues to forward packets based on pre-switchover *Cisco Express Forwarding (CEF)* information. The control-plane implements graceful restart routing protocol extensions to signal a supervisor restart to NSF-aware neighbor routers, reform its neighbor adjacencies, and rebuild its routing protocol database (in the background) following a switchover. Because the standby supervisor is "hot," the NSF/SSO switchover time is 0 to 3 seconds.

As previously described, neighbor nodes play a role in NSF function. A node that is capable of continuous packet forwarding during a route processor switchover is *NSF-capable*. Complementing this functionality, an *NSF-aware* peer router can enable neighbor recovery without resetting adjacencies and support routing database resynchronization to occur in the background. Figure 5-7 illustrates the difference between NSF-capable and NSF-aware routers. To gain the greatest benefit from NSF/SSO deployment, NSF-capable routers should be peered with NSF-aware routers (although this is not absolutely required for implementation) because only limited benefit will be achieved unless routing peers are aware of the capability of the restarting node to continue packet forwarding and assist in restoring and verifying the integrity of the routing tables after a switchover.

Cisco NSF and SSO are designed to be deployed together. NSF relies on SSO to ensure that links and interfaces remain up during switchover and that lower layer protocol state is

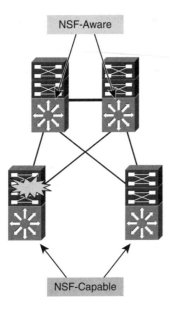

Figure 5-7 *NSF-capable versus NSF-aware routers*

maintained. However, it is possible to enable SSO with or without NSF because these are configured separately.

The configuration to enable SSO is simple, as shown here:

```
Router(config)# redundancy
Router(config-red)# mode sso
```

NSF, on the other hand, is configured within the routing protocol and is supported within EIGRP, OSPF, IS-IS and (to an extent) BGP. Sometimes NSF functionality is also called "graceful-restart."

To enable NSF for EIGRP, enter the following commands:

```
Router(config)# router eigrp 100
Router(config-router)# nsf
```

Similarly, to enable NSF for OSPF, enter the following commands:

```
Router(config)# router ospf 100
Router(config-router)# nsf
```

Continuing the example, to enable NSF for IS-IS, enter the following commands:

```
Router(config)# router isis level2
Router(config-router)# nsf cisco
```

And finally, to enable NSF/graceful-restart for BGP, enter the following commands:

```
Router(config)# router bgp 100
Router(config-router)# bgp graceful-restart
```

You can see from the example of NSF that the line between device-level availability technologies and network availability technologies sometimes is blurry. A discussion of more network availability technologies follows.

Network Availability Protocols

Network availability protocols, which include link integrity protocols, link bundling protocols, loop detection protocols, *first-hop redundancy protocols (FHRP)*, and routing protocols, increase the resiliency of devices connected within a network. Network resiliency relates to how the overall design implements redundant links and topologies and how the control-plane protocols are optimally configured to operate within that design. The use of physical redundancy is a critical part of ensuring the availability of the overall network. If a network device fails, having a path means the overall network can continue to operate. The control-plane capabilities of the network provide the capability to manage the way in which the physical redundancy is leveraged, the network load balances traffic, the network converges, and the network is operated.

You can apply the following basic principles to network availability technologies:

■ Wherever possible, leverage the capability of the device hardware to provide the primary detection and recovery mechanism for network failures. This ensures both a faster and a more deterministic failure recovery.

■ Implement a *defense-in-depth* approach to failure detection and recovery mechanisms. Multiple protocols, operating on different network layers, can complement each other in detecting and reacting to network failures.

■ Ensure that the design is self-stabilizing. Use a combination of control-plane modularization to ensure that any failures are isolated in their impact and that the control plane prevents any flooding or thrashing conditions from arising.

These principles are intended to be a complementary part of the overall structured modular design approach to the network architecture and primarily serve to reenforce good resilient network design practices.

Note   A complete discussion of all network availability technologies and best practices could easily fill an entire volume. Therefore, this discussion introduces and provides only an overview of the network availability technologies most relevant to TelePresence enterprise network deployments.

The protocols discussed in this section can be subdivided between Layer 2 (L2) and Layer 3 (L3) network availability protocols. Each layer's technologies are overviewed in turn.

L2 Network Availability Protocols

L2 network availability protocols that particularly relate to TelePresence network design include the following:

- Unidirectional Link Detection (UDLD) Protocol

- IEEE 802.1d Spanning Tree Protocol (STP)

- Cisco Spanning Tree Protocol enhancements

- IEEE 802.1w Rapid Spanning-Tree Protocol (RSTP)

- Trunks, Cisco Inter-Switch Link, and IEEE 802.1Q

- EtherChannels, Cisco Port Aggregation Protocol, and IEEE 802.3ad

- Cisco Virtual Switching System

The following sections discuss each of these L2 protocols.

UniDirectional Link Detection

In TelePresence campus networks, a link can transmit in one direction only, causing a lengthy delay in fault detection and, thus, excessive packet loss.

UniDirectional Link Detection (UDLD) protocol is a Layer 2 protocol that uses a keepalive to test that the switch-to-switch links connect and operate correctly. Enabling UDLD is a prime example of how to implement a *defense-in-depth* approach to failure detection and recovery mechanisms because UDLD (a L2 protocol) acts as a backup to the native Layer 1 unidirectional link detection capabilities provided by IEEE 802.3z (Gigabit Ethernet) and 802.3ae (Ten Gigabit Ethernet) standards.

The UDLD protocol allows devices connected through fiber-optic or copper Ethernet cables connected to LAN ports to monitor the physical configuration of the cables and detect when a unidirectional link exists. When a unidirectional link is detected, UDLD shuts down the affected LAN port and triggers an alert. Unidirectional links, such as shown in Figure 5-8, can cause a variety of problems, including spanning tree topology loops.

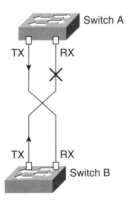

Figure 5-8 *Unidirectional link failure*

You can configure UDLD to be globally enabled on all fiber ports by entering the following command:

```
Switch(config)# udld enable
```

Additionally, you can enable UDLD on individual LAN ports in interface mode by entering the following commands:

```
Switch(config)# interface GigabitEthernet8/1
Switch(config-if)# udld port
```

Interface configurations override global settings for UDLD.

IEEE 802.1D Spanning Tree Protocol

In TelePresence campus networks, redundant paths are encouraged within the network design; however, redundant paths might cause Layer 2 loops and, thus, recursive forwarding and packet drops.

The *IEEE 802.1D Spanning Tree Protocol (STP)* prevents loops from being formed when switches are interconnected through multiple paths. SPT implements the Spanning Tree Algorithm by exchanging *Bridge Protocol Data Unit (BPDU)* messages with other switches to detect loops and then removes the loop by blocking selected switch interfaces. This algorithm guarantees that there is one—and only one—active path between two network devices, as illustrated in Figure 5-9.

STP prevents a loop in the topology by transitioning all (STP-enabled) ports through four STP states:

- **Blocking:** The port does not participate in frame forwarding. STP can take up to 20 seconds (by default) to transition a port from Blocking to Listening.

- **Listening:** The port transitional state after the Blocking state when the spanning tree determines that the interface should participate in frame forwarding. STP takes 15 seconds (by default) to transition between Listening and Learning.

- **Learning:** The port prepares to participate in frame forwarding. STP takes 15 seconds (by default) to transition from Learning to Forwarding (provided such a transition does not cause a loop; otherwise, the port will be set to Blocking).

- **Forwarding:** The port forwards frames.

Figure 5-10 illustrates the STP states, including the disabled state.

You can enable STP globally on a per-VLAN basis (referred to as *Per-VLAN Spanning Tree [PVST]*) by entering the following command:

```
Switch(config)# spanning-tree vlan 100
```

The two main availability limitations for STP follow:

- To prevent loops, redundant ports are placed in a Blocking state and as such are not used to forward frames and packets. This significantly reduces the advantages of redundant network design, especially for network capacity and load-sharing.

- Adding up all the times required for STP port-state transitions shows that STP can take up to 50 seconds to converge on a loop-free topology. Although this might have been acceptable when the protocol was first designed, it is certainly unacceptable today.

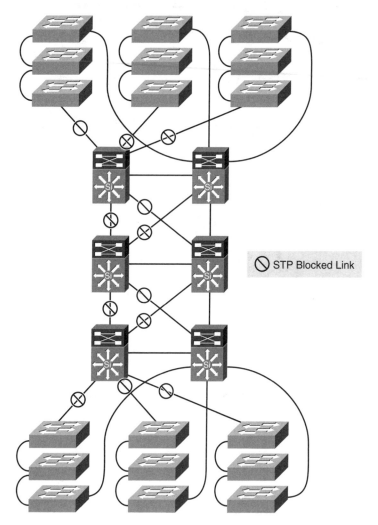

Figure 5-9 *STP-based redundant topology*

Both limitations are addressable using additional technologies. The first limitation can be addressed by using the Cisco Virtual Switching System (discussed later in this section), and the second limitation can be addressed by various enhancements that Cisco developed for STP, as discussed next.

Cisco Spanning Tree Enhancements

The STP 50-second convergence time results in TelePresence calls being self-terminated and is, therefore, unacceptable. Thus, if STP is to be used within a TelePresence campus network, STP convergence times need to be significantly improved.

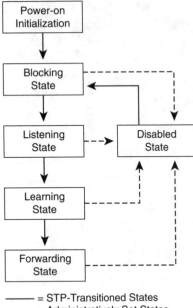

= STP-Transitioned States
= Administratively Set States

Figure 5-10 *STP port states*

To improve on STP convergence times, Cisco has made a number of enhancements to 802.1D STP, including the following:

- PortFast (with BPDU-Guard)

- UplinkFast

- BackboneFast

STP PortFast causes a Layer 2 LAN port configured as an access port to enter the Forwarding state immediately, bypassing the Listening and Learning states. You can use PortFast on Layer 2 access ports connected to a single workstation or server to allow those devices to connect to the network immediately instead of waiting for STP to converge because interfaces connected to a single workstation or server should not receive BPDUs. Because the purpose of PortFast is to minimize the time that access ports must wait for STP to converge, it should be used only on access ports. Optionally, for an additional level of security, PortFast can be enabled with BPDU-Guard, which immediately shuts down a port that has received a BPDU.

You can enable PortFast globally (along with BPDU-Guard) or on a per-interface basis by entering the following commands:

```
Switch(config)# spanning-tree portfast default
Switch(config)# spanning-tree portfast bpduguard default
```

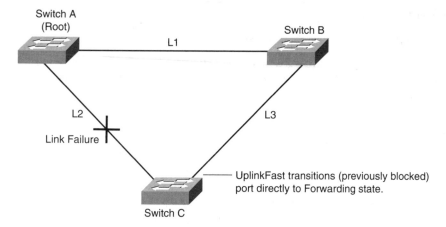

Figure 5-11 *UplinkFast recovery example after direct link failure*

UplinkFast provides fast convergence after a direct link failure and achieves load balancing between redundant Layer 2 links. If a switch detects a link failure on the currently active link (a *direct* link failure), UplinkFast unblocks the blocked port on the redundant link

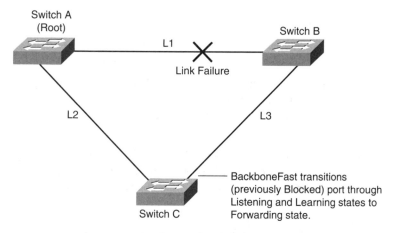

Figure 5-12 *BackboneFast recovery example after indirect link failure*

port and immediately transitions it to the Forwarding state without going through the Listening and Learning states, as illustrated in Figure 5-11. This switchover takes approximately one to five seconds.

You can enable UplinkFast globally, as follows:

```
Switch(config)# spanning-tree uplinkfast
```

In contrast, BackboneFast provides fast convergence after an *indirect* link failure, as shown in Figure 5-12. This switchover takes approximately 30 seconds (yet improves on the default STP convergence time by 20 seconds).

You can enable BackboneFast globally, as follows:

```
Switch(config)# spanning-tree backbonefast
```

These Cisco-proprietary enhancements to 802.1D STP were adapted and adopted into a new standard for STP, IEEE 802.1w or Rapid Spanning Tree Protocol (RSTP), which are discussed next.

IEEE 802.1w-Rapid Spanning Tree Protocol

Rapid Spanning Tree Protocol (RSTP) is an evolution of the 802.1D STP standard. RSTP is a Layer 2 loop prevention algorithm like 802.1D; however, RSTP achieves rapid failover and convergence times because RSTP is not a timer-based *Spanning Tree Algorithm (STA)* like 802.1D, but rather a handshake-based STA. Therefore, RSTP offers an improvement of 30 seconds or more (as compared to 802.1D) in transitioning a link into a Forwarding state.

The only three port states in RSTP are

■ Learning

■ Forwarding

■ Discarding

The Disabled, Blocking, and Listening states from 802.1D have been merged into a unique 802.1w *Discarding state*, which is a nonforwarding and nonparticipating RSTP port-state.

Rapid transition is the most important feature introduced by 802.1w. The legacy STA passively waited for the network to converge before moving a port into the Forwarding state. Achieving faster convergence was a matter of tuning the conservative default timers, often sacrificing the stability of the network.

RSTP can actively confirm that a port can safely transition to Forwarding without relying on any timer configuration. A feedback mechanism operates between RSTP-compliant bridges. To achieve fast convergence on a port, the RSTP relies on two new variables:

■ **Edge ports:** The *edge port* concept basically corresponds to the PortFast feature. The idea is that ports that directly connect to end stations cannot create bridging loops in the network and can, thus, directly transition to Forwarding (skipping the 802.1D Listening and Learning states). An edge port does not generate topology changes when its link toggles. Unlike PortFast though, an edge port that receives a BPDU immediately loses its edge port status and becomes a normal spanning-tree port.

■ **Link type:** RSTP can achieve only rapid transition to Forwarding on edge ports and on point-to-point links. The link type is automatically derived from the duplex mode of a port. A port operating in full-duplex will be assumed to be point-to-point, whereas a half-duplex port will be considered as a shared port by default. In today's switched networks, most links operate in full-duplex mode and are, therefore, treated as point-to-point links by RSTP. This makes them candidates for rapid transition to forwarding.

Like STP, you can enable RSTP globally on a per-VLAN basis, also referred to as *Rapid-Per-VLAN-Spanning Tree (Rapid-PVST)* mode, using the following command:

```
Switch(config)# spanning-tree mode rapid-pvst
```

Beyond STP, many other L2 technologies also play a key role in available network design, such as trunks, discussed in the following section.

Trunks, Cisco Inter-Switch Link, and IEEE 802.1Q

TelePresence codecs are assigned to the Voice VLAN, whereas most endpoint devices operate within the Data VLAN. It would be inefficient, costly, and administratively complex to use dedicated Ethernet ports and cables for each VLAN. Therefore, a logical separation of VLANs over a physical link is more efficient, cost-effective, and simpler to administer.

A *trunk* is a point-to-point link between two networking devices (switches and routers) capable of carrying traffic from multiple VLANs over a single link. VLAN frames are encapsulated with trunking protocols to preserve logical separation of traffic while transiting the trunk.

There are two trunking encapsulations available to Cisco devices:

- **Inter-Switch Link (ISL):** A Cisco-proprietary trunking encapsulation

- **IEEE 802.1Q:** An industry-standard trunking encapsulation and the trunking protocol used by TelePresence codecs

You can configure trunks on individual links or on EtherChannel bundles (discussed in the following section).

ISL encapsulates the original Ethernet frame with both a header and a Field Check Sequence (FCS) trailer, for a total of 30 bytes of encapsulation.

You can configure ISL trunking on a switch port interface, as demonstrated in Example 5-1. The trunking mode is set to ISL, and the VLANs permitted to traverse the trunk are explicitly identified. In this example VLANs 2 and 102 are permitted over the ISL trunk.

Example 5-1 *ISL Trunk Example*

```
Switch(config)#interface GigabitEthernet8/3
Switch(config-if)# switchport
Switch(config-if)# switchport trunk encapsulation isl
Switch(config-if)# switchport trunk allowed 2, 102
```

In contrast with ISL, 801.1Q doesn't actually encapsulate the Ethernet frame, but rather inserts a 4-byte tag after the Source Address field and recomputes a new FCS, as shown in Figure 5-13. This tag not only preserves VLAN information, but also includes a 3-bit field for Class of Service (CoS) priority (discussed in more detail in the Chapter 6, "Network Quality of Service Technologies").

IEEE 802.1Q also supports the concept of a native VLAN. Traffic sourced from the native VLAN is not tagged but is rather simply forwarded over the trunk. As such, only a single native VLAN can be configured for an 802.1Q trunk, to preserve logical separation.

Original Ethernet Frame

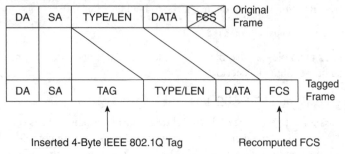

Inserted 4-Byte IEEE 802.1Q Tag   Recomputed FCS

Figure 5-13 *IEEE 802.1Q tagging*

Note Because traffic from the native VLAN is untagged, it is important to ensure that the same native VLAN be specified on both ends of the trunk. Otherwise, this can cause a routing black-hole and potential security vulnerability.

IEEE 802.1Q trunking is likewise configured on a switch port interface, as demonstrated in Example 5-2. The trunking mode is set to 802.1Q, and the VLANs permitted to traverse the trunk are explicitly identified. (In this example VLANs 3 and 103 are permitted over the 802.1Q trunk.) Additionally, VLAN 103 is specified as the native VLAN.

Example 5-2 *IEEE 802.1Q Trunk Example*

```
Switch(config)# interface GigabitEthernet8/4
Switch(config-if)# switchport
Switch(config-if)# switchport trunk encapsulation dot1q
Switch(config-if)# switchport trunk allowed 3, 103
Switch(config-if)# switchport trunk native vlan 103
```

Trunks are typically (but not always) configured in conjunction with EtherChannels, which allow for network link redundancy and are described next.

EtherChannels, Cisco Port Aggregation Protocol, and IEEE 802.3ad

Ethernet link speeds are standardized in factors of 10 (Ethernet, FastEthernet, GigabitEthernet, and Ten Gigabit Ethernet). When switch-to-switch links within TelePresence campus networks become congested, however, it might be costly to upgrade by a full factor of 10. It is generally more cost-effective to add another parallel link at the same speed; however, as more parallel links are added, these might become operationally complex to administer. Therefore, administration of multiple redundant links can be simplified through the use of EtherChannels.

EtherChannel technologies create a single logical link by bundling multiple physical Ethernet-based links (such as Gigabit Ethernet or Ten Gigabit Ethernet links) together, as shown in Figure 5-14. As such, EtherChannel links can provide for increased redundancy, capacity, and load-balancing. To optimize the load balancing of traffic over multiple links, it is recommended to deploy EtherChannels in powers of two (two, four, or eight) physical links. EtherChannel links can operate at either L2 or L3.

EtherChannel

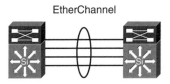

Figure 5-14   *EtherChannel bundle*

EtherChannel links can be created using *Cisco Port Aggregation Protocol (PAgP)*, which performs a negotiation prior to forming a channel, to ensure compatibility and administrative policies.

You can configure PAgP in four channeling modes:

■ **On:** Forces the LAN port to channel unconditionally. In the **on** mode, a usable EtherChannel exists only when a LAN port group in the **on** mode is connected to another LAN port group in the **on** mode. Ports configured in the **on** mode do not negotiate to form EtherChannels: They just do or do not, depending on the other port's configuration.

■ **Off:** Precludes the LAN port from channeling unconditionally.

■ **Desirable:** Places a LAN port into an active negotiating state in which the port initiates negotiations with other LAN ports to form an EtherChannel by sending PAgP packets. A port in this mode forms an EtherChannel with a peer port that is in either auto or desirable PAgP mode.

■ **Auto:** (Default) Places a LAN port into a passive negotiating state in which the port responds to PAgP packets it receives but does not initiate PAgP negotiation. A port in this mode forms an EtherChannel with a peer port that is in desirable PAgP mode (only).

PAgP, when enabled as an L2 link, is enabled on the physical interface (only). Optionally, you can change the PAgP mode from the default "auto" negotiation mode, as follows:

```
Switch(config)# interface GigabitEthernet8/1
Switch(config-if)# channel-protocol pagp
Switch(config-if)# channel-group 15 mode desirable
```

Alternatively, EtherChannels can be negotiated with the IEEE 802.3ad Link Aggregation Control Protocol (LACP), which similarly allows a switch to negotiate an automatic bundle by sending LACP packets to the peer. LACP supports two channel negotiation modes:

■ **Active:** Places a port into an active negotiating state in which the port initiates negotiations with other ports by sending LACP packets. A port in this mode forms a bundle with a peer port that is in either active or passive LACP mode.

■ **Passive:** (Default) Places a port into a passive negotiating state in which the port responds to LACP packets it receives but does not initiate LACP negotiation. A port in this mode forms a bundle with a peer port that is in active LACP mode (only).

Similar to PAgP, LACP requires only a single command on the physical interface when configured as a L2 link. Optionally, you can change the LACP mode from the default "passive" negotiation mode, as follows:

```
Switch(config)# interface GigabitEthernet8/2
Switch(config-if)# channel-protocol lacp
Switch(config-if)# channel-group 16 mode active
```

Note that PAgP and LACP do not interoperate with each other; ports configured to use PAgP cannot form EtherChannels with ports configured to use LACP, and can ports configured to use LACP cannot form EtherChannels with ports configured to use PAgP.

EtherChannel plays a critical role in provisioning network link redundancy, especially at the campus distribution and core layers. Furthermore, an evolution of EtherChannel technology plays a key role the Cisco Virtual Switching System, discussed in the following section.

Cisco Virtual Switching System

The Cisco Virtual Switching System (VSS) can achieve the lowest convergence times—and thus highest levels of availability—for Layer 2 TelePresence campus distribution block networks, as detailed in Chapter 9.

The Cisco Catalyst 6500 Virtual Switching System represents a major leap forward in device (and network) availability technologies by combining many of the technologies that have been discussed thus far into a single, integrated system. VSS allows for the combination of two switches into a single, logical network entity from the network control-plane and management perspectives. To the neighboring devices, the VSS appears as a single, logical switch or router.

Within the VSS, one chassis is designated as the active virtual switch, and the other is designated as the standby virtual switch. All control-plane functions, Layer 2 protocols, Layer 3 protocols, and software data path are centrally managed by the active supervisor engine of the active virtual switch chassis. The supervisor engine on the active virtual switch is also responsible for programming the hardware forwarding information onto all the *Distributed Forwarding Cards (DFC)* across the entire Cisco VSS as well as the policy feature card (PFC) on the standby virtual switch supervisor engine.

From the data plane and traffic forwarding perspectives, both switches in the VSS actively forward traffic. The PFC on the active virtual switch supervisor engine performs central forwarding lookups for all traffic that ingresses the active virtual switch, whereas the PFC on the standby virtual switch supervisor engine performs central forwarding lookups for all traffic that ingresses the standby virtual switch.

The first step to creating a VSS is to define a new logical entity called the *Virtual Switch Domain*, which represents both switches as a single unit. As switches can belong to one or more virtual switch domains, a unique number must define each switch virtual domain, as Example 5-3 demonstrates.

Example 5-3 *VSS Virtual Domain Configuration*

```
VSS-sw1(config)# switch virtual domain 100
Domain ID 100 config will take effect only
after the exec command 'switch convert mode virtual' is issued
VSS-sw1(config-vs-domain)# switch 1
```

Note   You need to configure a corresponding set of commands on the second switch, with the difference being that "switch 1" becomes "switch 2." However, the switch virtual domain number must be identical (in this example, 100).

Additionally, to bond the two chassis together into a single, logical node, special signaling and control information must be exchanged between the two chassis in a timely manner. To facilitate this information exchange, a special link is needed to transfer both data and control traffic between the peer chassis. This link is referred to as the *virtual switch link (VSL)*. The VSL, formed as an EtherChannel interface, can comprise links ranging from 1 to 8 physical member ports. Example 5-4 shows the configuration and conversion commands required to create a VSS.

Example 5-4 *VSL Configuration and VSS Conversion*

```
VSS-sw1(config)# interface port-channel 1
VSS-sw1(config-if)# switch virtual link 1
VSS-sw1(config-if)# no shut
VSS-sw1(config-if)# exit
VSS-sw1(config)# interface range tenGigabitEthernet 5/4 - 5
VSS-sw1(config-if-range)# channel-group 1 mode on
VSS-sw1(config-if-range)# no shut
VSS-sw1(config-if-range)# exit
VSS-sw1(config)# exit
VSS-sw1# switch convert mode virtual
This command will convert all interface names to naming convention "interface-
type switch-number/slot/port", save the running config to startup-config and
reload the switch.
Do you want to proceed? [yes/no]: yes
Converting interface names
Building configuration...
[OK]
Saving converted configurations to bootflash ...
[OK]
```

Note   As previously stated, a corresponding set of commands need to be configured on the second switch, with the difference being that "switch virtual link 1" becomes "switch virtual link 2." Additionally, "port-channel 1" becomes "port-channel 2."

VSL links carry two types of traffic: the VSS control traffic and normal data traffic. Figure 5-15 illustrates the Virtual Switch Domain and the VSL.

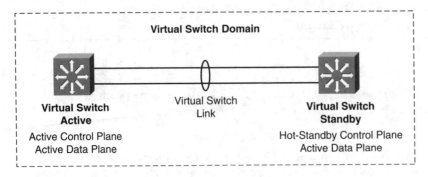

Figure 5-15   *Virtual Switch Domain and VSL*

Furthermore, VSS allows for an additional twist on EtherChannel technology, namely *Multi-chassis EtherChannel (MEC)*. Prior to VSS, Etherchannels were restricted to reside within the same physical switch. However in a VSS environment, the 2 physical switches form a single logical network entity, and, therefore, Etherchannels can be extended across the two physical chassis, forming a MEC.

MEC allows for an EtherChannel bundle to be created across two separate physical chassis (although these two physical chassis are operating as a single, logical entity), as shown in Figure 5-16.

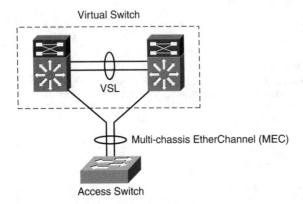

Figure 5-16   *Multi-chassis EtherChannel topology*

Therefore, MEC allows all the dual-homed connections to and from the upstream and downstream devices to be configured as EtherChannel links, as opposed to individual links. From a configuration standpoint, the commands to form a MEC are the same as a regular EtherChannel; it's just that these are applied to interfaces that reside on two separate physical switches, as shown in Figure 5-17.

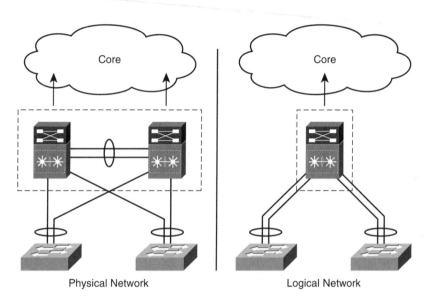

Figure 5-17   *MEC–physical and logical campus network blocks*

As a result, MEC links allow for implementation of network designs where true Layer 2 multipathing can be implemented without the reliance on Layer 2 redundancy protocols such as Spanning Tree Protocol, as contrasted in Figure 5-18.

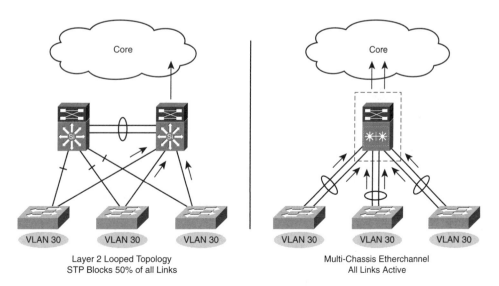

Figure 5-18   *STP topology versus VSS topology*

The advantage of VSS over STP is highlighted further by comparing Figure 5-19, which shows a full campus network design using VSS, with Figure 5-9, which shows a similar campus network design using STP.

Fully Redundant Virtual
Switch Topology

Figure 5-19   *VSS campus network design*

The capability to remove physical loops from the topology and no longer be dependent on Spanning Tree is one of the significant advantages of the virtual switch design. However, it is not the only difference. The virtual switch design allows for a number of fundamental changes to be made to the configuration and operation of the distribution block. By simplifying the network topology to use a single virtual distribution switch, many other aspects of the network design are either greatly simplified or, in some cases, no longer necessary. Furthermore, network designs using VSS can be configured to converge in under 200 ms, which is 250 times faster than STP!

This section covered many key Layer 2 network availability technologies. The next section continues the discussion, but at Layer 3.

L3 Network Availability Protocols

L3 network availability technologies that particularly relate to TelePresence network design include the following:

- Hot Standby Router Protocol (HSRP)

- Virtual Router Redundancy Protocol (VRRP)

- Gateway Load Balancing Protocol (GLBP)

- IP Event Dampening

Each of these L3 technologies are discussed in turn.

Hot Standby Router Protocol

TelePresence codecs route all traffic through their default gateway router. If (for whatever reason) the default gateway router fails, TelePresence calls hang or self-terminate, depending on the amount of time it takes for the default gateway router to recover (or be replaced).

The *Cisco Hot Standby Router Protocol (HSRP)* is the first of three First-Hop Redundancy Protocols (FHRP) discussed in this chapter (the other two being VRRP and GLBP). An FHRP provides increased availability by allowing for transparent failover of the first-hop (or default gateway) router.

HSRP is used in a group of routers for selecting an active router and a standby router. In a group of router interfaces, the active router is the router of choice for routing packets; the standby router is the router that takes over when the active router fails or when preset conditions are met.

Endpoint devices, or IP hosts, have an IP address of a single router configured as the default gateway. When HSRP is used, the HSRP virtual IP address is configured as the host's default gateway instead of the actual IP address of the router.

When HSRP is configured on a network segment, it provides a virtual MAC address and an IP address that is shared among a group of routers running HSRP. The address of this HSRP group is referred to as the *virtual IP address*. One of these devices is selected by the HSRP to be the active router. The active router receives and routes packets destined for the MAC address of the group.

HSRP detects when the designated active router fails; at which point, a selected standby router assumes control of the MAC and IP addresses of the Hot Standby group. A new standby router is also selected at that time.

HSRP uses a priority mechanism to determine which HSRP configured router is to be the default active router. To configure a router as the active router, you assign it a priority that is higher than the priority of all the other HSRP-configured routers. The default priority is 100, so if just one router is configured to have a higher priority, that router will be the default active router.

Devices that run HSRP send and receive multicast *User Datagram Protocol (UDP)*-based hello messages to detect router failure and to designate active and standby routers. When the active router fails to send a hello message within a configurable period of time, the standby router with the highest priority becomes the active router. The transition of packet forwarding functions between routers is completely transparent to all hosts on the network.

Multiple Hot Standby groups can be configured on an interface, thereby making fuller use of redundant routers and load sharing.

Figure 5-20 shows a network configured for HSRP. By sharing a virtual MAC address and IP address, two or more routers can act as a single *virtual router*. The virtual router does not physically exist but represents the common default gateway for routers that are configured to provide backup to each other. All IP hosts are configured with the IP address of the virtual router as their default gateway. If the active router fails to send a hello message within the configurable period of time, the standby router takes over and responds to the virtual addresses and becomes the active router, assuming the active router duties.

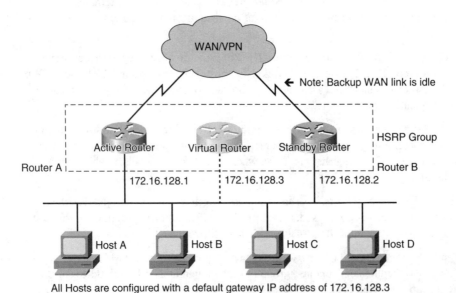

Figure 5-20   *HSRP topology*

HSRP also supports object tracking so that the HSRP priority of a router can dynamically change when an object that is tracked goes down. Examples of objects that can be tracked are the line protocol state of an interface or the reachability of an IP route. If the specified object goes down, the HSRP priority is reduced.

Furthermore, HSRP supports SSO awareness so that HRSP can alter its behavior when a router with redundant *Route Processors (RP)* is configured as SSO redundancy mode. When an RP is active and the other RP is standby, SSO enables the standby RP to take over if the active RP fails.

With this functionality, HSRP SSO information is synchronized to the standby RP, allowing traffic that is sent using the HSRP virtual IP address to be continuously forwarded during a switchover without a loss of data or a path change. Additionally, if both RPs fail on the active HSRP router, the standby HSRP router takes over as the active HSRP router.

Note   SSO awareness for HSRP is enabled by default when the RP's redundancy mode of operation is set to SSO (as shown in the "NSF with SSO" section of this chapter).

Example 5-5 demonstrates the HSRP configuration that you can use on the LAN interface of the active router from Figure 5-20. Each HSRP group on a given subnet requires a unique number; in this example the HSRP group number is set to 10. The virtual router's IP address (which is what each IP host on the network uses as a default-gateway address) is set to 172.16.128.3. The HRSP priority of this router has been set to 105, and preemption has been enabled on it; preemption allows for the router to immediately take over as the virtual router (provided it has the highest priority on the segment). Finally, object tracking has been configured so that if the line protocol state of interface Serial0/1 goes down (the WAN link for the active router, which is designated as object-number 110), the HSRP priority for this interface dynamically decrements (by a value of 10, by default).

Example 5-5   *HSRP Example*

```
Router(config)# track 110 interface Serial0/1 line-protocol
Router(config)# interface GigabitEthernet0/0
Router(config-if)# ip address 172.16.128.1 255.255.255.0
Router(config-if)# standby 10 ip 172.16.128.3
Router(config-if)# standby 10 priority 105 preempt
Router(config-if)# standby 10 track 110
```

As HRSP was the first FHRP and because it was invented by Cisco, it is Cisco proprietary. However, to support multivendor interoperability, aspects of HSRP were standardized in the Virtual Router Redundancy Protocol, which is discussed next.

Virtual Router Redundancy Protocol

The *Virtual Router Redundancy Protocol (VRRP)*, defined in RFC 2338, is a FHRP that is similar to HSRP but capable of supporting multivendor environments. A VRRP router is configured to run the VRRP protocol in conjunction with one or more other routers attached to a LAN. In a VRRP configuration, one router is elected as the *virtual router master*, with the other routers acting as backups if the virtual router master fails.

VRRP enables a group of routers to form a single *virtual router*. The LAN clients can then be configured with the virtual router as their default gateway. The virtual router, representing a group of routers, is also known as a VRRP group.

Figure 5-21 shows a LAN topology with VRRP configured. In this example, two *VRRP routers* (routers running VRRP) comprise a virtual router. However, unlike HSRP, the IP address of the virtual router is the same as that configured for the LAN interface of the virtual router master, in this example 172.16.128.1.

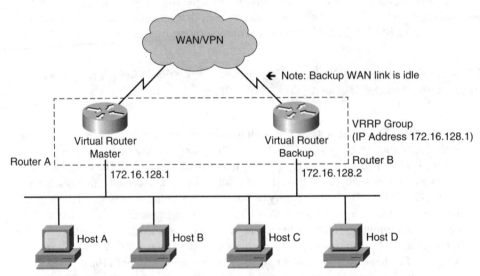

All Hosts are configured with a default gateway IP address of 172.16.128.1.

Figure 5-21   *VRRP topology.*

Router A assumes the role of the *virtual router master* and is also known as the *IP address owner* because the IP address of the virtual router belongs to it. As the virtual router master, Router A is responsible for forwarding packets sent to this IP address. Each IP host on the subnet is configured with the default gateway IP address of the virtual route master, in this case 172.16.128.1.

Router B, on the other hand, functions as a *virtual router backup*. If the virtual router master fails, the router configured with the higher priority becomes the virtual router master and provides uninterrupted service for the LAN hosts. When Router A recovers, it becomes the virtual router master again.

Additionally, like HSRP, VRRP supports object tracking and preemption and SSO awareness.

Note   SSO awareness for VRRP is enabled by default when the route processor's redundancy mode of operation is set to SSO (as was shown in the "NSF with SSO" section of this chapter).

Example 5-6 shows a VRRP configuration that can be used on the LAN interface of the virtual router master from Figure 5-21. Each VRRP group on a given subnet requires a unique number; in this example the VRRP group number is set to 10. The virtual IP address is set to the actual LAN interface address, designating this router as the virtual router master. The VRRP priority of this router has been set to 105. Unlike HSRP, preemption for VRRP is enabled by default. Finally, object tracking has been configured so that should the line protocol state of interface Serial0/1 go down (the WAN link for this router, which is designated as object-number 110), the VRRP priority for this interface dynamically decrements (by a value of 10, by default).

Example 5-6   *VRRP Example*

```
Router(config)# track 110 interface Serial0/1 line-protocol
Router(config)# interface GigabitEthernet0/0
Router(config-if)# ip address 172.16.128.1 255.255.255.0
Router(config-if)# vrrp 10 ip 172.16.128.1
Router(config-if)# vrrp 10 priority 105
Router(config-if)# vrrp 10 track 110
```

A drawback to both HSRP and VRRP is that the standby/backup router is not used to forward traffic and wastes both available bandwidth and processing capabilities. This limitation can be worked around by provisioning two complementary HSRP/VRRP groups on each LAN subnet, with one group having the left router as the active/master and the other group having the right router as the active/master router. Then, approximately half of the hosts are configured to use the virtual IP address of one HSRP/VRRP group, and remaining hosts are configured to use the virtual IP address of the second group. Obviously, this requires additional operational and management complexity. To improve the efficiency of these FHRP models without such additional complexity, Gateway Load Balancing Protocol can be used, which is discussed next.

Gateway Load Balancing Protocol

Cisco Gateway Load Balancing Protocol (GLBP) improves the efficiency of FHRP protocols by allowing for automatic load balancing of the default gateway. The advantage of GLBP is that it additionally provides load balancing over multiple routers (gateways) using a single virtual IP address and *multiple* virtual MAC addresses per GLBP group. (In contrast, both HRSP and VRRP used only *one* virtual MAC address per HSRP/VRRP group.) The forwarding load is shared among all routers in a GLBP group rather than handled by a single router while the other routers stand idle. Each host is configured with the same virtual IP address, and all routers in the virtual router group participate in forwarding packets.

Members of a GLBP group elect one gateway to be the *active virtual gateway (AVG)* for that group. Other group members provide backup for the AVG if that AVG becomes unavailable. The function of the AVG is that it assigns a virtual MAC address to each member of the GLBP group. Each gateway assumes responsibility for forwarding packets sent to the virtual MAC address assigned to it by the AVG. These gateways are known as *active virtual forwarders (AVF)* for their virtual MAC address.

The AVG is also responsible for answering *Address Resolution Protocol (ARP)* requests for the virtual IP address. Load sharing is achieved by the AVG replying to the ARP requests with different virtual MAC addresses (corresponding to each gateway router).

In Figure 5-22, Router A is the AVG for a GLBP group and is primarily responsible for the virtual IP address 172.16.128.3; however, Router A is also an AVF for the virtual MAC address 0007.b400.0101. Router B is a member of the same GLBP group and is designated as the AVF for the virtual MAC address 0007.b400.0102. All hosts have their default gateway IP addresses set to the virtual IP address of 172.16.128.3. However, when these are an ARP for the MAC of this virtual IP address, Host A and Host C receives a gateway MAC address of 0007.b400.0101 (directing these hosts to use Router A as their default gateway), but Host B and Host D receive a gateway MAC address 0007.b400.0102 (directing these hosts to use Router B as their default gateway). In this way the gateway routers automatically load share.

If Router A becomes unavailable, Hosts A and C do not lose access to the WAN because Router B assumes responsibility for forwarding packets sent to the virtual MAC address of Router A and for responding to packets sent to its own virtual MAC address. Router B also assumes the role of the AVG for the entire GLBP group. Communication for the GLBP members continues despite the failure of a router in the GLBP group.

Additionally, like HSRP and VRRP, GLBP supports object tracking and preemption and SSO awareness.

Note   SSO awareness for GLBP is enabled by default when the route processor's redundancy mode of operation is set to SSO (as was shown in the "NSF with SSO" section of this chapter).

However, unlike the object tracking logic used by HSRP and VRRP, GLBP uses a weighting scheme to determine the forwarding capacity of each router in the GLBP group. The weighting assigned to a router in the GLBP group can be used to determine whether it forwards packets and, if so, the proportion of hosts in the LAN for which it forwards packets. Thresholds can be set such that when the weighting for a GLBP group falls below a certain value, and when it rises above another threshold, forwarding is automatically reenabled.

The GLBP group weighting can be automatically adjusted by tracking the state of an interface within the router. If a tracked interface goes down, the GLBP group weighting is reduced by a specified value. Different interfaces can be tracked to decrement the GLBP weighting by varying amounts.

Example 5-7 shows a GLBP configuration that can be used on the LAN interface of the AVG from Figure 5-22. Each GLBP group on a given subnet requires a unique number; in this example the GLBP group number is set to 10. The virtual IP address for the GLBP group is set to 172.16.128.3. The GLBP priority of this interface has been set to 105, and like HSRP, preemption for GLBP must be explicitly enabled (if desired). Finally, object tracking has been configured so that should the line protocol state of interface Serial0/1

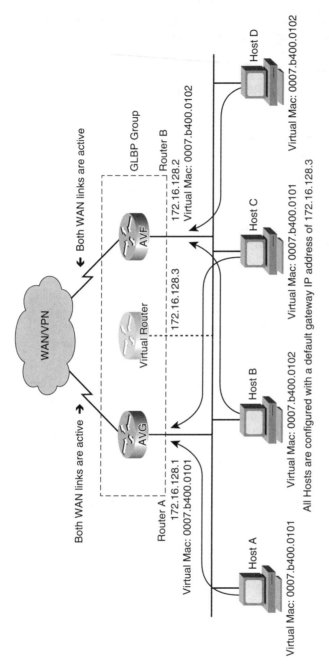

Figure 5-22   *GLBP topology*

go down (the WAN link for this router, which is designated as object-number 110), the GLBP priority for this interface dynamically decrements (by a value of 10, by default).

Example 5-7   *GLBP Example*

```
Router(config)# track 110 interface Serial0/1 line-protocol
Router(config)# interface GigabitEthernet0/0
Router(config-if)# ip address 172.16.128.1 255.255.255.0
Router(config-if)# glbp 10 ip 172.16.128.3
Router(config-if)# glbp 10 priority 105
Router(config-if)# glbp 10 preempt
Router(config-if)# glbp 10 weighting track 110
```

Having concluded an overview of these FHRPs, a discussion of another type of L3 network availability feature, IP Event Dampening, follows.

IP Event Dampening

Routing protocols provide network convergence functionality in IP networks, including TelePresence campus and branch networks. However, these protocols are impeded by links that "flap" or change state repeatedly. Although not a protocol in itself, *IP Event Dampening* complements the functioning of routing protocols to improve availability by minimizing the impact of flapping on routing protocol convergence.

Whenever the line protocol of an interface changes state, or flaps, routing protocols are notified of the status of the routes affected by the change in state. Every interface state change requires all affected devices in the network to recalculate best paths, install or remove routes from the routing tables, and then advertise valid routes to peer routers. An unstable interface that flaps excessively can cause other devices in the network to consume substantial amounts of system processing resources and cause routing protocols to lose synchronization with the state of the flapping interface.

The IP Event Dampening feature introduces a configurable exponential decay mechanism to suppress the effects of excessive interface flapping events on routing protocols and routing tables in the network. This feature allows the network administrator to configure a router to automatically identify and selectively dampen a local interface that is flapping. Dampening an interface removes the interface from the network until the interface stops flapping and becomes stable.

Configuring the IP Event Dampening feature improves convergence times and stability throughout the network by isolating failures so that disturbances are not propagated, which reduces the utilization of system processing resources by other devices in the network and improves overall network stability.

IP Event Dampening uses a series of administratively defined thresholds to identify flapping interfaces, to assign penalties, to suppress state changes (if necessary), and to make stabilized interfaces available to the network. These thresholds are as follows:

■ **Suppress threshold:** The value of the accumulated penalty that triggers the router to dampen a flapping interface. The flapping interface is identified by the router and assigned a penalty for each up and down state change, but the interface is not automatically dampened. The router tracks the penalties that a flapping interface accumulates. When the accumulated penalty reaches the default or preconfigured suppress threshold, the interface is placed in a dampened state. The default suppress threshold value is 2000.

■ **Half-life period:** Determines how fast the accumulated penalty can decay exponentially. When an interface is placed in a dampened state, the router monitors the interface for additional up and down state changes. If the interface continues to accumulate penalties and the interface remains in the suppress threshold range, the interface remains dampened. If the interface stabilizes and stops flapping, the penalty is reduced by half after each half-life period expires. The accumulated penalty reduces until the penalty drops to the reuse threshold. The default half-life period timer is five seconds.

■ **Reuse threshold:** When the accumulated penalty decreases until the penalty drops to the reuse threshold, the route is unsuppressed and made available to the other devices on the network. The default value is 1000 penalties.

■ **Maximum suppress time:** Represents the maximum amount of time an interface can remain dampened when a penalty is assigned to an interface. The default maximum penalty timer is 20 seconds.

IP Event Dampening is configured on a per-interface basis (where default values are used for each threshold) as follows:

```
Router(config-)# interface FastEthernet0/0
Router(config-if)# dampening
```

IP Event Dampening can be complemented with the use of route summarization, on a per-routing protocol basis, to further compartmentalize the effects of flapping interfaces and associated routes.

With device and network availability technologies having been discussed, the final section introduces operational availability technologies.

Operational Availabilities Technologies

As has been shown, the predominant way that availability of a network can be improved is to improve its MTBF by using devices that have redundant components and by engineering the network to be as redundant as possible, leveraging many of the technologies discussed in the previous sections.

However, glancing back to the general availability formula from Figure 5-1, another approach to improving availability is to reduce MTTR. Reducing MTTR is primarily a factor of operational resiliency.

MTTR operations can be significantly improved in conjunction with device and network redundant design. Specifically, the capability to make changes, upgrade software, and replace or upgrade hardware in a production network is extensively improved due to the implementation of device and network redundancy. The capability to upgrade individual devices without taking them out of service is based on having internal component redundancy complemented with the system software capabilities. Similarly, by having dual active paths through redundant network devices designed to converge in subsecond timeframes, you can schedule an outage event on one element of the network and allow it to be upgraded and then brought back into service with minimal or no disruption to the network as a whole.

You can also improve MTTR by reducing the time required to perform any of the following operations:

- Failure detection

- Notification

- Fault diagnosis

- Dispatch and Arrival

- Fault repair

Some technologies that can help automate and streamline these operations include the following:

- General Online Diagnostics (GOLD)

- Embedded Event Manager (EEM)

- In Service Software Upgrade (ISSU)

- Online Insertion and Removal (OIR)

Each of these technologies are briefly introduced next.

Generic Online Diagnostics

Cisco *General Online Diagnostics (GOLD)* defines a common framework for diagnostic operations for Cisco IOS Software-based products. GOLD has the objective of checking the health of all hardware components and verifying the proper operation of the system data plane and control plane at boot-time, as well as run-time.

GOLD supports the following:

- Bootup tests (includes online insertion)

- Health monitoring tests (background nondisruptive)

- On-Demand tests (disruptive and nondisruptive)

- User scheduled tests (disruptive and nondisruptive)

- CLI access to data through management interface

GOLD, in conjunction with several of the technologies previously discussed, can reduce device failure detection time.

Event Manager

The Cisco *IOS Embedded Event Manager (EEM)* offers the capability to monitor device hardware, software, and operational events and take informational, corrective, or any desired action—including sending an email alert—when the monitored events occur or when a threshold is reached.

EEM can notify a network management server and an administrator (via email) when an event of interest occurs. Events that can be monitored include the following:

- Application-specific events

- CLI events

- Counter- and interface-counter events

- Object-tracking events

- Online insertion and removal events

- Resource events

- GOLD events

- Redundancy events

- SNMP events

- Syslog events

- System manager and system monitor events

- IOS Watchdog events

- Timer events

Capturing the state of network devices during such situations can be helpful in taking immediate recovery actions and gathering information to perform root-cause analysis, reducing fault detection and diagnosis time. Notification times are reduced by having the device send email alerts to network administrators. Furthermore, availability is also improved if automatic recovery actions are performed without the need to fully reboot the device.

In Service Software Upgrade

The Cisco *In Service Software Upgrade (ISSU)* provides a mechanism to perform software upgrades and downgrades without taking a switch out of service. ISSU leverages the capabilities of NSF and SSO to allow the switch to forward traffic during supervisor IOS upgrade (or downgrade). With ISSU, the network does not reroute, and no active links are taken out of service. ISSU thereby expedites software upgrade operations.

Online Insertion and Removal

Online Insertion and Removal (OIR) allows linecards to be added to a device without affecting the system. Additionally with OIR, linecards can be exchanged without losing the configuration. OIR thus expedites hardware repair and replacement operations.

Summary

The goal of this chapter was to provide context for Chapter 9 by introducing general availability concepts, metrics, and technologies.

Availability is a factor of two components: the mean time between failures (MTBF) and the mean time to repair (MTTR) such failures. You can improve availability by increasing MTBF (which is primarily a function of device and network resiliency/redundancy) or by reducing MTTR (which is primarily a function of operational resiliency).

Device availability technologies were discussed, including Cisco Catalyst StackWise/StackWise Plus technologies that provide 1:n control-plane redundancy to Catalyst 3750G/3750E switches and nonstop forwarding (NSF) with stateful switch over (SSO), which similarly provides hot standby redundancy to network devices with multiple route processors.

Network availability protocols were also discussed, beginning with Layer 2 protocols, such as spanning-tree protocols, trunking protocols, EtherChannel protocols, and the Cisco Virtual Switching System. Additionally, Layer 3 protocols, such as HSRP, VRRP, GLBP, and IP Event dampening were overviewed.

Finally, operational availability technologies were introduced to round out how availability could be improved by automating and streamlining MTTR operations, including GOLD, EEM, ISSU, and OIR.

Further Reading

IETF Standards:

Virtual Router Redundancy Protocol http://www.ietf.org/rfc/rfc2338

Cisco Technology White Papers:

Enterprise Campus 3.0 Architecture: Overview and Framework: http://www.tinyurl. com/4bwr33

Cisco StackWise and StackWise Plus Technology: http://www.tinyurl.com/c4hncw

Nonstop Forwarding with Stateful Switchover on the Cisco Catalyst 6500: http://www. tinyurl.com/2xdgf5

Cisco Nonstop Forwarding with Stateful Switchover Deployment Guide: http://www. tinyurl.com/29pe94

Cisco Catalyst 6500 Series Virtual Switching System: http://www.tinyurl.com/5zph8e

Generic Online Diagnostics on the Cisco Catalyst 6500 Series Switch: http://www.tinyurl. com/dztzqs

EEM Configuration for Cisco Integrated Services Router Platforms: http://www.tinyurl. com/6kbldd

Cisco IOS Documentation:

Configuring HSRP: http://www.tinyurl.com/dcccjx

Configuring VRRP: http://www.tinyurl.com/bdp9ms

Configuring GLBP: http://www.tinyurl.com/bk55vs

Configuring IP Event Dampening: http://www.tinyurl.com/cp9g5y

A major competitive advantage of the Cisco TelePresence solution is that it supports the transport of real-time, high-definition video and audio over a converged IP network, rather than requiring a dedicated network for TelePresence. (Although dedicated networks are also supported.) The key enabling technology to accomplish this convergence is quality of service (QoS), which refers to the set of tools and techniques to manage network resources, such as bandwidth, while mitigating the adverse effects of latency, jitter, and loss. QoS technologies enable different types of traffic to intelligently contend for network resources. For example, voice and real-time video—such as TelePresence—might be granted strict priority service, whereas some critical data applications might receive (nonpriority) preferential services, and other undesired applications might even be assigned deferential levels of service.

QoS tools have been around for 30 years in one form or another. Even the Cisco QoS toolset is quite large and varied with many legacy hangovers. Therefore, rather than trying to cover all QoS tools, this chapter focuses on the tools that are most relevant to TelePresence network deployments—whether directly required for provisioning TelePresence or as part of a more comprehensive QoS policy—including the following:

- Classification tools

- Marking tools

- Policing tools

- Shaping tools

- Queuing tools

- Dropping tools

CHAPTER 6

Network Quality of Service Technologies

An overview of these QoS tools provides a foundational context for the platform-specific QoS design recommendations for TelePresence networks detailed in Chapter 10, "TelePresence Network Design Part 2: QoS Design."

Before discussing these tools in turn, the section that follows examines the Cisco IOS Software syntax structure that all these tools fall under, namely the Modular QoS Command-Line Interface (MQC).

Modular QoS Command-Line Interface

As the Cisco QoS tools evolved, they became increasingly platform idiosyncratic. Commands that worked on one platform wouldn't quite work on another, and there were always platform-specific requirements and constraints that had to be kept in mind. These idiosyncrasies made deploying QoS a laborious and often frustrating exercise, especially when deploying networkwide QoS policies, such as required by TelePresence. As an attempt to make QoS more consistent across platforms, Cisco introduced the MQC, which is a consistent, cross-platform command syntax for QoS.

Any QoS policy requires at least three elements:

1. Identification of what traffic the policy is to be applied to
2. What actions should be applied to the identified traffic
3. Where (that is, which interface) should these policies be applied, and in which direction

To correspond to these required elements, MQC has three main parts:

1. One or more *class maps* that identify what traffic the policies are to be applied to
2. A *policy map* that details the QoS actions that are to be applied to each class of identified traffic
3. A *service policy* statement that attaches the policy to specific interfaces and specifies the direction (input or output) that the policy is to be applied

As you see in the examples throughout this chapter, although the syntax of MQC might seem simple enough, it allows for nearly every type of QoS policy to be expressed within it and allows these policies, for the most part, to be portable across platforms.

Classification Tools

Classification tools serve to identify traffic flows so that specific QoS policies can be applied to specific flows, such as TelePresence media and control flows. Often the terms *classification* and *marking* are used interchangeably (yet incorrectly so); therefore, you need to understand the distinction between classification and marking operations:

- *Classification* refers to the inspection of one or more fields in a packet (the term *packet* is used loosely here to include all Layer 2 to Layer 7 fields, not just Layer 3 fields) to identify the type of traffic that the packet is carrying. When identified, the traffic is directed to the applicable policy-enforcement mechanism for that traffic type, where it receives predefined treatment (either preferential or deferential). Such treatment can include marking/remarking, queuing, policing, shaping, or any combination of these (and other) actions.

- *Marking*, on the other hand, refers to changing a field within the packet to preserve the classification decision that was reached. When a packet has been marked, a *trust boundary* is established, upon which other QoS tools later depend. Marking is only necessary at the trust boundaries of the network and (as with all other QoS policy actions) cannot be performed without classification. By marking traffic at the trust boundary edge, subsequent nodes do not have to perform the same in-depth classification and analyses to determine how to treat the packet.

MQC performs classification based on the logic defined within the class map structure. Such logic can include matching criteria at the data link, network, or transport Layer (Layers 2 to 4) or even at the application layer (Layer 7), through *Network Based Application Recognition (NBAR)* technology, as discussed in the next sections.

Class Maps

The primary classification tool within MQC is the class map. Each class map contains one or more **match** statements, which specify criteria that must be met for traffic identification

Because classmaps can contain multiple **match** statements, when a class map is defined, a logical operator for the discrete **match** statements also needs to be defined. Two options exist as follows:

- **match-all** (a logical AND operator), meaning that *all* **match** statements must be true at the same time for the class map condition to be true; **match-all** is the default operator; it is important not to use mutually exclusive match criteria when a **match-all** operator is defined within the class map, as this combination can never yield a positive match.

- **match-any** (a logical OR operator), meaning that *any* of the **match** statements might be true for the class map condition to be true.

These **match** statements specify the criteria for traffic identification. These can include the following:

- **Layer 1 parameters:** Physical interface, subinterface, PVC, or port

- **Layer 2 parameters:** MAC address, 802.1Q/p class of service (CoS) bits, Multiprotocol Label Switching (MPLS) Experimental (EXP) bits

- **Layer 3 parameters:** Differentiated Services Code Points (DSCP), source/destination IP address

- **Layer 4 parameters:** TCP or UDP ports

- **Layer 7 parameters:** Application signatures and URLs in packet headers or payload through Network Based Application Recognition (NBAR)

Figure 6-1 illustrates the Layer 2 to Layer 7 packet classification criteria; however, due to space limitations, the diagram is not to scale, nor are all fields indicated.

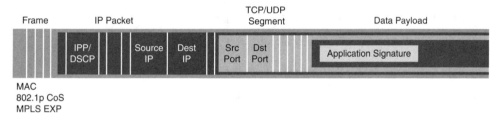

Figure 6-1   *Layer 2 to Layer 7 packet classification criteria*

Network Based Application Recognition

Although the majority of applications can be identified using Layer 3 or Layer 4 criteria (such as discrete IP addresses or well-known TCP/UDP ports), there are applications that cannot be identified by such criteria alone. This might be due to legacy limitations but more likely is due to deliberate design. For example, peer-to-peer media-sharing applications deliberately negotiate ports dynamically with the objective of penetrating firewalls.

When Layer 3 or Layer 4 parameters are insufficient to positively identify an application, NBAR might be a viable alternative solution. NBAR is the most sophisticated classifier in the IOS tool suite. NBAR can recognize packets on a complex combination of fields and attributes; however, you need to recognize that NBAR is merely a classifier, nothing more. NBAR can identify flows by performing deep-packet inspection, but it is the job of the policy map to determine what needs to be done with these flows when identified (that is, whether they should be marked, policed, dropped, and so on).

The NBAR deep-packet classification engine examines the data payload of stateless protocols and identifies application-layer protocols by matching them against a *Protocol Description Language Module (PDLM)*, which is essentially an application signature. There are more than 80 PDLMs embedded into Cisco IOS; furthermore, because PDLMs are modular, they can be downloaded from http://www.cisco.com/pcgi-bin/tablebuild.pl/pdlm and added to a system without requiring an IOS upgrade.

NBAR is dependent on *Cisco Express Forwarding (CEF)* and performs deep-packet classification only on the first packet of a flow. The remainder of the packets belonging to the flow is then CEF-switched.

The NBAR classifier is triggered by the **match protocol** command within a class map definition and is a more CPU-intensive classifier than classifiers that match traffic by DSCPs or access control lists (ACL).

NBAR can classify packets based on Layer 4 through Layer 7 protocols, which dynamically assign TCP/UDP ports. By looking beyond the TCP/UDP port numbers of a packet (known as subport classification), NBAR examines the packet payload and classifies packets on the payload content, such as transaction identifiers, message types, or other similar data. For example, HTTP traffic can be classified by Universal Resource Locators (URL) or *Multipurpose Internet Mail Extension (MIME)* types using regular expressions within the CLI. NBAR uses the UNIX filename specification as the basis for the URL specification format, which it converts into a regular expression.

Example 6-1 demonstrates classifying traffic by L2, L3, L4, and L7 parameters.

Example 6-1   *Classifying Traffic by Layer 2, 3, 4, and 7 Parameters*

```
Router(config)# class-map match-all L2-CLASSIFIER
Router(config-cmap)# match cos 3
Router(config-cmap)#!
Router(config-cmap)# class-map match-all L3-CLASSIFIER
Router(config-cmap)# match access-group name STANDARD-ACL
Router(config-cmap)# !
Router(config-cmap)# class-map match-all L4-CLASSIFIER
Router(config-cmap)# match access-group name EXTENDED-ACL
Router(config-cmap)# !
Router(config-cmap)# class-map match-any L7-CLASSIFIER
Router(config-cmap)# match protocol exchange
Router(config-cmap)# match protocol citrix
Router(config-cmap)# !
Router(config-cmap)#
Router(config-cmap)# ip access-list standard STANDARD-ACL
Router(config-std-nacl)# permit 10.200.200.0 0.0.0.255
Router(config-std-nacl)#
Router(config-std-nacl)# ip access-list extended EXTENDED-ACL
Router(config-ext-nacl)# permit tcp any any eq ftp
Router(config-ext-nacl)# permit tcp any any eq ftp-data
```

In this example, the class maps classify traffic as follows:

- **class-map match-all L2-CLASSIFIER:** Traffic is classified by matching on (Layer 2) 802.1p class of service (CoS) values (discussed in more detail in the next section).

- **class-map match-all L3-CLASSIFIER:** Traffic is classified, through a standard ACL, by (Layer 3) source IP address.

- **class-map match-all L4-CLASSIFIER:** Traffic is classified, through an extended ACL, by (Layer 4) TCP ports identifying FTP traffic.

- **class-map match-any L7-CLASSIFIER:** Traffic is classified, with the **match-any** operator, by NBAR PDLMs that identify SQLNET or Citrix traffic types.

Marking Tools

Marking tools change fields within the packet, either at Layer 2 or at Layer 3 so that in-depth classification does not have to be performed at each network QoS decision point. For example, TelePresence packets are typically marked at both Layer 2 (with 802.1p CoS values of 4 for media and 3 for signaling) and Layer 3 (with DSCP values CS4/32 for media and CS3/24 for signaling).

The primary tool within MQC for marking is *Class-Based Marking,* though policers (sometimes called markers) can also be used. You can use Class-Based Marking to set the CoS fields within an 802.1Q/p tag (over Ethernet networks), the Experimental bits within a MPLS label (over MPLS VPNs), or the Differentiated Services Code Points (DSCP) within an IPv4 or IPv6 header, and other packet fields. Class-Based Marking, like NBAR, is CEF-dependent. The command for Class-Based Marking is **set**, within a policy map per-class action.

Ethernet 802.1Q/p CoS

Native Ethernet does not support any fields that can be marked for QoS purposes. However, when trunked with the 802.1Q protocol, three bits of the 802.1Q tag are made available for setting User Priority, referred to as 802.1p. These bits are more commonly referred to as *CoS bits*. Three bits allow for eight binary combinations for marking, represented by values 0 to 7.

Figure 6-2 illustrates the Ethernet frame with an 802.1Q tag, which includes the following fields:

- **PRI:** The Priority field, which is a 3-bit field that refers to the IEEE 802.1p priority. It indicates the frame priority level from 0 (lowest) to 7 (highest), which prioritizes different classes of traffic (such as voice, video and data).

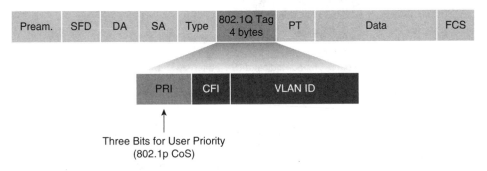

Figure 6-2   *Ethernet frame: 802.1Q/p CoS field*

- **CFI:** The Canonical Format Indicator, which is a 1-bit field. CFI is used for compatibility between Ethernet and Token Ring networks. It is always set to zero for Ethernet switches (and 1 for Token Ring networks).

- **VLAN ID:** The VLAN Identifier, which is a 12-bit field specifying the VLAN to which the frame belongs.

You can set CoS fields with Class-Based Marking by using the **set cos** command. To use Class-Based Marking to set the 802.1Q/p Class of Service field to 2, enter the following:

```
Router(config-cmap)# policy-map L2-MARKER
Router(config-pmap)# class MARK-COS-2
Router(config-pmap-c)# set cos 2
```

MPLS EXP

MPLS is a tunneling technology that prepends labels to IP packets to enable more efficient packet switching and virtual private networking. More than one MPLS label can be prepended, or "stacked," onto an IP packet.

> **Note** Typically, two labels are used in most MPLS VPN scenarios (one to identify each customer's traffic and another to perform local switching with a service provider's cloud); however, in some scenarios, such as MPLS Traffic Engineering, three or more labels are used.

MPLS labels contain 3 bits for CoS marking, which are referred to as the MPLS Experimental (EXP) bits. The possible values of the MPLS EXP bits for CoS are the same as those for 802.1Q/p CoS. Figure 6-3 shows the MPLS EXP bits within an MPLS label.

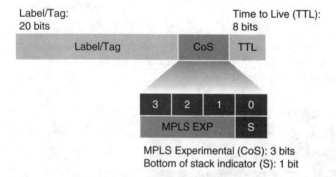

Figure 6-3 *MPLS EXP bits within an MPLS label*

Because MPLS labels include three bits for QoS marking, it is possible to *tunnel DiffServ*—that is, preserve Layer 3 DiffServ markings through a service provider's MPLS VPN cloud while still performing re-marking (through MPLS EXP bits) within the cloud to indicate in- or out-of-contract traffic.

RFC 3270 defines three distinct modes of MPLS DiffServ tunneling:

- **Uniform Mode:** Generally used when the customer and service provider share the same DiffServ domain, as in the case of an enterprise deploying its own MPLS VPN core. The provider can re-mark at either Layer 2 (MPLS EXP) or at Layer 3 (IPP/DSCP). The key point is that in uniform mode, the Layer 3 marking value that a packet has when exiting the MPLS VPN might be different from the value it had when entering the VPN.

- **Short-Pipe Mode:** Both Pipe and Short-Pipe modes preserve DiffServ transparency; that is, under these modes, Layer 3 packet marking values never change as a packet enters, transits, and exits the MPLS VPN. The key difference between Short-Pipe and Pipe mode relates to the final egress queuing policies as the packet exits the VPN. In Short-Pipe mode, these queuing policies are based on the customer's Layer 3 markings.

- **Pipe Mode:** Identical to Short-Pipe mode, but with the final egress queuing policies based on the service provider's Layer 2 markings.

The enterprise network administrator needs to understand these basic differences between MPLS DiffServ Tunneling modes, especially as they relate to how traffic can be marked and re-marked over the MPLS VPN.

Differentiated Services Code Points

The original IP protocol specification (RFC 791) included three bits for marking within the IP Type-of-Service (ToS) field, referred to as *IP Precedence (IPP)* bits. A general problem that all three-bit marking schemes have is that they simply do not have enough granularity to support the many classes of traffic traversing today's networks: For instance, with two values (6 and 7) reserved for network/internetwork control protocols, 5 generally used for voice, 4 for (all forms of) video, 3 for call-signaling, and 0 for best-effort, only 2 marking values (2 and 1) are available for all other classes of traffic.

The coarseness and insufficiency of 3-bit marking granularity led to the definition of a newer set of IP marking standards: the Differentiated Services Architecture (RFC 2474 and 2475). DiffServ standards supersede and replace IP Precedence. The Differentiated Services (or DiffServ, for short) Architecture uses 6 bits for IP marking (whether IPv4 or IPv6), allowing for 64 levels of marking granularity (values 0 through 63); however, note that these 64 levels do not in themselves represent or reflect application priority; they serve only to distinguish flows one from another. Each discrete marking value is a Differentiated Services Code Point (DSCP). Figure 6-4 shows the IP ToS Byte (for an IPv4 packet), including the (former) IP Precedence bits and the current DSCP bits.

The Class-Based Marking command to mark DSCP is to **set dscp**, which marks DSCP values for both IPv4 and IPv6 packets (whereas the command **set ip dscp** marks only IPv4 DSCP values). To set IPv4 and IPv6 DSCP values to 16 using DSCP marking, enter the following:

```
Router(config)# policy-map L3-DSCP-MARKER
Router(config-pmap)# class MARK-DSCP-16
Router(config-pmap-c)# set dscp 16
```

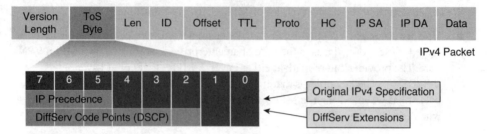

Figure 6-4   *IPv4 type of service byte (IP precedence bits and DSCP)*

You might encounter scenarios when 6-bit Layer 3 (DSCP) markings are attempted to be reflected by 3-bit Layer 2 (CoS or MPLS EXP) markings. Remember, however, that when such L3-to-L2 marking conversions are done, information is almost inevitably lost in translation (as abstracting 6 bits to 3 bits represents an 8:1 mapping; in other words, up to 8 DSCP values can be represented by a single CoS/MPLS EXP value). Even if such scenarios might be required throughout the network, marking at Layer 3 with DSCP should be preserved end-to-end to maintain granularity.

Generally speaking, the best place to mark packets is within the IP header's ToS byte, using DSCP values. This is for three main reasons:

- IP is end-to-end, whereas Layer 2 marking fields (CoS or MPLS EXP) might be lost when the media changes.

- As has been shown, DSCP has greater marking granularity and flexibility than 3-bit L2 marking schemes.

- When marking with DSCP, administrators can follow industry Per-Hop Behaviors (PHB), which are marking values, combined with standard-defined QoS treatments.

Per-Hop Behaviors (PHB) enable a network administrator to extend the reach of his QoS strategy, even across networks over which he does not have administrative control. As mentioned, with DSCP, there are 64 possible marking combinations (0 to 63). Some of these combinations have specific standardized QoS treatments assigned to them. The following section considers a well-known example to illustrate the PHB concept: Expedited Forwarding.

Expedited Forwarding PHB (RFC 3246)

The Expedited Forwarding PHB, defined in RFC 3246, is a strict-priority treatment for packets that have been marked to a DSCP value of 46 (101110), which is also termed *Expedited Forwarding (EF)*. Any packet marked 46/EF that encounters congestion at a given network node is to be moved to the front of the line and serviced in a strict priority manner. It doesn't matter how such behavior is implemented—whether in hardware or software—if the behavior is met for the given platform at the network node.

Incidentally, RFC 3246 does not specify which application is to receive such treatment; this is open to the network administrator to decide, although the industry norm over the last decade has been to use the EF PHB for VoIP.

The EF PHB provides an excellent case-point of the value of standardized PHBs. For example, if a network administrator decides to mark his VoIP traffic to EF and service it with strict priority over his networks, he can extend his policies to protect his voice traffic even over networks of which he does not have direct administrative control. He can do this by partnering with service providers and extranet partners who follow the same standard PHB (RFC 3246) and who will thus continue to service his (EF marked) voice traffic with strict priority over their networks.

Assured Forwarding PHB Group (RFC 2597)

RFC 2597 defines four Assured Forwarding groups, denoted by the letters "AF" followed by two digits.

The first digit denotes the AF class number and can range from 1 through 4. (Incidentally, these values correspond to the three most-significant bits of the codepoint, or the IPP value that the codepoint falls under.) Incidentally, the AF class number does not in itself represent priority. (That is, AF class 4 does not necessarily get any preferential treatment over AF class 1.)

The second digit refers to the level of drop preference within each AF class and can range from 1 (lowest drop preference) through 3 (highest drop preference). For example, during periods of congestion on an RFC 2597-compliant node, AF33 (representing the highest drop preference for AF class 3) would (statistically) be dropped more often than AF32, which in turn would (statistically) be dropped more often than AF31. Figure 6-5 shows the Assured Forwarding PHB encoding scheme.

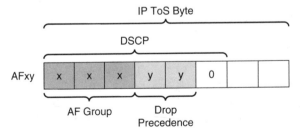

Figure 6-5   *DiffServ Assured Forwarding PHB encoding scheme*

Figure 6-6 shows the full table of Assured Forwarding PHBs with their decimal and binary equivalents.

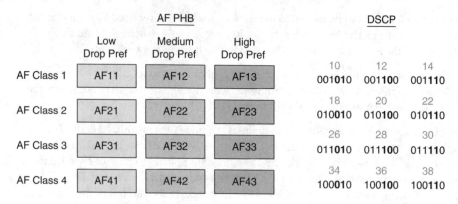

Figure 6-6   *Assured Forwarding PHBs with decimal and binary equivalents*

All AF traffic is initially marked to a drop preference value of 1. So for example, traffic for AF class 1 will initially be marked AF11; traffic for AF class 2 will be initially marked AF21, and so on. Only if AF traffic is policed by a DSCP-based policer (as will be discussed) can it be re-marked to a higher-drop preference, such as AF12 or AF13.

Assured Forwarding PHBs are most effective when applied to TCP-based traffic classes. This is because if such traffic exceeds the predefined rates, enforced by DSCP policers, exceeding and violating traffic might be re-marked to a higher drop preference value (either drop preference 2 or 3).

Consequentially, on congested nodes enabled with DSCP-based dropping algorithms, such re-marked traffic has a higher likelihood of being dropped. Dropped traffic, in turn, affects TCP windowing operations so that senders will adjust their transmission rates to optimize flows without dropping traffic, which is one of the objectives of the AF PHB.

Class Selector Code Points (RFC 2474)

Class Selectors, defined in RFC 2474, are not Per-Hop Behaviors, per se, but rather were defined to provide backward compatibility to IP Precedence. Each Class Selector corresponds to a given IP Precedence value, with its three least-significant bits set to 0. For example, IP Precedence 1 (001) is referred to as Class Selector 1 (001000 or DSCP 8); IP Precedence 2 (010) is referred to as Class Selector 2 (010000 or DSCP 16). Table 6-1 shows the IP Precedence to Class Selector mappings.

Table 6-1   *IP Precedence to Class Selector/DSCP Mappings*

IP Precedence Value	IP Precedence Name	IPP Binary Equivalent	Class Selector	CS Binary Equivalent	DSCP Value (Decimal)
0	Normal	000	CS0	000 000	0
1	Priority	001	CS1	001 000	8
2	Immediate	010	CS2	010 000	16
3	Flash	011	CS3	011 000	24
4	Flash-Override	100	CS4	100 000	32
5	Critical	101	CS5	101 000	40

Table 6-1 *IP Precedence to Class Selector/DSCP Mappings*

IP Precedence Value	IP Precedence Name	IPP Binary Equivalent	Class Selector	CS Binary Equivalent	DSCP Value (Decimal)
6	Internetwork Control	110	CS6	110 000	48
7	Network Control	111	CS7	111 000	56

*Class Selector 0 is a special case, as it represents the default marking value (defined in RFC 2474-Section 4.1); it is not typically called Class Selector 0 but rather Default Forwarding or DF.

Lower Effort Per-Domain Behavior (Scavenger) (RFC 3662)

Although most of the PHBs discussed so far represent manners in which traffic can be treated *preferentially*, there are cases where you might want to treat traffic *deferentially*. For example, certain types of nonbusiness traffic, such as gaming, video-downloads, peer-to-peer media sharing, and so on might dominate network links if left unabated.

To address such needs, a Lower Effort Per-Domain Behavior is described in RFC 3662 to provide a *less than Best Effort* service to undesired traffic. Two things should be noted about RFC 3662 from the start:

■ RFC 3662 is in the "informational" category of RFCs (not the standards track) and is not necessary to implement to be DiffServ standard-compliant.

■ A Per-*Domain* Behavior (PDB) has a different and larger scope than a Per-*Hop* Behavior (PHB). A PDB does not require that undesired traffic be treated within a "less than Best Effort service" at necessarily *every* network node (which it would if this behavior were defined as a Per-*Hop* Behavior); but rather, as long as one (or more) nodes within the administrative domain provide a "less than best effort service" to this undesired traffic class, the Per-Domain Behavior requirement has been met.

The reason a PDB is sufficient to provision this behavior, as opposed to requiring a PHB, is that the level of service is *deferential*, not *preferential*. To expand: When dealing with priority or preferential QoS policies, sometimes it is said that *a QoS chain of policies is only as strong as the weakest link*. For example, if provisioning an EF PHB for voice throughout your network and only one node in the path does not have EF properly provisioned on it, the overall quality of voice is (potentially) ruined. On the other hand, if you're objective is to provide a deferential level of service, all you need is one *weak link* in the path to lower the overall quality of service for a given class. Thus, if only a single *weak link* is required per administrative domain, a Per-Domain Behavior, rather than a Per-Hop Behavior, better suits the requirement.

The marking value suggested in RFC 3662 for *less than best effort* service is Class Selector 1 (DSCP 8). This marking value is typically assigned and constrained to a minimally provisioned queue so that it will be dropped most aggressively under network congestion scenarios.

Policing Tools

Policers monitor traffic flows and identify and respond to traffic violations. For example, policers can monitor TelePresence flows at the campus access edge. Because TelePresence flows are bounded (to typically 5 Mbps per screen at 1080p), flows in excess of such bounds would be indicative of network abuse and can be immediately identified and responded to by policers.

Policers achieve these objectives by performing ongoing checks for traffic violations and taking immediate prescribed actions when such violations occur. For example, a policer can determine if the offered load is in excess of the defined traffic rate and then drop the out-of-contract traffic, as illustrated in Figure 6-7.

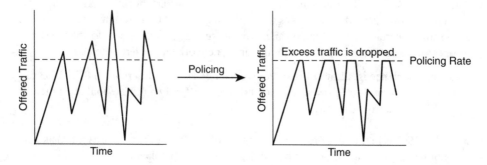

Figure 6-7   *A generic policer*

Additionally, policers can re-mark excess traffic to identify (but not necessarily drop) traffic that exceeds a given traffic contract, which might be valuable for reporting, billing, or capacity planning purposes. In such a role, the policer is called a *marker*. Figure 6-8 illustrates a policer functioning as a marker.

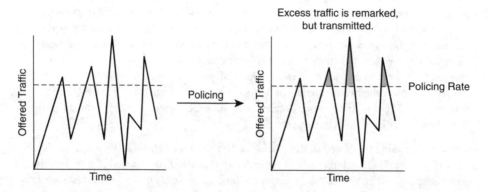

Figure 6-8   *A policer as a marker*

Cisco IOS policers are modeled after *token bucket* algorithms. Essentially, these algorithms are metering engines that keep track of how much traffic might be sent to conform to the specified traffic rates.

A *token*, in everyday use, is an item given to an individual that represents the right to use a given service, such as to ride on the subway or to play a video game, and so on. In QoS terminology, a *token* permits the policing algorithm to send a single bit (or in some cases, a byte) of traffic. Typically, these tokens are granted at the beginning of a second, according to the defined policing rate, referred to as the *Committed Information Rate (CIR)*.

Tokens granted at the beginning of each second of operation are placed in a logical cache, referred to as the *bucket*. A key difference in policing algorithms is how unused tokens are dealt with at the end of each second: Some policers allow unused tokens to accumulate in the bucket, whereas others force unused tokens to be discarded. These differences, and the effects on traffic policing, is discussed in more detail shortly.

For example, if the CIR is set to 8000 bps, then 8000 tokens are placed in the bucket at the beginning of each second. Each time a bit of traffic is offered to the policer, the bucket is checked for tokens. If there are tokens in the bucket, the traffic is passed. One token is removed from the bucket for each bit of traffic that is passed, and such traffic is viewed to *conform* the rate, and the specified action for conforming traffic is taken. (The conforming traffic is typically transmitted unaltered.) When the bucket runs out of tokens, any additional offered traffic is viewed to *exceed* the rate, and the exceed action is taken. (The exceeding traffic is either re-marked or dropped.)

In addition to defining the CIR, policers require that a committed burst (Bc) also be defined. The *committed burst*, also known as the *normal burst*, refers to the bytes allowed in a subsecond traffic burst before packets will be considered to exceed the rate limit.

Single-Rate Policers

The earliest policers use a *Single-Rate Two-Color Marker/Policer* model with a single token bucket algorithm. In this model, traffic is identified as one of two states (colors): *conforming* (to the CIR) or *exceeding* (the CIR). Marking and dropping actions are performed on each of these two states of traffic. Any unused tokens left in the bucket at the end of the second/cycle are discarded. In other words, one CIR worth of tokens is granted at the beginning of a second, and at the end of the second, the bucket is emptied. This type of marker/policer is fairly crude and, when defined to drop, rather than re-mark packets, can result in the traffic policing pattern illustrated previously in Figure 6-7 (A generic policer).

Note Although a policer can be deployed at ingress or egress interfaces, they are generally deployed at the network edge on traffic ingress. After all, there is little point in spending valuable CPU cycles routing and processing packets that are only going to be dropped.

Dual-Rate Policers

Random traffic patterns, whether network traffic or otherwise, generally do not respond well to crude single-rate policers. As an analogy, consider automobile traffic that is "policed" by traffic lights at intersections that have only two states/colors: green (for go) and red (to stop). Additionally, these lights could fluctuate from one state to the other without any warning or allowance. Some drivers would be arbitrarily penalized when the lights changed from one moment to the next, and the overall traffic flow would be inefficient.

However, as with traffic lights, if a third state (the yellow light) is introduced, traffic flows much better. The yellow light indicates to drivers that they are approaching the limit and allows them to react accordingly. Similarly with network traffic, a moderate allowance for burst, allows for the possibility of feeding back to the application that the transmission limits are being reached (that is, by re-marking some exceeding traffic) and allows for the applications to react accordingly (whether they do is a different matter, but at least the possibility is presented).

Therefore, with dual rate policers, there are three traffic states. Continuing the traffic light analogy, these follow:

- **Conform (green light):** Traffic is within the defined rate and is transmitted without any penalty.

- **Exceed (yellow light):** Traffic is surpassing the defined rate, yet an allowance for burst allows for a moderate penalty (typically re-marking) to be applied.

- **Violate (red light):** Traffic is surpassing both the defined rate and any burst allowances and should, thus, have the maximum penalty applied (which might be a second-degree of re-marking or dropping).

There are two standards-defined Dual-Rate policers (as defined in RFC 2697 and 2698, respectively). The sections that follow take a closer look at each of these.

A Single-Rate Three-Color Marker (RFC 2697)

With the Single-Rate Policer, the token bucket is emptied at the end of the second, and any unused tokens are wasted. An improvement to this algorithm is defined in RFC 2697, which details the logic of a Single-Rate Three-Color Marker.

The Single-Rate Three-Color Marker/Policer uses a two token bucket algorithm. Any unused tokens are not discarded at the end of a second, but rather are placed in a second token bucket to be used as credits later for temporary bursts that might exceed the CIR. The initial allowance of tokens placed in this second bucket is called the *Excess Burst (Be)*. This is the maximum number of bits that can exceed the burst size.

This model allows three possible traffic conditions to be identified (hence the term "Three-Color"): conform, exceed, or violate. And, in turn, specific actions can be defined for each of these three states, including transmit, re-mark, or drop.

The Single-Rate Three-Color Marker uses the following definitions within the RFC:

- **CIR:** Committed Information Rate; the policed rate

- **CBS:** Committed Burst Size (CBS); maximum size of the first token bucket (referred to as Bc within Cisco IOS syntax)

- **EBS:** Excess Burst Size (EBS); maximum size of the second token bucket (referred to as Be within Cisco IOS syntax)

- **Tc:** Token count of CBS; the instantaneous number of tokens left in the CBS bucket

- **Te:** Token count of EBS; the instantaneous number of tokens left in the EBS bucket

- **B:** Byte size of offered packet

Figure 6-9 illustrates the logical flow of the Single-Rate Three-Color Marker/Policer.

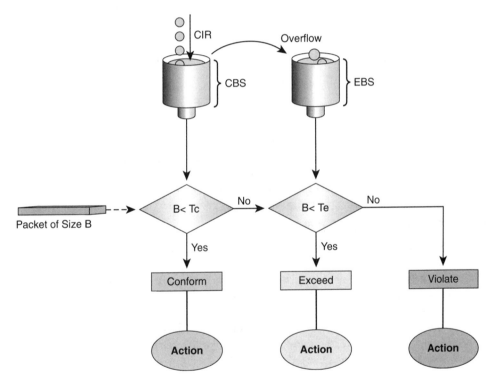

Figure 6-9   *RFC 2697 Single-Rate Three-Color Policer logic*

The Single-Rate Three-Color Policer's tolerance of temporary bursts, shown in Figure 6-10, results in fewer TCP retransmissions and thus more efficient bandwidth utilization. Furthermore, it is a highly suitable tool for marking according to RFC 2597 AF classes, which have three "colors" (or drop preferences) defined per class (AFx1, AFx2, or AFx3).

Example 6-2 shows the configuration to police traffic in class-default to a CIR of 256 kbps with a Bc of 1500 bytes and a Be of 3000 bytes. Note that for this policer, the CIR is defined in bps, but Bc and Be are defined in bytes. Additionally, the policer is configured to function as a marker that complies with the Assured Forwarding PHB for AF class 3.

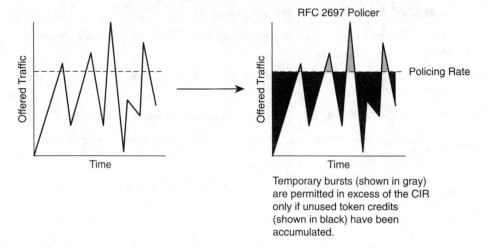

Temporary bursts (shown in gray)
are permitted in excess of the CIR
only if unused token credits
(shown in black) have been
accumulated.

Figure 6-10 *RFC 2697 Single-Rate Three-Color Policer effect on traffic flow*

Example 6-2 *RFC 2697 Single-Rate Three-Color Policer Example*

```
Router(config)# policy-map RFC2697-POLICER
Router(config-pmap)# class class-default
Router(config-pmap-c)# police cir 256000 bc 1500 be 3000
Router(config-pmap-c-police)# conform-action set-dscp-transmit af31
Router(config-pmap-c-police)# exceed-action set-dscp-transmit af32
Router(config-pmap-c-police)# violate-action set-dscp-transmit af33
```

A Two-Rate Three-Color Marker (RFC 2698)

The Single-Rate Three-Color Marker/Policer presented a significant improvement for policers, in that it made an allowance for temporary traffic bursts (if the overall average transmitted rate was equal to or below the CIR). However, the variation in the amount of accumulated excess burst credits could cause a degree of unpredictability in traffic flows. To improve on this, a Two-Rate Three-Color Marker/Policer was defined in RFC 2698. This policer addresses the Peak Information Rate (PIR), which is unpredictable in the RFC 2697 model. Furthermore, the Two-Rate Three-Color Marker/Policer allows for a sustainable excess burst (negating the need to accumulate credits to accommodate temporary bursts).

The Two-Rate Three-Color Marker/Policer uses the following parameters to meter the traffic stream:

- **PIR:** Peak Information Rate; the maximum rate traffic ever allowed

- **PBS:** Peak Burst Size; the maximum size of the first token bucket (referred to as Be within Cisco IOS syntax)

- **CIR:** Committed Information Rate; the policed rate

- **CBS:** Committed Burst Size; the maximum size of the second token bucket (referred to as Bc within Cisco IOS syntax)

- **Tp:** Token count of CBS; the instantaneous number of tokens left in the PBS bucket

- **Tc:** Token count of EBS; the instantaneous number of tokens left in the CBS bucket

- **B:** Byte Size of Offered Packet

The Two-Rate Three-Color Policer also uses a two-token bucket algorithm, but the logic varies slightly. Rather than transferring unused tokens from one bucket to another, this policer has two separate buckets that are filled each second with two separate token rates. The first bucket is filled with the PIR amount of tokens, and the second bucket is filled with the CIR amount of tokens. Any unused tokens are discarded (from both buckets) at the end of each second. In this model, the Be works the same as the Bc, except for the PBS bucket (not the CBS bucket). This means that Be represents the peak limit of traffic that can be sent during a subsecond Interval. The logic varies further in that the initial check is to see if the traffic is within the PIR, and only then is the traffic compared against the CIR. (That is, a violate condition is checked for first, then an exceed condition, and finally a conform condition, which is the reverse of the logic of the previous model.) Figure 6-11 illustrates this logic.

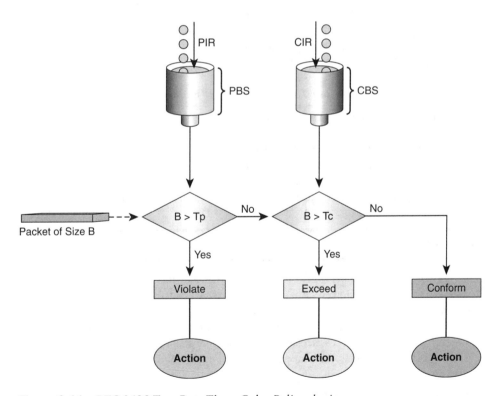

Figure 6-11   *RFC 2698 Two-Rate Three-Color Policer logic*

The Two-Rate Three-Color Marker allows for sustainable excess bursts (and is not dependent on accumulating credits) and has a hard-top peak limit, as shown in Figure 6-12.

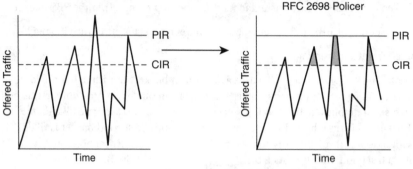

Figure 6-12   *RFC 2698 Two-Rate Three-Color policer effect on traffic flow*

Example 6-3 shows the configuration to police traffic on class-default to a CIR of 256 kbps with a Bc of 1500 bytes and a PIR of 512 kbps with a Be of 3000 bytes. Note that for this policer, CIR and PIR are defined in bps, but Bc and Be are defined in bytes. As before, the policer is configured to function as a marker that complies with the Assured Forwarding PHB, but this time for AF class 4.

Example 6-3   *RFC2698 Two-Rate Three-Color Policer Example*

```
Router(config)# policy-map RFC2698-POLICER
Router(config-pmap)# class class-default
Router(config-pmap-c)# police cir 256000 bc 1500 pir 512000 be 3000
Router(config-pmap-c-police)# conform-action set-dscp-transmit af41
Router(config-pmap-c-police)# exceed-action  set-dscp-transmit af42
Router(config-pmap-c-police)# violate-action set-dscp-transmit af42
```

Shaping Tools

Shapers operate in a manner similar to policers in that they invoke token bucket algorithms to meter traffic. However, the principle difference between a policer and a shaper is that where a policer re-marks or drops traffic as a policy action, a shaper merely *delays* traffic. Even though TelePresence is a real-time application, you might encounter scenarios, such as subline rate access scenarios, which require shaping policies to be included within a comprehensive TelePresence QoS policy. Figure 6-13 illustrates generic traffic shaping.

Shapers are particularly useful when traffic must conform to a specific rate of traffic to meet a service-level agreement (SLA) or to guarantee that traffic offered to a service provider is within a contracted rate. Additionally, shapers have long been associated with *Non-Broadcast Multiple-Access (NBMA)* WAN topologies, such as ATM and Frame Relay, where potential speed-mismatches exist. However, shapers are becoming increasingly

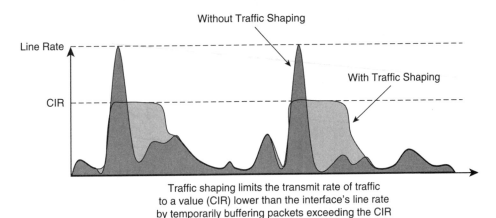

Traffic shaping limits the transmit rate of traffic
to a value (CIR) lower than the interface's line rate
by temporarily buffering packets exceeding the CIR

Figure 6-13 *Generic traffic shaping effect on traffic flow*

popular on newer Layer 3 WAN access circuits, such as Ethernet-based handoffs, to conform to subline access rates.

Shapers, like policers, use token bucket algorithms. On most platforms, by default, IOS shapers set the Bc to equal CIR/8, which yields an interval (Tc) of 125 ms. Although this interval value might be adequate for data applications, it introduces unnecessary interpacket delays for real-time networks. Consider the example shown in Figure 6-14.

A shaper uses the CIR, Bc, and Be to smooth a traffic stream to a specified rate. It achieves the given CIR by taking the line speed of the interface and dividing it into equal length timeslots (Intervals, or Tc) and then sends a smaller portion (Bc) of the traffic during each timeslot. The timeslot size is governed by the Bc parameter (Tc = Bc / CIR). In Figure 6-14, a line rate of 128 kbps is shaped to 64 kbps. The Bc, by default, is one eighth of the CIR (or eight kbps). Each second is divided into eight timeslots of 125 ms each, and the shaped rate of 64,000 bps is divided into eight bursts of 8000 bps each (Bc). Each burst will take 62.5 ms to transmit (at a 128 kbps line rate). So the shaper transmits information for the first 62.5ms of each 125 ms timeslot and is silent for the remaining 62.5 ms of the timeslot. Over the span of a second, this achieves the *average* rate of CIR.

Additionally, you can use the Be value to determine the *peak* Rate of sending, which is calculated as follows:

Peak Rate = CIR (1 + Be / Bc)

Peak-rate shaping allows the router to burst higher than average-rate shaping. However, when peak-rate shaping is enabled, any traffic exceeding the CIR can be dropped if the network becomes congested.

A router interface might be configured to shape using average rates, through the **shape average** policy-action command, or to a peak rate, through the **shape peak** policy-action command. The configuration for a basic Class-Based Shaping policy to shape to an average rate of 5 Mbps is as follows:

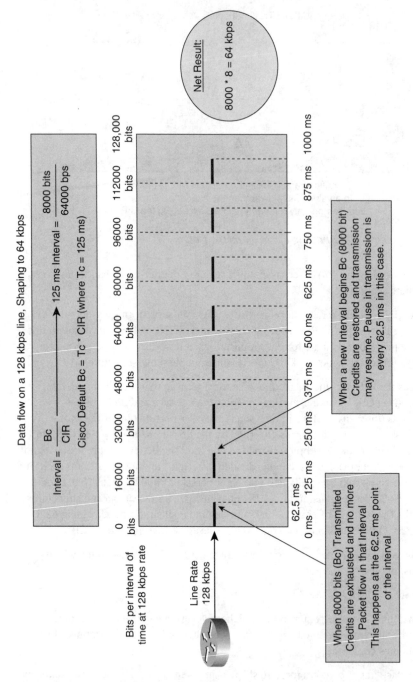

Figure 6-14   *Shaping behavior with default Bc values*

```
Router(config)# policy-map CB-SHAPING-5MBPS
Router(config-pmap)# class class-default
Router(config-pmap-c)# shape average 5000000
```

Because shaping involves buffering, various queuing techniques might be activated when the shaping buffer has been filled to capacity. Such queuing techniques are discussed in more detail in the next section.

Queuing Tools

Queuing policies (particularly priority queuing policies) are critical to providing the levels of service that TelePresence requires. Normally, on uncongested interfaces, packets are transmitted in order on a First-In-First-Out (FIFO) basis. However, if packets arrive at an interface faster than they can be transmitted out the interface, excess packets might be buffered. When packets are buffered, they might be reordered prior to transmission according to administratively defined algorithms, which are generally referred to as queuing policies. It is important to recognize that queuing policies are engaged *only* when the interface is experiencing congestion and are deactivated shortly after the interface congestion clears.

Queuing might be performed in software or in hardware. Within Cisco IOS Software there are two main queuing algorithms available:

■ Class-Based Weighted-Fair Queuing (CBWFQ)

■ Low-Latency Queuing (LLQ)

Within Cisco Catalyst hardware, queuing algorithms fall under a 1PxQyT model. These software and hardware queuing algorithms are discussed in the following sections.

CBWFQ

Class-Based Weighted-Fair Queuing (CBWFQ) is a queuing algorithm that combines the capability to guarantee bandwidth with the capability to dynamically ensure fairness to other flows within a class of traffic.

CBWFQ allows for the creation of up to 64 classes of traffic, each with its own reserved queue. Each queue is serviced in a weighted-round-robin (WRR) fashion based on the bandwidth assigned to each class. Bandwidth might be assigned to a class in terms of absolute kbps (with the **bandwidth** command), as a percentage of a link's bandwidth (with the **bandwidth percent** command), or as a percentage of bandwidth remaining, after the strict-priority Low-Latency Queue has been serviced (with the **bandwidth remaining** command).

To better understand how CBWFQ works, Example 6-4 begins by constructing a simple CBWFQ policy.

Example 6-4   *CBWFQ Policy Example*

```
Router(config)# policy-map CBWFQ
Router(config-pmap)# class NETWORK-CONTROL
Router(config-pmap-c)# bandwidth percent 5
Router(config-pmap-c)# class TRANSACTIONAL-DATA
Router(config-pmap-c)# bandwidth percent 20
Router(config-pmap-c)# class BULK-DATA
Router(config-pmap-c)# bandwidth percent 10
Router(config-pmap-c)# class class-default
Router(config-pmap-c)# fair-queue
```

Next, look at the underlying CBWFQ mechanisms that correspond with this policy, as illustrated in Figure 6-15.

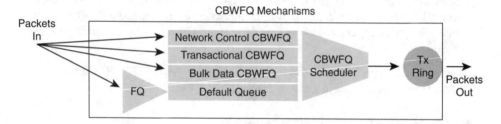

Figure 6-15   *Class-Based Weighted-Fair Queuing mechanisms*

In Figure 6-15, you see a router interface that has been configured with a 4-class CBWFQ policy, with an explicit CBWFQ defined for Network Control, Transactional Data, and Bulk Data, respectively, and the default CBWFQ queue, which has a Fair-Queuing (FQ) pre-sorter assigned to it.

Note   CBWFQ is a bit of a misnomer because the pre-sorter that can be applied to certain CBWFQs, such as class-default, is not actually a Weighted-Fair Queuing (WFQ) pre-sorter, but rather a Fair-Queuing (FQ) pre-sorter, and as such, it ignores any IP Precedence values when calculating bandwidth allocation traffic flows. To be more technically accurate, this queuing algorithm would be better named Class-Based Fair-Queuing or CBFQ.

Another underlying queuing mechanism is a final (FIFO) output buffer called the *Tx-Ring*, which serves the purpose of always having packets ready to be placed onto the wire so that link utilization can be driven to 100 percent. The Tx-Ring also serves to indicate congestion to IOS. Specifically, when the Tx-Ring fills to capacity, the interface is known to be congested, and a signal is sent to engage any LLQ/CBWFQ policies that have been configured on the interface.

CBWFQ works in the following manner:

1. Packets are classified according to the class maps and assigned to either explicitly defined CBWFQs or to the default queue. If the packets are assigned to the default queue and fair-queuing has been enabled on the default class with the **fair-queue** subcommand, packets receive a proportionately equal share of the available bandwidth for the default queue. For example, if there is 100 kbps assigned to the default queue and there are 10 IP flows that are contenting for the default queue, each flow is assigned an equal share (10 kbps) of bandwidth by the FQ pre-sorter.

2. Next, the CBWFQ scheduler dequeues the packets from each CBWFQ in a weighted-round-robin (WRR) manner that reflects the proportionate bandwidth allocations per-class.

3. These packets are then enqueued into the Tx-Ring.

4. Finally, the packets exit the Tx-Ring in a FIFO manner as they are transmitted across the physical interface media.

CBWFQ is a highly efficient queuing algorithm for data applications but lacks the capability to provide strict-priority servicing to real-time applications, such as voice or interactive video. This is because it provides a bandwidth guarantee but not a latency/jitter guarantee. Therefore, to service such real-time applications, a strict-priority queue was added to the CBWFQ algorithm, and the resulting algorithm was named Low-Latency Queuing.

LLQ

Low-Latency Queuing (LLQ) is essentially CBWFQ combined with a strict priority queue. Traffic assigned to the strict priority queue, using the **priority** command, is completely serviced before all other CBWFQ queues are serviced. LLQ bandwidth, like CBWFQ bandwidth, can be assigned either in absolute kbps or as a percentage of the link's bandwidth (using the **priority percent** command).

Note The original name for the LLQ algorithm was Priority-Queue-Class-Based Weighted-Fair Queuing (PQ-CBWFQ). Although this name was technically more descriptive, it was obviously clumsy from a marketing perspective, hence, the algorithm was renamed LLQ.

To better understand how LLQ works, Example 6-5 adds a strict priority queue, to support VoIP, to the previous (CBWFQ) configuration from Example 6-4.

Example 6-5 *LLQ/CBWFQ Policy Example*

```
Router(config)# policy-map LLQ
Router(config-pmap)# class VOICE
Router(config-pmap-c)# priority 100
Router(config-pmap-c)# class CALL-SIGNALING
```

```
Router(config-pmap-c)# bandwidth percent 5
Router(config-pmap-c)# class TRANSACTIONAL-DATA
Router(config-pmap-c)# bandwidth percent 20
Router(config-pmap-c)# class BULK-DATA
Router(config-pmap-c)# bandwidth percent 10
Router(config-pmap-c)# class class-default
Router(config-pmap-c)# fair-queue
```

Next, look at Figure 6-16 to see what has changed in the underlying queuing mechanisms when LLQ has been combined with CBWFQ.

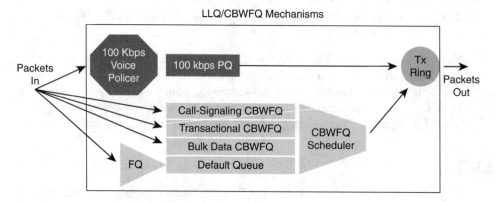

Figure 6-16   *LQ and CBWF Q mechanisms*

Note   For the sake of simplicity, some Layer 2 subsystems (including Link Fragmentation and Interleaving) have been omitted from Figure 6-16 because these mechanisms simply aren't relevant at the link speeds required by TelePresence.

In Figure 6-16, you see a router interface that has been configured with a 5-class LLQ/CB-WFQ policy, with voice assigned to a 100-kbps LLQ, and additional three explicit CB-WFQs defined for Call-Signaling, Transactional Data, and Bulk Data respectively, and a default queue that has a Fair-Queuing pre-sorter assigned to it. However, an underlying mechanism that might not be obvious from the configuration, but is shown in the illustration, is an implicit policer attached to the LLQ.

The threat posed by any strict priority-scheduling algorithm is that it can completely starve lower-priority traffic. To prevent this, the LLQ mechanism has a built-in policer. This policer (like the queuing algorithm itself) engages only when the LLQ-enabled interface is experiencing congestion. Therefore, it is important to provision the priority classes properly. In this example, if more than 100 kbps of voice traffic was offered to the interface, and the interface was congested, the excess voice traffic would be discarded by the implicit policer. However, traffic that is admitted by the policer gains access to the strict priority queue and is handed off to the Tx-Ring ahead of all other CBWFQ traffic.

Now, consider the case of servicing not just voice with strict-priority LLQ, but also real-time interactive-video (which, for these two following examples, is abbreviated simply as *video*).

Two options exist to the network administrator. The first is to admit both voice and video to the same LLQ. Thus the second LLQ example policy becomes what is shown in Example 6-6.

Example 6-6   *Aggregate LLQ for Voice and Video Policy Example*

```
Router(config)# class-map match-any REALTIME
Router(config-cmap)# match dscp ef
Router(config-cmap)# ! Matches VoIP on DSCP EF (per RFC4594)
Router(config-cmap)# match dscp cs4
Router(config-cmap)# ! Matches Realtime-Interactive Video on CS4 (per RFC4594)
Router(config-cmap)#
Router(config-cmap)# policy-map LLQ2
Router(config-pmap)# class REALTIME
Router(config-pmap-c)# priority 500
Router(config-pmap-c)# ! Combined LLQ for VoIP and Video
Router(config-pmap-c)# class CALL-SIGNALING
Router(config-pmap-c)# bandwidth percent 5
Router(config-pmap-c)# class TRANSACTIONAL-DATA
Router(config-pmap-c)# bandwidth percent 20
Router(config-pmap-c)# class BULK-DATA
Router(config-pmap-c)# bandwidth percent 10
Router(config-pmap-c)# class class-default
Router(config-pmap-c)# fair-queue
```

Figure 6-17 illustrates the corresponding IOS mechanisms for this second LLQ example.

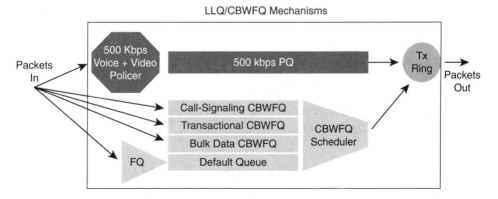

Figure 6-17   *Aggregate LLQ for voice and video policy mechanisms*

In Figure 6-17, you can see that not only has the LLQ been expanded in size (to 500 kbps), but also the implicit policer (for the combined VoIP and TelePresence class) has been increased to 500 kbps. Such a policy can continue to protect voice from data and video from data. However, this policy does potentially allow video to interfere with voice. This is because traffic offered to the LLQ class is serviced on a first-come, first-serve basis. Therefore, should video traffic suddenly burst, it is possible (even likely) that voice traffic would be dropped.

At this point, you can realize another benefit of the implicit policer for the LLQ—not only does this mechanism protect nonreal-time queues from bandwidth-starvation, but also it allows for Time-Division Multiplexing (TDM) of the LLQ. TDM of the LLQ allows for the configuration and servicing of *multiple* LLQs, while abstracting the fact that there is only a single LLQ "under-the-hood," so to speak. Pertinent to the example, by configuring two LLQs, not only are voice and video protected from data applications, but also voice and video are protected from interfering with each other.

Example 6-7 provides the final policy example to cover this point, wherein a dual-LLQ design is used, one each for voice and video.

Example 6-7   *Dual-LLQ for Voice and Video Policy Example*

```
Router(config)# class-map match-all VOICE
Router(config-cmap)# match dscp ef
Router(config-cmap)# ! Matches VoIP on DSCP EF (per RFC4594)
Router(config-cmap)# class-map match-all VIDEO
Router(config-cmap)# match dscp cs4
Router(config-cmap)# ! Matches Realtime-Interactive Video on CS4 (per RFC4594)
Router(config-cmap)# !
Router(config-cmap)# policy-map LLQ3
Router(config-pmap)# class VOICE
Router(config-pmap-c)# priority 100
Router(config-pmap-c)# ! Provisions 100 kbps of LLQ for VoIP
Router(config-pmap-c)# class VIDEO
Router(config-pmap-c)# priority 400
Router(config-pmap-c)# ! Provisions 400 kbps of LLQ for Realtime-Interactive Video
Router(config-pmap-c)# class CALL-SIGNALING
Router(config-pmap-c)# bandwidth percent 5
Router(config-pmap-c)# class TRANSACTIONAL-DATA
Router(config-pmap-c)# bandwidth percent 20
Router(config-pmap-c)# class BULK-DATA
Router(config-pmap-c)# bandwidth percent 10
Router(config-pmap-c)# class class-default
Router(config-pmap-c)# fair-queue
```

Figure 6-18 illustrates the corresponding IOS mechanisms for this third LLQ example.

In Figure 6-18, you see that two separate implicit policers have been provisioned, one each for the VoIP class (to 100 kbps) and another for the Video class (to 400 kbps), yet

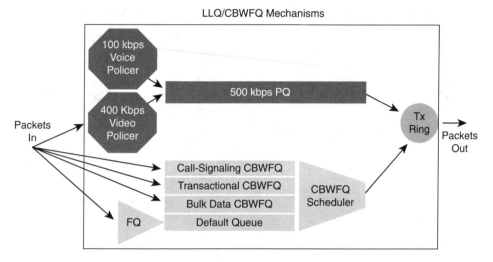

Figure 6-18   *Dual-LLQ for vice and video policy mechanisms*

there remains only a single strict-priority queue, which is provisioned to the sum of all LLQ classes, in this case to 500 kbps (100 kbps + 400 kbps). Traffic offered to either LLQ class is serviced on a first-come, first-serve basis until the implicit policer for each specific class has been invoked. For example, if the video class attempts to burst beyond its 400 kbps rate, it will be dropped.

Therefore, when considering designs to support real-time applications, such as VoIP and TelePresence (an Interactive-Video application, as defined in RFC 4594), a dual-LLQ design can provide the best levels of service for VoIP and TelePresence, while preventing these from interfering with each other.

Hardware Queuing: 1PxQyT

To scale QoS functionality to campus speeds (like Gigabit Ethernet or 10 Gigabit Ethernet), Catalyst switches must perform QoS operations, including queuing, within hardware. For the most part, classification, marking, and policing policies (and syntax) are consistent in both Cisco IOS Software and Catalyst hardware; however, queuing and dropping are significantly different when implemented in hardware. Hardware queuing across Catalyst switches is implemented in a model that can be expressed as **1PxQyT**, where

- **1P** represents the support of a strict-priority hardware queue (which is usually disabled by default)

- x**Q** represents x number of nonpriority hardware queues (including the default, Best-Effort queue)

- y**T** represents y number of drop-thresholds per nonpriority hardware queue

For example, a Catalyst 6500 48-port 10/100/1000 RJ-45 Module (WS-X6748-GE-TX) has a 1P3Q8T queuing structure, meaning that it has

- One strict priority hardware queue (which, incidentally, on this linecard is Queue 4)

- Three additional nonpriority hardware queues, each with eight configurable Weighted Random Early Detect (WRED) drop thresholds per queue

Traffic assigned to the strict-priority hardware queue is treated with an *Expedited Forwarding Per-Hop Behavior (EF PHB)*. That being said, it bears noting that on some platforms, there is no explicit limit on the amount of traffic that can be assigned to the PQ, and as such the potential to starve nonpriority queues exists. However, this potential for starvation can be effectively addressed by explicitly configuring input policers that limit (on a per-port basis) the amount of traffic that can be assigned to the priority queue (PQ). Incidentally, this is the recommended approach defined in RFC 3246 (Section 3).

Traffic assigned to a nonpriority queue will be provided with bandwidth guarantees, subject to the PQ being either fully-serviced or bounded with input policers.

For most platforms, there are typically multiple, configurable drop-thresholds per nonpriority queue. These are provided to allow for selective dropping policies (discussed in more detail in the next section) and to accommodate intraqueue QoS, which is more important in hardware queuing structures (where the number of queues is few and fixed) than in software queuing structures (where generally-speaking there are more queues available than needed). For example, if a campus network administrator had 12 classes of traffic to provision, yet had to work within a 1P3Q8T queuing structure, he could configure the drop thresholds to provide intraqueue QoS inline with his overall service-level objectives. In other words, he is not constrained to only provision four classes of traffic because that is the total number of queues his hardware supports.

To better understand the operation of a Catalyst hardware queuing, consider a simple example where the hardware supports a 1P2Q2T queuing structure, meaning one strict priority queue, two nonpriority queues each with two configurable drop-thresholds per nonpriority queue. In this example, bandwidth to these queues can be allocated so that Q1 (the default queue) is allocated 85 percent, Q2 (the network control queue) is allocated 10 percent, and Q3 (the priority queue) is allocated 5 percent.

Additionally, consider the use of *Weighted Tail Drop (WTD)* as the dropping algorithm. In this example, a drop threshold has been configured at 40 percent of Q1's depth (Q1T1), and another drop threshold has been configured at 40 percent of Q2's depth (Q2T1). Each queue also has a nonconfigurable drop threshold that corresponds to the tail of the queue (Q1T2 and Q2T2, respectively).

With these queues and thresholds thus provisioned, traffic can be assigned to these queues and thresholds based on CoS values; specifically CoS 5 (representing VoIP) is assigned to Q3, CoS 7 (representing network control protocols, such as Spanning Tree) is mapped to Q2T2, CoS 6 (representing internetworking protocols, such as routing protocols) is mapped to Q2T1, CoS values 2-4 (representing video and data applications) are mapped to Q1T2, and CoS values 0 and 1 are mapped to Q1T1.

Figure 6-19 illustrates this 1P2Q2T hardware queuing example, with WTD.

As shown in Figure 6-19, packets marked CoS 5 are assigned to the strict priority queue (Q3) and are serviced ahead of all other traffic. Additionally, packets with CoS values 0

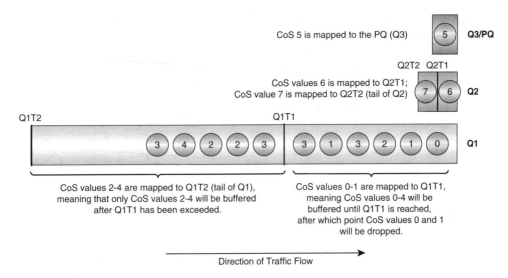

Figure 6-19   *1P2Q2T hardware queuing with WTD example*

through 4 are assigned on a first-come, first-serve basis to Q1 until Q1T1 is reached. At this point, the queuing algorithm no longer buffers packets marked with CoS values 0 and 1, but drops these; therefore, the remainder of Q1 is exclusively reserved for packets marked to CoS values 2 to 4 (representing higher-priority traffic). Similarly, packets with CoS values 6 and 7 are assigned to Q2, but packets marked CoS 6 are dropped if Q2T1 is exceeded.

Additionally, on some platforms and linecards, queuing is possible not only on egress, but also on ingress. This is because some platforms and linecards are engineered based on oversubscriptions ratios. This engineering approach is often taken as most campus links have average utilization rates far below link capacity and, therefore, can be more economically provisioned for with architectures based on oversubscription.

For example, the Cisco Catalyst 3750G is a fixed-configuration switch that supports up to 48 10/100/1000 ports, plus 4 Small Form-Factor Pluggable (SFP) ports for either GE or 10GE uplinks, representing a (minimum) total input capacity of (48 Gbps + 4 Gbps) 52 Gbps. The *backplane* of the 3750G is a dual 16 Gbps counter-rotating ring, with a total capacity of 32 Gbps. Thus, this 3750G architecture is engineered with a minimum over-subscription ratio of 52:32 or 13:8 or 1.625:1. However, when 10GE SFP uplinks are used or when (up to 9) 3750G switches are *stacked* (through Cisco Stackwise technology) into one logical grouping sharing the same dual-ring backplane, the oversubscription ratio be-comes much higher. Thus, to protect real-time and critical traffic from being potentially dropped during extreme scenarios, when input rates exceed ring capacity, ingress queuing can be enabled on this platform through a 1P1Q3T queuing structure.

Remember that hardware queuing is (as the name implies) hardware-specific; therefore, there is considerable disparity in ingress and egress queuing structures and feature support across Catalyst switches platforms. For example, hardware egress queuing structures include the following:

- **1P3Q3T** (Catalyst 2960 and 3560 or 3750)

- **1P3Q1T** (Catalyst 4500 or 4900) and **1P7Q1T,** (Catalyst 4500-E or 4900M)

- **1P2Q1T, 1P2Q2T, 1P3Q1T, 1P3Q8T, 1P7Q4T,** and **1P7Q8T** (Catalyst 6500, module-dependent)

> **Note** Some older Cisco Catalyst 6500 linecards also support 2Q2T, but these linecards are considered legacy and not recommended for IP Telephony and TelePresence deployments. For the full matrix of Catalyst 6500 queuing structures by module, refer to http://tinyurl.com/bgjkr5.

Additionally, some switches support CoS-to-Queue mappings only (like the Catalyst 6500), others support either CoS- or DSCP-to-Queue mappings (like the Catalyst 2960, 3560 and 3750, and 4500 and 4900). Similarly, when it comes to dropping algorithms, some platforms support CoS-based WRED (Catalyst 6500), others support CoS- or DSCP-based Weighted-Tail Drop (WTD) (Catalyst 2960 and 3560 and 3750), or even platform-specific dropping algorithms, such as Dynamic Buffer Limiting (DBL) (Catalyst 4500 and 4900).

Long story short—network administrators need to be thoroughly familiar with the mapping, queuing, and dropping features of their Catalyst switches and linecard platforms to properly provision QoS policies within the campus.

Dropping Tools

Although generally dropping policies is not applicable for TelePresence flows, these do play an important part in the overall QoS policy design on TelePresence networks. Dropping tools are complementary to (and dependent on) queuing tools; specifically, queuing algorithms manage the front of a queue (that is, how a packet *exits* a queue), whereas congestion avoidance mechanisms manage the tail of a queue (that is, how a packet *enters* a queue).

Dropping tools, sometimes called congestion avoidance mechanisms, are designed to optimize TCP-based traffic. TCP has built-in flow control mechanisms that operate by increasing the transmission rates of traffic flows until packet loss occurs. At this point, TCP abruptly squelches the transmission rate and gradually begins to ramp the transmission rates higher again. Incidentally, this behavior makes a strong case against the statement that "QoS isn't necessary; just throw more bandwidth at it." Because if left unchecked, lengthy TCP sessions (as are typical with bulk data and scavenger applications) will consume any and all available bandwidth, simply due to the nature of TCP windowing.

When no congestion avoidance algorithms are enabled on an interface, the interface is said to *tail drop*. That is, after the queuing buffers have filled, all other packets are dropped as they arrive.

In a constricted channel, such as in a WAN or VPN, all the TCP connections eventually synchronize with each other as they compete for the channel. Without congestion avoidance mechanisms, they all ramp up together, lose packets together, and then back off together. This behavior is referred to as *global synchronization*. In effect, waves of TCP traffic flow through the network nodes, with packets overflowing the buffers at each wave peak and lulls in traffic between the waves.

Figure 6-20 illustrates TCP global synchronization behavior attributable to tail-dropping and the suboptimal effect this behavior has on bandwidth utilization.

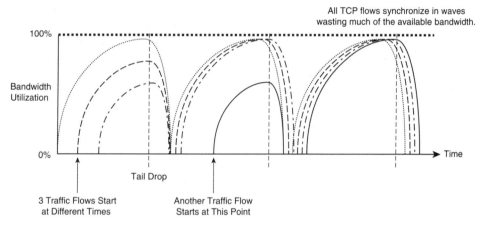

Figure 6-20   *TCP global synchronization*

Random Early Detect (RED) counters the effects of TCP global synchronization by randomly dropping packets before the queues fill to capacity.

Instead of waiting for queuing buffers to fill before dropping packets, RED causes the router to monitor the buffer depth and perform early discards (drops) on random packets when the defined queue threshold has been exceed.

RED drops occur within the operational bounds of TCP retry timers, which slow the transmission rates of the sessions but prevent these from slow-starting. Thus RED optimizes network throughput of TCP sessions.

Because UDP does not have any retry logic, congestion avoidance techniques such as RED (and variants) do not optimize UDP-based traffic.

Note   Cisco IOS Software does not (directly) support Random Early Detect (RED), only Weighted-RED (WRED), discussed in the next section. However, if all packets assigned to a WRED-enabled queue have the same IP Precedence or DSCP markings, the effective policy is simply RED.

WRED

WRED is an enhancement to RED that enables a degree of influence over the *randomness* of the selection of packets to be dropped. WRED factors the *weight* of the packet into the drop selection process; in Cisco IOS routers, the weight is based on the IP Precedence (IPP) value of the packet, whereas in Cisco Catalyst switches, the weight might be the CoS value of the packet (which is termed CoS-based WRED). To simplify the discussion, IP Precedence-based WRED is discussed, but the principles apply equally to CoS-based WRED.

Within the WRED algorithm, a *minimum threshold* for a given IPP value determines the queue depth at which packets of a given IPP value will *begin to be randomly dropped*. The *maximum threshold* determines the queue depth at which *all packets* of a given IPP value *will be dropped*. These thresholds are configurable, as is the Mark Probability Denominator (MPD), which determines how aggressively the packets of a given IPP value will be dropped. (For example, a mark probability denominator value of 10 indicates that up to 1 in 10 packets of a certain precedence value will be randomly dropped.)

By default, WRED drops packets with lower IPP values sooner than packets with higher IPP values. Figure 6-21 provides a simplified illustration of WRED operation.

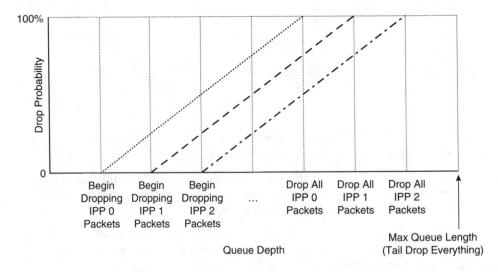

Figure 6-21   *Weighted RED operation*

WRED is enabled on a per-class basis with the **random-detect** command, as demonstrated in Example 6-8. As previously noted, WRED is dependent on queuing; therefore, before WRED can be enabled on a class of traffic, a CBWFQ queuing option, with or without a FQ pre-sorter, needs to be applied to the class. (WRED is not appropriate on the LLQ, which is intended for latency and drop-sensitive traffic.)

Example 6-8   *Enabling WRED on a Per-Class Basis*

```
Router(config)# policy-map WRED
Router(config-pmap)# class TCP
Router(config-pmap-c)# bandwidth percent 30
Router(config-pmap-c)# random-detect
Router(config-pmap-c)# class UDP
Router(config-pmap-c)# bandwidth percent 20
Router(config-pmap-c)# class class-default
Router(config-pmap-c)# fair-queue
Router(config-pmap-c)# random-detect
```

DSCP-Based WRED

As previously discussed, IP Precedence marking has been made obsolete by Differentiated Services, and as such, tools based on IPP, such as WRED, need to be modified accordingly. To achieve DiffServ compliance, the WRED algorithm can be optionally modified to operate based on the Assured Forwarding (AF) drop-preference values (as defined in RFC 2597) to influence its drop probability as queues fill. Such operation is referred to as *DSCP-based WRED*. Remember, the second digit of an AF codepoint indicates drop preference and can range from 1 (lowest drop preference) to 3 (highest drop preference). For example, if DSCP-based WRED is enabled on a queue servicing AF class 2 traffic, AF23 would be statistically dropped more often than AF22, which, in turn, would be statistically dropped more often than AF21. Figure 6-22 illustrates a simplified example of DSCP-based WRED for AF class 2.

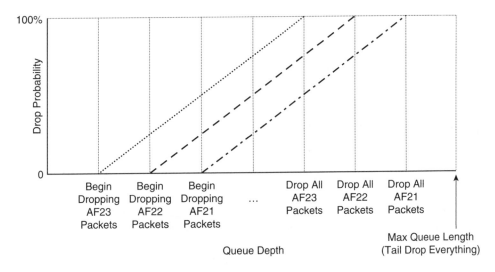

Figure 6-22   *DSCP-based WRED operation for AF class 2*

DSCP-based WRED can be enabled on a CBWFQ—with or without a FQ pre-sorter—with the **dscp-based** keyword in conjunction with the **random-detect** command, as demonstrated in Example 6-9.

Example 6-9   *Enabling DSCP-Based WRED on a CBWFQ*

```
Router(config)# policy-map DSCP-WRED
Router(config-pmap)# class TCP
Router(config-pmap-c)# bandwidth percent 30
Router(config-pmap-c)# random-detect dscp-based
Router(config-pmap-c)# class UDP
Router(config-pmap-c)# bandwidth percent 20
Router(config-pmap-c)# class class-default
Router(config-pmap-c)# fair-queue
Router(config-pmap-c)# random-detect dscp-based
```

Additionally, DSCP-based WRED thresholds and mark probability denominators are tunable on a per-codepoint basis using the **dscp** keyword in conjunction with the **random-detect** command. In Example 6-10, the minimum threshold is set to begin dropping AF11-marked packets at 5 (meaning as soon as the queue depth reaches 5 packets, WRED randomly begins dropping AF11 packets). The maximum threshold for AF11 (at which all AF11-marked packets drop) is set to 20 packets. And the mark probability denominator is set to 8 (meaning that between these thresholds, up to 1 in 8 packets that are marked with AF11 drop).

Example 6-10   *Tuned DSCP-Based WRED Example*

```
Router(config)# policy-map TUNED-DSCP-WRED
Router(config-pmap)# class AF1
Router(config-pmap-c)# bandwidth percent 10
Router(config-pmap-c)# random-detect dscp-based
Router(config-pmap-c)# random-detect dscp af11 5 20 8
```

Explicit Congestion Notification

Traditionally, the only way to inform sending hosts that there was congestion on the network and that the hosts should slow their transmission rates was by dropping TCP packets.

RFC 3168, however, defined a new and more efficient way that the network could communicate congestion to sending hosts, namely the "The Addition of Explicit Congestion Notification (ECN) to IP." By marking the final two bits of the ToS byte of the IP header, devices can communicate to each other and to endpoints that they are experiencing congestion. These two bits have been defined as follows:

■   **ECN-capable Transport (ECT) bit:** This bit indicates whether the device and the transport protocol supports ECN.

■ **Congestion Experienced (CE) bit:** This bit (in conjunction with the ECT bit) indicates whether congestion was experienced en route.

Figure 6-23 shows the location of the ECN bits in the TOS byte of an IP packet header.

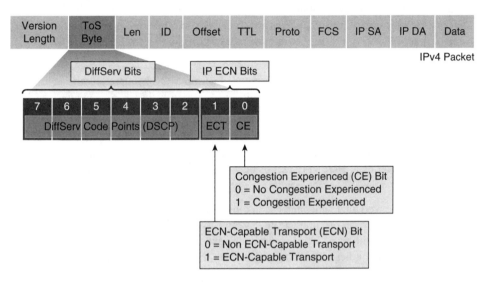

Figure 6-23 *IP ToS byte ECN bits*

During periods of congestion, WRED/DSCP-based WRED drops packets when the average queue length exceeds a specific threshold value. ECN is an extension to WRED, such that *ECN marks packets, instead of dropping them*, to communicate the existence of congestion when the average queue length exceeds a specific threshold value. Routers configured with the WRED ECN feature use this marking as a signal to application endpoints that the network is congested. This way, TCP transmission rates can be adjusted by the application endpoints without dropping packets, (or at least with dropping far fewer packets).

WRED ECN is enabled with the **ecn** keyword with the **random-detect** command. WRED ECN can be enabled by itself or in conjunction with WRED or DSCP-based WRED (as shown in Example 6-11).

Example 6-11 *DSCP-Based WRED ECN Policy Example*

```
Router(config)# policy-map WRED-ECN
Router(config-pmap)# class class-default
Router(config-pmap-c)# fair-queue
Router(config-pmap-c)# random-detect dscp-based
Router(config-pmap-c)# random-detect ecn
```

HQoS

A final element to consider about MQC-based QoS tools is that these can be combined in a hierarchical fashion, meaning, MQC policies can contain other "nested" QoS policies within them. Such policy combinations are commonly referred to as *Hierarchal QoS policies* or *HQoS policies*. HQoS policies are crucial in some TelePresence deployment scenarios, particularly with respect to subline rate services like Metro Ethernet or MPLS VPN services (with Ethernet handoffs).

Syntactically, HQoS policies can be constructed within MQC by attaching the **service-policy** command to a per-class action within a policy map, rather than to an interface. Incidentally, the **output** keyword is not required for such a policy because this is implied.

Consider a couple of examples where HQoS policies might be useful. First, look at an example of nested HQoS policies using the same QoS tool (such as a hierarchical policer), and then take a look at HQoS policies using a combination of different QoS tools (such as an HQoS shaping with queuing policy).

In the first case, you might encounter scenarios where some applications require policing at multiple levels. For example, it might be desirable to limit all TCP traffic to 5 Mbps, while, at the same time, limiting FTP traffic (which is a subset of TCP traffic) to no more than 1.5 Mbps. To achieve this nested policing requirement, Hierarchical Policing can be used.

The policer at the second level in the hierarchy acts on packets transmitted or marked by the policer at the first level. Therefore, any packets dropped by the first level are not seen by the second level. Up to three nested levels are supported by the Cisco IOS Hierarchical Policing feature.

Example 6-12 shows the configuration for the nested, two-level, hierarchical policing of TCP and FTP traffic.

Example 6-12   *Hierarchical Policing Policy Example*

```
Router(config)# policy-map FTP-POLICER
Router(config-pmap)# class FTP
Router(config-pmap-c)# police cir 1500000
Router(config-pmap-c-police)# conform-action transmit
Router(config-pmap-c-police)# exceed-action   drop
Router(config-pmap-c-police)# violate-action drop
Router(config-pmap-c)# exit
Router(config-pmap)# exit
Router(config)# policy-map TCP-POLICER
Router(config-pmap)# class TCP
Router(config-pmap-c)# police cir 5000000
Router(config-pmap-c-police)# conform-action transmit
Router(config-pmap-c-police)# exceed-action   drop
Router(config-pmap-c-police)# violate-action drop
Router(config-pmap-c-police)# service-policy FTP-POLICER
```

Figure 6-24 illustrates the logic of this hierarchical policing example.

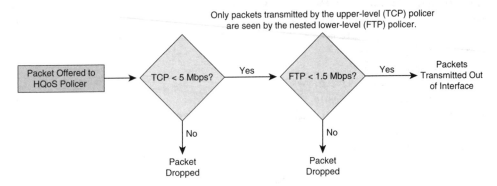

Figure 6-24 *Hierarchical policing logic example*

Additionally, it is often useful to combine shaping and queuing policies in a hierarchical manner, particularly over subline rate access scenarios.

As previously discussed, queuing policies only engage when the physical interface is congested (as is indicated to IOS Software by a full Tx-Ring). This means that queuing policies never engage on media that has a contracted subline rate of access, whether this media is Frame Relay, ATM, or Ethernet. In such a scenario, queuing can be achieved only at a subline rate by introducing a two-part HQoS policy wherein

■ Traffic is shaped to the subline rate.

■ Traffic is queued according to the LLQ/CBWFQ policies within the subline rate.

With such an HQoS policy, it is not the Tx-Ring that signals IOS Software to engage LLQ/CBWFQ policies, but rather it is the Class-Based Shaper that triggers software queuing when the shaped rate has been reached.

Consider a practical example: A service provider offers an enterprise subscriber a GigabitEthernet handoff, but with a (subline rate) contract for only 60 Mbps, over which he wants to deploy IP Telephony and TelePresence and data applications. Normally, queuing policies will engage only on this GE interface when the offered traffic rate exceeds 1000 Mbps. However, the enterprise administrator wants to ensure that traffic within the 60 Mbps contracted rate is properly prioritized prior to the handoff so that both VoIP and TelePresence are given the highest levels of service. Therefore, he configures an HQoS policy so that the software shapes all traffic to the contracted 60 Mbps rate *and* attaches a nested LLQ/CBWFQ queuing policy *within* the shaping policy so that traffic is properly prioritized within this 60 Mbps subline rate. Finally, the shaping policy (with the nested queuing policy) is attached to the GE interface, as shown in Example 6-13.

Example 6-13 *Hierarchical Shaping and Queuing Policy Example*

```
Router(config)# class-map match-all VOIP
Router(config-cmap)# match dscp ef
Router(config-cmap)# ! Matches VoIP on DSCP EF
```

```
Router(config-cmap)# exit
Router(config)# class-map match-all TELEPRESENCE
Router(config-cmap)# match dscp cs4
Router(config-cmap)# ! Matches TelePresence on DSCP CS4 (per RFC4594)
Router(config-cmap)# exit
Router(config)#
Router(config)# policy-map LLQ-CBWFQ
Router(config-pmap)# class VOIP
Router(config-pmap-c)# priority percent 10
Router(config-pmap-c)# ! Provisions 6 Mbps of LLQ for VoIP
Router(config-pmap-c)# class TELEPRESENCE
Router(config-pmap-c)# priority percent 25
Router(config-pmap-c)# ! Provisions 15 Mbps of LLQ for TelePresence
Router(config-pmap-c)# class CALL-SIGNALING
Router(config-pmap-c)# bandwidth percent 5
Router(config-pmap-c)# class TRANSACTIONAL-DATA
Router(config-pmap-c)# bandwidth percent 20
Router(config-pmap-c)# class BULK-DATA
Router(config-pmap-c)# bandwidth percent 10
Router(config-pmap-c)# class class-default
Router(config-pmap-c)# fair-queue
Router(config-pmap-c)# exit
Router(config-pmap)# exit
Router(config)#
Router(config)# policy-map HQoS-60MBPS
Router(config-pmap)# ! HQoS Shaping policy
Router(config-pmap)# class class-default
Router(config-pmap-c)# shape average 60000000 1200000
Router(config-pmap-c)# ! Rate=650Mbps; Bc=1.2Mb, Tc=20ms
Router(config-pmap-c)# service-policy LLQ-CBWFQ
Router(config-pmap-c)# ! Forces queuing policy to engage at sub-line rate
Router(config-pmap-c)# exit
Router(config-pmap)# exit
Router(config)#
Router(config)# interface GigabitEthernet0/1
Router(config-if)# description Access Edge (60 Mbps CIR over GE)
Router(config-if)# service-policy output HQoS-60MBPS
Router(config-if)# ! Attaches HQoS policy to GE interface
Router(config-if)# exit
```

Figure 6-25 illustrates the underlying mechanisms for this HQoS policy.

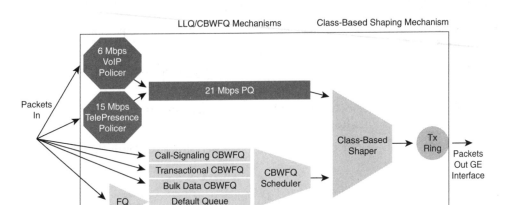

Figure 6-25   *HQoS Policy: Shaping to a Subline Rate with Queuing Within the Shaped Rate*

Summary

To guarantee the service levels required by real-time applications, such as VoIP or TelePresence, and critical data applications, QoS tools must be used throughout the network. These tools include classification and marking tools, policing tools, shaping tools, queuing tools, and dropping tools. The Cisco QoS toolset falls within a common syntax referred to as the Modular QoS Command-Line Interface (MQC), which consists of three elements:

- Class maps (for classification)

- Policy maps (which define the actions to be performed on a specific traffic type)

- Service policy statement

Additionally, MQC policies can be nested or arranged in a hierarchical manner, allowing for more policy flexibility. Furthermore, some QoS tools can be implemented in hardware (such as in Catalyst switches) or in software (such as in Cisco IOS routers). Because hardware varies from one platform to another, network administrators must fully understand the hardware QoS features and functionality for a given platform and linecard.

Further Reading

DiffServ Standards:

RFC 2474, "Definition of the Differentiated Services Field (DS Field) in the IPv4 and IPv6 Headers" http://www.ietf.org/rfc/rfc2474

RFC 2475, "An Architecture for Differentiated Services" http://www.ietf.org/rfc/rfc2475

RFC 2597, "Assured Forwarding PHB Group" http://www.ietf.org/rfc/rfc2597

RFC 2697, "A Single Rate Three Color Marker" http://www.ietf.org/rfc/rfc2697

RFC 2698, "A Two Rate Three Color Marker" http://www.ietf.org/rfc/rfc2698

RFC 3246, "An Expedited Forwarding (PHB) Per Hop Behavior" http://www.ietf.org/rfc/rfc3246

RFC 3662, "A Lower Effort Per Domain Behavior (PDB) for Differentiated Services" http://www.ietf.org/rfc/rfc3662

RFC 3270, "Multi-Protocol Label Switching (MPLS) Support of Differentiated Services" http://www.ietf.org/rfc/rfc3270

RFC 4594, "Configuration Guidelines for DiffServ Service Classes" http://www.ietf.org/rfc/rfc4594

Cisco IOS Documentation:

Modular QoS CLI (MQC) syntax: http://www.tinyurl.com/cyc56u

Classification and Marking tools: http://www.tinyurl.com/bj2xbn

Policing and Shaping tools: http://www.tinyurl.com/afc3rv

Congestion Management (Queuing) tools: http://www.tinyurl.com/crrmdt

Congestion Avoidance (Dropping) tools: http://www.tinyurl.com/adndep

Cisco Catalyst QoS Documentation:

Catalyst 2960: http://www.tinyurl.com/d2gncw

Catalyst 3560: http://www.tinyurl.com/aw6smw

Catalyst 3750: http://www.tinyurl.com/asx9xj

Catalyst 4500 & 4900: http://www.tinyurl.com/3mtyuf

Catalyst 6500: http://www.tinyurl.com/2y725o

Design Guides:

Enterprise Quality of Service Solution Reference Network Design Guide: http://www.cisco.com/go/srnd

Books:

Szigeti, Tim and Christina Hattingh. *End-to-End QoS Network Design: Quality of Service in LANs, WANs, and VPNs.* Cisco Press, 2005. ISBN: 1-58705-176-1.

This chapter covers various protocols required by the Cisco TelePresence Solution to operate over an IP network infrastructure. These protocols are separated into four broad categories; the specific protocols covered within this chapter include the following:

- **Network control protocols:** These include IEEE 802.1p/Q VLAN tagging and class of service (CoS); IEEE 802.3af Power over Ethernet (PoE); Network Time Protocol (NTP); and Dynamic Host Configuration Protocol (DHCP).

- **Signaling protocols:** These include Session Initiation Protocol (SIP); Extensible Markup Language/Simple Object Access Protocol (XML/SOAP), Application XML/SOAP (AXL/SOAP); Telephony Application Programming Interface/Java TelePhony Application Programming Interface (TAPI/JTAPI) over Computer Telephony Integration Quick Buffer Encoding (CTIQBE); Web-based Distributed Authoring and Versioning (WebDAV); and Lightweight Directory Access Protocol (LDAP).

- **Network management protocols:** These include Cisco Discovery Protocol (CDP); Trivial File Transfer Protocol (TFTP); and Simple Network Management Protocol (SNMP).

- **Security protocols:** These include Transport Layer Security (TLS) Protocol; Datagram Transport Layer Security (dTLS) Protocol; Secure Real-time Transport Protocol (sRTP), Secure Shell (SSH) Protocol, and Secure Hypertext Transfer Protocol (HTTPS).

This chapter does not cover every protocol used by Cisco TelePresence; however, most of the important ones are discussed.

CHAPTER 7

TelePresence Control and Security Protocols

Network Control Protocols

The protocols covered within this section primarily provide network connectivity and control services for Cisco TelePresence.

IEEE 802.1p/Q: VLAN Tagging and CoS

The IEEE 802.1Q specification defines a standards-based mechanism for providing VLAN tagging and class of service (CoS) across Ethernet networks. This is accomplished through an additional 4-byte tag, which carries VLAN and frame prioritization information, inserted within the header of a Layer 2 Ethernet frame, as shown in Figure 7-1.

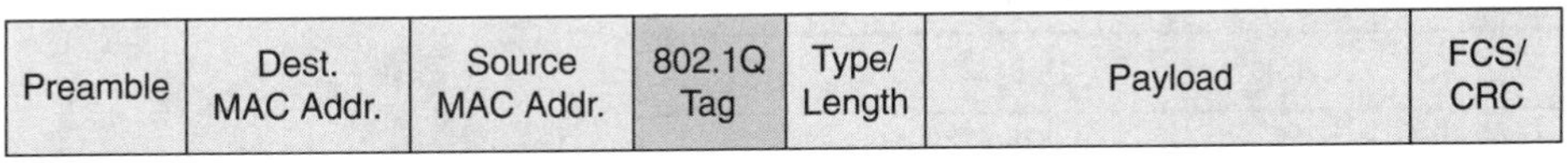

Preamble	Dest. MAC Addr.	Source MAC Addr.	802.1Q Tag	Type/ Length	Payload	FCS/ CRC

Figure 7-1 *Ethernet frame with 802.1Q tag*

The 802.1Q tag has a specific format, consisting of four fixed-length fields. Two of the four fields carry the frame prioritization and VLAN information. Figure 7-2 illustrates the format of the 802.1Q tag itself.

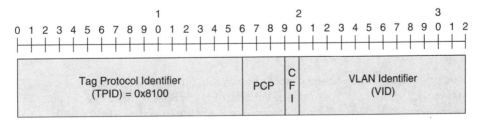

Figure 7-2 *IEEE 802.1Q tag format*

The following are the fields within the 802.1Q tag:

- **Tag Protocol Identifier (TPID):** 802.1Q tagged Ethernet frames are indicated by a value of 0x8100 within this 16-bit field.

- **Priority Code Point (PCP):** A 3-bit field that indicates the frame priority level.

- **Canonical Format Indicator (CFI):** A 1-bit field set to 0 for Ethernet. Used for compatibility between Ethernet and Token Ring.

- **VLAN Identifier (VID):** A 12-bit field that specifies the VLAN to which the frame belongs.

The IEEE 802.1Q standard allows up to 4096 VLANS. To ensure interoperability with devices that do not support 802.1Q, the concept of the native VLAN was also introduced. Frames belonging to the native VLAN are not modified by the sending device (that is, the 4-byte 802.1Q tag is not added to the frame) when they are sent over a trunk. Likewise, any frames received over a trunk that does not have an 802.1Q tag are put into the native VLAN of the receiving device.

The operation of the three bits of the Priority Code Point (PCP) field is defined within the IEEE 802.1p standard, which is an extension of 802.1Q. The IEEE 802.1p and 802.1Q standards, therefore, work together to provide expedited traffic capabilities at the Layer 2 frame level. The IEEE 802.1p standard establishes eight levels of priority, referred to as CoS values. Table 7-1 illustrates the mapping of the CoS value to the bit field.

Table 7-1 *CoS Value to PCP Bit Field Mapping*

COS Value	Bit Field
CoS 7	111
CoS 6	110
CoS 5	101
CoS 4	100
CoS 3	011
CoS 2	010
CoS 1	001
CoS 0	000

Common practice is to map different classes of traffic into different CoS values as they are sent across VLAN trunks. For example, VoIP traffic might be sent with a CoS 5 value, TelePresence sent with a CoS 4 value, and normal data traffic sent with a default CoS 0 value. Separate queues within network infrastructure devices that send and receive the frames then implement prioritization of the traffic classes.

IEEE 802.1p/Q Utilization Within Cisco TelePresence Networks

When a TelePresence endpoint is configured to utilize a Voice VLAN (VVLAN) (consistent with current best practice recommendations for IP telephony deployments), the switch port to which the endpoint is connected effectively operates as a VLAN trunk. All traffic (voice, video, signaling, and management) received from the primary codec of the TelePresence endpoint includes an IEEE 802.1Q header with the VLAN tag corresponding to the VVLAN number. Likewise, all traffic sent to the primary codec from the Cisco Catalyst access edge switch also includes a VLAN tag corresponding to the VVLAN number. VLAN tagging is also extended to all traffic to and from the associated IP Phone attached to the primary codec of a CTS endpoint. Figure 7-3 shows an example of this.

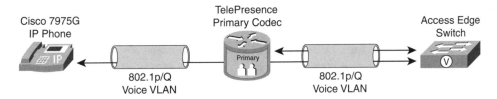

Figure 7-3   *Voice VLAN tagging of TelePresence traffic*

The implementation of the Voice VLAN that includes TelePresence traffic and traditional VoIP traffic can be used to both isolate access to devices on the Voice VLAN and to provide a separate and consistent quality of service (QoS) for all traffic corresponding to the VVLAN across the network infrastructure. Traffic isolation can be accomplished by access control lists (ACL) defined on network infrastructure devices, which restrict access to the VVLAN only to those devices that require such access. Consistent QoS can be provided by trusting the CoS value of ingress frames from the VVVLAN and mapping CoS values to ingress or egress queues for prioritization. CoS values can also be mapped to DSCP values to provide a consistent QoS and prioritization as the TelePresence traffic flows across Layer 3 uplinks that do not use VLAN trunking.

The implementation of a VVLAN for TelePresence deployments is optional. If a VVLAN is not defined on the Cisco Catalyst access edge switch, all traffic to and from the TelePresence endpoint is sent without any IEEE 802.1Q VLAN tags. In such cases, the switch can be configured to trust the DSCP value within the Layer 3 IP header of the TelePresence traffic and then map the DSCP values into appropriate ingress or egress queues for prioritization across the network infrastructure.

IEEE 802.3af: Power over Ethernet

The IEEE 802.3af specification defines a standards-based mechanism for providing *Power over Ethernet (PoE)* to devices. Power is provided inline, using two of the four available pairs (4 wires) of the 8-pin modular jack used for twisted-pair Ethernet connections. The standard introduces two types of devices:

- **Power Sourcing Equipment (PSE):** Includes devices such as Ethernet switches and power injectors that provide inline power to powered devices

- **Powered Devices:** Includes devices such as IP Phones, access points, and IP cameras that receive power from PSE

The specification defines a nominal voltage of 48 volts direct current (min 44 Vdc to max 57 Vdc), with a maximum power output of 15.4 watts per PSE (switch) port. To support more intelligent power management, the PSE might optionally classify powered devices. Table 7-2 shows the currently defined power classifications.

Table 7-2   *IEEE 802.3af Power Classifications*

Class	Max Output Power (Watts)
0	15.4
1	4.0
2	7.0
3	15.4
4	Treat device as Class 0

If the PSE cannot determine the power classification of a powered device, it should default to a Class 0 device with a maximum of 15.4 Watts. Class 4 is reserved for future use. The IEEE 802.3af task force is currently working on an extension to PoE, commonly referred to as PoE+, which might extend the amount of power supplied by a PSE to 24 watts per port.

In Cisco TelePresence deployments, IEEE 802.3af-based PoE is supplied by the primary codec to the attached IP 7975G Phone (Class 3 device) associated with the CTS endpoint. Power can also be provided locally to the IP 7975G Phone if desired. PoE is also supplied to the primary and auxiliary cameras connected to the primary codec. If the CTS endpoint supports multiple codecs, such as with the CTS-3200 or CTS-3000, the secondary codecs supply PoE to their associated primary camera Ethernet connections as well.

Network Time Protocol (NTP)

Network Time Protocol (NTP) is a protocol for synchronizing device clocks across TCP-based computer networks. The latest documented version is NTP v3, defined in IETF RFC 1305. NTP uses UDP port 123 for the distribution of *Coordinated Universal Time (UTC)* in a hierarchical tree structure. Clocks are synchronized based on their Stratum level, which indicates their precision. Stratum 0 clocks refer to devices that keep highly accurate time, such as atomic clocks. Stratum 1 clocks refer to computers that receive time directly from stratum 0 clocks. Stratum 2 clocks refer to computers that receive time from Stratum 1 computers, and so forth. Network administrators typically synchronize the clocks of network infrastructure devices to synchronize timestamps of event logs collected from routers and switches through SYSLOG and SNMP Traps.

Cisco TelePresence endpoints (CTS devices, CTS-MAN, and the CTMS) all support NTP for time synchronization, which is necessary within a TelePresence deployment for scheduling the resources for a meeting. Further, time must also be synchronized with any email and calendaring systems, such as Microsoft Exchange or IBM/Lotus Domino, used to schedule meetings. Finally, it should be noted that Cisco TelePresence deployments also rely on the use of digital certificates for secure communication; such as Secure Shell (SSH) and Hypertext Transer Protocol over Secure Socket Layer (HTTPS) for secure management, and Transport Layer Security (TLS) for secure SIP signaling. These security protocols often rely on the use of digital certificates, which have a range of dates for which the certificate is valid. Therefore, to prevent any issues with these security protocols due to incorrect dates configured within TelePresence equipment, time synchronization through mechanisms such as NTP are recommended.

Dynamic Host Configuration Protocol (DHCP)

The *Dynamic Host Configuration Protocol (DHCP)* provides a means to centrally manage and assign parameters to devices within an IP network. These parameters include IP address, subnet mask, default gateway, DNS server, and TFTP server, among others. DHCP operates in client/server mode, in which a host functioning as the DHCP client sends a DHCPDISCOVER UDP packet with source port of 68 and destination port of 67 to the MAC-layer broadcast address (0xffffffff). If the DHCP server is not on the same LAN segment, a Layer 3 device such as a Cisco IOS router can perform a DHCP relay function to relay the packet to a DHCP server located on another IP subnet. The DHCP server then returns a DHCPOFFER message containing the requested parameters, using UDP source port 67 and destination port 68. If the parameters are acceptable to the DHCP client, it issues a DHCPREQUEST directly to the DHCP server, using the source IP address handed to it by the DHCP server. The DHCP server follows up with a DHCPACK. At this point, the DHCP server binds the IP address with the particular host for the duration of the DHCP lease, which can be specified by the network administrator on most DHCP server platforms. Figure 7-4 shows an example of the operation of DHCP from a high level.

When a relay function sits between the DHCP client and the DHCP server, the relay inserts a gateway address into the DHCPDISCOVER, allowing the DHCP server to understand what subnet the request came from. This allows the DHCP server to pick an address from the correct pool of addresses to assign the DHCP client.

Both the primary codec of the TelePresence endpoint and its associated IP 7975G Phone can use DHCP to receive their IP addresses and be informed of the location of the TFTP server that holds their configuration and operating system files. When the primary codec and IP Phone have completed booting and have performed a SIP registration with the *Cisco Unified Communications Manager (CUCM)* cluster, the IP addresses of the devices will be visible from the administrative interface of CUCM, which also binds the phone number of the TelePresence endpoint with its IP address when it registers. Therefore, fixed IP addresses are not needed for management and operation of TelePresence endpoints. Static IP addressing is, however, recommended for devices such as the CTMS, Cisco TelePresence Manager, and, of course, the CUCM server.

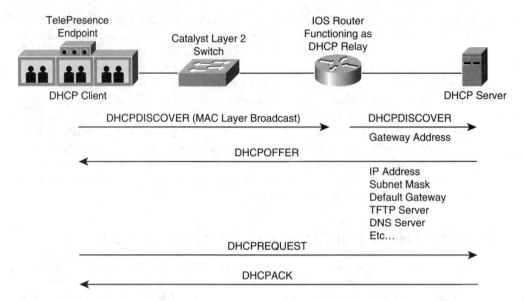

Figure 7-4 *High-level overview of DHCP operation*

Signaling Protocols

The protocols covered in this section are primarily used for scheduling and initiating TelePresence meetings.

Session Initiation Protocol (SIP)

The *Session Initiation Protocol (SIP)* is a text-based protocol for initiating, modifying, and terminating interactive sessions between devices. The protocol was originally developed by the *IETF Multiparty Multimedia Session Control (MMUSIC)* working group and proposed in 1999 in RFC 2543. The current proposed standard for SIP is defined in IETF RFC 3261 that obsoletes the earlier RFC.

SIP is a peer-to-peer protocol, meaning that all parties are equals, versus a master-slave re-lationship. SIP defines multiple physical and logical entities, some of which are discussed in Table 7-3.

Table 7-3 *SIP Entities*

Entity	Description
User Agent (UA)	A logical entity, typically within an end device, that can both initiate SIP requests and generate responses to SIP requests. User agents consist of two parts: a user agent client (UAC) and a user agent server (UAS).
User Agent Client (UAC)	The part of the user agent that initiates SIP requests.

Table 7-3   *SIP Entities*

Entity	Description
User Agent Server (UAS)	The part of the user agent that receives SIP requests and generates responses.
Back-to-Back User Agent (B2BUA)	A logical entity that receives and processes SIP requests as a user agent server and then functions as a user agent client by generating SIP requests as a response. The B2BUA maintains the dialog state and participates in all SIP requests for the dialog.
Proxy	An intermediary that receives requests from a user agent or a proxy and forwards the requests to another proxy or user agent. Their primary purpose is for routing SIP requests to other locations. A proxy can be either stateful or stateless.
Registrar	An entity that receives SIP registration requests from user agents and places the information from the user agents into the location service or the domain that it handles.

Figure 7-5 shows the relationship between the SIP entities as they relate to Cisco TelePresence components.

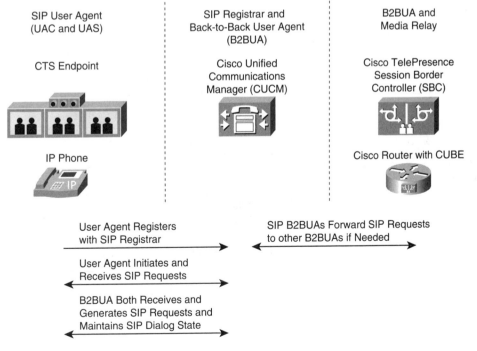

Figure 7-5   *SIP entities as they relate to Cisco TelePresence components*

SIP signaling is handled through a series of requests and responses in a client/server manner. The SIP specification defines multiple request types (also known as SIP methods). RFC 3261 defined six original methods: REGISTER, INVITE, ACK, BYE, CANCEL, and OPTIONS. Additional RFCs have extended the methods supported by SIP. Table 7-4 defines some of the more utilized SIP methods.

Table 7-4   *SIP Methods*

SIP Method	Description
REGISTER	Creates a binding between a user agent's URI with a contact address, used for location of endpoints within a SIP network.
INVITE	Initiates a SIP session between SIP endpoints.
ACK	Acknowledgement of the final response to an INVITE method.
BYE	Terminates a SIP session between endpoints.
CANCEL	Cancels a pending session between endpoints.
OPTIONS	Allows a SIP endpoint to query the options and capabilities supported by another endpoint.
REFER	Transfers a user to a different URI, used for call transfer.
SUBSCRIBE	Allows a SIP endpoint to request notification of an event.
NOTIFY	Used to inform the endpoint of the occurrence of an event to which the endpoint is subscribed.

The responses to SIP methods are similar to those found in HTTP, using numerical codes to indicate the response. Table 7-5 provides a high level overview of the response code classes within SIP signaling.

Table 7-5   *SIP Response Code Classes*

Response Code Class	Description
1xx	Informational: Indicates the SIP request is progressing.
2xx	Success: Indicates the SIP request has completed successfully.
3xx	Redirection: Indicates the SIP request needs to be redirected to another user agent server for processing.
4xx	Client Error: Indicates the request failed because of a client error.
5xx	Server Error: Indicates the request failed because of a server error.

Table 7-5 *SIP Response Code Classes*

Response Code Class	Description
6xx	Global Failure: Indicates the request has failed and should not be tried again.

Figure 7-6 shows an example flow of SIP requests and responses within an SIP INVITE, as it relates to Cisco TelePresence.

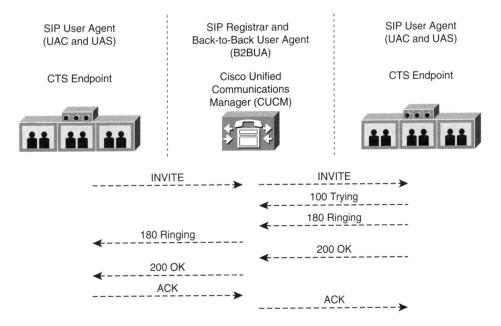

Figure 7-6 *Example SIP INVITE message flow*

In Figure 7-5, the Cisco Unified Communications Manager (CUCM) functions as a B2BUA, receiving the initial SIP INVITE from one TelePresence endpoint and generating its own SIP INVITE to the other TelePresence endpoint. The reader should note that SIP allows direct signaling between endpoints (user agents), although this is not utilized by Cisco TelePresence.

SIP messages follow a standard format. The first line contains the request method itself, followed by a series of headers, and then finally the body of the SIP message. Example 7-1 shows a sample SIP INVITE.

Example 7-1 *Example SIP Message Format*

```
! Request Line
INVITE sip:6019@10.16.1.10 SIP/2.0
! Headers
```

```
Via: SIP/2.0/TCP 10.19.1.11:51317;branch=z9hG4bK40016297
From: "1010" <sip:1010@10.16.1.10>;tag=0019aa044fec52f71f6dede8-78b77acc
To: <sip:6019@10.16.1.10>
Call-ID: 0019aa04-4fec005e-55db26f2-19a0f56a@10.19.1.11
Max-Forwards: 70
Date: Wed, 10 Sep 2008 18:18:25 GMT
CSeq: 101 INVITE
User-Agent: Cisco-Telepresence-#375/1.0
Contact: <sip:101051317;transport=tcp>
Expires: 180
Accept: application/sdp
Allow: ACK,BYE,CANCEL,INVITE,NOTIFY,OPTIONS,REFER,REGISTER,UPDATE,INFO,SUBSCRIBE
Remote-Party-ID: "1010" <sip:1010@10.19.1.11>;party=calling;id-
type=subscriber;privacy=off;screen=yes
Allow-Events: kpml,dialog
Content-Length: 561
Content-Type: application/sdp
Content-Disposition: session;handling=optional
! Message Body (Session Description Protocol)
v=0
o=Cisco-SIPUA 26362 0 IN IP4 10.19.1.11
s=SIP Call
c=IN IP4 10.19.1.11
t=0 0
a=sendrecv
m=audio 16384 RTP/AVP 96 0 101
b=TIAS:128000
a=rtpmap:96 mpeg4-generic/48000
a=fmtp:96 profile-level-id=16;streamtype=5;mode=AAC-
hbr;config=11B0;sizeLength=13;indexLength=3;indexDeltaLength=3;constantDuration=480
a=rtpmap:0 PCMU/8000
a=rtpmap:101 telephone-event/8000
a=fmtp:101 0-15
m=video 16388 RTP/AVP 112
b=TIAS:4000000
a=rtpmap:112 H264/90000
a=fmtp:112 profile-level-id=4d0028;sprop-parameter-
sets=R00AKAmWUgDwBDyA,SGE7jyA=;packetization-mode=1
```

Table 7-6 provides a description of some of the more common headers found within the
SIP message displayed in Example 7-1.

Table 7-6 *SIP Header Descriptions*

Header	Description
Via:	The Via: header indicates the version of SIP (currently SIP 2.0), the transport protocol (TCP or UDP), the IP address or name of the originator of the request and the port number, and a transaction identifier, which always begins with branch=z9hG4bK.
From:	The From: header includes an optional display name, the URI of the request originator enclosed in < >, and a pseudo-random tag generated uniquely for each dialog.
To:	The To: header includes and optional a display name and the URI of the request recipient enclosed in < >.
Call-ID:	The Call-ID: header includes a pseudo-random string used uniquely identify all requests and responses within a given dialog.
Max-Forwards:	The Max-Forwards: header is a hop count that is decremented by each proxy server that forwards the request.
Cseq:	Cseq: contains a command sequence number, which is incremented by one for each successive request, as well as the SIP request method. It is used to determine retransmissions within SIP call sequences.
Contact:	The Contact: header contains one or more SIP or SIPS URIs, which provide information for the other party to contact this user agent.
Allow:	The Allow: header lists all of the SIP methods supported by this user agent.
Content Length:	The Content Length: header is a count of the message body length in bytes, which follows the SIP headers.

SIP can operate over UDP or TCP, using port 5060 in both cases. The stateless nature of UDP allowed SIP over UDP to scale well in large deployments. Today, however, many deployments use SIP over TCP in order to take advantage of the use of Transport Layer Security (TLS) along with SIP, provide confidentiality and authentication of the SIP signaling. TLS requires a stateful protocol, such as TCP, to operate over.

XML/SOAP

Extensible Markup Language (XML) is a recommendation from the World Wide Web Consortium (W3C) initially derived as a subset of the Standard Generalized Markup Language (SGML) to address the challenges of large scale electronic publishing. The goal of XML is to simplify the sharing of structured data between information systems, particularly over the Internet. The latest version of the XML specification is version 1.0.

XML describes a class of data objects referred to as *XML documents* and to some extent describes how computer applications process those documents. Other markup languages, such as HTML, have a specific tag set that does not allow arbitrary structure within a document. XML comes with no specified tag set. Instead, XML provides a means for defining tags and the relationships between them. Because of this, the semantics of a particular XML document can be defined individually by the user or through a Document Type Definition (DTD) or XML schema.

XML documents typically begin with an XML declaration <?xml... ?> signifying the document is an XML document. The most common form of markup found within an XML document is an *element*. An element within an XML document begins with a start-tag and ends with an end-tag, such as the following:

```
<element>
</element>
```

Another common form of markup is an attribute. Attributes are case-sensitive name-value pairs that can occur within the start-tags after the element name. The following is an example of an element with attributes:

```
<video type="H.264" framerate="30 fps"> telepresence </video>
```

The two categories of XML documents are

- Well-formed

- Valid

A document is well-formed if it obeys the syntax of XML. This includes the following:

- There can only be one root element.

- All open tags must have a corresponding closing tag.

- No attribute can appear more than once in a start tag.

- Non-empty tags must be properly nested.

- Parameter entries must be declared before they are used.

An XML document is valid if it refers to a proper DTD or XML Schema and it obeys the constraints of the DTD or XML Schema. Examples of constraints include the correct elements, element sequence, and nesting of elements and whether required attributes are provided and the attribute values are of the correct type. XML documents often appear within the body of an HTTP POST message.

SOAP is a lightweight protocol that uses the extensibility of XML, primarily intended for exchanging structured information for messaging within a decentralized and distributed environment. SOAP is often used in the implementation of web services within the network. A SOAP message consists of a mandatory SOAP <Envelope> root element, an optional <Header> element, and a mandatory <body> element. SOAP messages often appear within the body of an XML document.

The Cisco TelePresence Manager (CTS-MAN) uses XML/SOAP over HTTP in order to exchange messages with CTS Endpoints regarding the scheduling of TelePresence meetings, as well as to inform the CTS-MAN of the beginning and ending of scheduled TelePresence meetings. Example 7-2 demonstrates such an XML/SOAP exchange, in which a

TelePresence endpoint is notifying the CTS-MAN of the start of a call, with the corresponding response shown in Example 7-3.

Example 7-2   *Example XML/SOAP Message Between CTS Endpoint and the CTS-MAN*

```
! HTTP
POST /cdm/services/CalendarSRService HTTP/1.1
Host: 10.16.1.7:8080
User-Agent: gSOAP/2.7
Content-Type: text/xml; charset=utf-8
Content-Length: 947
Connection: close
SOAPAction: "cdm/sendCallStartNotificationOutbound"
! XML Message
<?xml version="1.0" encoding="UTF-8"?>
! SOAP Message
<SOAP-ENV:Envelope
    xmlns:SOAP-ENV="http://schemas.xmlsoap.org/soap/envelope/"
    xmlns:SOAP-ENC="http://schemas.xmlsoap.org/soap/encoding/"
    xmlns:xsi="http://www.w3.org/2001/XMLSchema-instance"
    xmlns:xsd="http://www.w3.org/2001/XMLSchema"
    xmlns:ns2="http://tempuri.org/ns2.xsd"
    xmlns:ns1="http://calendarsrservice.soap.cdm.ts.cisco.com">
<SOAP-ENV:Header>
    <ns2:Authentication>
      <swVersion>1.0</swVersion>
      <ipAddress>10.19.1.11</ipAddress>
      <userName>admin</userName>
      <passWord>Y2lzY28=</passWord>
    </ns2:Authentication>
  </SOAP-ENV:Header>
  <SOAP-ENV:Body>
    <ns1:sendCallStartNotificationOutbound>
      <parameters>
        <CallID>0019aa04-4fec005e-55db26f2-19a0f56a@10.19.1.11</CallID>
        <RoomName>room-a0@tp.com</RoomName>
        <UTCTime>2008-09-10T11:18:25</UTCTime>
        <DialedNumber>6019</DialedNumber>
        <CallMode>telepresence</CallMode>
        <DialMode>manual</DialMode>
      </parameters>
    </ns1:sendCallStartNotificationOutbound>
  </SOAP-ENV:Body>
</SOAP-ENV:Envelope>
```

Example 7-3 *Corresponding XML/SOAP Response Between CTS-MAN and the CTS Endpoint*

```
! HTTP
HTTP/1.1 200 OK
Server: Apache-Coyote/1.1
Content-Type: text/xml;charset=utf-8
Date: Wed, 10 Sep 2008 18:18:25 GMT
Connection: close
! XML Message
<?xml version="1.0" encoding="utf-8"?>
! SOAP Message
<soapenv:Envelope
    xmlns:soapenv="http://schemas.xmlsoap.org/soap/envelope/"
    xmlns:xsd="http://www.w3.org/2001/XMLSchema"
    xmlns:xsi="http://www.w3.org/2001/XMLSchema-instance">
  <soapenv:Body>
    <sendCallStartNotificationOutboundResponse
            xmlns="http://calendarsrservice.soap.cdm.ts.cisco.com">
      <parameters xmlns="">
        <responseCode>1</responseCode>
        <responseString>OK</responseString>
      </parameters><
    /sendCallStartNotificationOutboundResponse>
  </soapenv:Body>
</soapenv:Envelope>
```

AXL/SOAP

Application XML (AXL) is a Cisco application programming interface (API) designed to give applications access to Cisco Unified Communications Manager (CUCM) configuration and provisioning services. AXL is implemented as a SOAP over HTTP web service. Requests, in the form of XML/SOAP documents, are sent from an application to the internal web server of the CUCM, which responds with an XML-formatted SOAP response. Cisco TelePresence Manager (CTS-MAN) uses AXL/SOAP in order to discover the TelePresence endpoints configured within CUCM.

JTAPI, TAPI, and CTIQBE

The Java Telephony API (JTAPI) is a portable, object-oriented application programming interface (API) that provides computer telephony integration (CTI) call control. JTAPI was designed by a consortium of industry-leading computer and telecommunications companies. JTAPI is both scalable and extensible, integrating both first-party and third-party call control models. The Telephony API (TAPI) is a Microsoft API that provides similar computer telephony integration functionality for Microsoft Windows. Both JTAPI and TAPI use Computer Telephony Integration Quick Buffering Encoding (CTIQBE) to communicate with CUCM. CTIQBE is a Cisco-specific protocol that runs over TCP. CTS-MAN uses JTAPI over CTIQBE to register with Cisco Unified Communications Manager CTI Manager service, to receive device event status of Cisco TelePresence endpoints.

WebDAV

Web-based Distributed Authoring and Versioning (WebDAV) is an extension to the Hypertext Transfer Protocol version 1.1 (HTTP1/1) defined in IETF RFC 4918. WebDAV provides a set of methods, headers, and content types used for the management of resource properties; the creation and management of resource collections; the manipulation of URL namespaces; and for locking resources in order to avoid collisions. CTS-MAN uses WebDAV to communicate with Microsoft Exchange servers in order to extract information regarding scheduled meetings that involve TelePresence rooms. CTS-MAN then uses this information to reserve resources on any applicable Cisco TelePresence Multipoint Switch (CTMS); and push scheduled meetings down to the IP 7975G Phones associated with TelePresence endpoints, via XML/SOAP.

LDAP

The Lightweight Directory Access Protocol (LDAP) is a lightweight alternative to the Directory Access Protocol (DAP) used for accessing X.500 directory services through TCP/IP. The LDAP protocol itself is defined under IETF RFC 4511. LDAP operates in client/server mode. A client starts an LDAP session by connecting to an LDAP server. LDAP requires a reliable transport protocol. By default, the protocol runs on TCP port 389. The client then sends an operation request to the server, using Abstract Syntax Notation One (ASN.1) Basic Encoding Rules (BER), and the server replies in turn. Confidentiality of the information can be preserved through the use of TLS along with LDAP.

To support scheduled TelePresence meetings, Cisco TelePresence rooms must be configured within directory servers such as Active Directory. Mailboxes for the TelePresence rooms are then created by mail applications such as Microsoft Exchange and/or IBM/Lotus Domino. CTS-MAN uses LDAP to communicate with directory servers to learn about the configured TelePresence rooms so that meeting scheduling information can be accessed from the mail server.

Figure 7-7 provides a high-level summary of the TelePresence signaling protocols between CTS endpoints, CUCM, CUBE, SBC, CTS-MAN, CTMS, email servers (that is, Microsoft Exchange or IBM/Lotus Domino), and directory servers (that is, Microsoft Active Directory).

Network Management Protocols

The protocols listed in this section are primarily for configuring and managing Cisco TelePresence deployments.

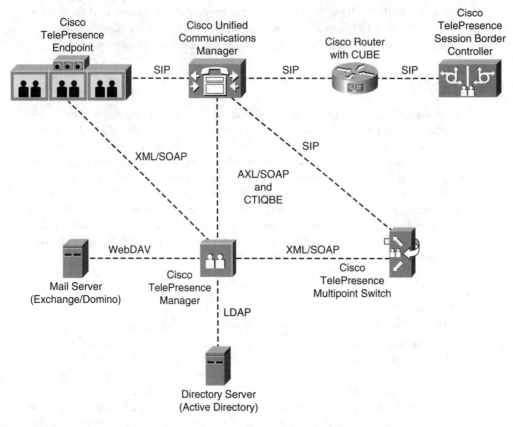

Figure 7-7   *TelePresence signaling summary*

Cisco Discovery Protocol

Cisco Discovery Protocol (CDP) is a data link layer (Layer 2) device discovery protocol that runs on Cisco-manufactured equipment, including routers, switches, access points, IP phones, and TelePresence endpoints. CDP provides similar functionality to the IEEE 802.1AB Link Layer Discovery Protocol (LLDP) and the enhanced Link Layer Discovery Protocol – Media Endpoint Discovery (LLDP-MED). However, CDP pre-dates LLDP/LLDP-MED by several years.

By default, Cisco devices send CDP packets every 60 seconds on each interface that supports the protocol. CDP runs on all media that supports *Subnetwork Access Protocol (SNAP)*; including LANs, Frame Relay, and ATM. On Ethernet networks, packets are sent to the multicast address 01:00:0C:CC:CC:CC. The same multicast address is also used for other protocols such as VLAN Trunking Protocol (VTP), Dynamic Trunking Prototol (DTP), Port Aggregation Protocol (PagP), and UniDirectional Link Detection (UDLD); however, a Protocol ID value of 0x20 signifies a CDP packet.

Information within CDP announcements is sent as a series of entries, each in type-length-value (TLV) format. Figure 7-8 shows the format of a CDP packet.

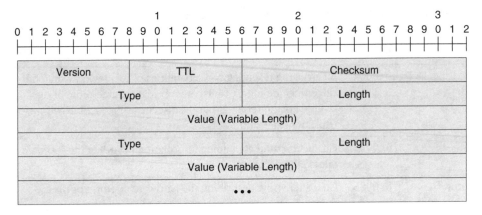

Figure 7-8 *CDP packet format*

The following are the fields within the CDP packet:

- **Version:** An 8-bit field that contains the current version of CDP, which is 0x02

- **Time-To-Live (TTL):** An 8-bt field containing the length of time in seconds that a device that receives the announcement should keep the information

- **Checksum:** A 16-bit checksum on the CDP packet

- **Type:** A 16-bit field containing TLV types. Table 7-7 lists many current TLV type values

- **Length:** A 16-bit field containing the length in bytes of the Type, Length, and Value fields combined

- **Value:** A variable length field that includes values of TLV entries

Table 7-7 shows some of the defined TLV types that are more relevant to TelePresence deployments.

Table 7-7 *CDP TLV Types Relevant to TelePresence*

TLV Type	Hex Value	Description
Device ID	0x0001	Character string unique to the sending device. Typically either the MAC address or hardware serial number along with the manufacturer's Organizationally Unique Identifier (OUI).
Address	0x0002	List of network layer addresses configured on the device. The first address in the list is the address at which Simple Network Management Protocol (SNMP) messages can be received, if SNMP is supported.
Port ID	0x0003	Character string identifying the port that the CDP packet was sent from.

continues

Table 7-7   *CDP TLV Types Relevant to TelePresence (continued)*

TLV Type	Hex Value	Description
Capabilities	0x0004	Bit string representing the capabilities of the device. Common values include router, transparent bridge, source-route bridge, switch, host, Internet Group Management Protocol (IGMP)-capable, repeater, and so on.
Version	0x0005	Character string containing information regarding the software release the device runs.
Platform	0x0006	Character string describing the hardware platform of the device.
VTP Management Domain	0x0009	Contains the name of the VTP management domain for those devices that run VTP.
Native VLAN	0x000a	Used to indicate to the remote device the native (untagged) VLAN and whether the port sending the CDP updates functions as a trunk port or a host/edge port.
Appliance VLAN-ID	0x000e	Contains one or more tuples that contain a 1-byte Appliance ID and a 2-byte VLAN-ID. Can be used to signal that the port has been configured to support VoIP devices using a VVLAN. The receiving device, such as an IP Phone, can subsequently modify its configuration to send voice traffic using the VVLAN tag.
Power Consumption	0x0010	Can be sent by devices that utilize inline power. This TLV indicates the maximum amount of power, in milliwatts, expected to be obtained and used by the device over the interface that the CDP packet is sent.
Extended Trust	0x0012	When a port is configured to be "trusted" from a QoS perspective, packets received on the port are not re-marked. This TLV can be used to indicate to devices such as IP Phones that the "trust" is extended to the device connected to the PC port of the IP Phone.
CoS for Untrusted Ports	0x0013	Indicates the CoS value with which all packets received on an untrusted port should be marked by a simple switching device, such as an IP Phone, which cannot itself classify individual packets.
Power Requested	0x0019	Sent by powerable devices to negotiate a suitable power level from the supplier of the inline power.
Power Available	0x001a	Sent by the device supplying inline power to negotiate a suitable power level for the device requiring inline power.

Note that if a device does not recognize a TLV value, it silently discards it. This ensures backward-compatibility with older versions. Because CDP is an extensible protocol, new TLV values can be added in future versions as well.

CDP Utilization Within Cisco TelePresence Networks

When the 7975G IP Phone associated with a TelePresence endpoint starts up, it sends CDP messages to the primary codec. The codec receives these CDP messages and passes them along to the Catalyst access-edge switch. The primary codec also generates its own CDP messages, which are sent to the access-edge switch. Likewise, the Catalyst access-edge switch also generates CDP messages that are sent to the primary codec and forwarded to the IP 7975G Phone. Figure 7-9 shows an example of CDP message exchange between the IP Phone and the Catalyst access-edge switch.

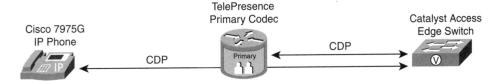

Figure 7-9   *CDP messages between TelePresence devices*

The primary benefit of CDP within Cisco TelePresence deployments is to allow the Catalyst access-edge switch port to inform both the primary codec and its associated IP 7975G Phone of the configuration of a VVLAN. The access-edge switch informs the primary codec and IP 7975G Phone through the Appliance VLAN-ID TLV, shown previously in Table 7-7. Upon receiving the Appliance VLAN-ID TLV within CDP messages from the access-edge switch, both the primary codec and its associated IP Phone can modify their configurations to send traffic with the 802.1Q VLAN tag corresponding to the VVLAN. This allows the Cisco Catalyst access-edge switch to identify the correct VLAN and, therefore, the correct IP subnet for the traffic to and from the Cisco TelePresence endpoint.

Although not implemented in current versions of Cisco TelePresence, CDP could also be used by the primary codec to negotiate a suitable power level for its associated IP Phone when the phone uses inline power. This can be accomplished through CDP packet exchanges that include the Power Consumption, Power Requested, and Power Available TLVs. Other potential extensions include the capability of the Catalyst access-edge switch to automatically identify a Cisco TelePresence device and apply policy to the port, based on CDP packet exchanges that include the Platform and Device ID TLVs.

Trivial File Transfer Protocol (TFTP)

Trivial File Transfer Protocol (TFTP), specified in IETF RFC 1350, is a simple file transfer protocol. Other RFCs extend the functionality of TFTP, which is often used to download firmware, operating system, and configuration files to network devices. Figure 7-10 shows an example of how TFTP operates to download IP Phone operating system and configuration files from the CUCM server.

The IP Phone (TFTP client) initiates a TFTP read request (RRQ) to the CUCM server (TFTP server) using UDP port 69. Because UDP is the transport layer protocol, no three-way handshake (as found with TCP) is needed to initiate a session. For read requests, the TFTP server simply begins sending blocks of data using a high-numbered UDP port. This port, often allocated from the IANA range of dynamic and private ports (from 49152 to 65535), is referred to as an *ephemeral port*. The file is then transferred as a sequence of

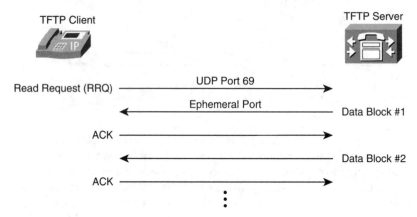

Figure 7-10   *TFTP protocol operation for downloading IP Phone files*

full-sized blocks of data, one packet at time, using the ephemeral port. Each block of data (that is, packet) is acknowledged before the next packet is sent. The end of the file transfer is signified by receipt of either a packet with less than a full block of data or a packet with no data. Because TFTP has no authentication or encryption mechanisms built into the protocol itself, it should be used cautiously over networks that are not private. TFTP also has a write request (WRQ) function, although this function is not used by Cisco TelePresence.

As shown in Figure 7-10, TFTP is used by Cisco IP Phones to download both their operating system firmware loads and their configuration files. This includes the 7975G IP Phone attached to the primary codec of a TelePresence endpoint. The TFTP server function can be integrated within the CUCM cluster, as shown in Figure 7-10, or offloaded to a separate TFTP server. The location of the TFTP server for Cisco IP Phones is often indicated by Option 150 within DHCP replies when DHCP is implemented across the network. Alternatively, the TFTP server location can also be hard-coded within IP Phones if DHCP is not used. Cisco offers the capability to download firmware loads, which are secured by an authentication algorithm across the file. Cisco also offers the capability to encrypt configuration files while on the CUCM server, which bypasses the need for TFTP to support authentication and encryption. Because TFTP uses ephemeral ports, any firewalls deployed between the IP Phones and the TFTP server (CUCM) might require application-level inspection of TFTP packets to determine and dynamically open the ephemeral port used for the TFTP file transfer.

Cisco TelePresence primary codecs do not use TFTP to download their operating system and configuration files. Instead, the primary codec of a CTS endpoint initiates an HTTP session, using TCP port 6970 to its download server (typically the CUCM). Operating system images and configuration files are downloaded to the primary codec. If the TelePresence endpoint supports secondary codecs, they are upgraded through the image downloaded to the primary codec. This ensures that all codecs of a single TelePresence endpoint run the same operating system image.

Simple Network Management Protocol

The Simple Network Management Protocol (SNMP) refers both to a specific protocol used to collect information and configure devices over an IP network, as well as an overall Internet-standard network management framework. The SNMP network management framework consists of the following components:

- **Network Management Stations (NMSs):** An NMS is typically a server that runs network management applications, which in turn uses SNMP to monitor and control network elements.

- **Network Elements:** Network elements are the actual managed devices (routers, switches, TelePresence codecs, and so on) on the IP network.

- **Agents:** Agents are software components running within network elements that collect and store management information.

- **Managed Objects:** Managed objects are specific characteristics of network elements that can be managed. Objects can be single entities or entire tables. Specific instances of managed objects are often referred to as variables.

- **Management Information Bases (MIBs):** MIBs are collections of related management objects that define the structure of the management data through a hierarchical namespace using Object Identifiers (OIDs). Each OID describes a particular variable that can either be read from a managed object or set on a managed object. MIBs can be standards-based or proprietary. Because SNMP management information utilizes a hierarchical namespace, individual vendors can extend management capabilities of their products through proprietary MIBs, which are typically published.

There are currently three versions of SNMP commonly deployed—SNMPv1, SNMPv2c, and SNMPv3. SNMPv1 was the initial version introduced in the late 1980s. It is currently defined primarily under IETF RFC 1155, RFC 1157, and RFC 1213. The security model used by SNMPv1 consists of authentication only, using community strings (read-only and read/write), which are sent in clear text within SNMP messages. Because of this, SNMPv1 is considered inherently insecure, and read/write capability should be used with caution, even over private networks.

SNMPv2c was proposed around the mid 1990s and is currently defined primarily under IETF RFCs 1901–1908. The "c" in SNMPv2c indicates a simplified version of SNMPv2, which also uses a security model based on community strings. SNMPv2 improved performance of SNMPv1 by introducing features such as the get-bulk-request PDU and notifications, both discussed in Table 7-8. However, because it still uses the same security model as SNMPv1, read/write capability should be used with caution. SNMPv1 and SNMPv2 use different header and PDU formats, as well as support different procedures; therefore, compatibility is achieved only by agents that can proxy between the two versions or through network management stations that can send and receive both SNMPv1 and SNMPv2c messages.

SNMPv3 was introduced in the early 2000s and is currently defined primarily under IETF RFCs 3411–3418. A primary benefit of SNMPv3 is its security model, which eliminates the community strings of SNMPv1 and SNMPv2c. SNMPv3 supports message integrity, authentication, and encryption of messages; allowing both read and read/write operation over both public and private networks.

As mentioned previously, SNMP protocol defines a number of Protocol Data Units (PDUs), some of which are shown in Table 7-8, along with the particular version of SNMP that supports them. These PDUs are essentially the commands for managing objects through SNMP.

Table 7-8 *Commonly Used PDUs Based on SNMP Version*

Version	PDU	Description
SNMPv1	get-request	Command/response mechanism by which an NMS queries a network element for a particular variable.
SNMPv1	response	Command/response mechanism by which an NMS receives information about a particular variable from a network element, based upon a previously issued SNMP request message.
SNMPv1	get-next-request	Command/response mechanism that can be used iteratively by an NMS to retrieve sequences of variables from a network element.
SNMPv1	set-request	Issued by an NMS to change the value of a variable on a network element or initialize SNMP traps or notifications to be sent from a network element.
SNMPv1	trap	Asynchronous mechanism by which a network elements issues alerts or information about an event to an NMS.

Table 7-8 *Commonly Used PDUs Based on SNMP Version*

Version	PDU	Description
SNMPv2	get-bulk-request	Improved command/response mechanism which can be used by an NMS to retrieve sequences of variables from a network element with a single command.
SNMPv2	inform-request	Provides similar functionality as the trap PDU, but the receiver acknowledges the receipt with a response PDU.

As of the time this book was written (CTS version 1.4), CTS, CTMS, and CTS Manger support the MIBs listed in Table 7-9. Future versions of Cisco TelePresence will add additional SNMP MIB support.

Table 7-9 *MIB Support in TelePresence Endpoints (CTS, CTMS, and CTS-MAN)*

MIB Name	Description
CISCO-SYSLOG-MIB	Provides an SNMP interface into syslog messages.
CISCO-CDP-MIB	Provides Ethernet neighbor information, such as the attached IP Phone and upstream switch.
HOST-RESOURCES-MIB	Provides system operating system information such as system CPU, memory, disk, clock, and individual process information.
RFC-1213-MIB	Provides basic MIB2 structure / information such as system uptime, system description, snmp location, and snmp contact.
IF-MIB	Provides Ethernet interface statistics, such as bytes and packets transmitted and received, as well as interface errors.
UDP-MIB	Provides the number of inbound and outbound UDP packets, as well as drops.
TCP-MIB	Provides the number of inbound and outbound TCP packets, connections, and number of TCP retransmissions.
SNMP Protocol Specific MIBs: SNMP-FRAMEWORK-MIB, SNMP-MPD-MIB, SNMP-NOTIFICATION-MIB, SNMP-TARGET-MIB, SNMP-USM-MIB, SNMP-VACM-MIB	Provides information relating to the SNMP daemon configuration and current state.

In addition to the MIBs listed in Table 7-9, CTS devices support the additional MIBs listed in Table 7-10.

Table 7-10   *Additional MIBs Supported by CTS Devices*

MIB Name	Description
CISCO-TELEPRESENCE-MIB	Provides notification on peripheral and user authentication failures. Also allows for the remote restart of the CTS device.
CISCO-ENVMON-MIB	Provides system temperature.

TelePresence Security Protocols

The protocols listed within this section are used primarily to provide secure communications between TelePresence devices. The secure communications could be for management purposes, signaling, or for the actual media streams themselves.

Transport Layer Security (TLS)

The Transport Layer Security (TLS) protocol is designed to provide authentication, data integrity, and confidentiality for communications between two applications. TLS is based on SSL version 3.0, although the two protocols are not compatible. The initial version, TLS 1.0, was defined under IETF RFC 2246 in 1999. TLS 1.1, defined in IETF RFC 4346, and obsoleted TNS 1.0 in 2006. The latest version, TLS 1.2, was proposed for standardization in 2008 and is defined in IETF RFC 5246.

TLS operates in a client/server mode with one side acting as the "server" and the other side acting as the "client." TLS requires a reliable transport layer protocol such as TCP to operate over. The protocol has two primary layers:

- The TLS Handshake Protocol layer
- The TLS Record Protocol layer

The TLS Handshake Protocol layer provides the following functionality:

■   Allows the client and server to authenticate each other using asymmetric or public key cryptography (that is, digital certificates). Authentication can be one-sided—the client authenticates the server; or mutual—the client/server authenticate each other.

■   Allows the client/server to reliably negotiate a compression algorithm, message authentication algorithm, encryption algorithm, and the necessary cryptographic keys before any application data is sent.

Figure 7-11 shows a high level overview of the message flows in a TLS handshake from the perspective of the TelePresence endpoint being the client and the CUCM being the server.

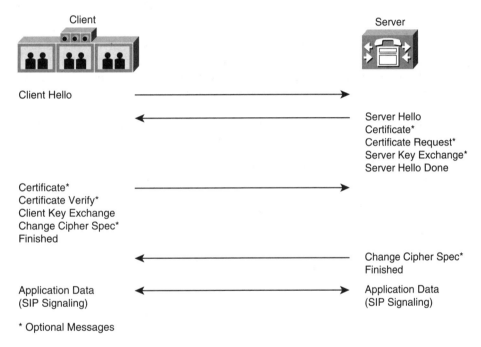

Figure 7-11   *Message flows for TLS handshake*

The TLS Handshake protocol layer is designed to operate in a lock-step manner, meaning that messages received in incorrect order will cause the TLS handshake to fail. Because TLS is fairly flexible in terms of one-sided authentication versus, mutual authentication, and whether encryption and message authentication are utilized or not, many of the messages within the TLS handshake are optional. Bulk encryption of the application data is typically done via encryption algorithms such as Advanced Encryption Standard (AES), using symmetric keying. The negotiation of these keys is done securely within the TLS Handshake Protocol layer through the Client and Server Key Exchange messages. The multiple TLS handshake messages (that is, Certificate, Certificate Request, Server Hello Done) can appear within a single TCP packet in order to minimize the number of packets sent during the handshake.

The TLS Record Protocol layer runs directly on top of a reliable transport layer protocol, such as TCP. It takes application data and fragments it into manageable blocks. The TLS Record Protocol then optionally compresses the block, applies a Message Authentication Code (MAC), and encrypts it, depending upon what was negotiated during the TLS Handshake Protocol for the particular TLS session.

Cisco TelePresence devices use TLS to secure the SIP signaling between the TelePresence primary codec and the CUCM server, as well as between the associated IP 7975G Phone and the CUCM server when SIP signaling utilizes TCP as the transport protocol. TelePresence endpoints can operate in one of three device security modes:

- **Non Secure:** Neither message authentication nor encryption is enabled for SIP signaling of the RTP voice and video media and the RTCP control streams.

- **Authenticated:** Message authentication is enabled for SIP signaling between the TelePresence device and CUCM via TLS, however, encryption is not enabled. Further, in Authenticated mode, neither message authentication or encryption is enabled for the RTP voice and video media and the RTCP control streams.

- **Encrypted:** Message authentication and encryption are enabled for SIP signaling via TLS. Message authentication and encryption are enabled for the RTP voice and video media and the RTCP control streams via secure RTP (sRTP).

At press time, the current version of the Cisco Session Border Controller (SBC) does not support SIP signaling secured with TLS. Secure signaling is supported only between the CTS endpoint and CUCM, but not across the SIP trunk between the CUCM and SBC. Therefore, secure signaling is not currently supported for intercompany B2B TelePresence deployments. However, secure media transport is still supported through the use of sRTP with the dTLS key exchange mechanism, discussed in the following section.

Secure Real-Time Transport Protocol (sRTP)

Secure RTP (sRTP), defined in IETF RFC 3711, details the methods of providing confidentiality and data integrity for both Real-time Transport Protocol (RTP) voice and video media, as well as their corresponding Real-time Transport Control Protocol (RTCP) streams. sRTP accomplishes this through the use of encryption and message authentication headers. Indirectly sRTP also provides replay protection. Figure 7-12 shows the format of an sRTP packet.

As you can see in Figure 7-12, encryption applies only to the payload of the RTP packet. Message authentication, however, is applied to both the RTP header as well as the RTP

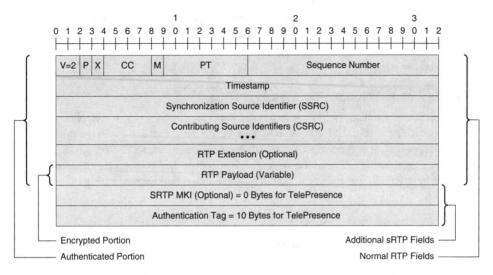

Figure 7-12 *sRTP packet format*

payload. Because message authentication applies to the RTP sequence number within the header, sRTP indirectly provides protection against replay attacks as well.

sRTP defines two additional fields that do not appear in normal RTP packets, the Master Key Identifier (MKI) field, and the Authentication Tag field. The MKI field is an optional field of configurable length, used to indicate the master key, from which the individual session keys were derived for encryption and/or authentication, within a given cryptographic context. This field is not used with Cisco TelePresence currently. The Authentication Tag is a recommended field of configurable length, used to hold the message authentication data for the RTP header and payload for the particular packet.

The default cipher for encryption defined within RFC-3711 is AES with a 128-bit encryption key. The protocol is extensible, so other ciphers can be used. The default cipher yields no expansion of the RTP payload itself. The default authentication transform is HMAC-SHA1 which results in an 80-bit (10-byte) Authentication Tag appended to the RTP packet. Therefore, the minimum expansion of the RTP packet through the addition of SRTP is only 10 bytes when the Authentication Tag field is use and the MKI field is not used.

sRTP Key Exchange

Symmetric keying is normally used for encryption algorithms such as AES, as well as for authentication transforms such as Hash Message Authentication Code-Secure Hash Algorithm version 1 (HMAC-SHA1). The actual process for exchanging keying material for sRTP is outside the scope of RFC 3711. The two methods used by Cisco TelePresence include the use of SIP Session Description Protocol (SDP) messages (sometimes referred to as *S-descriptors*) to exchange keying material during call establishment, and the use of datagram TLS (dTLS) within the media flows after call establishment to exchange keying material. Cisco TelePresence uses both methods of key exchange. However TelePresence endpoints will prioritize the use of keying material derived from dTLS over keying material derived from SDP messages if both methods succeed. The sections that follow discuss each of these methods.

Key Exchange Through SDP Messages

This method of exchanging keying material, used primarily by Cisco IP Telephony devices, is defined within IETF RFC-4568. The RFC defines a method for exchanging the cryptographic suite and keying material information for unicast sRTP flows through SIP SDP messages during call establishment. This is accomplished through the "crypto" attribute (a=crypto) under the particular media type (m=video or m=audio) within the SDP. The format of the "crypto" attribute is as follows:

a=crypto:<tag> <crypto-suite> <key-params> [<session-params>]

The *tag* field is a decimal number used to uniquely distinguish multiple crypto attributes from each other. The *crypto-suite* field contains the cipher and message authentication algorithms for the particular crypto attribute. The *key-params* field itself has the following format:

key-params = *<key-method>* *":"* *<key-info>*

The *key-method* field indicates the method by which keying material is exchanged. For example, **inline** indicates the keying information is contained within the SDP. For inline keying, the *key-info* field can contain further information in the following format:

<key‖salt> ["|" lifetime] ["|" MKI ":" length]

The **key ‖ salt** field is a concatenation of the master key and master salt. The **lifetime** field indicates the lifetime in terms of packets that can use the master key. The **MKI** field indicates whether the Master Key Identifier will be included within SRTP packets or not. Finally the **length** field indicates the length of the MKI field within SRTP packets.

An example of the use of the crypto attribute within an SDP as follows:

m=video 16386 RTP/SAVP 112
a=crypto:1 AES_CM_128_HMAC_SHA1_80
  inline:d0RmdmcmVCspeEc3QGZiNWpVLFJhQX1cfHAwJSoj|2^20|1:32

In the preceding example, the first line has been included to show that the following crypto attribute applies only to the video media flow, which will use sRTP over UDP port 16386, with an RTP payload type of 112.

The second line contains the crypto attribute itself, which indicates that encryption algorithm used for the sRTP stream will be AES in Counter Mode (CM), with a 128-bit key. The authentication algorithm will be the Hashed Message Authentication Code – Secure Hash Algorithm 1 (HMAC-SHA1) with an 80-bit authentication code.

The third line contains three fields, each separated by a "|." The first field indicates that the master key and salt are sent inline, followed by the actual key and salt. The second field indicates that the master key is good for a lifetime 2^{20} packets. The final field indicates that a Master Key Identifier will be sent within the sRTP packet, and its length will be 32 bytes.

This is a generic example for illustration purposes of the protocol and not taken from a Cisco TelePresence endpoint.

You should review IETF RFC 4568 regarding the use of the crypto attribute for this purpose. Because keying material is sent within SIP signaling, encryption of the SIP signaling itself via TLS is necessary to secure the key exchange. Cisco IP Telephony devices support only the method of sRTP key exchange discussed in this section. When an IP Phone is added to an existing TelePresence meeting, the encryption keys used for the sRTP media flows between the TelePresence primary codec and the add-on IP Phone are exchanged via SDP messages within the SIP signaling.

Key Exchange via dTLS

The datagram Transport Layer Security (dTLS) protocol, defined in IETF RFC 4347, is designed to provide authentication, data integrity, and confidentiality for communications between two applications over a datagram transport protocol such as UDP. dTLS is based on TLS and is designed to provide equivalent security guarantees. However, in order to account for the underlying unreliable transport, mechanisms such as sequence numbers and retransmission capability have been added to the dTLS handshake.

Figure 7-13 shows a high level overview of the message flows in a dTLS handshake from the perspective of two TelePresence endpoints, both functioning as client and server to each other.

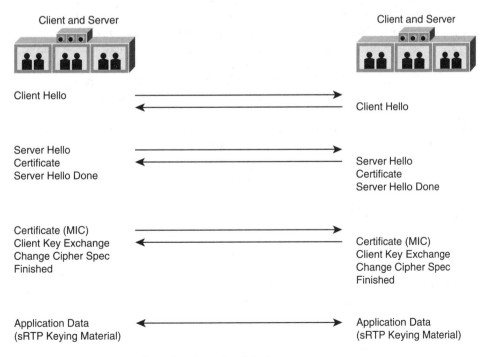

Figure 7-13 *Message flows for dTLS handshake*

The first difference that should be noted from the TLS handshake shown in Figure 7-11 is that the dTLS handshake occurs directly between the TelePresence endpoints. There is no "transitive trust" issue where the SIP B2BUA within the CUCM participates within the sRTP key exchange and therefore has knowledge of the sRTP keying material. Although this might not be a significant issue in a TelePresence deployment within a single corporate entity, it is important from a business-to-business TelePresence perspective; where additional components such as Session Border Controllers (SBCs) are outside the administrative control of the corporate entity. This issue is discussed further in Chapter 14, "Intercompany TelePresence Design."

Only the TelePresence primary codecs perform dTLS handshakes. Because all voice and video media originate from the primary codec during a TelePresence meeting, sRTP keying material needs to be exchanged only between primary codecs and not their associated IP 7975G phones. However, because both voice and video media streams exist, two dTLS handshakes occur—one over each media stream—and keying material is exchanged for encryption of both the voice and the video media. This was not shown in Figure 7-13. Future versions of Cisco TelePresence might include additional key exchange mechanisms such as the sRTP Encrypted Key Transport (EKT), as well.

Bandwidth Impact of Enabling TelePresence Encryption

Because the average TelePresence voice RTP packet is approximately 220 bytes in size before using sRTP, the use of encryption represents an increase in voice packet size of roughly 4.5%. Because the average TelePresence video RTP packet is approximately 1,100 bytes in size; use of encryption represents an increase in video packet size of only about 0.9%. Because the amount of video traffic greatly exceeds the amount of voice traffic in terms of bandwidth usage during a TelePresence meeting, the effect of enabling sRTP on the overall bandwidth utilization estimates for TelePresence meetings is considered negligible. The use of SIP over TLS does result in an increase in packet sizes and number of packets sent for SIP signaling between the TelePresence endpoints and CUCM server. However, the amount of SIP signaling messages sent between devices is also considered negligible from a bandwidth perspective compared to the amount of video traffic. Therefore, the rough estimate of approximately 20% network protocol overhead for TelePresence meetings is considered to hold for both encrypted and non-encrypted calls.

Secure Shell (SSH)

Secure Shell (SSH) is a protocol that provides confidentiality, host authentication, and data integrity between two hosts. SSH operates in client/server mode across the network, typically using TCP port 22. The protocol was intended originally as a secure alternative to protocols such as Telnet, which sends passwords in clear text across network. The most current version of secure shell, SSH-2, is defined under IETF RFC 4250 through RFC-4256.

SSH-2 defines three layers within the protocol:

■ **The transport layer:** Responsible for the initial key exchange (typically via Diffie-Hellman); server authentication (typically via public-key cryptography); and setting up encryption, message authentication, and optionally compression. Although not specified within SSH-2, encryption is typically done through bulk symmetric-key encryption algorithms such as 3DES and AES. Message authentication is accomplished via strong message authentication codes (MACs).

■ **The user authentication layer:** Authenticates the end-user via methods such as passwords, public key cryptography, or one-time password tokens. The user authentication layer relies on the transport layer.

■ **The connection layer:** The connection layer allows multiple channels to be supported across a single SSH connection; thus, the connection layer relies on the user authentication layer.

Cisco CTS endpoints (CTS-3200s, CTS-3000s, CTS-1000s, and CTS-500s), the Cisco TelePresence Manager (CTS-MAN), and the CTMS all support SSH-2 connectivity. This provides an additional means of securely managing TelePresence endpoints in addition to the normal administrative web interface that can be accessed via Secure HTTP (HTTPS). When accessing TelePresence endpoints via SSH, the administrator userid and password utilized for the administrative web interface are also used for SSH access.

Secure Hypertext Transfer Protocol (HTTPS)

Secure Hypertext Transfer Protocol (HTTPS) is simply the Hypertext Transfer Protocol (HTTP) secured through the use of either SSL or TLS. HTTPS is discussed in informational IETF RFC 2818 and typically uses TCP port 443. Because HTTP is a well-known client/server protocol used for access to resources through a web browser, it will not be covered in detail within this chapter. Read IETF RFC 2616 regarding HTTP v1.1 if you are not familiar with the protocol operation.

Cisco CTS endpoints (CTS-3200s, CTS-3000s, CTS-1000s, and CTS-500s), the Cisco TelePresence Manager (CTS-MAN), and the CTMS all support HTTPS connectivity for web-based device management. Because HTTPS is based on SSL / TLS security, digital certificates are used to authenticate the CTS endpoint to the client web browser. When a client web browser connects to the CTS endpoint, the web server running within the CTS endpoint may send a self-signed certificate to the client. Because this self-signed certificate is not from a trusted root certificate authority, the client web browser might display a warning message, claiming the certificate to be invalid. The end user will need to accept the certificate in this case in order to establish the HTTPS session with the CTS endpoint.

Summary

This chapter has provided a fairly high level overview of some of the various protocols required by the Cisco TelePresence Solution in order to operate over an IP network infrastructure. These protocols were organized into four broad categories:

■ **Network control protocols:** Primarily provide network connectivity and control services for Cisco TelePresence. They include IEEE 802.1p/Q, IEEE 802.3af POE, NTP, and DHCP.

- **Signaling protocols:** Primarily used for scheduling and initiating TelePresence meetings. They include SIP, XML/SOAP, AXL/SOAP, JTAPI over CTIQBE, WebDAV, and LDAP.

- **Network management protocols:** Primarily used for configuring and managing Cisco TelePresence deployments. They include CDP, TFTP, and SNMP.

- **Security protocols:** Primarily used to provide secure communications between TelePresence devices. The secure communications could be for management purposes, signaling, or for the actual media streams themselves. Security protocols include TLS, dTLS, sRTP, SSH, and HTTPS.

Not every protocol utilized by Cisco TelePresence has been discussed within this chapter; however, through reading this chapter, you should have a better understanding of how the Cisco TelePresence Solution makes use of standardized protocols to operate over network infrastructures.

Further Reading

IETF Standards:

Session Initiation Protocol (SIP): http://www.ietf.org/rfc/rfc3261

Trivia File Transfer Protocol (TFTP): http://www.ietf.org/rfc/rfc1350

Dynamic Host Configuration Protocol (DHCP): http://www.ietf.org/rfc/rfc2131

Network Time Protocol (NTP v3): http://www.ietf.org/rfc/rfc1305

Simple Network Management Protocol (SNMP v3): http://www.ietf.org/rfc/rfc3411 - rfc3418

Transport Layer Security (TLS v1.2): http://www.ietf.org/rfc/rfc5246

Datagram Transport Layer Security (dTLS): http://www.ietf.org/rfc/rfc4347

Secure Real-time Transport Protocol (sRTP): http://www.ietf.org/rfc/rfc3711

Secure Shell Protocol (SSH): http://www.ietf.org/rfc/rfc4251

Hypertext Transfer Protocol (HTTP v1.1): http://www.ietf.org/rfc/rfc2616

Web-Based Distributed Authoring and Versioning (WebDAV): http://www.ietf.org/rfc/rfc4918

Lightweight Directory Access Protocol (LDAP): http://www.ietf.org/rfc/rfc4911

HTTP over TLS: http://www.ietf.org/rfc/rfc2818

Encrypted Key Transport for Secure RTP: http://www.tools.ietf.org/id/draft-mcgrew-srtp-ekt-03.txt

IEEE Standards:

IEEE 802.3af (PoE): http://www.standards.ieee.org/getieee802/802.3.html

IEEE 802.1p/Q (COS/VLAN): http://www.standards.ieee.org/getieee802/802.1.html

W3C Standards:

Simple Object Access Protocol (SOAP): http://www.w3.org/TR/soap/

Extensible Markup Language (XML): http://www.w3.org/XML/

Part III: Telepresence System Design

To sufficiently reproduce the experience of a live, in-person, face-to-face meeting, you must design the environment where you install the TelePresence systems to provide a near-perfect replication of lighting, sound, and ambiance. Careful adherence to the design principles and specifications provided here can result in an experience that is so lifelike, realistic, and free from technological distractions that participants can focus 100 percent of their attention on the people they meet with and the meeting content, and experience most of the same emotional and psychological interactions that occur when people meet face-to-face.

Proper design of a TelePresence environment involves a number of different aspects, each of which by itself is critical to the experience, and some aspects are inter-related and can influence each other. For example, even if the network performs perfectly, an improperly lit room can lead to grainy and pixilated video quality. As another example, if the acoustical behavior of the room, such as the amount of ambient noise and reverberation within the environment, is not controlled, the quality of the audio might sound muffled, reverberant, and even choppy, and the audio detection algorithms used to facilitate switching in multipoint meetings could fail, resulting in false switching to a participant who is not speaking, or a failure to switch to a participant who is speaking. Many of the audio and video issues that at first glance might seem to be attributed to system hardware and software quality or network performance can actually be the result of an improperly designed room environment.

Although the examples that illustrate the principles discussed in this chapter are specific to Cisco TelePresence CTS-3000 and CTS-1000 model systems, most of these principles are adaptive and can be applied to any TelePresence system, regardless of the size, shape, number of screens and cameras, or vendor. As the market introduces

CHAPTER 8

TelePresence Room Design

new systems, you need to focus on the principles discussed in this chapter and how you can apply them to each type of system.

This chapter covers the following topics:

- **Room Dimensions, Shape, and Orientation:** Discusses the physical size, shape, and orientation of the room and the location of doors, windows, columns, and furniture within the room.

- **Wall, Floor and Ceiling Surfaces:** Discusses the recommended colors, patterns, and materials of wall, floor, and ceiling surfaces within the room.

- **Lighting and Illumination:** Discusses overall illumination considerations and specific lighting requirements and recommendations.

- **Acoustics:** Discusses the concepts of sound reproduction and the effects of ambient noise and reverberation within the environment and how they are measured.

- **HVAC:** Discusses the heating, ventilation, and air conditioning (HVAC) requirements and the recommended types and locations of air-conditioning registers within the room.

- **Power Requirements:** Discusses power consumption requirements for the equipment and participants and the recommended types and locations of electrical receptacles within the room.

- **Network Connectivity:** Discusses the network connectivity required within the room for the equipment and the participants and the recommended ways to provide network access to the participants.

Room Dimensions, Shape, and Orientation

The primary criteria for selecting a room is to find one that meets the recommended width, depth, and height requirements and is free from obstructions such as pillars and columns. The dimensions also play a critical role in how much lighting is required, how the room appears visually on the screen, and the acoustic properties of the room.

The following sections provide details on each aspect of room dimensions, including width, depth, height, angles, and shapes, such as curved or concaved walls and asymmetric geometries, protruding entrances and vestibules, and the orientation of the TelePresence within the room.

Tip   Each dimensional measurement has minimum, recommended, and maximum values. You should strive to find a room that meets the recommended dimensions for maximum flexibility and performance. Choosing a room that is either too small or too big can have negative side effects as explained within each section.

Width Requirements

The room needs to be wide enough to comfortably fit the TelePresence system and any peripherals that might be located on its left or right sides, with enough extra space on each side for service personnel to access the back of the system to service it. You might also want extra space for furniture, such as cabinets, coffee tables, couches, sofas, or storage space for extra chairs.

Determining Room Width

To begin, find the width of the TelePresence system itself and add at least 1 foot (30.48 centimeters) on each side to enable service personnel to access the sides and back of the system. The Cisco TelePresence CTS-3000, for example, measures precisely 18-feet (5.486-meters) wide. Adding 1 foot (30.48 centimeters) of access space on each side brings the minimum width to 20 feet (6.096 meters). Figure 8-1 illustrates the minimum room width of a CTS-3000.

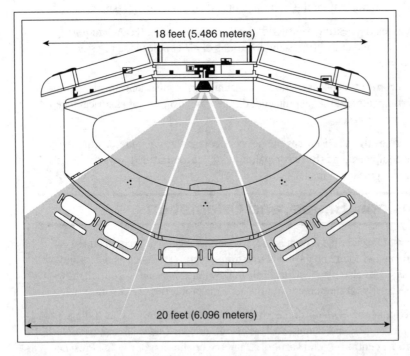

Figure 8-1   *CTS-3000 minimum room width*

The CTS-1000 measures precisely 5.11-feet (1.557-meters) wide. Adding one foot (30.48 centimeters) of access space on each side brings the minimum width to 7.11 feet (2.167 meters). Figure 8-2 illustrates the minimum room width of a CTS-1000.

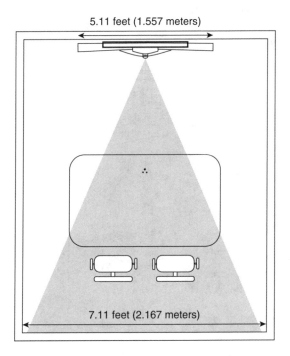

5.11 feet (1.557 meters)

7.11 feet (2.167 meters)

Figure 8-2   *CTS-1000 minimum room width*

Tip   The illustrations in this chapter are not necessarily to scale. The measurements clarify the scale of the objects within the illustrations.

Factoring in Peripherals

The second step is to factor in any additional peripherals such as auxiliary data displays or document cameras that might be located on the left or right sides of the system. Both the CTS-3000 and CTS-1000 systems support the use of auxiliary LCD displays and document cameras for use with the Auto Collaborate feature. You can often find these optional peripherals on the left or right sides of the system to obtain the total width of the system. Following are some specific examples to illustrate how to approach these considerations.

LCD displays come in different sizes and can be mounted to the ceiling above the TelePresence system; mounted to the wall on the left or right sides of the system; mounted to a vertical stand with a base located to the right or left sides of the system; or placed on a piece of furniture such as a cabinet or cart to the right or left sides of the system. The section "Height Requirements," covers ceiling-mounted scenarios in greater detail. This current section focuses on left- and right-side mounting options. Consider the example of a customer who wants to install a 52-inch (132.08 centimeter) Sharp 525U LCD on the left side of the CTS-3000. The 52 inches is the diagonal measurement of the display. The actual width of this particular display is 49.4 inches (125.476 centimeters). The bezel of the display might be a few inches away from the edge of the TelePresence system and might be mounted on a stand that has a slightly wider base than the actual width of the display. The recommendation in this example would be to round up 6 inches to 12 inches (15.24 centimeters to 30.48 centimeters) to allow for flexibility in the exact placement of the display. Figure 8-3 illustrates this arrangement.

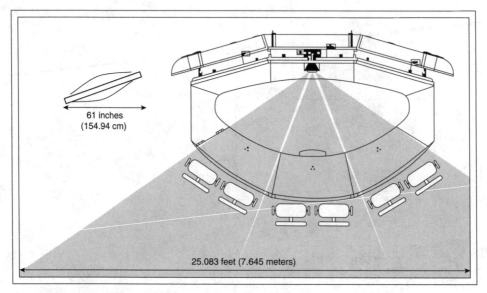

Figure 8-3 *CTS-3000 with optional auxiliary LCD display on left side*

Document cameras can be mounted within the ceiling or located on a flat surface such as a cabinet or table on the left or right sides of the TelePresence system. For the CTS-3000, the optimal solution is to ceiling-mount the document camera above the table where the participants sit. However, on a CTS-1000 it is popular to use a desktop document camera located off to one side or the other. The Wolfvision VZ-9plus Desktop Visualizer, for example, measures 12.6-inches (32.004-centimeters) wide and would likely be located on a cabinet or table surface at least a few inches larger than the actual base of the visualizer. Figure 8-4 illustrates this arrangement, where the cabinet that the WolfVision camera is sitting on measures 2–feet (60.96-centimeters) in width.

Factoring in Additional Participants

The third step is to add enough space for participants sitting on the left or right sides of the TelePresence system. This does not apply to the CTS-3000 model system, but on the CTS-1000 it might come into play depending on the orientation of the system within the room. Figure 8-5 illustrates a CTS-1000 with additional seating on the left and right sides of the table.

The chairs depicted as silhouetted would not be used during an active TelePresence meeting but could be located within the room like this to maximize seating capacity when us-

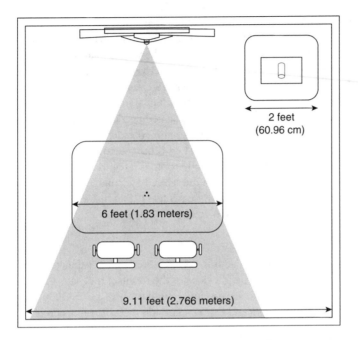

Figure 8-4   *CTS-1000 with optional desktop document camera on right side*

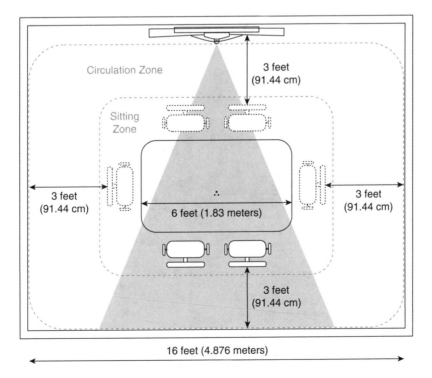

Figure 8-5   *Example of CTS-1000 seating arrangement*

ing the room for non-TelePresence meetings. Interior Design standards specify recommended measurements for the distance from the edge of the table to the back of the participant's chair and from the back of the participant's chair to the wall behind them. These are referred to as the *sitting zone* and *circulation zone*, respectively. The recommended sitting zone is 2 feet (60.96 centimeters), and the recommended circulation zone is 3 feet (91.44 centimeters). The circulation zone provides enough distance for people to get in and out of their chairs and for others to circulate behind a seated participant and accounts for wheelchair accessibility. The third measurement to take into consideration is *elbow room*. Each chair position needs a minimum of 3 feet (91.44 centimeters) of width. For this reason, the recommended table width for a CTS-1000 room is 6 feet (1.828 meters) to comfortably accommodate two participants seated at the table. To accommodate the extra chairs on each side of the table, you need an additional 5 feet (1.524 meters) on both sides of the table, for a total width of 16 feet (4.876 meters).

Factoring in Additional Furniture

The fourth step is to add enough space for any additional furniture, such as cabinetry that might be located along the walls on the left or right sides of the room, extra chairs that might be placed on the side of the room, and so on. Figure 8-6 illustrates a CTS-3000 with cabinets located on the left side of the room and extra chairs stored on the right side of the room.

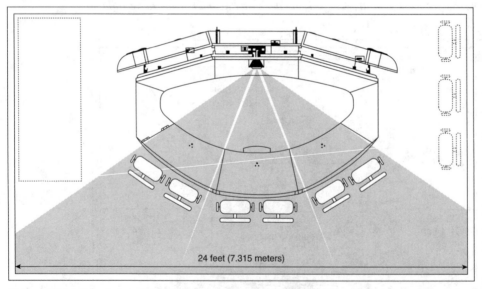

24 feet (7.315 meters)

Figure 8-6   *Example of CTS-3000 with cabinets and extra chairs*

Understanding Maximum Width Constraints

Now that you are aware of the minimum and recommended width requirements, you need to understand why Cisco specifies a maximum width. In the case of width, the maximum recommendation comes primarily from the acoustic effects of reverberation within the room. When the width of the room is significantly wider than the recommended value, sound traveling through the air might take longer to reflect off of the walls, resulting in high levels of reverberation. Mitigating reverberation caused by excessively wide rooms can occur a number of different ways. Of course, you can always build false walls on the left or right sides to reduce the width of the room, but this is not always necessary. You can usually achieve the desired results simply by placing furniture within the room such as overstuffed chairs or couches, or covering portions of the walls in acoustically dampening materials such as fabrics or oil paintings. The section "Acoustics," later in the chapter, covers reverberation in more detail.

The other negative effect of excessively wide rooms is the amount of light needed to sufficiently cover the entire room in even, well-distributed light. Avoid dark areas and shadows, even if they are not within the view of the cameras. The wider the room, the more light fixtures you need to blanket the room in light. The section "Lighting and Illumination," later in the chapter, covers lighting in greater detail.

Width Requirements Summary

Based on all of the information covered in this section, Table 8-1 summarizes the minimum, recommended, and maximum width requirements for the CTS-3000 and CTS-1000 model systems.

Table 8-1   *Minimum, Recommended, and Maximum Room Width for CTS-1000 and CTS-3000*

Model	Minimum Width	Recommended Width	Maximum Width
CTS-3000	20 feet (6.096 meters)	22 feet (6.7056 meters)	31 feet (9.448 meters)
CTS-1000	7.11 feet (2.167 meters)	12 feet (3.657 meters)	20 feet (6.096 meters)

Depth Requirements

The room should be deep enough to comfortably fit the TelePresence system, with enough extra space behind the participants for people to walk to and from their seats. You might also want extra space for furniture, such as cabinets and sofas, or for extra chairs behind the primary participants.

Determining Room Depth

To begin, find the depth of the TelePresence system and add at least 5 feet (1.524 meters) past the edge of the table to allow for minimum seating and circulation zones. The CTS-3000, for example, measures precisely 10.07 feet (3.069 meters) from the back of the light façade structure to the edge of the table, and recommended specifications dictate that it be installed at least 12 inches (30.48 centimeters) away from the wall to allow service personnel to access the back of the system. Adding 5 feet (1.524 meters) beyond the table edge for the participant's chairs and a circulation zone behind them brings the minimum depth to 16 feet (4.876 meters). Figure 8-7 illustrates the minimum room depth of a CTS-3000.

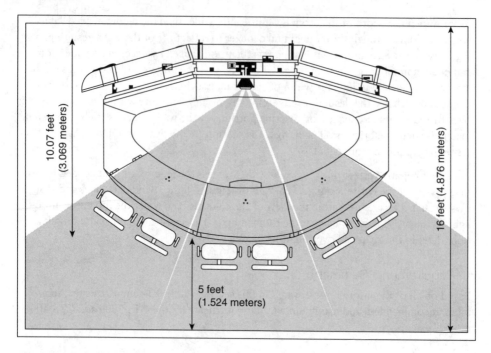

Figure 8-7   *CTS-3000 minimum room depth*

The CTS-1000 is a little different because it does not include an integrated table, so the customer must supply a table and must understand how far away the table should be placed from the system. The system itself measures precisely 9 inches (22.86-centimeters) deep and is bolted flush to the wall. But the distance from the camera to the edge of the table is a critical measurement because the camera on the CTS-1000 has a fixed focal length and depth of field. If the participants sit too close to the system, they will appear out of focus, and the vertical angle of the camera to their faces will be skewed, resulting in a distorted view. Likewise, if they sit too far away from the system, they will also be out of focus and will appear smaller than life size. The distance from the camera to the edge of the table should be precisely 8.5 feet (2.59 meters). Adding 5 feet (1.524 meters) beyond the table edge for the participants' chairs and a circulation zone behind them brings the minimum depth to 14.25 feet (4.343 meters). Figure 8-8 illustrates the minimum room depth of a CTS-1000.

Caution   The minimum depth is a critical measurement that should not be compromised.

It is common for customers to want to sacrifice the service access zone behind the system or the circulation zone behind the participants' chairs to fit the system into a room that is slightly smaller than the minimum measurements previously specified. For example, many customers have asked if the CTS-3000 can be made to fit within a room that is only 14-feet (4.267 meters) deep, or a CTS-1000 into a room that is only 10-feet (3.048 meters) deep. However, you need to understand several critical aspects that should dissuade you from doing this.

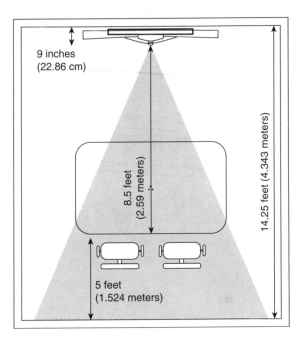

Figure 8-8   *CTS-1000 minimum room depth*

Camera Focal Length and Depth of Field Considerations

First, the focal length and depth of field of the cameras on the CTS-3000 and CTS-1000 model systems are precisely designed to capture a subject that is 8.5 feet to 14.5 feet (2.59 to 4.419 meters) away from the camera. When the wall is too close behind the seated participants, it has two negative side effects:

■   The participants appear "painted" onto the wall behind them because you have no depth between them and the wall.

■   The wall appears to be "crawling" because it's so close to the camera that it is within the depth of field, and the pattern of the wall surface is visible on camera. Even relatively smooth wall surfaces such as painted gypsum drywall exhibit this behavior.

In addition to these two visual side effects, the walls become marred and scratched over time from participants bumping the backs of their chairs up against them.

Camera Vertical Viewing Angle Considerations

Second, the vertical angle of the camera's field of view is designed to be precisely 7 degrees above the participants' eyes (give or take a degree or two to accommodate different people's heights when seated). This provides optimal vertical eye gaze alignment. On the CTS-3000, it is not possible to sit too close to the camera because it comes with an integrated table, but on the CTS-1000, if the participants sit too close to the system, they appear out of focus and too low on the screen. The natural inclination is for the installer to adjust the vertical angle of the camera slightly downward and pull the focus as far in as it will go to get the participants within the camera's field of view. By angling the camera down, however, you distort the angle of the camera to the subject resulting in a "down-ward" appearance of the participant on screen and a misalignment of the vertical eye gaze. Figure 8-9 illustrates this concept.

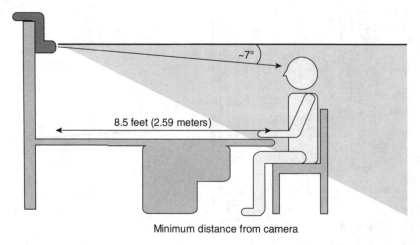

Minimum distance from camera

Figure 8-9 *CTS-1000 minimum distance from camera*

Factoring in Additional Furniture, Seating Capacity, and Wall Adornments Behind the Participants

Now that you understand the absolute minimum depth requirements, consider the space required for optional furniture, extra seating, and wall adornments in the back of the room behind the primary participants. It is highly desirable that customers consider doing this because placing adornments and furniture behind the participants creates a sensation of "depth" on the screen and makes the participants and their environment look as lifelike as possible. You might want to place cabinetry or artwork on the back wall, some couches or overstuffed chairs for decorative purposes, or a combination of both. Figure 8-10 illustrates these concepts.

Tip If you add furniture and adornments to provide the sensation of depth within the view of the camera, take caution to choose patterns and colors that look good on camera and complement people's skin tones. Avoid highly reflective surfaces such as glass picture frames and certain colors such as deep reds and mahoganies or extremely bright colors such as fluorescent signs. The section "Wall Surfaces," later in the chapter, covers this in more detail.

Understanding Maximum Depth Constraints

The last thing to consider is the maximum room depth. As with the maximum width discussed previously, the maximum depth requirement is due primarily to lighting and acoustic considerations, although the lighting consideration is even more severe in this case because the back wall is within the view of the cameras, making shadows and dark areas even more pronounced and undesirable. In addition, objects further than 15 feet

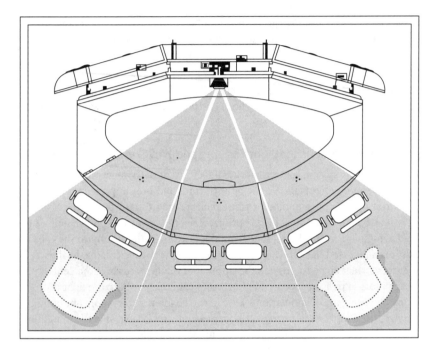

Figure 8-10 *CTS-3000 with cabinet and chairs along back wall*

(4.572 meters) or so away from the cameras will become increasingly out of focus. There-fore, although it is desirable to have slightly more than the minimum depth to allow for the placement of furniture and artwork to create the sensation of depth in the image, if the room is too deep, this will backfire on you because the objects on the back wall will be completely out of focus.

Depth Requirements Summary

Based on all the preceding information, Table 8-2 summarizes the minimum, recommended, and maximum depth requirements for the CTS-3000 and CTS-1000 model systems.

Table 8-2 *Minimum, Recommended, and Maximum Room Depth*

Model	Minimum Depth	Recommended Depth	Maximum Depth
CTS-3000	16 feet (4.876 meters)	20 feet (6.096 meters)	23 feet (7.01 meters)
CTS-1000	14.5 feet (4.419 meters)	16 feet (4.876 meters)	20 feet (6.096 meters)

Height Requirements

The ceiling height of the room should be high enough to comfortably fit the TelePresence system and any peripherals that might be located above the system and be within local construction codes for fire suppression systems, suspended light fixtures, and so on.

These codes vary by location and the age of the building, but in general, a minimum ceiling height of 8 feet (2.438 meters) is necessary for a TelePresence system.

Determining Room Height

To begin, find the height of the TelePresence system. The CTS-3000, for example, measures precisely 6.76-feet (2.060-meters) high. The CTS-1000 measures precisely 6.48-feet (1.975-meters) high.

Vertical Clearance Considerations for Light Fixtures and Fire Suppression Systems

However, the height of the system is not the critical factor that determines the minimum ceiling height. What's more important are the light fixtures and fire suppression systems. Suspended light fixtures require a minimum vertical clearance from the top of the fixture to the ceiling from which it hangs to achieve optimal reflectivity of the light bouncing off the ceiling, and a minimum vertical clearance from the bottom of the fixture to the tops of people's heads. Even recessed light fixtures have a minimum vertical clearance to throw the light out at the correct angle to provide the optimal coverage pattern. If the ceiling is too low, even the most-expensive recessed light fixture cannot distribute the light properly. The section "Lighting and Illumination," later in the chapter, covers more about light fixtures. Likewise, fire suppression systems have regulations that determine the minimum vertical clearance from the sprinkler head to the equipment and people below it. Consult your local city or state ordinances to understand this better.

Factoring in Vertical Clearance for Peripherals

Second, additional peripherals such as auxiliary data displays or document cameras might be located in the ceiling or suspended from the ceiling. Both the CTS-3000 and CTS-1000 systems support the use of optional LCD displays that you can mount to the ceiling above the system or locate on the right or left sides of the system. If the LCD display is above the system, you need to allow sufficient space between the light façade structure of the system and the ceiling to accommodate the additional overhead display.

Consider the example of a customer who wants to install a 40-inch (101.6-centimeter) NEC 4010-BK LCD display mounted to the ceiling above the CTS-3000. The 40 inches is the diagonal measurement of the display. The actual height of this particular display is 24 inches (60.96 centimeters), and you might want to leave a couple of inches between the bottom bezel of the LCD display and the top edge of the TelePresence system to allow for flexibility in the exact vertical placement of the display. Figure 8-11 illustrates this arrangement.

However, note that in Figure 8-11, if you suspend light fixtures that hang down 24 inches (60.96 centimeters) below the ceiling, they might obstruct the participants' view of the overhead LCD display. Therefore, the ceiling must be high enough so that the angle of the participants' view of the LCD display clears the bottom of the light fixture by a comfortable number of inches (centimeters).

Document cameras, such as LCD displays, can also be mounted from, or within, the ceiling. You can install the Wolfvision VZ-32 Ceiling Visualizer, for example, within a plenum housing recessed within a dropped ceiling, or from a pole in situations where recessing it

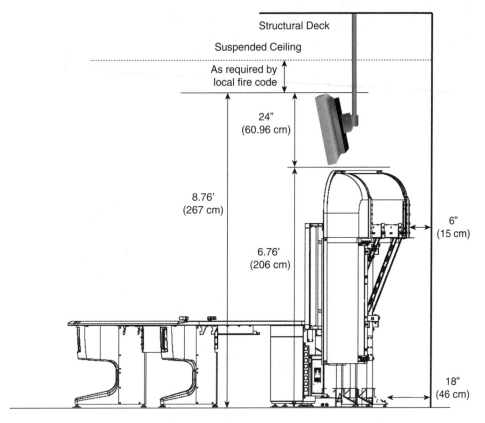

Figure 8-11   *CTS-3000 with optional auxiliary LCD display on top*

is not an option. In either case, the Wolfvision VZ-32 Ceiling Visualizer has a minimum height requirement to properly capture a document or other object located on the table surface of the TelePresence system. This is because you must install this particular camera at an 18-degree angle from the area of table it will be capturing. Figure 8-12 illustrates this arrangement.

Tip   Mount the Visualizer to the structural deck in such a way as to eliminate vibrations. Vibrations caused by Heating, Ventilation, and Air Conditioning (HVAC) systems can cause the image on the Visualizer to "shake." Refer to the manufacturer's documentation for recommended ceiling installation procedures.

Based on all the preceding information, the recommended ceiling height of a Cisco TelePresence CTS-3000 and CTS-1000 room is 10 to 12 feet (3.048 to 3.657 meters).

Understanding Maximum Height Constraints

The last thing to consider is the maximum ceiling height. Like the maximum width and depth discussed previously, the maximum height is primarily a function of lighting and

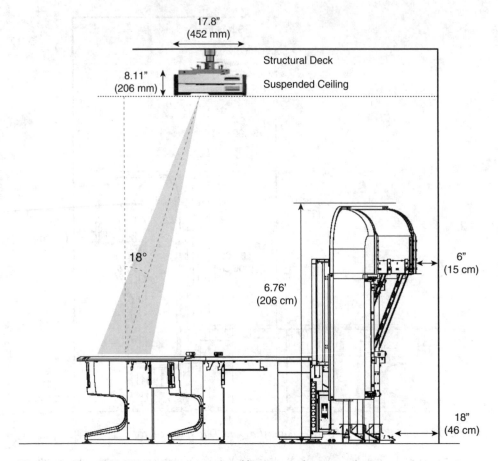

Figure 8-12 *CTS-3000 with optional wolfVision ceiling visualizer*

acoustic considerations. Excessively high ceilings might make it extremely difficult to provide the correct amount of light throughout the room and might cause severe shadowing and dark areas, which must be avoided. Light fixtures take advantage of the reflective properties of the ceiling material (for example, the ceiling tiles of a dropped ceiling reflect light off their surface) to allow light emitted from the fixture to be spread evenly throughout the room. Likewise, the ceiling materials also reflect some percentage of sound. If the sound takes a long time to travel to and from the ceiling, it can result in high levels of reverberation within the room.

The most effective method of mitigating a ceiling that is too high is to install a dropped ceiling to reduce its height. However, if the ceiling is only a few feet too high, to mitigate lighting and acoustic issues, it might be adequate to simply use higher wattage bulbs in your light fixtures and use ceiling tiles that have a high Noise Reduction Coefficient (NRC) Rating to reduce reverberation. The sections "Lighting and Illumination" and "Acoustics" cover more about light fixtures and reverberation. You might need to consult a lighting expert to determine the most optimal type and quantity of light fixtures and bulb wattage required based on the height of your ceiling.

Height Requirements Summary

Based on all of the preceding information, Table 8-3 summarizes the minimum, recommended, and maximum height requirements for the CTS-3000 and CTS-1000 model systems.

Table 8-3 *Minimum, Recommended, and Maximum Room Height*

Minimum Height	Recommended Height	Maximum Height
8 feet (2.438 meters)	10 feet (3.048 meters)	12 to 14 feet (3.657 to 4.267 meters)

Angles, Shape, and Orientation

Rooms are not always square or rectangular in shape, often have protruding entrances, vestibules, or columns, and the walls can be curved or concaved. Walls and ceilings can also be vertically or horizontally asymmetrical.

These types of geometric patterns can be good or bad, depending on the orientation of the TelePresence system within the room. Consider the three primary factors:

■ How angles and shapes within the field of view of the camera appear on screen

■ Whether obstructions, such as protruding entrances and columns, interfere with the location of the TelePresence system within the room

■ How the acoustics might be affected by curved, concaved, or asymmetric wall and ceiling angles

Considering the Effects of Protruding Walls

First, consider how objects appear within the camera's field of view. Figures 8-13 and 8-14 illustrate the horizontal and vertical fields of view on the CTS-3000.

From a top-down perspective (horizontal field of view), the cameras capture a portion of the side walls and the entire back of the room. From the side perspective (vertical field of view), the cameras capture everything from just above the participants' heads all the way down to the baseboards and even the floor, depending on how far away the back wall is from the cameras. Refer back to the "Depth Requirements" section in this chapter for guidance on how deep the room should be.

The point of these illustrations is to highlight that everything within the camera's field of view will show up on screen. Vertical and horizontal lines and shapes on the walls and floor can appear on camera and be distracting; inverted corners can cause undesirable shadowing because light from the ceiling fixtures might not reach it; and protruding walls can interfere with the placement of the system.

For example, consider what would happen if a protruding wall or column were placed within the room. Figure 8-15 illustrates this arrangement.

Not only would this protruding wall become an obstacle for the two participants seated on the right side of the system and interfere with the circulation zone behind them, but

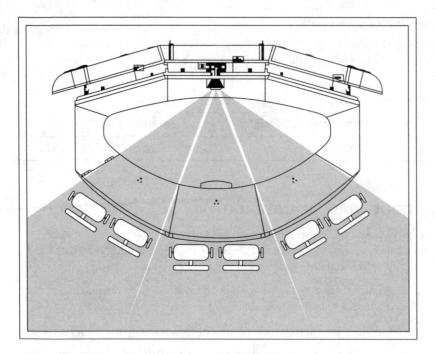

Figure 8-13   *CTS-3000 horizontal field of view*

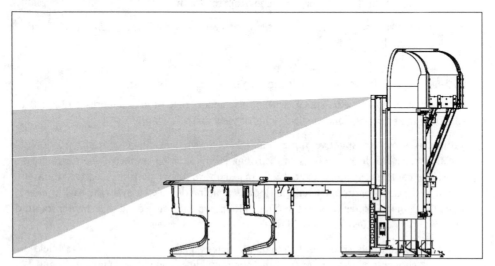

Figure 8-14   *CTS-3000 vertical field of view*

also the vertical edges of the wall would appear on camera and could be distracting. Most important, in this particular example, the corners where the back and side walls meet the protruding wall will likely be darker than the other wall surfaces because light from the ceiling fixtures will not illuminate them as well. Depending on the dimensions of the room, it might be possible to reorient the system to avoid this situation. Figure 8-16

24 feet (7.315 meters)

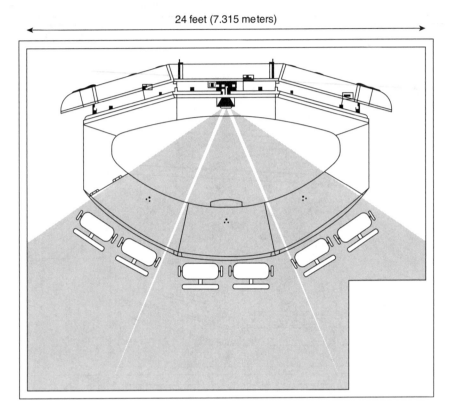

Figure 8-15 *CTS-3000 with protruding wall within the horizontal field of view*

illustrates one example of how this can be achieved, provided that the walls are wide enough the fit the system and depending on the location of the door.

This example arrangement sacrifices access to the back of the system from the left side of the system to place the system as close to the middle of the room as possible, but access is still available from the right side, so it might be the best compromise in this example. This arrangement also leaves no room on the left or right sides of the system for optional peripherals such as auxiliary LCD displays; however, if the ceiling is high enough, the customer might opt to mount the auxiliary LCD display from the ceiling above the system. Also, depending on the location of the door, this arrangement might not be possible at all, or the door would need to be moved to an alternative location. The customer must weigh the pros and cons of these trade-offs. The best solution might be to simply find a different room or investigate how much it would cost to have the protruding wall removed.

Considering the Effects of Curved and Concave Walls

Next, consider the effect of curved and concaved wall surfaces. Depending on their shape and the orientation of the system within the room, curved and concaved wall surfaces can produce unfavorable acoustic side effects because sound reverberating off their surfaces could converge at a certain place within the room. Figure 8-17 illustrates an example of this effect.

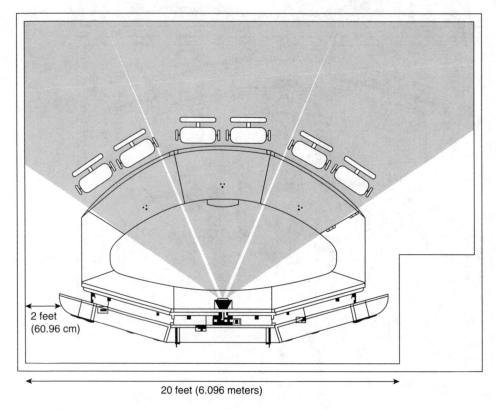

2 feet
(60.96 cm)

20 feet (6.096 meters)

Figure 8-16   *CTS-3000 reoriented to eliminate protruding wall*

The arrows within the diagram illustrate how sound emanating from the system reflects off the walls in such a way that it converges in the center of the room. Reverberation levels in the center are higher than on the outsides, which can throw off the echo-cancellation algorithms of the system and cause a negative acoustic experience for the participants. Simple tactics for reducing this effect include placing furniture or hanging acoustic-dampening material, such as fabrics or oil paintings, on or near the back wall to either absorb the sound or cause it to reflect in a different direction. The section "Acoustics" later in the chapter, covers reverberation in greater detail.

Considering the Effects of Asymmetric Wall and Ceiling Angles

Finally, consider the effect of asymmetric wall and ceiling angles. Walls can be asymmetrical both vertically (the angle of the wall from floor to ceiling is not straight up and down) or horizontally (the length of the wall goes in toward the room or out away from the room at an angle). Ceilings can also be at asymmetrical angles. Figures 8-18 and 8-19 illustrate asymmetric wall surfaces from a top-down and side perspective.

These types of geometries can actually have a positive effect on the acoustic properties of the room because sound emanating from the system reflects in different directions. However, the wall surfaces that appear within the camera's field of view might be at odd

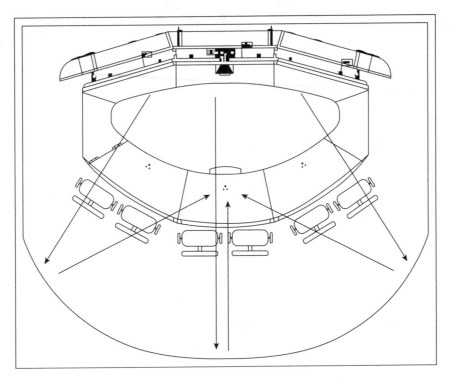

Figure 8-17 *CTS-3000 with concaved wall surfaces*

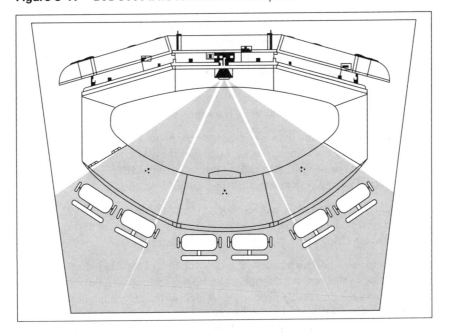

Figure 8-18 *CTS-3000 with horizontally asymmetric wall surfaces*

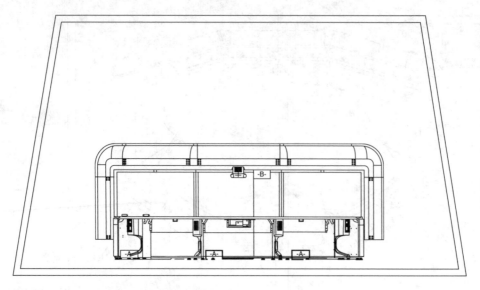

Figure 8-19   *CTS-3000 with vertically asymmetric wall surfaces*

angles and end up being a distraction. You might also find it more difficult to achieve a consistent level of illumination along the wall surfaces because of the odd-shaped corners.

Doors and Windows

The primary goal is to keep all doors and windows outside of the view of the cameras. However, this is not always possible and should not be considered a strict requirement. Doors should ideally be located so as to maximize the circulation zone around partici-pants' chairs and should not be located behind or on the sides of the system. Figure 8-20 illustrates the recommended door locations on a CTS-3000.

The ideal arrangement is to have a vestibule, although this is seldom feasible given standard conference room dimensions. Figure 8-21 illustrates an example vestibule arrangement.

Remember that any surface within the view of the cameras should be made of a material that looks good on camera and complements the décor of the room. Therefore, steel and wood grain doors should be avoided, particularly if they are within the view of the cam-eras. Painted surfaces free of any distracting textures are the best choice.

Door jambs should be sealed to block ambient sound from outside the room from leaking through the cracks in the door jamb or the space underneath the door. The section "Acoustics," later in the chapter, covers ambient noise in greater detail.

Cover windows, regardless of their location, to block out all sunlight and reduce acoustic reverberation. Windows that face the interior of the building and do not allow any sun-light into the room do not necessarily need to be covered, although you might still want to do so for purposes of acoustics and aesthetics. When windows are within the view of the cameras, special care needs to be taken to choose a window covering that looks good on camera. Horizontal and vertical blinds are not recommended. Loose, billowy drapes

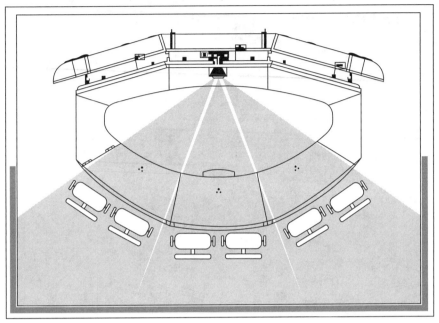

▬▬▬▬▬▬ **Recommended door and window locations**

Figure 8-20 *CTS-3000 recommended door locations*

and curtains are also not the best choice. Drapes made from a straight or taut material are the most suitable and should ideally be a solid color, free of any distracting patterns or textures, look good on camera, and complement the décor of the room.

Wall, Floor, and Ceiling Surfaces

Now that you have an idea of the necessary size, shape, and orientation of a TelePresence room, the following sections discuss the importance of colors, textures, patterns, and the acoustical behavior of the wall, floor, and ceiling surfaces within the environment.

Wall Surfaces

The color, Light Reflectivity Value (LRV), texture, and patterns of visible wall surfaces greatly influence the quality of the video experience and the capability of the TelePresence system to accurately reproduce human skin tones. In addition, certain wall surface materials provide better acoustic behavior than others. Some materials reflect sound, whereas others absorb it. The most common types of wall surface construction materials are gypsum drywall, wood paneling, brick or cinder block, and glass.

Considering Surface Pattern and Texture

The first element to consider is the pattern and texture of the material. The patterns and textures of wood grain surfaces and brick and cinder block materials can create odd visual disturbances in the video and therefore should be avoided on all wall surfaces that are

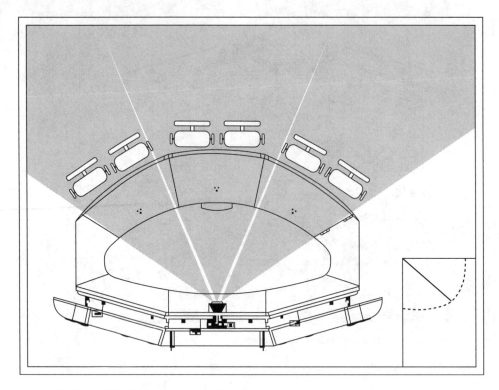

Figure 8-21 *CTS-3000 with vestibule entry way*

within the camera's field of view. Likewise, surfaces with horizontal or vertical lines, such as wood paneling, should ideally be avoided. Finally, surfaces with busy patterns such as wallpaper are discouraged. The optimal choice is painted gypsum drywall.

Considering Surface Acoustic Properties

The second aspect is the acoustic behavior of the material. The wall surfaces should absorb sound from within the room and from outside the room. Sound emanating from within the room should be absorbed by the wall material rather than reverberate off of it. The amount of sound reflected by a material is the Noise Reduction Coefficient (NRC). The higher the NRC rating, the more sound is absorbed by the material. In addition, sound emanating from within the room should not transfer through the wall material, nor should sound emanating from outside the room transfer through the wall material into the room. The amount of sound absorbed as it penetrates through a material is the Sound Transmission Class (STC). The higher the STC rating, the more sound is absorbed as it passes through the walls. This also applies to doors and windows. Doors should be solid, not hollow, and the door jambs should be sealed to reduce the amount of noise allowed to transfer through the cracks around the sides, top, and under the door. The section "Acoustics," later in the chapter, covers NRC and STC ratings in greater detail.

Although wood and gypsum drywall tend to absorb sound, materials such as brick or cinder block and glass surfaces tend to reflect sound. Finished wood surfaces such as paneling can also be highly reflective. Therefore, even if the wall surface in question is outside the view of the cameras, it might still be undesirable from an acoustical perspective. However, an acoustically reflective surface on one side of the room can be offset by an acoustically absorptive surface on another, so just because the material is acoustically reflective does not mean you shouldn't use it in certain portions of the room for its aesthetic appeal.

Considering Surface Color and Light Reflectivity Value

The third aspect is the color and Light Reflectivity Value (LRV) of the surface. LRV is a measure of how much light is reflected off a painted surface and, conversely, how much is absorbed. Figure 8-22 illustrates a simple LRV scale.

LRV Scale

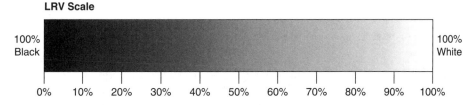

Figure 8-22   *Light Reflectivity Value (LRV) scale*

Depending on the amount of pigment within the paint, deep, dark colors tend to absorb certain light spectrums while reflecting others. For example, a cherry or mahogany wood desk or cabinet can create a reddish hue on objects within the camera's field of view and cause certain people's skin tones to look too red. Other colors can give people a greenish or yellowish hue making them look ill. People who work with cameras and video equipment, such as studio camera crews, newscasters, and the like know full well the effects that different paint colors have on people's skin tones. The behavior of the paint color also depends on the color temperature and intensity of the light within the room. The section "Lighting and Illumination," later in this chapter, provides more detail about light color temperature and luminosity.

For the uninitiated, rather than delving into the theory behind these concepts and expecting TelePresence customers to become overnight experts in paint colors, Cisco has attempted to simplify this entire issue by defining a palette of recommended colors to choose from that provide optimal flesh tone depiction within the Cisco-specific camera, codec, and plasma technology. For the specific color temperature and luminosity of a CTS-3000 or CTS-1000 environment, Cisco has found that the best choice of paint colors are those that are of a neutral tone, are chromatically tame, and fall within an LRV range of 18 to 20 percent. Other TelePresence vendors and even future models of Cisco TelePresence solutions might provide slightly different color recommendations based on the design of their systems and the type of virtual experience they want to create. For example, a TelePresence solution designed for a doctor's office or a hospital's surgery room, or a solution designed for a presenter on stage in front of a virtual audience might have radically different paint color and lighting recommendations.

However, because of the vast number of different color systems and paint manufacturers throughout the world, it has not been possible for Cisco to specify exact color reference indexes on a global level. Therefore, Cisco took the approach of selecting several paint colors from Benjamin Moore and providing those as "example" recommended colors. The list that follows provides the currently recommended Benjamin Moore colors:

- Wilmington Tan: HC-34

- Huntington Beige: HC-21

- Woodstock Tan: HC-20

- Cork: 2153-40

- Classic Caramel: 1118

- Fairmont Gold: 1071

- Peach Brandy: 112

Tip Do not rely on electronic or printed color samples. Computer monitors and printers are not calibrated to accurately reproduce these colors; therefore, these should be considered as examples only. Customers are encouraged to order physical color samples (also known as color swatches) from Benjamin Moore and take those to their local paint supplier to have them matched.

Considering Surfaces in Camera Field of View

The last item to discuss is any other wall surface treatments or adornments that might be within the camera's field of view. This includes door and window frames, cabinetry, recessions and other aesthetic wall construction, paintings, signs and company logos, or any other object that has a surface that is within the camera's field of view. The same principles of color, texture, and pattern described previously apply to these objects as well. In addition, avoid bright contrasts, such as neon lights within a sign or company logo, and reflective surfaces, such as glass picture frames and dry-erase boards; however, some amount of contrast is encouraged. For example, window treatments, a company logo, or an oil painting that complements the look and feel of the room can provide just the right amount of contrast to complement a large surface of painted gypsum drywall.

Flooring Surfaces

The type of flooring material used within the TelePresence room can greatly affect the acoustical experience of the system. The most common types of flooring surface material are carpet, wood, tile and marble, and raised plenum floors. To be blunt, all materials other than carpet are terrible from an acoustic perspective and should be covered with carpeting. This can be an unfortunate yet necessary step for customers who have invested a lot of money installing beautiful marble floors or those wanting to install a TelePresence system in a room that has a raised plenum floor. There are two aspects to the acoustic behavior of flooring materials that you need to consider:

- The amount of ambient sound that bounces off the surface versus being absorbed by the surface is the Noise Reduction Coefficient (NRC). All flooring surfaces have an

NRC rating assigned to them. The higher the NRC rating, the more sound is absorbed by the surface. Carpet provides the highest NRC rating of all flooring surfaces.

- The amount of noise created by walking on the surface. This is the Impact Insulation Class (IIC) and is also commonly referred to as *foot fall*. All flooring surfaces have an IIC rating assigned to them. The clicking and thumping sounds produced when people walk across a floor surface can reverberate throughout the room. This is especially important for raised plenum floors because the sounds reverberate within the hollow space underneath the floor.

Note The section "Acoustics," later in this chapter, covers NRC and IIC ratings in more detail.

Consider the type of carpet you should use, given that carpet is the inevitable choice:

- Portions of the carpet might be visible within the camera's field of view, depending on the depth of the room. (Refer back to Figure 8-14 in the Depth Requirements section earlier in this chapter.) Therefore, the same principles discussed in the previous section for paint colors, textures, and patterns apply to this portion of floor surface as well. You need to choose a color for your carpet that looks good on camera, is complementary to the rest of the room, and is free of loud or busy patterns. If the carpet is not within the field of view of the camera, you are free to choose whatever colors and patterns suit your artistic desires, although most corporate environments tend to use warm or neutral tones.

- The carpet should not be excessively thick or else the participants will have difficulty rolling their chairs in and out from the table. Standard industrial-strength, short carpeting, typical of what is found in the average corporate conference room is recommended.

- The carpet does not have to be laid in one solid piece. You can use tiled carpet that is applied in sections. This is especially useful on raised plenum floors so that you can still access the floor tiles to run conduit or cabling. However, tiled carpeting can tend to wear around the edges because of foot traffic, so you need to consider how and where it is applied and solicit the advice of a carpeting expert for assistance.

Ceiling Surfaces

The type of ceiling material used within the TelePresence room can greatly affect the acoustical experience of the system and the illumination. The most common type of ceiling material in corporate environments is dropped ceiling tiles (also known as suspended ceilings). However, metal, wood, gypsum drywall, and cement ceiling surfaces are also found in some locations.

Before analyzing different ceiling materials, it is worth stating that every TelePresence room, regardless of size, needs a ceiling over it. This might seem like an odd thing to say, but some customers have tried to install TelePresence systems in rooms that have an open ceiling. For example, this has been an issue when attempting to demonstrate a TelePresence system in a trade show environment such as a convention center where they build a booth to contain the system.

A ceiling is necessary for two reasons:

■   To isolate the room from outside noise, such as foot traffic and conversations in adjacent rooms and hallways.

■   Overhead, ceiling-mounted light fixtures are mandatory to provide the proper levels of ambient light throughout the room.

Trade show environments have special ceiling considerations because anytime you put a ceiling over something, all sorts of fire and electrical codes come into play. These subjects are outside the scope of this book. You should consult a company that specializes in constructing trade show booths for details.

Dropped ceilings with removable tiles provide the best acoustical and illumination performance. They also provide the most flexibility for rearranging objects within the ceiling such as light fixtures, air conditioning registers, ceiling-mounted document cameras, and the like. However, dropped ceilings might not be possible if the height of the ceiling is too low. Customers should be aware of the negative consequences and what features they might lose by installing a system in a room that does not have a dropped ceiling. After reviewing this section and referring back to the "Room Height Requirements" section previously in this chapter, when you take all factors into perspective, the best choice might be to find an alternative room.

Two primary considerations when choosing a ceiling material follow:

■   **Acoustic properties:** How much sound is absorbed by the ceiling material?

■   **Reflectivity:** How much light is reflected off the ceiling surface?

Considering the Acoustic Properties of the Ceiling

First, the ceiling material should absorb sound from within the room and from outside the room. Sound emanating from within the room should be absorbed by the ceiling material rather than reflecting off of it. The amount of sound absorbed by a material is the Noise Reduction Coefficient (NRC). The higher the NRC rating, the more sound is absorbed by the material, which, in turn, reduces the amount of acoustic reverberation within the room. In addition, sound emanating from within the room should not transfer through the ceiling material, nor should sound emanating from outside the room transfer through the ceiling material into the room. The amount of sound absorbed as it penetrates through a material is the Sound Transmission Class (STC). The higher the STC rating, the more sound is absorbed as it permeates through the ceiling. These concepts are further explained in the "Acoustics" section later in this chapter. Ceiling tiles with an NRC rating of .80 or greater and an STC rating of 60 or greater are recommended, as described in Table 8-4 and illustrated in Figures 8-40 and 8-41.

Considering the Light Reflectivity of the Ceiling

Second, as discussed in the "Lighting and Illumination" section, the goal of the light fixtures in the ceiling is to fill the room with just the right amount of ambient light. The ceiling material chosen can either complement or detract from this goal. Ceiling materials that are bright in color tend to reflect light off their surface, allowing the light fixtures in the ceiling to reach their full potential. Conversely, ceiling materials that are dark in color tend to absorb light, reducing the effectiveness of the light fixtures in the ceiling and making it more difficult to achieve the proper amount of illumination within the room. Ceiling tiles illustrated that are white or beige in color are reflective in nature. A surface that is too reflective can cause the amount of light bouncing off the ceiling to be uncomfortably bright. The reflectivity of the ceiling surface should not be as reflective as a mirror, for example. It should diffuse the light, while reflecting it to produce a soft glow unnoticeable to the human eye.

Lighting and Illumination

Lighting is the single most critical element that can influence the quality of the perceived video. It is affected by the dimensions (width, depth, and height) and angles of wall surfaces of the room; the diameter of the camera lens (known as the aperture); and the color and reflectivity of wall, floor, and ceiling surfaces. Too much light, and the room will feel like a recording studio and will be uncomfortable for the participants to sit in for long durations of time. Conversely, a room that is not lit well enough will appear dark on camera, shadows will appear around the face and neck of participants and in the corners of the room, and the perceived quality of the video will suffer.

Have you ever wondered how television and movie directors record such vibrant looking scenes, or how camera crews can take a picture of a room that looks so stunning and realistic? The secret is in how they illuminate the environment. Film and camera crews use special studio-quality lighting to illuminate their subjects in just the right way to produce the richest, most vibrant images possible. If you've ever been on stage, in a recording studio, or in a photo shoot, you'll probably recall how warm, bright, and uncomfortable it was under those lights. The primary goal of these environments is to illuminate the face of the subjects, along with their background environment, so that they look good on camera.

Conversely, the average conference room or meeting room and cubicle and hallway environments in office buildings are generally designed to provide a warm, soft lighting environment that is comfortable to work in for long durations. The primary goal of these environments is to illuminate table and work surfaces where people write or type on computer keyboards.

The goal of a TelePresence room is to strike just the right balance between studio-quality lighting and comfort for the participants. The participants and the environment around them must be illuminated properly to produce the most realistic, lifelike video quality. However, the environment should be comfortable enough for the participants to sit in it for hours without developing a headache or eye strain.

The three aspects to the design of lighting within a TelePresence room follow:

- The angles and direction of the light and which surfaces it illuminates

- The temperature or color of the light

- The strength or intensity of the light

The following section begins by investigating the angles and direction of light required.

Considering Light Angles and Direction

In a *three-point lighting* system, three points, or directions, of light influence what the camera sees:

- First, the light that fills the entire environment is ambient light, or fill light. This light generally comes from fixtures in the ceiling to blanket the room in even, well-distributed light.

- Second, the light that falls on a participant's face is participant light, or point light. This light illuminates the face to reduce shadows around the eyes, neck, and other such surfaces that directly face the camera. Point lighting generally does not exist in the average conference room and, therefore, must be supplied as part of the TelePresence system.

- Third, the perceived depth in an image as viewed by a camera is best when the subjects' shoulders and the tops of their heads are gently illuminated, causing them to "pop out" from the background behind them. This is shoulder lighting, or "rim lighting and is optional for a high-quality TelePresence image. You can also use rim lighting to illuminate the wall behind the participants to achieve a similar effect (depth in the perceived image).

Figures 8-23 through 8-26 illustrate the effects of fill, point, and rim lighting on a subject.

The critical types of light for a TelePresence solution are ambient (fill) and participant (point) lighting. Shoulder (rim) lighting is optional and left to the discretion of the customer whether to implement it. The remainder of this section focuses on ambient and participant lighting.

Before getting into the details of how to design the proper amount of ambient and participant light into the room, let's quickly touch on the concepts of light color temperature and intensity.

Considering Light Color Temperature

The color temperature of a light source is effectively a measure of how yellow, white, or blue it appears. The system of measurement used for rating the color temperature of light bulbs is the Kelvin (K). Incandescent light bulbs produce a yellowish light, with a Kelvin rating of approximately 2800K. The average fluorescent light bulb used in commercial construction is 3500K. Studio environments typically use 5000K fluorescent bulbs that produce a white light. Lower color temperatures are easier on the eyes and, hence, their popularity in homes and office buildings; however, they do a poor job of illuminating things sufficiently to make a subject look good on camera. By contrast, a room lit with

Figure 8-23   *A subject on camera with fill lighting only*

Figure 8-24   *A subject on camera with point lighting only*

5000K fluorescent bulbs will make you look fantastic on camera but will be uncomfortable to sit in for long durations. After much trial and error during the early phases of design on the CTS-3000, Cisco found that the best color temperature to use in TelePresence rooms is 4000K to 4100K. Incandescent light bulbs do not produce this temperature of

Figure 8-25   *A subject on camera with rim lighting only*

Figure 8-26   *A subject on camera with 3-point lighting*

light, and, therefore, fluorescent bulbs and fixtures are recommended. Fluorescent light bulb manufacturers use different "friendly" terms to describe the temperature of their bulbs, such as "cool white," but in most cases they also print the Kelvin rating on the bulb.

For those that do not print the Kelvin on the bulb, you can usually look it up on the manufacturer's website based on the part number printed on the bulb.

Measuring Light Intensity

The intensity or strength of a light source such as a fluorescent bulb is effectively a function of its wattage. There are various systems of measurement for this, including lumens, lux, foot candles, and candela. Cisco has chosen to standardize on the lux measurement in all TelePresence-related documentation. Lux is a measure of the intensity of light within a volume of space. It is also a measure of the intensity of light that hits a surface, such as a wall, a subject's face, or a table surface. The lumen, by contrast, is a measure of how much light is emitted by a source. So although a bulb produces light in terms of lumens, what you're actually concerned with in a TelePresence room is how much lux it provides at various points within the room. The average conference room or meeting room found in corporate environments is approximately 150 lux to 300 lux. This is much too dark for the aperture of a camera to sufficiently capture a human subject in good detail. By contrast, the average studio environment is approximately 700 lux, which is much too bright for humans to be comfortable for long durations. After much trial and error during the early phases of design on the CTS-3000, Cisco found that the ideal light intensity for a TelePresence room is 400 lux.

To summarize, the goal is to fill the room with 400 lux of well-distributed ambient light, using fluorescent bulbs with a color temperature of 4100K. However, when measuring the light within the room, it is critical to understand the angles from which lux is measured within a TelePresence room.

Cisco uses a tool called a lux meter to measure the intensity of light at various points within the room. There are essentially four different angles from which light should be measured:

■ From the camera's point of view, looking toward the participants

■ From the participant's point of view, looking toward the cameras

■ From the participant's point of view, facing upward toward the ceiling

■ From the perspective of the side and back walls

Cisco divides the room into sections, or zones, to measure light from all these different perspectives. Figure 8-27 illustrate the zones of a CTS-3000 room.

Zones 1 to 3 provide a measure of how much light is seen from the perspective of the cameras. Zones 4 to 6 provide a measure of how much light is seen from the perspective of the participants, and hence how well lit the participants will look on camera. Zones 4 to 6 also measure how much downward light strikes the shoulders of the participants and the table surface. Zones 7 to 9 provide a measure of how much light reaches the back wall. Within each zone, it is important to note the direction from which the light should be measured. In zones 1 to 3, the measurement is taken with the lux meter facing the participants. In zones 4 to 9, the measurement is taken with the lux meter facing the cameras. In zones 4 to 6, there is an additional measurement taken with the lux meter facing up toward the ceiling at shoulder height. Figure 8-28 illustrates the direction the lux meter should be facing within each of the zones.

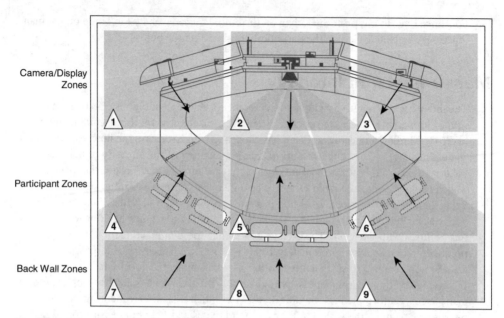

Figure 8-27   *CTS-3000 illumination zones—top down view*

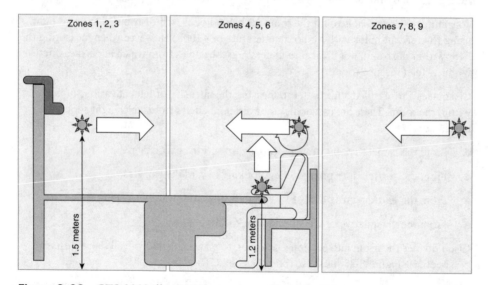

Figure 8-28   *CTS-3000 illumination zones—side view*

In zones 1 to 3, the light is measured with the lux meter facing toward the participants at approximately 5 feet (1.5 meters) from the floor. In zones 4 to 6, two separate measurements are taken:

- One with the lux meter facing toward the cameras at approximately 5 feet (1.5 meters) from the floor.

- The second with the lux meter facing up toward the ceiling at approximately 4 feet (1.2 meters) from the floor.

Finally, in zones 7 to 9, the light is measured with the lux meter facing toward the cameras at approximately 5 feet (1.5 meters) from the floor. Throughout all 9 zones, the light should measure approximately 400 lux, except for the second measurement in zones 4 to 6, in which the light should measure approximately 600 to 700 lux. No point in the room should measure lower than 150 lux or higher than 700 lux. Areas that are lower than 150 lux appear completely black on camera, and areas that are higher than 700 lux appear washed out on camera.

By following this methodology for measuring light within your TelePresence environment, you can achieve the best quality video and consistent, reproducible results. Although the illustrations provided are specific to the CTS-3000, you can use the same methodology in smaller or bigger rooms by simply shrinking or increasing the size and number of zones.

Light Fixture and Bulb Considerations

Fluorescent bulb manufacturers specify bulb intensity in terms of how many lumens they produce, but you are concerned with how much light they provide (in terms of lux) at various places throughout the room. The challenge, therefore, is to identify the number of bulbs per fixture, the number of fixtures, and the wattage per bulb required to achieve the desired amount of lux throughout the room. An expert lighting consultant can assist you to determine the best lighting configuration for any given room, and there are lighting design software applications on the market to help you determine precisely which type of fixture, how many bulbs per fixture, and what wattage of bulb you should use. Cost is obviously an important factor as well, so the ultimate goal is to find the right combination at the best possible price. This can also vary by city and by country because of the variety of fixture manufactures and construction costs in various parts of the world. The following sections provide some recommendations on the types and quantity of light fixtures that have been used successfully in Cisco TelePresence rooms to date.

The two most common types of ceiling light fixtures used within TelePresence rooms are pendant-style fixtures that hang down from the ceiling and recessed fixtures that are recessed within the ceiling. Both types are further broken down into three subtypes based on what direction the light is thrown: 100 percent direct, 100 percent indirect, and direct-indirect. Figure 8-29 and Figure 8-30 illustrate these various types of fixtures.

One hundred-percent direct light fixtures direct the light straight down instead of dispersing it evenly throughout the room. Therefore, the light will be more intense directly under the fixture compared to the perimeter of the area, or zone, in which it's measured. This results in hot spots on camera where the tops of people's heads and table surfaces is extremely bright and washed out, but the background areas such as wall surfaces are darker and shadowed. Therefore, 100-percent direct light fixtures are not recommended.

One hundred-percent indirect light fixtures function by directing light upward toward the ceiling or by refracting the light off a reflective surface within the fixture. This allows the light to be more evenly distributed throughout the room. As illustrated in Figure 8-30, indirect light fixtures can either be hung from the ceiling as a pendant-style fixture or recessed in the ceiling. Both types are recommended, but which one you ultimately decide to use depends on the dimensions (width, depth, and height) of the room.

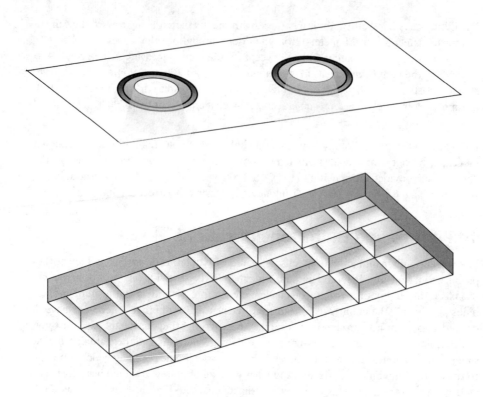

Figure 8-29   *Example of 100 percent direct light fixtures*

Both pendant-style and recessed-style fixtures are also available in direct-indirect configurations, where a portion of the light (for example, 20 percent) is directed downward while
the remaining portion (for example, 80 percent) is directed upward toward the ceiling or
reflective surface within the fixture. These are not recommended for the same reason that
100-percent direct fixtures are not—the portion of light that is directed downward could
create hot spots. Figure 8-31 illustrates the difference between a direct and indirect fixture and a 100-percent indirect fixture.

Another aspect of indirect light fixtures is the degree of dispersion, which is a measure of
the angle at which light is thrown from the fixture. The greater the degree of dispersion,
the less fixtures are required to provide the same coverage of an area. Figure 8-32 illustrates the difference between a standard fixture that has a degree of dispersion less than 60
degrees and a higher-end fixture that has a degree of dispersion greater than 60 degrees.

Now, consider some example 100-percent indirect ceiling fixture arrangements, based on
different room dimensions. These examples assume the use of a CTS-3000 room measuring 20-feet wide x 15 feet to 20-feet deep (6.096 meters wide x 4.572 meters to 6.096 meters deep). Figure 8-33 illustrates the recommended number and placement of fixtures
using standard quality 2-feet x 4-feet (.609 meters x 1.219 meters) recessed fixtures.

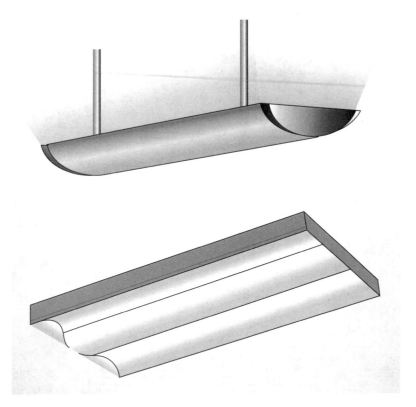

Figure 8-30 *Example of 100 percent indirect light fixtures*

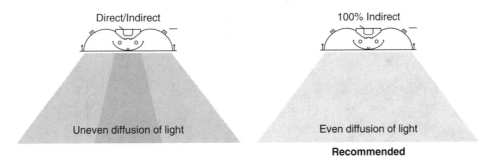

Figure 8-31 *Direct and indirect light fixture versus 100-percent indirect light fixture*

You can also achieve the same results using a higher-end model of fixture that provides either more bulbs per fixture (for example, four bulbs instead of two), run at a higher wattage level per bulb (for example, 80 watts instead of 40 watts) or with a higher degree of dispersion. Figure 8-34 illustrates this arrangement.

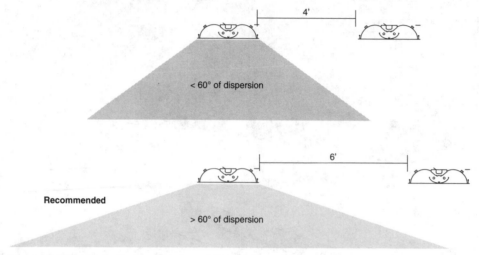

Figure 8-32   *Light fixture degrees of dispersion*

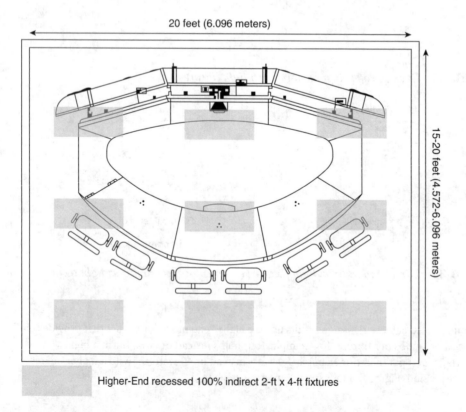

Figure 8-33   *Example CTS-3000 using standard recessed light fixtures*

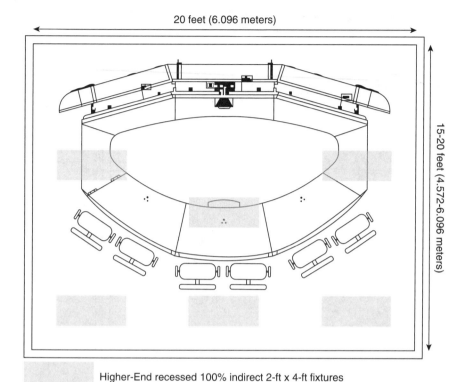

20 feet (6.096 meters)

15-20 feet (4.572-6.096 meters)

Higher-End recessed 100% indirect 2-ft x 4-ft fixtures

Figure 8-34 *Example CTS-3000 using higher-end recessed light fixtures*

Likewise, you can achieve the same results using 100-percent indirect standard suspended light fixtures. Figure 8-35 illustrates this arrangement for a room that is 15-feet deep (4.572 meters deep), while Figure 8-36 illustrates this arrangement for a slightly deeper room.

Light Fixture Ballast Considerations

The last item to consider when choosing a light fixture is the type of ballast it uses. The ballast is the device within the fixture that regulates the flow of power through the bulb. Fluorescent light fixtures have two types of ballasts: magnetic and electronic. Although magnetic ballasts are frequently preferred for their durability and long life, they produce a flickering effect on the TelePresence video because the cameras operate at a different frequency than the light fixtures. Therefore, electronic ballasts are required for Cisco TelePresence rooms.

Tip It is important that you use light fixtures with electronic ballasts. It is common to overlook this when designing the TelePresence room;, when the system is installed and first used, the customer sees the flickering on the screen, and then the light fixtures have to be swapped out. This can cause the installation to be delayed and the costs of the installation to increase.

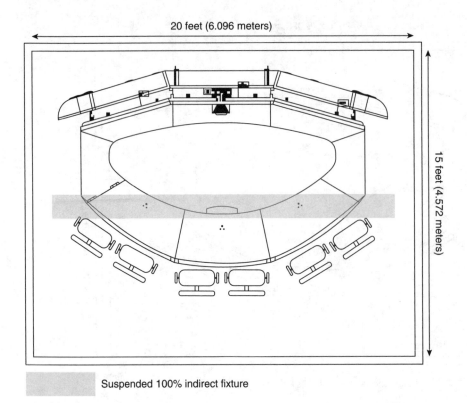

Suspended 100% indirect fixture

Figure 8-35   *Example CTS-3000 suspended light fixture for a 15-foot deep room*

Acoustics

One of the most impressive aspects of the Cisco TelePresence solution is its audio quality. The sound is spatial (emanates from the direction of the person who is speaking) and is full-duplex. (You can talk over each other with no clipping.) The microphones are directional and have a coverage pattern designed to capture the voice of the participants sitting directly in front of them. The microphones also filter out certain background frequencies. The audio compression board in the system encodes the voice from the participants at 48KHz using the Advanced Audio Coding—Low Delay compression algorithm. On the receiving end, the speakers are specifically designed to reproduce the frequency range and decibel levels of human speech so that it feels life-like, as if the person is sitting 8 feet (2.438 meters) or so away from you on the other side of the virtual table.

Other capabilities within the Cisco TelePresence portfolio exploit the acoustic properties of the Cisco TelePresence system. In multipoint meetings for example, the Cisco TelePresence Multipoint Switch (CTMS) relies on the signal strength of the audio coming from each microphone to determine which segment should be displayed at any given time.

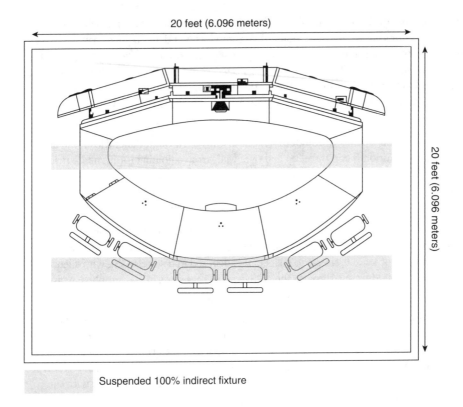

20 feet (6.096 meters)

20 feet (6.096 meters)

Suspended 100% indirect fixture

Figure 8-36 *Example CTS-3000 recessed light fixtures for a 20-foot deep rooms*

Background noise and reverberation in the room can degrade these acoustic qualities and even disrupt the switching behavior in multipoint meetings. Therefore, careful engineering of the environment must be done to ensure that ambient noise and reverberation levels within the room are kept in check. However, you don't want the TelePresence room to be so flat and sterile acoustically speaking that it feels like you're in a sound chamber or recording studio. The goal is to re-create the experience of an in-person meeting, so some amount of ambient noise and reverberation is tolerable—even desirable. Cisco has defined precise targets and thresholds for ambient noise and reverberation levels within a TelePresence room, providing a comprehensive test methodology for measuring those levels and recommendations for remediating typical sources of higher than desired ambient noise and reverberation.

Measuring Ambient Noise

Ambient noise is everywhere and is generated by numerous things. Take a moment to pause and listen to the background noises around you. Have you ever noticed the sound of the air whooshing through the air-conditioning ventilation vents in your room, the gentle humming of the air-conditioning machinery in the ceiling, the buzzing of fluorescent light fixtures above you, the sound of cars and buses and ambulances passing by on the street outside your building, the people talking in the room next door, or the sounds of phones ringing in the offices and cubicles around yours? You probably haven't because your brain has become accustom to those sounds and unconsciously tunes them out, but those are exactly the types of sounds we are interested in measuring and, to the degree possible, eliminating inside the TelePresence room.

Ambient noise can emanate through thin, hollow walls or through the cracks in the door jamb around the door. It can travel up and over walls from adjoining rooms and corridors and permeate through the ceiling into your room. This section discusses methods for treating the walls, doors, flooring, and ceiling materials to remediate these sources of noise, but first, consider how these noise sources are measured.

Cisco uses a Sound Pressure Level (SPL) meter to measure the level of ambient sound within the room. SPL is a logarithmic measurement of the root square mean (or average power) pressure of sound relative to silence. It is denoted in decibels (dB), with silence equal to 0dB. Sound travels through the air in waves. Therefore, SPL is simply a measure of the strength, or pressure, of that wave.

The SPL of human speech is generally 60dB to 65dB. Because of the way the human ear and brain work, background sound that is 25dB to 30dB less than human speech generally goes unnoticed. Therefore, the goal is create a room where the average SPL of ambient background noise is no greater than approximately 36dB. Noise levels exceeding 42dB are cause for concern, and levels exceeding 50dB can cause significant problems with the TelePresence experience.

When measuring the SPL level of a room, the average measurement across the entire environment (that is, throughout the room) is used. This establishes a baseline measurement referred to as the *noise floor average*. However, because sound dissipates over distance, when measuring the SPL of a specific source, such as an air conditioning vent or fluorescent light fixture, the SPL is taken from a defined distance from the source (for example, SPL = 30dB at 1 meter away from the vent).

As with the lighting measurement techniques discussed in the previous sections, Cisco divides the room into sections, or zones, to measure the ambient noise floor average at various points within the room. Figure 8-37 illustrates the acoustic zones of a CTS-3000 room.

Within each of the six zones, the ambient noise is measured with the decibel meter approximately 5 feet (1.5 meters) from the floor using a slow sweeping motion to capture the average SPL for that zone. These measurements are done using an A-weighted test. A seventh measurement is taken using a C-weighted test within the middle of the room (front of zone 5) to capture the C-weighted average SPL for the entire room. Note that the C-weighted target is approximately 52dB, compared to the A-weighted target of 36dB mentioned previously. Finally, specific measurements are taken of any particular source of noise, such as each of the air conditioning vents in the room, at a distance of 3 feet (1 meter) from the source, using an A-weighted test. You should be concerned with any A-weighted measurements that exceed 36dB, a C-weighted measurement that exceeds 56dB, or any specific source such as HVAC vents that exceed 36dB at 3 feet (1 meter) distance from the

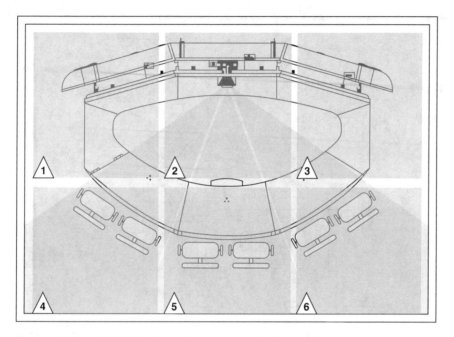

Figure 8-37   *CTS-3000 acoustic zones: top down view*

source. For all these tests, you should choose a time of the day that represents the high average, ideally, when the HVAC is actively producing air flow through the vents.

Measuring Reverberation

Reverberation is essentially a measurement of how long a sound continues to bounce around the room before decaying to the point that it can no longer be heard. The measurement used to denote reverberation is called RT60, which is a measurement of the time required for a sound to decay by 60dB. For example, if you have a source generating sound at 65dB, and it takes 200ms for that sound to dissipate to 5dB, the RT60 measurement for that sound is 200ms. The more the sound can reflect off of walls, ceiling, flooring, and other surfaces, the longer it will take for that sound to decay. Figure 8-38 illustrates this concept.

The ideal reverberation level for a Cisco TelePresence room is 150ms to 300ms. Levels ranging from 300ms to 500ms are cause for concern, and levels exceeding 500ms can cause significant problems with the TelePresence experience. Reverberation is measured for each of the following frequency ranges independently: 125Hz, 250Hz, 500Hz, 1kHz, 2kHz, and 4kHz. Different frequencies of sound reflect off of (or are absorbed by) wall, ceiling, and flooring surfaces differently. Although the human ear cannot discern all these frequencies, the microphones of the TelePresence system might. Therefore, measuring the reverberation of all these frequencies ensures that we understand the acoustic behavior of the room for all types of sounds, from the low frequency sounds generated by building machinery, through the frequencies of human speech and music, up into the higher

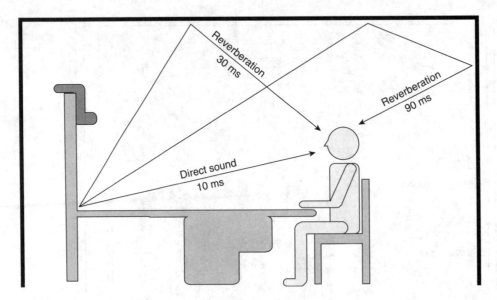

Figure 8-38   *Reverberation illustrated*

pitched sounds generated by electronic devices. For each of these tests, you want to measure from the center of the room, as illustrated in Figure 8-39.

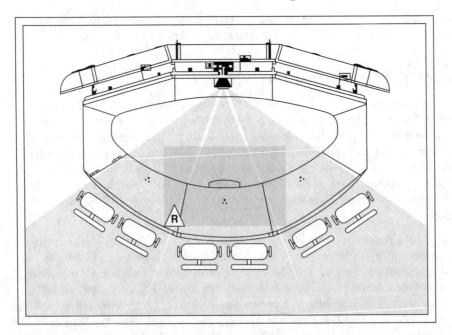

Figure 8-39   *Reverberation zone: top down view*

To measure reverberation, place the decibel meter in RT60 mode in the center of the room on a table surface approximately 5 feet (1.5 meters) off the floor. Use a tone generator and amplified speaker to completely fill the room with > 70dB of white or pink noise for several seconds and then instantly silence the tone generator. The decibel meter measures the time it takes (in milliseconds) for the noise to decay by 60dB. Repeat the test for each of the six frequency levels. For accuracy, several measurements should be taken with the tone generator and amplified speaker at different locations within the room for each of the frequency ranges to ensure that your measurements represent a true average for the room.

> **Tip** White and pink noise are patterns of sound produced by a tone generator for the purpose of testing reverberation. They sound like static to the human ear. Pink noise is generally used for TelePresence RT60 tests because pink noise more accurately emulates the way the human auditory system works and, therefore, provides a more precise measurement of how reverberation would be detected by the human ear.

Targeted and Maximum Ambient Noise and Reverberation Levels

Table 8-4 summarizes the targets and thresholds for ambient noise and reverberation.

Table 8-4 *Target and Maximum Ambient Noise and Reverberation Levels*

Measurement	Target	Maximum	Notes
Ambient Noise Floor Average (A-Weighted)	36dB	42dB	Within each of the six zones
Ambient Noise Floor Average (C-Weighted)	56dB	62dB	In the front of zone 5
Specific noise source (@ 1 meter from the source)	36dB	42dB	Air-conditioning vents, light fixtures, or any other specific device such as the fan on a UPS or Ethernet switch
Reverberation (RT60)	150ms–300ms	500ms	For each of the six frequency levels

Controlling Ambient Noise and Reverberation Levels

The primary method of controlling ambient noise and reverberation levels within the room is to use the appropriate wall, flooring, and ceiling building materials. All types of building material have ratings associated with them for the following three acoustic properties:

- **Noise Reduction Coefficient (NRC):** The NRC is a rating that represents the amount of sound energy absorbed upon striking a surface. An NRC of 0 indicates perfect reflection; an NRC of 1 indicates perfect absorption. NRC generally pertains to sound within the room and, therefore, applies to wall, flooring, and ceiling surfaces. The target NRC for a TelePresence room is .60.

- **Sound Transmission Class (STC):** The STC is a rating that represents the amount of sound energy required to transfer through a surface or structure. An STC of 40 requires greater than 40 decibels of sound energy to transfer through the structure. STC generally pertains to sound leaking into the room from adjacent rooms and corridors and, therefore, pertains to wall and ceiling surfaces and items such as doors and windows that can leak audio. The target STC for a TelePresence room is 60 for internal walls, doors, and windows and 90 for external walls, doors, and windows.

- **Impact Insulation Class (IIC):** The IIC is a rating similar to STC but pertains specifically to flooring surfaces. IIC measures the resistance to the transmission of impact noise such as footfall, chairs dragging, and dropped items. This measurement is especially important in multifloor buildings and with plenum flooring. The IIC represents the amount of sound energy required to transfer sound through a surface or structure. An IIC of 40 would require greater than 40 decibels of sound energy to travel through a surface or structure. The target IIC for a TelePresence room is 60.

Table 8-5 summarizes the target and maximum ratings for common construction surfaces within the TelePresence room. The Notes column provides examples of the types of materials you can use to achieve these ratings.

Table 8-5   *Target and Maximum NRC, STC, and IIC Ratings*

Material	Acoustic Property	Target	Maximum	Notes
Walls	NRC	.40	.30	Acoustic fabric on gypsum or moderate-weighted curtains
	STC	60	40	1/2-in. gypsum drywall on both sides with heavy insulation or acoustic panels
Flooring	NRC	.40	.30	Padded carpeting over cement
	IIC	60	40	Standard commercial construction practices
Ceiling Tile	NRC	.80	.70	Commercial acoustic ceiling tile
	STC	60	40	Commercial acoustic ceiling tile
Doors	STC	60	40	Solid core door with gasket on top, bottom, and sides
Interior Windows	STC	60	40	1/4-in. double pane windows or acoustical treated coverings
Exterior Windows	STC	90	70	Location near high traffic or airports might want highest ratings

Scenarios for Mitigating Ambient Noise and Reverberation

This section concludes with a few common scenarios for how these ratings apply and what type of remediation tactics you can use.

First, by far the most common problem encountered by customers is the noise created by the HVAC registers. The challenge is that because the TelePresence equipment and the human bodies within the room produce so much heat, either a high level of air flow or a low temperature air flow is required to achieve a comfortable temperature within the room. Finding the proper balance of temperature, air flow, and SPL can be tricky. On one hand, increasing the air flow generally causes the SPL of the register to go well above the maximum of 46dB, either as a result of the air flow through the register or the machinery noise created by the motors and fans traveling through the ducting. On the other hand, decreasing the temperature can cause the air flowing out of the register to be uncomfortably cold for people who happen to stand or sit directly beneath it. It is recommended that you consult an HVAC specialist for assistance in finding the proper balance for your room. However, one general piece of advice is to always use NC30-rated air registers, which diffuse the air flowing out of the register to reduce the air flow noise. The next section "HVAC" reviews the BTU requirements and recommended types and locations of HVAC registers in greater detail.

The second most common area of problems are ambient noise and reverberation levels caused by low NRC and STC values of walls, doors, and windows. Noise can also come up and over the walls from adjoining rooms and corridors and permeate through the ceiling. Figure 8-40 illustrates some of these common scenarios.

Simple tactics for remediating these issues include increasing the thickness of the walls (for example, installing a second layer of gypsum drywall to double its thickness), adding sound-absorbing insulation within the walls, installing an acoustic blanket or foam tile inserts above the ceiling to eliminate the sound traveling up and over the wall, and using ceiling tiles with high NCR and STC ratings. Figure 8-41 illustrates some examples of these materials.

For rooms that exhibit high levels of reverberation, the best remediation tactic is generally to cover the wall surfaces with acoustically dampening materials, such as small fabric panels placed in strategic locations on one or more walls in the room. Refer back to the "Wall, Floor, and Ceiling Surfaces" section earlier in this chapter for additional considerations.

HVAC

The HVAC design goals for Cisco TelePresence rooms boil down to three primary criteria:

- Generating enough air flow to keep the temperature of the room comfortable for the participants. This is measured in terms of British Thermal Units per hour (BTU/hr) and is a function of the heat generated by the TelePresence system and other electronic devices within the room, plus the heat generated by the human bodies within the room.

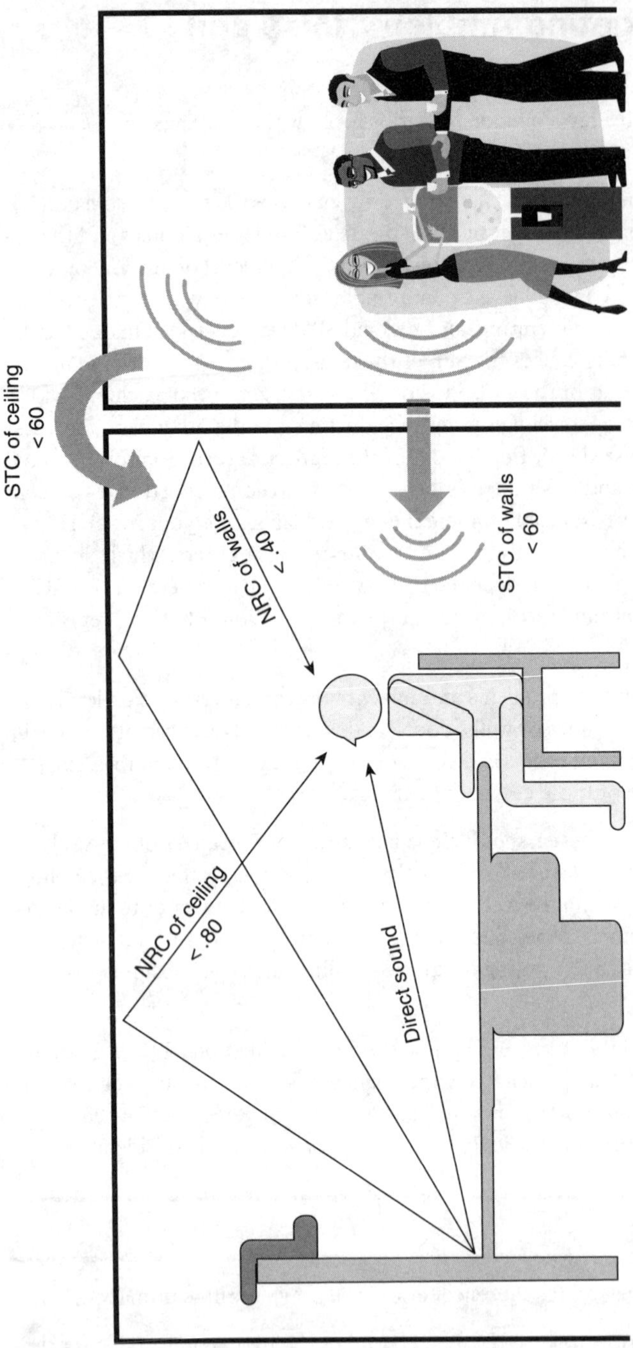

Figure 8-40 *Example NRC and STC scenarios*

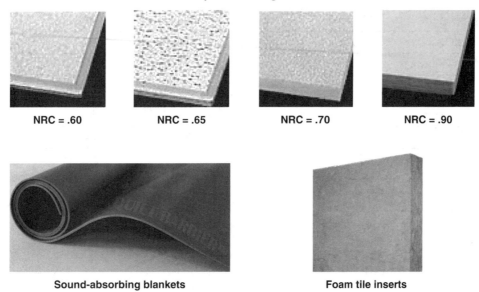

Figure 8-41 *Example ceiling materials used to increase NRC and STC ratings*

- Achieving the above BTU/hr performance without generating high levels of ambient noise. Simply cranking up the air conditioning is rarely the best solution because it can result in a higher volume of wooshing sound coming through the HVAC registers (the vents that supply air to the room). You must strive to achieve a balance of the air flow:noise ratio.

- Positioning the HVAC registers to maximize the efficiency of the air flow between the supply registers and the return registers. This is critical as it can effectively reduce the total amount of BTU/hr capacity required by as much as 25%, thereby reducing or eliminating the costs associated with upgrading the capacity of the HVAC system.

Tables 8-6, 8-7, and 8-8 summarize the BTU requirements for the CTS-3000, CTS-3200, and CTS-1000. These values include all the equipment and lighting provided with the system and the participants within the room. Note that the CTS-500 is designed to be deployed within an existing room with no HVAC modifications, and, therefore, a power consumption table for that model is not provided here.

Tip The total BTU/hr provided at the bottom of each table can be reduced by 25% (multiply by .75) if the HVAC registers are positioned properly, as illustrated in Figure 8-42. This is because we can take advantage of the efficiency of the HVAC system to displace the warm air generated by the TelePresence System and the people, thereby reducing the amount of BTU capacity required, potentially saving the customer thousands of dollars in HVAC system upgrades.

Table 8-6 *BTU Requirements for the CTS-3000*

Component	Maximum[1]	Typical[1]	Minimum[1]	Idle[1]
Plasma Displays	2,880w	2,658w	2,658w	9w
Primary Codec	120w	113w	113w	113w–120w
Secondary Codec (108w max / 101 average each)	216w	202w	202w	202w–216w
Light Façade	348w	348w	348w	0w
Laptop Power (240w max / 144w average each)	1,440w	864w	144w	0w
Projector	288w	225w	0w	0w–5w
Auxiliary LCD[2] (325w max / 230w average each)	975w	230w	0w	0.6w
Auxiliary Document Camera[2]	200w	200w	0w	0w
Total Wattage	6,467w	4,840w	3,465w	324w–350w
Total Amperage (wattage / volts)	54A @ 120V 27A @ 240V	41A @ 120V 21A @ 240V	28A @ 120V 14A @ 240V	3A @ 120V 2A @ 240V
People (450 BTU/hr each)	2,700 BTU/hr	2,700 BTU/hr	450 BTU/hr	0 BTU/hr
Total BTU/hr (wattage * 3.413) + people[3]	24,772 BTU/hr	19,218 BTU/hr	12,276 BTU/hr	1,106–1,195 BTU/hr

Table 8-7 *BTU Requirements for the CTS-3200*

Component	Maximum[1]	Typical[1]	Minimum[1]	Idle[1]
Plasma Displays	2,880w	2,658w	2,658w	9w
Primary Codec	120w	113w	113w	113w–120w
Secondary Codec (108w max / 101 average each)	216w	202w	202w	202w–216w
Light Façade	348w	348w	348w	0w
Laptop Power (240w max / 144w average each)	4,320w	2,592w	144w	0w
Projector	288w	225w	0w	0w–5w
Auxiliary LCD (325w max / 230w average each)	975w	230w	0w	0.6w
Auxiliary Document Camera[2]	200w	0w	0w	0w
Total Wattage	9,347w	6,368w	3,465w	324w–350w
Total Amperage (wattage / volts)	54A @ 120V 27A @ 240V	41A @ 120V 21A @ 240V	28A @ 120V 14A @ 240V	3A @ 120V 2A @ 240V
People (450 BTU/hr each)	8,100 BTU/hr	5,400 BTU/hr	450 BTU/hr	0 BTU/hr
Total BTU/hr (wattage * 3.413) + people[3]	40,000 BTU/hr	27,134 BTU/hr	12,276 BTU/hr	1,106–1,195 BTU/hr

Table 8-8   *BTU Requirements for the CTS-1000*

Component	Maximum[1]	Typical[1]	Minimum[1]	Idle[1]
Plasma Displays	960w	886w	886w	3w
Primary Codec	120w	113w	113w	113w–120w
Light Façade	80w	80w	80w	0w
Laptop Power (240w max / 144w average each)	480w	288w	144w	0w
Auxiliary LCD[2]	325w	36w	0w	0w–5w
Auxiliary Document Camera[2]	200w	0w	0w	0w
Total Wattage	2,165w	1,403w	1,223w	116w–128w
Total Amperage (wattage / volts)	19A @ 120V 10A @ 240V	12A @ 120V 6A @ 240V	10A @ 120V 5A @ 240V	2A @ 120V 1A @ 240V
People (450 BTU/hr each)	900 BTU/hr	450 BTU/hr	450 BTU/hr	0 BTU/hr
Total BTU/hr (wattage * 3.413) + people[3]	8,289 BTU/hr	5,238 BTU/hr	4,624 BTU/hr	396–437 BTU/hr

[1] Maximum values represent fully utilizing every possible feature to the maximum supported configurations and filling the room with people. Typical represents what most customers tend to use and also represents average load versus max load on the components. Minimum represents little to no use of auxiliary LCD displays, document cameras, laptops, and number of participants in attendance and average load on the components. Idle represents what the system uses during nonbusiness hours when the displays are put into sleep mode and the lights are turned off.

[2] Varies by model. Table 8-9 provides the maximum and idle power requirements for certain models that Cisco has specifically tested.

[3] Reduce by 25% (multiply by .75) if HVAC registers are positioned properly.

Table 8-9 *Power Requirements for Auxiliary Displays and Document Cameras*

Vendor – Model	Maximum	Idle
NEC LCD1770NX	36w	<3w
NEC LCD2070NX	50w	<3w
NEC LCD4010	230w	<5w
NEC LCD4020	240w	<5w
NEC LCD4610	260w	<5w
NEC LCD4620	240w	<5w
Samsung 400PXN	230w	<1w
Samsung 460PXN	310w	<1w
Sharp PN-525U	325w	<1w
WolfVision VZ-9plus	55w	0w
WolfVision VZ-C12²	200w	0w
WolfVision VZ-C32	200w	0w

HVAC Air Noise Diffusion Considerations

As mentioned previously in the "Acoustics" section, to meet these BTU requirements without exceeding the ambient noise threshold of 46dB, the recommendation is that you always use NC30-rated air registers, which diffuse the air flowing out of the register to reduce the air flow noise. To maximize the efficiency of the air flow through the room, you should locate the supply registers behind the participants and the return registers directly over the 65-inch plasma displays of the TelePresence system. Doing so can reduce the capacity requirements of the HVAC substantially. Figure 8-42 illustrates such an arrangement for a CTS-3000 room.

Finally, measure the temperature of the air flowing out of the register. (Use a laser thermometer pointed directly at the register from 3 feet [1 meter] away.) If the temperature of the air is warmer than 70-degrees Fahrenheit (21-degrees Celsius), it is probably too warm to be effective, and your HVAC system might need to be recharged. However, if the tem-

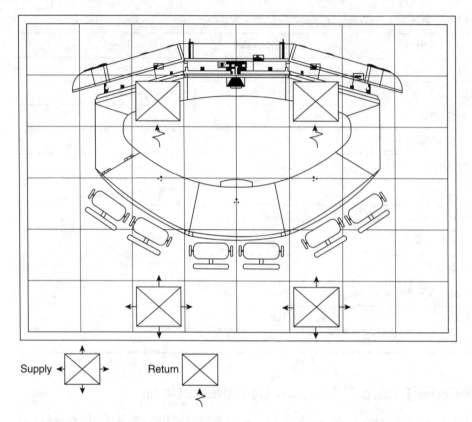

Figure 8-42 *Reflected ceiling plan showing recommended HVAC register locations*

perature of the air is colder than 55-degrees Fahrenheit (12° Celsius), it might cause discomfort for the participants standing or sitting directly beneath the register. An HVAC specialist can further assist you in measuring and designing the HVAC system.

Power Requirements

Cisco TelePresence systems—especially the larger models such as the CTS-3000 and CTS-3200—have unique power requirements that must be taken into account during the room evaluation and design phase. The chances of your room already containing the correct type and quantity of electrical circuits and receptacles are slim. Therefore, the services of a qualified electrician will be required for every room you deploy.

First, take the amount of wattage consumed by the system to ascertain the quantity and amperage of electrical circuits required to power the equipment. These calculations were provided previously in Tables 8-6, 8-7, and 8-8.

Now that you know the total wattage and total amperage required by the system, you can ascertain the number of circuits and amperage per circuit. Cisco TelePresence systems are rated for 10amps@240v or 20amps @120v. Electrical codes in use suggest that only 80 percent of a circuit's capacity should be used. Therefore, on a 20-amp circuit running at 120v in the U.S., only 16 amps of it are useable, and on a 10-amp circuit running at 240V in Europe, only 8 amps are useable. Therefore, a CTS-3000 for example that requires a total of 54amps@120V, divided by 16amps per circuit, requires a minimum of four 16amp circuits on the wall.

The components are attached to Power Distribution Units (PDU). Each PDU, in turn, is attached to one of the power circuits on the wall. The CTS-3000 requires four PDUs. Table 8-10 shows which of the four PDUs each component is attached to and, hence, how the power is distributed across the circuits.

Table 8-10 *Power Distribution for CTS-3000*

Component	PDU #1	PDU #2	PDU #3	PDU #4
Three 65-in. Plasma Displays	1 @ 960 Watts	1 @ 960 Watts	1 @ 960 Watts	
One Primary Codec		1 @ 120 Watts		
Two Secondary Codecs	1 @ 108 Watts		1 @ 108 Watts	
Three Lighting Façade Fixtures (Top)	1 @ 80 Watts	1 @ 80 Watts	1 @ 80 Watts	
Two Lighting Façade Fixtures (Sides)	1 @ 54 Watts		1 @ 54 Watts	
One Projector				1 @ 288 Watts
(optional) Auxiliary LCD displays	1 @ 240 Watts	1 @ 240 Watts	1 @ 240 Watts	
(optional) WolfVision document camera		1 @ 200 Watts		
Six Participant A/C power jacks in table legs				6 @ 240 Watts each
Total Watts	1442 Watts	1600 Watts	1442 Watts	1728 Watts
Amperage Required	12.02A @ 120V or 6.01A @ 240V	13.34A @ 120V or 6.67A @ 240V	12.02A @ 120V or 6.01A @ 240V	14.4A @ 120V or 7.2A @ 240V

Tip Always check your country's electrical regulations to determine the appropriate number of amps permitted per circuit.

Tip   The circuits to which the TelePresence equipment is attached should be dedicated circuits not controlled by a light switch.

Again, remember that things can change from one product release to another, so the information in Table 8-10 is given as an example and is highly subject to change. For instance, when Cisco first released the CTS-3000, only four *dedicated* circuits were needed, and the light façade was connected to the same circuits as the other components. But that meant that the light façade remained on 24 hours a day, 7 days a week. To improve this, Cisco Technical Marketing came out with a recommendation that the light façade be connected to a fifth *switched* electrical circuit that was controlled by the same switch on the wall that controlled the overhead/ceiling lights in the room, and Cisco manufacturing started including a fifth PDU in every CTS-3000 shipment to facilitate customers doing this. However, because most ceiling light fixtures operate at 277V, additional electrical conditioning components were required to extend a receptacle of that circuit to the wall behind the system so that the light façade could be plugged into it. Now, at the time of this writing, Cisco is coming out with a third, better option—a separate, custom-designed PDU called the Auxiliary Control Unit (ACU), which is attached to a fifth *dedicated* circuit. The ACU is controlled by the Primary Codec and controls the individual receptacles on the ACU to turn the light façade on/off automatically. The system can be configured to turn the lights on/off per call, or on at the beginning of business hours (by default, at 7 a.m. local time) and off after business hours (by default, at 6 p.m. local time). These settings are configurable. The ACU also provides an RS-232 serial port, which is connected to the projector to automate the configuration of the projector settings.

Tip   Don't forget to include any auxiliary components in your calculation, such as document cameras and LCD displays.

Next, when you have your calculations for the amount of amperage per circuit and the number of circuits required, the electrician needs to know where in the room these circuits should be installed. A floor plan and reflected ceiling plan is the most accurate way to specify this. For example, Figure 8-43 shows five dedicated 20A circuits installed along the wall behind the system, with additional receptacles from circuit#5 extended to the ceiling and walls for the WolfVision document camera and Auxiliary LCD displays.

Finally, remember that one of the primary goals of Cisco TelePresence is ease of use. Therefore, the system is designed to be left on 24 hours a day, 7 days a week so that people can walk in and use it anytime, without trying to figure out how to turn the system on before they can use it. To facilitate this, Cisco has introduced three improvements to reduce the power consumption during off hours:

- In the 1.1 release, the system began automatically putting the plasma displays and projector into standby mode during off hours.

- In the 1.2 release, the system began controlling the WolfVision document camera programmatically to enable us to put it into standby mode during off hours as well.

- In release 1.4, the Auxiliary Control Unit (ACU) was introduced to allow the light façade to be turned on/off automatically, as previously described.

More improvements are likely to be made in the future, so check with Cisco for the latest specifications and power recommendations.

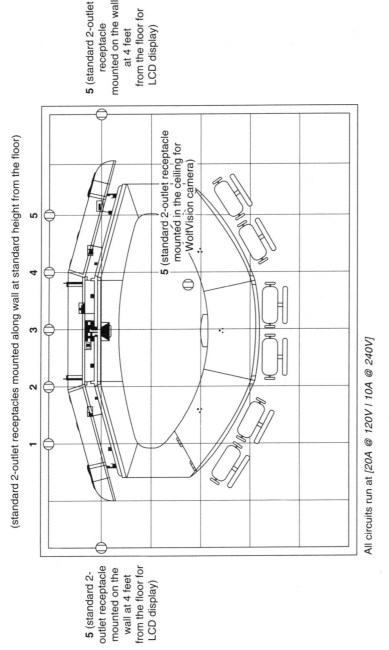

Figure 8-43   *Reflected ceiling plan showing recommended power outlet locations*

Some customers have asked whether the system can be shut down at night. Doing so will not damage the equipment in any way. The system is designed to be powered off without requiring a soft shutdown. However, it is still not advised because it will reduce the usefulness of the system. Because TelePresence promotes global meetings, it is not uncommon for users to have meetings with colleagues in another country at 10 p.m., or even at 2 a.m.

Network Connectivity

Cisco TelePresence systems use a unique multiplexing technique so that even though there are multiple codecs, cameras, microphones, speakers, displays, and auxiliary accessories, the entire system requires a single Category 5e or Category 6, Unshielded Twisted Pair (UTP) Gigabit Ethernet port to attach it to the network. These topics are covered in detail in Chapter 3, "TelePresence Audio and Video Technologies," and Chapter 4, "Connecting TelePresence Systems."

In addition to the single Gigabit Ethernet port required by the TelePresence system, network connectivity must also be provided for the participants, who might want to bring laptop computers into the meeting. There are two ways to accommodate this:

- Built-in Ethernet and Power Receptacles

- Providing 802.11 wireless Ethernet coverage within the TelePresence room

First, for Cisco TelePresence systems that provide integrated furniture, such as the CTS-3000 and CTS-3200 models, Ethernet and power receptacles are provided as built into the table legs. Note that these Ethernet ports do not connect to the back of the primary codec. Instead, a separate Ethernet switch (sold separately) must be provided to terminate all these Ethernet ports and then attach upstream to the network. A 1RU high and 19-inch (48.26 centimeters) wide mounting bracket is provided with the CTS-3000 and CTS-3200 that provides a convenient location for the Ethernet switch to be rack-mounted to the back of the system, and a second Category 5e or Category 6, Unshielded Twisted Pair (UTP) Gigabit Ethernet port must be provided for this switch to uplink to the network.

When using this method, follow two important guidelines:

- For acoustic purposes, the Ethernet switch you choose must generate as little ambient noise as possible.

- This switch should provide a software feature set that meets your organization's requirements and policies for LAN security, quality of service (QoS), and manageability.

Finding this combination of features in an Ethernet switch can be difficult. On the one hand, low-cost, fanless Ethernet switches might not provide adequate security and management functions. On the other hand, a Cisco Catalyst switch with the appropriate enterprise class feature set might be too loud. At the time of writing, Cisco TelePresence Technical Marketing identified the following models of Cisco Catalyst 2960 Series switches as the most suitable for use with a CTS-3000 or CTS-3200 model system:

- Cisco Catalyst 2960G-8TC-L with RCKMNT-19-CMPCT=

- Cisco Catalyst 2960-8TC-L with RCKMNT-19-CMPCT=

Because new switch products are always coming out, you should check with Cisco for the latest recommendations.

The second method you can use is to deploy an 802.11 wireless Ethernet solution within the room. Chances are high that a customer deploying TelePresence will already have an 802.11 solution deployed, so this is the ideal way to do it, not only because it's silent, but also because it's generally easier to secure a wireless network and provide differentiated access for guest users versus regular employees. Within the Cisco internal deployment of TelePresence, this has been the method of choice. The Ethernet ports in the table legs are left physically disconnected, and wireless is provided to all users. In addition to providing reliable and secure access to Cisco employees, guestnet access is provided to customers and other guests. The guestnet provides them with a connection that is outside the corporate firewall and quarantined from the rest of the internal network.

In summary, each Cisco TelePresence system requires either two Ethernet ports (one for the system and one for the participant access switch) on the wall located behind the system, or one Ethernet port with wireless network access for the participants.

Summary

The advanced audio, video, and networking technologies of TelePresence comprise only one half of the equation. The room and environment you use it in is equally important as the technology itself to delivering a TelePresence experience. Network engineers who are familiar with deploying other Cisco technologies will find TelePresence a fascinating new venture because it incorporates environmental, aesthetic, and acoustical concepts that many network engineers might not have been introduced to before. This chapter provided a detailed view into the design considerations for the room in which a TelePresence system will be deployed. In it, the following topics were discussed, providing both the theory behind each concept along with specific examples and recommendations:

- **Room Dimensions, Shape, and Orientation:** Discussed the physical size, shape, and orientation of the room and the location of doors, windows, columns, and furniture within the room.

- **Wall, Floor and Ceiling Surfaces:** Discussed the recommended colors, patterns, and materials of wall, floor, and ceiling surfaces within the room.

- **Lighting and Illumination:** Discussed overall illumination considerations and specific lighting requirements and recommendations.

- **Acoustics:** Discussed the concepts of sound reproduction and the effects of ambient noise and reverberation within the environment and how they are measured.

- **HVAC:** Discussed the heating, ventilation, and air conditioning (HVAC) requirements and the recommended types and locations of air-conditioning registers within the room.

- **Power Requirements:** Discussed power consumption requirements for the equipment and participants and the recommended types and locations of electrical receptacles within the room.

- **Network Connectivity:** Discussed the network connectivity required within the room for the equipment and the participants and the recommended ways of providing network access to the participants.

For TelePresence conferences to be natural, realistic, and effective, the network infrastructure must service the high-definition audio and video packets sent between TelePresence endpoints with high availability and quality.

From an availability standpoint, TelePresence is one of the most sensitive applications to packet loss on the network and is up to 100 times more sensitive to packet loss than VoIP. As such, networks supporting TelePresence need to have correspondingly higher availability built into their designs.

From a quality of service (QoS) viewpoint, TelePresence requires stricter service levels than virtually any other application and as such needs to be provisioned accordingly on a device-by-device basis; however, TelePresence provisioning is not to interfere with VoIP. Therefore, extensive attention needs to be given to the QoS designs of the network.

This chapter and Chapter 10, "TelePresence Network Design Part 2: QoS Design," discuss in detail the design considerations and best-practice recommendations for both campus and branch networks deploying TelePresence. This chapter focuses on network availability designs, whereas Chapter 10 examines QoS designs.

CHAPTER 9

TelePresence Network Design Part 1: Availability Design

TelePresence Availability Considerations and Targets

TelePresence is highly sensitive to packet loss, especially the HD video component (which is the primary and dominant component of TelePresence). This is due to the high degree of compression used by the TelePresence codecs to process HD video.

For example, HD video is not practically deployable without efficient compression schemes such as MPEG4 or H.264. To illustrate this point, consider a high-definition 1080p30 video stream, such as used by TelePresence systems. The three parameters of 1080p30 are as follows:

- **1080:** Refers to 1080 lines of horizontal resolution, which are matrixed with 1920 lines of vertical resolution (as per the 16:9 widescreen aspect ratio used in HD video formatting), resulting in 2,073,600 pixels per screen.

- **p:** Indicates a progressive scan, which means that every line of resolution is refreshed with each frame (as opposed to an interlaced scan, which would be indicated with an "i" and would mean that every other line is refreshed with each frame).

- **30:** Refers to the transmission rate of 30 frames per second.

Although video sampling techniques might vary, each pixel has approximately 3 bytes of color and luminance information. When all this information is factored together (2,073,600 pixels $\times$ 3 bytes $\times$ 8 bits per byte $\times$ 30 frames per second), it results in approximately 1.5 Gbps of information per screen! However, H.264-based TelePresence codecs transmit this information at under 5 Mbps per screen, which translates to over 99 percent compression. Thus, the overall effect of packet loss is proportionally magnified so that dropping even one packet in 10,000 (0.01 percent packet loss) is noticeable to end users in the form of pixelization. This is simply because a single packet represents a hundred or more packets' worth of information, due to the extreme compression ratios applied, as illustrated in Figure 9-1.

If packet loss sensitivity is defined as the level of packet loss at which the end user notices the impact on the application quality, TelePresence is more than 100 times more sensitive to packet loss than VoIP.

This is because VoIP networks are typically designed to have a packet loss requirement of no more than 1 percent. Specifically, VoIP codecs include Packet Loss Concealment (PLC) algorithms that hide the loss of a single voice packet (in a row). They do this by playing

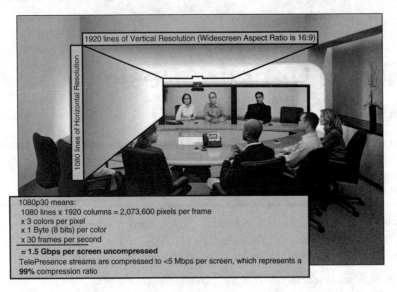

1920 lines of Vertical Resolution (Widescreen Aspect Ratio is 16:9)

1080 lines of Horizontal Resolution

1080p30 means:
1080 lines x 1920 columns = 2,073,600 pixels per frame
x 3 colors per pixel
x 1 Byte (8 bits) per color
x 30 frames per second
= 1.5 Gbps per screen uncompressed
TelePresence streams are compressed to <5 Mbps per screen, which represents a
99% compression ratio

Figure 9-1   *TelePresence data compression*

out the last packet's audio sample for an additional packetization interval (typically 20 ms). However, if two VoIP packets are lost (in a row), the PLC algorithms can no longer cover up the loss, and an audible clip is heard in the conversation. This "no two lost packets in a row" requirement is actually difficult to express as a percentage, as theoretically VoIP codecs could conceal up to 50 percent packet loss (provided the packets lost were every other packets and never two in a row). Nonetheless, the packet loss target for VoIP is generally held to be 1 percent.

In contrast, as previously noted, end users of TelePresence systems can visually detect quality issues with the HD video streams when experiencing only 0.01 percent packet loss. Therefore, from an end-user perspective, TelePresence is 100 times more sensitive to packet loss than VoIP. However, it should be noted that a small allowance for minor pixelization can be made, and as such the recommended packet loss target for TelePresence networks is 0.05 percent.

However, an absolute target for packet loss is not the only consideration in high availability network design. Loss, during normal network operation, should effectively be 0 percent over a properly designed network. In such a case, it is generally only during network events, such as link failures and route-flaps, where packet loss would occur. Therefore, it is usually more meaningful to express availability targets not only in absolute terms, such as <0.05 percent, but also in terms of network convergence targets.

Statistical analysis on speech and communications have shown that overall user satisfaction with a conversation (whether voice or interactive video) begins to drop when latency exceeds 200 ms. This is because 200 ms is about the length of time it takes for one party to figure out that the other person has stopped talking and thus, it is their turn to speak. This value (200 ms) provides a subjective "conversation disruption" metric. Put another way, a delay in excess of 200 ms, whether network transmission delay or network convergence delay, would impact the naturalness of a voice or video conversation. This is not to say that a loss of packets for 200 ms is unnoticeable to end users (as already mentioned, a loss of a single packet in 10,000 might be noticeable as minor pixelization); however, a temporary interruption of 200 ms would likely not be considered intolerable, should it happen, and would not significantly impact a conversation. This is because a disruption within 200 ms (which translates to seven frames of video, or less) would likely only result in a momentary video image freeze. By the time the eight frames of video arrive, the image will likely be lost, and the RTCP protocol will request a resync, which can take at least three additional seconds to recover.

Note   One such statistical analysis of speech and communication is the ITU G.114 (E-Model). Although the primary application of the ITU G.114 E-Model is to target one-way transmission latency, these observations and metrics can also be applied to the context of network convergence latency.

Thus, to maintain naturalness in TelePresence conversations, even during network events, the network convergence target for highly available campus and data center networks is 200 ms. On other network topologies, such as WAN/VPN branch networks, this target is likely unattainable, given the technologies and constraints involved (as discussed in more detail later in this chapter), in which case the network should be designed to converge in the lowest achievable amount of time (which is recommended in the 5 second to 15 second range).

Note   Convergence times aren't uniform for all network events. For instance, upstream versus downstream network outages might take different amounts of time to recover from. Thus, these convergence targets represent the worst-case scenario convergence times.

To summarize these considerations: The targets for TelePresence campus and data center networks in terms of packet loss is 0.05 percent with a network convergence target of 200 ms; on WAN/VPN branch networks, loss should still be targeted to 0.05 percent, but convergence targets (which should be minimized) will inevitably be considerably higher and will be dependent on topologies, geographies, service-level agreements (SLA), and other constraints.

Designing the underlying network infrastructure to support these levels of network availability will benefit all applications on the converged network, not just TelePresence.

Highly Available Campus Design for TelePresence

Designing a highly available campus network is much like laying a foundation for a house: If engineering work is skipped at the foundation level, the house will crack and eventually fail. On the other hand, if a reliable foundation is engineered and built, the house will stand for years, growing with the owner through alterations and expansions to provide safe and reliable service throughout its lifecycle. The same is true for a campus network. If the foundation of availability is properly engineered from the start, it can support today's advanced applications, like TelePresence, and tomorrow's.

The three main principles that relate to campus design architectures are as follows:

- Redundancy

- Hierarchy

- Modularity

The following sections address each of these campus network design considerations

Redundancy

As discussed in Chapter 5, "Network Availability Technologies," the key design principle to improving availability is to engineer with redundancy. However, although redundancy is good, it's the case where "more is not always better." Multiple levels of redundancy (overredundancy) might prove disadvantageous. Specifically, when network resources have more than one backup, the law of diminishing returns begins to apply, as network configuration, operation, and troubleshooting complexity outweigh the incremental value that additional levels of redundancy might achieve. Figure 9-2 illustrates a campus network with three levels of redundancy.

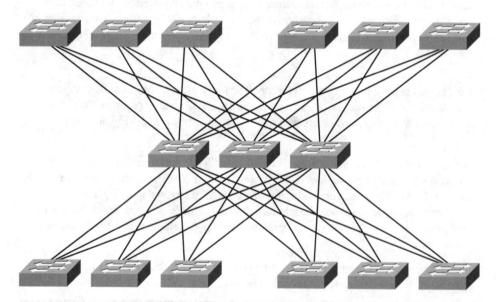

Figure 9-2 *Over redundant campus network design*

In Figure 9-2, if any given link failed, there would be at least two alternate paths to the next node. Although this provides an incremental level of availability, it also makes it more difficult to determine which backup path will be chosen, which might increase the time to troubleshoot and repair a problem. In contrast, if only two paths existed between nodes, the network failure would be deterministic, or predictable. Deterministic network failover is a design objective that facilitates troubleshooting, reducing Mean Time To Repair (MTTR) and increasing overall availability. Therefore, for most enterprise networks, it is recommended to design with only a single level of redundancy (with only one backup for every link or device).

Nonetheless, with even a single level of redundancy, campus networks can quickly become large and complex; however, applying the design principles of hierarchy and modularity can do much to efficiently scale and simplify these networks, as discussed in the following sections.

Hierarchy

Hierarchical design, which closely relates to modular design, significantly enhances scalability and availability.

For example, one network design option is to fully mesh all devices. In a fully meshed network, the number of links required to interconnect a given number of devices or nodes, is

n(n-1) / 2

where n represents the number of nodes.

For example, if there are 8 switches within the campus network and these are fully meshed, 28 links are required [8(8-1)/2] to fully interconnect these, as illustrated in Figure 9-3.

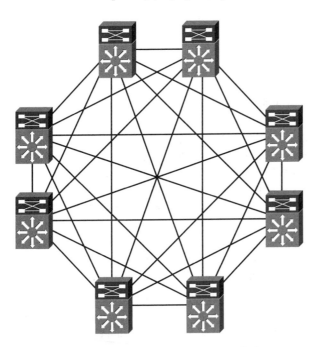

Figure 9-3   *Fully meshed campus network design*

Adding another pair of switches to the fully meshed topology illustrated in Figure 9-3 would require an additional 17 links [[10(10-1)/2]-28], for a total of 45 links. Adding yet another pair would require an additional 21 links [[12(12-1)/2]-45], bringing the total number of links required to 66, and so on.

An alternative approach would be to use a level of hierarchy within the design, namely a common pair of switches that all other switches would connect to. These common switches form a "core" layer, as illustrated in Figure 9-4. In such a design, each pair of switches added to the network requires only 5 links; specifically, each switch requires a link to each core switch (4 links per pair), plus one link joining the pair. Additionally, there is a single link between the core switches, which brings the total number of links to connect 8 switches to 21 (4 pairs × 5 links per pair + 1 core-interconnect).

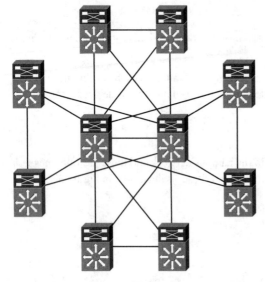

Figure 9-4   *(Two-level) hierarchical campus network design*

Although using a core layer has saved only a modest 7 links under an 8-switch topology, scalability gains are better demonstrated as additional pairs are added to the network. Because adding an incremental pair of switches requires only 5 new links, adding two more pairs of switches to the topology illustrated in Figure 9-4 would require only 10 additional links, bringing the total number of links to 31 (as opposed to 66 under a fully meshed design).

In short, a hierarchical design requires a linear increase in the number of links required to interconnect devices (in this example, 5 links per incremental pair), as opposed to an exponential increase in the number of links, as required by a fully meshed design.

More than one level of hierarchy is often required in most enterprise campus networks, delineating three distinct layers of the campus network. These layers not only contribute to increased scalability, but also lend themselves to specific roles within the network architecture:

- **Access layer:** The edge of the campus network, where endpoints-such as TelePresence codecs, IP Phones, wireless access points, PCs, and printers attach to the network. The access layer provides the intelligent demarcation between the network infrastructure and the computing devices that leverage that infrastructure. As such it might be required to provide infrastructure services (such as PoE), security services (such as 802.1x and/or 802.1Q), QoS (such as trust boundary enforcement and other services discussed in more detail in the following chapter), and management services (such as CDP and SNMP).

- **Distribution layer:** Has a unique role in that it acts as an aggregation, which services and controls the boundary between the access and the core layers of the network. The distribution layer serves three main purposes: First, it is the aggregation point for access switches providing connectivity and policy services for traffic flows; second, it provides an isolation and demarcation point between the distribution building block (building blocks are discussed in the next section) and the rest of the network; and third, it is an element in the core of the network and participates in the core routing design, providing a summarization boundary for network routing protocols.

- **Core layer:** In some ways the simplest yet most critical part of the campus. The core campus is the backbone that glues together all the elements of the campus architecture, serving as the common aggregator for all elements of the campus. As such, the core provides a limited set of services and is designed to be highly available and operate in an always-on mode. The key design objective for the campus core is to provide the appropriate level of redundancy to allow for immediate data-flow recovery if any component (switch, supervisor, line card, or fiber) fails. The network design must also permit the occasional, but necessary, hardware and software upgrade and change to be made without disrupting any network applications. The core of the network should not implement any complex policy services, nor should it have any directly attached user and server connections. The core should also have the minimal control plane configuration combined with highly available devices configured with the correct amount of physical redundancy to provide for this nonstop service capability.

Figure 9-5 illustrates the three layers of campus hierarchy.

Beyond enhancing and simplifying scalability, hierarchical network design enables a modularity to be incorporated within the network architecture, as be discussed next.

Modularity

Any large complex network (or system) can be built using a set of modularized components that can be assembled in a structured, hierarchical manner. Dividing any system into subcomponent modules provides a number of immediate benefits. For example, each of the modules can be designed with some degree of independence from the overall design and can be operated as semi-independent elements providing for overall higher system availability and for simpler management and operations.

Thus, the campus network can modularize into building blocks that can be assembled in a hierarchical fashion to achieve a higher degree of stability, flexibility, and manageability, not only for these individual modules, but also for the campus network as a whole.

The primary building block of campus design is the access-distribution block (also referred to as the distribution block); however, there are other role-specific blocks also, such as services blocks (for providing WLAN and UC services), WAN/VPN edge blocks, and

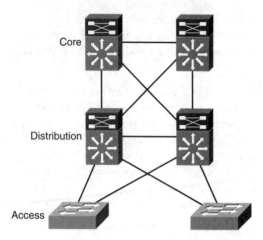

Figure 9-5   *(Three-level) hierarchical campus network design: access, distribution, and core layers*

Internet edge blocks. Additionally, the data center, as a whole, could be considered a modular block within the campus network. Figure 9-6 illustrates a modular campus architecture with multiple types of building blocks.

> **Note**   As TelePresence endpoints connect to the distribution block, this block will be the focus of the designs to follow. However, the design principles and recommendations likewise apply to various other campus building blocks.

Properly designing the distribution block goes a long way to ensuring the success and stability of the overall campus architecture. It is the network topology control plane design choices, such as Layer 2 or Layer 3 network control protocols, that are central to determining how the distribution block glues together and fits within the overall architecture. The three main design options for the distribution block are as follows:

- Multitier design

- Virtual switching system (VSS) design

- Routed access design (either EIGRP or OSPF)

Although all three of these designs use the same basic physical topology and cabling plan, there are differences in where the Layer 2 and Layer 3 boundaries exist, how the network topology redundancy is implemented, and how load-balancing works, and other differences, which are presented in the following sections.

Multitier Campus Distribution Block Design

The multitier distribution block design, illustrated in Figure 9-7, is the traditional campus distribution block design. All the access switches are configured to run in Layer 2 forwarding mode, and the distribution switches are configured to run both Layer 2 and Layer 3 forwarding. VLAN-based trunks extend the subnets from the distribution switches

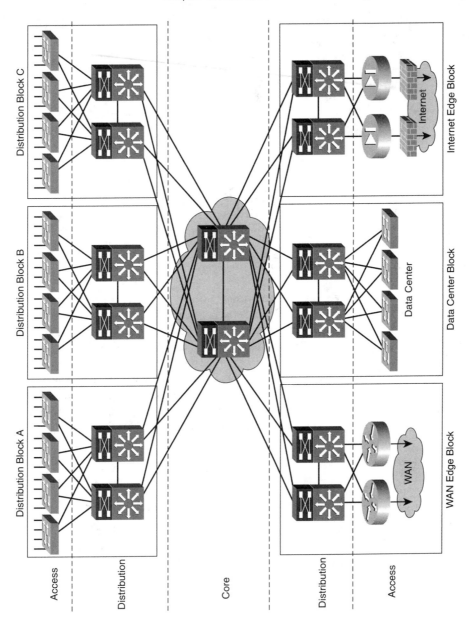

Figure 9-6 *Modular campus architecture*

down to the access layer. Either Spanning Tree Protocol (STP), with Cisco STP enhancements, such as PortFast with BPDU Guard, UplinkFast and BackboneFast, or RSTP is configured between the access and distribution switches. A First-Hop Redundancy Protocol (preferably Gateway Load Balancing Protocol [GLBP] to provide automatic load-balancing) is run on the distribution layer switches with a routing protocol to provide upstream routing to the core of the campus. The distribution switches are interconnected with a Layer 3 EtherChannel link.

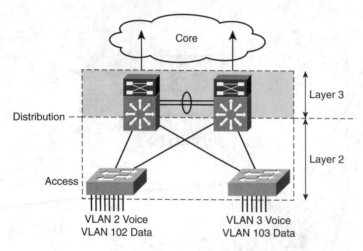

Figure 9-7   *Multitier campus distribution block design*

The multitier design has two basic variations, as shown in Figure 9-8, which primarily differ only in the manner in which VLANs are defined. In the looped design, one-to-many VLANs are configured to span multiple access switches. As a result, each of these spanned VLANs has a Spanning Tree or Layer 2 looped topology. The other alternative, the loop-free design, follows the best practice for the multitier design and defines unique VLANs for each access switch. The removal of loops in the topology provides a number of benefits, including per device uplink load balancing with the use of GLBP, a reduced dependence on the Spanning Tree to provide for network recovery, reduction in the risk of broadcast storms, and the capability to avoid unicast flooding.

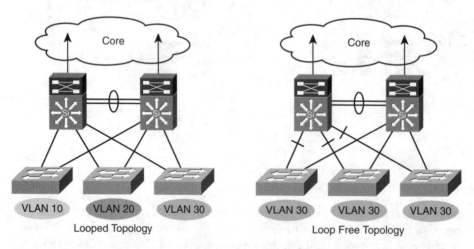

Figure 9-8   *Two variations of the multitier campus distribution block design*

Many campus networks today use the multitier campus block design; however, this design will not meet the availability targets for TelePresence (of 0.05 percent packet loss with

200 ms convergence times). This is simply due to the convergence times required by RSTP (which can be tuned to converge within 800 ms) and STP (which requires up to 50 seconds to converge).

Therefore, for campus networks supporting TelePresence, it is recommended to deploy (or consider deploying) either a VSS design or a routed access design, as detailed in the following sections.

Virtual Switch Campus Distribution Block Design

The Cisco Virtual Switch System (VSS), overviewed in Chapter 5, allows for the multitier distribution block design to be significantly improved in the areas of availability, efficiency, and manageability.

Following are the main design elements of a VSS distribution block design:

■ Virtual switch domain on the distribution switches

■ Virtual switch link between the distribution switches

■ Multi-chassis EtherChannel links on the distribution (virtual) switch

■ EtherChannel uplinks on the access switches

Figure 9-9 illustrates each of these design elements labeled 1 through 4, respectively.

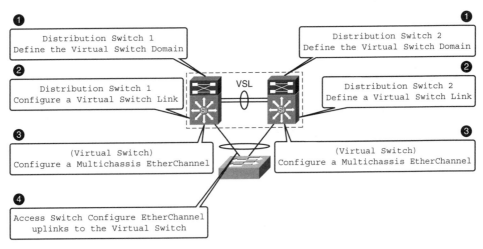

Figure 9-9 *Virtual switching system distribution block design*

Example 9-1 shows the configuration of the distribution/virtual switch part of the VSS distribution block design, and Example 9-2 shows the configuration of the access switch component of the design.

Example 9-1 *Distribution/Virtual Switch Design for VSS Distribution Block*

```
Distribution-VSS-Switch# show run
! Output omitted for brevity.
!
! Configure SSO
redundancy
 keepalive-enable
 mode sso
 main-cpu
   auto-sync running-config
!
! Define the Virtual Switch Domain
switch virtual domain 10
switch mode virtual
! Assign higher priority to primary switch
 switch 1 priority 110
! Assign lower priority to backup switch
 switch 2 priority 100
 dual-active detection pagp trust channel-group 202
!
!
! Define the Virtual Switch Link
interface Port-channel1
 description VSL link from Switch 1
 no switchport
 no ip address
 load-interval 30
 switch virtual link 1
!
<repeat for other end of VSL>
!
! Assign physical links to VSL
interface TenGigabitEthernet1/1/1
 description VSL link (member) from Switch 1
 no switchport
 no ip address
 logging event link-status
 logging event bundle-status
! Associate physical port with VSL EtherChannel bundle
 channel-group 1 mode on
!
<repeat for each physical link within VSL>
!
! Define a Multi-Chassis EtherChannel (MEC) to access-switch
interface Port-channel202
```

```
  description MEC downlink to Access Switch
  switchport
! Configure 802.1Q trunking options
  switchport trunk encapsulation dot1q
  switchport trunk native vlan 202
  switchport trunk allowed vlan 2,102
  switchport mode trunk
  logging event link-status
  logging event trunk-status
  logging event bundle-status
  logging event spanning-tree status
  load-interval 30
! Enable PortFast
  spanning-tree portfast trunk
  hold-queue 2000 out
!
! Assign physical interfaces to MEC
interface GigabitEthernet1/8/1
  description MEC downlink (member) to Access Switch
  switchport
! Configure 802.1Q trunking options
  switchport trunk encapsulation dot1q
  switchport trunk native vlan 202
  switchport trunk allowed vlan 2,102
  switchport mode trunk
  logging event link-status
  logging event spanning-tree status
  load-interval 30
  channel-protocol lacp
! Associate physical port with EtherChannel bundle 202
  channel-group 202 mode active
  hold-queue 2000 out
!
<repeat for each physical link within MEC>
!
!
router eigrp 100
  passive-interface default
  no passive-interface Port-channel200
  no passive-interface Port-channel201
  network 10.0.0.0
  distribute-list Default out Port-channel255
  distribute-list Default out Port-channel256
  no auto-summary
  eigrp router-id 10.122.102.1
```

```
 eigrp event-log-size 3000000
! Enable NSF (with SSO) for distribution-to-core neighbor adjacencies
 nsf
!
```

Example 9-2   *Access Switch Design for VSS Distribution Block*

```
Access-Switch# show run
! Output omitted for brevity.
!
! Enable Rapid Spanning Tree
spanning-tree mode rapid-pvst
spanning-tree loopguard default
spanning-tree logging
spanning-tree extend system-id
!
vlan internal allocation policy ascending
!
! Define Access Data VLAN
vlan 2
 name ACCESS-DATA-VLAN
!
! Define Access Voice VLAN
vlan 102
 name ACCESS-VOICE-VLAN
!
!
interface GigabitEthernet0/1
 description Access edge port
! Configure 802.1Q trunking options on access port
 switchport access vlan 2
 switchport mode access
 switchport voice vlan 102
 load-interval 30
! Enable PortFast and BPDU Guard
 spanning-tree portfast
 spanning-tree bpduguard enable
!
...
!
! Define EtherChannel uplink to Distribution/Virtual Switch
interface Port-channel1
 description EtherChannel uplink to VSS Distribution Switch
! Configure 802.1Q trunking options
 switchport trunk encapsulation dot1q
```

```
 switchport trunk native vlan 202
 switchport trunk allowed vlan 2,102
 switchport mode dynamic desirable
 logging event spanning-tree
 logging event status
 load-interval 30
 carrier-delay msec 0
!
! Assign physical interfaces to EtherChannel uplink
interface GigabitEthernet0/27
 description EtherChannel uplink (member) to VSS Distribution Switch
! Configure 802.1Q trunking options
 switchport trunk encapsulation dot1q
 switchport trunk native vlan 202
 switchport trunk allowed vlan 2,102
 switchport mode dynamic desirable
 logging event trunk-status
 logging event bundle-status
 logging event spanning-tree
 logging event status
 load-interval 30
 carrier-delay msec 0
 channel-protocol pagp
! Associate physical port with EtherChannel bundle 1
 channel-group 1 mode desirable
!
```

Virtual switching systems can provide convergence times within 200 ms (the target for TelePresence campus convergence). However, another design option to achieve similar levels of convergence times is routed access design, discussed next.

Routed Access Campus Distribution Block Design

An alternative configuration to the traditional multitier distribution block model is routed access design, in which the access switch acts as a full Layer 3 routing node (providing both Layer 2 and Layer 3 switching), and the access to distribution Layer 2 uplink trunks are replaced with Layer 3 point-to-point routed links. This alternative design moves the Layer 2/3 demarcation to the access layer (from the distribution layer in the multitier design), as shown in Figure 9-10. As with the multitier design, however, the distribution switches are interconnected with a Layer 3 EtherChannel link.

In best practice multitier and routed access design, each access switch is configured with unique voice and data VLANs (and any other required VLANs). In the routed access design, the default gateway and root bridge for these VLANs is simply moved from the distribution switch to the access switch. Addressing for all end stations and for the default gateway remains the same. VLAN and specific port configuration remains unchanged on the access switch. Router interface configuration, access lists, and any other configurations

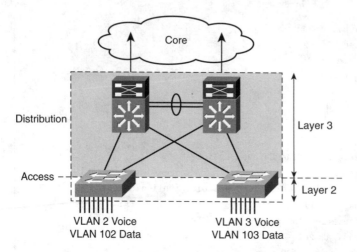

Figure 9-10   *Routed access campus distribution block design*

for each VLAN remain identical. However, these are now configured on the VLAN Switched Virtual Interface (SVI) on the access switch, instead of on the distribution switches. A notable configuration change associated with the move of the Layer 3 interface down to the access switch is that it is no longer necessary to configure a First-Hop Redundancy Protocol (FHRP), as the router interfaces for all subnets/VLANs are now local.

The routed access distribution block design has a number of advantages over the multitier design, including faster convergence times (within 200 ms), the use of a single network control protocol (either EIGRP or OSPF), the support of common end-to-end troubleshooting tools (such as ping and traceroute), and the removal of any FHRP requirement.

Note   Although routed access designs are suitable for most environments, these might not be suitable for all because these require that no VLAN span multiple access switches.

Routed access designs can be deployed using either EIGRP or OSPF, as detailed in following sections. However, there are a few design elements that both approaches hold in common, as discussed next.

Routed Access Design: Common Elements

There are several elements that EIGRP and OSPF routed access designs have in common, including

- Point-to-Point IP addressing scheme
- Point-to-Point fiber connections
- Link debounce timer settings
- Carrier-delay settings
- IP event dampening support

Each of these common design elements will be addressed in turn.

Point-to-Point IP Addressing Scheme

The first of these common design elements involves the IP addressing scheme of the point-to-point subnets between the distribution and the access switches (which, if converting from a multitier design, means allocating new subnets for these links). For each access switch, this entails the allocation of two new subnets, one for each uplink. Subnets can be divided and subdivided by using variable-length subnet masking (VLSM). However, these subnets should be contained within the summarized address block advertised upstream to the core of the network and not increase the number of routes contained within the core of the network. Additionally, in this manner, network events can be compartmentalized within subnets and masked from the distribution and core networks, reducing the need for any superfluous convergence events. Two efficient VLSM options exist to provide IP addresses for these point-to-point links:

- **VLSM addressing using /30 subnets:** Using 30-bit subnet masking (255.255.255.252) provides an efficient use of VLSM address space. A single Class C address block chosen out of the summarized address range for the distribution block addresses links to 32 access switches, which is sufficient for all but the largest distribution block.

- **VLSM addressing using /31 subnets:** It might be desirable to use 31-bit masking (255.255.255.254) on the distribution-to-access point to provide an even more efficient usage of address space. The 31-bit prefixes, as defined in RFC 3021, provide for twice as many subnets to be created out of the same block of addresses as would be available using /30 addressing.

Note   For more information on /31 addressing, see RFC 3021 at: http://www.ietf.org/rfc/rfc3021

Point-to-Point Fiber Connections

A second common design element relates to the recommended best practice for campus design to use point-to-point fiber connections for all links between switches. In addition to providing better electromagnetic and error protection, fewer distance limitations and higher capacity fiber links between switches provide for improved fault detection. In a point-to-point fiber campus design using GigE and 10GigE fiber, remote node and link loss detection is normally accomplished using the remote fault detection mechanism implemented as a part of the IEEE 802.3z (GigE) and 802.3ae (10GigE) link negotiation protocols. If you have physical link failure, local or remote transceiver failure, or remote node failure, the remote fault detection mechanism triggers a link down condition that then triggers software and hardware routing and forwarding table recovery. The rapid convergence in the Layer 3 campus design is largely because of the efficiency and speed of this fault detection mechanism.

Link Debounce Timer Settings

When tuning the campus for optimal convergence, you need to review the status of the link debounce and carrier delay configuration. By default, GigE and 10GigE interfaces operate with a 10 ms debounce timer that provides for optimal link failure detection. The default debounce timer for 10/100 fiber and all copper link media is longer than that for GigE fiber, which is one reason for the recommendation of a high-speed fiber deployment for switch-to-switch links in a routed campus design. It is good practice to review the status of this configuration on all switch-to-switch links to ensure the desired operation, as shown in the following sample output:

```
L3-Access-Switch# show interfaces tenGigabitEthernet 4/2 debounce
Port   Debounce time   Value(ms)
Te4/2   disable
```

The default and recommended configuration for debounce timer is "disabled," which results in the minimum time between link failure and notification of the upper layer protocols.

Carrier-Delay Settings

A third common design element is to ensure that the carrier-delay behavior is configured to a value of zero (0) to ensure no additional delay in the notification of link down. In the current Cisco IOS levels, the default behavior for Catalyst switches is to use a default value of 0 ms on all Ethernet interfaces for the carrier-delay time to ensure fast link detection. It is still recommended as best practice to hard code the carrier-delay value on critical interfaces with a value of 0 ms to ensure the desired behavior, as shown in the following interface configuration example:

```
L3-Access-Switch(config)# interface GigabitEthernet1/1
L3-Access-Switch(config-if)# description Uplink to Distribution 1
L3-Access-Switch(config-if)# carrier-delay msec 0
```

IP Event Dampening Support

A final common design element relates to IP event dampening. When tightly tuning the interface failure detection mechanisms, it is a best practice to configure IP event dampening on any routed interface. As discussed in Chapter 5, IP event dampening provides a mechanism to control the rate at which interface state changes are propagated to the routing protocols if a flapping link condition occurs, by assigning a penalty and penalty decay mechanism on link state transitions. If a rapid series of link status changes occur, the penalty value for an interface increases until it exceeds a threshold, at which time no additional interface state changes are propagated to the routing protocols until the penalty value associated with the interface is below the reuse threshold. IP event dampening can be configured to operate with default values for the suppress, reuse, and maximum penalty values, as shown in the following interface configuration example:

```
L3-Access-Switch(config)# interface GigabitEthernet1/1
L3-Access-Switch(config-if)# description Uplink to Distribution 1
L3-Access-Switch(config-if)# dampening
```

Having covered these common settings for both EIGRP and OSPF routed access design, each design option is now detailed.

EIGRP Routed Access Design

The four design elements required for EIGRP routed access design are as follows:

- EIGRP stub routing at the access layer

- EIGRP route filtering at the distribution layer

- EIGRP route summarization at the distribution layer

- EIGRP hello and hold timer tuning at the access and distribution layers.

Note This section assumes a working knowledge of EIGRP operation and configuration. For additional details relating to EIGRP, refer to the Cisco Press book *Routing TCP/IP*, Volume 1, Second Edition by Jeff Doyle and Jennifer Carroll.

The length of time it takes for EIGRP (or in fact, any routing protocol) to restore traffic flows within the campus is bounded by the following three main factors:

- The time required to detect the loss of a valid forwarding path

- The time required to determine a new best path

- The time required to update software and associated hardware forwarding tables

In the cases where the switch has redundant equal-cost paths, all three of these events are performed locally within the switch and controlled by the internal interaction of software and hardware. In the case where there is no second equal-cost path nor a feasible successor for EIGRP to use, the time required to determine the new best path is variable and primarily dependent on EIGRP query and reply propagation across the network. To minimize the time required to restore traffic in the case where a full EIGRP routing convergence is required, it is necessary to provide strict bounds on the number and range of the queries generated.

Although EIGRP provides a number of ways to control query propagation, the three main methods that are best suited to routed access design are the use of the EIGRP stub feature, route-filtering, and route summarization.

EIGRP Stub Routing at the Access Layer

The design of the Layer 3 access campus is similar to a branch WAN. The access switch provides the same routing functionality as the branch router, and the distribution switch provides the same routing functions as the WAN aggregation router. In the branch WAN, the EIGRP stub feature is configured on all the branch routers to prevent the aggregation router from sending queries to the edge access routers. In the campus, configuring EIGRP stub on the Layer 3 access switches also prevents the distribution switch from generating downstream queries, as shown in the following example:

```
EIGRP-L3-Access-Switch(config)# router eigrp 100
EIGRP-L3-Access-Switch(config-router)# network 10.0.0.0
EIGRP-L3-Access-Switch(config-router)# eigrp stub connected
```

Configuring the access switch as a "stub" router enforces hierarchical traffic patterns in the network. In the campus design, the access switch is intended to forward traffic only to and from the locally connected subnets. The size of the switch and the capacity of its uplinks are specified to meet the needs of the locally connected devices. The access switch is never intended to be a transit or intermediary device for any data flows that are not to or from locally connected devices. The hierarchical campus is designed to aggregate the lower speed access ports into higher-speed distribution uplinks, and then to aggregate that traffic up into high-speed core links. The network is designed to support redundant capacity within each of these aggregation layers of the network but not to support the reroute of traffic through an access layer. Configuring each of the access switches as EIGRP stub routers ensures that the large aggregated volumes of traffic within the core are never forwarded through the lower bandwidth links in the access layer and also ensures that no traffic is ever mistakenly routed through the access layer, bypassing any distribution layer policy or security controls.

Each access switch in the routed access design should be configured with the EIGRP stub feature to aid in ensuring consistent convergence of the campus by limiting the number of EIGRP queries required if a failure occurs, and to enforce engineered traffic flows to prevent the network from mistakenly forwarding transit traffic through the access layer.

EIGRP Route Filtering at the Distribution Layer

A second EIGRP routed access design element is route filtering, which serves as a complement to the use of EIGRP stub routing. Cisco recommends applying a distribute list to all the distribution downlinks to filter the routes received by the access switches. The combination of stub routing and route filtering ensures that the routing protocol behavior and routing table contents of the access switches are consistent with their role, which is to forward traffic to and from the locally connected subnets only. Cisco recommends that a default or "quad zero" route (0.0.0.0 mask 0.0.0.0) be the only route advertised to the access switches, as shown in Example 9-3.

Example 9-3 *Distribution Switch EIGRP Route Filtering*

```
EIGRP-Distribution-Switch(config)# router eigrp 100
EIGRP-Distribution-Switch(config-router)# network 10.120.0.0 0.0.255.255
EIGRP-Distribution-Switch(config-router)# network 10.122.0.0 0.0.0.255
EIGRP-Distribution-Switch(config-router)# distribute-list QUAD-ZERO out
GigabitEthernet3/3
EIGRP-Distribution-Switch(config-router)# exit
EIGRP-Distribution-Switch(config)# ip access-list standard QUAD-ZERO
EIGRP-Distribution-Switch(config-std-nacl)# permit 0.0.0.0
```

EIGRP Route Summarization at the Distribution Layer

Configuring EIGRP stub (with distribution route filtering) significantly reduces the number of queries generated by a distribution switch if a downlink failure occurs, but it does not guarantee that the remaining queries are responded to quickly. If a downlink failure occurs, the distribution switch generates three queries: one sent to each of the core switches and one sent to the peer distribution switch. The queries generated ask for information about the specific subnets lost when the access switch link failed. The peer distribution switch has a successor (valid route) to the subnets in question through its downlink to the access switch and can return a response with the cost of reaching the destination through this path.

The fast response from the peer distribution switch does not (in itself) ensure a fast convergence time, which necessitates a third EIGRP routed design element: route summarization. This is because EIGRP recovery is bounded by the longest query response time. The EIGRP process has to wait for replies from all queries to ensure that it calculates the optimal loop-free path. Responses to the two queries sent toward the core need to be received before EIGRP can complete the route recalculation. To ensure that the core switches generate an immediate response to the query, it is necessary to summarize the block of distribution routes into a single summary route advertised toward the core, as shown in the following example:

```
EIGRP-Distribution-Switch(config)# interface TenGigabitEthernet4/1
EIGRP-Distribution-Switch(config-if)# description Distribution 10 GigE uplink to
Core 1
EIGRP-Distribution-Switch(config-if)# ip summary-address eigrp 100 10.120.0.0
255.255.0.0 5
```

With the upstream route summarization in place, whenever the distribution switch generates a query for a component subnet of the summarized route, the core switches reply that they do not have a valid path (cost = infinity) to the subnet query.

Using a combination of stub routing and summarizing, the distribution block, routing upstream to the core, both limits the number of queries generated and bounds those that are generated to a single hop in all directions. Keeping the query period bounded to less than 100 ms keeps the network convergence similarly bounded under 200 ms (the target for TelePresence campus networks).

EIGRP Hello and Hold Timer Tuning at the Access and Distribution Layers

A fourth EIGRP routed access design element relates to the tuning of EIGRP timers. As previously discussed, the recommended practice is to use point-to-point fiber connections for all links between switches. Link failure detection through 802.3z and 802.3ae remote fault detection mechanism provides for recovery from most campus switch component failures. However, Cisco recommends in the Layer 3 campus design that the EIGRP hello and dead timers be reduced to 1 and 3 seconds, respectively, as shown in Example 9-4. The loss of hellos and the expiration of the dead timer do provide a backup to the Layer 1/2 remote fault detection mechanisms. Reducing the EIGRP hello and hold timers from defaults of 5 seconds and 15 seconds provides for faster routing convergence in the rare event that Layer 1/2 remote fault detection fails to operate, and hold timer expiration is required to trigger a network convergence because of a neighbor failure.

Example 9-4   *Access Switch EIGRP Timer Tuning*

```
EIGRP-L3-Access-Switch(config)# interface TenGigabitEthernet4/3
EIGRP-L3-Access-Switch(config-if)# description 10 GigE to Distribution-Left
EIGRP-L3-Access-Switch(config-if)# ip address 10.122.0.26 255.255.255.254
EIGRP-L3-Access-Switch(config-if)# ip hello-interval eigrp 100 1
EIGRP-L3-Access-Switch(config-if)# ip hold-time eigrp 100 3
```

Note   It is important to ensure that both the EIGRP hello and hold timers are set identically on both ends of each link; otherwise, EIGRP neighbor adjacencies will not form properly.

EIGRP Routed Access Design Configuration

Putting all these elements together yields the access and distribution switch configurations for EIGRP routed access design for TelePresence campus networks, as shown in Examples 9-5 and 9-6, respectively.

Example 9-5   *Access Switch EIGRP Routed Access Design*

```
EIGRP-L3-Access-Switch# show run
! Output omitted for brevity.
!
key chain eigrp
 key 100
!
! Configure spanning tree as a redundant protective mechanism
spanning-tree mode rapid-pvst
spanning-tree loopguard default
!
! Create a local Data and Voice VLAN
vlan 2
 name ACCESS-DATA-VLAN
!
vlan 102
 name ACCESS-VOICE-VLAN
!
!
! Define the uplink to the Distribution switches as a point to point Layer 3 link
interface GigabitEthernet1/1
 description Uplink to Distribution 1
! Enable IP Event Dampening with default values
```

```
  dampening
! Configure the switch-to-switch link using a /30 or /31 subnet>
  ip address 10.120.0.205 255.255.255.254
! Reduce EIGRP hello and dead timers to 1 and 3 seconds
  ip hello-interval eigrp 100 1
  ip hold-time eigrp 100 3
! Enable EIGRP MD5 authentication (optional, but recommended)
  ip authentication mode eigrp 100 md5
  ip authentication key-chain eigrp 100 eigrp
  logging event link-status
  load-interval 30
! Hard-code the link carrier-delay to 0 ms
  carrier-delay msec 0
!
!
! Define Switched Virtual Interfaces's for both access Data and Voice VLANs
interface Vlan2
  ip address 10.120.2.1 255.255.255.0
  ip helper-address 10.121.0.5
  no ip redirects
  load-interval 30
!
interface Vlan102
  ip address 10.120.102.1 255.255.255.0
  ip helper-address 10.121.0.5
  no ip redirects
  load-interval 30
!
! Configure Access switch as an EIGRP stub router
router eigrp 100
  network 10.120.0.0 0.0.255.255
  no auto-summary
  eigrp stub connected
  eigrp router-id 10.122.0.22
!
```

Example 9-6   *Distribution Switch EIGRP Routed Access Design*

```
EIGRP-Distribution-Switch# show run
! Output omitted for brevity.
!
key chain eigrp
!
key-string 7 01161501
!
```

```
! Configure spanning tree as a redundant protective mechanism
spanning-tree mode rapid-pvst
spanning-tree loopguard default
!
!Configure point to point Layer 3 links to each of the access switches
interface GigabitEthernet3/1
 description Link to Access Switch
! Enable IP Event Dampening with default values
 dampening
! Configure the switch to switch link using a /30 or /31 subnet>
 ip address 10.120.0.204 255.255.255.254
! Reduce EIGRP hello and dead timers to 1 and 3 seconds
 ip hello-interval eigrp 100 1
 ip hold-time eigrp 100 3
! Enable eigrp MD5 authentication (optional, but recommended)
 ip authentication mode eigrp 100 md5
 ip authentication key-chain eigrp 100 eigrp
 logging event link-status
 load-interval 30
! Hard-code the link carrier-delay to 0 ms
 carrier-delay msec 0
!
!
! Configure point to point L3 links to each of the core switches
interface TenGigabitEthernet4/1
 description 10 GigE to Core 1
! Enable IP Event Dampening with default values
 dampening
! Configure the switch to switch link using a /30 or /31 subnet>
 ip address 10.122.0.26 255.255.255.254
! Reduce EIGRP hello and dead timers to 1 and 3 seconds
 ip hello-interval eigrp 100 1
 ip hold-time eigrp 100 3
! Enable eigrp MD5 authentication (optional, but recommended)
 ip authentication mode eigrp 100 md5
 ip authentication key-chain eigrp 100 eigrp
! Advertise a summary address for the entire distribution block upstream to the
core>
 ip summary-address eigrp 100 10.120.0.0 255.255.0.0 5
 logging event link-status
 load-interval 30
! Hard-code the link carrier-delay to 0 ms
 carrier-delay msec 0
!
!
```

```
! Configure a point to point Layer 3 link between distribution switches
interface TenGigabitEthernet4/3
 description 10 GigE to Distribution 2
! Enable IP Event Dampening with default values
 dampening
! Configure the switch to switch link using a /30 or /31 subnet>
 ip address 10.122.0.21 255.255.255.254
! Reduce EIGRP hello and dead timers to 1 and 3 seconds
 ip hello-interval eigrp 100 1
 ip hold-time eigrp 100 3
! Enable eigrp MD5 authentication (optional, but recommended)
 ip authentication mode eigrp 100 md5
 ip authentication key-chain eigrp 100 eigrp
 logging event link-status
 load-interval 30
! Hard-code the link carrier-delay to 0 ms
 carrier-delay msec 0
!
!
router eigrp 100
! Set all interfaces not connected to another Layer 3 switch to passive
 passive-interface GigabitEthernet2/1
! Specify which networks should be routed by EIGRP
 network 10.120.0.0 0.0.255.255
 network 10.122.0.0 0.0.0.255
! Apply a route filter to block all routes other than the default to the
access-switches
 distribute-list QUAD-ZERO out GigabitEthernet3/1
 distribute-list QUAD-ZERO out GigabitEthernet3/2
 ...
 eigrp router-id 10.122.0.3
!
...
ip access-list standard QUAD-ZERO
 permit 0.0.0.0
!
```

Note   A helpful trick to remember when configuring Layer 3 switches is to use the **passive-interface default** router configuration command coupled with the **no passive-interface** interface configuration command because this can save dozens (if not hundreds) of passive interface commands.

The alternative routing protocol that you can use for routed access designs is OSPF, which is discussed next.

OSPF Routed Access Design

There are six design elements required from OSPF routed access design:

- OSPF area 0 designation of the core layer

- OSPF totally stubby configuration at the distribution and access layer

- OSPF route summarization at the distribution layer

- OSPF SPF and LSA throttle tuning

- OSPF Hello and dead timer tuning

- OSPF designated router configuration at the distribution layer

The first four elements are configured within the OSPF router configuration; the last two are interface-specific OSPF configurations.

Note   This section assumes a working knowledge of OSPF operation and configuration. For additional details relating to OSPF, refer to the Cisco Press book *Routing TCP/IP*, Volume 1, Second Edition by Jeff Doyle and *Cisco OSPF Command and Configuration Handbook* by William R. Parkhurst.

OSPF Area 0 Designation of the Core Layer

The first OSPF routed access design element is the designation of the campus core as OSPF area 0. OSPF implements a two-tier hierarchical routing model that uses a core or backbone tier known as area zero (0). Attached to that backbone through area border routers (ABR) are a number of secondary tier areas. The hierarchical design of OSPF areas is well-suited to the hierarchical campus design. The campus core provides the backbone function supported by OSPF area 0, and the distribution building blocks with redundant distribution switches can be configured to be independent areas with the distribution switches acting as the ABRs, as shown in Figure 9-11.

Mapping a unique OSPF area to each distribution block directly maps the basic building block of the OSPF routing design (the area) onto the basic building block of the campus network (the distribution block). The function of the distribution switch as a point of control for traffic to and from all access segments is directly supported by the functions of the ABR to control routing information into and out of the area. The boundary for route convergence events provided by the ABR supports the desire to have the distribution block provide for fault containment and also serves to aid in controlling the time required for routing convergence by restricting the scope of that routing convergence. Additionally,

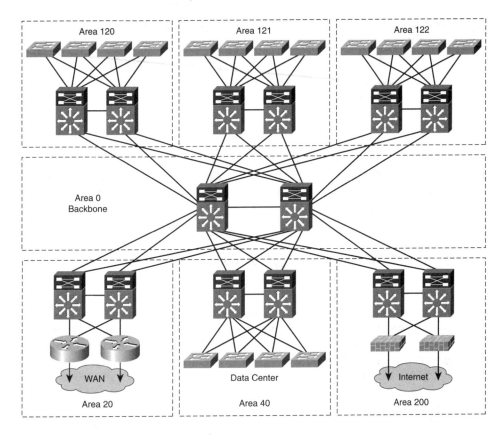

Figure 9-11 *Campus OSPF area design*

leveraging the properties of an OSPF stub area makes it relatively simple to enforce the rule that traffic not destined to an address within the distribution block is never forwarded into or through the area. Configuring each distribution block as a unique area ensures that the large aggregated volumes of traffic within the core are never forwarded through the lower bandwidth links in the access layer and also ensures that no traffic is ever mistakenly routed through the access layer, bypassing any distribution layer policy or security controls.

OSPF Totally Stubby Configuration at the Distribution and Access Layer

Closely related to ensuring that the access layer never becomes a transit link is the second OSPF routed access design element of configuring the access switches to be totally stubby OSPF areas, which is achieved by including the **no-summary** keyword in conjunction with the **area stub** OSPF command. Although many types of stub areas exist, Cisco recommends that totally stubby area configurations be used for the campus distribution blocks to minimize the size of the routing and forwarding tables in the access switches, as shown in the following example:

```
OSPF-L3-Access-Switch(config)# router ospf 100
OSPF-L3-Access-Switch(config-router)# area 120 stub no-summary
```

Note   Configuring a totally stubby area automatically injects an artificial default route (sourced from the ABR) as the sole route propagated into the area. Therefore, a route filter (with a quad-zero network), as used in the EIGRP example, is not explicitly required in OSPF routed access design.

OSPF Route Summarization at the Distribution Layer

The third design element in OSPF routed access is to implement a well-structured summarization scheme to reduce the scope of network topology updates if link or node failures occur. Route summarization aids in route control by reducing the number of routes and associated topology table information propagated by Link State Advertisements (LSA) in each network node. Without route summarization in place at the distribution ABR, each intra-area network prefix LSA in the local area is converted to a matching type-3 summary network LSA in the backbone area. A change in the cost or the deletion of a link in the local area needs to be propagated throughout the network as a summary route LSA update. With the appropriate route summarization in place, a single summary LSA is advertised into the backbone from the local area. Changes to specific intra-area LSAs within a summary range are not propagated to the backbone and the rest of the network.

Summarization of distribution area routes is accomplished through the use of the **area range** command. The **range** command defines which subnets within the specified distribution area are summarized into a single outbound summary network advertisement.

Cisco recommends that the cost of the advertised summary network route be specified with a static or hard-coded cost, as shown in the following configuration:

```
OSPF-Distribution-Switch(config)# router ospf 100
OSPF-Distribution-Switch(config-router)# area 120 range 10.120.0.0 255.255.0.0
cost 10
```

OSPF SPF and LSA Throttle Tuning

The fourth OSPF routed access design element relates to tuning OSPF throttle timers to optimize convergence. There are two throttle timers that affect the shortest-path-first (SFP) algorithm: the SPF throttle timer and the LSA throttle timer.

The SPF throttle timers implement an exponential back-off mechanism if multiple triggers for sequential SFP runs occur. The SPF throttle timer is configured with three values: spf-start, spf-hold, spf-max-wait. The first wait interval between SPF calculations is the amount of time in milliseconds specified by the spf-start argument. Each consecutive wait interval is two times the current hold level in milliseconds until the wait time reaches the maximum time in milliseconds as specified by the spf-max-wait argument. Subsequent wait times remain at the maximum until the values are reset or a link-state advertisement (LSA) is received between SPF calculations.

The Cisco recommended values for SPF throttle tuning are 10 ms (spf-start), 100 ms (spf-hold), and 5 seconds (spf-max-wait).

Operating with SPF throttle timers, LSA throttle timers limit the generation of LSAs to further optimize convergence. The LSA throttle timer is configured with three values:

- **start-interval:** Specifies the minimum delay in generating LSAs. The Cisco recommended value for this timer is 10 ms.

- **hold-interval:** Calculates the rate-limiting times for subsequent LSA generation. The Cisco recommended value for this timer is 100 ms.

- **max-interval:** Specifies the maximum wait time between generation of the same LSA. The Cisco recommended value for this timer is 5 ms.

Additionally, in tuning the throttle timer controlling the generation of LSAs, it is necessary to make a similar configuration to the throttle timer controlling the receipt of LSAs. The **lsa arrival** timer controls the rate at which a switch accepts a second LSA with the same LSA ID. It is considered best practice to tune the arrival rate at some value less than the generated rate to accommodate for any buffering or internal process timer scheduling delays. When using an LSA throttle hold-interval of 100 ms, it is recommended to use an LSA arrival value of 80 ms.

The SPF and LSA throttle timers and the LSA arrival timer are tuned to these recommended values in Example 9-7.

Example 9-7 *OSPF SPF and LSA Throttle Tuning*

```
OSPF-L3-Access-Switch(config)# router ospf 100
OSPF-L3-Access-Switch(config-router)# timers throttle spf 10 100 5000
OSPF-L3-Access-Switch(config-router)# timers throttle lsa all 10 100 5000
OSPF-L3-Access-Switch(config-router)# timers lsa arrival 80
```

OSPF Hello and Dead Timer Tuning

The fifth element in OSPF routed access design is OSPF Hello and Dead timer tuning; however, unlike SPF and LSA throttle tuning, these Hello and Dead timers are configured on the interface (and not within the OSPF router configuration mode). Because the recommended best practice for campus design uses point-to-point GigE and 10GigE fiber connections for all links between switches, link loss detection is normally accomplished by 802.3z and 802.3ae link protocols. However, the recommendation in the Layer 3 campus design is that the OSPF Hello and Dead timers be reduced to 250 ms and 1 second, respectively. Such tuning provides a backup to the Layer 1/2 remote fault detection mechanisms, in the rare case where a routed interface remains up after link loss. These timers are tuned with the **ip ospf dead-interval** interface command, as shown in the interface configuration example that follows. Notice, however, that the Hello interval is not explicitly configured but is calculated by taking the minimal Dead interval, 1 second, as specified by the **minimal** keyword, and then dividing by the **hello-multiplier** value configured (which is 4 by default).

```
OSPF-L3-Access-Switch(config)# interface GigabitEthernet3/11
OSPF-L3-Access-Switch(config-if)# ip ospf dead-interval minimal hello-multiplier 4
```

Note   It is important to ensure that both the OSPF Hello and Dead timers are set identically on both ends of each link; otherwise, OSPF neighbor adjacencies will not form properly.

OSPF Designated Router Configuration at the Distribution Layer

The six and final element of OSPF routed access design is to designate the distribution switch as the OSPF designated router (DR) on the access-to-distribution links. Although the campus is configured with point-to-point GigE links, OSPF still negotiates the DR and backup DR on each of the switch-to-switch links. In the campus environment, the selection of which switch is selected as DR has no impact on the stability or speed of convergence of the network. However, it is still recommended that the distribution switch be configured to act as DR on each of the access-distribution uplinks. If an access-distribution uplink fiber failure occurs, the distribution switch acting as the DR can directly propagate updated network LSAs to all connected access and distribution switch peers in the area. The distribution switch can be configured to act as the DR by setting the **ip ospf priority** on its distribution-to-access interface to 255; conversely, the access switch can be configured to never become a DR by setting the **ip ospf priority** on its access-to-distribution link to 0, as shown in Examples 9-8 and 9-9, respectively.

Example 9-8   *Distribution Switch Designated Router Configuration*

```
OSPF-Distribution-Switch(config)# interface GigabitEthernet3/11
OSPF-Distribution-Switch(config-if)# description Link to Access Switch
OSPF-Distribution-Switch(config-if)# dampening
```

```
OSPF-Distribution-Switch(config-if)# ip address 10.120.0.204 255.255.255.254
OSPF-Distribution-Switch(config-if)# ip ospf dead-interval minimal hello-
multiplier 4
OSPF-Distribution-Switch(config-if)# ip ospf priority 255
```

Example 9-9   *Access Switch Nondesignated Router Configuration*

```
OSPF-L3-Access-Switch(config)# interface GigabitEthernet1/1
OSPF-L3-Access-Switch(config-if)# description Uplink to Distribution 1
OSPF-L3-Access-Switch(config-if)# dampening
OSPF-L3-Access-Switch(config-if)# ip address 10.120.0.205 255.255.255.254
OSPF-L3-Access-Switch(config-if)# ip ospf dead-interval minimal hello-multiplier 4
OSPF-L3-Access-Switch(config-if)# ip ospf priority 0
```

OSPF Routed Access Design Configuration

Putting all these elements together yields the access and distribution switch configurations for OSPF routed access design for TelePresence campus networks, as shown in Examples 9-10 and 9-11, respectively.

Example 9-10   *Access Switch OSPF Routed Access Design*

```
OSPF-L3-Access-Switch# show run
! Output omitted for brevity.
!
!Configure spanning tree as a redundant protective mechanism
spanning-tree mode rapid-pvst
spanning-tree loopguard default
!
!
! Create a local Data and Voice VLAN
vlan 2
 name ACCESS-DATA-VLAN
!
vlan 102
 name ACCESS-VOICE-VLAN
!
!
! Define the uplink to the Distribution switches as a point to point Layer 3 link
interface GigabitEthernet1/1
 description Uplink to Distribution 1
! Enable IP Event Dampening with default values
 dampening
! Configure the switch-to-switch link using a /30 or /31 subnet>
 ip address 10.120.0.205 255.255.255.254
! Tune OSPF hello and dead timers to 250 ms and 1 second
```

```
 ip ospf dead-interval minimal hello-multiplier 4
 ! Disable access-switch from becoming OSPF DR on uplink
 ip ospf priority 0
 logging event link-status
 load-interval 30
 ! Hard-code the link carrier-delay to 0 ms
 carrier-delay msec 0
 !
 !
 ! Define Switched Virtual Interfaces for both Access Data and Voice VLANs
 interface Vlan2
 ip address 10.120.2.1 255.255.255.0
 ip helper-address 10.121.0.5
 no ip redirects
 load-interval 30
 !
 interface Vlan102
 ip address 10.120.102.1 255.255.255.0
 ip helper-address 10.121.0.5
 no ip redirects
 load-interval 30
 !
 router ospf 100
 router-id 10.120.250.6
 log-adjacency-changes
 ! Modify the OSPF reference BW to support 10GigE links
 auto-cost reference-bandwidth 10000
 ! Configure the access switch as a member of the OSPF Totally Stubby Area
 area 120 stub no-summary
 ! Tune SPF Throttle Timers
 timers throttle spf 10 100 5000
 ! Tune LSA Throttle Timers
 timers throttle lsa all 10 100 5000
 ! Tune LSA Arrival Timer
 timers lsa arrival 80
 network 10.120.0.0 0.0.255.255 area 120
 !
```

Example 9-11   *Distribution Switch OSPF Routed Access Design*

```
OSPF-Distribution-Switch# show run
 ! Output omitted for brevity.
 !
 ! Configure point-to-point L3 links to each of the access switches
 interface GigabitEthernet3/1
```

```
 description Downlink to Access Switch
! Enable IP Event Dampening with default values
 dampening
! Configure the switch-to-switch link using a /30 or /31 subnet>
 ip address 10.120.0.204 255.255.255.254
! Tune OSPF hello and dead timers to 250 ms and 1 second
 ip ospf dead-interval minimal hello-multiplier 4
! Configure distribution-switch to be OSPF DR on downlink
 ip ospf priority 255
 logging event link-status
 logging event spanning-tree status
 logging event bundle-status
 logging event trunk-status
 load-interval 30
! Hard-code the link carrier-delay to 0 ms
 carrier-delay msec 0
!
!
! Configure point-to-point L3 links to each of the core switches
interface TenGigabitEthernet4/1
 description 10 GigE to Core 1
! Enable IP Event Dampening with default values
 dampening
! Configure the switch-to-switch link using a /30 or /31 subnet>
 ip address 10.122.0.26 255.255.255.254
! Tune OSPF hello and dead timers to 250 ms and 1 second
 ip ospf dead-interval minimal hello-multiplier 4
 logging event link-status
 logging event spanning-tree status
 logging event bundle-status
 load-interval 30
! Hard-code the link carrier-delay to 0 ms
 carrier-delay msec 0
!
!
! Configure point-to-point L3 links to the peer distribution switch
interface TenGigabitEthernet4/3
 description L3 link to peer distribution
! Enable IP Event Dampening with default values
 dampening
! Configure the switch-to-switch link using a /30 or /31 subnet>
 ip address 10.120.0.23 255.255.255.254
! Tune OSPF hello and dead timers to 250 ms and 1 second
 ip ospf dead-interval minimal hello-multiplier 4
 logging event link-status
```

```
 logging event spanning-tree status
 logging event bundle-status
 load-interval 30
! Hard-code the link carrier-delay to 0 ms
 carrier-delay msec 0
!
!
router ospf 100
 router-id 10.122.102.1
 log-adjacency-changes
! Modify the OSPF reference BW to support 10GigE links
 auto-cost reference-bandwidth 10000
! Configure the distribution block area as an OSPF Totally Stubby Area
 area 120 stub no-summary
! Summarize the distribution block subnets into a single route advertised into core
 area 120 range 10.120.0.0 255.255.0.0 cost 10
! Tune SPF Throttle Timers
 timers throttle spf 10 100 5000
! Tune LSA Throttle Timers
 timers throttle lsa all 10 100 5000
! Tune LSA Arrival Timer
 timers lsa arrival 80
 network 10.120.0.0 0.0.255.255 area 120
 network 10.122.0.0 0.0.255.255 area 0
!
```

Having covered these recommended distribution block designs for TelePresence-enabled campus networks, branch designs for TelePresence are presented next.

Highly Available Branch Designs for TelePresence

In the branch, availability targets are significantly impacted and limited not only by the increased distances between devices (resulting in longer convergence times due to increased network latency), but also by the increased cost of bandwidth (resulting in longer and more frequent periods of congestion), and the cost to scale hardware redundancy to the number of branches required, which can often be in the hundreds, if not thousands. Therefore, network administrators are required to factor in relevant business costs and constraints with their availability targets when deploying branch networks.

Following are two main recommended branch profile designs that an administrator can choose from in deploying TelePresence over the WAN/VPN:

■ Dual-tier branch profile

■ Multitier branch profile

Each of these profiles are presented with their pros and cons relating to network availability.

Dual-Tier Branch Profiles

Figure 9-12 illustrates the dual-tier branch profile.

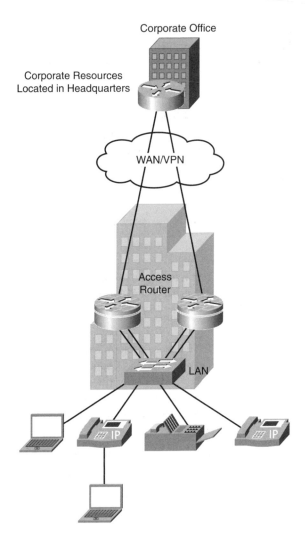

Figure 9-12 *Dual-tier branch profile*

The dual-tier branch profile consists of two access routers connected to an external switch. Dual WAN/VPN links and access router redundancy provide increased levels of network availability, as opposed to having a single WAN/VPN edge device.

The access routers serve to terminate WAN/VPN connections, and the LAN connectivity is performed by a desktop switch. For additional user capacity, additional switches might be added, or alternatively, Integrated Services Routers (ISR) with integrated switch modules can be used.

If an external switch is used, the access routers can be configured to leverage HSRP, VRRP, or GLBP as a FHRP. Additionally, (as discussed in Chapter 5) GLBP can provide the extra benefit of automatic load-balancing over the links to more efficiently use expensive WAN/VPN bandwidth.

Nonetheless, the increased availability that this model delivers is achieved at the cost of additional equipment and additional ongoing bandwidth expenses, and increased management complexity of the branch, as now there are more devices to administer. For the highest levels of availability, dual service providers are recommended.

An additional consideration relating to TelePresence WAN/VPN links is that there must be sufficient bandwidth across both WAN/VPN links to carry the entire traffic load if one circuit fails. Because a standard recommendation is to have average traffic utilization rates within 75 percent of capacity, this would mean provisioning no more than (approximately) 35 percent (half of 75 percent) for TelePresence calls per WAN/VPN link. This allows sufficient bandwidth for TelePresence calls to continue, even if a single link failure occurs.

Note Chapter 10 covers additional TelePresence bandwidth provisioning considerations and recommendations.

Routing protocols are likewise recommended to be tuned to optimize convergence times. Although subsecond convergence is rarely, if ever, achievable over WAN/VPN circuits, an adjusted convergence target needs to be set. (Five seconds to 15 seconds is generally viewed as acceptable.)

You can use many types of WAN/VPN media. For TelePresence deployments, a minimum of 10-Mbps circuits are recommended, as discussed in more detail in Chapter 10. Therefore, media options include point-to-point, ATM, Packet Over SONET (POS), and Ethernet (Metro/MPLS VPN line-rate or subline rate) circuits, among others. The examples that follow demonstrate each of these main WAN/VPN media interface configurations, which would be configured on both access router WAN/VPN interfaces.

Example 9-12 shows a point-to-point DS3 circuit interface configuration optimized for TelePresence.

Example 9-12 *Point-to-Point DS3 WAN Circuit Interface Configuration*

```
Router(config)# interface Serial6/0
Router(config-if)# description P2P-DS3-to-CAMPUS
Router(config-if)# ip address 192.168.2.9 255.255.255.252
Router(config-if)# tx-ring-limit 10
Router(config-if)# dsu bandwidth 44210
Router(config-if)# framing c-bit
Router(config-if)# cablelength 10
Router(config-if)# serial restart-delay 0
```

Example 9-13 shows an ATM PVC circuit interface and subinterface configuration for TelePresence branches.

Example 9-13 *Point-to-Point ATM PVC Circuit Interface and Subinterface Configuration*

```
Router(config)# interface ATM1/0
Router(config-if)# description ATM-to-CAMPUS
Router(config-if)# no ip address
Router(config-if)# no atm ilmi-keepalive
Router(config-if)# interface ATM1/0.135 point-to-point
Router(config-subif)# description 45MBPS-ATM-PVC-to-CAMPUS
Router(config-subif)# ip address 192.168.2.1 255.255.255.252
Router(config-subif)# pvc 0/35
Router(config-subif-atm-vc)# vbr-nrt 44760 44760
Router(config-subif-atm-vc)# encapsulation aal5snap
```

Example 9-14 shows a POS interface that you can use to carry TelePresence to the branch.

Example 9-14 *POS Circuit Interface Configuration*

```
Router(config)# interface POS3/0/0
Router(config-if)# description POS-to-CAMPUS
Router(config-if)# ip address 192.168.1.1 255.255.255.252
Router(config-if)# clock source internal
```

Example 9-15 shows an Ethernet interface that you can use to connect a TelePresence-enabled branch to either MPLS VPN or Metro Ethernet service provider at full line-rate or subline rates.

Example 9-15 *Ethernet Circuit Interface Configuration*

```
Router(config)# interface GigabitEthernet0/1
Router(config-if)# description GE-to-MPLS/METRO-SP-to-CAMPUS
Router(config-if)# ip address 192.168.1.50 255.255.255.252
Router(config-if)# no ip redirects
Router(config-if)# no ip proxy-arp
Router(config-if)# duplex auto
Router(config-if)# speed auto
Router(config-if)# media-type rj45
Router(config-if)# negotiation auto
```

An alternative to the dual-tier branch profile design would be a multitier branch design

Multitier Branch Profiles

Figure 9-13 illustrates the multitier branch profile.

The multitier branch profile consists of dual access routers for WAN/VPN termination, dual Adaptive Security Appliances (ASA) for security and firewall services, dual ISRs for services integration (such as mobility and IP communication services), and several desktop

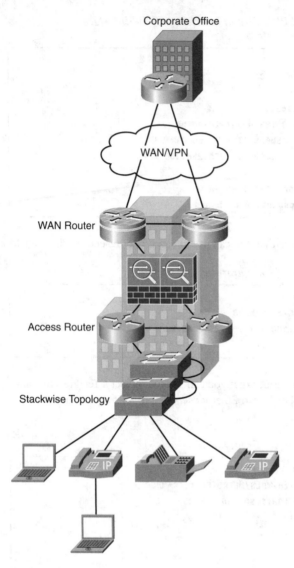

Figure 9-13 *Multitier branch profile*

switches connected through Cisco Stackwise technology. The multitier branch model offers the highest levels of availability and redundancy but requires the most hardware costs
and management complexity.

From an availability perspective, the multitier model doesn't introduce new concepts or
configurations, but rather redistributes elements of the dual-tier design over additional
hardware components.

Summary

This chapter discussed the network availability requirements and related design recommendations for TelePresence. Notably, it was shown that TelePresence has one of the highest requirements of network availability of any application, which is primarily due to the extreme degree of compression utilized within the TelePresence codecs on the HD video streams (more than 99 percent). Thereby, the overall effect of packet loss is proportionally magnified so that dropping even one TelePresence packet in 10,000 (0.01 percent packet loss) is noticeable to end users in the form of pixelization. This means that from a user perspective, TelePresence is 100 times more sensitive to packet loss than even VoIP. However, it should be noted that a small allowance for minor pixelization can be made, and as such the recommended packet loss target for TelePresence networks is 0.05 percent.

Consideration was also given to the network convergence targets. As statistical analysis on speech has shown, 200 ms is about the length of time it takes for one party to figure out that the other person has stopped talking. This value provides a subjective "conversation disruption" metric, which can be used as a convergence target for campus and data center networks deploying TelePresence.

TelePresence campus designs were presented that used the principles of redundancy, hierarchy, and modularity. For redundancy, it was shown that "more is not always better" because overredundant designs negate deterministic failover. Hierarchical designs were shown to simplify network scalability, and modular designs were demonstrated to provide higher system availability by compartmentalizing and by simplifying management and operations.

Three design options were presented for the campus access-distribution block: multitier design, virtual switching system design, and routed access design (either with EIGRP or OSPF). However, only VSS and routed access designs can achieve 200 ms convergence times, and detailed design recommendations for these design options were presented.

TelePresence branch designs were also discussed, and it was noted that branch availability targets are significantly impacted due to technical, geographic, bandwidth, and service provider constraints so that convergence targets for WAN/VPN networks would likely be in the 5 second to 15 seconds range. Two branch profile designs were presented: dual-tier branch profile and multitier branch profile. These profiles vary in respective availability, scalability, functionality, size, and cost. The dual-tier profile incorporates some high availability with distributed LAN connectivity through desktop switches and WAN connectivity through branch routers. The multitier profile offers the most availability but offers no integration of services in a single platform. Ultimately network administrators must asses their branch availability targets, and their costs and constraints, when selecting a branch model to support TelePresence.

Finally, availability is not the only element to consider when deploying networks to support TelePresence, but rather QoS also is a major component of the network design, as discussed in detail in the following chapter.

Further Reading

Standards:

ITU G.114 "One-way transmission time": http://tinyurl.com/ae53pp

ITU-T H.264 "Advanced video coding for generic audiovisual services": http://tinyurl.com/56g22e

IETF RFC 3201 "Using 31-Bit Prefixes on IPv4 Point-to-Point Links": http://www.ietf.org/rfc/rfc3021

Cisco IOS Documentation:

Configuring Virtual Switching Systems: http://www.tinyurl.com/yqg97w

Cisco Design Guides:

Campus Network for High Availability Design Guide: http://www.tinyurl.com/d3e6dj

Enterprise Campus 3.0 Architecture: Overview and Framework: http://www.tinyurl.com/4bwr33

High Availability Campus Network Design–Routed Access Layer using EIGRP or OSPF: http://www.tinyurl.com/cqwwzq

Enterprise Branch Architecture Design Overview: http://www.tinyurl.com/dls398

Cisco Press Books:

Doyle, Jeff and Jennifer Carroll. *Routing TCP/IP*, Volume 1, Second Edition. Cisco Press, 2005. ISBN: 1-58705-202-4.

Parkhurst, William R. *Cisco OSPF Command and Configuration Handbook*. Cisco Press, 2008. ISBN: 1-58705-540-6.

For TelePresence conferences to be natural, realistic, and effective, the network infrastructure must service the high-definition audio and video packets sent between TelePresence endpoints with high availability and quality. The previous chapter focused on availability designs for TelePresence networks; this chapter focuses on quality of service (QoS) designs for TelePresence networks.

A major benefit of the Cisco TelePresence Solution over competitive offerings is that the real-time, high-definition video and audio are transported over a converged IP network rather than a dedicated network (although dedicated networks are also supported). The key enabling technology to achieve convergence is QoS.

From a QoS viewpoint, TelePresence requires stricter service levels for loss, latency, and jitter than virtually any other application on the network. Additionally, TelePresence requires detailed bandwidth and burst provisioning on a device-by-device basis. Furthermore, priority servicing of TelePresence must not interfere or degrade IP Telephony servicing.

Therefore, to meet these design challenges, extensive attention needs to be given to the QoS designs of the network, as detailed in this chapter.

CHAPTER 10

TelePresence Network Design
Part 2: Quality of Service Design

TelePresence QoS Considerations

Before a network administrator can design QoS policies to provision TelePresence traffic, he must consider the service level requirements of TelePresence and define an end-to-end Differentiated Services (DiffServ) strategy. Each of these branches of considerations will now be discussed.

TelePresence Service Level Requirements

The first consideration of QoS design is to fully understand the service level requirements of the applications being provisioned. Service level requirements are defined in terms of the following:

- Bandwidth
- Burst
- Latency
- Jitter
- Loss

Each of these service level requirements for TelePresence are discussed in turn.

TelePresence Bandwidth Requirements

There are several factors that influence the amount of bandwidth required by a Cisco TelePresence system. The first is the type of CTS system: For instance, a three-screen CTS system (such as a CTS-3000/3200) requires correspondingly more bandwidth than a single-screen system (such as a CTS-500/1000). Another bandwidth requirement factor is the video resolution level: CTS systems can operate at 720p or 1080p (with 1080p requiring, on average, twice the bandwidth of 720p, holding everything else constant). Correspondingly, TelePresence codecs can operate at three levels of motion handling (labeled simply "Good," "Better," and "Best") within a given video resolution; the better the level of motion handling, the more bandwidth is required. Additionally, TelePresence systems can support auxiliary audio and video components, such as tying in an audio bridge or sharing a presentation through the data projector, each of which require additional amounts of bandwidth. Furthermore, TelePresence software releases generally include support for additional optional features (such as an interoperability feature with H.323-based video conferencing) which, if enabled, require incremental bandwidth.

Therefore, bandwidth provisioning for TelePresence becomes an exercise of adding up all these bandwidth-requiring elements for a given CTS system. To illustrate, consider the bandwidth requirements of a CTS-1000 configured with 720p-Good resolution and motion handling, with an auxiliary video stream (a 5 frame-per-second video channel for sharing presentations or other collateral via the data-projector) and an auxiliary audio stream (for at least one additional person conferenced in by an audio-only bridge). Table 10-1 breaks down the bandwidth requirements by component.

Table 10-1 *Bandwidth Requirements of a CTS-1000 at 720p (Good)*

1 primary video stream @ 1 Mbps	1000 kbps
1 primary audio stream @ 64 kbps	64 kbps
1 auxiliary video stream (5 fps)	500 kbps
1 auxiliary audio stream	64 kbps
Total audio and video bandwidth (at Layer 7)	1628 kbps

The total bandwidth requirements, without network overhead, for such a system would be 1.628 Mbps. However, network overhead must also be taken into account, such as IP/UDP/RTP overhead (which combined, amounts to 40 bytes per packet) and media-specific Layer 2 overhead. In general, video (unlike VoIP) does not have clean formulas for calculating network overhead. This is because video packet sizes and rates vary proportionally to the degree of motion within the video image itself. Cisco TelePresence video packets average 1100 bytes per packet. However, a conservative rule of thumb that has been thoroughly tested and widely deployed is to overprovision video bandwidth by 20 percent. With this 20 percent overprovisioning rule applied, the requisite bandwidth for a CTS-1000 running at 720p-Good becomes 2 Mbps (rounded).

Next, consider the bandwidth requirements of a CTS-3000 system running at full 1080p-Best, with an auxiliary video stream and an auxiliary audio stream. Table 10-2 shows the detailed bandwidth requirements.

Table 10-2 *Bandwidth Requirements of a CTS-3000 at 1080p-Best*

3 primary video streams @ 4 Mbps each	12,000 kbps
3 primary audio streams @ 64 kbps each	192 kbps
1 auxiliary video stream	500 kbps
1 auxiliary audio stream	64 kbps
Total audio and video bandwidth (at Layer 7)	12,756 kbps

With the 20 percent overprovisioning rule applied, the requisite bandwidth for a CTS-3000 running at 1080p-Best becomes approximately 15 Mbps (with a bit of rounding applied). Incidentally, this value of 15 Mbps for a CTS-3000 at 1080p-Best is used in most of the CTS-3000 examples throughout this chapter.

Table 10-3 shows the core bandwidth requirements of CTS systems at each resolution and motion handling level.

Table 10-3 *Cisco TelePresence 500/1000/3000/3200 Bandwidth Requirements*

Resolution	1080p	1080p	1080p	720p	720p	720p
Motion Handling	*Best*	*Better*	*Good*	*Best*	*Better*	*Good*
Video per Screen (kbps)	4000	3500	3000	2250	1500	1000
Primary audio streams @ 64 kbps each	64	64	64	64	64	64
(5 fps) Auto Collaborate Video Channel (kbps)	500	500	500	500	500	500
Auto Collaborate Audio Channel (kbps)	64	64	64	64	64	64
CTS-500/1000 Total Audio and Video BW (kbps)	4628˙	4128˙	3628˙	2878˙	2128˙	1628˙
CTS-3000/3200 Total Audio and Video BW (kbps)	12,756	11,256	9756	7506	5256	3756
CTS-500/1000 max bandwidth, including network overhead (kbps)	5.554˙	4954˙	4354˙	3454˙	2554˙	1954˙
CTS-3000/3200 max bandwidth, including network overhead (kbps)	15,307	13,507	11,707	9007	6307	4507

˙The CTS-1000 transmits up to 128 kbps of audio but can receive up to 256 kbps when participating in a meeting with a CTS-3000.

Note These bandwidth numbers represent worst-case maximum bandwidth scenarios, which are generated during periods of maximum motion and contrast within the encoded video (such as all meeting participants wearing plaid or Hawaiian shirts and dancing all at the same time). Normal use, or average bandwidth utilization scenarios (with users sitting and talking and gesturing naturally), typically generate only about 60 percent to 80 percent of these maximum bandwidth rates.

Additionally, remember that as Cisco TelePresence software continues to evolve and adds new feature support, the bandwidth requirements for TelePresence will correspondingly evolve and expand. For example, a feature was added in CTS software release 1.3 that enabled TelePresence systems to interoperate with older H.323 video conferencing systems. This interoperability feature adds an additional 768 kbps of video bandwidth and an additional 64 kbps of audio bandwidth, plus network overhead, to TelePresence flows.

Similarly, a feature was added in CTS software release 1.4 that enables the auto-collaborate video channel to transmit at full 30 fps. This feature adds an additional 3500 kbps of bandwidth (plus network overhead) to TelePresence flows. (The total required bandwidth for 30 fps of auto-collaborate video is 4000 kbps, but this replaces the 5 fps auxiliary video channel that requires 500 kbps, for a net incremental bandwidth requirement of 3500 kbps.)

Suffice it to say, as new features are supported in future releases of TelePresence software, these also need to be factored into the bandwidth provisioning calculations for TelePresence flow.

TelePresence Burst Requirements

So far, bandwidth has been discussed in terms of bits per second, or (in other words) how much TelePresence traffic is sent over a one-second interval. However, when provisioning bandwidth and configuring queuing, shaping, and policing commands on routers and switches, burst must also be taken into account. Burst is defined as the amount of traffic (generally measured in bytes) transmitted over a (variable) subsecond interval. In the context of TelePresence provisioning, the interval of interest is 33 ms; this is because TelePresence codecs operate at 30 fps and, therefore, transmit a video frame every 33 ms. This 33-ms period is also referred to as a *frame interval*.

Each frame consists of several thousand bytes of video payload, and therefore each frame interval consists of anywhere from a few to several dozen packets (per video display) with an average packet size of 1100 bytes per packet. However, because video is variable in size (due to the variability of motion in the encoded video frame image), the packets transmitted by the codec are not always spaced evenly over each 33-ms frame interval, but rather are transmitted in bursts measured in shorter intervals. Therefore, although the overall (maximum) bandwidth for a CTS-300 @ 1080p (Best) might average to 15 Mbps over one second, when measured on a per millisecond basis, the packet transmission rate might be highly variable.

In H.264 video, which TelePresence systems use, the worst-case burst scenario would be the full screen of (spatially compressed) video, which is periodically sent, which is known as the *Instantaneous Decode Refresh (IDR)* frame. The IDR frame is the key frame that subsequent video frames reference, sending only differential information between subsequent frames and the IDR frame, rather than the full picture again.

Note For more information about H.264 video encoding, refer to RFC 3964 "RTP Payload Format for H.264 Video" at http://www.ietf.org/rfc/rfc3984.

The maximum IDR frame size is approximately 64 KB. Therefore, the maximum burst parameter should be configured to permit up to 64 KB of burst per video display within a 33-ms video frame interval.

Adequate burst tolerance must be accommodated by all switch and router interfaces in the path, as discussed on a per-platform basis throughout this chapter.

Note The earliest versions of Cisco TelePresence software were quite bursty. However, starting with CTS software version 1.2 and later, traffic smoothing algorithms were implemented to space out frame interval bursting, resulting in more "network-friendly" TelePresence traffic patterns. Nonetheless, burst requirements are still an important factor to consider when provisioning QoS policies for TelePresence.

TelePresence Latency Requirements

Cisco TelePresence has a network latency target of 150 ms, based on the ITU-T G.114 one-way latency target for real-time transmissions. This target does not include codec processing time but represents purely network flight time.

This latency target might not always be possible to achieve, however, simply due to the laws of physics and the geographical distances involved. Therefore, TelePresence codecs have been designed to sustain high levels of call quality even up to (and even beyond) 200 ms of latency. As latency increases beyond these levels, *visually* the call quality remains the same, but *aurally*, the lagtime between one party speaking and the other party responding becomes unnaturally excessive. However, with an adjustment in user expectations, TelePresence is even supported over satellite circuits (with latency in the range of 500 ms to 2000 ms) if each party waits a few extra moments before responding to ensure that the other party has finished speaking.

Note The earliest versions of Cisco TelePresence software included thresholds for latency, which (if exceeded) would trigger a message to be displayed across the bottom of the screen to this effect. However, starting with CTS software version 1.5, these latency thresholds have been completely removed.

Network latency time can be broken down further into fixed and variable components:

- Serialization (fixed)

- Propagation (fixed)

- Queuing (variable)

Serialization refers to the time it takes to convert a Layer 2 frame into a serial stream of bits, represented by Layer 1 electrical or optical pulses over a transmission media. Therefore, serialization delay is fixed and is a function of the line rate (that is, the clock speed of the link). For example, a 45 Mbps DS3 circuit would require 266 µs to serialize a 1500-byte Ethernet frame onto the wire. At the circuit speeds required for TelePresence serialization, delay is not a significant factor in the overall latency budget.

The most significant network factor in meeting the latency targets for TelePresence is propagation delay, which can account for more than 90 percent of the network latency time budget. Propagation delay is also a fixed component and is a function of the physical distance that the signals have to travel between the originating endpoint and the receiving endpoint. The gating factor for propagation delay is the speed of light: 300,000 km/s (or 186,000 miles per second). Roughly speaking, the speed of light in an optical fiber is slightly less than one half the speed of light in a vacuum. Thus, the propagation delay works out to be approximately 6.3 µs per km (or 8.2 µs per mile).

Another point to keep in mind when calculating propagation delay is that optical fibers are not always physically placed over the shortest path between two geographic points, especially over transoceanic links. Due to installation convenience, circuits might be hundreds or thousands of kilometers longer than theoretically necessary.

Nonetheless, the network flight-time budget of 150 ms allows for nearly 24,000 km (or 15,000 miles) worth of propagation delay (which is approximately 60 percent of the earth's circumference); the theoretical worst-case scenario (exactly half of the earth's circumference) would require only 126 ms. Therefore, the latency target of 150 ms is generally achievable for virtually any two locations on the planet, given relatively direct (terrestrial) transmission paths. However, for some scenarios, such as extreme terrestrial links or satellite links or business-to-business connections over multiple SP exchanges, user expectations might have to be set accordingly because there is little a network administrator can do about increasing the speed of light.

Given the end-to-end latency targets and thresholds for TelePresence, the network administrator also must know how much of this budget to b allocate to the service provider and how much to the enterprise. A general recommendation for this split is 80:20, with 80 percent of the latency budget allocated to the service provider (edge-to-edge), and 20 percent to the enterprise (10 percent codec-to-edge on one side and 10 percent edge-to-codec on the other). However, some enterprise networks might not require a full 20 percent of the latency budget and, thus, might reallocate their allowance to a 90:10 service provider-to-enterprise split, or whatever the case might be. The main point is that a fixed budget needs to be clearly apportioned to both the service provider and to the enterprise so that the network administrators can design their networks accordingly.

Note   Another point to remember here is the additional latency introduced by multipoint resources. Latency is always measured from end-to-end (for example, from codec 1 to codec 2). However, in a multipoint call, the path between the two codecs traverses a Cisco TelePresence Multipoint Switch (CTMS). The multipoint switch introduces approximately 10 ms of latency, and the path from codec 1 to the CTMS and from the CTMS to codec 2 might be greater than the path between codec 1 and codec 2 directly, depending on the physical location of the CTMS. Therefore, when engineering the network with respect to latency, the network administrator must calculate both scenarios for every TelePresence system deployed:

■   One for the path between each system and every other system for point-to-point call

■   One for the path between each system, through the CTMS, to every other system

These latency considerations are examined in more detail in Chapter 13, "Multipoint TelePresence Design."

The final TelePresence latency component to be considered is queuing delay, which is variable. Queuing delay is a function of whether a network node is congested and what the scheduling QoS policies are to resolve congestion events. Given that the latency target for TelePresence is tight and, as has been shown, the majority of factors contributing to the latency budget are fixed, careful attention must be given to queuing delay because this is the only latency factor that is directly under the network administrator's control through QoS policies.

Figure 10-1 illustrates the TelePresence latency targets, components, and budgets.

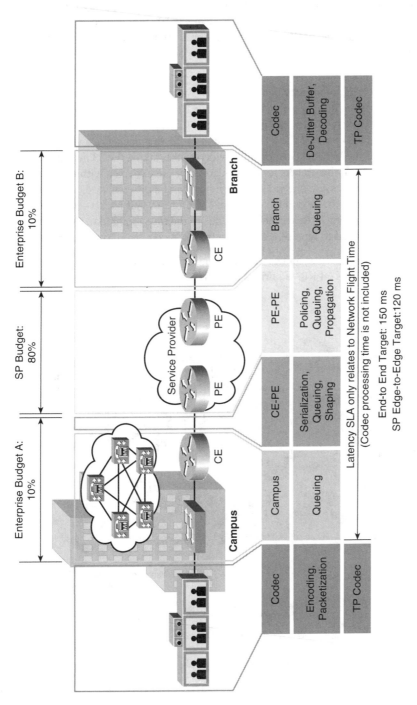

Figure 10-1 *TelePresence latency targets, components, and budgets*

TelePresence Jitter Requirements

Cisco TelePresence has a (video frame) jitter target of 10 ms, peak-to-peak. *Jitter* is the variance in network latency. Thus, if the average latency is 100 ms and packets arrive between 95 ms and 105 ms, the peak-to-peak (packet-level) jitter is 10 ms. Measurements within the Cisco TelePresence codecs use peak-to-peak jitter but at the video frame level (and not the packet level).

Video frame jitter is a bit of a tricky concept because most network administrators are accustomed to considering jitter at the packet level only. However, CTS codecs don't measure jitter at the *packet* level (Layer 3), but rather at the *video frame* level (Layer 7). Specifically, the codecs compare the RTP timestamp of the first packet of a video frame to the timestamp of the last packet of the same video frame, taking the 33 ms video frame interval into account. All the packets for each video frame are expected within 33 ms. However, as already discussed, one video frame might be of a different size (and thus require more packets) than the next, and vice versa. Therefore, even if packet-level jitter is held to be zero, video frame jitter can still exist, due to the time required to serialize the additional packets needed to represent one video frame, as compared to the next.

To illustrate, consider the video frames shown in Figure 10-2, specifically video frames #3 and #4. Video frame #3 is 64 KB, requiring (at least) 59 packets (of an average size of 1,100 bytes).

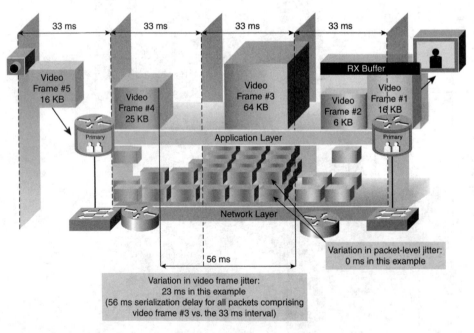

Figure 10-2   *TelePresence video frame jitter versus packet jitter example*

Note TelePresence uses a maximum video payload size of 1100 bytes because this allows for network overhead plus encryption overhead to be added to the packet while still being within the Maximum Transmission Unit (MTU) of Ethernet (1500 bytes).

Assuming a 10-Mbps Ethernet circuit, each packet would be 1154 bytes in size (1100-byte payloads + 40 bytes of IP/UDP/RTP headers and 14 bytes of Ethernet overhead), resulting in a bit rate of 544,688 bps (59 packets × 1,154 Bytes × 8 bits/byte). At a 10-Mbps rate, approximately 55 ms would be required to serialize these packets (assuming that there is absolutely zero packet-level jitter). The receiving codec is expecting the first packet of video frame #4 exactly 33 ms after the first packet of video frame #3; however, because it takes 55 ms to serialize all the packets representing video frame #3, there will be 22 ms of video frame jitter between video frames #3 and #4 (55 ms serialization time minus the 33-ms frame interval). Therefore, it can be seen that even without any (Layer 3) packet level jitter, video frame jitter can still exist, simply due to the serialization times required to send variable numbers of packets that represent subsequent video frames.

Cisco TelePresence codecs have two built-in thresholds for jitter to ensure a high-quality user experience: Jitter Threshold 1 and Jitter Threshold 2.

Note At the time of writing (CTS software version 1.5), Jitter Threshold 1 is set to 125 ms, and Jitter Threshold 2 is set to 165 ms. These threshold values have changed in previous software releases and thus might yet change again in future software releases.

If video frame jitter exceeds Jitter Threshold 1 for several seconds, two things occur:

- A warning message appears at the bottom of the video display indicating that the network is experiencing congestion and that call quality might be affected.

- The TelePresence codecs downgrade to a lower level of motion-handling quality within the given resolution.

As previously mentioned, Cisco TelePresence codecs have three levels of motion handling quality within a given resolution, specifically 720p-Good, 720p-Better, and 720p-Best; and 1080p-Good, 1080p-Better, and 1080p-Best. Therefore, for example, if a call at 1080p-Best would exceed Jitter Threshold 1 (125 ms) for several seconds, the codec would display the warning message and would downgrade the motion handling quality to 1080p-Good. Similarly a call at 720p-Best would downgrade to 720p-Good. Incidentally, downgraded calls do not automatically upgrade should network conditions improve because this could cause a "flapping" effect where the call upgrades and then downgrades again, over and over.

Continuing the scenario, if a TelePresence call exceeds Jitter Threshold 2 for several seconds, two additional things occur. The TelePresence codecs

- Self-terminate the call

- Display an error message on the 7975G IP Phone indicating that the call was terminated due to excessive network congestion

Finally, as with latency, the jitter budget is proportioned between the service provider and enterprise networks. Unfortunately, unlike latency or packet loss, jitter is not necessarily additive. Nonetheless, simply for the sake of setting a jitter target for each party, the recommended split is 50/50 between the service provider and enterprise so that each group of network administrators can design their networks to a clear set of jitter targets and thresholds. Also like latency, this split can be negotiated differently between the service provider and enterprise to meet certain unique scenarios, such as satellite connections. Again, the main point is that a fixed jitter budget needs to be clearly apportioned to both the service provider and to the enterprise so that the end-to-end target and thresholds are not exceeded.

It is recommended that service providers engineer their networks to meet the jitter target of 10 ms but base their SLA on Jitter Threshold 1, which provides global coverage between any two sites on the planet (through terrestrial links).

TelePresence Loss Requirements

Cisco TelePresence is highly sensitive to packet loss and so has an end-to-end packet loss target of 0.05 percent.

The packet loss sensitivity of TelePresence is discussed in the previous chapter (Chapter 9, "TelePresence Network Design Part 1: Availability Design").

Similar to jitter, TelePresence codecs have built-in thresholds for packet loss to ensure a high-quality user experience: Loss Threshold 1 and Loss Threshold 2.

Note   At the time of writing (CTS software version 1.5), Loss Threshold 1 is set to 1 percent, and Loss Threshold 2 is set to 10 percent. These threshold values have changed in previous software releases and thus might yet change again in future software releases.

If Loss Threshold 1 is exceeded for several seconds, two things occur:

- A warning message appears at the bottom of the video display indicating that the network is experiencing congestion and that call quality might be affected.

- The TelePresence codecs downgrade to a lower level of motion handling quality within the given resolution.

As previously mentioned, Cisco TelePresence codecs have three levels of motion handling quality within a given resolution, specifically 720p-Good, 720p-Better, and 720p-Best; and 1080p-Good, 1080p-Better, and 1080p-Best. Therefore, for example, if a call at 1080p-Best would exceed Loss Threshold 1 for several seconds, the codec would display the warning message and would downgrade the motion-handling quality to 1080p-Good. Similarly, a call at 720p-Best would downgrade to 720-Good in the same scenario. Incidentally, downgraded calls do not automatically upgrade should network conditions improve because this could cause a "flapping" effect where the call upgrades and then downgrades again, over and over.

Continuing the scenario, if a TelePresence call exceeds Loss Threshold 2 for several seconds, two additional things occur. The TelePresence codecs

- Self-terminate the call

- Display an error message on the 7975G IP Phone indicating that the call was terminated due to excessive network congestion

Finally, as with previously defined service level requirements, the loss budget is proportioned between the service provider and enterprise networks. The recommend split is 50/50 between the service provider and enterprise so that each group of network administrators can design their networks to a clear set of packet loss targets and thresholds. Of course, this split might be negotiated differently between the service provider and enterprise to meet certain unique scenarios, such as satellite connections. Again, the main point is that a fixed packet loss budget needs to be clearly apportioned to both the service provider and to the enterprise so that the end-to-end target and thresholds are not exceeded.

With the service level requirements of TelePresence having been duly considered, an end-to-end DiffServ strategy must be formulated before place-in-the-network QoS policies can be configured, as discussed next.

TelePresence DiffServ Strategy

As QoS is an end-to-end technology, an end-to-end QoS strategy must be articulated prior to configuring platform-specific designs so that there will be policy consistency at each network node. The Differentiated Services (DiffServ) strategy should include an end-to-end marking value, policing guidelines, queuing guidelines, and shaping guidelines, among other elements.

Hardware Versus Software QoS Policies

A primary best-practice that should be reflected in the DiffServ strategy is to always deploy QoS in hardware, rather than software, whenever a choice exists. Cisco Catalyst switches perform QoS operations in hardware Application Specific Integrated Circuits (ASICS) and have zero CPU impact; Cisco IOS routers, on the other hand, perform QoS operations in software, resulting in a marginal CPU impact, the degree of which depends on the platform, policies, link speeds, and traffic flows involved. So whenever supported, QoS policies such as classification, marking/remarking, and policing can all be performed at line rates with zero CPU impact in Catalyst switches (as opposed to IOS routers), which makes the overall QoS design more efficient.

A practical example of how this principle is applied is as follows: Although all nodes in the network path must implement queuing policies, classification policies should be implemented in Cisco Catalyst switches (which perform QoS in *hardware*) as close to the source of the traffic as possible, for example, on the access edge switch to which the TelePresence System is attached, rather than waiting until the traffic hits the WAN routers (which perform QoS in *software*) to be classified.

TelePresence Marking Recommendation

Another design element within the TelePresence DiffServ strategy is to follow industry standards whenever possible because this extends the effectiveness of your QoS policies beyond your direct administrative control. For example, if a real-time application, such as

VoIP, is marked to the industry standard recommendation as defined in RFC 3246 (An Expedited Forwarding Per-Hop Behavior, which was discussed in Chapter 6, "Network Quality of Service Technologies"), it will be provisioned with strict priority servicing at every node within the enterprise network. Additionally, as it's handed-off to a service provider following this same industry standard, the VoIP traffic will be similarly provisioned and serviced in a strict priority manner. Therefore, even though the enterprise administrator does not have direct control of the QoS policies within the service provider's cloud, he has extended the influence of their QoS designs to include their service provider's cloud, simply by following the industry standard recommendations.

A relevant industry reference for marking and provisioning TelePresence traffic (along with many other types of traffic) is RFC 4594, "Configuration Guidelines for DiffServ Service Classes," which is categorized as an *informational* RFC.

Note   It is important to comment on the difference between the IETF RFC categories of informational and standard: An informational RFC is an industry recommended best practice, whereas a standard RFC is an industry requirement. Therefore RFC 4594 is a set of formal DiffServ QoS configuration best practices, not a requisite standard.

RFC 4594 puts forward 12 application classes and matches these to RFC-defined Per-Hop Behaviors (PHB). Table 10-4 summarizes these application classes and recommended PHBs.

Table 10-4   *RFC 4594 DiffServ Application Classes and PHBs*

Application	Layer 3 Classification		IETF RFC
	PHB	*DSCP*	
Network Control	CS6	48	RFC 2474
VoIP Telephony	EF	46	RFC 3246
Call Signaling	CS5	40	RFC 2472
Multimedia Conferencing	AS41	34	RFC 2597
Real-Time Interactive	CS4	32	RFC 2474
Multimedia Streaming	AF31	26	RFC 2597
Broadcast Video	CS3	24	RFC 2474
Low-Latency Data	AF21	18	RFC 2597
Operations/Administration/Management (OAM)	CS2	16	RFC 2474
High-Throughput Data	AF11	10	RFC 2597
Best Effort	DF	0	RFC 2474
Low-Priority Data	CS1	8	RFC 3662

Some of the application class names in RFC 4594 are a little different (but compatible) with application class names that Cisco has used extensively in its design guides, as summarized in Table 10-5. It's a matter of administrative preference as to which names are used; although the RFC 4594 names might be more technically accurate, they're a bit wordier. (For example, "High-Throughput Data" can be shortened to "Bulk Data," and "Low-Priority Data" can be simplified to "Scavenger.")

Table 10-5 *Cisco Application Class Names and RFC 4594 Counterparts*

Cisco Application Class Names	RFC 4594 Application Class Names
Routing	Network Control
Voice	VoIP Telephony
Interactive Video	Multimedia Conferencing
Streaming Video	Multimedia Streaming
Transactional Data	Low-Latency Data
Network Management	Operations/Administration/Management (OAM)
Bulk Data	High-Throughput Data
Scavenger	Low-Priority Data

Because RFC 4594 is an informational RFC and not a standard, modifications can be made in the implementation of this RFC to suit specific business needs and constraints. This has been the case in the Cisco adoption of RFC 4594. Specifically, RFC 4594 recommends call signaling to be marked CS5; however, all Cisco IP Telephony products (including TelePresence) mark call signaling to CS3. Lacking a compelling business case to justify an expensive, time-consuming, and customer-impacting marking migration to CS5, Cisco plans to continue marking call signaling traffic as CS3, until future business requirements might require otherwise. Therefore, for the remainder of this chapter, RFC 4594 marking values are used throughout, with the one exception of swapping call signaling marking (to CS3) and broadcast video (to CS5), as summarized in Table 10-6.

Table 10-6 *Cisco-Modified Implementation of RFC 4594*

Application Class	Per-Hop Behavior	Admission Control	Queuing and Dropping	Application Examples
VoIP Telephony	EF	Required	Priority Queue (PQ)	Cisco IP Phones (G.711, G.729)
Broadcast Video	CS5	Required	(Optional) PQ	Cisco IP Video Surveillance / Cisco Enterprise TV
Real-time Interactive	CS4	Required	(Optional) PQ	Cisco TelePresence
Multimedia Conferencing	AF4	Required	BW Queue + DSCP WRED	Cisco Unified Personal Communicator
Multimedia Streaming	AF3	Recommended	BW Queue + DSCP WRED	Cisco Digital Media System (VoD)
Network Control	CS6	—	BW Queue	EIGRP, OSPF, BGP, HSRP, IKE
Call-Signaling	CS3	—	BW Queue	SCCP, SIP, H.323
Ops / Admin / Mgmt (OAM)	CS2	—	BW Queue	SNMP, SSH, Syslog
Transactional Data	AF2	—	BW Queue + DSCP WRED	Cisco WebEx / MeetingPlace / ERP Apps
Bulk Data	AF1	—	BW Queue + DSCP WRED	E-mail, FTP, Backup Apps, Content Distribution
Best Effort	DF	—	Default Queue + RED	Default Class
Scavenger	CS1	—	Min BW Queue (Deferential)	YouTube, iTunes, BitTorent, Xbox Live

Note Some of the classes have been re-ordered in Table 10-6 to group together (for emphasis) the applications requiring Admission Control.

As has been discussed, TelePresence has unique (and higher/tighter) service level requirements than does generic video conferencing applications; therefore, TelePresence requires a dedicated class with a dedicated classification marking value.

Video conferencing applications have traditionally been marked to (RFC 2597) Assured Forwarding Class 4, which is the recommendation from RFC 4594. However, the AF PHB (discussed in Chapter 6) includes policing (to conforming, exceeding, and violating traffic rates), and correspondingly increasing the Drop Preferences (to Drop Preference 1, 2, and 3 respectively), and ultimately dropping traffic according to the Drop Preference markings. TelePresence traffic has a low tolerance to drops (0.05 percent) and, therefore, would not be appropriately serviced by an AF PHB.

Because of the low latency and jitter service-level requirements of TelePresence, it might seem attractive to assign it an EF PHB (RFC 3246); after all, there is nothing in RFC 3246 that dictates that only VoIP can be assigned to this PHB. However, it is important to recognize that VoIP behaves considerably differently than video. As previously mentioned, VoIP has constant packet sizes and packet rates, whereas video packet sizes vary, and video packet rates also vary in a random and bursty manner, as illustrated in Figure 10-3. Thus, if both TelePresence and voice were assigned to the same marking value and class, (bursty) TelePresence video could easily interfere with (well-behaved) voice. Therefore, for both operational and capacity planning purposes, RFC 4594 recommends using separate marking values for voice and video.

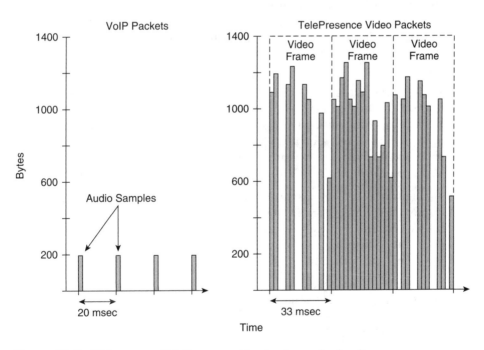

Figure 10-3 *Voice versus TelePresence video (at the packet level)*

What should TelePresence be marked to? The best formal guidance is provided in RFC 4594, where a distinction is made between a Multimedia Conferencing (which is well-suited for generic video conferencing) service class and a Real-Time Interactive service class. The Real-Time Interactive service class is intended for inelastic video flows, such as TelePresence, with the recommended marking value of Class Selector 4 (CS4).

TelePresence Policing Recommendations

In general, policing TelePresence traffic should be avoided whenever possible due to its high sensitivity to packet loss, although three notable exceptions to this exist:

- The first place where policing TelePresence might prove beneficial in the network is at the campus access edge. (This is an optional policy and not required in all cases.) Administrators can deploy access-edge policers for security purposes to mitigate the damage caused by the potential abuse of trusted switch ports. Because TelePresence endpoints can mark TelePresence flows to the recommended 802.1Q/p CoS value (CoS 4) and DSCP codepoint value (CS4), the network administrator might choose to trust the CoS or DSCP values received from these ports. However, if a disgruntled employee gains physical access to the TelePresence switch ports, she can send whatever traffic she chooses to over these ports and their flows are trusted over the network. Such rogue traffic flows might hijack voice or video queues and easily ruin call or video quality over the QoS-provisioned network infrastructure. Therefore, the administrator can choose to limit the scope of damage that such network abuse might present by configuring access-edge policers on TelePresence switch ports to re-mark (to Scavenger: DSCP CS1) or drop out-of-profile traffic originating on these ports (for example, CS4 traffic exceeding 15 Mbps). Supporting this approach, RFC 4594 recommends edge policing the Real-Time Interactive service class through a single-rate policer.

- The second place TelePresence traffic might be policed is if TelePresence is assigned to a Low-Latency Queue (LLQ) within Cisco IOS routers at the WAN or VPN edge. This is because any traffic assigned to an LLQ is automatically policed by an implicit policer set to the exact value as the LLQ rate (as discussed in Chapter 6). For example, if TelePresence is assigned an LLQ of 15 Mbps, it is also implicitly policed by the LLQ algorithm to exactly 15 Mbps; any excess TelePresence traffic is dropped.

- The third place that TelePresence is likely to be policed in the network is at the service provider's provider edge (PE) routers in the ingress direction. Service providers need to police traffic classes, especially real-time traffic classes, to enforce service contracts and prevent possible oversubscription on their networks and thus ensure service-level agreements (SLA).

Whenever TelePresence is policed, sufficient attention must be given to the burst parameters so that TelePresence traffic is not dropped when adhering to policy requirements.

TelePresence Queuing Recommendations

As for queuing guidelines, to achieve the high levels of service required by TelePresence, queuing policies must be enabled on every node along the path to provide service guarantees, regardless of how infrequently congestion might occur on certain nodes. RFC 4594 specifies the minimum queuing requirement of the Real-Time Interactive service class to be a rate-based queue (a queue that has a guaranteed minimum bandwidth rate). However, RFC 4594 also makes an allowance that while the PHB for Real-Time Interactive service class should be configured to provide high bandwidth assurance, it *might* be configured as a *second EF PHB*—although using a CS4 DSCP marking value.

This means that, for example, TelePresence, which has been assigned to this Real-Time Interactive service class, can be queued with either a guaranteed rate nonpriority queue (such as a Cisco IOS Class-Based Weighted Fair Queue [CBWFQ]) or a guaranteed-rate strict priority queue (such as a Cisco IOS Low-Latency Queue [LLQ]); in either case, TelePresence is to be marked as Class Selector 4 (and not EF).

Therefore, because RFC 4594 allows for the Real-Time Interactive service class to be given a second EF PHB (in other words, a second strict priority treatment) and because of the low latency, low jitter, and low loss requirements of TelePresence, it is recommended to place TelePresence in a strict-priority queue, such as a Cisco IOS LLQ or a Cisco Catalyst hardware priority queue whenever possible. However, exceptions to this recommendation are discussed in more detail in the "Branch QoS Design: LLQ versus CBWFQ" section of this chapter.

However, an additional provisioning consideration must be taken into account when provisioning TelePresence with a second EF PHB, which relates to the amount of bandwidth of a given link that should be assigned for strict priority queuing. The well-established and widely deployed Cisco best practice recommendation is to limit the amount of strict priority queuing configured on an interface to no more than one third of the link's capacity. This has often been referred to as the "33% LLQ Rule."

The rationale behind this rule is that if an administrator assigns too much traffic for strict priority queuing, the overall effect is a dampening of QoS functionality for nonreal-time applications. Remember, the goal of convergence is to enable voice, video, and data to *transparently* coexist on a single network. When real-time applications such as voice and TelePresence dominate a link (especially a WAN/VPN link), data applications fluctuate significantly in their response times when TelePresence calls are present versus when they are absent, thus destroying the transparency of the converged network.

For example, consider a 45-Mbps DS3 link configured to support two separate CTS-3000 calls, both configured to transmit at full 1080p-Best resolution. Each such call requires 15 Mbps of real-time traffic. Prior to TelePresence calls being placed, data applications have access to 100 percent of the bandwidth. (To simplify the example, assume there are no other real-time applications, such as VoIP, on this link.) However, after these TelePresence calls are established, all data applications would suddenly be contending for less than 33 percent of the link. TCP windowing would take effect, and many data applications would hang, time-out, or become stuck in a nonresponsive state, which usually translates into users calling the IT help desk complaining about the network (which, ironically, happens to be functioning properly, albeit in a poorly configured manner).

To obviate such scenarios, Cisco technical marketing has done extensive testing and has found that a significant decrease in data application response times occurs when real-time traffic exceeds one third of link bandwidth capacity. Similarly, extensive testing and customer deployments have shown that a general best queuing practice is to limit the amount of strict priority queuing to 33 percent of link bandwidth capacity. This strict priority queuing rule is a conservative and safe design ratio for merging real-time applications with data applications.

Note As Cisco IOS Software allows the abstraction (and thus configuration) of multiple strict priority LLQs, in such a multiple LLQ context, this design principle would apply to the sum of all LLQs to be within one third of link capacity.

TelePresence Shaping Recommendations

For shaping guidelines, it is recommended to avoid shaping TelePresence flows unless necessary. This is because the objective of shapers is to delay traffic bursts above a certain rate and to smooth out flows to fall within contracted rates. Therefore, shapers could have a negative effect on jitter values for TelePresence.

However, in certain situations, shapers are a necessity. One such case is subline-rate circuits, where the only way to force queuing policies to engage at a subline rate is to implement a hierarchical shaping policy with a nested queuing policy (as discussed later in this chapter).

TelePresence Link Efficiency Recommendations

It is recommended to not enable compressed RTP (cRTP) for TelePresence. This is because of the large CPU impact of cRTP and the negligible returns in bandwidth savings it entails at TelePresence circuit speeds.

And finally, it is recommended not to use Link Fragmentation and Interleaving (LFI) on TelePresence flows. This is because, like cRTP, LFI is useful only on slow-speed links (usually 768 kbps or less), over which TelePresence could not be deployed anyway.

Having discussed the marking, policing, queuing, and shaping recommendations that form the end-to-end QoS strategy for TelePresence, specific place-in-the-network designs for the campus and branch will now be detailed.

Campus QoS Design for TelePresence

The campus is the primary place-in-the-network (PIN) where TelePresence endpoints connect to the network infrastructure. Specifically, the 10/100/1000 NIC on the TelePresence primary codec connects, typically through an Intermediate Distribution Frame (IDF), to the campus access layer edge switch port. It is at this switch port that the initial QoS policies required to support TelePresence are enabled. Additional QoS policies are also required on all campus interswitch links, such as uplinks and downlinks between the access and distribution layers, and uplinks and downlinks from the distribution-to-core layers and all core-layer links.

The first QoS operation that needs to be performed is to define the trust boundary. The trust boundary is the point in the network at which 802.1Q/p CoS markings and IP DSCP markings are accepted or overridden by the network.

At the access layer, the network administrator can enable the infrastructure to

- Trust the endpoints (CoS and DSCP)

- Not trust the endpoints and manually re-mark TelePresence traffic using administratively defined policies within the access-edge switch

- Conditionally trust the endpoints (trust is extended only after a successful CDP negotiation)

If a dedicated Cisco Unified Communications Manager (CUCM) is used for managing TelePresence endpoints, the recommendation is to configure it to mark video (TelePresence) traffic to DSCP CS4. This then instructs all TelePresence primary codecs to mark all TelePresence call traffic (both video and audio) to CS4. (But all call-signaling traffic continues to be marked CS3). The Cisco 7975G IP Phone, in turn, will be instructed (by default) to mark VoIP traffic to EF and call-signaling to CS3. Therefore, the switch port connecting to the TelePresence primary codec can be configured to trust DSCP.

Alternatively, the access switch ports can be set to trust CoS, as both the Cisco 7975G IP Phone and the TelePresence primary codec are assigned to the Voice VLAN (VVLAN) and tag their traffic with 802.1Q/p CoS values. The 7975G IP Phone marks VoIP traffic to CoS 5 and call-signaling traffic to CoS 3. The Cisco TelePresence codec marks TelePresence traffic (both video and audio) to CoS 4 and call-signaling traffic to CoS 3. However, if the switch port is configured to trust CoS, it generates an internal DSCP value for all traffic flows through the CoS-to-DSCP map. Only one change is recommended to be made to the default CoS-to-DSCP map, which is to map CoS 5 to EF (46) instead of leaving the default mapping of CoS 5 to CS5 (40), as this makes the DSCP marking for VoIP inline with RFC 3246 and 4594.

Finally, the access switch might be set to conditionally trust the TelePresence endpoint. This is because Cisco IP Telephony devices, including the Cisco Unified 7979G IP Phone that is an intrinsic part of the TelePresence endpoint system, have the capability to identify themselves, through Cisco Discovery Protocol (CDP), to the network infrastructure. Upon a successful CDP negotiation, the network infrastructure dynamically extends trust to the endpoints, which include both the Cisco Unified 7975G IP Phone and the TelePresence primary codec. The primary functionality that conditional trust brings is to allow for user mobility within the IP Telephony-enabled enterprise. (Users can add/move/change where their IP Phones connect, and the network automatically adapts without requiring an administrator to manually change switch port trust policies.) This user mobility is not a crucial functionality to support TelePresence because TelePresence units are rarely moved around (due to sheer size). Nonetheless, this conditional trust functionality is supported by TelePresence codecs and adds a minor element of security if the TelePresence codec is physically disconnected from the wall network jack by an unknowing and disgruntled individual, who then connects some other device (such as a laptop) to this trusted switch port. In this case, by using a conditional trust policy, the abuser's traffic would no longer be trusted. However, it should be noted that CDP is neither an authenticated nor an encrypted protocol, and as such, CDP-spoofing tools are readily available on the Internet for downloading and hacking purposes.

Figure 10-4 illustrates the operation of conditional trust policies and endpoint CoS markings and the CoS-to-DSCP mappings of the access-edge switch for TelePresence scenarios.

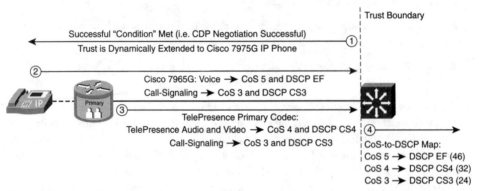

Figure 10-4   *Conditional trust, CoS markings, and mappings for TelePresence*

Note   Note that if trust CoS is used (as opposed to conditional trust), steps 2, 3, and 4 in Figure 10-4 would still apply. The only difference is that the switch would skip step 1, as the port CoS values would always be trusted, regardless of CDP.

An optional recommendation for the access-edge switch port connecting to a TelePresence primary codec is to configure a policer to prevent network abuse in case of a compromise of this trusted port. Similar to the previous example, this recommendation is to prevent an unknowing and disgruntled individual that gains physical access to the TelePresence switch port from sending rogue traffic over the network that can hijack voice or video queues and easily ruin call or video quality. Therefore, the administrator can choose to limit the scope of damage that such network abuse might present by configuring access-edge policers on TelePresence switch ports to drop (or re-mark to Scavenger/CS1) out-of-profile traffic originating on these ports. This is not only a Cisco recommended best practice but is also reflected in RFC 4594 that recommends edge policing the Real-Time Interactive service class through a single-rate policer. If such a policer is configured, it is recommended to use Per-Port/Per-VLAN policers whenever supported. In this manner, a set of policers can be applied to the Voice VLAN to ensure that voice, video, and call signaling traffic are performing within normal levels, and a separate, more stringent, policer can be applied to the data VLAN. TelePresence policing details are discussed later in this chapter.

Finally, to ensure guaranteed levels of service, queuing needs to be configured on all nodes where the potential for congestion exists, regardless of how infrequently it might occur. In campus networks, placing TelePresence in the strict-priority hardware queues yields optimal results, especially in terms of protection against packet loss during momentary periods of congestion, which can occur regularly in campus networks even under normal operating conditions. Additionally, placing TelePresence traffic in these strict-priority queues does not involve any incremental or ongoing monetary expense (beyond initial configuration) because this potential for strict-priority servicing already exists within the campus network infrastructure, and the exercise simply becomes a matter of reconfiguring existing queuing structures to enable strict-priority queuing for TelePresence.

Therefore, it is highly recommended that all Catalyst switches and linecards within a Cisco TelePresence campus design support a 1PxQyT queuing model, as discussed in Chapter 6.

Looking beyond the campus access edge, when the trust boundary has been established and optimal access-edge policers have been enabled, the DSCP values on all other inter-switch links and campus-to-WAN hand-off links can be trusted. Therefore, it is recommended to trust DSCP (not CoS) on all inter-switch links, whether these are uplinks/downlinks to/from the distribution layer, uplinks/downlinks to/from the core layer, intracore links, or links to WAN Aggregation routers. The reason it is recommended to trust DSCP and not CoS is two-fold:

- First, because marking granularity is lost every time a node is set to trust CoS. For example, if TelePresence endpoints are marking traffic to CS4 and Unified Video Advantage (or other Videoconferencing/Video Telephony endpoints) are marking their traffic to AF41 and the distribution-layer is set to trust CoS from the access-layer, these flows both appear the same (as CoS 4) to the distribution-layer switch and are indistinguishable from each other from that node forward.

- Second, trusting CoS implies using 802.1Q trunking between switches; however, as discussed in Chapter 9, most enterprise campus networks are designed to be Layer 3 (especially in the Distribution and Core layers), and thus 802.1Q is not used on these interswitch links. Also, queuing policies, with TelePresence assigned to the PQ (along with VoIP), are likewise recommended to be enabled on every node along the path, including all interswitch links.

Figure 10-5 summarizes the QoS design requirements and recommendations within an enterprise campus supporting TelePresence.

Although there is a wide array of platform and linecard combinations that you can use for TelePresence campus networks, only a cross-section of GE/10GE platforms are presented in this chapter to limit the scope but still illustrate how you can implement these recommendations across platforms, including the Cisco Catalyst 3560/3750, the 4500/4900, and the 6500 families of switches. Each of these platform families will be now considered.

Note For a complete discussion of Catalyst switch platform QoS design guidance for TelePresence, refer to the latest TelePresence Network Design Guide at http://www.tinyurl.com/ce7twk.

Catalyst 3560/3750 QoS Design for TelePresence

The Cisco Catalyst 3560G is a fixed-configuration switch that supports up to 48 10/100/1000 ports with integrated Power over Ethernet (PoE), plus four Small Form-Factor Pluggable (SFP) ports for uplinks. The 3560G has a 32-Gbps backplane, which is moderately oversubscribed (52 Gbps theoretical maximum input versus 32-Gbps backplane

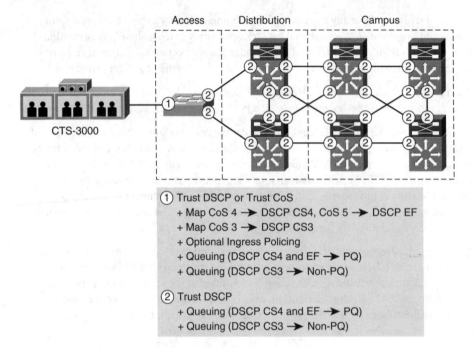

Figure 10-5 *Campus QoS design recommendations for TelePresence*

yields an oversubscription ratio of 1.625:1). Additionally, the 3560G supports IP routing (including IPv6), multicast routing, and an advanced QoS and security feature set.

The Catalyst 3750G is nearly identical, with only a few additional key features, including the support for a stackable configuration (through Stackwise technology), allowing for the 32-Gbps backplane (composed of dual counter-rotating 16-Gbps rings) to be extended over multiple 3750G switches (up to 9). Additionally, the 3750G provides support for 10 Gigabit Ethernet (10GE) connectivity. Obviously, however, the more switches in the stack, and the use of 10GE connectors, increases the oversubscription ratio accordingly.

The 3560-E and 3750-E represent the next evolution of these switches. As before, the 3560-E is a fixed configuration switch, but now with a 128-Gbps backplane and 10GE port support. Similarly, the 3750-E supports a 128-Gbps backplane with dual 10GE port support and the support for a stackable configuration (through Stackwise Plus technology, allowing a 64-Gbps interconnect between stacked switches).

As the 3560G, 3750G, 3560-E, and 3750-E share virtually identical feature parity (the main differences being the backplane throughput and uplink port speeds), these can be considered (in this QoS design context) as a single switch, with the abbreviated reference of simply C3560/3750.

Note As only GE/10GE platforms are relevant and recommended for TelePresence campus networks, the original Catalyst 3560/3750 switches are not included in this context and discussion, as these support only Fast Ethernet or 10/100 interfaces.

From a QoS perspective, some of the relevant features of the Catalyst 3560G/3750G/E include conditional trust, Per-Port/Per-VLAN policers (through Hierarchical QoS policies), DSCP-to-Queue mapping, 1P1Q3T ingress queuing, and 1P3Q3T egress queuing. Additionally, these platforms provide (minimally) 750 KB of receive buffers and 2 MB of transmit buffers for each set of four ports. These buffers can be allocated, reserved, or dynamically borrowed from a common pool on a port-port, per-queue basis, depending on the administrative configurations chosen.

As QoS is disabled by default on these switches, the first configuration step is to enable QoS globally:

```
C3750(config)# mls qos
```

With QoS enabled, the access-edge trust boundaries can be defined. As discussed previously, there are three trust options:

- Trust DSCP

- Trust CoS

- Conditional trust

It is recommended that ports used for data and VoIP Telephony be configured to conditionally trust CoS, whereas ports used for TelePresence be configured to either trust DSCP, trust CoS, or conditionally trust CoS. Trusting DSCP on these ports is the simplest operationally. The interface command to configure DSCP trust is fairly straightforward:

```
C3750(config-if)# mls qos trust dscp
```

Alternatively, if an administrator chooses to trust CoS or conditionally trust CoS, he must ensure that the fifth parameter in the global CoS-to-DSCP map, which corresponds to the DSCP mapping for CoS 4, is set to 32 (CS4). Additionally, to support IP Telephony properly, the global CoS-to-DSCP mapping table should be modified such that CoS 5 (the sixth parameter in the CoS-to-DSCP map) is mapped to 46 (EF), which is not the default. (The default setting is 40/CS5.) These settings are achieved through the following global and interface commands:

```
C3750(config)# mls qos map cos-dscp 0 8 16 24 32 46 48 56
C3750(config)# interface GigabitEthernet1/0/1
C3750(config-if)# mls qos trust cos
```

Finally, if an administrator chooses to implement conditional trust on the TelePresence ports, this feature can be enabled with the following interface command:

```
C3750(config-if)# mls qos trust device cisco-phone
```

These trust-boundary configurations can be verified with the following commands:

- show mls qos

- show mls qos map cos-dscp

- show mls qos interface

Catalyst 3560/3750 1P1Q3T Ingress Queuing

As the C3560/3750 platforms have architectures based on oversubscription, they have been engineered to guarantee QoS by protecting critical traffic trying to access the backplane/stack-ring through ingress queuing. Ingress queuing on this platform can be configured as 2Q3T or 1P1Q3T. However, as VoIP and TelePresence require strict-priority servicing in the campus, it is recommended to enable the 1P1Q3T ingress queuing structure with DSCP EF (VoIP) and CS4 (TelePresence) mapped to the ingress PQ (Q2).

Note Catalyst 1PxQyT queuing structures were overviewed in Chapter 6.

The configurable thresholds in the nonpriority queue can protect control traffic. For example, network control traffic (such as Spanning Tree Protocol) associated with DSCP CS7 and internetwork control traffic (such as Interior Gateway Protocols, including EIGRP and OSPF) marked DSCP CS6 can be explicitly protected by assigning these to Q1T3. Additionally, a degree or protection can be offered to call-signaling traffic (which is essentially control traffic for the IP Telephony infrastructure), which is marked CS3. All other traffic types can be provisioned in Q1T1. Figure 10-6 illustrates the recommended ingress 1P1Q3T queuing configuration for the C3560/3750 platforms.

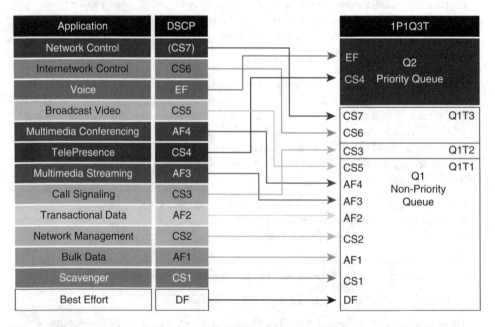

Figure 10-6 *Catalyst 3560/3750 (1P1Q3T) ingress queuing diagram for TelePresence deployments*

Based on Figure 10-6, Example 10-1 outlines the recommended configuration for ingress queuing on the C3560/3750 for TelePresence deployments.

Example 10-1 *C3560/3750 (1P1Q3T) Ingress Queuing Configuration for TelePresence Deployments*

```
C3750# show run
! Output omitted for brevity.
!
! This section modifies the CoS-to-DSCP mapping table
mls qos map cos-dscp 0 8 16 24 32 46 48 56
 ! Modifies CoS-to-DSCP mapping to map CoS 5 to DSCP EF
!
! This section configures the Ingress Queues and Thresholds for 1P1Q3T
mls qos srr-queue input buffers 70 30
 ! Configures the Ingress Queue buffers such that Q2 (PQ) gets 30% of buffers
mls qos srr-queue input priority-queue 2 bandwidth 30
 ! Configures the Ingress PQ (Q2) to be guaranteed 30% BW on stack ring
mls qos srr-queue input bandwidth 70 30
 ! Configures SRR weights between Ingress Q1 and Q2 for remaining bandwidth
mls qos srr-queue input threshold 1 80 90
 ! Configures Ingress Queue 1 Threshold 1 to 80% and Threshold 2 to 90%
 ! Ingress Queue 1 Threshold 3 remains at 100% (default)
 ! Ingress Queue 2 Thresholds 1, 2 and 3 remain at 100% (default)
!
! This section configures the Ingress DSCP-to-Queue Mappings
mls qos srr-queue input  dscp-map queue 1 threshold 1 0 8 10 12 14
 ! Maps DSCP 0, CS1 and AF1 to Ingress Queue 1 Threshold 1 (Q1T1)
mls qos srr-queue input  dscp-map queue 1 threshold 1 16 18 20 22
 ! Maps DSCP CS2 and AF2 to Ingress Queue 1 Threshold 1 (Q1T1)
mls qos srr-queue input  dscp-map queue 1 threshold 1 26 28 30 34 36 38 40
 ! Maps DSCP AF3 and AF4 and CS5 to Ingress Queue 1 Threshold 1 (Q1T1)
mls qos srr-queue input  dscp-map queue 1 threshold 2 24
 ! Maps DSCP CS3 to Ingress Queue 1 Threshold 2 (Q1T2)
mls qos srr-queue input  dscp-map queue 1 threshold 3 48 56
 ! Maps DSCP CS6 and CS7 to Ingress Queue 1 Threshold 3 (Q1T3)
mls qos srr-queue input  dscp-map queue 2 threshold 1 32 46
 ! Maps DSCP CS4 (TelePresence)& EF (VoIP) to Ingress-PQ Threshold 1 (Q2T1)
!
```

Note Nonstandard DSCP values can also be mapped to their respective queues; however, to simplify these configurations, nonstandard DSCP-to-Queue mappings have not been shown in the example configurations in this chapter.

These ingress queuing configurations can be verified with the following commands:

■   show mls qos queue-set

■   show mls qos maps cos-input-q

■   show mls qos maps dscp-input-q

Catalyst 3560/3750 1P3Q3T Egress Queuing

Having provisioned ingress queuing to prioritize TelePresence traffic, attention can now be shifted to egress queuing design for the Catalyst 3560/3750. Although the Catalyst 3560/3750 supports either 4Q3T or 1P3Q3T egress queuing configurations, it is recommended to enable the 1P3Q3T egress queuing configuration, where Q1 serves as the PQ. Then both VoIP (DSCP EF) and TelePresence (DSCP CS4) can be mapped to Q1 (the PQ). Default traffic can be assigned to Q3, and Q4 can be designated as a less than Best Effort queue, servicing Bulk (AF1) and Scavenger (DSCP CS1) traffic, being assigned to Q4T2 and Q4T1, respectively. Network Control (DSCP CS7) and Internetwork Control (DSCP CS6) can be mapped to the highest threshold of the preferential nonpriority queue (Q2T3), while Call-Signaling (DSCP CS3) can be mapped to the second highest threshold in that queue (Q2T2). All other applications can be mapped to Q2T1. Figure 10-7 shows the recommended 1P3Q3T egress queuing configuration for the C3560/3750 platforms.

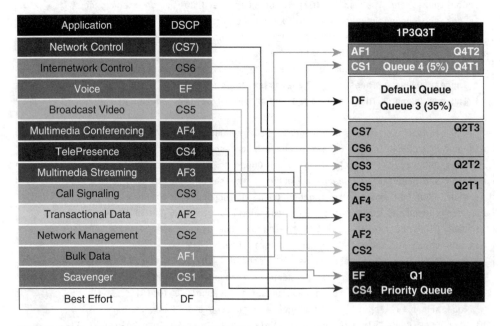

Figure 10-7 *Catalyst 3560/3750 (1P3Q3T) egress queuing diagram for TelePresence deployments*

Based on Figure 10-7, Example 10-2 details the recommended configuration for egress queuing on the Catalyst 3560/3750 for TelePresence deployments.

Example 10-2 *C3560/3750 (1P3Q3T) Egress Queuing Configuration for TelePresence Deployments*

```
C3750# show run
! Output omitted for brevity.
!
! This section configures the Output DSCP-to-Queue Maps
```

```
mls qos srr-queue output dscp-map queue 1 threshold 3 32 46
 ! Maps DSCP CS4 (TelePresence) and EF (VoIP) to Egress Queue 1 (PQ)
mls qos srr-queue output dscp-map queue 2 threshold 1 16 18 20 22
 ! Maps DSCP CS2 and AF2 to Egress Queue 2 Threshold 1 (Q2T1)
mls qos srr-queue output dscp-map queue 2 threshold 1 26 28 30 34 36 38 40
 ! Maps DSCP AF3 and AF4 and CS5 to Egress Queue 2 Threshold 1 (Q2T1)
mls qos srr-queue output dscp-map queue 2 threshold 2 24
 ! Maps DSCP CS3 to Egress Queue 2 Threshold 2 (Q2T2)
mls qos srr-queue output dscp-map queue 2 threshold 3 48 56
 ! Maps DSCP CS6 and CS7 to Egress Queue 2 Threshold 3 (Q2T3)
mls qos srr-queue output dscp-map queue 3 threshold 3 0
 ! Maps DSCP DF to Egress Queue 3 Threshold 3 (Q3T3 - Default Queue)
mls qos srr-queue output dscp-map queue 4 threshold 1 8
 ! Maps DSCP CS1 to Egress Queue 4 Threshold 1 (Q4T1)
mls qos srr-queue output dscp-map queue 4 threshold 2 10 12 14
 ! Maps DSCP AF1 to Egress Queue 4 Threshold 2 (Q4T2)
!
! This next section configures the WRED min and max thresholds for Q1
mls qos queue-set output 1 threshold 2 80 90 100 100
 ! Sets Egress Queue 2 Threshold 1 (Q2T1)Ò 80% and Threshold2 (Q2T2)Ò 90%
mls qos queue-set output 1 threshold 4 60 100 100 100
 ! Sets Egress Queue 4 Threshold 1 (Q4T1) Ò 60% and Threshold 2 (Q4T2)Ò 100%
!
! This section configures trust-DSCP and queuing on TP access ports & uplink ports
interface GigabitEthernet1/0/1
 description TelePresence Access Port or Uplink port
mls qos trust dscp
  ! Assigns the TelePresence port and/or uplink port to trust DSCP
 queue-set 1
  ! Assigns interface to Queue-Set 1 (default)
 srr-queue bandwidth share 1 30 35 5
  ! Q2 gets 30% of remaining BW (after PQ); Q3 gets 35% & Q4 gets 5%
priority-queue out
  ! Expedite queue is enabled for TelePresence and VoIP
!
```

You can verify these egress queuing configurations with the following commands:

- show mls qos queue-set

- show mls qos maps cos-output-q

- show mls qos maps dscp-output-q

- show mls qos interface

- show mls qos interface buffers

- show mls qos interface queueing

- show controllers ethernet-controller port-asic statistics

Catalyst 4500/4900 QoS Design for TelePresence

From a QoS standpoint, there are two radically different branches within the Catalyst 4500/4900 family of switches: the Classic Supervisor branch, which includes the Supervisor II+, II+10GE, IV, V and V-10GE supervisors, and the Supervisor 6-E branch.

Catalyst 4500 Classic Supervisors with 1P3Q1T Egress Queuing

The Cisco Catalyst 4500 series switches with Classic Supervisors are midrange modular platforms with chassis options to support 3, 6, 7, and 10 slots; these models include the Catalyst 4503, 4506, 4507R, and 4510R, respectively (the latter two models supporting a redundant supervisor option).

Within the Catalyst 4500 Classic Supervisor branch, oversubscription and buffering capabilities vary by linecard. Some linecards are entirely nonblocking, whereas others, such as the 4448 and the 4548, provision a single 1-Gbps uplink to the switch fabric for every 4 or 8 (10/100/1000) ports, which equates to a 4:1 (for the 4524) or an 8:1 (4448 and 4548) theoretical oversubscription ratio. Unlike the Catalyst 3560/3750, the Catalyst 4500/4900 does not support ingress queuing to offset oversubscription scenarios. As such, the 4448 and 4548 series linecards, although suitable at the campus access-edge, would not be recommended to be used as uplinks nor within the distribution and core layers of a TelePresence-enabled campus.

In contrast, the Catalyst 4948 has a completely nonblocking architecture and would be suitable at any layer (access, distribution, or core) within a TelePresence-enabled campus network. Specifically, the Catalyst 4948 provides 96 Gbps of switching fabric for its fixed configuration 48 x 10/100/1000 ports plus 4 SFP ports (that might be GE or 10GE). Additionally, the Catalyst 4948 provides approximately 16 MB of buffering that is shared among all 48 ports.

As the Catalyst 4500 Classic Supervisors and the 4948 share virtually identical QoS feature parity (the main differences being the backplane throughput and buffer architectures), these can be considered as a single switch and abbreviated as C4500/4900 for this discussion.

From a QoS perspective, some of the relevant features of the C4500/4900 include conditional trust, an elegant Per-Port/Per-VLAN policer implementation, DSCP-to-Queue mapping, 4Q1T or 1P3Q1T queuing support, and an advanced congestion algorithm (Dynamic Buffer Limiting [DBL]).

It bears mentioning that there is a minor syntactical difference when configuring QoS features on the C4500/4900, as compared to other switching platforms; specifically, QoS commands on this platform do not include the **mls** prefix used on the Catalyst 3560/3750 and the Catalyst 6500 series platforms. For example, to globally enable QoS on the C4500/4900 (which is disabled by default), the command is not **mls qos** but simply **qos**.

With QoS enabled, access-edge trust boundaries can be defined. As discussed previously, there are three options for trust: trust DSCP, trust CoS, or conditional trust. The recommendation is that ports used for data and VoIP Telephony be configured to conditionally trust CoS, whereas ports used for TelePresence be configured to either trust DSCP, trust CoS, or conditionally trust CoS. Trusting DSCP on these ports is the simplest operationally and is enabled with the following interface command:

```
C4500(config-if)# qos trust dscp
```

Alternatively, if the interface is set to trust CoS, CoS 5 must be explicitly mapped to DSCP EF. All other CoS-to-DSCP mappings can be left at their respective default values. These functions can be achieved through the following global and interface commands:

```
C4500(config)# qos map cos 5 to 46
C4500(config)# interface GigabitEthernet1/1
C4500(config-if)# qos trust cos
```

Finally, if the interface can be set to conditional trust, you can enter the following interface command:

```
C4500(config-if)# qos trust device cisco-phone
```

As with configuration commands, the C4500/4900 omits the **mls** prefix in the corresponding verification commands. These trust-boundary configurations can be verified with the following commands:

- show qos
- show qos maps
- show qos interface

The C4500/4900 can be configured to operate in a 4Q1T mode or a 1P3Q1T mode, the latter of which is recommended for VoIP and TelePresence deployments. On the C4500/4900, however, the strict priority queue, when enabled, is Q3. As the C4500/4900 supports DSCP-to-Queue mappings, it can distinguish between applications such as generic Videoconferencing/Video Telephony (AF4) and TelePresence (CS4), even though these share the same CoS and IP Precedence values (CoS/IPP 4). Given these capabilities, the recommendation is to enable 1P3Q1T queuing on the C4500/4900, with VoIP (EF) and TelePresence (CS4) assigned to the strict-priority queue (Q3). Q2 can be dedicated to service default traffic, and Q1 can be used to service less than Best Effort Scavenger (CS1) and Bulk (AF1) traffic. All other applications can be mapped to Q4, the preferential queue. Figure 10-8 illustrates the recommended (1P3Q1T + DBL) egress queuing configuration for the C4500/4900 platform.

As previously mentioned, the C4500/4900 supports an advanced congestion avoidance algorithm, Dynamic Buffer Limiting (DBL), rather than Weighted Tail Drop (WTD) or Weighted-Random Early-Detect (WRED). Therefore, no DSCP-to-Threshold mappings are required on the C4500/4900. However, to leverage DBL, it must be globally enabled (as it is disabled by default) with the following global command:

```
C4500(config)# qos dbl
```

Optionally, DBL can be configured to operate to support RFC 3168, "IP Explicit Congestion Notification" (IP ECN, which was discussed in Chapter 6), which utilizes the remaining

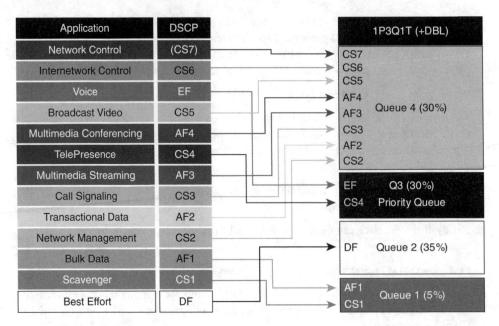

Figure 10-8 *Catalyst 4500/4900 classic supervisor (1P3Q1T) egress queuing diagram for TelePresence deployments*

2 bits of the IPv4/IPv6 Type of Service (ToS) byte. (The DSCP value uses the first 6 bits of the ToS byte.) The following global command enables ECN for DBL:

```
C4500(config)# qos dbl exceed-action ecn
```

Additionally, to leverage DBL (with/without IP ECN) on a per-interface basis, a service policy applying DBL to all flows must be constructed and applied to each interface. This can be done by using the following basic policy map shown in Example 10-3.

Example 10-3 *C4500/4900 Class-default DBL Configuration*

```
C4500(config)# policy-map DBL
C4500(config-pmap)# class class-default
C4500(config-pmap-c)# dbl
C4500(config-pmap-c)# exit
C4500(config-pmap)# exit
C4500(config)# interface GigabitEthernet1/1
C4500(config-if)# service policy output DBL
```

However, at this point, an important consideration pertaining to DBL must be taken into account, namely DBL (when enabled and configured as per the preceding recommendations) is active on *all* flows, including flows destined to the PQ (Q3), which in this case includes VoIP and TelePresence traffic. As DBL introduces dynamic drops, especially on bursty, large-packet flows, this is detrimental to TelePresence call quality. Therefore, to explicitly disable DBL on PQ traffic, the amendments can be made to the previous, generic DBL policy, as shown in Example 10-4.

Example 10-4 *C4500/4900 Class Default DBL Configuration, with DBL Disabled on PQ*

```
C4500(config)# class-map match-any PQ
C4500(config-cmap)# match dscp ef
C4500(config-cmap)# match dscp cs4
C4500(config-cmap)# exit
C4500(config)# policy-map DBL
C4500(config-pmap)# class PQ
C4500(config-pmap-c)# exit
C4500(config-pmap)# class class-default
C4500(config-pmap-c)# dbl
C4500(config-pmap-c)# exit
C4500(config-pmap)# exit
C4500(config)# interface GigabitEthernet1/1
C4500(config-if)# service policy output DBL
```

In this modified policy, the class map PQ identifies traffic destined to the Priority Queue, specifically EF (VoIP) and CS4 (TelePresence) traffic. In the policy map, the PQ-class receives no action (DBL or otherwise) and serves only to exclude these flows from the following class-default policy of applying DBL to all (other) flows. Recommended practice dictates that you should use this modified policy on C4500/4900 platforms supporting TelePresence in conjunction with DBL; otherwise DBL drops negatively impact TelePresence call quality.

Based on Figure 10-8 and Example 10-4, Example 10-5 shows the recommended configuration for 1P3Q1T egress queuing on the C4500/4900 for TelePresence deployments.

Example 10-5 *C4500/4900 (1P3Q1T) Egress Queuing Configuration for TelePresence Deployments*

```
C4500# show run
! Output omitted for brevity.
!
!This section enables DBL globally and excludes DBL on PQ flows
qos dbl
 ! Globally enables DBL
qos dbl exceed-action ecn
 ! Optional: Enables DBL to mark RFC 3168 ECN bits in the IP ToS Byte
class-map match-any PQ
 match dscp ef
 match dscp cs4
  ! Classifies traffic mapped to PQ for exclusion of DBL-policy
policy-map DBL
class PQ
 ! No action (DBL or otherwise) is applied on traffic mapped to PQ
 class class-default
  dbl
```

```
   ! Enables DBL on all (other) traffic flows
 !
 ! This section configures the DSCP-to-Transmit Queue Mappings
 qos map dscp 0 to tx-queue 2
  ! Maps DSCP 0 (Best Effort) to Q2
 qos map dscp 8 10 12 14 to tx-queue 1
  ! Maps DSCP CS1 (Scavenger) and AF11/AF12/AF13 (Bulk) to Q1
 qos map dscp 16 18 20 22 to tx-queue 4
  ! Maps DSCP CS2 (Net-Mgmt) and AF21/AF22/AF23 (Transactional) to Q4
 qos map dscp 24 26 28 30 to tx-queue 4
  ! Maps DSCP CS3 (Call-Sig) and AF31/AF32/AF33 (MultiMedia) to Q4
 qos map dscp 34 36 38 40 to tx-queue 4
  ! Maps DSCP AF41/AF42/AF43 (Interactive-Video) and CS5 (Broadcast Video) to Q4
 qos map dscp 32 46 to tx-queue 3
  ! Maps DSCP CS4 (TelePresence) and EF (VoIP) to Q3 (PQ)
 qos map dscp 48 56 to tx-queue 4
  ! Maps DSCP CS6 (Internetwork) and CS7 (Network Control) to Q4
 !
 ! This section configures queues, activates the PQ and applies DBL
 interface range GigabitEthernet1/1 - 48
  tx-queue 1
   bandwidth percent 5
   ! Q1 gets 5% BW
  tx-queue 2
   bandwidth percent 35
   ! Q2 gets 35% BW
  tx-queue 3
   priority high
   ! Q3 is PQ
   bandwidth percent 30
   ! Q3 (PQ) gets 30% BW
  tx-queue 4
   bandwidth percent 30
   ! Q4 gets 40%
  service-policy output DBL
   ! Applies DBL to all flows except VoIP & TelePresence
 !
```

You can verify these egress queuing configurations with the following commands:

- show qos dbl

- show qos maps dscp tx-queue

- show qos interface

Catalyst 4500 Supervisor 6-E with 1P7Q1T Egress Queuing

Starting with Cisco IOS Release 12.2(40)SG, the Catalyst 4500 Supervisor Engine 6-E (Sup 6-E) series radically broke away from the Classic Supervisors method of deploying QoS and instead employs the Modular QoS Command-Line Interface (MQC) model of QoS (MQC is discussed in Chapter 6).

Note   QoS functionality and syntax on the Catalyst 4500 Supervisor 6-E and the Catalyst 4900M are equivalent.

From a trust-boundary perspective, the MQC model does not support the *trust* feature, but rather, the incoming traffic is considered trusted by default. In this default mode, a Sup 6-E trusts both the CoS value of packet and the DSCP value. This means that both TelePresence and VoIP packets from a CTS system can be accepted without any explicit mapping requirement. (For instance, the VoIP packets from the 7975G IP Phone are marked CoS 5 and DSCP 46; because both values are trusted by default, there is no CoS 5-to-DSCP 46 mapping required.)

The Sup 6-E hardware supports (up to) eight transmit queues per port. Queues are assigned when an output policy is attached to a port with one or more queuing related actions for one or more classes of traffic. Because there are only eight queues per port, there can be at most eight classes of traffic (including the reserved class, class-default) with queuing actions defined.

On Sup 6-E, only one transmit queue on a port can be configured as *strict priority* queue (which, in effect, constitutes a hardware LLQ) with the **priority** policy map class action command. The priority queue is serviced first until it is empty or until it is under its shape rate. Only one traffic stream can be destined for the priority queue per class-level policy. (In other words, multiple hardware LLQs are not supported on the Sub 6-E.) The hardware LLQ can starve other queues unless it is rate limited, and as such, the Sup 6-E supports an unconditional (explicit) policer to rate limit packets enqueued to the strict priority queue. When the priority queue is configured on one class of a policy map, only **bandwidth remaining** is accepted on other classes, guaranteeing a minimum bandwidth for other classes from the remaining bandwidth of what is left after using the priority queue. When the priority queue is configured with a policer, either **bandwidth** or **bandwidth remaining** is accepted on other classes.

Additionally, as with the Classic Supervisors, DBL can be enabled on a per-class basis but is most effective when applied against TCP-based traffic flows (as opposed to UDP-based traffic flows).

Thus, the Sup 6-E can be configured to operate in a 1P7Q1T mode. VoIP (EF) and TelePresence (CS4) can be assigned to the strict-priority queue. Network and Internetwork Control (CS6 and CS7, respectively), along with Call Signaling and Network Management (CS3 and CS2, respectively), can share a Control/Management queue. This enables dedicated queues to be provisioned for Broadcast Video (CS5), Multimedia Conferencing (AF4), Multimedia Streaming (AF3), and Transactional Data (AF2). Bulk Data (AF1) and Scavenger (CS1) can share a bandwidth-constrained "less than Best Effort" queue, while all other traffic is assigned to the default/Best Effort queue. Figure 10-9 illustrates the recommended 1P7Q1T Sup 6-E egress queuing configuration for the C4500/4900M platform.

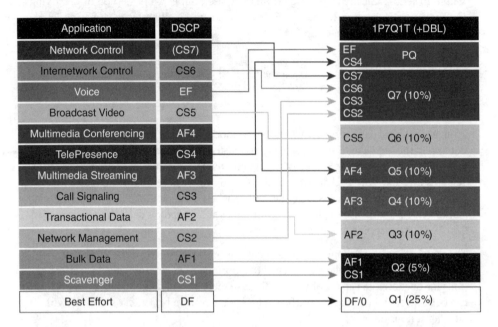

Figure 10-9　*Catalyst 4500/4900M Supervisor 6-E (1P7Q1T) egress queuing diagram for TelePresence deployments*

Based on Figure 10-9, Example 10-6 provides the recommended configuration for egress queuing on the 4500/4900M Supervisor 6-E for TelePresence deployments.

Example 10-6　*Catalyst 4500/4900M Supervisor 6-E (1P7Q1T) Egress Queuing Configuration for TelePresence*

```
C4500-SUP6E# show run
! Output omitted for brevity.
!
!This section define the class-maps
class-map match-any PQ
 match dscp ef
 match dscp cs4
  ! Classifies traffic mapped to PQ (VoIP and TelePresence, respectively)
class-map match-any CONTROL-MGMT
 match dscp cs7
 match dscp cs6
 match dscp cs3
 match dscp cs2
  ! Classifies traffic mapped to CONTROL-MGMT queue
```

```
   ! Includes Network + Internetwork Control (CS7 & CS6), respectively
   ! Includes Call-Signaling and Net-Mgmt (CS3 & CS2), respectively
class-map match-all BROADCAST-VIDEO
 match dscp cs5
   ! Classifies Broadcast Video traffic
class-map match-all MULTIMEDIA-CONFERENCING
 match dscp af41 af42 af43
   ! Classifies Multimedia Conferencing traffic
class-map match-all MULTIMEDIA-STREAMING
 match dscp af31 af32 af33
   ! Classifies Multimedia Streaming traffic
class-map match-all TRANSACTIONAL-DATA
 match dscp af21 af22 af23
   ! Classifies Transactional Data traffic
class-map match-any BULK-SCAVENGER
 match dscp cs1
 match dscp af11 af12 af13
   ! Classifies Scavenger and Bulk Data traffic, respectively
!
!This section define the policy-map
policy-map 1P7Q1T
 class PQ
  priority
  police cir percent 20 bc 33 ms
   conform-action transmit
   exceed-action drop
   ! Enables the hardware LLQ (PQ)
   ! Explicit policer for the PQ to prevent BW starvation for other queues
 class CONTROL-MGMT
  bandwidth percent 10
   ! Provisions a BW guarantee for the CONTROL-MGMT queue
 class BROADCAST-VIDEO
  bandwidth percent 10
   ! Provisions a BW guarantee for the BROADCAST-VIDEO queue
 class MULTIMEDIA-CONFERENCING
  bandwidth percent 10
   ! Provisions a BW guarantee for the MULTIMEDIA-CONFERENCING queue
 class MULTIMEDIA-STREAMING
  bandwidth percent 10
   ! Provisions a BW guarantee for the MULTIMEDIA-STREAMING queue
 class TRANSACTIONAL-DATA
  bandwidth percent 10
  dbl
   ! Provisions a BW guarantee for the TRANSACTIONAL-DATA queue
   ! DBL is applied on the TRANSACTIONAL-DATA queue
```

```
 class BULK-SCAVENGER
  bandwidth percent 5
  dbl
   ! Provisions a BW constraint for the BULK-SCAVENGER queue
   ! DBL is applied on the BULK-SCAVENGER queue
 class class-default
  bandwidth percent 25
 dbl
   ! Provisions a BW guarantee for the default/Best Effort queue
   ! Enables DBL on all Best Effort traffic flows
 !
 ! This section configures applies the 1P7Q1T queuing policy to an interface range
 interface range GigabitEthernet2/1 - 48
  service-policy output 1P7Q1T
   ! Applies the 1P7Q1T queuing policies to all interfaces within the range
 !
```

You can verify these egress queuing configurations with the following commands:

■   show policy-map

■   show policy-map interface GigabitEthernet

Catalyst 6500 QoS Design for TelePresence

The Cisco Catalyst 6500 series switches represent the flagship of the Cisco switching portfolio and are available in 3, 4, 6, 9, or 13 slot combinations; these models include the 6503, 6504, 6506, 6509 (regular or Network Equipment Building System [NEBS] compliant), and 6513. Additionally, most of these chassis options are also available in Enhanced models, designated by a -E suffix (such as 6503-E, 6504-E, and so on) for additional feature functionality and performance.

Overall, the Catalyst 6500 provides the highest performance switching plane, supporting a 720-Gbps switching fabric and the option to run either centralized or distributed forwarding to achieve optimal performance. Additionally, the Catalyst 6500 provides leading-edge Layer 2 to Layer 7 services, including rich high-availability, manageability, virtualization, security, and QoS feature sets, and integrated PoE, allowing for maximum flexibility in virtually any role within the campus.

The queuing and buffering capabilities of Catalyst 6500 supervisors and linecards vary according to type. Some linecards, such as the 6148A-GE and the 6548-GE, are engineered with oversubscription ratios (in these cases, 8:1 oversubscription ratios), and as such, although suitable at the access layer, such linecards would not be recommended to be deployed as uplinks or within the distribution and core layers of the TelePresence-enabled campus network.

Note   You can find a summary of the ingress and egress queuing structures, and ingress, egress, and total buffering capabilities for Catalyst 6500 supervisors and linecards at http://www.tinyurl.com/cljup7.

From a TelePresence QoS design perspective, the most relevant features of the C6500 include port-trust, linecard-dependent queuing options, and WRED support.

The commands and syntax to enable QoS and to define trust boundaries are identical to those detailed in the Catalyst 3560/3750 section of this chapter and so will not be repeated here.

For linecard-queuing design, most queuing structures on the Catalyst 6500, both ingress and egress, are CoS-based (with the sole exception, at the time of writing, of the WS-X6708-10GE linecards, which support DSCP-based queuing). This presents a challenge to network administrators deploying both TelePresence (CS4) and Multimedia Conferencing (AF41) because these applications both share the same CoS value of 4. As such, TelePresence and Multimedia Conferencing traffic are indistinguishable from one another with a CoS-based queuing scheme, with both applications always mapped to the same queue. A similar problem exists for administrators deploying Broadcast Video (CS5/CoS 5) with VoIP (EF/CoS 5). Therefore, on CoS-based linecards, administrators are encouraged to configure the hardware strict-priority queues on their C6500 platforms to adequately provision for their VoIP, Broadcast Video, TelePresence, and Multimedia Conferencing traffic. Although this might seem like a lot of bandwidth destined to the PQ, at GE/10GE campus speeds, there is typically more than adequate bandwidth to service these applications in the PQ and still stay within the 33% LLQ Rule.

As space does not permit every Catalyst 6500 queuing model to be detailed in this chapter (of which there are nine ingress and eight egress, at the time of writing), only two will be presented to illustrate how CoS-based and DSCP-based queuing can be implemented on the C6500 series switches; specifically the 1P3Q8T CoS-based queuing model (used by the 6148A and 6748 series linecards) and the 1P7Q4T DSCP-based queuing model used by the 6708-10GE series linecards.

Note   For a more comprehensive set of detailed Catalyst 6500 queuing model design recommendations, refer to the latest TelePresence Network Design Guide at http://www.tinyurl.com/ce7twk.

Egress Queuing Design: 1P3Q8T

Both the 6148A and 6748 linecards support a CoS-based egress queuing structure of 1P3Q8T, which uses WRED as a congestion avoidance mechanism. Under such a queuing structure, CoS 5 (VoIP and Broadcast Video) and CoS 4 (TelePresence and Multimedia Conferencing) are recommended to be mapped to the strict-priority queue. CoS 6 and 7 (Internetwork and Network Control), CoS 3 (Call-Signaling and Multimedia Streaming) and CoS 2 (Network Management and Transactional Data) can all be assigned to Q3; however, in Q3 the WRED thresholds can be set to give incremental preference to CoS 7 and 6, followed by CoS 3, and finally by CoS 2. CoS 1 (Scavenger/Bulk) can be constrained to a less than Best Effort queue (Q1). Q2 can then be dedicated for the default class (CoS 0). To minimize TCP global synchronization, WRED can be enabled on the nonreal-time queues for congestion avoidance. (Technically, the congestion avoidance behavior is RED, as only one CoS weight is assigned to each queue.) Figure 10-10 illustrates the recommended egress 1P3Q8T queuing configuration for Catalyst 6500 6148A and 6748 linecards.

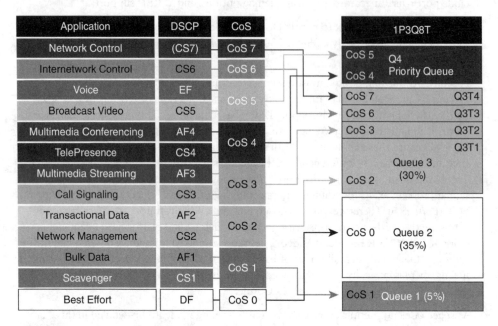

Figure 10-10 *Catalyst 6500 1P3Q4T CoS-based egress queuing diagram for TelePresence deployments*

Based on Figure 10-10, Example 10-7 shows the recommended configuration for egress queuing on the Catalyst 6500 6148A and 6748 linecards for TelePresence deployments.

Example 10-7 *Catalyst 6500 1P3Q4T CoS-Based Egress Queuing Configuration for TelePresence Deployments*

```
C6500# show run
! Output omitted for brevity.
!
! This section configures the queues and enables the PQ
interface range GigabitEthernet4/1 - 48
 wrr-queue queue-limit 5 35 30
   ! Allocates 5% for Q1, 35% for Q2 and 30% for Q3
priority-queue queue-limit 30
   ! Allocations 30% for the Strict-Priority Queue
 wrr-queue bandwidth 5 35 30
   ! Sets the WRR weights for 5:35:30 (Q1:Q2:Q3) bandwidth servicing
```

```
!
! This section enables WRED on the queues and configures WRED thresholds
wrr-queue random-detect 1
wrr-queue random-detect 2
wrr-queue random-detect 3
 ! WRED is enabled on Q1, Q2 and Q3, respectively
wrr-queue random-detect min-threshold 1 80 100 100 100 100 100 100 100
 ! Sets Min WRED Threshold for Q1T1 to 80% and all others to 100%
wrr-queue random-detect max-threshold 1 100 100 100 100 100 100 100 100
 ! Sets Max WRED Threshold for Q1T1 to 100% and all others to 100%
wrr-queue random-detect min-threshold 2 80 100 100 100 100 100 100 100
 ! Sets Min WRED Threshold for Q2T1 to 80% and all others to 100%
wrr-queue random-detect max-threshold 2 100 100 100 100 100 100 100 100
 ! Sets Max WRED Threshold for Q2T1 to 100% and all others to 100%
wrr-queue random-detect min-threshold 3 60 70 80 90 100 100 100 100
 ! Sets Min WRED Threshold for Q3T1 to 60%, Q3T2 to 70%, Q3T3 to 80%, Q3T4 to 90%
wrr-queue random-detect max-threshold 3 70 80 90 100 100 100 100 100
 ! Sets Max WRED Threshold for Q3T1 to 70%, Q3T2 to 80%, Q3T3 to 90%, and all
others to 100%
 !
 ! This section maps CoS values to their respective queues
wrr-queue cos-map 1 1 1
 ! Maps CoS 1 (Scavenger & Bulk Data) to Q1T1
wrr-queue cos-map 2 1 0
 ! Maps CoS 0 (Best Effort) to Q2T1
wrr-queue cos-map 3 1 2
 ! Maps CoS 2 (Transactional Data & Net-Mgmt) to Q3T1
wrr-queue cos-map 3 2 3
 ! Maps CoS 3 (Multimedia Streaming & Call-Signaling) to Q3T2
wrr-queue cos-map 3 3 6
 ! Maps CoS 6 (Internetwork Control) to Q3T3
wrr-queue cos-map 3 4 7
 ! Maps CoS 7 (Network Control) to Q3T4
priority-queue cos-map 1 4 5
 ! Maps CoS 4 (TelePresence and MM-Conferencing) and CoS 5 (VoIP + Bdcst Video)
to the PQ
mls qos trust dscp
 ! Sets interface to trust DSCP
!
```

You can verify these egress queuing configurations with the **show queueing interface Gi-gabitEthernet x/y** command.

Egress Queuing Design: 1P7Q4T

The 6708-10GE linecards support a CoS- or DSCP-based egress queuing structure of 1P7Q4T, which uses WRED as a congestion avoidance mechanism.

The increased granularity in queue mapping that is presented by the support of DSCP-to-Queue mapping enables TelePresence traffic to be separated from Multimedia Conferencing traffic (and for VoIP traffic to be separated from Broadcast Video traffic, and so forth). As such, TelePresence can be assigned to the strict priority queue, along with VoIP.

Queue 7 can be used to service control and management traffic, including (in respective order):

1. Network Control traffic (DSCP CS7)
2. Internetwork Control traffic (DSCP 6)
3. Call Signaling traffic (DSCP CS3)
4. Network Management traffic (CS2)

This respective order can be enforced by leveraging the four drop thresholds that can be assigned per the nonpriority queue. Specifically, CS2 can be mapped to Q7T1, CS3 can be mapped to Q7T2, CS6 can be mapped to Q7T3, and CS7 can be mapped to Q7T4 (the tail of the queue).

This allows for dedicated queues to be provisioned for Broadcast Video (CS5 to Q6), Multimedia Conferencing (AF4 to Q5), Multimedia Streaming (AF3 to Q4), and Transactional Data (AF2 to Q3).

This leaves Q2 to serve as a default/Best Effort queue and Q1 to serve as a "less than Best Effort" queue to service Bulk Data (AF1) and Scavenger (CS1) traffic, respectively. Again, the respective priority of Bulk Data over Scavenger traffic in Q1 can be enforced by leveraging the configurable WRED drop thresholds for the queue, such that Scavenger is mapped to Q1T1 and Bulk Data to Q1T2.

To minimize TCP global synchronization, WRED can be enabled on the nonreal-time queues for congestion avoidance. Additionally, as this platform supports DSCP-to-Queue/Threshold mappings, the Assured Forwarding Per-Hop Behavior (AF PHB) can be fully implemented on all AF traffic classes by enabling DSCP-based WRED (so that AFx3 drops before AFx2, which [respectively] is dropped before AFx1).

Figure 10-11 illustrates the recommended egress 1P7Q4T (DSCP-to-Queue) queuing configuration for Catalyst 6500 6708-10GE linecards.

Based on Figure 10-11, Example 10-8 shows the recommended configuration for egress queuing on the Catalyst 6500 6708-10GE linecards for TelePresence deployments.

Example 10-8 *Catalyst 6500 1P7Q4T DSCP-Based Egress Queuing Configuration for TelePresence Deployments*

```
C6500# show run
! Output omitted for brevity.
!
! This section configures the queues and enables the PQ
interface range TenGigabitEthernet4/1 - 8
 wrr-queue queue-limit 5 25 10 10 10 10 10
```

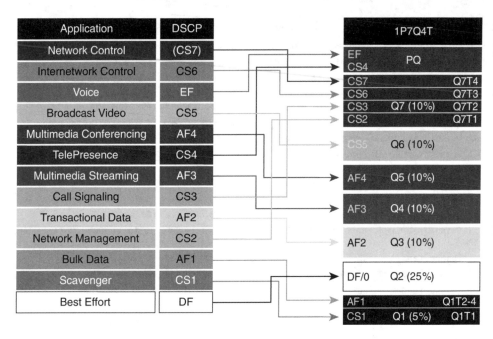

Figure 10-11   *Catalyst 6500 1P7Q4T DSCP-based egress queuing diagram for TelePresence deployments*

```
  ! Allocates 5% to Q1, 25% to Q2, 10% to Q3, 10% to Q4,
  ! Allocates 5% to Q5, 5% to Q6 and 10% to Q7
wrr-queue bandwidth 5 25 10 10 10 10 10
  ! Sets the WRR weights for 5:25:10:10:10:10:10 (Q1 through Q7)
priority-queue queue-limit 20
  ! Limits PQ to 20%
  !
  ! This section enables WRED and configures WRED thesholds
wrr-queue random-detect 1
wrr-queue random-detect 2
wrr-queue random-detect 3
wrr-queue random-detect 4
wrr-queue random-detect 5
wrr-queue random-detect 6
wrr-queue random-detect 7
  ! Enables WRED on Q1-Q7
wrr-queue random-detect min-threshold 1 60 70 80 90 100 100 100 100
  ! Sets Min WRED Thresholds for Q1T1 to 60%, Q1T2 to 70%, Q1T3 to 80%, Q1T4 to 90%
wrr-queue random-detect max-threshold 1 70 80 90 100 100 100 100 100
  ! Sets Max WRED Thresholds for Q1T1 to 70%, Q1T2 to 80%, Q1T3 to 90%, Q1T4 to
100%
wrr-queue random-detect min-threshold 2 80 100 100 100 100 100 100 100
  ! Sets Min WRED Threshold for Q2T1 to 80% and all others to 100%
```

```
wrr-queue random-detect max-threshold 2 100 100 100 100 100 100 100 100
  ! Sets all Max WRED Thresholds for Q2 to 100%
wrr-queue random-detect min-threshold 3 70 80 90 100 100 100 100 100
  ! Sets Min WRED Thresholds for Q3T1 to 70%, Q3T2 to 80%, Q3T3 to 90%, Q3T4 to
100%
wrr-queue random-detect max-threshold 3 80 90 100 100 100 100 100 100
  ! Sets Max WRED Thresholds for Q3T1 to 80%, Q3T2 to 90%, Q3T3 & Q3T4 to 100%
wrr-queue random-detect min-threshold 4 70 80 90 100 100 100 100 100
  ! Sets Min WRED Thresholds for Q4T1 to 70%, Q4T2 to 80%, Q4T3 to 90%, Q4T4 to
100%
wrr-queue random-detect max-threshold 4 80 90 100 100 100 100 100 100
  ! Sets Max WRED Thresholds for Q4T1 to 80%, Q4T2 to 90%, Q4T3 & Q4T4 to 100%
wrr-queue random-detect min-threshold 5 70 80 90 100 100 100 100 100
  ! Sets Min WRED Thresholds for Q5T1 to 70%, Q5T2 to 80%, Q5T3 to 90%, Q5T4 to
100%
wrr-queue random-detect max-threshold 5 80 90 100 100 100 100 100 100
  ! Sets Max WRED Thresholds for Q5T1 to 80%, Q5T2 to 90%, Q5T3 & Q5T4 to 100%
wrr-queue random-detect min-threshold 6 80 100 100 100 100 100 100 100
  ! Sets Min WRED Threshold for Q6T1 to 80% and all others to 100%
wrr-queue random-detect max-threshold 6 100 100 100 100 100 100 100 100
  ! Sets all Max WRED Thresholds for Q6 to 100%
wrr-queue random-detect min-threshold 7 60 70 80 90 100 100 100 100
  ! Sets Min WRED Thresholds for Q7T1 to 60%, Q7T2 to 70%, Q7T3 to 80%, Q7T4 to 90%
wrr-queue random-detect max-threshold 7 70 80 90 100 100 100 100 100
  ! Sets Max WRED Thresholds for Q7T1 to 70%, Q7T2 to 80%, Q7T3 to 90%, Q7T4 to
100%
  !
  ! This section sets trust, DSCP-to-Queue mapping mode and maps DSCP-to-
Queue/Thresholds
mls qos trust dscp
  ! Sets interface to trust DSCP
mls qos queue-mode mode-dscp
  ! Enables DSCP-to-Queue mapping mode
wrr-queue dscp-map 1 1 8
  ! Maps Scavenger (CS1)to Q1T1
wrr-queue dscp-map 1 2 14
  ! Maps Bulk Data (AF13) to Q1T2 - AF13 PHB
wrr-queue dscp-map 1 3 12
  ! Maps Bulk Data (AF12) to Q1T3 - AF12 PHB
wrr-queue dscp-map 1 4 10
  ! Maps Bulk Data (AF11) to Q1T4 - AF11 PHB
wrr-queue dscp-map 2 1 0
  ! Maps Best Effort to Q2T1
wrr-queue dscp-map 3 1 22
  ! Maps Transactional Data (AF23) to Q3T1 - AF23 PHB
wrr-queue dscp-map 3 2 20
```

```
   ! Maps Transactional Data (AF22) to Q3T2 - AF22 PHB
wrr-queue dscp-map 3 3 18
   ! Maps Transactional Data (AF21) to Q3T3 - AF21 PHB
wrr-queue dscp-map 4 1 30
   ! Maps Multimedia Streaming (AF33) to Q4T1 - AF33 PHB
wrr-queue dscp-map 4 2 28
   ! Maps Multimedia Streaming (AF32) to Q4T2 - AF32 PHB
wrr-queue dscp-map 4 3 26
   ! Maps Multimedia Streaming (AF31) to Q4T3 - AF31 PHB
wrr-queue dscp-map 5 1 38
   ! Maps Multimedia Conferencing (AF43) to Q5T1 - AF43 PHB
wrr-queue dscp-map 5 2 36
   ! Maps Multimedia Conferencing (AF42) to Q5T2 - AF42 PHB
wrr-queue dscp-map 5 3 34
   ! Maps Multimedia Conferencing (AF41) to Q5T3 - AF41 PHB
wrr-queue dscp-map 6 1 40
   ! Maps Broadcast Video (CS5) to Q6T1
wrr-queue dscp-map 7 1 16
   ! Maps Net-Mgmt (CS2) to Q7T1
wrr-queue dscp-map 7 2 24
   ! Maps Call-Signaling (CS3) to Q7T2
wrr-queue dscp-map 7 3 48
   ! Maps IP Routing (CS6) to Q7T3
wrr-queue dscp-map 7 4 56
   ! Maps Spanning-Tree (CS7) to Q7T4
priority-queue dscp-map 1 32 46
   ! Maps TelePresence (CS4) and Voice (EF) to the PQ
!
```

You can verify these egress queuing configurations with the **show queueing interface TenGigabitEthernet x/y** command.

Branch QoS Designs for TelePresence

The primary business advantages of TelePresence systems include the following:

- Reduced travel time and expense

- Improved collaboration and productivity

- Improved quality of work/life (due to reduced travel)

- The green advantage of a reduced carbon footprint

These business advantages, however, are not fully realized if TelePresence systems are connected solely through an Intra-Campus Deployment Model (as illustrated in Figure 4-11 in Chapter 4, "Connecting TelePresence Systems"); rather, gaining these advantages requires

TelePresence systems to be deployed over WANs, whether these are private WANs or virtual private networks (VPNs).

WANs or VPNs can interconnect large campuses to each other or can connect one or more large campuses with smaller branch offices (as illustrated in Figure 4-12 in Chapter 4). To simplify these permutations, all TelePresence connections over a wide area can be referred to as "branch" places-in-the-network (PIN). Branch PINs serve as boundary points between LANs and WANs and, as such, these are often the most bottlenecked PINs and therefore have the most critical QoS requirements within the network infrastructure, as illustrated in Figure 10-12.

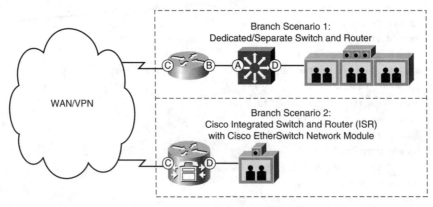

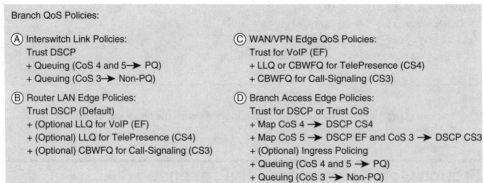

Branch QoS Policies:

Ⓐ Interswitch Link Policies:
   Trust DSCP
   + Queuing (CoS 4 and 5 ➤ PQ)
   + Queuing (CoS 3 ➤ Non-PQ)

Ⓑ Router LAN Edge Policies:
   Trust DSCP (Default)
   + (Optional LLQ for VoIP (EF)
   + (Optional) LLQ for TelePresence (CS4)
   + (Optional) CBWFQ for Call-Signaling (CS3)

Ⓒ WAN/VPN Edge QoS Policies:
   Trust for VoIP (EF)
   + LLQ or CBWFQ for TelePresence (CS4)
   + CBWFQ for Call-Signaling (CS3)

Ⓓ Branch Access Edge Policies:
   Trust for DSCP or Trust CoS
   + Map CoS 4 ➤ DSCP CS4
   + Map CoS 5 ➤ DSCP EF and CoS 3 ➤ DSCP CS3
   + (Optional) Ingress Policing
   + Queuing (CoS 4 and 5 ➤ PQ)
   + Queuing (CoS 3 ➤ Non-PQ)

Figure 10-12 *Branch QoS design recommendations for TelePresence*

A comparison of Figure 10-12 with Figure 10-5 shows that the LAN policies are the same in both the campus and branch; although, the actual nodes at which some of these policies are deployed might vary according to whether a separate switch and router are used at the branch or an Integrated Switch Router (ISR) is used at the branch.

However, the QoS policies at the branch WAN edge (and correspondingly at the campus WAN aggregation edge) are a new element. To help select the best policies to be used at these critical edges, it is beneficial to review some additional considerations, including the politically charged decision of whether to use LLQ or CBWFQ over the WAN/VPN.

LLQ Versus CBWFQ over the WAN/VPN?

Probably the most controversial decision relating to TelePresence deployments is whether to provision TelePresence traffic over the WAN/VPN in a strict-priority LLQ or in a dedicated bandwidth-guaranteed CBWFQ.

In campus networks, placing TelePresence in the strict-priority hardware queues yields optimal results, without incurring any additional, ongoing costs, making the decision to service TelePresence with strict-priority queues within the campus relatively straightforward.

However, the corresponding decision becomes more complicated over the WAN/VPN due to three main considerations:

- The cost of subscribing to real-time SP services

- The 33% LLQ Rule

- The potential effect of TelePresence on VoIP

Considering the Cost of Subscribing to Real-time SP Services

The first and foremost consideration in the LLQ versus CBWFQ decision is the ongoing cost of subscribing to real-time services from an SP. Service providers generally charge enterprise customers premium rates for the amount of traffic they want serviced within a real-time class. At times, these additional premiums might make it cost prohibitive to provision TelePresence traffic within a real-time SP class. At the very least, such expensive premiums could diminish the overall business cost savings that TelePresence can provide an enterprise (versus employee travel expenses).

Considering the 33% LLQ Rule

The second consideration is the potential impact of the 33% LLQ Rule, as discussed earlier in this chapter. At times, administrators cannot provision adequate amounts of bandwidth for TelePresence and remain within this conservative design recommendation. This is generally the case when dealing with (45-Mbps) T3/DS3 links. According to the 33% LLQ Rule, no more than 15 Mbps of traffic of such a link should be assigned for strict-priority servicing. However, if a network administrator already has VoIP provisioned (quite properly) in an LLQ on such a link and is looking to also provision TelePresence with strict-priority servicing, he or she has a decision to make. For example, if they want to deploy a CTS-3000 at 1080p-Best (requiring 15 Mbps just for TelePresence), they either need to upgrade the link's bandwidth capacity (which is often cost-prohibitive, as the next tier of bandwidth might be OC3), or they violate this design rule to accommodate all their real-time traffic.

Remember that the 33% LLQ Rule is a conservative design recommendation, with the intent of reducing the variance in application response times of nonreal-time applications during periods that the real-time classes are utilized at maximum capacity. And also that the 33% LLQ Rule rule is not to be viewed as a mandate but is simply a best practice design recommendation. There might be cases where specific business objectives cannot be met while holding to this recommendation. In such cases, enterprises must provision according to their detailed requirements and constraints. However, you need to recognize the tradeoffs involved with overprovisioning real-time traffic classes in conjunction with the negative performance impact this has on nonreal-time-application response times.

Quite naturally then, to make such provisioning decisions, a network administrator might wonder about the tradeoffs involved in TelePresence application performance when TelePresence is placed in an LLQ versus a CBWFQ. In such a comparison, the most sensitive service level attribute is jitter because both policies can be configured to completely prevent packet loss. As you might predict, provisioning TelePresence in an LLQ results in lower peak-to-peak jitter values, as compared to provisioning TelePresence in a CBWFQ.

Note   Newer versions of CTS software have superior traffic smoothing capabilities (as compared to the earliest versions) and deeper de-jitter buffering, both of which amount to less overall sensitivity of TelePresence to jitter. Therefore, the advantage of LLQ over CBWFQ queuing policies is less with the latest versions of CTS software.

Therefore, although a moderate performance advantage to TelePresence can be observed when it is provisioned in an LLQ versus a CBWFQ, the advantage is not so great as to preclude recommending provisioning TelePresence in a CBWFQ when it is not viable to be provisioned with an LLQ. In other words, from a purely technical standpoint, the best performance levels for TelePresence can be achieved when it is provisioned in an LLQ. However, when other factors (such as additional ongoing costs or over-provisioning constraints for real-time bandwidth, and so on) need to be taken into account and render provisioning TelePresence in an LLQ unviable, acceptable of service can be achieved by provisioning TelePresence in a dedicated CBWFQ.

Considering the Potential Effect of TelePresence on VoIP

The third main consideration of whether to use LLQ or CBWFQ is the potential effect of TelePresence traffic on VoIP traffic if both are to be serviced in a strict-priority queue. As discussed in Chapter 6, the Cisco IOS LLQ feature supports the deployment of dual- or multiple-LLQs (even though "under-the-hood," there is only a single strict-priority queue, which is being time-division multiplexed). A dual-LLQ design can protect VoIP from bursty video applications (such as TelePresence) while at the same time provisioning both applications with strict-priority servicing. Therefore, if VoIP has already been provisioned in an LLQ and the decision has been made to provision TelePresence with strict priority, a dual-LLQ design would be recommended to protect VoIP and TelePresence from interfering with each other.

Each design option, LLQ and CBWFQ, will be detailed in the following sections.

TelePresence Branch WAN Edge LLQ Policy

If TelePresence is to be assigned to an LLQ, then in addition to adequately provisioning priority bandwidth to the LLQ, one additional design parameter needs to be calculated: the burst parameter of the implicit policer of the LLQ.

The implicit policer for the LLQ is a token-bucket algorithm policer (like any other Cisco IOS or Catalyst QoS policer, as discussed in Chapter 6) and needs a burst parameter to be defined to police to a subline rate.

TelePresence codecs, whether operating at 720p or 1080p resolution, display 30 frames per second; alternatively phrased, TelePresence codecs send information representing one frame of video every 33 ms. However, to configure the policing burst so that it does not drop TelePresence traffic, the maximum transmission (in bytes) within a 33-ms interval must be analyzed. In other words, the burst needs to accommodate the worst-case scenario per frame of TelePresence video. As previously mentioned, in H.264 video, which TelePresence systems use, this worst-case scenario would be the full screen of (spatially compressed) video, which is periodically sent, which is known as the IDR frame. The IDR frame is the key frame that subsequent video frames reference, sending only differential information between subsequent frames and the IDR frame, rather than the full picture again.

The maximum IDR frame size is approximately 64 KB. Therefore, the LLQ burst parameter should be configured to permit up to 64 KB of burst per frame per screen. In the case of triple-display CTS-3000 systems (such as the CTS-3000/3200), 192 KB of burst (3 × 64 KB) should be provisioned to accommodate the rare event of a "triple-IDR storm," where all three codecs send IDR frames simultaneously.

Furthermore, if the auxiliary video and auto-collaborate video channel are also used, an additional 64 KB of burst must be included.

Note If Cisco design recommendations for TelePresence room lighting and other environmental variables (as discussed in detail in Chapter 8, "TelePresence Room Design") are not followed, IDR frame sizes might vary in size beyond 64 KB, which might, in turn, affect the network QoS policies.

For example, consider first a CTS-500/1000 system: applying the IDR as the worst-case burst scenario for TelePresence primary video (at 64 KB) coupled with an allowance of auxiliary video bursting of the same amount (64 KB). Example 10-9 shows the configuration to provision a branch WAN edge queuing policy that provisions a TelePresence CTS-1000 system running at 1080p-Best (with the optional support of an auxiliary video stream) to an LLQ with an optimal burst parameter (of 128 KB).

Example 10-9 *Dual-LLQ Branch WAN Edge Policy for VoIP and TelePresence (CTS-1000 at 1080p-Best with Auxiliary Video)*

```
Router(config)# policy-map WAN-EDGE
Router(config-pmap)# class VOIP
Router(config-pmap-c)# priority percent 10
! LLQ for VoIP
Router(config-pmap-c)# class TELEPRESENCE
Router(config-pmap-c)# priority 5500 128000
 ! LLQ for CTS-1000 (1080p-Best + aux video)
 ! Burst: 64 KB for primary video + 64 KB for auxiliary video
```

Likewise, Example 10-10 shows the configuration to provision a branch WAN Edge queuing policy that provisions a TelePresence CTS-3000 system running at 1080p-Best (with the optional support of an auxiliary video stream) to an LLQ with an optimal burst parameter (of 256 KB).

Example 10-10 *Dual-LLQ Branch WAN Edge Policy for VoIP and TelePresence (CTS-3000 at 1080p-Best with Auxiliary Video)*

```
Router(config)# policy-map WAN-EDGE
Router(config-pmap)# class VOIP
Router(config-pmap-c)# priority percent 10
! LLQ for VoIP
Router(config-pmap-c)# class TELEPRESENCE
Router(config-pmap-c)# priority 15000 256000
! LLQ for CTS-3000 (1080p-Best + aux video)
! Burst: 3x 64 KB for primary video + 64 KB for auxiliary video
```

On some interfaces, such as OC3-POS interface, an explicit policer needs to be configured in conjunction with the LLQ priority statement. In such cases, the same calculations for policing burst parameters apply.

Consider a full case-study example with a CTS-3000 system (running at 1080p-Best with auxiliary video) deployed, along with VoIP, in a dual-LLQ policy over an OC3-POS WAN edge. An RFC 4594-based 12-class model is used, with the bandwidth allocations illustrated in Figure 10-13.

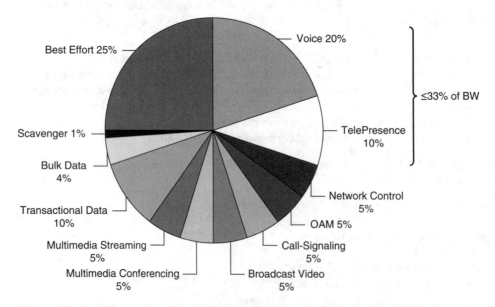

Figure 10-13 *Case study example bandwidth allocations of a dual-LLQ branch WAN edge policy for VoIP and TelePresence over an OC3-POS branch interface*

Example 10-11 shows the configuration for this dual-LLQ case-study example.

Example 10-11 *Case Study Example Configuration of a Dual-LLQ Branch WAN Edge Policy for VoIP and TelePresence over an OC3-POS Branch Interface*

```
Router# show run
! Output omitted for brevity.
!
! This section defines the class-maps
class-map match-all VOICE
 match dscp ef
  ! Voice marking
class-map match-all TELEPRESENCE
 match dscp cs4
  ! TelePresence marking
class-map match-all NETWORK-CONTROL
 match dscp cs6
  ! IP Routing marking
class-map match-all OAM
 match dscp cs2
  ! Operations / Administration / Management marking
class-map match-all CALL-SIGNALING
 match dscp cs3
  ! Call-Signaling (Cisco-marking)
class-map match-all BROADCAST-VIDEO
 match dscp cs5
  ! Broadcast Video (Cisco-marking)
class-map match-all MULTIMEDIA-CONFERENCING
 match dscp af41 af42 af43
  ! Multimedia Conferencing markings
class-map match-all MULTIMEDIA-STREAMING
 match dscp af31 af32 af33
  ! Multimedia Streaming markings
class-map match-all TRANSACTIONAL-DATA
 match dscp af21 af22 af23
  ! Transactional Data markings
class-map match-all BULK-DATA
 match dscp af11 af12 af13
  ! Bulk Data markings
class-map match-all SCAVENGER
 match dscp cs1
  ! Scavenger marking
!
! This section defines the policy-map
policy-map WAN-EDGE-OC3-POS
 class VOICE
  police cir 30000000 bc 37500 conform-action transmit exceed-action drop
  priority
```

```
 ! LLQ command for OC3-POS
 ! Voice is policed to 30 Mbps (20%)
 ! Bc for VoIP is optimally set to CIR/100 (after conversion to Bytes)
 ! Single-Rate Policing action
class TELEPRESENCE
police cir 15000000 bc 256000 conform-action transmit exceed-action drop
  priority
 ! LLQ command for OC3-POS
 ! TelePresence is policed to 15 Mbps (10%) for CTS-3000 (1080p-Best + aux video)
 ! Burst: 3x 64 KB for primary video + 64 KB for auxiliary video
 ! Single-Rate Policing action
class NETWORK-CONTROL
 bandwidth percent 5
 ! CBWFQ for Routing
class OAM
 bandwidth percent 5
 ! CBWFQ for Network Management
class CALL-SIGNALING
 bandwidth percent 5
 ! CBWFQ for Call-Signaling
class BROADCAST-VIDEO
 bandwidth percent 5
 ! CBWFQ for Broadcast Video
class MULTIMEDIA-CONFERENCING
 bandwidth percent 5
 random-detect dscp-based
 ! CBWFQ for Multimedia Conferencing
 ! DSCP-WRED for Multimedia Conferencing
class MULTIMEDIA-STREAMING
 bandwidth percent 5
 random-detect dscp-based
  ! CBWFQ for Multimedia Streaming
  ! DSCP-WRED for Multimedia Streaming
class TRANSACTIONAL-DATA
 bandwidth percent 10
 random-detect dscp-based
  ! CBWFQ for Transactional Data
  ! DSCP-WRED for Transactional Data
class BULK-DATA
 bandwidth percent 4
 random-detect dscp-based
  ! CBWFQ for Bulk Data
  ! DSCP-WRED for Bulk Data
class SCAVENGER
 bandwidth percent 1
```

```
    ! Minimum CBWFQ for Scavenger
class class-default
  bandwidth percent 25
  random-detect
    ! CBWFQ for Best Effort
    ! WRED for Best Effort
!
! This section applies the service policy to the OC3 POS interface
interface POS3/0/1
 description BRANCH-TO-CAMPUS-OC3-POS
 ip address 192.168.5.1 255.255.255.252
 clock source internal
 service-policy output WAN-EDGE-OC3-POS
   ! Attaches policy to OC3-POS
!
```

You can verify these WAN edge queuing configurations with the **show policy-map interface** command.

TelePresence Branch WAN Edge CBWFQ Policy

If, on the other hand, TelePresence is to be assigned to a CBWFQ, in addition to adequately provisioning guaranteed bandwidth to the CBWFQ, one additional design parameter needs to be considered: the length of the CBWFQ.

By default, CBWFQs are 64-packets deep. Extensive testing has shown that this default queue-depth has at times resulted in tail-drops when provisioned to protect TelePresence flows. Therefore, on most interfaces it is recommended to increase the default queue-depth for the TelePresence queue to 128 packets, using the **queue-limit 128** command in conjunction with the CBWFQ **bandwidth** command.

Example 10-11 shows a sample policy provisioning a TelePresence CTS-3000 system running at 1080p-Best (with the optional support of an auxiliary video stream) to a CBWFQ, with an extended queue-depth to 128 packets.

Example 10-11 *CBWFQ Branch WAN Edge Policy for TelePresence (CTS-3000 at 1080p-Best with Auxiliary Video)*

```
Router(config)# policy-map WAN-EDGE
Router(config-pmap)# class VOIP
Router(config-pmap-c)# priority percent 10
! LLQ for VoIP
Router(config-pmap-c)# class TELEPRESENCE
Router(config-pmap-c)# bandwidth 15000
Router(config-pmap-c)# queue-limit 128
! CBWFQ for CTS-3000 (1080p-Best + aux video)
! Extended queue-limit for TelePresence CBWFQ
```

Consider another full case study example; however, this time with TelePresence serviced in a CBWFQ. In this case, a 12-class RFC 4594-based WAN edge policy is used, with TelePresence serviced in a CBWFQ over the branch T3 WAN edge (because provisioning both VoIP and TelePresence in a dual-LLQ design would, in this case, require 45 percent of priority queuing, which would cause excessive variations in application response times to the other 10 application classes). Figure 10-14 shows the WAN edge bandwidth allocations for this case study.

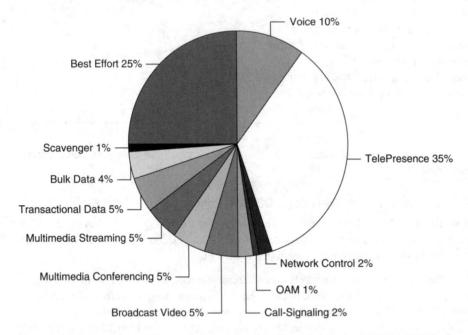

Figure 10-14 *Case study example bandwidth allocations of a CBWFQ WAN edge policy for TelePresence over a T3 branch WAN interface*

Example 10-12 shows the configuration for this CBWFQ case study example.

Example 10-12 *Configuration of a CBWFQ Branch WAN Edge Policy for TelePresence over a T3 Branch WAN Interface*

```
Router# show run
! Output omitted for brevity.
!
! [The class maps are identical to those in Example 10-11]
! This section defines the policy-map
policy-map WAN-EDGE-T3
 class VOICE
  priority percent 10
   ! LLQ for VoIP
```

```
class TELEPRESENCE
 bandwidth percent 35
 queue-limit 128
   ! CBWFQ for TelePresence (CTS-3000) as a ratio of T3 (45 Mbps)
   ! Queue-Limit is expanded for TelePresence to 128 packets (from 64 packet
default)
class NETWORK-CONTROL
 bandwidth percent 2
   ! CBWFQ for Routing
class OAM
 bandwidth percent 1
   ! CBWFQ for Ops/Admin/Mgmt
class CALL-SIGNALING
 bandwidth percent 2
   ! CBWFQ for Call-Signaling
class BROADCAST-VIDEO
 bandwidth percent 5
   ! CBWFQ for Broadcast Video
class MULTIMEDIA-CONFERENCING
 bandwidth percent 5
 random-detect dscp-based
   ! CBWFQ for Multimedia Conferencing
   ! DSCP-WRED for Multimedia Conferencing
class MULTIMEDIA-STREAMING
 bandwidth percent 5
 random-detect dscp-based
   ! CBWFQ for Multimedia Streaming
   ! DSCP-WRED for Multimedia Streaming
class TRANSACTIONAL-DATA
 bandwidth percent 5
 random-detect dscp-based
   ! CBWFQ for Transactional Data
   ! DSCP-WRED for Transactional Data
class BULK-DATA
 bandwidth percent 4
 random-detect dscp-based
   ! CBWFQ for Bulk Data
   ! DSCP-WRED for Bulk Data
class SCAVENGER
 bandwidth percent 1
   ! Minimum CBWFQ for Scavenger
class class-default
 bandwidth percent 25
 random-detect
   ! CBWFQ for Best Effort
```

```
    ! WRED for Best Effort
!
! This section applies the service policy to the T3 interface
interface Serial6/0
 description BRANCH-TO-CAMPUS-T3
 ip address 192.168.2.9 255.255.255.252
 tx-ring-limit 10
  ! Tuned T3 Tx-Ring for TelePresence
 dsu bandwidth 44210
 framing c-bit
 cablelength 10
 serial restart-delay 0
 max-reserved-bandwidth 100
  ! >75% Explicitly defined BW Override
 service-policy output WAN-EDGE-T3
  ! Attaches policy to T3 interfact
!
```

These WAN edge queuing configurations can be verified with the **show policy-map interface** command.

Branch MPLS VPN QoS Considerations and Design

The advent of MPLS VPN service offerings that inherently offer full-mesh connectivity has shifted the QoS administration paradigm. Under traditional hub-and-spoke Layer 2 WAN designs, the enterprise network administrator controlled all the QoS policies by configuring these on the WAN edges of WAN aggregator and branch routers, as previously discussed. However, under a full-mesh topology, it is the SP's QoS policies on the provider edge (PE) routers that ultimately determine how traffic enters a branch, and these SP policies might be different from the enterprise's policies on the (unmanaged) customer edge (CE) routers.

Therefore, to ensure end-to-end service levels, enterprise administrators must choose SPs that offer compatible policies to meet their business objectives. Furthermore, enterprises must fully understand the SP's QoS policies and map their policies to match in a complementary manner.

A primary consideration is the SP's SLA. Earlier in this chapter, the bandwidth and service level requirements of TelePresence (including latency, jitter, and loss requirements) were shown to be high and tight. Therefore, to achieve these tight end-to-end SLAs, it is mandatory that the SP guarantee a subset of these SLAs from PE-edge-to-PE-edge.

However, additional enterprise-to-service provider considerations for MPLS VPN deployments also apply, including the following:

■   The number of enterprise traffic classes versus the number of SP traffic classes; and if collapsing is required, how to perform this efficiently.

- Marking or re-marking requirements on CE egress to gain admission to the desired SP traffic class; and (optional) re-marking requirements on CE ingress to restore enterprise traffic markings for provisioning, accounting, or management purposes.

- Nontraditional WAN access media, such as subline-rate Ethernet access, and the QoS implications these pose.

Each of these considerations is discussed next.

SP Class-of-Service Models

Regarding SP class-of-service models, at the time of writing, in North America, most SPs offer 4-class QoS models, and a few also offer 6-class models. In EMEA or Asia Pacific, some providers offer even more classes. SPs strive to offer service differentiation by varying the details of their models, so there is no one-size-fits-all recommendation that covers all cases. However, the principles applied in the following 4- and 6-class enterprise-to-SP mapping examples can be extended to other traffic class models as well.

As there are generally fewer SP traffic classes than enterprise classes, this requires that more than one enterprise traffic class be assigned to the same SP class. When such collapsing has to be done, it is recommended to avoid mixing TCP-based applications with UDP-based applications within a single SP class. This is due to the behavior of these respective protocols during periods of congestion. Specifically, due to TCP transmission guarantees and its windowing behavior, TCP transmitters throttle back flows when drops are detected. In contrast, most UDP transmitters are completely oblivious to drops and, therefore, never lower transmission rates because of dropping. When TCP flows are combined with UDP flows within a single SP class and the class experiences congestion, TCP flows continually lower their transmission rates, potentially giving up their bandwidth to UDP flows that are oblivious to drops. This effect is called *TCP starvation/UDP dominance*. Even if WRED is enabled on the SP class, the same behavior would be observed because WRED (for the most part) manages congestion only on TCP-based flows. Granted, it is not always possible to separate TCP-based flows from UDP-based flows, but it is beneficial to be aware of this behavior when making such application-mixing decisions within a single SP class.

SP Traffic Marking/Remarking Requirements

Another related consideration is traffic marking/re-marking requirements. Most providers use DSCP values as the admission criteria per SP class. These DSCP values likely vary from one provider to another; therefore, it is important for the enterprise subscriber be fully informed of the DSCP admission criteria for each SP class. At times applications might need to be re-marked to gain admission to the desired SP class. When such is the case, re-marking should be done as the final operations on the (unmanaged) CE *egress* edge. Otherwise, if re-marking is done at an earlier node, say the campus access edge, changes to the SP QoS policies or migration to another SP would be much more difficult to manage, as would using multiple SPs for redundancy (each with its own marking scheme).

Also, there might be times when the enterprise has a business requirement to maintain DSCP markings in the branch, perhaps for traffic accounting purposes or for other reasons. In such cases, the enterprise subscriber might choose to make the MPLS VPN appear DSCP-transparent by restoring enterprise DSCP markings on the CE *ingress* edge.

Additionally, each SP class is likely policed on the PE ingress edge. Excess traffic can either be re-marked or dropped. Again, it is important for the enterprise subscriber to know exactly how excess traffic is treated on a per-class basis. Understanding SP policing policies is an especially important consideration for the TelePresence class. As we have already discussed, some TelePresence configurations require up to 256 KB of committed burst from a policer. Therefore, in such a deployment scenario, it is essential to confirm with the SP that whatever class TelePresence traffic is assigned to is policed with at least 256 KB of burst.

Nontraditional WAN Access Media QoS Considerations

Finally, the QoS implications of nontraditional WAN access media, such as Ethernet, need to be considered. Queuing policies engage only when the physical interface is congested (which is indicated to Cisco IOS Software by a full interface Tx-Ring). This means that queuing policies never engage on media that has a contracted subline rate of access, whether this media is Frame Relay, ATM, or Ethernet. In such a scenario, queuing can be achieved only at a subline rate by introducing a two-part policy, sometimes referred to as Hierarchical QoS (HQoS) policy or nested QoS policy, wherein

- Traffic is shaped to the subline rate.

- Traffic is queued according to the LLQ/CBWFQ policies within the subline rate.

With such an HQoS policy, it is not the Tx-Ring that signals Cisco IOS Software to engage LLQ/CBWFQ policies, but rather it is the Class-Based Shaper that triggers software queuing when the shaped rate has been reached (as discussed in the HQoS section of Chapter 6 and later in this chapter).

Enterprise and SP MPLS VPN QoS TelePresence Design Recommendations

Figure 10-15 shows how all these QoS considerations and policies fit together for a TelePresence-enabled branch subscribing to an MPLS VPN SP.

As shown in Figure 10-15, the enterprise subscriber provisions LLQ/CBWFQ policies for VoIP and TelePresence (in conjunction with HQoS subline rate shapers, if required) and performs any application-class remarking on the CE egress edges. Optionally, if required, the enterprise can restore their markings on the CE ingress edges for any traffic that required re-marking over the MPLS VPN.

In turn, the SP polices traffic on a per-class basis on their PE ingress edges and provisions LLQ/CBWFQ policies according to their class-models on the PE egress edges. They can also perform QoS and MPLS Traffic Engineering within their core; however, such policies are beyond the scope of the enterprise-centric designs.

Note   Due of the explicit ingress policing on PE edges of MPLS VPNs, it cannot be overemphasized that the enterprise subscriber needs a comprehensive Call Admission Control system in place to limit the amount of TelePresence traffic over the MPLS VPN;

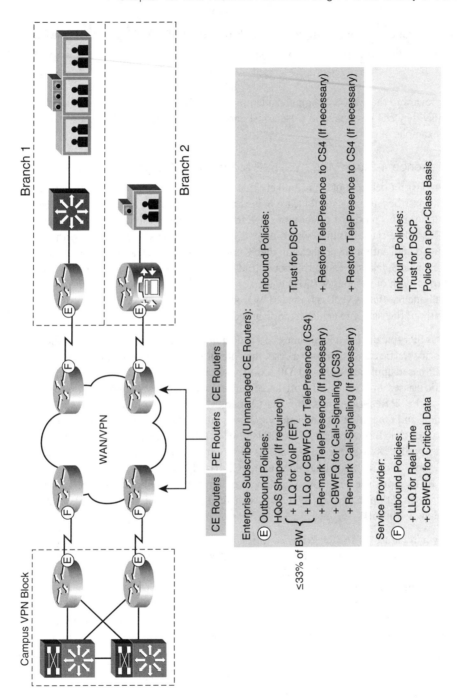

Figure 10-15 *Enterprise and SP MPLS VPN QoS design recommendations for TelePresence*

otherwise the call quality of *all* TelePresence calls over the MPLS VPN might degrade to the point of unusability.

Having reviewed these QoS design considerations for MPLS VPNs, the following sections show how they can be applied to a 4-class SP model, a 6-class SP model, and a subline rate access example.

TelePresence 4-Class MPLS VPN SP Model QoS Design

In the 4-class model example, it is unlikely that TelePresence can be assigned to a dedicated SP class because this would leave only three classes for all other applications. Therefore, within such a model, it is recommended to combine TelePresence with VoIP within the SP-Real-time class. It is highly recommended not to combine TelePresence with any unbounded application (an application that is not governed by call admission control) within a single SP class because this could lead to class congestion resulting in TelePresence drops (with or without WRED enabled on the SP class), which would ruin TelePresence call quality. But as VoIP is bounded by CAC, as is TelePresence, these can share a class without the risk of oversubscription and drops.

A 4-class SP typically has a Real-time class, a default Best Effort class, and two additional nonpriority traffic classes. In such a case, the enterprise administrator can elect to separate TCP-based applications from UDP-based applications by using these two nonpriority SP traffic classes. Specifically, if VoIP and TelePresence are the only applications to be assigned to the SP Real-time class, Broadcast Video, Multimedia Conferencing, Multimedia Streaming, and Operations/Administration/Management (OAM) traffic (which is largely UDP-based) can all be assigned to the UDP SP-class (SP-Critical 2). This leaves the other nonpriority SP class (SP-Critical 1) available for control plane applications, such as Network Control and Call-Signaling, along with TCP-based Transactional Data applications. Figure 10-16 shows the per-class re-marking requirements from the CE edge to gain access to the classes within the 4-class SP model, with TelePresence assigned to the SP-Real-time class, along with VoIP.

As shown in Figure 10-16, TelePresence traffic must be re-marked on the CE egress edge to CS5 to gain access to the SP's Real-time class. Also, Broadcast Video must be re-marked to CS2 to assign it to the UDP SP class (SP-Critical 2). Similarly, Multimedia Conferencing and Multimedia Streaming must be re-marked to AF2 to assign these also to the UDP SP class. Correspondingly, Transactional Data traffic must be re-marked to AF3 to gain access into the TCP SP class (SP-Critical 1). No other traffic requires re-marking to gain admission to the desired SP classes; this includes Bulk and Scavenger because these default to the SP-Best Effort class without any explicit re-marking.

Based on Figure 10-16, Example 10-13 presents the recommended configuration for 4-class enterprise-to-SP mapping. Explicit remarking requirements (to gain admission to the correct SP class) are highlighted within the example.

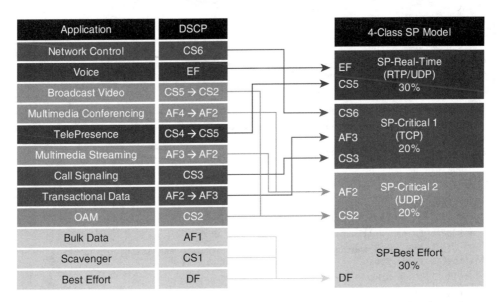

Figure 10-16 *Enterprise-to-SP Mapping: 4-class SP Model example with TelePresence assigned to the Real-time class along with voice*

Example 10-13 *Enterprise-to-SP Mapping: 4-Class SP Model Example with TelePresence Assigned to the Real-time Class Along with Voice*

```
Router# show run
! Output omitted for brevity.
!
! [The class maps are identical to those in Example 10-11]
! This section defines the policy-map
policy-map CE-EDGE-4CLASS-OC3-POS
 class VOICE
   police cir 30000000 bc 37500 conform-action transmit exceed-action drop
   priority
   ! LLQ command for OC3-POS
   ! Voice is policed to 30 Mbps (20%)
   ! Bc for VoIP is set to CIR/100 (after conversion to Bytes)
   ! Single-Rate Policing action
 class TELEPRESENCE
   police cir 15000000 bc 256000 conform-action transmit exceed-action drop
   priority
   set dscp cs5
   ! LLQ command for OC3-POS
   ! TelePresence is policed to 15 Mbps (10%) for CTS-3000 (1080p-Best + aux video)
   ! Burst: 3x 64 KB for primary video + 64 KB for auxiliary video
   ! Single-Rate Policing action
   ! TelePresence is remarked to CS5 to gain admission to the SP-Realtime Class
 class NETWORK-CONTROL
```

```
   bandwidth percent 5
   ! CBWFQ for Routing
 class BROADCAST-VIDEO
   bandwidth percent 5
   set dscp cs2
   ! CBWFQ for Broadcast Video
   ! Broadcast Video is remarked to CS2 to gain admission to the SP-Critical 2
 (UDP) Class
 class MULTIMEDIA-CONFERENCING
   bandwidth percent 5
   random-detect dscp-based
   set dscp af21
   ! CBWFQ for Multimedia Conferencing
   ! DSCP-WRED for Multimedia Conferencing
   ! Multimedia Conferencing is remarked to AF2 to gain admission to the SP-
 Critical 2 (UDP) Class
 class MULTIMEDIA-STREAMING
   bandwidth percent 5
   random-detect dscp-based
   set dscp af21
     ! CBWFQ for Multimedia Streaming
     ! DSCP-WRED for Multimedia Streaming
     ! Multimedia Streaming is remarked to AF2 to gain admission to the SP-Critical
 2 (UDP) Class
 class CALL-SIGNALING
   bandwidth percent 5
   ! CBWFQ for Call-Signaling
 class TRANSACTIONAL-DATA
   bandwidth percent 10
   random-detect dscp-based
   set dscp af31
     ! CBWFQ for Transactional Data
     ! DSCP-WRED for Transactional Data
     ! Transactional Data is remarked to AF3 to gain admission to the SP-Critical 1
 (TCP) Class
 class OAM
   bandwidth percent 5
   ! CBWFQ for Network Management
  class BULK-DATA
   bandwidth percent 4
   random-detect dscp-based
     ! CBWFQ for Bulk Data
     ! DSCP-WRED for Bulk Data
  class SCAVENGER
   bandwidth percent 1
     ! Minimum CBWFQ for Scavenger
```

```
class class-default
  bandwidth percent 25
  random-detect
    ! CBWFQ for Best Effort
    ! WRED for Best Effort
!
```

These 4-class enterprise-to-service provider MPLS VPN queuing configurations can be verified with the **show policy-map interface** command.

TelePresence 6-Class MPLS VPN SP Model QoS Design

In contrast to a 4-class SP model, a 6-class model offers additional flexibility because it supports not only a Real-time class and a default Best Effort class, but also a less-than Best Effort Scavenger class and three additional nonpriority traffic classes. To illustrate more design options, TelePresence can be assigned to a nonpriority (CBWFQ) SP-class in this example; but of course TelePresence can also be assigned, in combination with VoIP, to the SP-Real-time class, as detailed in the previous section.

In this case, the enterprise administrator can dedicate one of the nonpriority classes (such as SP-Critical 1) for TelePresence. Again, it bears reiteration that it would not be recommended to assign TelePresence in conjunction with any unbounded application into a single SP class because the other application could potentially cause the combined class to congest, resulting in TelePresence drops and loss of call quality.

This leaves two additional nonpriority classes, which again enables the administrator to separate TCP-based applications from UDP-based applications. Specifically, Broadcast Video, Multimedia Conferencing, Multimedia Streaming, and Operations/Administration/Management (OAM) traffic can all be assigned to the UDP SP-class (SP-Critical 3). This leaves the other nonpriority SP class (SP-Critical 2) available for control plane applications, such as Network Control and Call-Signaling, along with TCP-based Transactional Data applications. Figure 10-17 shows the per-class re-marking requirements from the CE edge to gain access to the classes within the 6-class SP model with TelePresence assigned to a nonpriority SP class.

As shown in Figure 10-17, TelePresence traffic does not need to be re-marked to gain access to the dedicated, nonpriority SP class to which it is assigned (SP-Critical 1). However as before, Broadcast Video must be re-marked to CS2 to be admitted into the UDP SP class (SP-Critical 3); Multimedia Conferencing and Multimedia Streaming must be re-marked to AF2 to be admitted also to the UDP SP class. Correspondingly, Transactional Data traffic must be re-marked to AF3 to gain access into the TCP SP class (SP-Critical 2). No other traffic requires re-marking to gain admission to the desired classes. However, Bulk and Scavenger no longer default to the SP-Best Effort class, but rather now default to the SP-Scavenger class, which is the desired policy to bind these potentially bandwidth-hogging applications.

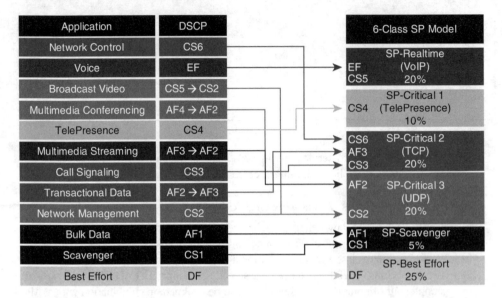

Figure 10-17 *Enterprise-to-SP mapping: 6-class SP model example with TelePresence assigned to a non-real-time class*

Based on Figure 10-17, Example 10-14 provides a sample configuration for 6-class enter-prise-to-SP mapping. Explicit re-marking requirements (to gain admission to the correct SP class) are highlighted within the example.

Example 10-14 *Enterprise-to-SP Mapping: 6-Class SP Model Example with TelePresence Assigned to a Non-Real-time Class*

```
Router# show run
! Output omitted for brevity.
!
! [The class maps are identical to those in Example 10-11]
! This section defines the policy-map
policy-map CE-EDGE-6CLASS-OC3-POS
 class VOICE
  police cir 30000000 bc 37500 conform-action transmit exceed-action drop
  priority
   ! LLQ command for OC3-POS
   ! Voice is policed to 30 Mbps (20%)
   ! Bc for VoIP is set to CIR/100 (after conversion to Bytes)
   ! Single-Rate Policing action
 class TELEPRESENCE
  bandwidth percent 10
  queue-limit 128
    ! CBWFQ for TelePresence (CTS-3000) as a ratio of OC3 (155 Mbps)
    ! Queue-Limit is expanded for TelePresence to 128 packets (from 64 packet
default)
```

```
    ! Note: No remarking required for TelePresence to gain admission to SP-
Critical 1 Class
class NETWORK-CONTROL
  bandwidth percent 5
  ! CBWFQ for Routing
class BROADCAST-VIDEO
  bandwidth percent 5
  set dscp cs2
  ! CBWFQ for Broadcast Video
  ! Broadcast Video is remarked to CS2 to gain admission to the SP-Critical 3
(UDP) Class
class MULTIMEDIA-CONFERENCING
  bandwidth percent 5
  random-detect dscp-based
  set dscp af21
  ! CBWFQ for Multimedia Conferencing
  ! DSCP-WRED for Multimedia Conferencing
  ! Multimedia Conferencing is remarked to AF2 to gain admission to the SP-
Critical 3 (UDP) Class
class MULTIMEDIA-STREAMING
  bandwidth percent 5
  random-detect dscp-based
  set dscp af21
   ! CBWFQ for Multimedia Streaming
   ! DSCP-WRED for Multimedia Streaming
   ! Multimedia Streaming is remarked to AF2 to gain admission to the SP-Critical
3 (UDP) Class
class CALL-SIGNALING
  bandwidth percent 5
  ! CBWFQ for Call-Signaling
class TRANSACTIONAL-DATA
  bandwidth percent 10
  random-detect dscp-based
  set dscp af31
   ! CBWFQ for Transactional Data
   ! DSCP-WRED for Transactional Data
   ! Transactional Data is remarked to AF3 to gain admission to the SP-Critical 2
(TCP) Class
class OAM
  bandwidth percent 5
  ! CBWFQ for Network Management
 class BULK-DATA
  bandwidth percent 4
  random-detect dscp-based
   ! CBWFQ for Bulk Data
   ! DSCP-WRED for Bulk Data
```

```
class SCAVENGER
  bandwidth percent 1
   ! Minimum CBWFQ for Scavenger
class class-default
  bandwidth percent 25
  random-detect
   ! CBWFQ for Best Effort
   ! WRED for Best Effort
!
```

You can verify these 6-class enterprise-to-SP MPLS VPN queuing configurations with the **show policy-map interface** command.

TelePresence Subline Rate Ethernet Access QoS Designs

As previously discussed, to enforce CE edge queuing policies at subline rates, an HQoS policy must be used so that a shaper smoothes out traffic to the subline rate and forces queuing to occur if this rate is exceeded.

As with policers, Cisco IOS shapers operate on a token-bucket principle, achieving subline rates by allowing traffic through in specified bursts (Bc) per subsecond intervals (Tc). As shaping introduces delay to packets above the burst value, it is important to properly size the bursts and intervals to minimize potential shaping jitter. For example, as previously discussed, 1080p sends 30 frames of video per second or, phrased differently, a video frame's worth of information every 33 ms. However, if the shaping interval is set too low, say to 5 ms, a frame's worth of information might be delayed over three to five shaping intervals (depending on the amount of frame information). Extensive testing has shown that configuring a shaping interval of 20 ms has resulted in the most consistent and minimal jitter values to support a TelePresence call.

The interval parameter cannot be set directly but is set indirectly by explicitly configuring the burst parameter. The relationship between the interval, burst, and shaped rate is given as

$$Tc = Bc \text{ / Shaped Rate}$$

Or

$$Bc = \text{Shaped Rate} \times Tc$$

For example, on a GE interface configured to support a subline rate of 50 Mbps, a burst value of 1 megabit (50 Mbps × 20 ms) would result in an optimal shaping interval for TelePresence.

Note   The burst parameter for a TelePresence hierarchical shaper might not necessarily be the same value as the burst parameter set for a TelePresence policer. This is because shapers and policers use burst parameters differently and also have different objectives within the network. Specifically, shapers use time constants and bursts (according to the preceding formula) to smooth traffic flows to conform to subline rates, whereas policers do not.

(These simply drop or re-mark packets.) Furthermore, the role of hierarchical shapers in such network designs is to ensure that the ingress policers on the SP's PE are *not* exceeded, which could cause TelePresence to be dropped. Thus, even though these parameters are both referred to as burst, they are different, both in function and in purpose.

Translating this into an HQoS policy yields the following configuration, as shown in Example 10-15.

Example 10-15 *HQoS Policy to Queue and Shape TelePresence Traffic to a 50 Mbps Subline Rate over a Gigabit Ethernet Interface*

```
Router# show run
! Output omitted for brevity.
!
! [The class maps are identical to those in Example 10-11]
! [The CE-EDGE policy-maps are identical to either Example 10-14 or 10-15]
! This section defines the HQoS shaping policy with the nested CE-Edge queuing
policy
policy-map HQoS-50MBPS
 class class-default
  shape average 50000000 1000000
  service-policy CE-EDGE
    ! Shaping Rate=50 Mbps; Bc=1 Mbps, Tc=20 ms
    ! Nested CE-EDGE queuing policy forces queuing at sub-line rate
!
! This section applies the HQoS service policy to the GE interface
interface GigabitEthernet0/1
 description CE-EDGE-GE
 ip address 192.168.1.50 255.255.255.252
 no ip redirects
 no ip proxy-arp
 duplex auto
 speed auto
 media-type rj45
 negotiation auto
 service-policy output HQoS-50MBPS
  ! Attaches HQoS policy to GE int
!
```

You can verify this HQoS policy configuration with the **show policy-map interface** command.

Note As mentioned throughout this chapter, additional design detail for TelePresence QoS policies can be found within the latest TelePresence Network Design Guide at http://tinyurl.com/ce7twk.

Summary

This chapter began by defining the service level requirements of TelePresence solutions, including bandwidth, burst, latency, jitter, and loss. Bandwidth requirements were shown to vary from 2 Mbps to 20 Mbps, depending on system configuration, resolution and motion-handling levels, and optional components. Maximum bursts were shown to correspond to H.264 Instantaneous Decode Refresh (IDR) frames, which yield 64 KB per video display, within 33 ms video frame intervals. Latency was shown to be a function of serialization, propagation, and queuing, with the latency target for TelePresence defined as 150 ms, based on G.114. Jitter was examined at Layer 3 (packet-level jitter) and at Layer 7 (video frame jitter); the peak-to-peak jitter target was set at 10 ms. The loss target, discussed extensively in the previous chapter, was reiterated to be 0.05 percent.

Next, consideration was given to an end-to-end DiffServ strategy, based on RFC 4594, with TelePresence marked as CS4 and provisioned with priority queuing (wherever viable).

This DiffServ strategy was first applied to campus networks, with detailed configuration recommendations for Cisco Catalyst 3560/3750, 4500/4900, and 6500 platforms and linecards.

Next, consideration was given to branch networks, with the option of provisioning TelePresence in either an LLQ or a CBWFQ. The advantages and trade-offs of each option were discussed, and the dual-LLQ option was also presented (to prevent TelePresence from interfering with VoIP provisioning). Additionally, MPLS VPN QoS policies for branch networks were also presented, including 4-class and 6-class enterprise-to-service provider mapping examples. Finally, subline access rate scenarios were considered, which necessitate hierarchical QoS policies, with queuing policies nested within shaping policies.

Further Reading

Standards and RFCs:

ITU G.114, "One-way Transmission Time": http://www.tinyurl.com/ae53pp

ITU-T H.264, "Advanced Video Coding for Generic Audiovisual Services": http://www.tinyurl.com/56g22e

IETF RFC 2474, "Definition of the Differentiated Services Field (DS Field) in the IPv4 and IPv6 Headers": http://www.ietf.org/rfc/rfc2474

IETF RFC 2597, "Assured Forwarding PHB Group": http://www.ietf.org/rfc/rfc2597

IETF RFC 3246, "An Expedited Forwarding PHB (Per-Hop Behavior)": http://www.ietf.org/rfc/rfc3246

IETF RFC 3984, "RTP Payload Format for H.264 Video": http://www.ietf.org/rfc/rfc3984

IETF RFC 4594, "Configuration Guidelines for DiffServ Service Classes": http://www.ietf.org/rfc/rfc4594

Cisco IOS Documentation:

Catalyst 3560 QoS Configuration Guide: http://www.tinyurl.com/4qmvyh

Catalyst 3750 QoS Configuration Guide: http://www.tinyurl.com/bxk6wd

Catalyst 3750-E and 3560-E QoS Configuration Guide: http://www.tinyurl.com/bvpog7

Catalyst 4500 and 4900 QoS Configuration Guide: http://www.tinyurl.com/c3lttk

Catalyst 4500 Supervisor 6-E and 4900M QoS Configuration Guide: http://www.tinyurl.com/dn5bty

Catalyst 6500 QoS Configuration Guide: http://www.tinyurl.com/ce5d33

Cisco IOS Quality of Service Solutions Configuration Guide, Release 12.4: http://www.tinyurl.com/6r6vql

Cisco Design Guides:

Cisco TelePresence Network Systems 2.0 Design Guide: http://www.tinyurl.com/cwmacq

Cisco Press Books:

Szigeti, Tim and Christina Hattingh. *End-to-End QoS Network Design: Quality of Service in LANs, WANs, and VPNs.* Cisco Press, 2005. ISBN: 1-58705-176-1.

This chapter discusses the deployment of Cisco TelePresence within an enterprise that implements internal firewalling within the company. Chapter 14, "Intercompany TelePresence Design," provides discussion about the deployment of external firewalling between companies. You implement internal firewalling within an organization for a number of reasons, including the following:

1. **Access control within an enterprise campus:** To provide access control for a corporate department, division, or service module within the campus network. This might be done for regulatory or internal security reasons.

2. **Access control between enterprise campus locations:** To provide NAT services between two campus locations. For example, when two companies merge, there might be a period of time where NAT is done because of an overlapping IP address space between the two sides of the company. You can also implement access control between the two campus locations if necessary.

3. **Access control from branch locations to corporate campus sites:** At WAN aggregation points within an enterprise organization to restrict inbound access from branch locations to certain protocols and resources within the corporate campus locations. You might do this to enhance the trust boundary between the branch locations and the corporate campus.

4. **Access control within enterprise branch locations:** To restrict access to certain devices within a branch. An example is the isolation of IP-based point-of-sale terminals within a store location.

CHAPTER 11

TelePresence Firewall Design

Figure 11-1 shows the deployment of firewalling in these four areas in relation to a TelePresence deployment.

You might need to enable the following flows through the firewall to support the TelePresence deployment:

- Device provisioning flows between the *Cisco Unified Communications Manager (CUCM)* cluster and *Cisco TelePresence Systems (CTS)* endpoints to successfully bring the CTS endpoints onto the network and register with CUCM.

- Call scheduling and service flows between the CTS Manager and the CTS endpoints.

- Call signaling flows between CTS endpoints and the CUCM cluster to initiate and terminate TelePresence meetings.

- The actual audio and video media flows between CTS endpoints in a point-to-point call.

- The actual audio and video media flows between CTS endpoints and the *Cisco TelePresence Multipoint Switch (CTMS)* in a multipoint call.

- Flows between network management stations and the CTS endpoints to successfully manage the TelePresence deployment.

Cisco Firewall Platforms

Cisco currently provides three firewall product lines:

- ASA 5500 Series of firewall appliances

- IOS Firewall running on Cisco IOS router platforms

- Firewall Service Module (FWSM) for the Catalyst 6500 switches and Cisco 7600 Series routers

Note that the Cisco PIX Firewall series is not listed because it has been replaced with the ASA 5500 Series of firewall appliances. The discussion in this chapter is primarily on the deployment of Cisco TelePresence with the ASA 5500 Series of firewall appliances; however, the concepts apply to other firewalls that provide similar capability as well.

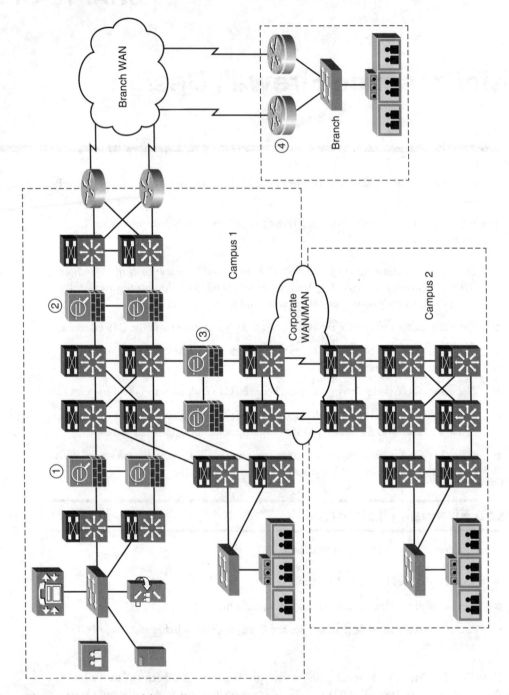

Figure 11-1 *Internal firewalling within an enterprise organization*

Firewall Deployment Options

The following sections discuss some of the options available when deploying a firewall within an enterprise network. Where appropriate, information about the effect of the choice of firewall deployment on TelePresence is discussed.

Transparent Versus Routed Mode

Firewalls such as the Cisco ASA 5500 Series can operate either as a Layer 2 (transparent mode) or Layer 3 (routed mode) device. A firewall operating in transparent mode does not mean that access control decisions are made based upon Layer 2 MAC address information. Access control decisions are still made based upon Layer 3 and higher (for Application Layer Protocol Inspection) information. A firewall operating in transparent mode has the same IP subnet on both sides of the firewall, as shown at the top of Figure 11-2. This is often beneficial for deploying firewalling in existing networks because you do not need to change IP addressing to insert the firewall. Note that Figure 11-2 and all subsequent examples within this chapter use RFC 1918 addressing.

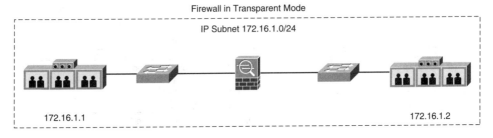

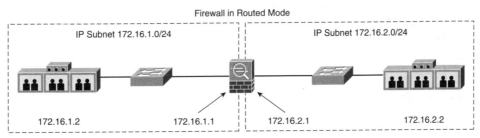

Figure 11-2 *Transparent mode versus routed mode firewall*

A firewall operating in routed mode has different IP subnets on both sides of the firewall, as shown at the bottom Figure 11-2. For brevity purposes, the examples in this chapter illustrate different firewall and NAT scenarios and configurations based on routed mode because that is the more traditional mode of operation for many customers. Transparent mode would, in principle, work similarly.

Equal Versus Unequal Interface Security Levels

Firewalls such as the Cisco ASA 5500 Series operate based upon the concept of levels of trust within the network. This is reflected through security levels configured on firewall interfaces. Security levels range from 100, which is the most secure interface, to 0, which is the least secure interface. These are often referred to as the *inside* and *outside* interfaces on a firewall with only two interfaces.

By default, traffic initiated from a device on an interface with a higher security level can pass to a device on an interface with a lower security level. Return traffic corresponding to that session can dynamically pass from the lower interface security level to the interface with the higher security level. The term *session* can also apply to return UDP-based traffic, although there is no actual session as with TCP-based traffic. The use of symmetric port numbering in point-to-point TelePresence calls can actually provide a benefit when traversing firewalls because of this behavior, as shown in Figure 11-3.

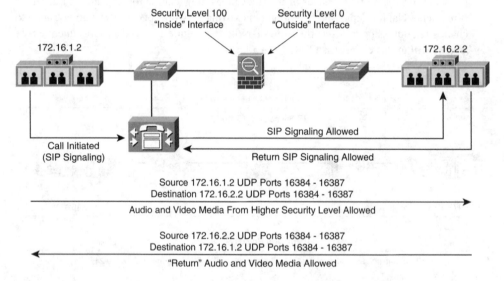

Figure 11-3 *Symmetrical port numbering with point-to-point TelePresence assists in firewall traversal*

In Figure 11-3, the audio RTP traffic and accompanying RTCP channel use UDP ports 16384 and 16385; whereas the video RTP traffic and accompanying RTCP channel use UDP ports 16386 and 16387. Because the UDP ports are symmetric, the audio and video generated by the CTS endpoint on the interface with the lower security level appears as if it is the return traffic of the CTS endpoint on the higher security level and is, therefore, allowed back through the firewall.

Note Symmetric use of ports does not currently hold true for multipoint TelePresence calls. Although each CTS endpoint sends media to the CTMS using UDP ports 16384 through 16387, the CTMS uses a separate port range for sending audio and video media to each CTS endpoint in a multipoint call. Therefore, the audio and video media ports are not symmetric within a multipoint call.

By default, traffic initiated from a device on an interface with a lower security level cannot pass to a device on an interface with a higher security level. You can modify this behavior with an ingress access control list (ACL) on the lower security interface level. For example, in Figure 11-3, an ingress ACL on the interface with the lower security level allows both the primary codec and the associated IP Phone of the CTS endpoint to register with the CUCM cluster through SIP. With an inbound ACL, you might need to configure static translations within the firewall to enable the devices on the inside network to be visible to the outside network. Depending upon the firewall deployment, an ingress ACL applied to the interface with the higher security level might also be desired to limit traffic going from higher level security interfaces to interfaces with lower security levels.

You can also enable Cisco ASA 5500 Series Firewalls to operate with interfaces having equal security levels. By default, traffic cannot pass between interfaces having the same security level unless the **same-security-traffic permit inter-interface** global command is also configured within the firewall. Again, you can use ingress ACLs applied on each interface and static translations to specifically enable access between certain devices and protocols connected to interfaces with equal security levels. The "TelePresence Protocol Requirements" section in this chapter discusses specific protocols that might be required within ACLs.

Network Address Translation

Network Address Translation (NAT) is normally used to hide the internal IP addressing of an enterprise organization when accessing resources on the Internet. It is not utilized often in internal firewall deployments, unless overlapping IP address ranges exist within the enterprise. These IP address duplications could be the temporary result of acquisitions and mergers between companies.

NAT utilizes the concept of dynamic address pools that translate local addresses to global addresses, and individual static translations between devices on the local side and the global side. Figure 11-4 provides an example of one-sided NAT within a TelePresence deployment, again using RFC 1918 addressing.

To simplify Figure 11-4, the ACLs enabling appropriate inbound and outbound addresses and protocols are not shown.

When deploying TelePresence within a one-sided NAT environment, you might need static translations between the inside or local IP addresses of the CTS endpoint, associated IP 7975G Phone, CUCM, and possibly DNS server. These translate to the global IP addresses that are visible to the network on the outside interface. In this type of deployment, the inside network is aware of the entire IP address range of the outside network, and proper IP routing must be configured for reachability. The outside network, however, is not aware of the inside IP addressing. All inside addresses translate to global IP addresses by the firewall. Therefore, IP routing on the outside must reach only the IP subnet of the global address pool.

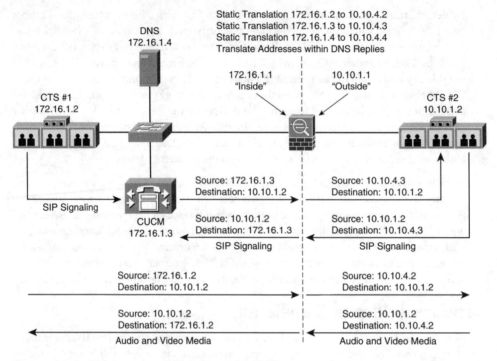

Figure 11-4   *TelePresence deployment with NAT*

Note   Many-to-one NAT, also referred to as Port Address Translation (PAT), does not work in this environment because of the requirements for static translations.

The ASA 5500 Series Firewall also has an option for translating IP addresses within DNS replies. This enables the DNS server to deploy on the inside of the NAT Firewall and still correctly hand out IP addresses to devices "outside" the firewall. Modifications to the configuration of the CTS endpoint are also required for this configuration to operate correctly. Referring to Figure 11-4, the DNS server entry in CTS#2 needs to be configured to point to the global address of the DNS server (10.10.4.4). The entry for the CUCM cluster configured in CTS#2 can use the hostname of the CUCM server. The DNS translation function of the firewall ensures that the local CUCM address translates to the global address before being handed to CTS#2. Otherwise, the configuration of CTS#2 would need to be modified to include the global address of the CUCM server as well.

An alternative to translation of DNS replies within the firewall is a split DNS implementation. In this configuration, you deploy a DNS server on both sides of the firewall with the appropriate records for the particular addressing used on that side of the firewall. However, this method doubles the amount of administrative work in maintaining DNS across the enterprise.

Application Layer Protocol Inspection

Application layer protocol inspection is required for services that embed IP addressing information within user data sections of a packet or that open secondary channels on dynamically assigned ports. These protocols require the firewall to perform a deep packet inspection to extract such information. The Cisco TelePresence solution embeds IP addressing information within the SIP signaling between CTS endpoints and the CUCM cluster. SIP signaling is also used to dynamically specify the RTP audio and video media ports, which range from UDP ports 16384 to ports 32766. The firewall, therefore, dynamically opens and closes the required audio and video media ports based upon inspection of the SIP signaling between the CTS endpoints and the CUCM cluster.

Without SIP inspection, the network administrator might have to statically open these UDP port ranges for the IP addresses corresponding to each CTS endpoint that needs to pass through the firewall. This presents a larger security vulnerability from a firewall perspective. Therefore, when possible, the use of application layer protocol inspection of SIP traffic for TelePresence deployments is recommended. Note also that DNS and TFTP application layer protocol inspection are enabled by default with the ASA 5500 Series of firewall appliances. It is recommended to leave these enabled.

TLS Proxy Functionality

When *Transport Layer Security (TLS)* encryption is enabled for SIP signaling, the firewall cannot inspect the SIP/SDP messages to dynamically open the necessary ports. In this scenario, the network administrator might be left with one of two alternatives:

■ Statically open the range of IP addresses and UDP ports that correspond to the RTP audio and video media streams that must cross the firewall.

■ Implement a firewall that uses TLS proxy functionality for CTS endpoints.

With TLS proxy functionality, the TLS session is established between the TelePresence endpoint and the firewall. A second TLS session is established between the firewall and the CUCM server. The firewall can then decrypt the TLS packets and inspect the SIP/SDP messages to determine the necessary dynamic UDP ports to open for audio and video media. The signaling is then re-encrypted and sent to its respective endpoint.

TelePresence Protocol Requirements

The following sections discuss some of the protocols that might need to be enabled through a firewall, depending upon the configuration of the network and CTS endpoints. See the Appendix, "Protocols Used in Cisco TelePresence Solutions," for a complete list of protocols used by TelePresence devices. The discussion in this chapter is geared toward identification of TelePresence protocol requirements based upon the following functions:

■ Provisioning the devices onto the network

■ Registering the devices with the CUCM

■ Call scheduling and services flows

- Call signaling flows needed to initiate and terminate a TelePresence meeting

- Support of the actual media flows across the network

- Management of the devices on the network

Device Provisioning Flows

Device provisioning flows are the signaling and data flows needed by CTS endpoints to boot and register with the CUCM cluster.

Dynamic Host Configuration Protocol (DHCP)

As discussed in Chapter 7, "TelePresence Control and Security Protocols," DHCP is used for dynamic IP address assignment. Client-sent DHCP packets have UDP source port 68 and destination port 67. Server-sent DHCP packets have UDP source port 67 and destination port 68. If both the primary codec of the CTS endpoint and its associated IP Phone use static IP addressing, DHCP is not required. If either the primary codec or its associate IP Phone use dynamic IP addressing, DHCP might be required to pass through the firewall, depending upon the network configuration. Figure 11-5 shows three DHCP deployment options where no firewall ACL entries are needed to support TelePresence.

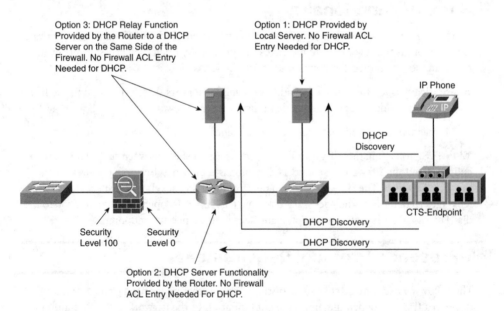

Figure 11-5 *DHCP deployments not requiring firewall ACL entries for TelePresence*

The initial DHCP DISCOVERY packet is sent by the CTS endpoint to the IP broadcast address (255.255.255.255). Therefore, either the DHCP server functionality must be local to the IP subnet, or a router can be configured to provide DHCP relay functionality to a DHCP server on another IP subnet. If the DHCP server functionality is on the same side of the firewall, no ACL entries are needed for DHCP flows from TelePresence devices.

Figure 11-6 shows two DHCP deployment options where firewall ACL entries are needed to support TelePresence.

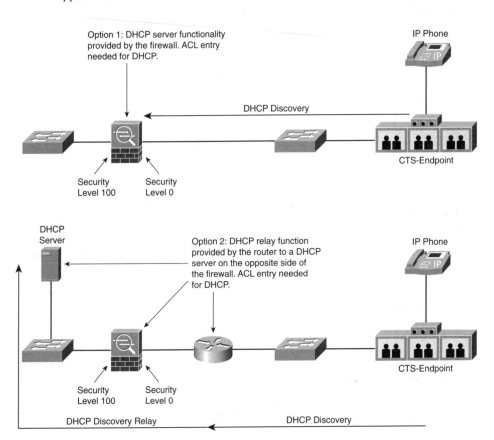

Figure 11-6 *DHCP deployments requiring firewall ACL entries for TelePresence*

Option 1 in Figure 11-6 shows that even if the firewall provides the DHCP server functionality, an ACL entry might be needed to enable the inbound DHCP DISCOVERY packet and further DHCP packet exchanges. If a router provides DHCP relay functionality to a DHCP server on the opposite side of a firewall, as shown in Option 2, an ACL entry might be needed to enable the relayed DHCP exchanged to occur as well.

Domain Name System

Domain Name System (DNS) uses UDP port 53 for the hostname to IP address resolution. If hostnames are included within DHCP provisioning flows or configuration files sent to the CTS endpoint or its associated IP Phone, DNS is required for the CTS endpoint or IP Phone to resolve the hostname to an IP address.

DNS might be required to pass through the firewall, depending upon the network configuration. DNS queries are initiated by the CTS endpoints. Therefore, if the DNS server is located on the same side of the firewall as the CTS endpoint, no ACL entry might be needed for DNS. However, if the DNS server is located on the opposite side of the firewall from the CTS endpoint, an ACL entry enabling DNS queries from the CTS endpoint might be needed. Figure 11-7 shows these two deployment options.

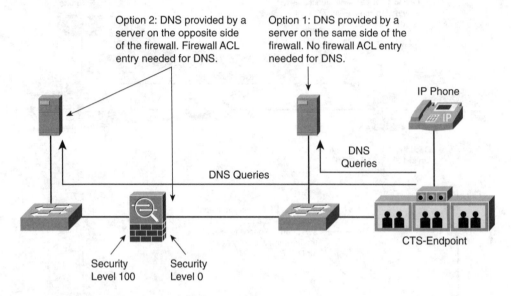

Figure 11-7   *DNS support for TelePresence in a firewall deployment*

Network Time Protocol (NTP)

NTP uses UDP port 123 for clock synchronization across the network infrastructure. If the NTP server to which the CTS endpoint synchronizes with is located on the opposite side of the firewall from the CTS endpoint, an ACL entry enabing NTP traffic generated from the CTS endpoint might be needed. Figure 11-8 provides an example of NTP within a TelePresence deployment.

Configuration Download and Device Registration Protocols

Configuration download protocols include those needed by the CTS codecs and their attached IP Phones to upgrade system load images and download device configuration files. The CUCM cluster often provides the download server functionality and is, therefore, the only example discussed within this chapter. Further, this section assumes that the CUCM cluster is on the opposite side of the firewall from the CTS endpoint.

Trivial File Transfer Protocol

The 7975G IP Phone, which serves as the user interface for TelePresence calls, requires *Trivial File Transfer Protocol (TFTP)* for downloading system images during upgrades and for downloading configuration files. TFTP servers listen on UDP port 69 but then dynamically assign a different port number for actual file transfers. Therefore, you need to

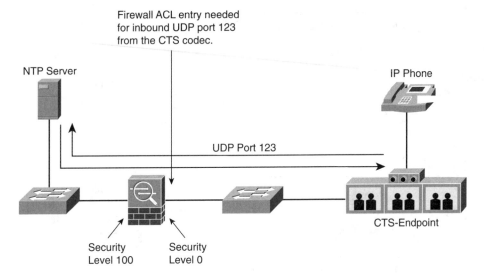

Figure 11-8 *NTP support for TelePresence in a firewall deployment*

leave application layer protocol inspection enabled for TFTP within the firewall, which is the default for ASA 5500 Series Firewall appliances. However, an ACL entry enabling the initial TFTP read request from the CTS endpoint to the CUCM cluster might be needed.

TCP Port 6970

Unlike IP Phones, TelePresence codecs do not use TFTP for download of system images and configuration files. TelePresence codecs use HTTP over TCP port 6970 to download system images and configuration files. An ACL entry enabling the session to be initiated by the CTS endpoint on the opposite side of the firewall from the CUCM cluster might be required. Figure 11-9 shows both protocols required by the CTS endpoints for system image upgrade and configuration download.

SIP Registration

When the CTS codec and associated IP Phone complete downloading their configuration files, and possibly upgrading their system images, both perform a SIP registration with the CUCM cluster. SIP signaling uses either TCP or UDP port 5060. The connection-oriented nature of TCP makes it preferred for TelePresence deployments and is the only protocol discussed within this chapter. If the SIP signaling is protected via TLS, TCP port 5061 is used. This section also assumes that the CUCM cluster is on the opposite side of the firewall from the CTS endpoint.

Because SIP REGISTER requests are initiated by the CTS primary codec and associated IP Phone, ACL entries on the firewall that enable the inbound traffic might be required. Figure 11-10 shows the SIP requirements for registration by both the CTS primary codec and associated IP Phone.

If additional IP Phones that support the Cisco SCCP protocol exist on the firewall interface with the lower security level, an ingress ACL entry on the firewall interface with the

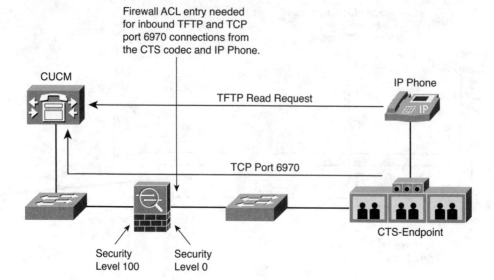

Figure 11-9   *Configuration download protocol support for TelePresence in a firewall deployment*

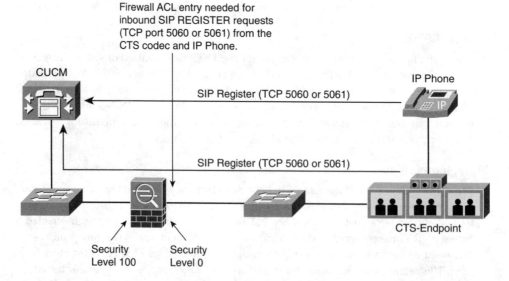

Figure 11-10   *SIP registration support for TelePresence in a firewall deployment*

lower security level will generally be needed to enable such devices to register with CUCM. These can be used because of the audio add-on feature of TelePresence meetings.

Call Scheduling and Services Flows

Call scheduling flows are data flows between the CTS Manager and CTS endpoints that update the meeting schedule information that appears on the 7975G IP Phone associated with the CTS endpoint. CTS Manager uses XML/SOAP to push scheduling information out to the CTS endpoints. CTS endpoints then push the content to the IP Phone GUI through XML. The CTS endpoint can also initiate XML/SOAP sessions to send messages to the CTS Manager.

From a firewall perspective, because the session can be initiated from the CTS endpoint on the lower security level interface to the CTS Manager on the higher security level interface, an ACL entry will generally be needed to support the call scheduling information flows, as shown in Figure 11-11.

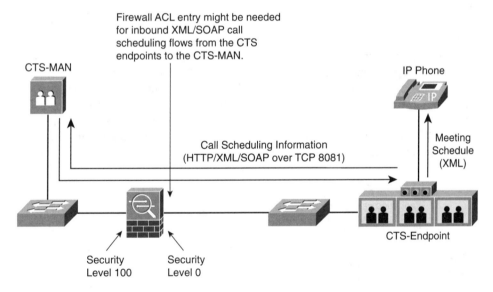

Figure 11-11   *Call scheduling flow support for TelePresence in a firewall deployment*

Call service flows include things such as directory lookup services available through the GUI of the IP Phone associated with the CTS endpoint. IP Phones use XML over HTTP port 8080 to communicate with the CUCM cluster and potentially other servers to provide these services, as shown in Figure 11-12.

Because these flows originate with the IP Phone associated with the CTS endpoint or other IP Phones that might be bridged onto a TelePresence meeting, an ingress ACL entry on the firewall interface with the lower security level might be required to enable these to pass through the firewall.

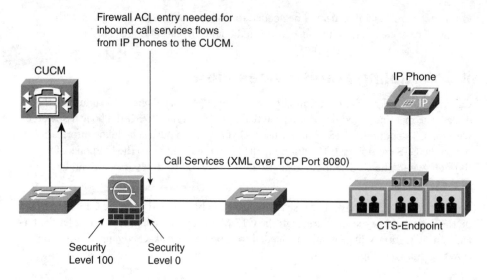

Figure 11-12   *Call services flows support for TelePresence in a firewall deployment*

Call service flows also include HTTP/XML/SOAP messages between the Cisco TelePresence Multipoint Switch (CTMS) and CTS codecs used for in-meeting controls during multipoint TelePresence meetings. The CTMS listens on TCP port 9501 for inbound connections initiated from the CTS endpoint. The CTS endpoints use an ephemeral (random high number) source port. The CTMS can also initiate connections to the CTS endpoints, using source port TCP 9501. Because requests can be initiated by the CTS primary codec, ACL entries on the firewall that enable the inbound traffic will generally be required, as illustrated Figure 11-13.

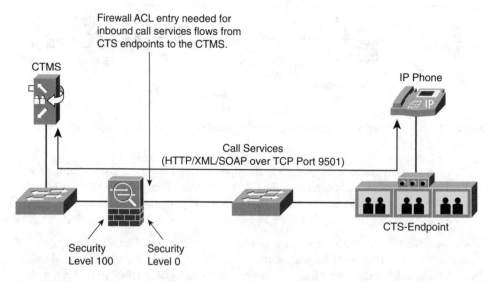

Figure 11-13   *Call services flows for multipoint TelePresence in a firewall deployment*

Call Signaling Flows

Call signaling flows are the SIP signaling (UDP and TCP Port 5060, or TCP Port 5061) flows between the CTS endpoints and the CUCM used to start, stop, and put calls on hold. From a firewall perspective, because SIP is already enabled through the firewall for the CTS endpoint to register with the CUCM cluster, no additional ACL entries are needed to support call signaling flows, as illustrated in Figure 11-14.

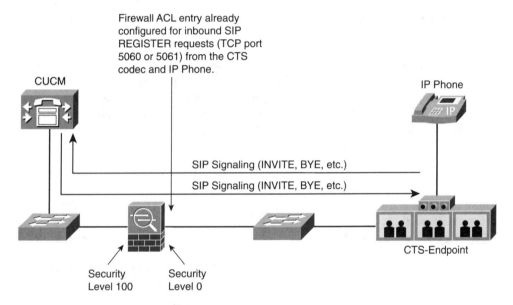

Figure 11-14 *Call signaling flow support for TelePresence in a firewall deployment*

In Figure 11-14, outbound call signaling from the CUCM to the CTS endpoint on the opposite side of the firewall is automatically enabled from an interface with a higher security level to an interface with a lower security level.

Media Flows

Media flows are the actual RTP/UDP streams that carry the audio and video of the TelePresence meeting. Video from individual cameras is carried within individual media streams. Likewise, audio from individual microphones is carried within individual media streams. All the audio media streams multiplex into a single audio RTP stream with a single UDP port before being sent over the network. Likewise, all the video media streams multiplex into a single video RTP stream with a single UDP port before being sent over the network. In addition, RTCP control information for each audio and video stream can also multiplex within each UDP stream. This eases firewall traversal because only a single UDP audio stream and single UDP video stream are sent from a CTS endpoint. Alternatively, the RTCP control information can be carried within the next higher odd-numbered UDP port.

Slight variations in media flows between point-to-point TelePresence calls and multipoint TelePresence calls exist, as covered in the following sections.

Point-to-Point TelePresence Calls

In point-to-point TelePresence calls, the audio and video UDP streams flow directly between the CTS endpoints. The flows are symmetric, as shown in Figure 11-15. Therefore, TelePresence can be deployed without any ACL entry on the lower security interface that enables the inbound UDP media streams (typically UDP ports 16384 through 16387). This assumes no application-level inspection of SIP traffic to dynamically open media ports either. When SIP signaling has completed, each CTS endpoint independently begins to send audio and video media. The audio and video media from the CTS endpoint on the lower security interface of the firewall are temporarily blocked by the firewall. However, when the audio and video media from the CTS endpoint on the higher security interface of the firewall passes through the firewall, it dynamically enables the reverse traffic through. This unblocks the audio and video media from the CTS endpoint on the lower security interface of the firewall. Figure 11-15 shows this functionality.

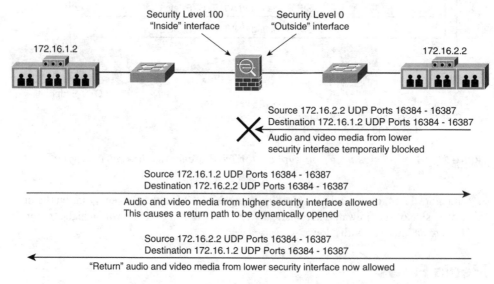

Figure 11-15   *Firewall behavior with symmetric TelePresence flows*

This behavior enables the network administrator to implement the firewall without having to open static RTP port ranges on the lower security interface, reducing the security vulnerability of the network. The network administrator can certainly configure an ingress ACL on the lower security interface enabling UDP ports 16384 to 16387 (or a larger range of ports from 16384 to 32766) if the initial blocking of video presents an issue. However, despite this functionality, this configuration is not recommended. Instead, it is recommended that the firewall administrator enable application-level protocol inspection of SIP traffic to enable the firewall to dynamically open and close the necessary UDP ports for the audio and video media, as shown in Figure 11-16.

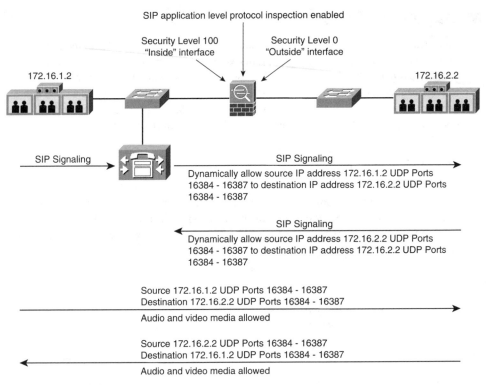

Figure 11-16 *TelePresence with SIP application-level protocol inspection*

Enabling SIP application level protocol inspection causes the firewall to inspect the SDP packets within SIP INVITE requests for the particular IP addresses and UDP ports required for audio and video media in each direction. The firewall continues to inspect any re-INVITES and inspects the SIP BYE message and dynamically closes the media ports as well. Dynamically closing the media ports causes temporary blocking of a large number of TelePresence audio and video media packets at the firewall because the codecs typically send SIP BYE messages before actually stopping the media flows.

Multipoint TelePresence Calls

In multipoint TelePresence calls, the audio and video UDP streams flow between the CTS endpoints and the CTMS. Again, only one UDP audio stream and one UDP video stream exist for each CTS endpoint, with the associated higher odd-numbered UDP stream carrying the RTCP traffic. However, because the CTMS has a single IP address and must support multiple UDP audio and video streams from multiple CTS endpoints, the flows are not symmetric from a UDP port numbering perspective. Therefore the network administrator might need to statically open a range of UDP ports to the IP address of the CTMS on the lower security interface of the firewall if SIP application-level protocol inspection is not utilized. However, as with point-to-point Telepresence, you need to enable SIP application-level protocol inspection to enable the firewall to dynamically open and close the necessary media ports.

Management Flows

Management flows are needed by management stations or end-user PCs to monitor, configure, and troubleshoot the CTS endpoints. CTS codecs currently support management connections using the HTTPS and SSH protocols. The associated IP Phone also supports management connections utilizing HTTP and HTTPS. In addition, CTS codecs can be configured to receive SNMP requests and generate SNMP responses, receive ICMP requests and generate ICMP responses, and send SNMP traps to a management station.

HTTP, HTTPS, and SSH

HTTP uses TCP port 80. HTTPS uses TCP port 443. SSH uses TCP port 23. Because all these protocols initiate from management stations on the interface with the higher security level toward the CTS endpoint on the interface with the lower security level, you do not need ingress ACL entry on the firewall interface with the lower security level, as illustrated in Figure 11-17.

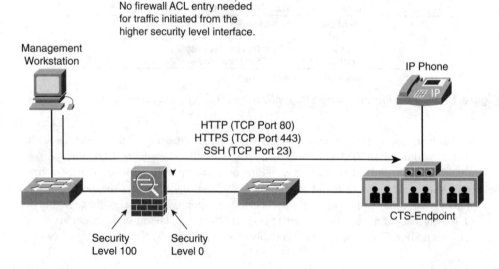

Figure 11-17 *Management station initiated protocols*

SNMP Requests and Responses

CTS endpoints listen on UDP port 161 for SNMP requests from management stations. SNMP responses are generated by the CTS endpoint with UDP source port 161 to the ephemeral port (high-numbered random port) used by the management station. Because SNMP requests initiate from management stations on the interface with the higher security level toward the CTS endpoint on the interface with the lower security level, you do not need ingress ACL entry on the firewall interface with the lower security level, as illustrated in Figure 11-18.

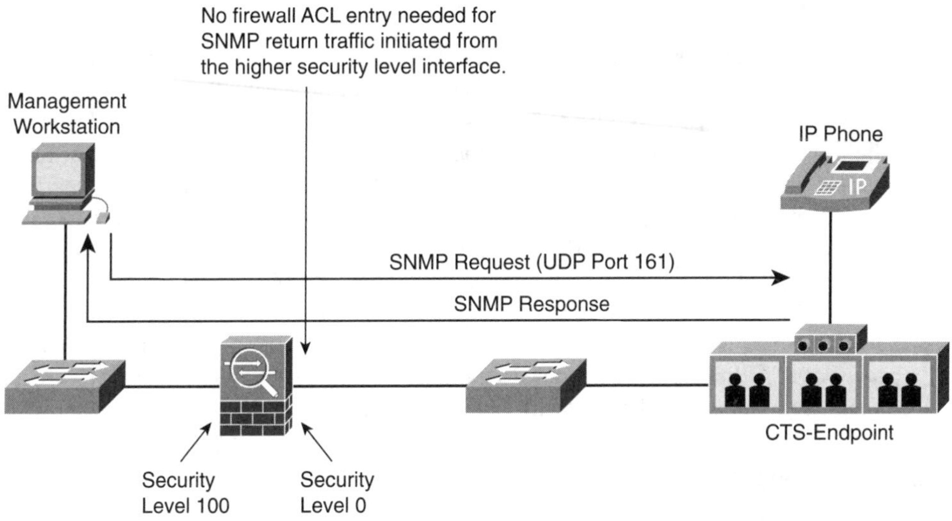

No firewall ACL entry needed for
SNMP return traffic initiated from
the higher security level interface.

Figure 11-18 *SNMP requests and responses*

SNMP Traps

SNMP management stations typically listen on UDP Port 162 for SNMP traps. Because
SNMP traps are unsolicited events from the CTS endpoints, an ingress ACL entry on the
firewall interface with the lower security level might be needed to enable them to pass to
the management server on the interface with the higher security level, as illustrated in
Figure 11-19.

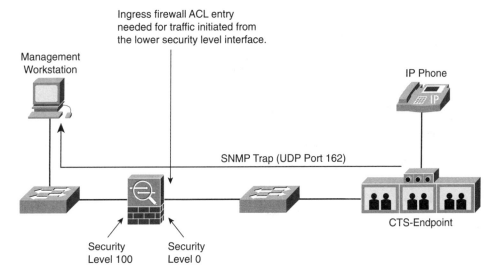

Figure 11-19 *CTS endpoint initiated management protocols*

ICMP

CTS endpoints and their associated 7975G IP Phones also send ICMP packets to each other occasionally, typically in the form of Destination Unreachable/Port Unreachable message types (ICMP Type 3 Code 3). These can be used to convey reachability/unreachability of services between CTS endpoints across the network. For example, because SIP signaling is sent between the CTS endpoints and CUCM to end a call; both CTS endpoints do not stop sending audio and video media at exactly the same time. One side can continue receiving media for a brief time, after it ends the call and closes its receiving media ports. In that situation, the CTS endpoint might send ICMP Destination Unreachable/Port Unreachable packets to the sending side, indicating that it has shut down those ports. Therefore ICMP packets might also need to be enabled through the firewall to the particular IP addresses corresponding to the TelePresence devices. Enabling SNMP through a firewall should be used with caution, however.

Additional Management Flows

As presented in Chapter 7, additional management flows might also exist between the CTS Manager, CUCM cluster, CTMS, email/calendaring servers, directory/LDAP servers, and management workstations, as shown in Figure 11-20.

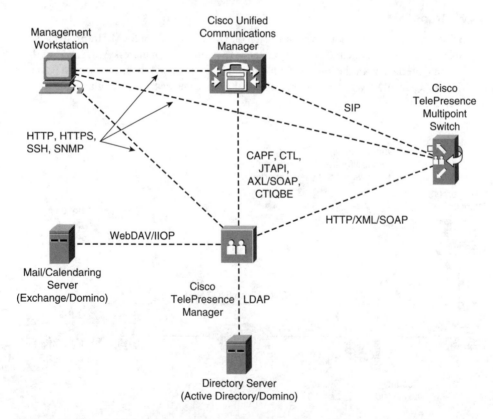

Figure 11-20 *Additional management flows*

Depending upon how the internal firewalling is deployed within the enterprise, it might or might not be necessary to enable these flows through the firewall for correct TelePresence operation.

Current best practices recommend deploying a dedicated CUCM cluster for TelePresence, so one design option would be to deploy the CUCM, CTS-Manager, and CTMS on one segment of a service module or data center deployed within the enterprise. Directory services and email/calendaring services can be deployed on a second segment. Finally, network management services can be deployed on a third segment. Internal firewalling can then be deployed, limiting access between the segments only to those protocols required. Figure 11-21 shows a simplified example of firewalling between segments of an enterprise service module or data center.

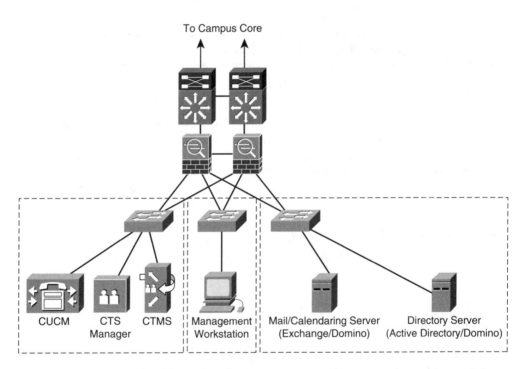

Figure 11-21 *Example of firewalling between segments of an enterprise service module or data center*

In Figure 11-21, no firewalling is needed between the CUCM cluster, CTS Manager, and CTMS because they exist on the same Layer 3 subnet. However, these devices are firewalled from the CTS endpoints deployed throughout the rest of the network and from the management workstation, directory server, and email/calendaring server. The management workstation is separated onto its own Layer 3 subnet. HTTP, HTTPS, SSH, and SNMP protocols need to be enabled through the firewall between the management workstation and the CUCM, CTS Manager, and CTMS. Likewise, these protocols need to be enabled through the firewall between the management workstation and the CTS endpoints deployed throughout the rest of the network. Finally, the directory server and email/calendaring server are separated onto another Layer 3 subnet within the service module or data center. Web-based Distributed Authoring and Versioning (WebDAV)/Internet Inter-ORB Protocol (IIOP) and the Lightweight Directory Access Protocol (LDAP) protocol need to be enabled through the firewall between these devices and the CTS Manager. WebDAV enables the CTS Manager to access scheduling information from Microsoft Exchange servers. IIOP provides similar access to IBM Domino Servers. Also, the necessary protocols need to be enabled through the firewall for normal email clients throughout the network to access directory services, download email, and access calendaring services. Virtual LAN (VLAN) subinterfaces can be deployed within the firewall, or separate physical interfaces can be utilized, as shown in the previous example. Finally, this is only one example method of implementing firewalling between these devices within a service module or data center deployed within an enterprise network. Other alternative approaches exist as well.

Example Firewall Configuration

Example 11-1 shows part of a Cisco ASA 5500 Series Firewall configuration between TelePresence devices on two campuses, as shown in Figure 11-22.

The firewall for this example has been configured for routed mode operation, with unequal interface security levels and no NAT, and with SIP application layer protocol inspection enabled. Note that neither the CTS Manager nor the CTMS are included within this example and that additional application layer protocol inspection for protocols (not discussed in this chapter) are defaults within the configuration example and not required for TelePresence operation.

Example 11-1 *Example Firewall Configuration*

```
! Interface Security Levels:
!
interface GigabitEthernet0/0
 description Connection to tp-c1-6500-2 Gig3/1
 speed 1000
 duplex full
 nameif CAMPUS
 security-level 50                          ! Higher security level
 ip address 10.16.7.2 255.255.255.0
!
!
interface GigabitEthernet1/0
 description Connection to tp-c1-6500-1 Gig0/2
 speed 1000
 duplex full
 nameif WAN
 security-level 40                          ! Lower security level
 ip address 10.16.8.2 255.255.255.0
!
```

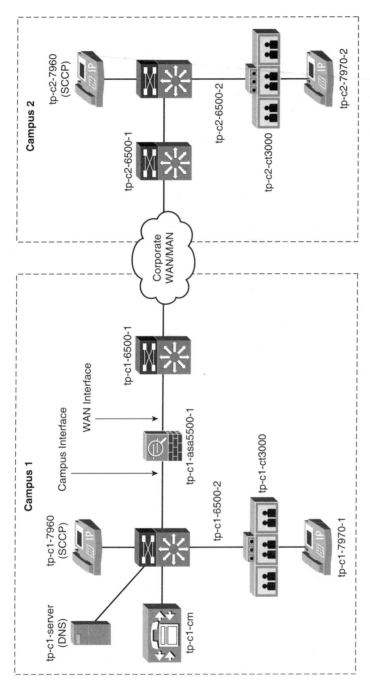

Figure 11-22 *Topology for example firewall configuration*

```
! Static Xlates:
!
static (CAMPUS,WAN) tp-c1-server tp-c1-server netmask 255.255.255.255 dns
! Allow the Campus 1 DNS server to be reachable from the lower security interface
static (CAMPUS,WAN) tp-c1-ct3000 tp-c1-ct3000 netmask 255.255.255.255 dns
! Allow the Campus 1 TelePresence unit to be reachable from the lower security
interface
static (CAMPUS,WAN) tp-c1-7960-1 tp-c1-7960-1 netmask 255.255.255.255 dns
! Allow the Campus 1 IP7960 phone to be reachable from the lower security
interface
static (CAMPUS,WAN) tp-c1-7975-1 tp-c1-7975-1 netmask 255.255.255.255 dns
! Allow the Campus 1 IP 7975G phone to be reachable from the lower security
interface
static (CAMPUS,WAN) tp-c1-cm tp-c1-cm netmask 255.255.255.255 dns
! Allow CUCM to be reachable from the lower security interface
! WAN ACL:
!
access-list NEW_WAN extended permit icmp any any unreachable
! Allow ICMP unreachables from all devices to be sent.
!
access-list NEW_WAN extended permit tcp host tp-c2-ct3000 host tp-c1-cm eq sip
access-list NEW_WAN extended permit tcp host tp-c2-7975-1 host tp-c1-cm eq sip
! Allow SIP devices to register with CUCM
!
access-list NEW_WAN extended permit tcp host tp-c2-7960-1 host tp-c1-cm eq 2000
! Allow SCCP devices to register with CUCM
!
access-list NEW_WAN extended permit udp host tp-c2-ct3000 host tp-c1-server eq
domain
access-list NEW_WAN extended permit udp host tp-c1-7960-1 host tp-c1-server eq
domain
access-list NEW_WAN extended permit udp host tp-c1-7975-1 host tp-c1-server eq
domain
! Allow devices to access the DNS server to translate names to valid IP
! addresses
!
access-list NEW_WAN extended permit udp host tp-c2-7975-1 host tp-c1-cm eq tftp
access-list NEW_WAN extended permit udp host tp-c2-7960-1 host tp-c1-cm eq tftp
! Allow devices to access the TFTP server within CUCM for downloading of
! configuration and OS
!
access-list NEW_WAN extended permit tcp host tp-c2-7975-1 host tp-c1-cm eq 8080
access-list NEW_WAN extended permit tcp host tp-c2-7960-1 host tp-c1-cm eq 8080
! Allow XML access from the IP Phones to CUCM
!
access-list NEW_WAN extended permit tcp host tp-c2-ct3000 host tp-c1-cm eq 6970
! TCP port used during firmware upgrades of the TelePresence CTS-3000 units.
```

```
!
! Note: ACL entry for SNMP traps not included in this configuration.
! Campus ACL:
!
access-list NEW_CAMPUS permit ip any any
! Default ACL shown in the example. This allows all traffic inbound
! on the higher level security interface.
! Application of ACLs Inbound on Interfaces:
!
access-group NEW_CAMPUS in interface CAMPUS
access-group NEW_WAN in interface WAN
!
! Global Policy Which Includes SIP Application Specific Protocol Inspection:
!
policy-map type inspect dns migrated_dns_map_1
 parameters
   message-length maximum 512
!
policy-map asa_global_fw_policy
 class inspection_default
   inspect dns migrated_dns_map_1
   inspect ftp
   inspect h323 h225
   inspect h323 ras
   inspect netbios
   inspect rsh
   inspect rtsp
   inspect http
   inspect esmtp
   inspect sqlnet
   inspect sunrpc
   inspect tftp
   inspect xdmcp
   inspect sip
   inspect skinny
! SIP, SCCP, TFTP and DNS application layer protocol inspection enabled.
!
service-policy asa_global_fw_policy global
!
```

Summary

This chapter provided a high-level overview of the deployment of Cisco TelePresence with firewalls deployed internally within a single organizational entity. Internal firewalling might be deployed for a number of reasons including access control within a service module or data center within the enterprise campus; NAT and possible access control between enterprise campuses; access control to and from branch locations to enhance the trust boundary between the enterprise campus and branches; and even access control within a branch location for certain devices. When deploying Cisco TelePresence within an environment with internal firewalling, the network and firewall administrators need to identify the various flows needed between devices to allow TelePresence to correctly operate. These flows include device provisioning flows, call scheduling and service flows, call signaling flows, actual media flows themselves, and management flows. It is hoped that this chapter provided you with a better understanding of these flows and how they need to be allowed through firewalls to successfully deploy the Cisco TelePresence Solution within an environment where internal firewalling is utilized.

Further Reading

Cisco ASA 5500 Series Adaptive Security Appliance Configuration Guides: http://www.tinyurl.com/yrhv8z

Cisco TelePresence uses the *Session Initiation Protocol (SIP)* for all call signaling. SIP is a peer-to-peer application layer protocol used for establishing, modifying, and terminating sessions between endpoints. It was developed by the *Internet Engineering Task Force (IETF) Multiparty Multimedia Session Control (MMUSIC) Working Group* and is currently documented in RFC 3261. This chapter assumes some familiarity with SIP. Chapter 7, "TelePresence Control and Security Protocols," provides a brief overview of SIP. If you are unfamiliar with SIP, review this information before continuing.

Cisco TelePresence can also use encrypted SIP signaling through the use of *Transport Layer Security (TLS)*. Chapter 7 provides an overview of TLS and the security modes in which a TelePresence endpoint can operate. From a SIP signaling standpoint, when the TLS session is established, the SIP signaling proceeds as discussed within this chapter; therefore, the discussion within this chapter also applies to SIP signaling secured with TLS.

CHAPTER 12

TelePresence Call-Signaling Design

Overview of TelePresence Call-Signaling Components

The Cisco TelePresence suite of virtual meeting solutions supports point-to-point and multipoint meetings, both within a single business entity and between businesses. Figure 12-1 shows the components involved in a TelePresence meeting from a signaling standpoint.

These components consist of the following:

- Cisco Unified Communications Manager (CUCM) Cluster

- Two or more Cisco TelePresence System (CTS) Endpoints

- One or more Cisco TelePresence Multipoint Switches (CTMS)

- IP network infrastructure over which the signaling, as well as the audio and video media, are transported

- Cisco Unified Border Element (CUBE)

- Cisco TelePresence Session Border Controller (SBC)

The optional meeting scheduling components that appear in Figure 12-1 are not part of the actual SIP call signaling process and are not be discussed within this chapter.

CUCM: SIP Registrar and Back-to-Back User Agent

CUCM is the core call processing software for the Cisco TelePresence solution and other Cisco IP Telephony devices. From a SIP signaling perspective, CUCM functions as both a Registrar and a *Back-to-Back User Agent (B2BUA)*. By default, CUCM listens on TCP and UDP port 5060 for SIP-related signaling. TCP provides greater reliability because it guarantees delivery of the call signaling packets to endpoints; however, UDP is also still used for endpoints. The benefit of UDP-based SIP signaling is less overhead because a session does not need to be established between endpoints prior to call signaling.

CUCM holds the database of all Cisco TelePresence devices within a particular network. CTS endpoints must first register with CUCM before they can participate within a TelePresence meeting. For CTS endpoints to successfully register, they must be preconfigured within the CUCM cluster. Device registration is accomplished through a SIP REGISTER method that is sent from each CTS endpoint to the CUCM cluster. Periodically the CTS endpoints also reregister with CUCM so that it knows the devices are still active.

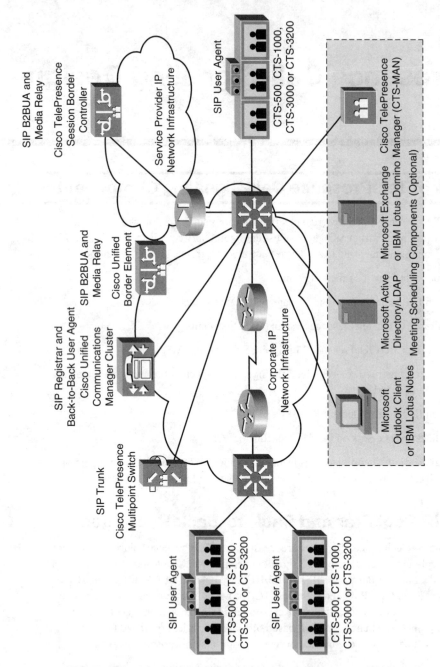

Figure 12-1 *Cisco TelePresence solution components*

CUCM also functions as a B2BUA, processing requests as a *user agent server (UAS)* and generating requests as a *user agent client (UAC)*. Unlike a proxy server, CUCM maintains dialog state and participates in all requests sent on the dialogs it establishes. All SIP call signaling occurs between CTS endpoints and the CUCM cluster; no SIP signaling occurs directly between CTS endpoints in a TelePresence meeting.

Examples of the signaling for a registration, call setup, call hold, and call termination appear within the "Single-Cluster Call Signaling Examples" section of this chapter.

CTS Endpoints: SIP User Agents

A Cisco TelePresence meeting consists of any combination of two or more CTS endpoints. From a signaling perspective, these devices function as SIP User Agents. Although some CTS endpoints, such as the CTS-3000, consist of a primary codec and multiple secondary codecs, only the primary codec of each CTS endpoint participates in SIP signaling. Each CTS endpoint also includes a Cisco Unified 7975G IP Phone, although not shown in Figure 12-1. The IP Phone functions as the user interface for launching, controlling, and concluding the TelePresence meeting. Both the primary codec and the IP Phone register with CUCM, sharing the same dial extension; therefore, for each TelePresence site, there are two devices defined within the CUCM database. Both the CTS endpoint and its associated IP Phone are configured as SIP line devices within CUCM.

CTMS: SIP Trunk

The CTMS connects to the CUCM cluster by way of a SIP trunk. SIP trunks are signaling interfaces and do not use the SIP REGISTER method. Therefore, the CTMS does not register with CUCM, although it does initiate and receive SIP INVITE requests. Thus for SIP trunks, CUCM functions solely as a B2BUA. Route patterns are configured within CUCM to route multipoint calls to the SIP trunks of the multipoint switches.

When configuring SIP trunks within CUCM, the design engineer needs to be aware of possible SIP protocol requirements of the device connected through the SIP trunk. For example, CTMS versions prior to Release 1.1 use only UDP for SIP signaling to and from CUCM. Therefore, the outgoing transport type on the CUCM SIP Trunk Security Profile Configuration must be set for UDP to support these versions. Figure 12-2 shows an example of how this is configured.

Cisco TelePresence SBC and CUBE: B2BUA and Media Proxy

The Cisco TelePresence Session Border Controller (SBC) and Cisco Unified Border Element (CUBE) are application layer gateways that provide SIP B2BUA signaling and media relay services. Typically the SBC will be deployed by a service provider organization, and CUBE will be deployed at the Internet edge of the enterprise organization to provide secure business-to-business TelePresence services. From the standpoint of CUCM, both the SBC and CUBE can appear as a SIP trunk. For TelePresence deployments within a single business entity, the SBC and CUBE are generally not required. The section "Business-to-

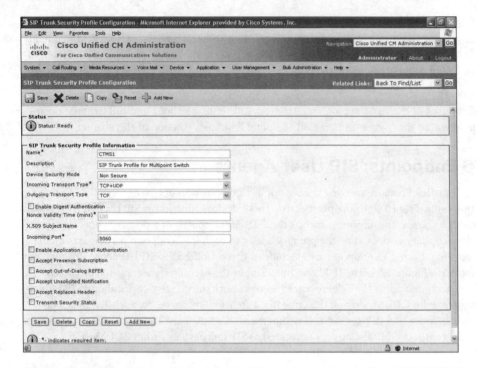

Figure 12-2 *Example configuration of a SIP trunk security profile within CUCM*

Business Signaling," later within this chapter discusses TelePresence deployments with both the SBC and CUBE.

The next sections explore some of the details contained within the SIP signaling between CTS endpoints.

Session Description Protocol

Within the initial SIP INVITE requests, the Cisco TelePresence codec uses the *Session Description Protocol (SDP)*, which IETF RFC 2327 discusses. SDP is a text-based protocol that allows two endpoints that are configured for different audio or video modes to negotiate a common set of media parameters for the call. This is accomplished primarily through the use of the bandwidth (b=...), media (m=...), and attribute (a=...) lines discussed next. The Quality parameter within the TelePresence device configuration in CUCM determines what media capabilities are offered in the initial SDP. The quality parameter has six possible settings:

- Highest Detail, Best Motion: 4 Mbps, 1080p

- Highest Detail, Better Motion: 3.5 Mbps, 1080p

- Highest Detail, Good Motion: 3 Mbps, 1080p

- High Detail, Best Motion: 2.25 Mbps, 720p

- High Detail, Better Motion: 1.5 Mbps, 720p

- High Detail, Good Motion: 1 Mbps, 720p

Because CUCM functions as a B2BUA, it sees the SDP information about the media capabilities of both sides of the TelePresence call. CUCM determines what audio and video parameters are used for the meeting based on the parameters that are common to both TelePresence devices and what is allowed through the configuration within CUCM. The configuration parameters for the allowed audio and video rates are based primarily on the region and location bandwidth settings of the device pool to which the TelePresence devices belong. This allows CUCM to set up a call between two TelePresence devices that are configured for different video modes. For example, if one TelePresence device is configured to support calls up to 1080p mode while another is configured to support only calls up to 720p mode, CUCM sets up the call using 720p mode.

Table 12-1 shows an example SDP session within a SIP INVITE from a CTS endpoint.

Table 12-1   *Example SDP Session Within a SIP INVITE*

SDP Attribute / Value Pair	Description
v=0	Protocol version
o=Cisco-SIPUA 5572 0 IN IP4 10.19.1.11	Originator and session identifier
s=SIP Call	Session name
c=IN IP4 10.19.1.11	Connection information
t=0 0	Time the session is active
a=sendrecv	Session attribute line

m=audio 16384 RTP/AVP 96 0 99 101
b=TIAS:64000
a=rtpmap:96 mpeg4-generic/48000
a=fmtp:96 profile-level-id=16;
streamtype=5;mode=AAC-hbr;config=11B0;
sizeLength=13;indexLength=3;
indexDeltaLength=3;constantDuration=480
a=rtpmap:0 PCMU/8000
a=rtpmap:99 L16/48000
a=rtpmap:101 telephone-event/8000
a=fmtp:101 0-15
	Audio media, bandwidth, and media-level attribute lines

continues

Table 12-1   *Example SDP Session Within a SIP INVITE (continued)*

SDP Attribute / Value Pair	Description
m=video 16388 RTP/AVP 112 b=TIAS:4000000 a=rtpmap:112 H264/90000 a=fmtp:112 profile-level-id=ABCDEF; sprop-parametersets=Z00AKAoWVAPAEPI=, aGFLjyA=;packetization-mode=1	Video media, bandwidth, and media-level attribute lines

Bandwidth Negotiation

The proposed bandwidth usage offered by the CTS endpoint for the TelePresence call is indicated for both audio and video media through the bandwidth (b=...) lines within the SDP. Cisco TelePresence system endpoints offer only a single audio and video stream in the initial SIP INVITE. For example, a CTS-3000 has three codecs, each capable of transmitting 4 Mbps of video simultaneously and up to a total of four 64-kbps audio streams. However, the initial SIP INVITE will propose only 4 Mbps for video and 64 kbps for audio. Upon successful call setup, the CTS endpoints discover each other's video and audio capabilities, which include the number of audio and video streams each is capable of transmitting and receiving. The bandwidth usage is then modified by way of a new SIP INVITE (or re-INVITE) with a new SDP. In this manner the Cisco TelePresence solution can accommodate calls between CTS endpoints with different numbers of screens and yet still have CUCM control overall bandwidth usage.

Media Negotiation

The proposed media usage offered by the CTS endpoint for the TelePresence call is indicated by the media (m=...) lines. The media lines indicate the media type, port by which the media will be transmitted, transport protocol, and one or more media formats. Two media types are transmitted in the SDP for a TelePresence call, one for audio and one for video. The range of ports used by the voice and video media is from 16384 to 32766. At the time this book was written, the proposed port by which the media will be transmitted is typically 16384 for audio and 16386 for video for a point-to-point TelePresence meeting. The transport protocol is the Realtime Transport Protocol using the *Audio/Video Profile (RTP/AVP)* over UDP. The media formats are typically media payload types defined within the RTP/AVP. The media attribute lines (a=...) discussed in the next section provide further information regarding media formats.

TelePresence uses a single RTP audio stream and a single H.264 over RTP video stream in each direction, for a total of four RTP media streams per bidirectional point-to-point TelePresence meeting. This holds true regardless of the model of CTS device. With CTS-3000 devices, the video streams from the multiple codecs multiplex into a single RTP stream. Likewise, the audio streams multiplex into a single audio stream. The auxiliary video and audio streams also multiplex into these streams.

> **Note:**   TelePresence endpoints also send an RTCP control stream for each RTP stream. RTCP streams can use the next higher (odd) UDP port associated with each RTP stream, or can muliplexed within the RTP stream as well.

Because CUCM functions as a B2BUA, it sees the SDP information about the media capabilities of both sides of the TelePresence call. If the CUCM location and region parameters for the allowed audio and video rates are configured with insufficient bandwidth to accommodate the video media but are configured with sufficient bandwidth for the audio media, CUCM might negotiate the call to go through as an audio-only call by way of the SDP it generates to the remote site—if configured to do so.

Other Negotiated Parameters

The media attribute lines (a=...) provide further information that might be required to decode certain media formats. These might include the encoding name and clock rate. For example, the line

```
a=rtpmap:112 H264/90000
```

from Table 12-1 indicates that video media is encoded using the ITU-T H.264 standard at a clock rate of 90,000 Hz. Other media attribute lines beginning with

```
a=fmtp...
```

provide even more information specific to the particular format that are not interpreted by SDP. These provide additional information such as the packetization mode that transmits the H.264 video media over RTP.

CTS Boot Process

Although the CTS boot process is technically not part of the SIP signaling, it has been included for reference within this chapter. Figure 12-3 shows an example of the high-level data flows in the boot process.

As Figure 12-3 shows, the 7975G IP Phone connects directly to the primary codec of the CTS unit. The power-over-Ethernet (PoE) connection powers the IP Phone. Therefore, when you power the primary codec on or restart, the IP Phone also starts. When the devices boot, they send *Cisco Discovery Protocol (CDP)* packets to advertise their existence to the upstream Cisco Catalyst switch to which the primary codec directly attaches. CDP is a Layer 2 protocol that, among other things, you use to learn with which VLAN the IP Phone and codec should tag their packets. For CTS systems with secondary codecs, such as the CTS-3000, the secondary codecs do not follow the process shown in Figure 12-3. Incidentally, the codec forwards CDP packets from the attached IP Phone to the Catalyst switch. The Catalyst switch also sends its own CDP packets out its interface, which both the codec and attached IP Phone receive.

After learning what VLAN to tag packets, the IP Phone and codec can each optionally send DHCP Requests to obtain IP addresses. If the network information, which includes the IP address, default gateway, DNS server, TFTP server, and so on, have been statically

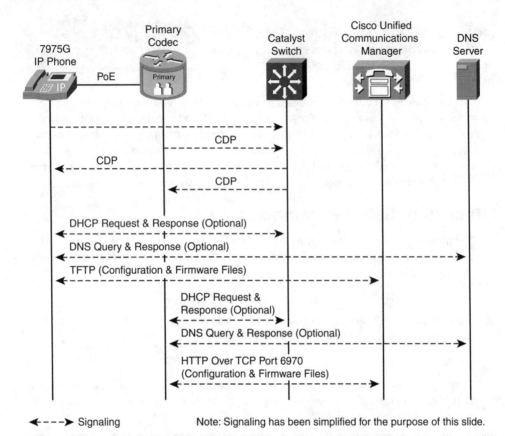

Figure 12-3   *Example Cisco TelePresence boot process*

configured within the devices, DHCP is not necessary and can be disabled within the devices. Figure 12-3 shows an example in which the Cisco Catalyst switch functions as a DHCP server. However, in many network deployments, the Catalyst switch relays DHCP to a centralized server within the data center. One of the critical parameters that the DHCP server provides is the location of the download server that contains the firmware and configuration files of the device. This can be sent to the device via DHCP Option 150, containing either the IP address or the hostname of the download server. In many Cisco IP Telephony deployments, the download server functionality is handled through the TFTP download service of the CUCM.

If the hostname of the CUCM server was provided to the device through DHCP Option 150, or if the hostname of the download server was statically configured within the IP Phone or codec, instead of an IP address, the device needs to query a DNS server to translate the hostname into an IP address, as shown in Figure 12-3.

When the IP address of the download server (CUCM) is known, the IP Phone and codec each request their specific configuration file. The configuration file typically takes the form of

```
SEPxxxxxxxxxxxx.cnf.xml
```

where

SEPxxxxxxxxxxxx

corresponds to the device configured within the CUCM database, and the

xxxxxxxxxxxx

is typically the MAC address of the codec or IP Phone. The IP Phone uses TFTP to download its configuration. The CTS unit, however, uses TCP to download its configuration file. The CTS unit establishes an HTTP connection over TCP port 6970 to the download server (CUCM) to get the specific XML file containing its configuration. Within the XML configuration file, there is an element similar to the following example:

```
<loadInformation>SIPTS.1-2-1-1025D-k9.sbn</loadInformation>
```

This contains the current firmware load that the codec or IP Phone should be running. If the firmware load that the device is currently running does not match this version, the codec and IP Phone proceed to download the new firmware version and reboot with the new version. Firmware loads are copied from the primary codec to the secondary codecs for those CTS units with secondary codecs.

The configuration file for the device generates automatically when you add the device to the CUCM database and dynamically updates when the configuration changes within CUCM. When the configuration changes within the CUCM database, the administrator has the option to reset or restart the device from CUCM. Changes to the device configurations are not dynamically pushed out to the devices themselves. The devices request the new configuration files only when they are reset or restarted. The one exception to this is when the codec or IP Phone first performs a SIP REGISTER with CUCM. Immediately after registration, CUCM sends a SIP NOTIFY message to the device containing a *service-control* event. The action specified within the event will be **action=check-version**, which instructs the codec or IP Phone to check its configuration file version to verify that it is the latest configuration. This action is necessary to maintain the current version in situations where the codec or IP Phone loses and then reestablishes connection to CUCM without rebooting.

When the codec and IP Phone receives its configuration and finishes booting, it can begin the SIP registration process with CUCM.

Single-Cluster Call Signaling Examples

The following sections provide examples of SIP signaling within a single CUCM cluster for registration, call setup, call hold, and call termination between Cisco TelePresence devices.

CTS Endpoint Registration

As mentioned previously, the 7975G IP Phones that function as the user interface for the TelePresence solution also register with CUCM, sharing the same dial extension as the TelePresence codecs. Figure 12-4 shows an example of the high-level data flows in the registration process.

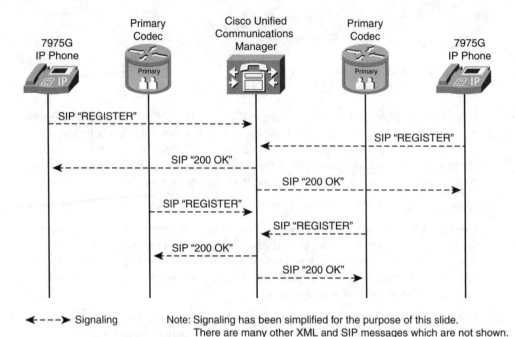

Figure 12-4 *Example Cisco TelePresence device registration*

Each TelePresence primary codec and its associated IP Phone send a SIP REGISTER request to CUCM, which acknowledges each request via a SIP 200 OK message sent back to the device. CUCM does not maintain an open TCP connection to each registered device; therefore, each device has to periodically reregister with CUCM. By default the registration period is 3600 seconds or 6 minutes. Table 12-2 shows some of the more relevant SIP

Table 12-2 *Example SIP Timers Within CUCM*

CUCM Timer	Value	Description
Timer Register Expires	Default: 3600 sec	Specifies the value that the SIP endpoint sends in the Expires header of the REGISTER message.
Timer Register Delta	Default: 5 sec Min: 0 sec Max: Less than the Timer Register Expires value	Parameter used in conjunction with the Timer Register Expires setting. The SIP endpoint reregisters at Timer Register Delta seconds before the registration period ends.
Timer Invite Expires	Default: 180 sec	Specifies the time after which a SIP INVITE expires.
Timer T1	Default: 500 msec	Specifies the lowest value of the retransmission timer for SIP messages.

Table 12-2 *Example SIP Timers Within CUCM*

CUCM Timer	Value	Description
Timer T2	Default: 4000 msec	Specifies the highest value of the retransmission timer for SIP messages.
Retry INVITE	Default: 6 times	Specifies the maximum number of times that an INVITE request retransmits.
Retry Non-INVITE	Default: 10 times	Specifies the maximum number of times that a SIP message, other than an INVITE request, retransmits.

timers and number of times a particular request is retried. These parameters can be set within CUCM through a SIP profile that associates with the TelePresence primary codec and IP Phone.

For the most part, simply accept the default timers and retry numbers in the Standard SIP Profile that is assigned by default to any SIP device created within CUCM.

The contact header within the SIP REGISTER method provides the IP address, transport protocol, port number, and dial extension for CUCM to reach the TelePresence Codecs and IP Phones. This information embeds at the application level. When working with address translation devices that might exist between the TelePresence endpoints and the CUCM cluster, these devices might also need to translate this information for registration to be successful.

Call Setup

When registration is complete, signaling can begin to establish a meeting between two Cisco TelePresence systems. Figure 12-5 shows a high-level overview of the call establishment signaling between TelePresence codecs, their associated IP Phones, and the CUCM cluster in a point-to-point call.

To make the SIP signaling easier to understand, it has been greatly simplified in Figure 12-5. SIP SUBSCRIBE and NOTIFY messages have been removed from the call flow. These messages primarily update the IP Phones and TelePresence codecs regarding the status of the call. Finally, HTTP messages between TelePresence codecs and the Cisco TelePresence Manager have also been removed. These messages inform the Cisco TelePresence Manager of the beginning and ending of a scheduled TelePresence meeting.

Call setup is initiated when the end user selects, through the interface GUI of the IP Phone, the remote TelePresence location to which to establish a meeting. This causes the IP Phone to generate an XML message to the TelePresence codec. The XML message instructs the TelePresence codec to generate a SIP INVITE request, which is sent to the CUCM cluster.

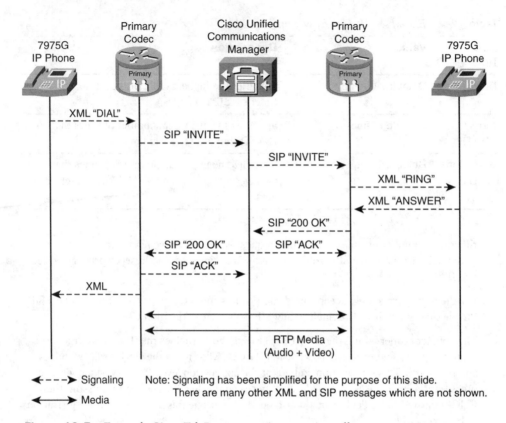

Figure 12-5 *Example Cisco TelePresence point-to-point call setup*

CUCM then generates a new SIP INVITE that is sent to the remote TelePresence codec. Upon receipt of the SIP INVITE, the TelePresence codec informs the IP Phone of the in-coming call through an XML message. The end user at the remote location accepts the in-coming call through the GUI of the IP Phone. This causes an XML message to be sent to the remote TelePresence codec, informing it to answer the call. Alternatively, the dial ex-tension is configured with the auto-answer feature enabled. This allows the remote site to answer the call without end user intervention. Note also that the XML service running on the IP Phone that initiated the call is updated when the call is established.

Within the call signaling, CUCM informs each CTS endpoint of the IP address of the other endpoint so that audio and video media can be sent directly between them. Because the same dial extension is shared between the remote TelePresence codec and the remote IP Phone that functions as its user interface, CUCM generates the new SIP INVITE mes-sage to both remote devices. However, only the TelePresence codec responds to the invite with a SIP 200 OK message.

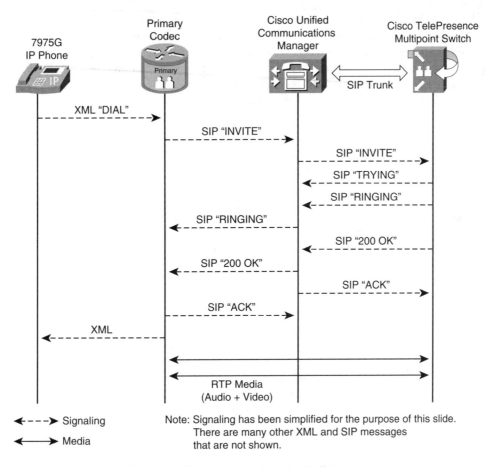

Figure 12-6   *Example Cisco TelePresence Multipoint Call Setup*

From a design perspective, you can locate the CUCM cluster anywhere within the network, although best practices suggest locating the CUCM cluster behind a firewall within the data center because the TelePresence video and audio media do not flow through the CUCM cluster. Therefore, the positioning of the CUCM cluster does not affect the end-to-end delay or jitter seen by the CTS units during TelePresence calls.

Figure 12-6 shows the SIP call signaling involved in the setup of a multipoint call.

From the perspective of SIP call signaling and the audio and video media flows, a multipoint TelePresence meeting appears similar to multiple point-to-point calls between CTS endpoints and the CTMS.

Finally, Cisco TelePresence embeds the audio and video media endpoint addresses within the SIP call signaling messages as well. This has implications for firewalls and network address translation. For a firewall to determine the IP addresses and ports to dynamically open to allow the audio and video media through, the firewall might need to monitor the SIP signaling flow. Also IP address translation might pose issues because the addressing received by the remote TelePresence device might not represent a routable IP address to the routers and Layer 3 switches at the remote site. This is of particular concern with business-to-business TelePresence deployments. Devices such as the CUBE and SBC might be necessary to facilitate call signaling. Chapter 11, "TelePresence Firewall Design," and Chapter 14, "Intercompany TelePresence Design," provide more detailed information regarding address translation and SIP inspection within intracompany and intercompany TelePresence deployments.

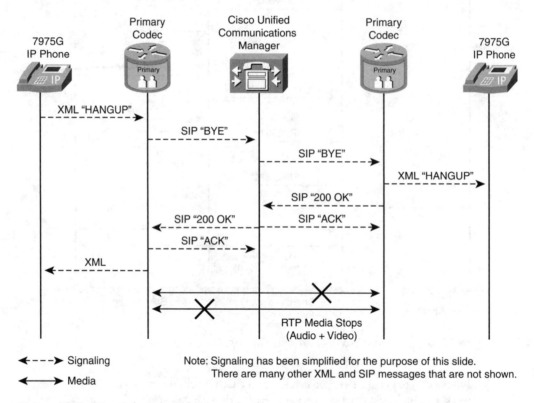

Figure 12-7   *Example Cisco TelePresence call termination*

Call Termination

Figure 12-7 shows a high-level overview of the call termination signaling between the TelePresence codecs, the IP Phones that function as their user interfaces, and the CUCM cluster.

To make the SIP signaling easier to understand, it has again been greatly simplified in Figure 12-7. Call termination begins when the end user at one end of a TelePresence meeting uses the GUI of the IP Phone to end the meeting. This causes the IP Phone to send an XML message to the TelePresence codec, instructing it to hang up the call by generating a SIP BYE message. The SIP BYE message is sent to CUCM, which then generates a new SIP

BYE message to the remote TelePresence codec. The remote TelePresence codec informs
the IP Phone at the remote site that the call is terminating. Upon receipt of the SIP 200
OK messages from the TelePresence codecs, the audio and video media streams stop.

Because CUCM functions as a B2BUA that maintains state of all SIP calls initiated and terminated through it, it can capture call detail records of when TelePresence meetings start
and stop. This might be necessary for management systems and for billing charges for
TelePresence meetings back to individual departments.

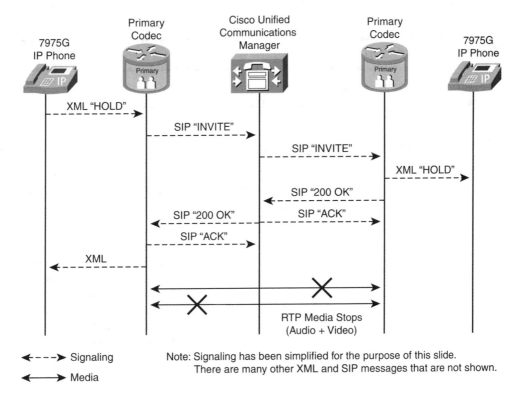

Figure 12-8   *Example Cisco TelePresence call hold*

Call Hold

Any modifications to the TelePresence call, such as a CTS endpoint going on hold, are signaled through a new SIP INVITE request that is sent to the CUCM. Figure 12-8 shows a
high-level overview of the call signaling when a point-to-point TelePresence call is placed
on hold.

A call hold is initiated when the end user selects the hold option, through the GUI of the
7975G IP phone. This causes the IP Phone to generate an XML message to the TelePresence codec. The XML message instructs the TelePresence codec to generate a new SIP IN-
VITE request, which is sent to the CUCM cluster. This new SIP INVITE modifies the

existing session between the two CTS endpoints. CUCM, in turn, generates a new SIP IN-VITE that is sent to the remote TelePresence codec. Upon receipt of the SIP INVITE, the remote TelePresence codec informs the IP Phone of the call going on hold through an XML message. Within the call signaling, CUCM informs each CTS endpoint to stop sending audio and video media between them.

When the end user takes the call off hold, another SIP INVITE method generates, again modifying the existing session between the two CTS endpoints. The SIP signaling instructs the CTS endpoints to again begin sending audio and video media between them.

Intercluster Call Signaling

The following sections discuss TelePresence call signaling between CUCM clusters, both within a single enterprise organization and between separate business entities.

Single Enterprise Signaling

TelePresence call signaling between CUCM clusters within a single enterprise organization can be accomplished by simply defining a SIP trunk between CUCM clusters. Figure 12-9 shows an example of the SIP signaling.

As with the multipoint configuration with a CTMS, route patterns are configured within each CUCM to route intercluster TelePresence calls to the SIP trunk that connects the two CUCM clusters. In Figure 12-9, the RTP streams carrying the audio and video media do not pass through the CUCM clusters but are sent directly between CTS endpoints, as in a single CUCM cluster TelePresence deployment. This example assumes unrestricted IP connectivity within the enterprise organization. Enterprise environments that implement firewalling and potentially even address translation internally within their networks might want to deploy a TelePresence call signaling model more similar to that shown in the next section.

Business-to-Business Signaling

Business-to-business TelePresence deployments require an application layer gateway to provide secure connectivity between separate business entities. Often, the TelePresence meeting is encrypted for additional security. As mentioned previously in the chapter, the CUBE and SBC are application layer gateways that provide B2BUA functionality and media relay services within a business-to-business TelePresence deployment. Figure 12-10 shows an example of the SIP signaling involved in a business-to-business TelePresence deployment.

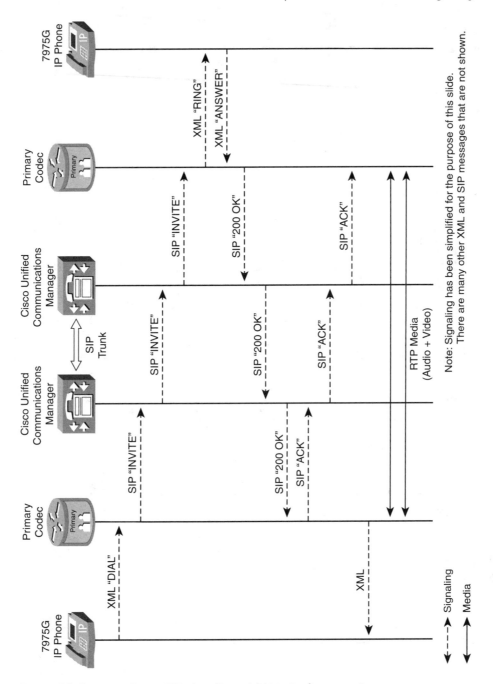

Figure 12-9 *Inter cluster SIP signaling within a single enterprise*

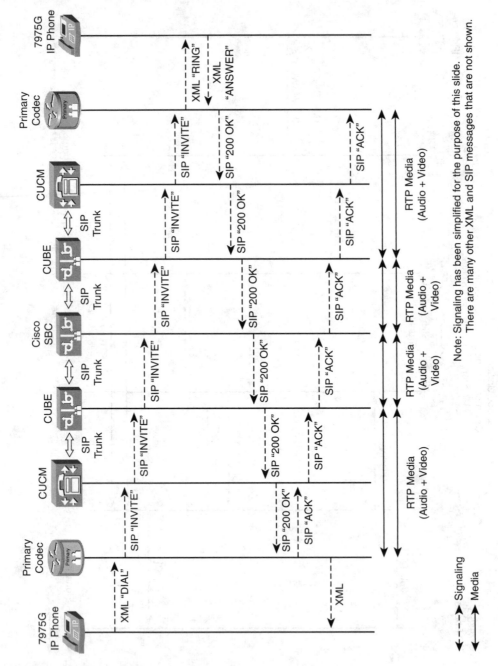

Figure 12-10 *Inter cluster SIP signaling between enterprises*

Typically the SBC is within the network of a service provider that provides business-to-business TelePresence services to enterprise customers. The CUBE, however, generally is within the enterprise Internet edge. Firewalls will typically be deployed at the Internet edge of the enterprise network to allow only SIP signaling and the RTP media connectivity between the enterprise CUBE and the SBC within the service provider network.

Within the business-to-business TelePresence deployment, a SIP trunk is defined between the CUCM cluster of each enterprise and the CUBE. Off-net route patterns are configured within CUCM to route business-to-business TelePresence calls to the SIP trunk and over to the SBC. In Figure 12-10, the RTP streams carrying the audio and video media do pass through the CUBE and SBC, which act as media relay points between the enterprise locations.

Summary

The Cisco TelePresence solution uses SIP for all call signaling, although an XML service is utilized between the IP 7975G phone and the primary codec of TelePresence endpoints to initiate and terminate calls. From a signaling perspective, CUCM functions as a SIP Registrar and a Back-to-Back User Agent (B2BUA). CTS endpoints function as SIP User Agents. Finally, the Cisco TelePresence Multipoint Switch (CTMS) appears to CUCM as a SIP trunk. TelePresence uses Session Description Protocol (SDP) within SIP INVITE messages to negotiate bandwidth, media, and other parameters between devices within a TelePresence meeting. Intercluster SIP signaling can be accomplished by defining SIP trunks between CUCM clusters for a single enterprise organization. For intercluster SIP signaling between multiple business entities, the Cisco Unified Border Element (CUBE) and Session Border Controller (SBC), which function as B2BUAs and media relay points, are necessary to ensure secure business-to-business TelePresence services.

Further Reading

IETF Standards:

Session Initiation Protocol (SIP): http://www.ietf.org/rfc/rfc3261
Session Description Protocol (SDP): http://www.ietf.org/rfc/rfc2327

Multipoint TelePresence extends the virtual meeting experience, allowing three or more CTS endpoints to participate in a single conference. Cisco Multipoint TelePresence uses a centralized switching model where each CTS endpoint sends unicast audio and video streams to a multipoint switch. The multipoint switch mixes the streams and transmits audio and video streams back to each CTS endpoint. Figure 13-1 shows the components involved in a multipoint meeting.

Depending upon whether the TelePresence virtual meeting includes only CTS endpoints or also includes traditional video conferencing or desktop video conferencing endpoints, the required components differ. The right side of Figure 13-1 shows the components required for a multipoint meeting that consists of Cisco TelePresence endpoints only. The components are as follows:

- **Cisco TelePresence Multipoint Switch (CTMS):** Provides switching of the audio and video media streams.

- **Cisco TelePresence Systems (CTS) endpoints:** Any combination of three or more CTS endpoints such as the CTS-500, CTS-1000, CTS-3000, or CTS-3200.

- **Cisco Unified Communications Manager (CUCM) cluster:** Provides call signaling and control for the CTS endpoints.

- **IP infrastructure:** Provides transport of the call signaling, voice, and video media.

- **Meeting scheduling components:** Optional components consisting of the Cisco TelePresence Manager (CTS-MAN), Microsoft Exchange or IBM Lotus Domino Server, LDAP/Microsoft Active Directory Server, and PCs running Microsoft Outlook or IBM Lotus Notes client.

CHAPTER 13

Multipoint TelePresence Design

If legacy or desktop video conferencing systems are required for the virtual meeting, the components on the left side of Figure 13-1 might be required in addition to the components in the preceding list. These additional components include the following:

- **Cisco Unified Video Conferencing (CUVC) 3500 Series Multipoint Control Unit (MCU):** Provides switching and transcoding of the legacy audio and video media streams.

- **Legacy video conferencing systems:** One or more LAN, PSTN, or ISDN-based systems.

- **Desktop video conferencing systems:** One or more hardware-based video conferencing systems such as the Cisco IP Phone 7985G, software-based video conferencing systems such as Cisco Unified Video Advantage (CUVA), or Cisco Unified Personal Communicator (CUPC) running on a PC. A separate IP Phone can be also used for audio with CUVA.

- **Cisco gateway:** Optional component for interoperability between H.323 (LAN-based) and H.320 (ISDN-based) or H.324 (POTS-based) video conferencing systems.

- **Cisco IOS gatekeeper:** Optional component for E.164 address resolution, call routing, and call admission control of H.323 based systems.

CTMS Overview

The *Cisco TelePresence Multipoint Switch (CTMS)* is the central component of all multipoint meetings. It is a purpose built appliance that provides low-latency video and audio switching, typically adding less than 10ms of delay to any multipoint meeting. CTMS provides a scalable architecture, supporting up to 48 simultaneous table segments in one or more meetings as of software version 1.1. A table segment is defined as a display and camera on any CTS system. For example, CTS-3000 and CTS-3200 systems consist of three table segments, whereas CTS-1000 and CTS-500 systems consist of a single table segment. CTMS provides system management through Secure Shell (SSH), Hypertext Transfer Protocol over Secure Sockets Layer (HTTPS), Simple Network Management Protocol (SNMP), and Cisco Discovery Protocol (CDP).

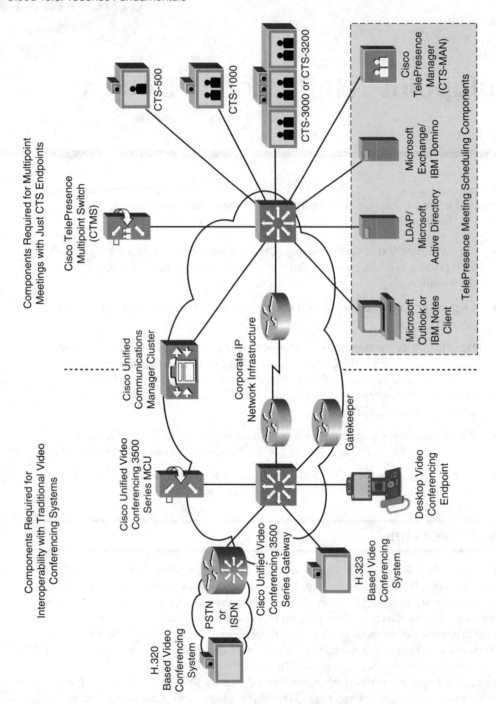

Figure 13-1   *Cisco multipoint TelePresence meeting components*

CTMS Meeting Types

The CTMS supports multiple meeting types, providing users with a number of scheduled and nonscheduled meetings to choose from based on their requirements. CTMS supports scheduled meetings, nonscheduled (static or ad hoc) meetings, or a combination of both meeting types in a single deployment environment. Figure 13-2 shows the Meetings Management screen of a CTMS, in which the various types of meetings can be configured.

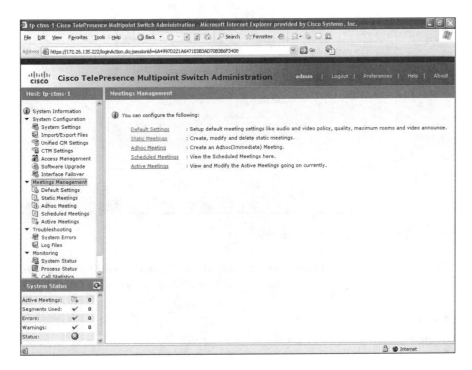

Figure 13-2 *CTMS Meetings Management screen*

Static Meetings

Static meetings are nonscheduled meetings configured on the CTMS through the administrative GUI. Static meetings are always available to any CTS room. They are accessed by manually dialing the static meeting telephone number or using a speed dial entry on the Cisco IP Phone associated with the CTS device within the TelePresence room. A meeting scheduler or administrator can add additional CTS rooms to the meeting at any time using the CTMS administrative GUI. The meeting scheduler or administrator also determines the meeting features for the static meeting. Figure 13-3 shows an example configuration of a static meeting.

Static meetings can be hosted or nonhosted. Hosted static meetings require the meeting scheduler or administrator to pre-assign a host room that is needed to start the meeting. All meeting rooms that dial in before the host room are placed on hold until the host room

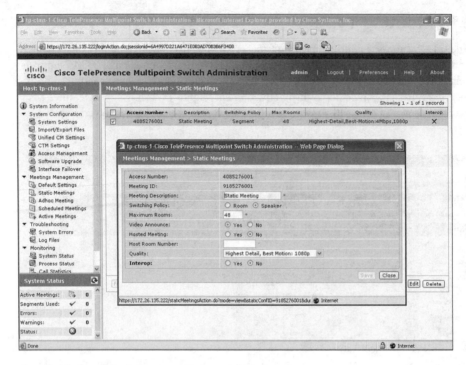

Figure 13-3   *CTMS Static Meetings configuration*

joins the meeting. All rooms are disconnected when the host room leaves the meeting. The CTMS Meeting Features section discusses the additional features shown in Figure 13-3.

Ad Hoc Meetings

Ad hoc meetings are nonscheduled, administrator-initiated, dial-out meetings. A meeting scheduler or administrator initiates the meeting through the CTMS administrative GUI. The CTMS dials out to each of the rooms, thereby requiring no end user interaction. Ad hoc meetings cannot be accessed by dialing in from a CTS system. Rooms must be added by the meeting scheduler or administrator using the CTMS administrative GUI.

Scheduled Meetings

Multipoint TelePresence meetings are scheduled by end users using any Microsoft Exchange or Lotus Domino client in the same manner that point-to-point meetings are scheduled. Scheduled meetings require no CTMS administrator interaction. CTS Manager is a required component for scheduled meetings. It provides the interface between Microsoft Exchange or IBM Lotus Domino and the CTMS, allowing the appropriate resources on the CTMS to be reserved for the multipoint meeting.

Scheduled meetings can be accessed by using the one-button-to-push meeting access feature. The meeting scheduler or administrator can add additional rooms to active scheduled meetings at any time during the meeting, using the CTMS administrative GUI.

CTMS Meeting Features

The CTMS supports a number of meeting features that provide flexibility and security for multipoint meetings. The following sections discuss these features in detail.

Switching Policy

The switching policy has two choices:

- **Room switching:** Applies to multipoint calls that include CTS endpoints with multiple cameras and displays, such as the CTS-3200 and the CTS-3000

- **Speaker switching:** Applies to all CTS endpoints

Room switching switches the video from all table segments of a particular room to all other rooms in the multipoint meeting. For CTS endpoints with multiple screens, if the active room changes, all table segments in the new active room display in all other rooms at the same time, replacing the previously active room. Figure 13-4 shows an example of room switching with CTS-3000s.

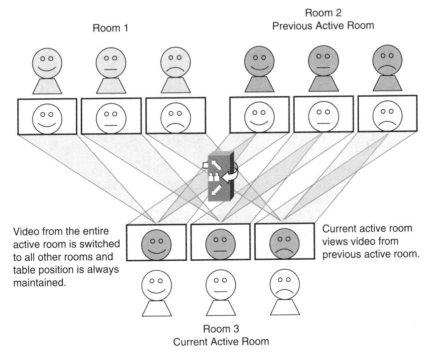

Figure 13-4 *Room switching with CTS-3000s*

Speaker switching enables each table segment to be switched independently so that at any given time a room might be viewing three different speakers in three different rooms. The new active speaker's table segment displays in all other rooms in its proper position. Figure 13-5 shows an example of speaker switching with CTS-1000s and CTS-3000s.

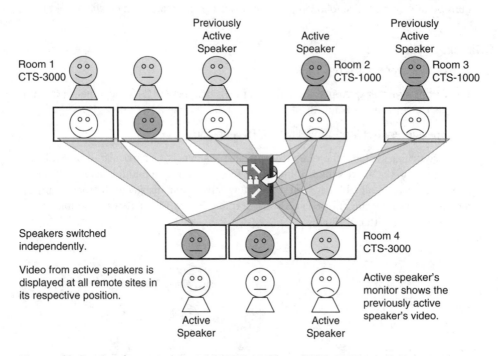

Figure 13-5 *Speaker switching with CTS-1000s and CTS-3000s*

Maximum Number of Rooms

The Maximum Rooms setting allows the administrator to limit the number of rooms allowed to join the meeting. The maximum number of rooms supported within a single meeting, and by the CTMS overall, is dependent upon the software version of the CTMS. For example, CTMS version 1.1 supports a maximum of 48 rooms, assuming single screen systems, or 16 rooms assuming three screen systems.

Video Announce

The Video Announce feature causes a Cisco TelePresence room that joins the conference to display to all other rooms for approximately two seconds. This prevents a muted room from joining without being noticed.

Lock Meeting

A meeting scheduler or administrator can lock a meeting through the administrative GUI only after a meeting is in progress. This prevents any additional rooms from joining the meeting. Additional TelePresence systems can be added to a meeting that is locked but only by the meeting scheduler or administrator through the administrative GUI. Figure

13-6 shows an example of how a meeting can be locked through the Active Meetings screen of the particular meeting, in this case an ongoing static meeting.

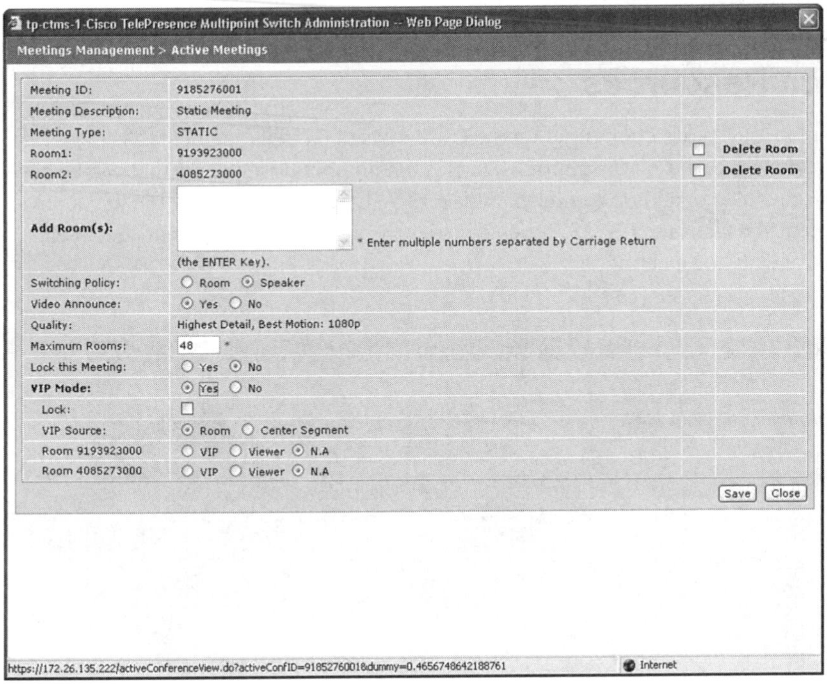

Figure 13-6   *Active Meetings detail screen*

Quality

The Quality setting enables the configuration of video resolution (1080p or 720p along with best, better, or good motion) on a per-call basis. Figure 13-3, shown previously, also shows the configuration of the Quality setting within a meeting. Meetings must be configured to support the lowest resolution Cisco TelePresence room participating in the multipoint meeting because the CTMS does not perform any transcoding or transrating. Cisco TelePresence systems have the capability to negotiate down from 1080p to 720p, enabling systems configured for 1080p to join a meeting configured for 720p. However, Cisco TelePresence Systems configured for 720p cannot negotiate up to 1080p and, therefore, will not connect to a meeting configured for 1080p.

VIP Mode

VIP Mode is a switching feature that is useful for meetings in which one room or table segment of a room is more important than the rest of the rooms. VIP Mode can be configured using either a *hard-lock* or *soft-lock*. When using a hard-lock, the video from the VIP room or table segment is always displayed at the other rooms, regardless of who is the active speaker. When using a soft-lock, the video from the VIP room or table segment is temporarily switched when a speaker at another room talks but is automatically switched back after the speaker stops talking, without the VIP site having to talk. This ensures the focus of the meeting is always on the VIP room. Figure 13-6, shown previously, also shows how the configuration of VIP Mode can be set within an active meeting by the meeting scheduler or administrator.

Multipoint Resources

Multipoint resources are configured on the CTMS based on table segments. As mentioned previously, each CTMS supports a maximum number of segments that can be allocated for scheduled or ad hoc meetings. Figure 13-7 shows an example of the Resource Management screen of the CTMS, which controls the allocation of segments between scheduled and ad hoc meetings.

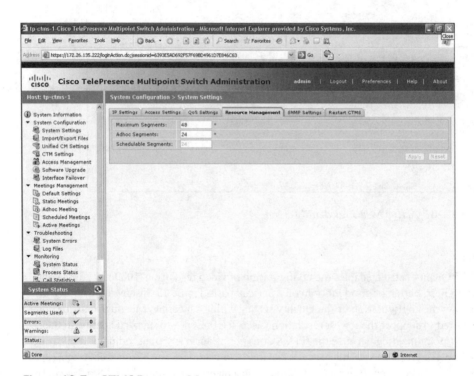

Figure 13-7 *CTMS Resource Management screen*

The CTMS Resource Management screen includes resources as follows:

- **Maximum segments:** The total number of segments supported on a CTMS. This field limits the number of segments supported on the CTMS below the maximum capacity if desired.

- **Ad hoc segments:** The number of segments available for nonscheduled meetings. Ad hoc segments are also used for any nonscheduled CTS endpoints added to a scheduled multipoint meeting through the CTMS administrative GUI.

■ **Schedulable segments:** The number of schedulable segments is used by CTS Manager to track available segments for scheduled multipoint meetings. This number is automatically calculated by subtracting the ad hoc segments from the maximum segments. Because of this, it is not possible to oversubscribe a CTMS such that the sum of the ad hoc segments and the schedulable segments exceed the maximum segments. The CTMS cannot dynamically reallocate segments between the two pools, either. For example, if the number of ad hoc segments required for meetings exceeds the configured capacity, the CTMS cannot temporarily "borrow" segments from the schedulable segments pool, even if they are not currently in use. Instead the sites that exceed the ad hoc segment pool will not be allowed to join their respective meetings.

Geographical Resource Management

Geographical resource management is an essential component for larger TelePresence deployments. When multiple CTMS devices are available in a multipoint deployment, multipoint meetings must be hosted on the appropriate CTMS based on proximity to CTS endpoints. This helps regionalize multipoint meetings, conserves bandwidth between regions, and ensures the lowest latency for each meeting.

Geographical resource management requires the Cisco TelePresence Manager (CTS-MAN) and is available only for scheduled meetings. As of CTMS version 1.1, geographical selection is based upon time zones. For each scheduled multipoint meeting, CTS-MAN calculates the arithmetic mean GMT of the scheduled CTS endpoints, checks for available resources on the selected CTMS, and schedules the meeting. If there are no resources available on the selected CTMS, CTS-MAN works its way down the list of CTMS devices until available resources are found. Figure 13-8 illustrates the CTMS selection process.

Note that the time zone of each CTS endpoint is determined by the Date/Time Group to which it is assigned within the CUCM configuration.

Although the current method for providing geographic resource management does provides significant benefits about selecting the appropriate CTMS for multipoint meetings, future versions might base geographical resource management on other factors. For instance, one method might be to base the decision upon predetermined relationships between the CTS endpoint region configuration and the region configuration of the CTMS within CUCM.

Quality of Service

The DSCP markings for CTS endpoint media (audio and video), signaling from the CTMS, and CUVC media for interoperability with legacy video conferencing systems, are controlled through the QoS Settings screen within the CTMS. Chapter 6, "Network Quality of Service Technologies," provides a discussion of the QoS recommendations around Cisco TelePresence. Cisco recommends the DSCP marking for audio and video media from the CTMS be CS4, based on IETF RFC 4594. Likewise the recommended DSCP marking for SIP signaling from the CTMS is CS3. This is consistent with recommendations for CTS endpoints defined within CUCM for point-to-point TelePresence meetings. Because the typical DSCP marking for standard definition legacy video conferencing systems is recommended to be AF41; the CTMS can mark media destined for the CUVC with a DSCP setting of AF41 as well.

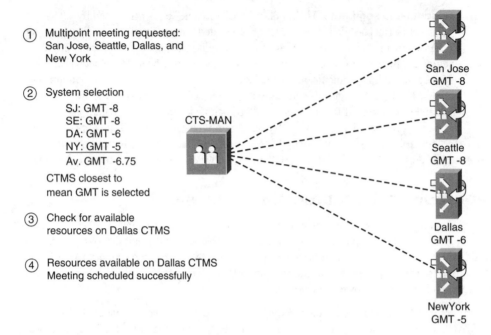

① Multipoint meeting requested:
San Jose, Seattle, Dallas, and
New York

② System selection
  SJ: GMT -8
  SE: GMT -8
  DA: GMT -6
  NY: GMT -5
  Av. GMT -6.75
CTMS closest to
mean GMT is selected

③ Check for available
resources on Dallas CTMS

④ Resources available on Dallas CTMS
Meeting scheduled successfully

CTS-MAN

San Jose
GMT -8

Seattle
GMT -8

Dallas
GMT -6

NewYork
GMT -5

Figure 13-8   *CTMS selection example*

Note   If no resources are available in Dallas, the next closest CTMS is selected (San Jose GMT-8)

Meeting Security

Meetings must provide the appropriate level of security for participants. TelePresence meeting security can be broken down into three broad categories:

- Administrative access control

- Meeting access control

- Meeting confidentiality

The sections that follow discuss these categories in greater detail.

Administrative Access Control

The CTMS includes three roles that provide three levels of administrative access control:

- Administrator

- Meeting scheduler

- Diagnostic technician

Multiple instances of each role (that is, multiple administrators, meeting schedulers, and diagnostic technicians) can be defined within a single CTMS. For each of the three administrative roles, passwords are stored through the local database within the CTMS.

Only the administrator and meeting scheduler roles have the ability to schedule meetings. Because administrators have full access to the CTMS, recommended practice dictates restricting this role to a limited set of individuals. Multiple meeting schedulers can be defined within the CTMS. Any meeting scheduler has access to all meeting resources within the CTMS.

Meeting Access Control

As previously stated, the CTMS provides static, ad hoc, and scheduled meetings, each providing different levels of access control to join the meeting. Scheduled and ad hoc meetings are inherently secure, not allowing uninvited Cisco TelePresence rooms to randomly dial into a meeting. Cisco TelePresence rooms can be added to these meetings after the call is in progress, but only by a meeting scheduler or administrator through the CTMS administrative GUI. Static meetings are less secure than scheduled and ad hoc meetings because any room can dial into them at any time. Configuring a hosted static meeting adds a measure of security, in that the host room must at least attend for the conference to begin.

Additional features can be added to multipoint meetings to provide a level of meeting access control. The Video Announce feature forces each new room entering the conference to be visible to the other rooms for approximately two seconds. This minimizes the chance of an unauthorized room "lurking" in the multipoint meeting. Selecting a static meeting in which the number of rooms defined for the static meeting, through the Maximum Rooms parameter, matches the number of rooms for the conference, minimizes the chance of an unauthorized room accessing the call. Finally, having a meeting scheduler or administrator lock the meeting guarantees that no unauthorized rooms can join a meeting when it is ongoing.

Meeting Confidentiality

CTMS software version 1.1 does not support encryption for multipoint meetings, although the CTS endpoints themselves do support encryption for point-to-point meetings. Therefore, one method of providing meeting confidentiality for multipoint TelePresence meetings running software version 1.1 and earlier is to provide encryption between sites through network components (that is, IPsec encryption). CTMS software version 1.5 will include the capability of the CTMS to support encryption.

Meeting Management

Multipoint meeting management is available through the CTMS Web interface, allowing administrators to monitor and or modify active multipoint meetings. The Active Meetings screen, shown in Figure 13-9, allows the administrator to view active meeting details and participants.

Administrators can also add or remove a room, change the switching policy, enable or disable video announce, and enable or disable VIP mode on any active multipoint meeting by selecting the meeting and editing it. Figure 13-6, shown previously, demonstrated an example of this.

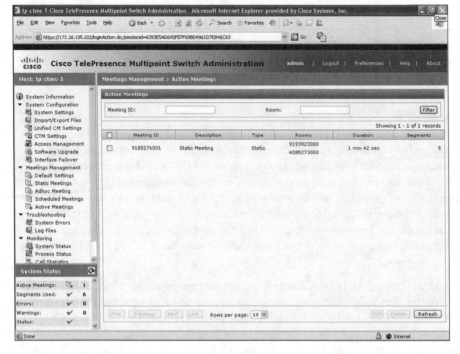

Figure 13-9　*CTMS Active Meetings screen*

Audio and Video Flows in a Multipoint TelePresence Design

To help control bandwidth utilization use during multipoint meetings, the CTMS implements a flow control feature. After the multipoint meeting is initiated and the active table segments have been established, the CTMS instructs CTS endpoints to stop transmitting video for table segments that are not currently displayed. CTMS uses audio to determine when an inactive table segment becomes active. At that point, the CTMS instructs the CTS system to start transmitting video again for the newly active table segment. This process is continued throughout the meeting, helping reduce overall bandwidth consumption for the multipoint meeting.

Audio in a Multipoint TelePresence Meeting

Audio from all TelePresence conference participants is always sent to the CTMS, regardless of whether the room has any audio energy (that is, someone is speaking). Each microphone of a CTS unit transmits a single 64-kbps RTP/AAC audio stream, excluding network protocol overhead. An additional audio stream can be sent from either the auxiliary audio input or through the audio add-in feature, which can add either a single phone or an audio conferencing bridge into the TelePresence virtual meeting. If multiple audio-only devices need to be added into a TelePresence multipoint meeting, it is more effective to add an audio bridge, rather than have multiple rooms each add individual phones.

Because audio is continuously sent from each CTS endpoint to the CTMS, there can be multiple simultaneous speakers in a multipoint conference. The CTMS replicates up to three audio streams to each CTS endpoint, even though the CTS endpoint might have only one speaker. Each CTS endpoint mixes the inbound audio to be sent to its speakers. Therefore, the number of audio streams outbound from the CTMS in a single multipoint meeting varies based upon how many speakers are talking.

Video in a Multipoint TelePresence Meeting

Unlike audio, video is not continuously transmitted from each CTS endpoint camera to the CTMS. Instead, the CTMS signals which camera should send its video. The CTMS determines which video stream to present to TelePresence meeting participants based on which speaker is currently talking. Figure 13-10 shows an example of this in a three-site CTS-1000 TelePresence call.

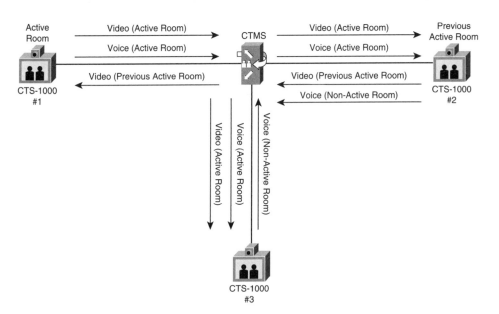

Figure 13-10 *Video flows in a three-site TelePresence call*

In the example illustrated in Figure 13-10, CTS-1000 #1 is the active room. Video from CTS-1000 #1 is, therefore, replicated on a packet-by-packet basis by the CTMS and sent to CTS-1000 #2 and CTS-1000 #3. However, the display of CTS-1000 #1 needs to continue showing video from the previous active room. In this example, the previous active room was CTS-1000 #2; therefore, video from CTS-1000 #2 continues to be sent to the CTMS, where it is replicated on a packet-by-packet basis and sent to CTMS-1000 #1.

Video from the camera inputs is transmitted through H.264 at 30 frames per second (fps). Unlike audio, TelePresence video can be sent at different overall data rates based upon the quality configuration of the CTS endpoints and the CTMS. The maximum data rate can burst up to approximately 4.4 Mbps per camera, excluding network overhead.

Auxiliary Video Input

Any CTS endpoint in a multipoint meeting can also function as a presenter for auxiliary video (for example, PowerPoint slides or video clips) and audio input. However, only one site can be the presenter at a time. The last device to physically connect to the auxiliary video input becomes the presenter. In a multipoint meeting, auxiliary audio and video from the presenter is sent to the CTMS, where it is replicated to all other CTS endpoints.

Cisco TelePresence currently supports two frame rates for auxiliary video input:

■ Low-speed auxiliary video that is transmitted through H.264 at 5fps. The maximum data rate can burst up to approximately 550kbps, excluding network overhead.

■ High-speed auxiliary video input requires a separate codec be added to existing CTS endpoints. High-speed auxiliary video is transmitted through H.264 at 30fps. The maximum data rate can burst up to approximately 4.4Mbps, excluding network overhead.

Note   CTMS software version 1.1 does not support the high-speed auxiliary video input for multipoint meetings, although the CTS endpoints do support it for point-to-point meetings. CTMS software version 1.5 will include the capability of the CTMS to support the high-speed auxiliary video input for multipoint meetings. The high-speed auxiliary video input will count as an additional segment against resources utilized within the CTMS.

The design engineer should be aware that due to the video flow control mechanism discussed earlier, the traffic pattern to and from the CTMS is highly asymmetrical in nature. More traffic will flow outbound from the CTMS site than inbound to the CTMS site. This asymmetric flow pattern is one of the major network differences between multiple point-to-point TelePresence meetings and multipoint TelePresence meetings.

Video Switchover Delay

The CTMS does not immediately signal CTS endpoints to send video upon seeing packets with audio energy. This could cause unnecessary flapping of video within the multipoint meeting and generate additional burstiness on the network. Instead, the CTMS implements a hold down timer before signaling the new active speaker or room to begin sending video. The hold down timer is designed to ensure that the new active speaker or room is indeed speaking, and it is not just random noise.

Participants within a TelePresence multipoint conference should be aware that they might need to talk for approximately two seconds before the video switches over. They should be particularly aware of this when taking a roll-call at the beginning of the meeting for their faces to be seen on the video displays. Note that the audio is never interrupted or delayed.

TelePresence Interoperability

Cisco TelePresence interoperability allows traditional room-based video conferencing systems and desktop video conferencing systems to participate within a Cisco TelePresence virtual meeting. TelePresence and traditional video conferencing are fundamentally different experiences and are typically maintained as separate environments today. Cisco TelePresence is specifically designed to maintain the in-person experience though life-size video of conference participants and spatial audio. However, most traditional room-based video conferencing systems are designed to show the entire room at once, often with only a single accompanying audio channel. As a result, conference participants are scaled to fit within the viewing display area. Likewise, desktop video conferencing systems are typically designed around limiting the amount of bandwidth utilized per device. Camera quality, acoustics, lighting, and background cannot be tightly controlled with desktop video conferencing—limiting the in-person experience.

The Cisco TelePresence interoperability solution retains the rich, immersive experience between Cisco TelePresence participants; while providing a bridge to existing room-based video conferencing and desktop video collaboration systems. This is accomplished by cascading (chaining) the CTMS and the CUVC together. CTMS software version 1.1, CTS software version 1.4, and CTS Manager version 1.4 or higher are required for both static and scheduled meeting support with interoperability.

The interoperability segment is limited to only Common Intermediate Format (CIF) resolution at 30fps in the initial release. CIF has a picture size of 352 x 288 pixels. The CIF video sent by the CUVC 3500 Series MCU, and switched by the CTMS to the CTS endpoint, is scaled to 4CIF (576 x 704 pixels) by the CTS endpoint codecs before being displayed on the TelePresence 65-inch 1080p display. The codec surrounds the remaining space with a black border, as seen in Figure 13-11.

Figure 13-11 *TelePresence interoperability: user experience*

Figure 13-12 shows a high-level view of the call signaling within a TelePresence call with interoperability.

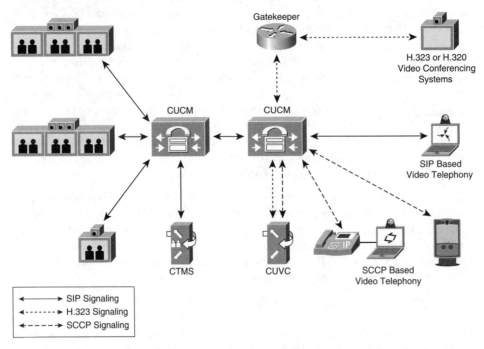

Figure 13-12   *Interoperability call signaling flows*

When the first CTS endpoint joins the static meeting, the CTMS dials out to the CUVC through the CUCM cluster. Separate CUCM clusters are deployed for TelePresence and legacy video conferencing systems. A SIP trunk is established between the CUCM clusters.

Figure 13-13 shows a high-level view of the media flows in a TelePresence virtual meeting that includes interoperability.

In a meeting that includes interoperability, each CTS endpoint sends an additional G.711 encoded audio stream to the CTMS. This is in addition to the normal AAC-LD audio streams sent for noninteroperable TelePresence meetings, previously discussed. The CTS endpoints also receive a G.711 encoded audio stream from the legacy video conferencing endpoints through the CUVC and CTMS.

When a CTS table segment becomes the active speaker, it also sends an additional H.264 Common Intermediate Format (CIF) stream to the CTMS. This standard definition video stream is then cascaded through the CTMS to the CUVC. The CUVC can then transcode that to any video format supported for the meeting by the legacy video conferencing endpoints. When any of the legacy video conferencing endpoints becomes the active speaker, an H.264 CIF stream is sent from the CUVC, through the CTMS, and switched to every CTS endpoint in the virtual meeting.

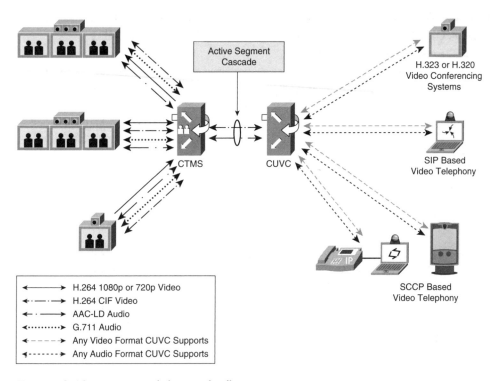

Figure 13-13 *Interoperability media flows*

The net effect of the additional G.711 audio stream and H.264 CIF video stream is approximately 768kbps, excluding network protocol overhead. Therefore, to support interoperability, the network design engineer should plan for approximately 768kbps plus protocol overhead (approximately 20 percent) of additional bandwidth to be provisioned for each CTS site.

The initial version of interoperability was designed this way because Cisco TelePresence endpoints that support multiple screens multiplex RTP streams into a single UDP stream. Many existing video conferencing endpoints currently support only a single screen and do not support the RTP multiplexing. Also, many existing video conferencing endpoints support only standard definition (SD) video. Future versions of Cisco TelePresence might support other methods of interoperability. For example, as more traditional video conferencing systems support high-definition (HD) video and multiple screens, they might interoperate directly with Cisco TelePresence endpoints using standards-based signaling. Alternatively, as more MCUs begin to support the RTP multiplexing of multiple screens, TelePresence endpoints might interoperate directly with these MCUs. These are just two of the possible ways that interoperability could evolve in the future.

Network Design Considerations for Multipoint TelePresence

The addition of multipoint meeting capability to a TelePresence deployment brings additional design decisions and considerations to the network engineer. Among the design decisions is the number of CTMS switches that need to be deployed and whether they are centralized or distributed throughout the network. The deployment model, in turn, influences the amount of additional latency induced within TelePresence meetings and the bandwidth requirements throughout the network. Finally, the introduction of multipoint switches adds additional burst considerations, which the network engineer must take into account. The sections that follow provide greater detail in each of these design decisions and considerations.

Note   Current recommendations are to deploy a separate CUCM cluster dedicated for Cisco TelePresence. The network engineer can deploy a SIP trunk between the TelePresence CUCM cluster and the IP TelePhony cluster, in a similar manner presented in the "Intercluster Call Signaling" section in Chapter 12, "TelePresence Call-Signaling Design." The deployment models discussed in the following sections assume a dedicated CUCM cluster for TelePresence.

Deployment Models

Several factors influence how multipoint TelePresence should be deployed within a network. The primary factors are the number of CTS endpoints and the geographic location of those endpoints. The number of CTS endpoints deployed determine whether more than one CTMS device is required. The geographic location of those CTS endpoints influences whether the CTMS devices should be centralized or distributed.

Centralized Deployment

Centralized designs are recommended for Cisco TelePresence deployments with six or fewer CTS units or for larger deployments that cover a limited geographic area. For centralized deployments, it is recommended that the CTMS be located at a regional or headquarters campus site with the necessary WAN bandwidth available to each of the remote sites and the necessary LAN bandwidth within the campus. The CTMS should be centrally located, based on the geographic location of the CTS rooms, although this might not be entirely possible due to the existing network layout. This prevents unnecessary latency caused by backhauling calls to a site at the far edge of the network.

Figure 13-14 illustrates a small TelePresence deployment with three regional/headquarter campus sites in North America and one site in Europe. In this example, the CTMS is placed centrally, located in New York, to minimize latency for multipoint meetings.

Distributed Deployments

A distributed deployment is recommended for large TelePresence deployments or smaller deployments with three or more CTS endpoints in separate geographical regions. As TelePresence networks grow, it is advantageous to localize CTMS devices if possible. Regionally

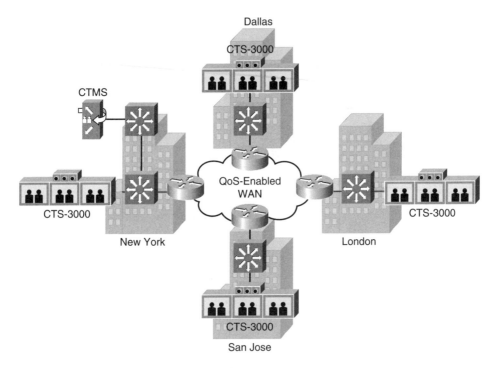

Figure 13-14 *Centralized multipoint design*

localizing CTMS devices minimizes latency and saves bandwidth. Figure 13-15 provides an example of a distributed deployment with a CTMS in New York providing multipoint services for North America and a CTMS in Paris providing multipoint services for Europe.

The current version of CTMS software does not support the cascading of multipoint calls through multiple CTMS devices; therefore, all participants in a single multipoint call need to use the same CTMS. However, future versions of CTMS software might provide support for a single multipoint call to be cascaded between multiple CTMS devices.

Additional Latency

Excessive latency in any Cisco TelePresence meeting degrades the in-person experience. Latency becomes an even larger issue with multipoint calls because all CTS systems dial in to a CTMS that might not be located in the same geographic location as the CTS endpoints. Due to the nature of multipoint, two CTS endpoints that provide low latency in a point-to-point meeting might have considerably higher latency in a multipoint meeting. Inserting any multipoint device in the media path of a Cisco TelePresence call introduces additional latency. However, proper placement of the CTMS helps minimize latency and preserve the Cisco TelePresence experience.

A Cisco TelePresence network should always be designed to target one-way, end-to-end, network latency of <150ms. However, in some cases this is not possible due to long distances between international sites. Therefore, the recommended upper limit allowed for one-way, end-to-end network latency is <200ms. Figure 13-16 illustrates a three-site multipoint deployment with the CTMS located in the hub site.

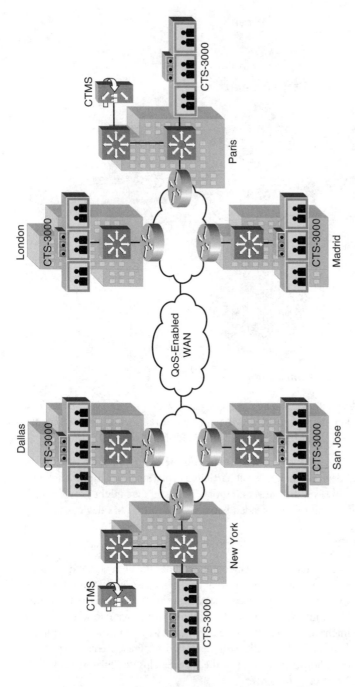

Figure 13-15　*Distributed multipoint design*

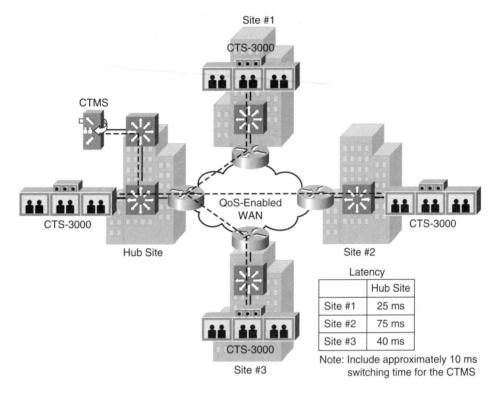

Figure 13-16 *Multipoint network latency example*

One way, network-only latency must stay below 200ms to maintain the TelePresence experience. In Figure 13-16, the hub site is chosen to deploy the CTMS. To calculate the highest latency for a multipoint deployment, take the two sites with the highest latency between themselves and the CTMS and add 10ms for CTMS switching delay. The worst case latency in Figure 13-16 is 75ms + 40ms + 10ms = 125ms.

Bandwidth Considerations

Sufficient bandwidth must be provisioned to the site that houses the CTMS to support the additional traffic required for multipoint meetings and the traffic required for point-to-point meetings.

Centralized Multipoint Design Bandwidth Requirements

Figure 13-17 highlights the bandwidth requirements of centralized multipoint designs by extending the simple multisite example shown in Figure 13-16 to include the bandwidth requirements for TelePresence for each site.

Calculating the amount of bandwidth required at the hub site is fairly straightforward. In Figure 13-17, the circuit to the hub site must have sufficient bandwidth to support three CTS-3000 systems at 1080p, with high-speed auxiliary input and interoperability with legacy video conferencing systems (60Mbps). Audio and video traffic from Site #1, Site

#2, and Site #3 must traverse the circuit during multipoint meetings. Note that the LAN infrastructure within the hub site must also be designed to support the cumulative bandwidth of all four TelePresence CTS endpoints (80Mbps).

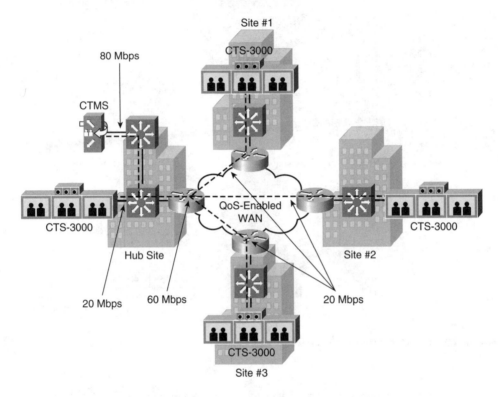

Figure 13-17   *Centralized multipoint design bandwidth example*

The design engineer should also keep in mind that the amount of bandwidth provisioned to the site that houses the CTMS might need to be increased for point-to-point meetings that occur at the same time as multipoint meetings.

Distributed Multipoint Design Bandwidth Requirements

Provisioning bandwidth for TelePresence deployments with a single CTMS and a limited number of CTS systems is fairly straightforward. However, in larger deployments with multiple CTMS devices and a mix of CTS-3200s, CTS-3000s, CTS-1000s, and CTS-500s, bandwidth provisioning becomes more difficult.

One approach is to simply provision sufficient bandwidth to accommodate the maximum amount of traffic from the CTMS at each regional location, assuming each CTMS is configured for its maximum of 48 segments (as of software version 1.1). For example, simply multiply 10.7Mbps per CTS-1000 (including high-speed auxiliary video input and interoperability with legacy video conferencing systems) by the maximum number of segments supported by the CTMS:

10.7Mbps x 48 table segments = 513.6Mbps

Additional bandwidth capacity might be required to handle additional point-to-point calls to and from each regional site.

The advantage of this method of bandwidth provisioning is that as networks grow, the network design engineer does not constantly need to increase bandwidth to each site. The downside is that for many customers, provisioning that much bandwidth is unfeasible from a cost perspective.

A second method of provisioning bandwidth is based on historical meeting patterns and knowledge of the specific CTS units within the network. This method relies on limiting the Maximum Segments defined within the CTMS to be at or below the bandwidth allocated for TelePresence meetings from that regional location. Figure 13-18 illustrates an example of this type of distributed multipoint TelePresence design.

As illustrated in Figure 13-18, the North America CTMS device is configured with a maximum of 36 table segments, based on WAN bandwidth and meeting patterns. The Europe CTMS device is configured with a maximum 17 of table segments, also based on WAN bandwidth and meeting patterns. The remaining multipoint devices are configured to support a maximum of 14 table segments.

When provisioning bandwidth using this method, it might be beneficial to base the bandwidth calculations for each site on the type of CTS system, the video resolution supported, whether interoperability is supported, and whether high-speed auxiliary video is supported to more accurately assess the bandwidth requirement.

For example, consider the following calculations for each multipoint device in Figure 13–18.

The calculations are based on all CTS endpoints running at 1080p best resolution, with high-speed auxiliary video input and interoperability. In environments with mixed resolutions, it is recommended that bandwidth be provisioned based on the highest resolution only.

Burst Considerations

In multipoint TelePresence calls, bursts are generated as a result of one of the following events:

- **Whenever a CTS endpoint joins a multipoint meeting:** If the call is configured with the Video Announce feature enabled, when a new CTS endpoint joins the call, it becomes the active speaker. This causes a new reference frame called an *Instantaneous Decode Refresh (IDR)* to be generated by the new CTS endpoint and replicated to every other CTS endpoint by the CTMS. In addition, the last active site sends an IDR to the CTMS, which is replicated and sent to the new CTS endpoint. Note that for CTS endpoints with multiple screens, multiple IDRs might be generated.

- **Normal transitioning of the active room or speaker from one CTS endpoint to another CTS endpoint:** This causes an IDR to be generated by the new active room or speaker and replicated by the CTMS to all the other CTS endpoints in the multipoint call.

- **One or more CTS endpoints or codecs reports loss in the received video:** This is reported back to the sending codec through RTCP packets from the receiver, indicating one or more video packets were not received. Packet loss causes the active room or speaker to generate an IDR to resynchronize all CTS endpoints. The IDR is replicated by the CTMS and sent to all CTS endpoints in the multipoint call.

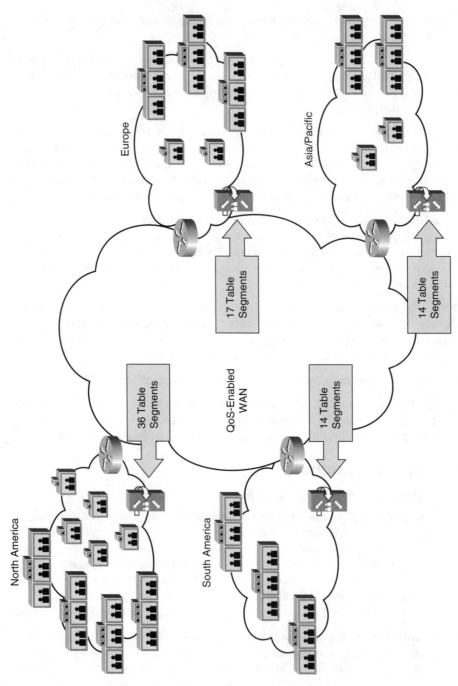

Figure 13-18 *Bandwidth provisioning based on historical meeting patterns*

```
North America region:
```

9 - CTS-1000 @ 10.7Mbps	= 96.3Mbps	9 table segments
9 - CTS-3000 @ 20.4Mbps	= 183.6Mbps	27 table segments
Multipoint bandwidth	= 279.9Mbps	36 table segments

```
South America and Asia/Pacific regions:
```

8 - CTS-1000 10.7Mbps	= 85.6Mbps	8 table segments
2 - CTS-3000 20.4Mbps	= 40.8Mbps	6 table segments
Multipoint bandwidth	= 126.4Mbps	14 table segments

```
Europe region:
```

8 - CTS-1000 10.7Mbps	= 85.6Mbps	8 table segments
3 - CTS-3000 20.4Mbps	= 61.2Mbps	9 table segments
Multipoint bandwidth	= 146.8 Mbps	17 table segments

■ **Periodic synchronization of the CTS endpoints by the active site:** Each active room or speaker periodically sends out an IDR to synchronize the CTS endpoints. This occurs approximately every 5 minutes with the current TelePresence solution. The IDR is replicated by the CTMS and sent to all CTS endpoints in the multipoint call.

■ **Normal transitioning of the video from a device connected to the auxiliary input of one of the CTS endpoints:** Only one CTS endpoint at a time can function as a presenter within a multipoint meeting through the use of the Auto-Collaborate feature. Whenever the presenting CTS endpoint changes the content of the auxiliary video input, such as transitioning a PowerPoint slide, the burst of content is replicated by the CTMS to all the other CTS endpoints within the multipoint call.

When designing the network to support multipoint TelePresence, a general rule of thumb is to allocate approximately 64kB of burst space per TelePresence screen and an additional 64kB of burst space for the auxiliary video input of the Auto-Collaborate feature. Figure 13-19 provides an example of calculating burst space required to support multipoint TelePresence.

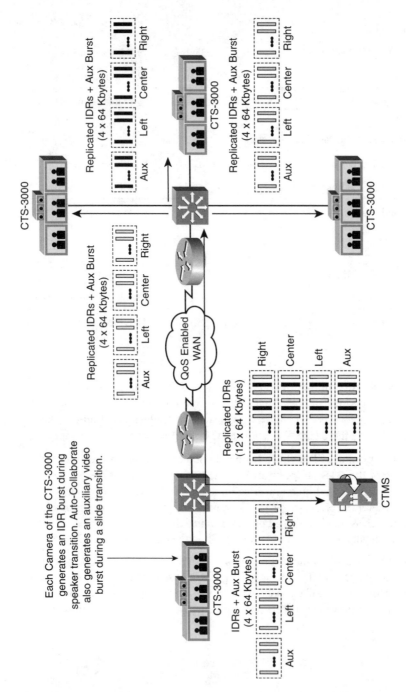

Figure 13-19   *TelePresence multipoint burst size estimation.*

In the example in Figure 13-19, when the CTS-3000 on the left side becomes the active room, video from each of its three cameras is sent to every other CTS endpoint. The initial video frame from each camera is a reference frame or IDR, which can be as large as 64kB. In addition, the CTS-3000 can function as a slide presenter. Any slide transition that occurs simultaneously to the speaker transition results in another burst of up to 64kB; therefore, the combined size of the burst sent from the CTS-3000 to the CTMS can be as large as 4 × 64kB = 256kB. This burst is replicated on a packet-by-packet basis by the CTMS to every other CTS endpoint within the multipoint meeting. In the example in Figure 13-19, there are three additional TelePresence rooms, each with a CTS-3000, in the meeting; therefore, a burst as large as 3 × 256kB = 768kB could be generated by the CTMS.

Although the probability of a slide transition occurring at exactly the same time as a speaker transition is low, the design engineer must recognize that the burst might occur within a single 33ms frame interval because TelePresence endpoints send video at 30 frames per second. Further, as the number of CTS endpoints in a single multipoint meeting increases, the size of the bursts generated by the CTMS increases. The network design engineer needs to deploy LAN switches and routers with sufficient buffering capacity to handle multipoint TelePresence bursts. Further, any shaping and policing done within the WAN also needs to accommodate such bursts. Failure to accommodate the bursts can result in an "IDR storm" that can degrade the quality of the meeting and might result in termination of the multipoint TelePresence call.

As mentioned previously, packet loss is reported back to the sender through RTCP packets. The sender generates an IDR in response to reports of packet loss. If some packets of the IDR are dropped by a policer, this is again reported to the sender through RTCP packets. The sender continues to generate new IDRs, which, in turn, are partially dropped by the policer. This causes the *IDR storm.*

Positioning of the CTMS Within the Network

Due to the total audio and video bandwidth requirements for a Cisco TelePresence CTMS, you need to consider its placement in the network.

Placement Within the Campus

Within a campus deployment, placement of the CTMS within a logical data center LAN segment might be desirable due to the availability of bandwidth, an uninterruptible power supply, and ease of monitoring. The downside is that all multipoint TelePresence traffic must be backhauled into and out of the logical data center LAN segment. The data center design might need to be adjusted to accommodate the necessary increase in traffic.

An alternative is to locate the CTMS at the access layer toward the logical WAN edge of the campus. This type of placement might minimize the amount of traffic that is backhauled through the campus LAN; however, this is dependent upon the location of the CTS endpoints. If the majority of the CTS endpoints within the multipoint TelePresence deployment are remote to the campus location, this design might provide some benefit. If the majority of the CTS endpoints are within the campus, this design might provide little benefit.

A third alternative is to simply locate the CTMS at the access layer within the campus network. This type of placement minimizes the amount of unnecessary traffic to the logical WAN edge and the logical data center if the majority of CTS endpoints are within the campus. The downside is that the likelihood of an uninterruptible power for the CTMS might be lower at the access layer. Figure 13-20 shows the three campus placement alternatives.

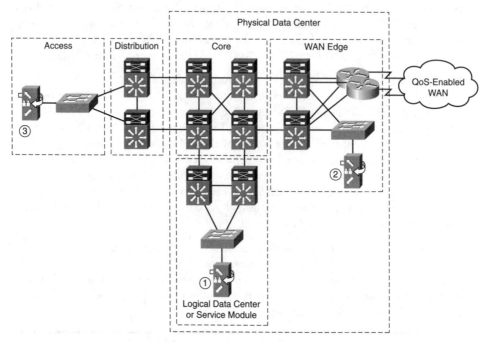

Figure 13-20   *Possible CTMS locations within the campus*

Placement within the Branch

Under some circumstances, it might be necessary to deploy a CTMS at a branch location. Due to limited bandwidth of branch locations, this design is not highly recommended. When deploying at a branch, the CTMS needs to be deployed at the distribution layer of any hierarchical LAN configuration, as shown in Figure 13-21.

This minimizes the amount of unnecessary traffic backhauled through the branch LAN network. An alternative is to place the CTMS at the access layer if no available LAN ports exist at the distribution layer.

LAN Switch Platform Considerations

The CTMS currently supports a single 10/100/1000Mbps Ethernet connection. The CTMS is capable of generating traffic loads in excess of 100Mbps; therefore, it is not recommended to place the CTMS on a 100Mbps Ethernet LAN port. Further, it is not recommended to connect the CTMS to a LAN switch port that is oversubscribed.

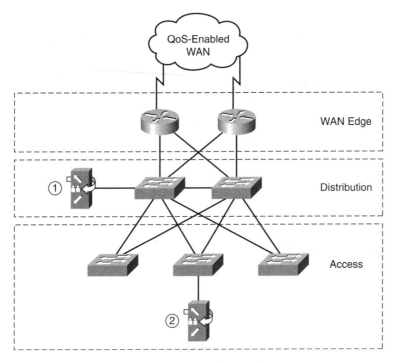

Figure 13-21 *Possible CTMS locations within the branch*

For example, some switch linecard or platform architectures provision groups of four or eight ports to share a single 1-Gbps connection to the switch fabric. This is often done to maintain a lower cost for the overall switch linecard or platform when transitioning to higher-speed connectivity. The CTMS needs to connect to a switch port that has a full 1Gbps connectivity to the switch fabric. Because multipoint TelePresence can generate large bursts, newer switch linecards and platforms that support buffer sizes in excess of 1MB per port are preferred for connecting the CTMS to the network.

Note Future versions of the CTMS might support multiple 10/100/1000-Mbps Ethernet connections to provide high availability through an active and standby interface configuration.

WAN Circuit Support

Multipoint TelePresence can be supported both on dedicated WAN circuits and converged WAN circuits. Dedicated circuit configurations are those in which TelePresence is the only traffic that exists on the WAN circuit. In other words, the design engineer deploys an overlay network designed exclusively for the support of TelePresence. Converged circuit configurations are those in which TelePresence integrates with data, voice, and other video applications over a WAN infrastructure.

Dedicated WAN Circuits

Multipoint TelePresence is recommended for only dedicated deployments that have E3 circuit rates (34 Mbps) and higher. When configured for a single multipoint call, the maximum number of CTS table segments for lower-speed WAN circuits, such as T3, E3, and OC-3 POS, is currently bounded not by the bandwidth of the circuits, but by the jitter induced by serialization delay of the multipoint bursts across the circuits.

For higher-speed circuits such as OC-12, OC-48, and Metro-Ethernet or MPLS with FastEthernet or GigabitEthernet handoff, the number of CTS table segments is more constrained by the total bandwidth of the circuit. When deploying over a Metro-Ethernet or MPLS handoff to a service provider network, it is critical that the service provider network is capable of handling the bursts generated by multipoint TelePresence.

Converged Circuits

When deploying over converged circuits, the design engineer can choose to configure multipoint TelePresence traffic in an LLQ configuration or a CBWFQ configuration. When deploying in an LLQ configuration, keep the total amount of LLQ traffic below approximately one-third of the bandwidth of the circuit. This ensures adequate bandwidth of nonreal-time traffic so that the performance of data applications is not adversely impacted. If TelePresence traffic is policed to a certain rate within the converged circuit, the policer must be configured to handle the bursts associated with multipoint TelePresence previously discussed. Finally, any shapers configured on the converged circuit, to match the contracted data rates to service provider networks, must also be configured to handle the bursts associated with multipoint TelePresence.

Basic Configuration Requirements for Multipoint TelePresence

The following sections discuss some of the basic configuration required for the CUCM to connect with the CTMS.

CUCM Configuration Requirements

From the perspective of CUCM, the CTMS appears as a SIP Trunk that must be configured on the CUCM cluster. The destination IP address configured within the SIP trunk points to the CTMS. In addition, a route pattern must be added to the CUCM cluster. This allows the CUCM cluster to route all calls to the extension or extensions corresponding to a multipoint call to the appropriate CTMS.

CTMS Configuration Requirements

In addition to getting the CTMS onto the network with an IP address, default gateway, DNS server, and domain name, the network administrator must also provide configuration information regarding the CUCM cluster to which the CTMS connects through the SIP Trunk configured within CUCM. Note that if a name is used for the CUCM cluster, the

CTMS must translate the name to an IP address through the DNS server. Next, if a Cisco TelePresence Manager (CTS-MAN) is deployed to support scheduled meetings, the CTMS must be configured with the CTS-MAN information. This requires not only the name or IP address of the CTS-MAN, but also the userid and password of an account configured on the CTS-MAN that accesses and schedules resources on the CTMS.

For further configuration information regarding the CTMS or CUCM, see the documents listed in the Further Reading section at the end of this chapter.

Summary

This chapter presented an overview of multipoint TelePresence. Multipoint extends the virtual meeting to three or more TelePresence rooms. Central to the multipoint design is the Cisco TelePresence Multipoint Switch (CTMS), which switches the audio and video media within a multipoint meeting. Three meeting types are currently supported by the CTMS: static, ad hoc, and scheduled meetings. In addition, the CTMS supports a wide range of features including switching policy, maximum rooms, video announce, locking a meeting, video quality, and VIP mode.

The CTMS has implemented a flow control mechanism to help control the use of bandwidth in a multipoint meeting. Audio, which is always sent to the CTMS in a multipoint meeting, determines which CTS endpoints send video. This results in an asymmetric flow of video, to and from the CTMS in a multipoint meeting. Cisco TelePresence also supports interoperability with traditional room-based video conferencing and desktop video collaboration systems through a cascade of the CTMS with the CUVC 3500 Series MCU.

Multipoint TelePresence can be deployed in centralized designs or distributed designs. Centralized designs consisting of a single CTMS are recommended for smaller TelePresence deployments. Distributed designs consisting of multiple CTMS units deployed regionally are recommended for larger designs to more effectively utilize available bandwidth. When deploying a multipoint TelePresence design, the network administrator must be aware of the additional bandwidth, latency, and burst requirements imposed by placement of the CTMS. If possible, place CTMS units in campus locations that are centrally located with respect to the TelePresence rooms that utilize the CTMS for multipoint meetings.

Finally, this chapter discussed the configuration of the CTMS, which appears as a SIP Trunk to CUCM. In addition to the SIP Trunk configuration, a route pattern must be added to the CUCM for it to route calls to the CTMS for multipoint meetings. In addition to basic IP addressing, the CTMS must be configured with the name or IP address of the CUCM. If scheduled meetings are supported, the CTMS must also be configured with the name or IP address of the CTS-MAN. In addition, the user ID and password of the CTS-MAN account that schedules resources on the CTMS must be configured.

Further Reading

Cisco TelePresence Multipoint Switch Documentation: http://www.tinyurl.com/3oyump

http://www.cisco.com/en/US/netsol/ns819/networking_solutions_program_home.html

The ability for different companies to communicate is fundamental to the value proposition of any collaborative technology. Deploying Cisco TelePresence within your own organization can help increase productivity and collaboration among the officers and employees within your company and drive down operating expenses, improve your organization's efficiency, decrease your time to market, and, therefore, improve both top- and bottom-line performance. When you add the ability to extend your reach beyond the boundary of your organization to meet face-to-face with customers, suppliers, partners, and shareholders through TelePresence, it can have explosive, business-revolutionizing implications.

This explosive impact has been articulated as Metcalfe's Law, which states that the value of a telecommunications network is proportional to the square of the number of connected users of the system. The law has often been illustrated using the example of fax machines: A single fax machine is useless, but the value of every fax machine increases with the total number of fax machines in the network because the total number of people with whom each user can send and receive documents increases. Now, imagine if TelePresence endpoints were as ubiquitous as fax machines: What would the impact on business communications be? Perhaps "explosive" and "revolutionary" might not even be strong enough terms to describe the impact. This law is, thus, a foundation principle of the Cisco Inter-Company TelePresence strategy.

Cisco TelePresence is not the first collaborative technology to require intercompany connectivity. Telephones, fax machines, email, instant messaging, video conferencing, web conferencing and several other communications technologies have solved the same problem: How to allow users at different companies to communicate with each other over this new medium without jeopardizing either organization's information security boundaries. What

CHAPTER 14

Inter-Company TelePresence Design

makes Cisco TelePresence unique is its requirement for extremely high bandwidth, end-to-end quality of service (QoS), and ease of use. The existing intercompany network architectures, such as the Public Switched Telephone Network (PSTN), Integrated Services Digital Network (ISDN), and the public Internet, are not capable of satisfying the end-to-end application requirements of Cisco TelePresence. We must invent a new generation of intercompany networks to support this application. That is the goal of the Cisco Inter-Company TelePresence architecture.

> **Note** Though subtle, there is an important distinction to be made in the use of the terms "intercompany" and "Inter-Company" in this chapter. The former refers to generic telecommunications systems between companies, such as PSTN, ISDN, and the Internet. The latter ("Inter-Company") refers to a Cisco branded solution that meets the security, quality, and application requirements to support Cisco TelePresence between companies.

This chapter discusses the end-to-end application requirements, solution components, network architecture design, and security necessary to enable Cisco TelePresence Inter-Company Communications. Specifically, this chapter covers the following topics:

- **End-to-end application requirements:** Briefly reviews the end-to-end application requirements that the intercompany architecture must possess to adequately replace a face-to-face meeting between users at different companies

- **Solution components:** Describes the various product components that comprise the Cisco TelePresence Inter-Company solution

- **Network architecture and security:** Describes the communications network architecture and the role of the various solution components within that architecture

- **Deployment models:** Reviews a few of the most popular deployment models that Cisco envisions its service provider partners to offer

End-to-End Application Requirements

The Cisco TelePresence solution was designed upon three simple tenets: quality, simplicity, and reliably. These requirements permeate all aspects of the product and are equally important to maintain when extending the solution to connect between different companies. In addition to these three primary tenets, three secondary requirements must be met to complete the solution: security, adherence to standards, and scalability.

Figure 14-1 illustrates this hierarchy of requirements for the Cisco TelePresence Inter-Company solution.

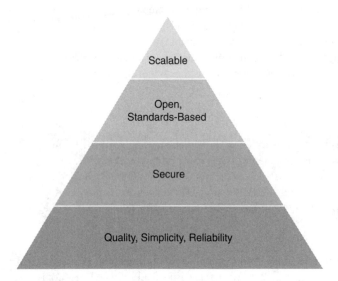

Figure 14-1   *Cisco TelePresence Inter-Company solution requirements hierarchy*

The following sections consider each of these requirements and their importance in the context of intercompany communications.

Experience Quality Requirements

First, the quality of the experience must be good enough to truly replace a face-to-face meeting. Cisco TelePresence provides the high-definition video and wideband audio necessary to deliver this level of experience; but relies on the underlying IP network transporting that traffic in order to deliver the packets in a consistent manner with low latency, jitter, and loss characteristics. Within each company's LANs and WANs, the administrator can employ Cisco IOS QoS tools to provide the end-to-end QoS required. However, when connecting different customer networks, the public Internet does not provide guaranteed QoS and is, therefore, not a viable transport network for Cisco TelePresence traffic. Likewise, the PSTN and ISDN networks do not provide enough bandwidth for TelePresence. This means that a new type of global intercompany network must be created: one that provides adequate bandwidth with quantifiable and guaranteed QoS.

Ease of Use Requirements

Second, the system must be incredibly simple to use, from arranging the meeting, to starting the meeting, to using the system during the meeting. It must be as natural to schedule and arrange as any other face-to-face meeting, preferably using existing tools and workflows that users are already accustomed to using. The user can launch the call and begin the meeting without having to navigate a complicated user interface or dialing nonintuitive addresses such as IP addresses or overly complex numerical numbers. This means that the global intercompany network must possess a logical intercompany addressing scheme that is intuitive for even the most nontechnical user to understand and navigate. Today primarily two such addressing schemes exist:

- The E.164 standard used by the Public Switched Telephone Network (PSTN)

- The Uniform Resource Identifier (URI) standard used by the public Internet

Humans are accustomed to dialing (globally unique) E.164 telephone numbers to call each other. They are also accustomed to sending each other emails using the (globally unique) URI addressing scheme such as user@domain.com. Therefore, users need to schedule meetings with a colleague at another company by sending them an email and launching the call at the scheduled time by dialing a globally unique and globally routable E.164 telephone number. The email messages sent between users at different companies might be routed over the public Internet. However, the call signaling and audio/video media associated with the TelePresence call must be routed over a QoS-enabled network, and there must be devices in the network that can handle E.164 numerical number routing between companies. In other words, the global intercompany network must emulate the E.164 routing functionality of the PSTN using a QoS-enabled IP network as the transport.

Reliability Requirements

Third, the system must be incredibly reliable. All it takes is one time where a user experiences a failure to start the meeting, or the system fails in the middle of an important meeting, for the user to stop trusting in the technology as a replacement for critical face-to-face meetings. The call must connect every time, must stay up and not fail (barring extreme failure scenarios such as a major network outage), and the audio/video quality must remain excellent throughout the entire meeting. This means that the global intercompany network must not only provide end-to-end QoS, but must also be highly resilient and highly available. In short, the network must be carrier-class.

Security Requirements

Fourth, the solution must be thoroughly secure. The users need to trust that the confidentiality of their discussion is maintained. Network administrators must trust that the TelePresence systems are not susceptible to attack from internal or external sources and that it does not compromise the security of the rest of their network. Extending the Cisco TelePresence solution beyond your enterprise network borders to include intercompany connectivity increases the importance of these requirements exponentially. All Cisco TelePresence signaling and media traffic must be encrypted end-to-end using the strongest possible authentication and encryption algorithms. Furthermore, the enterprise network borders must be protected by firewall and Network Address Translation (NAT) devices, and the security posture provided by those devices must not be weakened or bypassed to permit TelePresence traffic to flow between companies. This means that the global intercompany network must provide for a secure, yet scalable, method of firewall/NAT traversal and must support end-to-end encryption of all signaling and media packets.

Nonproprietary Requirements

Fifth, the solution must be open, flexible, and standards-based. Closed, proprietary architectures are not acceptable in today's competitive business and technical environments. It must leverage existing standards, technologies, protocols, and network architectures, and must extend to incorporate additional capabilities in the future. Specifically, the solution must be based on Session Initiation Protocol (SIP).

Scalability Requirements

Finally, and perhaps most important, the solution must be scalable to accommodate hundreds of thousands, or even millions of connections and must provide for global connectivity. An architecture that enables a select few companies to participate has limited value. Likewise, an architecture that requires each member company to manually peer with every other member company will not scale beyond a few dozen connections. By contrast, an architecture that provides for global connectivity and scalability can see Metcalf's law take effect.

Solution Components

The Cisco TelePresence Inter-Company Communications solution builds upon and is an extension of the existing Cisco TelePresence enterprise solution, the components of which are revisited in Figure 14-2 and detailed in the following list:

■ **Cisco TelePresence Systems:** The endpoints that reside within each company. The portfolio of endpoint models at the time this book was written include the CTS-500, CTS-1000, CTS-3000, and CTS-3200.

■ **Cisco Unified Communications Manager:** Performs the role of an enterprise-class, IP-based Private Branch Exchange (PBX) and manages all endpoint registration and call routing within a given enterprise network.

■ **Cisco TelePresence Multipoint Switch:** Enables three or more TelePresence systems to participate in a multipoint meeting. It can be located within the enterprise network, within the service provider network as a hosted service, or both.

■ **Cisco TelePresence Manager:** Provides the One-Button-to-Push (OBTP) ease of use by integrating with the enterprise's corporate groupware (such as Microsoft Exchange or Lotus Domino), enabling users to schedule TelePresence rooms within their companies using familiar workflow processes. TelePresence Manager resides within each enterprise network or can be located within the service provider network as a hosted service, or both.

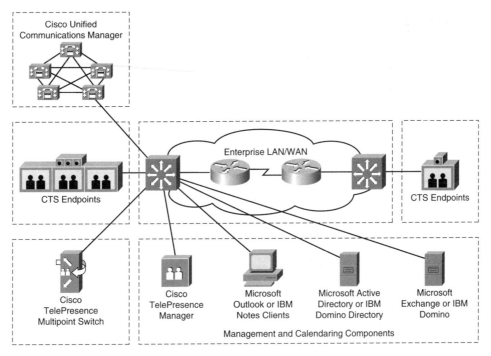

Figure 14-2 *Cisco TelePresence enterprise solution components*

- **Enterprise LAN/WAN:** Within each enterprise location, the TelePresence solution is intended to be implemented on a highly resilient, QoS-enabled, Gigabit Ethernet or faster LAN of switches and routers. Between locations of a given enterprise, a WAN composed of high-speed routers interconnect using reliable transport services, such as point-to-point leased line circuits or Multi-Protocol Label Switched Virtual Private Network (MPLS-VPN) services. Both the LAN and the WAN should be architected using the latest design recommendations and best practices, such as the Cisco Architecture for Voice, Video, and Integrated Data (AVVID) and the Cisco Secure Architecture for Enterprises (SAFE).

To this existing enterprise solution set, the Cisco TelePresence Inter-Company Communications solution adds the following components, as illustrated in Figure 14-3:

- **Cisco Session Border Controller (SBC):** A service provider-class softswitch running on Cisco IOS-XE or Cisco IOS-XR router platforms, such as the Cisco XR 12000, 7600, 7200-VXR, and ASR-1000. The SBC functions as an MPLS VRF-aware SIP Back-to-Back User Agent and media proxy, managing all call routing and media termination between different customer networks. The SBC can be further modularized into two subcomponents: a Signaling Border Element (SBE) and a Data Border Element (DBE). These elements reside within the service provider network and can be deployed in a decomposed fashion (SBE-only, DBE-only) or as a combined SBE + DBE running inside a Provider Edge (PE) router or as stand-alone devices connected to one or more PE routers.

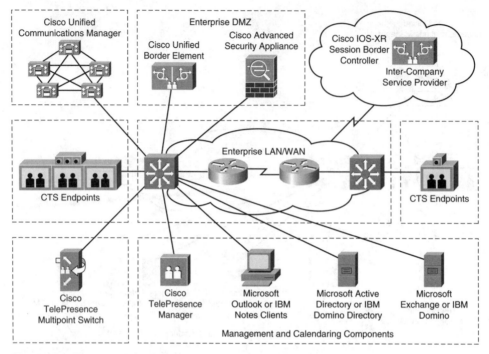

Figure 14-3   *Cisco TelePresence Inter-Company solution components*

- **Cisco Adaptive Security Appliance (ASA):** Provides firewall, NAT, and protocol inspection services on a dedicated appliance. It resides near the WAN edge boundary of each customer's network to provide a Demilitarized Zone (DMZ).

- **Cisco IOS or Cisco IOS-XE Firewall Services:** Provides firewall, NAT, and protocol inspection services on a Cisco IOS or IOS-XE router platform, such as a 2800 or 3800 Integrated Services Router (ISR), or the ASR-1000. It resides near the WAN edge boundary of each customer's network to provide a DMZ.

- **Cisco Unified Border Element (CUBE):** An enterprise-class SBC running on a Cisco IOS Integrated Services Router (ISR), such as the 2800 or 3800 series platforms. It provides an optional but highly recommended additional layer of security to hide and protect the enterprise network from the service provider. This device typically resides near the WAN edge boundary of each customer's network within the DMZ. Like the Cisco SBC, the CUBE can function either as an SBE-only, in which the signaling is routed through the CUBE, but the media flows around it, or as an SBE + DBE, in which both the signaling and media flow through the CUBE.

Network Architecture and Security

Let's begin with a simple goal: allowing two companies whose internal enterprise networks are otherwise totally isolated from each other to securely connect a TelePresence meeting between their two networks.

As Figure 14-4 illustrates, there are two companies that each have two office locations networked together using MPLS-VPN WAN service from a given service provider.

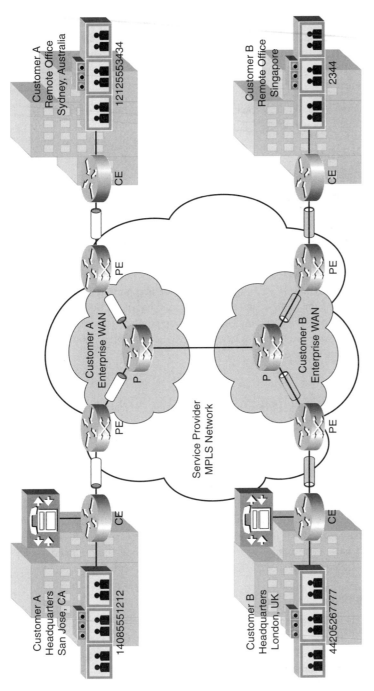

Figure 14-4 *Two companies using MPLS-VPN WANs*

Although both companies use the same service provider network, each company's VPN is completely autonomous, private, and secure. Each company has its own internal IP address space that can likely be RFC-1918 private addresses, routable only within their individual networks. Each company has its own Cisco Unified Communications Manager (CUCM) and Cisco TelePresence Systems using its own private dialing plan. These two companies are completely isolated from each other in every way; they have no route to each other's E.164 addresses, and they have no direct IP path between their two networks. It is entirely impossible for them to call each other.

To allow these two companies to talk to each other, several things must be solved.

Public E.164 Dialing

First, each company needs to dial a telephone number that is routable to the other customer's TelePresence Systems. Like any enterprise telephone system, a user at one company must reach a user at any other company by dialing a fully qualified E.164 number, such as 1(408)555-1212 (normally prefixed by an external access code such as a 9 in the United States or 00 in Europe and many parts of Asia to exit their Private Branch Exchange (PBX) and steer the call out to the public service provider network). When a user at Company A dials this number, the Communications Manager (which performs the role of an IP Private Branch Exchange, or IP-PBX, within that company) must strip the access code from the beginning of the number and route the remaining digits through a service provider that can determine which company that telephone number belongs to (in this case Company B). The service provider must then route the call down to Company B's Communications Manager.

Why E.164?

There are other standards for public addressing and call routing, such as SIP Uniform Resource Identifiers (URI) such as user@domain.com. The architecture must allow for the use of these standards, but for the initial roll-out of Inter-Company services, Cisco envisions customers and their service providers predominantly standardizing on E.164 addressing because it is the most familiar, easy to use, and ready to deploy on a global level. Note that in SIP, even a numeric E.164 number is converted into a URI. For example, when you dial 1(408)555-1212, it is converted under the hood to a URI format such as +14085551212@domain.com. So specifically, we are arguing that for the time being, numerical URIs are more appropriate than alphanumeric URIs for the Cisco TelePresence application. This is because the user interface of Cisco TelePresence is a telephone, and telephones are designed to dial numerical numbers, not letters and special characters such as the @ symbol.

Call Routing Scalability

By placing the responsibility of Inter-Company E.164 routing on the SBC or on the central call control within the SP exchange, the administrative burden on each enterprise is significantly reduced. This is the same model used by the PSTN. Each enterprise must simply install a default route to their Communications Managers to point all external calls to their service providers' SBC. The SBC is then responsible for managing the global Inter-Company dial plan between different enterprises. Some competing architectures place enterprise-class SBCs on customer premises and use a peer-to-peer dial plan model because there is no service provider offering Inter-Company routing for them at a global level. This is administratively burdensome because each enterprise would need to install routes to every other enterprise with which they want to communicate. By choosing to bring the Cisco TelePresence Inter-Company solution to market through its Tier-1 service provider partners, and by providing a service provider-class SBC, the Cisco architecture is superior in this aspect. Figure 14-5 illustrates the differences between these two approaches.

If the provider were merely providing the Layer 2 and Layer 3 physical connectivity, the task of managing the global dial plan would be left up to each participating enterprise. They would each need to install routes in their Communications Managers to every other customer in a fully meshed configuration with static entries. Each time a new customer joined the network, each enterprise would have to add a route to them. This obviously would not scale beyond a couple dozen customers at best.

> **Note**   Note that the SBC topology illustrated in the figures so far is grossly oversimplified. In reality, service providers can and should have dozens, even hundreds, of SBCs located throughout their network to provide redundancy and geographical scalability.

Inter-VPN Connectivity

By now, you should understand the high-level concept of each enterprise having a route to the service provider to provide Inter-Company dialing. However, if each customer's VPN is completely autonomous, private, and secure and there is no Layer 3 path between the Communications Managers and the SBC, how is this routing accomplished? Furthermore, after the call is established and the audio and video media begins flowing between the two endpoints, how will they reach other's IP addresses? There is no Layer 3 route between the two companies. Finally, each customer can use private, RFC-1918 addresses on the Communications Managers and TelePresence Systems. So even if a Layer 3 route exists, how can NAT requirements be addressed? The following sections answer these questions.

VPN Traversal

VPN Traversal is the second critical function provided by the Cisco Session Border Controller platform. The SBC is MPLS Virtual Route Forwarding (VRF)-aware, which enables it to provide Layer 2 to Layer 7 connectivity between otherwise isolated networks. By basing the solution on MPLS, Cisco is introducing a new type of architecture into the market and solving a difficult technical challenge. One approach is for each enterprise to extend their MPLS-VPN to the SBC, as illustrated in Figure 14-6.

The SBC, therefore, is now a Layer 3 entity on each customer's network, providing a method of traversing between those VPNs, as illustrated in the following example:

1. When Customer A calls Customer B, Customer A's Communications Manager sends a SIP INVITE to the SBC. Because the SBC is a Layer 3 entity on Customer A's VPN, there is a direct Layer 3 IP path between these two entities. The packet traverses Customer A's LAN and is routed by Customer A's CE router into the MPLS WAN. At the PE router handling Customer A's VPN, a MPLS VPN label is applied to the packet to

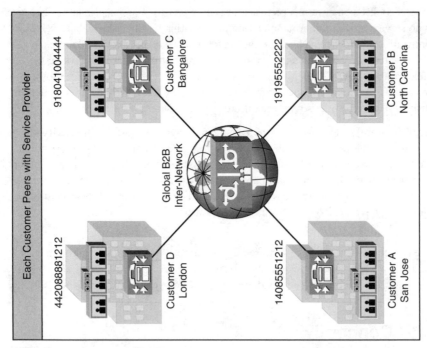

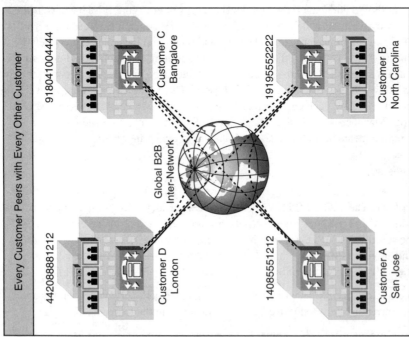

Figure 14-5   *Peer-to-peer versus service provider-based routing*

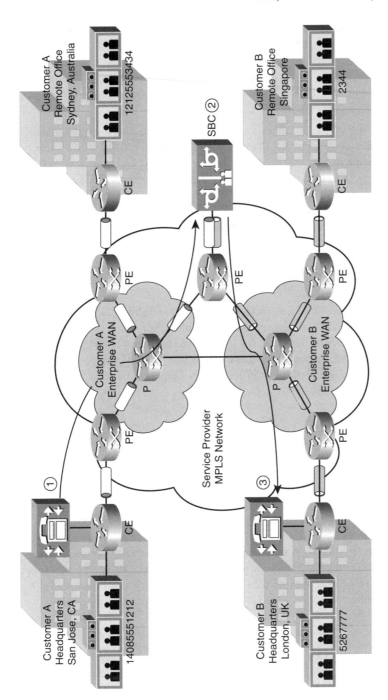

Figure 14-6 *SBC placed between customer VPNs*

place that packet onto that customer's VPN. It is label-switched across the MPLS network to the provider's SBC, which terminates that MPLS tunnel, pops the label off the packet, and processes the SIP message.

2. After performing an E.164 address lookup to find the destination IP address of Customer B's Communications Manager, the provider's SBC determines that the call must be routed to Customer B's VPN.

3. The SBC then constructs a new SIP message with Customer B's Communication Manager as the destination IP address, looks up that IP address in its MPLS VRF routing table for Customer B to locate the next hop for that IP address, and applies the MPLS label of Customer B's VPN to the packet. The packet is then label-switched across the MPLS network to the PE router handling Customer B's VPN. The PE router pops the MPLS label and forwards the packet down to Customer B's CE router, who, in turn, forwards it into Customer B's enterprise LAN to its Communications Manager. Because they are completely separate VPNs, each customer can use the same IP address space.

These three phases of call establishment are noted in Figure 14-6. Additionally, Figure 14-7 further breaks down this end-to-end call signaling exchange.

After the signaling messages have been exchanged and the media begins to flow between the two TelePresence endpoints, the DBE function within the SBC must provide the same Inter-VPN traversal for all the audio and video RTP packets between the two enterprises, as illustrated in Figure 14-8. In its simplest form, the packets would flow from Endpoint A to the SBC, be terminated by the SBC in VPN A, and then regenerated anew by the SBC in VPN B and forwarded to Endpoint B.

Note MPLS is not mandated by the architecture. Point-to-point leased lines and other WAN services are also supported, but MPLS provides the most elegant and scalable approach.

Inter-VPN Security

The traversal of SIP messages and audio/video RTP media packets through the SBC between different customers' MPLS-VPNs must be highly secure so as not to introduce unwanted leaks between them. The enterprise will likely not trust the SBC not to accidentally leak routes and information from its VPN to other VPNs, and vice versa. Likewise, the service provider who is managing the SBC will likely not trust the enterprises to control what types of packets are sent to the SBC. Layers of security must be applied along the path, including Layer 3 topology hiding, firewall, NAT, and SIP and RTP/RTCP protocol inspection.

Firewalls

First, the Layer 3 path between each customer's Communications Manager, their TelePresence systems, and the SBC must be protected by firewalls to control what type of traffic is permitted. Firewalls might exist at several points along the path, including at the customer WAN edge to protect the enterprise from the service provider and within the service provider network to protect the SBC from the enterprises. Let's begin by breaking down the path between Company A Headquarters and the SBC and layering in a firewall at the customer's WAN edge. Figure 14-9 illustrates the connections and devices along the path.

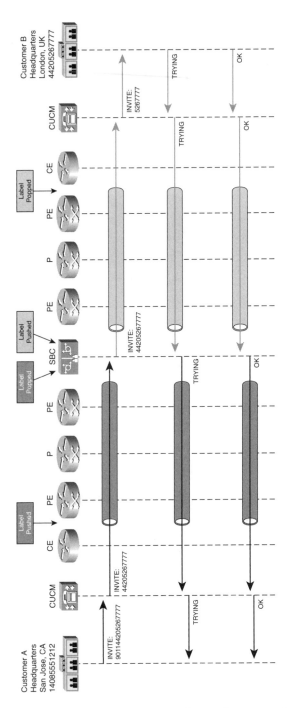

Figure 14-7   *Inter-VPN SBC call signaling example*

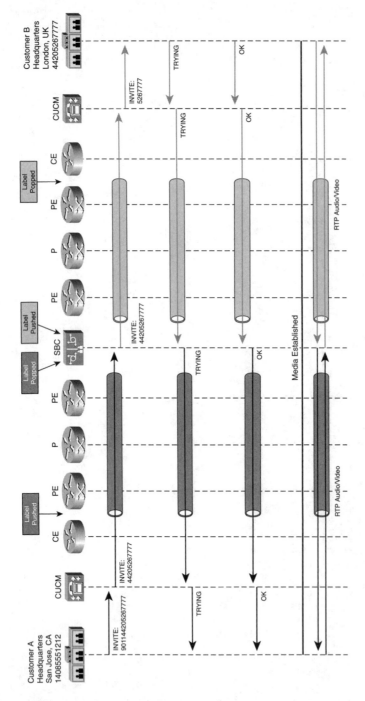

Figure 14-8 *Inter-VPN SBC media routing example*

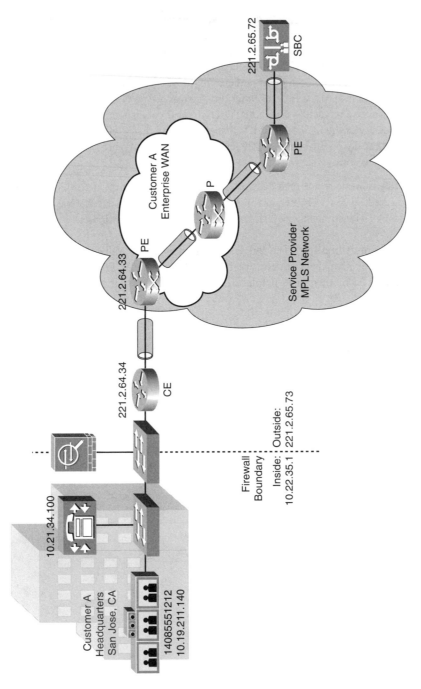

Figure 14-9   *Path from Company A headquarters to SBC: firewall only*

Now all SIP signaling packets originating from the customer's Communications Manager to the SBC and vice versa must traverse the firewall. Likewise, all audio and video media packets originating from the customer's TelePresence endpoints to the SBC and vice versa must traverse the firewall as well. The firewall can perform a medley of security features to protect these entities from each other and ensure the integrity of the communications. These features range from basic firewall functions, such as access control lists (ACL), to more advanced functions, such as SIP and RTP/RTCP protocol inspection services, which inspect the integrity of the SIP and RTP/RTCP messages and their conformance to standards, and dynamically open and close TCP and UDP ports based on the state of the SIP transactions and sessions.

The firewall function can reside on a dedicated security appliance such as the Cisco ASA, run on a dedicated Cisco IOS router, or run integrated on the customer's WAN edge router. Figure 14-10 illustrates these different firewall deployment options.

Basic Firewall Functionality   The simplest function of the firewall is to provide ACLs to explicitly or implicitly permit or deny certain IP addresses and TCP/UDP ports to communicate with each other. In its simplest form, the ACL would be constructed to do the following:

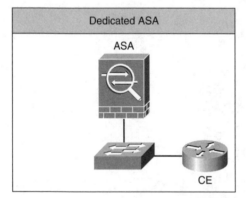

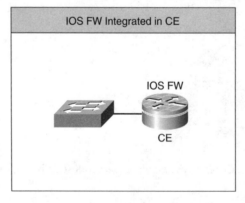

Figure 14-10   *Enterprise firewall deployment options*

- Explicitly permit the SBC to send SIP messages to the Communications Manager from the outside-in

- Implicitly permit the Communications Manager to send SIP messages to the SBC from the inside-out

- Implicitly permit the return flow of RTP/UDP packets from the outside-in to the TelePresence endpoints when they open the port by sending the first RTP/UDP packet from the inside-out

Figure 14-11 illustrates this functionality.

Advanced Firewall Functionality More advanced firewall functions include inspecting the SIP and RTP/RTCP messages for integrity and conformance and dynamically opening and closing TCP and UDP ports based on the state of the SIP transactions and sessions. However, if the SIP and RTP/RTCP packets are encrypted using TLS and Secure RTP (sRTP), the firewall cannot read them. At the time this book was written, a new feature called *TLS-Proxy* had been recently introduced on Cisco Firewall products, such as the ASA, which allows the firewall to participate in the TLS encryption between the Communications Manager and the SBC to decrypt and reencrypt the SIP messages and the RTP/RTCP packets. Work is under way to enable this feature throughout the various solution components so that the SIP and RTP/RTCP packets can be encrypted end-to-end while still

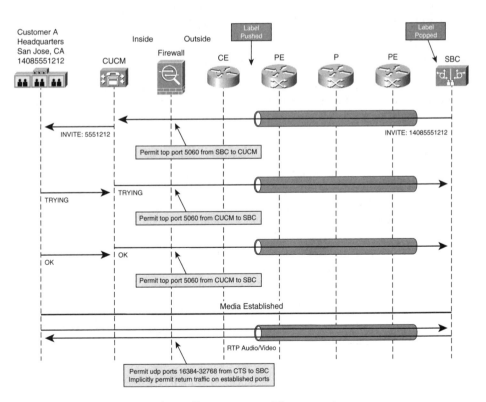

Figure 14-11 *Enterprise firewall access control list operation*

allowing the firewalls in the path to read them and provide the advanced functions previously mentioned. Until this capability is fully implemented in all the products end-to-end, the firewall must use ACLs to permit and deny the traffic. Other products within the solution provide SIP and RTP/RTCP protocol inspection, as you see in later sections.

Network Address Translation

Firewalls alone provide protection but require the Layer 3 IP addressing to be routable between the Communications Manager, TelePresence endpoints, and the SBC. If the customer wants to use RFC-1918 addressing on its Communications Manager or its TelePresence endpoints, NAT services must be provided at the customer edge in addition to firewall services. NAT provides an additional layer of security by hiding the IP addresses of the enterprise from the service provider. This is referred to as *topology hiding*. However, the SIP messages and RTP/RTCP packets need to traverse this NAT boundary.

Several different types of NAT exist in the industry. Likewise the industry standards bodies offer several competing architectures for NAT traversal, including the following:

■   Implementing SIP and RTP/RTCP Application Layer Gateway (ALG) services within the NAT so that the IP addresses and TCP/UDP ports contained within the body of the SIP messages can be "fixed up" as they pass through the NAT

■   Utilizing protocols such as Session Traversal Utilities for NAT (STUN), Interactive Connectivity Establishment (ICE), and Traversal Using Relay NAT (TURN) to work through NAT that do not provide SIP/RTP ALG functionality

■   Using Session Border Controllers (SBCs) to tunnel around or through NAT

Each approach has its associated pros and cons, depending on the specific situation being addressed. Because NAT is unable to read the SIP and RTP/RTCP messages because they are encrypted, Cisco has chosen to use the latter approach for now, using SBCs located within the service provider network and, optionally, also at the edge of the customer WAN.

Service Provider SBC-Based NAT Traversal   When Cisco set out to architect the Inter-Company solution, the design goal was to enable secure, transparent traversal of the enterprise NAT boundaries without dictating a specific type, vendor, model, or version of NAT. Cisco also did not want to dictate that the enterprise deploy an SBC at the enterprise edge, although that is supported as an optional, additional layer of protection as discussed later in the "Enterprise SBC-Based NAT Traversal" and "Enterprise Session Border Controllers" sections. Therefore, a nifty little feature was implemented in the Cisco SBC to allow it to solve the NAT traversal dilemma within the service provider network in a simple, yet elegant way, regardless of what model or version of NAT was used by the enterprise.

Figure 14-12 shows the same broken down path between Customer A Headquarters location and the service provider SBC. However, this time the enterprise has chosen not to export its internal RFC-1918 addresses to the SBC, and instead a NAT boundary is introduced at the customer edge.

The SBC does not have a route to the customer's RFC-1918 addresses in its routing table, and NAT cannot "fix up" the SIP messages either because the NAT model does not support SIP Application Layer Gateway (ALG) functionality or because the SIP messages are

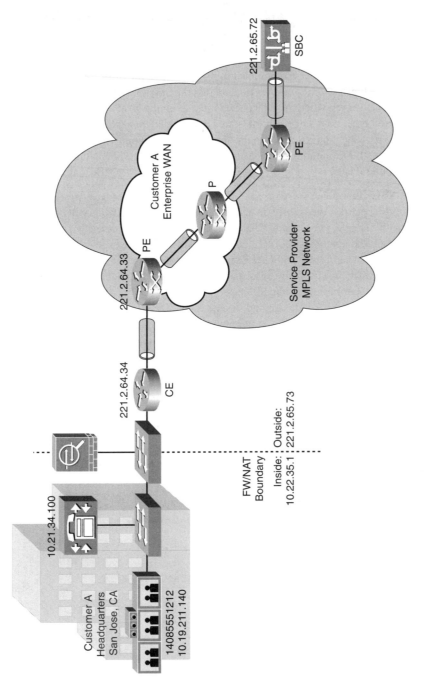

Figure 14-12   *Path from Company A headquarters to SBC: firewall and NAT*

encrypted between the Communications Manager and the SBC, or both. Figure 14-13 illustrates the exchange of SIP and RTP packets between the Communications Manager and the SBC and between the TelePresence endpoint and the SBC.

In the SIP INVITE sent from the Communications Manager to the SBC, the RFC-1918 IP address of the TelePresence endpoint was included in the Session Description Protocol (SDP) attributes. However, when the RTP packets sent from the TelePresence endpoint to the SBC traversed NAT, the source IP address and source UDP port was modified by NAT. The solution to this dilemma is actually quite simple. The SBC simply ignores the IP address and port that the Communications Manager told it to use in the SDP, and instead responds back to the IP address and port that it actually received the traffic from.

Enterprise SBC-Based NAT Traversal　The preceding examples have layered in a firewall and NAT between the enterprise network and the service provider SBC. By implementing this simple, yet elegant, NAT traversal feature in the Cisco SBC, the TelePresence Inter-Company solution can, in theory, work with any type, vendor, model, and version of NAT. The firewall and NAT significantly reduce the security exposure of the enterprise network, but for many customers this might not be enough. The service provider SBC is still permitted to send SIP messages through the firewall to the enterprise's Communications Manager and to send RTP/UDP messages through the firewall to the enterprise's TelePresence endpoints. These messages could be malformed or malicious, or the SBC could launch a medley of Denial of Service (DoS) type attacks

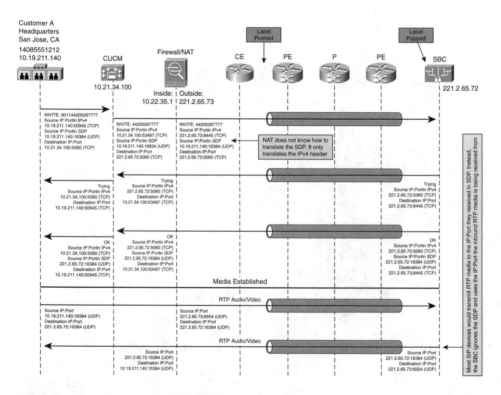

Figure 14-13　*Enterprise NAT operation*

against these IP addresses and ports, causing potential disruption to the enterprise's Communications Manager or TelePresence endpoints. Hence, a final layer of protection can be implemented by the enterprise customer using an enterprise-class SBC: the CUBE.

Enterprise Session Border Controllers

The Cisco enterprise-class SBC has been known by several names over the years: the Cisco Multimedia Conference Manager Proxy, the Cisco IOS IP-IP Gateway, and most recently the Cisco Unified Border Element (CUBE). The enterprise-class SBC is a feature of Cisco IOS Software running on an Integrated Services Router (ISR), such as the 2800 or 3800 series platforms, and can be implemented on a separate, stand-alone router within the DMZ or enabled on the WAN edge router. Figure 14-14 illustrates these deployment options.

CUBE functions as a SIP B2BUA and RTP/RTCP media proxy. It provides an additional layer of physical topology hiding; the SBC can communicate only with the CUBE, and CUBE in turn communicates with the Communications Manager and TelePresence endpoints hiding behind it. CUBE also performs SIP and RTP/RTCP protocol inspection and isolation. (That is, if malformed SIP or RTP/RTCP messages are sent from the SBC, the CUBE absorbs them instead of passing them on to the Communications Manager and TelePresence endpoints.) The CUBE can also provide an alternative method of NAT traversal.

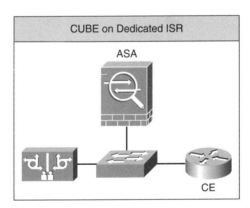

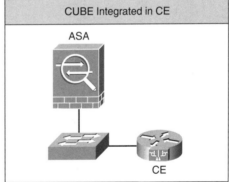

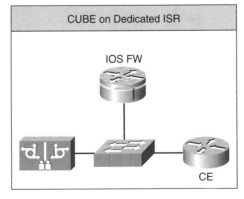

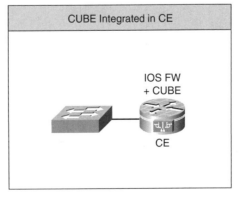

Figure 14-14 *Enterprise SBC deployment options*

(That is, the CUBE can have one interface inside the NAT and another interface outside the NAT, thereby negating the need for the NAT to "fix up" the messages.) Figure 14-15 illustrates one example of the CUBE in operation.

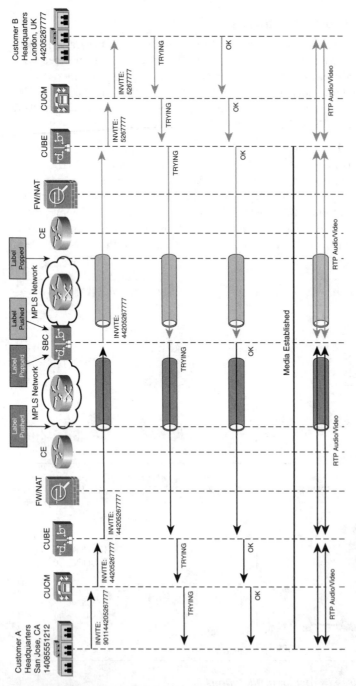

Figure 14-15 *Enterprise SBC operation*

SIP and RTP/RTCP Protocol Inspection

SIP and RTP/RTCP protocol inspection is the act of checking the headers and bodies of the messages for conformance to standards to mitigate the risk of malformed or malicious messages. Each of the components mentioned previously, including the firewall, the CUBE, and the SBC, provide this functionality, as illustrated in Figure 14-16.

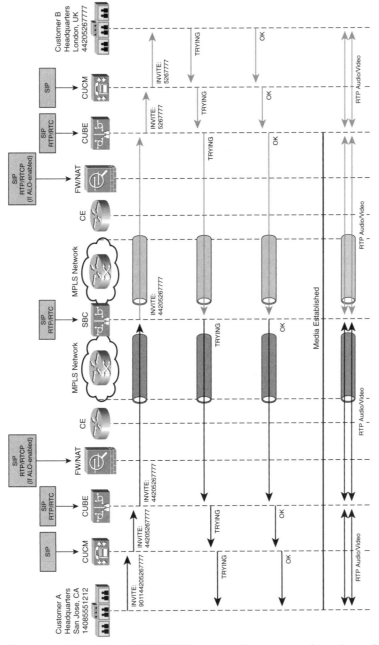

Figure 14-16   *SIP and RTP/RTCP protocol inspection along the path*

As the SIP message traverses from the TelePresence endpoint at Customer A, through the Communications Manager, through the CUBE, through the Firewall/NAT, through the SBC, through Customer B's firewall, NAT, CUBE, and Communications Manager, the SIP message is validated by each device that is capable of reading the contents of the message for conformance. Although the firewall can permit or deny certain IP addresses and ports, and NAT provides a layer of topology hiding and additional protection from rogue packets, these devices might not read the messages because they are encrypted or because the devices do not support the necessary SIP and RTP/RTCP ALG functionality, as discussed previously in the "Firewalls" and "Network Address Translation" sections. Therefore, the task of protocol conformance falls predominantly to the CUBE at each enterprise WAN edge and the SBC within the service provider network. Each of these run a medley of checks against the packet before forwarding it on to the next hop in that path. The actual checks performed vary by product and configuration, but some examples of the types of things these devices look for include, but are not limited to, the following:

- **SIP protocol inspection:** Verifies the headers and bodies of SIP and SDP messages for conformance with the standards.

- **RTP/RTCP protocol inspection:** Verifies the headers and bodies of RTP and RTCP audio and video media packets for conformance with the standards.

- **Rate of messages:** Protects against flooding attacks by restricting the number of SIP messages permitted from any one source.

- **Spoofed packets and rogue packets:** Drops packets that do not belong to a valid session based on IP addresses, TCP and UDP ports, and even SIP and RTP header information such as session ID, RTP sequence numbers, and so on.

- **Restrict codecs:** Restricts which audio and video encoding formats are permitted to be negotiated (for example, restrict audio to AAC-LD and restrict video to MPEG4/H.264).

- **Peer-based ACLs:** Restrict which IP addresses and hostnames are considered valid/authorized peers.

- **Digest authentication and hostname validation:** Authenticates the peer using a username/password authentication challenge/response and by validating the hostname in the SIP messages.

- **White lists/Black lists:** ALCs that permit or deny certain phone numbers (E.164 addresses) and SIP URIs from calling each other.

- **Call Admission Control:** Restricts the number of calls and the amount of bandwidth allowed to be used, either on a per call basis (for example, any given call can use only up to N Mbps) or on an aggregate basis (the sum of all calls from a given customer can use up to only N Mbps).

End-to-End Application-Layer Security

In addition to the myriad layers of protection provided by the components as discussed in the preceding section, all audio and video media packets must be authenticated and encrypted end-to-end for the users to trust that their conversations are indeed private and safe from eavesdropping.

However, encrypting the audio and video media packets is only the tip of the iceberg. The Cisco TelePresence solution provides a robust authentication and encryption framework encompassing much more than just media encryption. This framework was first invented in CUCM release 4.0 to support encryption of voice calls and has since proven to be a reliable and comprehensive security architecture supporting millions of Cisco Unified IP Phones deployed to date. Cisco TelePresence leverages this same Unified Communications architecture and extends it beyond the enterprise boundaries to provide end-to-end security for intercompany communications.

The following sections briefly describe each layer of this framework within the context of Cisco TelePresence Inter-Company Communications.

Digital Certificates

Before any secure communications can occur between a TelePresence endpoint and its Communication Manager or between two TelePresence endpoints, a framework of authentication and trust must first be established. Each TelePresence endpoint comes from the factory with an X.509v3 Digital Certificate installed in it, signed by the Cisco Manufacturing Certificate Authority. This is known as a Manufacturing Installed Certificate (MIC). This certificate provides the credentials used by the endpoints to perform a first-time authentication and enrollment into the security framework provided by the Communications Manager. Likewise, each Communications Manager also has a certificate, and this certificate authenticates the CM to the endpoint.

Certificate Authority Proxy Function

Within the Communications Manager is a Certificate Authority known as CAPF. This CA can create certificates under its own authority or can be used as a proxy to request certificates from an external CA and then proxy those certificates to the endpoints and the Communications Manager servers. The endpoints authenticate themselves to CAPF using their MICs. This enrollment process accomplishes the following:

- Allows the endpoint to download a new certificate known as a Locally Significant Certificate (LSC) that takes precedence over the MIC. This allows for new certificates to be distributed to the endpoints if the customer wants to use its own external CA, or if the Cisco Manufacturing CA were to ever be compromised, invalidating the integrity of the MIC. If the MIC were ever to be invalidated, the endpoint can alternatively use a one-time authentication string known only to the CAPF server and that endpoint to enroll with CAPF and download a new LSC.

- Allows the Communications Manager to learn the certificate of each endpoint, which it can later use to authenticate that endpoint in subsequent signaling protocol exchanges and to encrypt the endpoint configuration file.

- Allows the endpoint to learn the certificate of the Communications Manager Certificate Trust List Provider (CTL Provider).

Certificate Trust List

When CAPF has generated certificates for all the Communications Manager servers, the CTL Provider service builds a file called the Certificate Trust List (CTL). This file contains the list of Communications Manager hostnames, IP addresses, and certificates that the endpoints should trust for SIP signaling. The CTL Provider signs the CTL file using its own certificate and places the file on the Communications Manager to be downloaded by the endpoints. When the endpoint downloads the CTL, it authenticates the signature of the file and then reads the contents of the file to learn which Communications Manager servers it should trust.

Configuration File Integrity and Encryption

All endpoint configuration data is stored in the Communications Manager and is downloaded by the endpoints each time they boot up. It is also redownloaded automatically by the endpoints any time a change in the configuration is made within the Communications Manager Administration that would affect that endpoint's configuration. This configuration file must be encrypted so that only the intended endpoint can read it. Furthermore, it must be digitally signed by the Communications Manager so that the endpoint can trust that the file has not been manipulated by someone else. The Communications Manager encrypts the file using the endpoint's certificate and then signs the file using its own certificate. When the endpoint downloads its configuration file, it first verifies the signature of the file against the list of trusted servers contained in its CTL. If the signature is valid, it then proceeds to decrypt the file and read its contents.

Firmware File Integrity

Like configuration files, the firmware files (which contain the operating system and application software the endpoints execute) are also downloaded from the Communications Manager. To prevent an endpoint from downloading a firmware file that has been accidentally or maliciously modified or corrupted, the firmware files are digitally signed by Cisco when they are created. When the endpoint downloads its firmware file, it first verifies the signature of the file. If the signature is valid, it then proceeds to extract the firmware into its nonvolatile memory and boot to this new version.

Endpoint-Server Signaling Authentication and Encryption

The configuration file downloaded by the endpoints contains the list of Communications Managers that the endpoint should register to, which, in turn, are validated against the CTL file. The endpoint initiates a Tunneling Layer Security (TLS) handshake with its Communications Manager to establish a TLS connection over which it sends all SIP messages. During the handshake process, the endpoint provides the Communications Manager with its certificate as its credentials, and vice versa. Therefore, the TLS connection is mutually authenticated, and the two hosts use each other's certificates to encrypt all the SIP messages sent over this connection.

Server-Server Signaling Authentication and Encryption

For the SIP signaling channel between the Communications Manager, CUBE, and the service provider SBC, several options exist for authentication and encryption. Server-server relationships are a little different than endpoint-server relationships because server-server relationships are manually built by the administrators, whereas the endpoints automatically download their configurations.

Tunneling Layer Security and IPsec

TLS and IPsec are both viable means of encrypting all SIP signaling traffic between the servers. TLS works at the application layer, dynamically creating a secure tunnel between two applications whenever that application requests a socket. For example, the SIP call signaling stack running inside the Communications Manager can create a TLS connection to the SIP call signaling stack running on the CUBE. The TLS connection is, therefore, specific to that application.

IPsec, by contrast, works at the network or operating system layer, creating a secure tunnel between two hosts over which any application can travel. For example, the Communications Manager runs on top of the Linux operating system, whereas CUBE runs on top of Cisco IOS. These two operating systems can create an IPsec tunnel between each other, over which any application protocol, such as SIP, could be tunneled.

It's a subtle but distinct difference. From a practical point of view, both TLS and IPSec require the administrator to define the peer relationships and the credentials that establish the secure tunnel. The difference is *where* you administer that connection. For the Communications Manager, you configure TLS in the Communications Manager Administration pages, whereas you configure IPsec in the Operating System Platform Administration pages. Likewise, for CUBE, you configure TLS under the SIP dial-peer configuration, whereas you configure IPsec independently of the dial-peers using ACLs and IPsec policies that are then bound to one or more Layer 3 interfaces.

Another difference is that TLS is specific to TCP-based applications, whereas IPsec can be used for both TCP- and UDP-based applications. If the SIP connections between the Communications Manager, CUBE, and the SBC use UDP-based transport, TLS is not an option, and IPsec might be your best alternative.

Figure 14-17 helps illustrate the differences between TLS and IPsec.

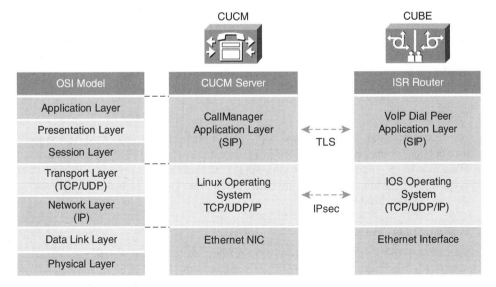

Figure 14-17 *Tunneling layer security versus IPsec*

Digest Authentication

If neither TLS nor IPsec are a viable option, simple Digest Authentication can be used. Like TLS, Digest Authentication operates at the application layer and allows each SIP request to be validated using a challenge/response method whereby the requestor provides its username and password to the receiver, and the receiver validates those credentials before accepting and responding to the request. For example, if CUBE initiates a request, such as a SIP INVITE to the Communications Manager, the Communications Manager can respond to the request with a digest challenge. CUBE responds to the challenge with its username and password credentials. The credentials are verified against the Communications Manager's Application User database, and assuming they pass, the Communications Manager responds to the original request (the INVITE). In turn, CUBE can do the same to the Communications Manager whenever the Communications Manager initiates a request. Although Digest Authentication is useful for validating the authenticity of the originator of every SIP request, it does not encrypt the message. Therefore, the SIP messages themselves can still be read, and potentially manipulated, by a man-in-the-middle eavesdropper. Therefore, Digest Authentication is the weakest form of security for SIP applications and should only be used if a superior method such as TLS or IPsec is not available.

Media Encryption

Now that you have secured all the signaling channels between the TelePresence endpoints and the Communications Managers, and between the Communications Managers and the CUBE, and between the CUBE and the service provider SBC, you are ready to activate media encryption. In the Cisco TelePresence Solution, as in its Unified Communications solution, media encryption is accomplished using Secure Real-Time Transport Protocol (sRTP), which simply scrambles the payload of the RTP message. The RTP, UDP, and IP headers are not encrypted. Therefore, sRTP adds virtually no overhead to each RTP packet, and only the two endpoints that are encoding and decoding the audio or video RTP packets need to support it. All other devices in the path that might proxy those RTP packets (such as the CUBE and Cisco SBC) need pass only the encrypted payload of the packet through transparently because they are not actually decoding and re-encoding the media. These devices rewrite the RTP header but do not decode or re-encode the RTP payload.

Key Exchange

For the two endpoints to encrypt and decrypt each other's media, keys must be negotiated between them. This must be done in a secure fashion over an encrypted tunnel, or else a man-in-the-middle could eavesdrop on the conversation and derive the keys for decrypting that session media. There are currently two methods of exchanging media session keys: S-Description and dTLS.

S-Description Versus dTLS

S-Description provides a means of exchanging keys through the SIP signaling messages, specifically within the body of the SDP offer and answer. These SIP/SDP messages follow the hop-by-hop path through every device in the path that reads and processes the contents of the SIP messages; from the source TelePresence endpoint to its Communications Manager, from the Communications Manager to CUBE, from CUBE to the SBC, from the SBC to CUBE, from CUBE to the Communications Manager, and finally down to the destination TelePresence endpoint. Each host in this chain must receive the S-Description field in the SDP body of its incoming SIP message and pass it in the SDP body of its outgoing SIP message to the next hop. This occurs in both directions so that the two endpoints know each other's keys.

There are two problems with this approach. First, it relies on the notion of *transitive trust*. Each host in this path must trust that the next-hop host has a secure connection to its next-hop host. For instance, the TelePresence endpoint must trust that the connection between the Communications Manager and CUBE is secured through TLS or IPsec. Likewise, the Communications Manager must trust that the connection between CUBE and the SBC is secured, and so forth. One enterprise administrator might ensure that TLS is configured between its TelePresence Endpoint all the way through to the service provider SBC, but there is no guarantee that the connection from the SBC to the other enterprise is secured. If the security of the end-to-end signaling path between two endpoints cannot be guaranteed, there is no way to trust that the S-Description keys are safe from eavesdropping.

Second, SIP enables many endpoints to share a common URI or telephone number. This enables a call to be extended to many endpoints so that it can be answered by any one of them. In Communications Manager vernacular, this is referred to as a *Shared Line Appearance*. In generic SIP vernacular, it is referred to as *forking*. Common uses of this feature include a user who has multiple devices that all share the same telephone number or a hunt group where multiple devices can answer inbound calls to a pilot number. Because the SIP/SDP message is forked to all the endpoints that share that number, the keys for encrypting that session's media are too. This is undesirable because any of the devices sharing that URI possess the media session keys and can, therefore, eavesdrop on the media.

Because of these two drawbacks in the S-Description method, Cisco TelePresence uses dTLS instead. S-Description is still supported, but dTLS takes precedence. After the SIP session is established end-to-end and the RTP media channels begin flowing between the two endpoints, the first thing the endpoints do before actually transmitting media is to initiate a dTLS handshake and establish a secure tunnel between themselves. This is done using the same UDP socket that was created to carry the RTP media, and because the RTP packets are passed transparently through devices such as CUBE and the SBC, the dTLS tunnel is end-to-end in nature between the two endpoints. The endpoints use their MIC certificates to establish the dTLS session and authenticate each other. They then exchange keys over this encrypted dTLS session and then proceed to encrypt the RTP messages using those keys. Any S-Description keys advertised or received by the endpoints are ignored in favor of the keys they negotiated directly between each other over dTLS. Figure 14-18 illustrates this end-to-end dTLS mechanism.

dTLS to S-Description Fallback

At the time this book was written, dTLS was used only by Cisco TelePresence endpoints. Other types of endpoints in the Unified Communications suite such as IP Phones and VoIP gateways continue to use S-Description. Therefore, if a Cisco TelePresence system calls a non-TelePresence device, such as an IP Phone or a gateway, the dTLS handshake

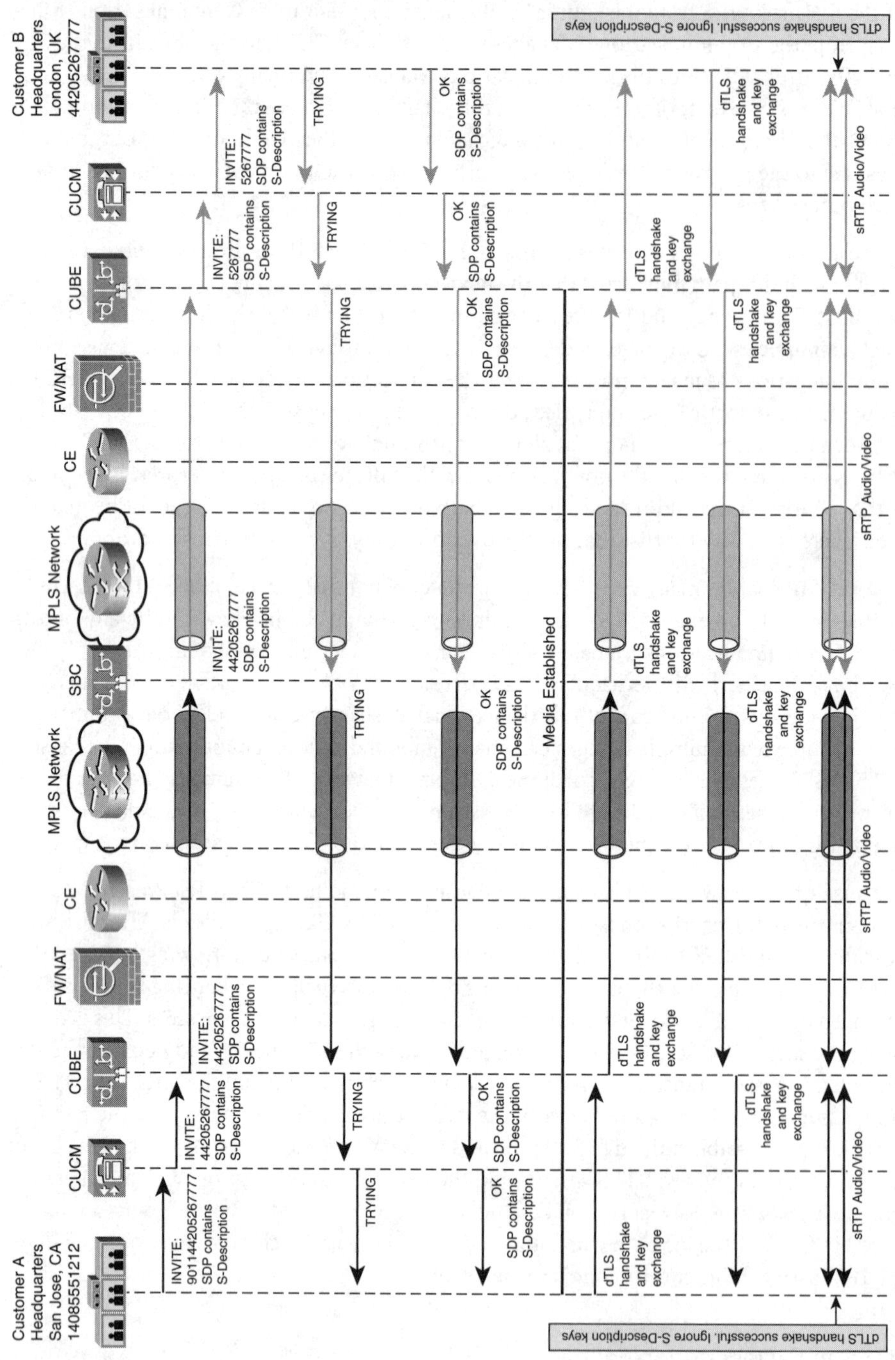

Figure 14-18 *dTLS key exchange operation*

fails, and the TelePresence system falls back to using the S-Description keys. This is referred to as *dTLS to S-Description fallback*, and it is automatic.

sRTP to RTP Fallback

Likewise, if both dTLS and S-Description fail for any reason, the TelePresence systems automatically fall back to using unencrypted RTP. This allows the call to proceed even if one end or the other is not configured for encryption. To ensure that the user knows whether their session is encrypted, icons are displayed on the screen to indicate the security level of the call. A Closed Lock icon means that the session's media is encrypted end-to-end. An Open Lock icon means that the SIP signaling between the TelePresence endpoint and its Communications Manager is encrypted, but both dTLS and S-Description negotiations failed for the current call and, therefore, the session's media is not encrypted. A Shield icon means that the SIP signaling between the TelePresence endpoint and its Communications Manager is authenticated but not encrypted, and neither is the media. Figure 14-19 illustrates these different icons and their meanings.

|Media is
encrypted|Media is not
encrypted|Signaling is
authenticated,
but not encrypted|

Figure 14-19   *Cisco TelePresence security icons and their meanings*

Inter-Company Deployment Models

Enterprise customers have a number of network design options to choose from when deploying Cisco TelePresence Inter-Company access circuits. The following sections step through these options, starting with the most simple deployment model consisting of a single access circuit to a single service provider and working up to the most scalable, yet most complex designs.

Service providers, in turn, have choices in the types of Inter-Company services they choose to offer and how those services are deployed.

Begin by examining a single enterprise customer who wants to connect to a single service provider so that it can meet with other customers connected to that same provider.

Converged Versus Overlay Access Circuits

The first choice every enterprise customer must make is whether to use a converged WAN circuit to access the inter-company network or to deploy a separate, overlay intercompany access circuit. The benefits of convergence are clear: maximize return on investment and achieve the lowest total cost of ownership by leveraging the same WAN circuits and bandwidth for all intra-company data, voice, video, and Inter-Company TelePresence communications.

However, some customer's WANs might not be ready for this level of integration, and upgrading their WAN to accommodate this level of convergence might require months of planning, so it might be more expedient for them in the short term to deploy a new circuit for intercompany communications. Even customers whose WANs are fully converged might need to modify their WAN to support Inter-Company TelePresence. Or their existing WAN circuits might not be from the same provider from whom they want to purchase intercompany services from, so they still might choose to deploy a separate, overlay circuit from their inter-company provider.

Consider the following scenario depicted in Figure 14-20 in which an Enterprise customer headquarters and three remote branch offices are interconnected using point-to-point, 45-Mbps T-3 leased-line WAN circuits from provider X.

This customer's WAN is fully converged; all data, voice, and video applications within its company ride over these leased-line circuits between its offices. The WAN circuits were recently upgraded from point-to-point, 1.544-Mbps T-1 circuits to 45-Mbps T-3 circuits when they deployed Cisco TelePresence between its branches, and now it would like to participate in Inter-Company TelePresence with some of its key partners, suppliers, and customers. However, provider X does not offer Cisco TelePresence Inter-Company services, so the customer must decide how to connect its offices to provider Y.

For this example, assume that re-architecting its WAN to migrate from point-to-point, T-3 leased lines to MPLS takes months of planning and reconfiguration, and the company's executives want intercompany TelePresence capabilities deployed immediately. Likewise, switching its existing WAN circuits from provider X to provider Y is not an option due to its existing contractual obligations with provider X. Therefore, the company has decided to keep its existing leased-line circuits from provider X and purchase a brand new, dedicated overlay access circuit from provider Y. Now it must decide where that circuit should terminate, how much bandwidth to provision on that circuit, and what the dial plan, IP routing, and Firewall/NAT traversal implications are.

Centralized Inter-Company Access Circuit

The natural first step, particularly for situations such as the one depicted in the preceding section, is to install a new, dedicated access circuit into a central location, such as the company's headquarters. Figure 14-21 illustrates this new arrangement.

This choice was the most expedient for this customer. It allowed the customer to get intercompany services up and running quickly at a relatively low up-front cost and minimal

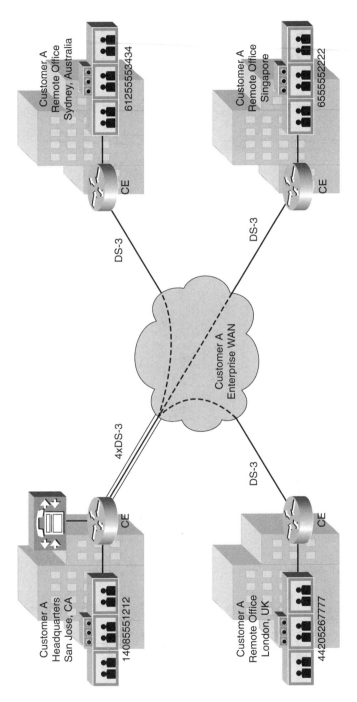

Figure 14-20   *Enterprise customer: existing WAN topology*

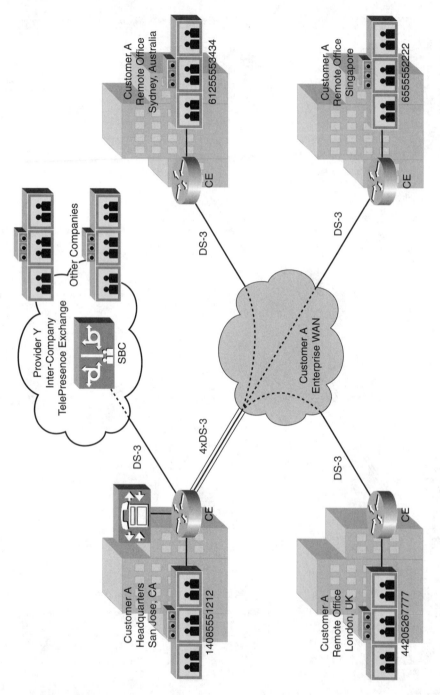

Figure 14-21 *Enterprise customer: new dedicated Inter-Company access circuit*

change to its existing network. However, there are some things to consider in terms of end-to-end latency, bandwidth capacity planning, dial plan design and firewall/NAT traversal.

Centralized Access Circuit: End-to-End Latency

The first and most critical aspect of choosing where this new circuit should be located is the additional latency caused by having to traverse the enterprise WAN before reaching the intercompany access circuit. For example, if location 4 were located in London, and the headquarters where the intercompany access circuit were located was California, and London wanted to have an intercompany meeting with a customer located somewhere else in the Europe, the call would need to traverse the enterprise leased-line WAN from London to California and then hop off to the intercompany service provider and travel all the way back across the Atlantic to Europe. This would introduce approximately 240 ms of unnecessary latency in each direction, assuming that it takes 120 ms to get from London to California and another 120 ms to get from California to Europe. This puts the end-to-end latency way above the 150 ms target for a good TelePresence experience. If the London location had an intercompany access circuit of its own, it could take a much more direct path, cutting the latency for that call by 75 percent or more.

Centralized Access Circuit: Bandwidth Capacity Planning

The second aspect to consider is how many intercompany calls might need to be sustained at any given time and, therefore, how much bandwidth should be provisioned on the intercompany access circuit. Intercompany service providers are most likely to sell bandwidth at a fixed rate per month in terms of simultaneous calls. For example, using the scenario depicted in the preceding figures, this customer could have four simultaneous intercompany calls at any given time. Assuming that each call from a CTS-3000 model TelePresence system requires approximately 15 Mbps, the customer needs to provision 60 Mbps on the intercompany access circuit.

Centralized Access Circuit: Dial Plan Design

The third aspect to consider is how a centralized access circuit might affect the company's dial plan and how to configure the routing of calls to and from the intercompany network. The sections that follow detail these considerations.

Route Lists and Route Groups

TelePresence Systems not only need to call other TelePresence Systems, but they also might need to make normal voice calls to the PSTN (such as when the Audio Add-In feature is used to bring a voice-only participant into a TelePresence meeting). Therefore, the dial plan must consist of routing entries that allow a TelePresence system to dial an external access code (such as 9 in the United States or 00 in Europe), followed by a fully qualified E.164 address of another company. The enterprise Communications Manager has no way of knowing whether that E.164 address is another company's TelePresence system or a PSTN phone number. One way to tackle this is to implement Route Groups and Route Lists in the Communications Manager. Route Group #1 would send the call to the intercompany service provider. If the intercompany provider does not recognize the E.164 address that was dialed, it rejects the call with SIP error code 404 Not Found. The customer's Communications Manager can then react to this error code by routing the call to the next Route Group in the Route List, Route Group #2, which could be a PSTN gateway, for example. Figure 14-22 illustrates this arrangement.

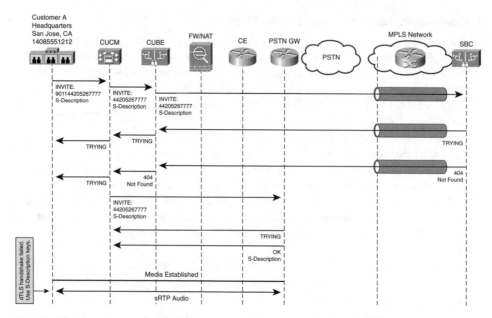

Figure 14-22   *Enterprise customer: Inter-Company and PSTN route groups*

E.164 Addressing

To mimic the familiar functionality of the PSTN, the TelePresence systems located around the world should be assigned E.164 addresses that correlate with their physical locations. For example, TelePresence systems in San Jose, California, would have an E.164 address beginning with country code 1 and area code 408. Likewise, TelePresence systems in London would begin with country code 44 and area code 20.

However, because the intercompany access circuit is physically located in a central location (in this case California), communicating the calling party and called party identification to the service provider might get a little convoluted. The provider might have rules about what calling party identifiers it accepts within each geography, and there also might be country-specific laws governing the use of VoIP that could be violated by routing a call from one country, through a U.S. service provider, and back to another company in the same country or another country. In addition, the users in other countries might need to be trained to dial the number as a long-distance call, even though they are calling another company in their same geography. For example, a user making an intercompany call from London to another company in London might have to dial the number as 9 011 44 20 5555 1234, whereas they would normally dial it as 0 5555 1234 when making a regular telephone call.

Centralized Access Circuit: Firewall/NAT Traversal

The forth aspect to consider is how to route the company's internal IP addresses to this new intercompany access circuit and how to deal with firewall and NAT boundaries between the enterprise network and service provider Y. Refer back to the "Inter-VPN Security" section earlier in this chapter for a discussion of these topics. There are innumerable possibilities here. For example, the customer might already have a DMZ at the location where the intercompany access circuit is installed, so it might run this new circuit through its existing firewall. Alternatively, a new firewall and DMZ might be deployed for this circuit. For sake of our example, the customer has chosen to terminate this new access circuit on a new, dedicated Cisco Integrated Services Router (ISR) that is managed by the service provider. Downstream from that router, a new Cisco Advanced Security Appliance (ASA) will be installed to the firewall communications between the intercompany network and the enterprise network. Finally, another ISR, managed by the customer, will run the CUBE services, which hide the customer's internal IP addresses from the service provider and provide an extra layer of protection between the service provider and the customer's Communications Manager. Figure 14-23 illustrates this arrangement.

Multiple, Decentralized Inter-Company Access Circuits

The previous examples illustrated the option of using a nonconverged, dedicated overlay circuit for accessing the intercompany TelePresence network from a centralized location. This was the expedient choice to get it up and running quickly with only four TelePresence rooms, but as it continues to deploy more and more TelePresence rooms around the globe, this model would result in high latency, bandwidth bottlenecks, and complicated dialing plans for the globally dispersed TelePresence locations. This section considers the possibilities if the enterprise customer's WAN was a fully converged, MPLS-based network.

Ideally, TelePresence calls should always take the shortest path to their destination from a physical and logical IP routing perspective to minimize end-to-end latency and reduce unnecessary bandwidth consumption. Furthermore, the experience of dialing TelePresence calls should ideally mimic, as closely as possible, the experience of dialing regular telephone calls with the same familiar access codes, international access codes, and other dialing rules and nomenclature users would intuitively be inclined to use.

Decentralized Access Circuits: Bandwidth Capacity Planning

Assume that the customer has now decided to convert its leased-line WAN circuits into an MPLS-based WAN, serviced by provider Y. Figure 14-24 illustrates this new arrangement.

Now that its WAN is MPLS-based, it can extend its MPLS VPN to connect each location to its service provider's Inter-Company SBCs. The SBCs are strategically located around the world, and new circuits are provisioned within the MPLS cloud to connect each of the SBCs to the customer's MPLS VPN. This arrangement provides shortest-path routing from each of the customer's locations to its nearest SBC. Figure 14-25 illustrates this arrangement.

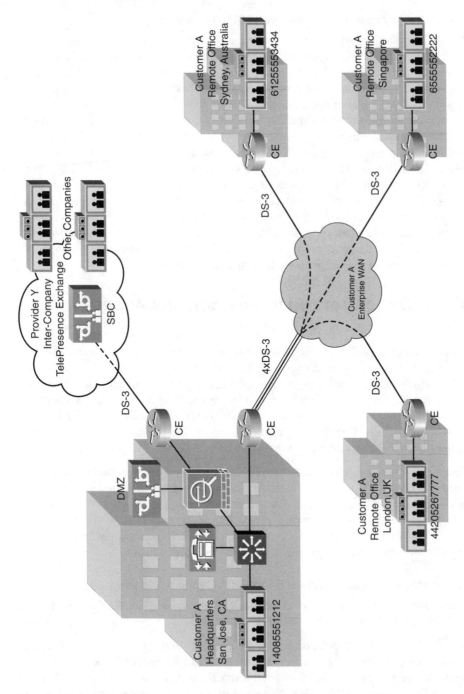

Figure 14-23 *Enterprise customer: centralized CUBE and firewall placement*

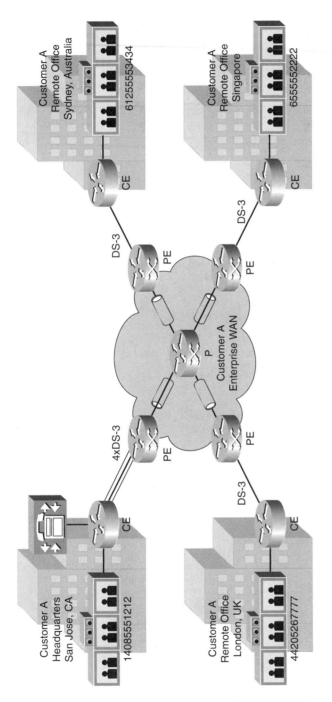

Figure 14-24 *Enterprise customer: new MPLS WAN topology*

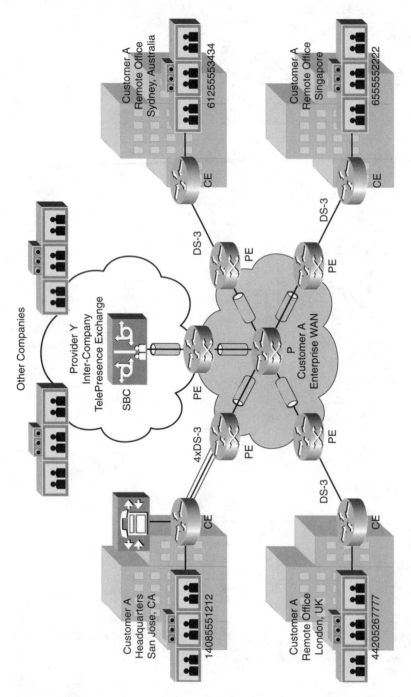

Figure 14-25 *Enterprise customer: MPLS VPN extended to service provider SBCs*

Now, when the London location calls another customer in Europe, the call traverses the London WAN circuit into the MPLS cloud and goes directly to the service provider's SBC, rather than hair pinning through the headquarters location, a much more expedient path.

Decentralized Access Circuits: Dial Plan Design

In reality, the intercompany service provider likely has several SBCs, located in strategic places around the globe. To steer the calls from each location to its nearest SBC, the dial plan in the Communications Manager must be constructed appropriately. For example, when the London location dials another customer in Europe, such as Hallbergmoos, Germany, they might do so by dialing 0 00 49 811 555 1234. This pattern, when dialed from the London location, should be routed by the Communications Manager to the SBC in Amsterdam. Conversely, when the California location dials that same customer in Germany, it might do so by dialing 9 011 49 811 555 1234, which can either be routed to the SBC in San Francisco and then traverse the service provider network to the SBC in Amsterdam, or it could be routed over the customer's MPLS VPN directly to the SBC in Amsterdam.

Route Lists, Route Groups, and Other Advanced Dial Plan Tools

CUCM is utterly flexible in its digit matching and routing configuration, and the configurations described in the preceding section can easily be achieved through the use of Route Patterns, Route Groups, and Route Lists to steer the calls to the correct destinations, while being filtered based on the source calling device using Calling Search Spaces, Partitions, Route Filters, and Translation Patterns (collectively referred to as *class of service permissions*). You can even use Time of Day Routing to steer calls one way during normal business hours for a given location, and another way outside of normal business hours for that location. You can also use these tools to provide multiple, preference-ordered routes to a given destination. For example, when the California location dials 9 011 49 811 555 1234 to call another company in Germany, this number could be routed to a Route List where preference #1 is to route the call to the Amsterdam SBC, preference #2 is to route the call to the San Francisco SBC, and preference #3 (if the intercompany provider offers such a service) is to route it to the intercompany provider's help desk so that an operator can assist the caller in reaching its desired destination. During regular business hours in California, preference #3 could route to the help desk in San Francisco, whereas outside of regular business hours that call could be routed to the help desk in Amsterdam.

Decentralized Access Circuits: Firewall/NAT Traversal

Because the TelePresence intercompany traffic now rides over the same converged WAN circuits from each office into the MPLS cloud, taking the most direct path to the service provider's SBC, the firewall and NAT boundaries should also be decentralized. Firewalls, NAT boundaries, and Unified Border Elements should be distributed at each office location at or near the WAN edge. This certainly adds a level of engineering complexity to the design but provides the highest level of security and the most efficient use of the converged network paths.

Most enterprises do not set up firewall and NAT boundaries between their remote offices because the WAN traffic is all internal to the company. But now, because intercompany traffic can ride over the same converged WAN circuits, firewalls and NAT boundaries need to be implemented at these locations. Intracompany traffic does not need to be fire-walled or translated, so ACLs can be constructed so that only traffic matching specific source/destination IP address ranges (traffic destined to/from the intercompany service provider) passes through the firewall and NAT. All intracompany traffic, including intra-company TelePresence calls, bypasses these devices and remains unaffected.

There are numerous options for which model and configuration of firewall and NAT to use and whether to implement the CUBE services on the existing WAN routers or deploy CUBE on new stand-alone routers. Refer back to the "Inter-VPN Security" section in this chapter for a discussion of these topics. The end goal is to design the solution so that TelePresence calls made from any office can be routed by the Communications Manager to that office's local CUBE, traverse the firewall and NAT boundary at that office's WAN edge, and go to the physically and logically closest service provider SBC. Likewise, in-bound calls from the service provider to any of the offices should be routed by the Com-munications Manager to that office's local CUBE and then down to the TelePresence endpoint at that office. Figure 14-26 illustrates these concepts.

Inter-Company Dialing Models

Throughout this chapter you have seen examples showing users directly dialing the TeleP-resence phone number of another company, similar to the way that regular telephone calls are made between companies today. In practice however, some companies might not want their users to directly dial external intercompany calls. This might be due, for example, to the way TelePresence Inter-Company services are financed internally within the company. Likewise, whether for privacy, security, or other policy-related reasons, some companies might not want to expose their TelePresence phone numbers to be directly dialed from the outside world.

Just like in enterprise telephone systems, the administrator has the choice whether to per-mit Direct Outward Dialing (DOD) or Direct Inward Dialing (DID) and has a great amount of control over how TelePresence phone numbers and names (Calling Line ID and Calling Name Display) are presented to the outside world.

Direct-Dialing Versus Indirect Meet-Me Dialing

Direct dialing presumes that the TelePresence room at one company is capable of directly dialing the TelePresence phone number of another company. This means that the company that is placing the call must have Direct Outward Dialing (DOD) enabled on their TeleP-resence rooms and that the company that is receiving the call must have Direct Inward Di-aling (DID) enabled on their TelePresence rooms.

Enabling DOD and DID is simply a matter of how the route patterns, route lists, route groups, and class of service permissions are configured in each company's Communica-tions Manager for each TelePresence room. As previously mentioned, the Communica-tions Manager provides the function of a Private Branch Exchange (PBX), and DOD is, therefore, typically enabled by dialing an external access code such as 9 in the United States or 0 in many other countries. These routes can be further restricted based on call-ing permissions to suit any political or financial policy the company might want. For example,

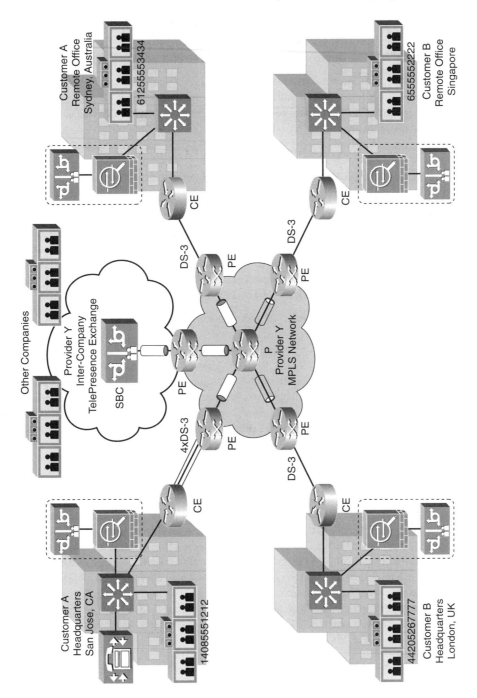

Figure 14-26 *Enterprise customer: decentralized firewalls and CUBEs*

the company might choose to allow CTS-3000s to directly dial external calls, whereas CTS-500s are not allowed to, or they might want to implement Time of Day Routing so that users are allowed to directly dial external calls only during business hours.

Likewise, enabling DID in the Communications Manager is simply a matter of the company purchasing a block of fully qualified E.164 DID numbers from its service provider and assigning those E.164 addresses to its TelePresence rooms so that external entities can directly dial into those rooms.

Direct Inward Dialing/Direct Outward Dialing Security Considerations

When enabling DID and DOD, a couple of security-related features are worth considering:

- **Auto-Answer Override:** For Intra-Company TelePresence calls, it is common practice to configure the TelePresence systems to automatically answer incoming calls. This allows the OBTP feature to work most conveniently. The first user to arrive at the meeting presses the button, and the other end automatically answers. However, when intercompany capabilities are enabled, this means that anybody outside your company can dial your TelePresence rooms, and the systems will automatically accept the call, which could result in serious privacy and confidentiality concerns.

    As of Cisco TelePresence Release 1.2 and higher, a feature was implemented in the TelePresence systems to override the auto-answer setting when the source of the call is an external party. This allows intracompany calls to be auto-answered, while intercompany calls are not. The Communications Manager decides whether the call is from an internal or external party based on the configuration of the SIP trunks inside the Communications Manager. If the SIP trunk is marked internal, the TelePresence System auto-answers the call. If the SIP trunk is marked External, the TelePresence System does not auto-answer the call and rings normally until a user accepts the inbound call by pressing the Answer softkey on the TelePresence IP Phone user interface.

- **White Lists and Black Lists:** Many customers want the capability to explicitly permit or deny specific Calling Party Numbers from dialing into their TelePresence rooms, and explicitly permit or deny their TelePresence rooms from dialing out to specific Called Party Numbers. There are a variety of places where these permit/deny lists can be maintained: in the service provider's Session Border Controller, in the enterprise customer's Unified Border Element, or in the enterprise customer's Communications Manager. Inbound permit/deny lists should ideally be located in the SBC or the CUBE to reduce the need to pass the call all the way down to the Communications Manager before deciding to reject it. Likewise, outbound permit/deny lists should ideally be located in the Communications Manager to reduce the need to pass the call all the way up to the CUBE or SBC before deciding to reject it.

In-Direct Meet-Me Dialing

For customers who do not want to enable direct dialing, the suggested alternative is to use the Cisco TelePresence Multipoint Switch (CTMS) as a centralized meeting place for all intercompany calls. Instead of dialing the TelePresence phone number of another company directly, users who want to have a meeting with another company must arrange for a CTMS dial-in number, and both parties must dial into the CTMS. This is referred to as

Meet-Me style conferencing and is a fully supported feature of CTMS. Alternatively, the CTMS administrator or help desk personnel can dial out from the CTMS to each of the parties at the scheduled time of the meeting. Refer to Chapter 13, "Multipoint TelePresence Design," for more details on CTMS functionality.

The CTMS can be located at one or the other company, or can be hosted by a service provider. Hosting the CTMS at your company provides the advantage of putting you in full control over your own multipoint resources, and you can use them whenever and however you want. You can deploy as many CTMS servers as you need, from a single server centrally located to dozens of servers distributed geographically around your network. You can assign each user his or her own dedicated CTMS meet-me number or allocate them from a pool on a per-meeting basis.

However, by hosting the CTMS, you voluntarily assume responsibility of managing those resources and putting in enough bandwidth into each CTMS location so that parties outside your company who want to meet with you can dial into your CTMS. You must also obtain an adequate range of DID numbers to be allocated to your CTMS for these Meet-Me style meetings. Many customers will prefer to outsource that function to their inter-company provider, who can host the CTMS resources inside the cloud and provide Meet-Me numbers as a service. This provides economies of scale because the service providers could host multiple customers on a pool of shared CTMS resources.

Scheduling Inter-Company Meetings

Cisco designed its TelePresence solution to ensure that TelePresence calls are just as easy and intuitive as dialing a regular telephone call. However, Cisco wanted to make it even easier than that and, therefore, developed a scheduling paradigm so that the users simply schedule their meeting as they normally would, using existing, familiar groupware applications such as Microsoft Outlook or Lotus Notes, and Cisco TelePresence Manager causes a button to appear on the TelePresence IP Phone so that the users simply push a single button to activate the meeting, eliminating the complexity of dialing numbers all together. Cisco refers to this as the OBTP feature.

Although OBTP works flawlessly within an organization, it doesn't work quite as fluidly when scheduling intercompany meetings because the user at company A who is using Microsoft Outlook or Lotus Notes to schedule the meeting does not have visibility into the availability of the people or TelePresence rooms at company B. Likewise, the Cisco TelePresence Manager at company A cannot push the meeting details down to the TelePresence IP Phones at company B. As a result, although scheduling the meeting between users at different companies is relatively straightforward, providing the OBTP feature for those meetings is challenging.

Cisco envisions inventing methods in the future whereby the TelePresence Managers at different companies can communicate and pass meeting details between each other to facilitate OBTP ease of use for intercompany meetings. For the time being, the following sections step through the different use cases and options available.

Direct Dialing Model

Consider the following use case: Rachael at company A wants to schedule a TelePresence meeting with three of her colleagues at company A and three of her colleagues at company B. Her Microsoft Outlook calendar shows her the availability, in real-time, of her colleagues at company A and the TelePresence rooms available to her at company A. However, she has no visibility into the availability of her colleagues or the TelePresence rooms at company B. She must email or call her colleagues at company B on the telephone to determine their availability before submitting the meeting request in Microsoft Outlook.

After discussing the meeting with her colleagues at company B over the telephone and determining their availability, she constructs a Microsoft Outlook meeting invitation that contains the following people and resources in the invitee field:

> To: racheal@companyA.com; bob@companyA.com; joe@companyA.com; sue@companyA.com; ralph@companyB.com; mark@companyB.com; janice@companyB.com
>
> Resources: TProom1@companyA.com

The Cisco TelePresence Manager at company A notices that only one TelePresence room has been invited to this meeting and responds by sending her an email asking for clarification. If Rachael ignores the email, the room will be reserved, but the OBTP feature will not be activated on the TelePresence IP Phone. Thus, when they arrive at the meeting, they will need to manually dial the TelePresence phone number of the other company. Alternatively, Rachael can respond to the email she received from her TelePresence Manager by following the hyperlink contained within the email to login to TelePresence Manager and specify a TelePresence number to be dialed for that meeting. Because she does not know the TelePresence phone number of company B, she must call one of her colleagues at that company to obtain it. OBTP will now be enabled on company A's TelePresence room for that meeting.

On the other side, the TelePresence room at company B has not been booked yet. One of the users at company B who received the meeting invitation (for example, Ralph, Mark, or Janice) must forward the invitation to their TelePresence room. So Janice forwards the meeting invitation to TProom1@companyB.com. The TelePresence Manager at the company notices that only one TelePresence at company B has been invited to this meeting and responds by sending Janice an email asking for clarification. Janice logs into her TelePresence Manager by following the hyperlink contained with the email and specifying the TelePresence number of the room at company A, calling Rachael back first to get that information. OBTP can now be enabled on company B's TelePresence room for that meeting as well. Now either side can initiate the meeting by pressing the button.

Obviously this workflow process is less than ideal. It requires that the users understand the behind-the-scenes behavior of Cisco TelePresence Manager and how to program it to provide OBTP for this type of meeting. They will likely need to open a case with their help desk to assist them through this process.

In-Direct Dialing Model

Until these scheduling complexities can be streamlined, many customers will choose to use the In-Direct Meet-Me model for intercompany calls and require that users contact the help desk to assist them in scheduling these types of meetings.

Enterprise-Hosted Multipoint Services

If the customer chooses to host the CTMS multipoint resources for intercompany meetings, they would presumably also create a staff of help desk personnel who are trained in the behind-the-scenes behavior of Cisco TelePresence Manager and how to coordinate the OBTP feature between companies. Instead of trying to navigate this process on her own, Rachael would call the help desk at her company to be consulted through the process. The help desk personnel can advise her on the availability of the TelePresence rooms at company A, how to obtain the availability of the users and TelePresence rooms at company B, and how to respond to the clarification emails that TelePresence Manager generated in the preceding scenario.

Service Provider-Hosted Multipoint Services

For customers who do not want to absorb the cost and complexity of maintaining and operating their own intercompany CTMS resources and help desk, outsourcing this entire process to an intercompany service provider is the most viable approach. Rachael would have coordinated with her colleagues to ascertain their availability but would have called the service provider's help desk for assistance in scheduling the TelePresence rooms at both companies and any CTMS resources required.

Multiple Service Provider Peering

So far, all the scenarios in this chapter have illustrated two companies connected to the same service provider. What if company A uses service provider X and company B uses service provider Y? The answer is service provider peering.

Just like the PSTN, Cisco envisions an Inter-Company TelePresence network where service providers around the globe participate in peering relationships, providing global reachability from any customer to any other customer, and the Cisco Inter-Company architecture provides for multiprovider peering. However, visions take time to come to fruition, and at the time this book was written, intercompany deployments were in their infancy, with several providers around the globe rolling out intercompany services to their customers and only beginning to contemplate the feasibility and preferred approach for peering with other providers.

Islands of Connectivity

To begin with, providers are likely to take their first steps in rolling out intercompany services within the boundaries of their own networks, deferring any peering relationships to a later date. Different providers will move at different speeds in different geographies. For example, provider X might be fully up and running in North America although just getting started in Europe, whereas provider Y is fully up and running in Europe and just getting started in North America. In addition, legislative and political boundaries might contribute to the complexities of delivering services within and between different providers and different countries. Therefore, there will be a period of time where islands of connectivity exist, and customers can call certain partners and customers but not others. Naturally, this can lead to frustration among those customers who cannot call the partner or customer they most want to do business with, which, in turn, can provide the necessary pressure on the providers to stimulate a resolution to this situation.

Single Tier, Direct Peering Model

Service providers have varying levels of relationships between each other; some partnering with each other, while others directly competing with each other. Therefore, providers are likely to move at different speeds when peering to various other providers. Provider X, for example, might welcome the opportunity to peer with Provider Y, while resisting the need to peer with Provider Z. Inevitably, its first step will be to peer with those it already has friendly relations with, and it is likely to peer directly with to each other, creating larger and larger islands of connectivity. For example, a provider in China might have good relations with two other providers in Singapore and Taiwan, and so they will peer to each other, creating a three-way relationship. This expands the island of connectivity for each of those three providers and the customers they service but still does not provide global connectivity to every other provider and customer.

Figure 14-27 illustrates such an arrangement, where customer A connects to provider X, and customer B connects to provider Y. SBCs are located within both providers' networks, providing connectivity down to the customers they serve and between one another.

A direct-dialed call from customer A to customer B would originate from the TelePresence room at customer A and be routed by customer A's Communications Manager to the CUBE at edge of its WAN, up to provider X's SBC attached to customer A's VPN, across provider X's network to its egress SBC, marking the demarcation point between provider X and provider Y, ingressing provider Y's network to its ingress SBC, traversing provider Y's network to the SBC that services customer B, down to customer B's CUBE, and routed by customer B's Communications Manager down to its TelePresence room.

Multitier, In-Direct Hierarchical Peering Model

Maintaining direct peering relationships between providers works quite well for a small number of interconnects but becomes costly and administratively burdensome as the number of peering relationships grows. It is a classic fully meshed problem, where each provider must maintain a peering relationship with every other provider, which at some point (beyond two or three relationships) becomes difficult to maintain (as the number of links to maintain would be $n(n-1)/2$, where n is the number of participating providers). As with any other fully meshed scenario, the answer is to establish a hierarchy to reduce the number of peering points each provider must maintain.

Hierarchies will naturally emerge out of this necessity, with some providers offering federated peering services to a number of other providers. Figure 14-28 illustrates this scenario

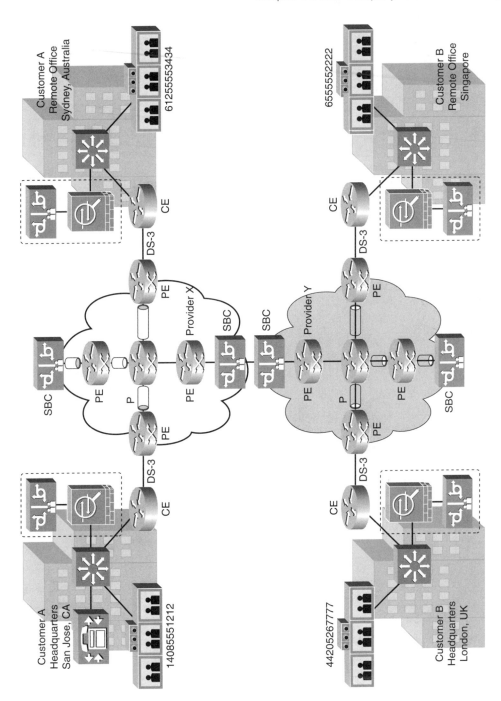

Figure 14-27 *Multiprovider peering: direct peering model*

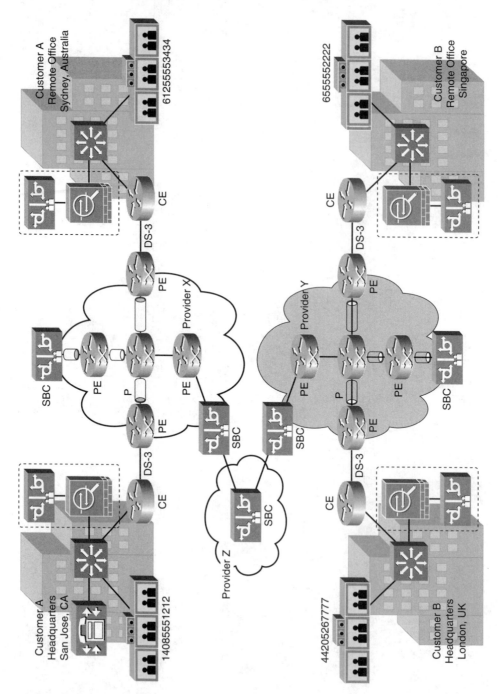

Figure 14-28 *Multiprovider peering: In-Direct hierarchical peering model*

where customer A connects to provider X, customer B connects to provider Y, and the providers are interconnected through a third provider Z.

It is too early to speculate on how and when these peering relationships will manifest in the market and which providers will peer with each other. However, the inevitable is obvious, Cisco TelePresence is radically changing the way businesses communicate and collaborate with each other, and intercompany connectivity is vital to the success of this new communications medium. It is only a matter of time before the global, high-speed, QoS enabled Inter-Company TelePresence network becomes a reality.

Summary

This chapter introduced the value of intercompany communications for TelePresence. Drawing on Metcalfe's Law, which states that the value of a telecommunications network is proportional to the square of the number of connected users, it was shown how radically TelePresence can transform business communications because it is more ubiquitously deployed. However, administrators deploying intercompany TelePresence face many challenges, including application requirements, security requirements, quality requirements, and scalability requirements. To meet these many challenges, the Cisco TelePresence Inter-Company solution was introduced.

Next, the Cisco TelePresence Inter-Company solution components were overviewed, including the Cisco Session Border Controller (SBC), the Cisco Adaptive Security Appliance (ASA), and the Cisco Unified Border Element (CUBE). The architecture of the Inter-Company solution was presented, with the signaling and media flows over the networks. The various elements necessary for end-to-end security were discussed in depth, including VPN and NAT traversal, encryption options, and signaling protocol inspection tools.

Next, Inter-Company deployment models were examined, including converged versus overlay models, centralized versus decentralized models, and Inter-Company dialing models. Multiple service provider peering was the final topic discussed because these initiatives are still in the early phases of solutions development.

Use this appendix as a reference. It contains tables that provide a consolidated list of the protocols that the Cisco TelePresence solution uses to operate. The six main categories of these protocols are:

- Protocols used by the TelePresence codecs

- Protocols used by the associated IP Phone 7975

- Protocols used by the Cisco TelePresence Manager when deployed with Microsoft Exchange

- Protocols used by the Cisco TelePresence Manager when deployed with IBM Domino

- Protocols used by the Cisco TelePresence Multi-point Switch

- Protocols used by Cisco IOS IP Service Level Agreement (IPSLA) devices

In each of the following tables, the columns include the protocol name; whether the specific protocol is UDP-based, TCP-based, or neither; the source IP address and port used for communication; the destination IP address and port used for communication; and a brief description of the protocol itself.

Protocols Used in Cisco TelePresence Solutions

Cisco TelePresence Codec Protocols

Table A-1 lists the protocols the codecs use to communicate with other devices within a Cisco TelePresence deployment. The codecs are the source of all video and audio media that is sent across the network in a TelePresence meeting. Note that this list of protocols is specific to the latest shipping version of the TelePresence codec software as of the time this appendix was written—software release 1.5(0). Previous software revisions might have slight differences in the protocols supported.

Table A-1 *Cisco TelePresence Codec (Release 1.5(0)) Protocols*

Protocol	TCP or UDP	Source Device: Port	Destination Device: Port	Description
CDP	—	CTS: —	Switch: —	Advertises its existence to the upstream Cisco Catalyst Ethernet Switch to which it attaches and to learn what VLAN it should tag its packets with. CDP is a Layer 2 protocol and, hence, does not use TCP or UDP for transport.
DHCP	UDP	0.0.0.0: 68 CTS: 68	Broadcast: 67	Requests an IP address from the DHCP server. It is recommended to use static IP addressing instead of DHCP on every CTS endpoint.
	UDP	0.0.0.0: 67 DHCP: 67	Broadcast: 68	Sent by the DHCP server in response to a request for an IP address.
ICMP	—	ANY: —	ANY: —	Sometimes determines whether a device is reachable (that is ICMP echo request/response), and ICMP unreachables can sometimes be sent by a device to indicate that a device or port is no longer reachable. ICMP time-exceeded might be sent by a device to indicate that the Time To Live (TTL) of a packet was exceeded.

continues

Table A-1 *Cisco TelePresence Codec (Release 1.5(0)) Protocols (continued)*

Protocol	TCP or UDP	Source Device: Port	Destination Device: Port	Description
NTP	UDP	CTS: 123	NTP: 123	Synchronizes the hardware clock on the CTS with an NTP server.
DNS	UDP	CTS: Ephemeral	DNS: 53	Resolves hostnames to IP addresses.
HTTP	TCP	CTS: Ephemeral	CUCM: 6970	Downloads configuration and firmware files from the CUCM TFTP service. The CTS uses HTTP instead of TFTP for accessing these files.
	TCP	CTS: Ephemeral CTS-MAN: Ephemeral	CTS-MAN: 8080 CTS: 8081	Uses XML/SOAP to coordinate meeting schedule and system operational status with CTS-MAN.
	TCP	ANY: Ephemeral	CTS: 80, 443	Accesses the administrative web interface of the CTS Codec. Port 80 is automatically redirected to port 443.
	TCP	CTS: Ephemeral	CTMS: 9501	Uses XML between each CTS and the CTMS for in-meeting controls such as Site/Segment Switching and Meeting Lock/Unlock.
SSH	TCP	ANY: Ephemeral	CTS: 22	Accesses the administrative CLI interface of the CTS Codec.
SNMP	UDP	ANY: Ephemeral	CTS: 161	Used to receive SNMP queries from a management station.
	UDP	CTS: Ephemeral	SNMP: 162	Sends SNMP traps to a management station.
CAPF	TCP	CTS: Ephemeral	CUCM: 3804	Registers its Manufacturing Installed Certificate (MIC) or obtains a Locally Significant Certificate (LSC) from the CUCM Certificate Authority Proxy Function (CAPF) service.
CTL	TCP	CTS: Ephemeral	CUCM: 2444	Downloads the Certificate Trust List (CTL) from the CUCM Certificate Trust List (CTL) Provider service.

Table A-1   *Cisco TelePresence Codec (Release 1.5(0)) Protocols*

Protocol	TCP or UDP	Source Device: Port	Destination Device: Port	Description
SIP	UDP	CTS: Ephemeral	CUCM: 5060	Used for registration and call signaling between the CTS and CUCM. Can be UDP port 5060, TCP port 5060, or TCP port 5061 if SIP over TLS is enabled. SIP over TLS is recommended.
	TCP		CUCM: 5060, 5061	
RTP	UDP	CTS: 16384 – 32768	ANY: ANY	Sends and receives audio and video media.

Cisco Unified IP Phone 7975 Protocols

Table A-2 lists the protocols used by the IP Phones associated with the codecs in a Cisco TelePresence deployment. The primary purpose of the IP Phone is to provide a GUI in which to begin, end, and control meetings from within the TelePresence room. Note that this list of protocols is specific to the latest shipping version of the IP Phone 7975 software as of the time this appendix was written—software release 8.4(3). Previous software revisions might have slight differences in the protocols supported.

Table A-2   *Cisco Unified IP Phone 797x (Release 8.4(3)) Protocols*

Protocol	TCP or UDP	Source Device: Port	Destination Device: Port	Description
CDP	—	Phone: —	Switch: —	Advertises its existence to the CTS Codec and to the upstream Cisco Catalyst Ethernet Switch to which it is attached to learn what VLAN it should tag its packets with and to negotiate Power over Ethernet. CDP is a Layer 2 protocol and, hence, does not use TCP or UDP.
DHCP	UDP	0.0.0.0: 68 Phone: 68	Broadcast: 67	Requests an IP address from the DHCP server.
	UDP	0.0.0.0: 67 DHCP: 67	Broadcast: 68	Sent by the DHCP server in response to a request for an IP address.

continues

Table A-2 *Cisco Unified IP Phone 797x (Release 8.4(3)) Protocols (continued)*

Protocol	TCP or UDP	Source Device: Port	Destination Device: Port	Description
ICMP	—	ANY: —	ANY: —	ICMP might sometimes to be used to determine whether a device is reachable (that is, ICMP echo request/response), and ICMP unreachables might sometimes be sent by a device to indicate that a device or port is no longer reachable. ICMP time-exceeded might be sent by a device to indicate that the Time To Live (TTL) of a packet was exceeded.
NTP	UDP	Phone: 123	NTP: 123	Synchronizes the hardware clock on the phone with an NTP server.
DNS	UDP	Phone: Ephemeral	DNS: 53	Resolves hostnames to IP addresses.
TFTP	UDP	Phone: Ephemeral	TFTP: 69	Downloads configuration and firmware files from the CUCM TFTP service.
	UDP	TFTP: Ephemeral	Phone: Ephemeral	The initial TFTP request to port 69 spawns unique sessions for each configuration and firmware file downloaded. These sessions are established using ephemeral source and destination ports.
HTTP	TCP	ANY: Ephemeral	Phone: 80	Accesses the administrative web interface of the phone (for troubleshooting purposes only).
SSH	TCP	ANY: Ephemeral	Phone: 22	Accesses the administrative CLI interface of the phone (for troubleshooting purposes only).
CAPF	TCP	Phone: Ephemeral	CUCM: 3804	Registers its Manufacturing Installed Certificate (MIC) or obtains a Locally Significant Certificate (LSC) from the CUCM Certificate Authority Proxy Function (CAPF) service.
CTL	TCP	Phone: Ephemeral	CUCM: 2444	Downloads the Certificate Trust List (CTL) from the CUCM CTL Provider service.

Table A-2 *Cisco Unified IP Phone 797x (Release 8.4(3)) Protocols*

Protocol	TCP or UDP	Source Device: Port	Destination Device: Port	Description
SIP	UDP	Phone: Ephemeral	CUCM: 5060	Used for registration and call signaling between the phone and CUCM. Can be UDP port 5060, TCP port 5060, or TCP port 5061 if SIP over TLS is enabled. SIP over TLS is recommended.
	TCP		CUCM: 5060, 5061	
RTP	UDP	Phone: 16384—32768	ANY: ANY	Sends and receives audio media.

Cisco TelePresence Manager for Microsoft Exchange Protocols

Table A-3 lists the protocols used by the Cisco TelePresence Manager (CTS-MAN) in a Cisco TelePresence deployment in which the email/calendaring server is Microsoft Exchange. The primary function of the CTS-MAN is to extract meeting scheduling information from the Microsoft Exchange servers and schedule the appropriate CTS endpoint and CTMS resources. Note that the list of protocols in Table A-3 is specific to the latest shipping version of the CTS-MAN software as of the time this appendix was written—software release 1.5(0). Previous software revisions might have slight differences in the protocols supported.

Table A-3 *Cisco TelePresence Manager (1.5 (0)) Protocols*

Protocol	TCP or UDP	Source Device:Port	Destination Device:Port	Description
CDP	—	—	—	Advertises its existence to the upstream Cisco Catalyst Ethernet Switch to which it is attached. CDP is a Layer 2 management protocol and, hence, does not use TCP or UDP.
DHCP	UDP	0.0.0.0: 68 CTS-MAN: 68	Broadcast: 67	Requests an IP address from the DHCP server. It is recommended to use static IP addressing instead of DHCP.
	UDP	0.0.0.0: 67 DHCP: 67	Broadcast: 68	Sent by the DHCP server in response to a request for an IP address.

continues

Table A-3 *Cisco TelePresence Manager (1.5 (0)) Protocols (continued)*

Protocol	TCP or UDP	Source Device:Port	Destination Device:Port	Description
ICMP	—	ANY: —	ANY: —	ICMP might sometimes to be used to determine whether a device is reachable (that is, ICMP echo request/response), and ICMP unreachables might sometimes be sent by a device to indicate that a device or port is no longer reachable. ICMP time-exceeded might be sent by a device to indicate that the Time To Live (TTL) of a packet was exceeded.
NTP	UDP	CTS-MAN: 123	NTP: 123	Synchronizes the hardware clock on the CTS-MAN with an NTP server.
DNS	UDP	CTS-MAN: Ephemeral	DNS: 53	Resolves hostnames to IP addresses.
HTTP	TCP	CTS: Ephemeral CTS-MAN: Ephemeral	CTS-MAN: 8080 CTS: 8081	Uses XML/SOAP to coordinate meeting schedule and system operational status between CTS-MAN and the CTS endpoints.
	TCP	CTMS: Ephemeral	CTS-MAN: 80	Uses XML/SOAP to coordinate meeting schedule and system operational status between CTS-MAN and the CTMS.
	TCP	CTS-MAN: Ephemeral	CUCM: 8443	Uses XML/SOAP to interrogate the CUCM database to discover the existence of CTS endpoints.
	TCP	ANY: Ephemeral	CTS-MAN: 80,443	Accesses the administrative web interface of CTS-MAN. Port 80 is automatically redirected to port 443.
SSH	TCP	ANY: Ephemeral	CTS-MAN: 22	Accesses the administrative CLI interface of CTS-MAN.
SNMP	UDP	ANY: Ephemeral	CTS-MAN: 161	Receives SNMP queries from a management station.
	UDP	CTS-MAN: Ephemeral	SNMP: 162	Sends SNMP traps to a management station.

Table A-3 *Cisco TelePresence Manager (1.5 (0)) Protocols*

Protocol	TCP or UDP	Source Device:Port	Destination Device:Port	Description
CAPF	TCP	CTS-MAN: Ephemeral	CUCM: 3804	Obtains a Locally Significant Certificate (LSC) from the CUCM Certificate Authority Proxy Function (CAPF) service.
CTL	TCP	CTS-MAN: Ephemeral	CUCM: 2444	Downloads the Certificate Trust List (CTL) from the CUCM CTL Provider service.
JTAPI	TCP	CTS-MAN: Ephemeral	CUCM: 2748	Uses JTAPI to register with CUCM CTI Manager service to receive device event status of CTS endpoints.
LDAP	TCP	CTS-MAN: Ephemeral	AD: 389,3268,636	Discovers the Microsoft Exchange mailbox name of each CTS endpoint and for authentication of users logging into CTS-MAN. Port 389 is used for single AD server deployments. If AD deployment uses a Global Catalogue Server; then port 3268 is used. If AD uses LDAP over Secure Sockets Layer (LDAP/SSL), port 636 is used. LDAP/SSL is recommended.
WebDAV	TCP	CTS-MAN: Ephemeral	Exchange: 80,443	Subscribes to the Microsoft Exchange mailbox of each CTS endpoint to process meeting requests. If Exchange is set up to support SSL, port 443 is used. Otherwise, port 80 is used. SSL is recommended.
	UDP	Exchange: Ephemeral	CTS-MAN: 3621	Notifies CTS-MAN of any events in the mailboxes it is subscribed to.

Cisco TelePresence Manager for IBM Domino Protocols

Table A-4 lists the protocols used by the Cisco TelePresence Manager (CTS-MAN) in a Cisco TelePresence deployment in which the email/calendaring server is IBM Domino. The primary difference between this table and Table A-3 is that the IBM Domino server uses the Internet Inter-ORB Protocol (IIOP) instead of the web-based Distributed Authoring and Versioning (WebDAV) protocol to communicate with CTS-MAN. This list of protocols is specific to the latest shipping version of the CTS-MAN software as of the time this appendix was written—software release 1.5(0). Previous software revisions might have slight differences in the protocols supported.

Table A-4 *Cisco TelePresence Manager (1.5 (0)) for IBM Domino Protocols*

Protocol	TCP or UDP	Source Device:Port	Destination Device:Port	Description
CDP	—	—	—	Advertises its existence to the upstream Cisco Catalyst Ethernet Switch to which it is attached. CDP is a Layer 2 management protocol and, hence, does not use TCP or UDP.
DHCP	UDP	0.0.0.0: 68 CTS-MAN: 68	Broadcast: 67	Requests an IP address from the DHCP server. It is recommended to use static IP addressing instead of DHCP.
	UDP	0.0.0.0: 67 DHCP: 67	Broadcast: 68	Sent by the DHCP server in response to a request for an IP address.
ICMP	—	ANY: N/A	ANY: —	Determines whether a device is reachable (that is, ICMP echo request/response), and ICMP unreachables might sometimes be sent by a device to indicate that a device or port is no longer reachable. ICMP time-exceeded might be sent by a device to indicate that the Time To Live (TTL) of a packet was exceeded.
NTP	UDP	CTS-MAN: 123	NTP: 123	Synchronizes the hardware clock on the CTS-MAN with an NTP server.
DNS	UDP	CTS-MAN: Ephemeral	DNS: 53	Resolves hostnames to IP addresses.

Table A-4   *Cisco TelePresence Manager (1.5 (0)) for IBM Domino Protocols*

Protocol	TCP or UDP	Source Device:Port	Destination Device:Port	Description
HTTP	TCP	CTS: Ephemeral CTS-MAN: Ephemeral	CTS-MAN: 8080 CTS: 8081	Uses XML/SOAP to coordinate meeting schedule and system operational status between CTS-MAN and the CTS endpoints.
	TCP	CTMS: Ephemeral	CTS-MAN: 80	Uses XML/SOAP to coordinate meeting schedule and system operational status between CTS-MAN and the CTMS.
	TCP	CTS-MAN: Ephemeral	CUCM: 8443	Uses XML/SOAP to interrogate the CUCM database to discover the existence of CTS endpoints.
	TCP	ANY: Ephemeral	CTS-MAN: 80,443	Accesses the administrative web interface of CTS-MAN. Port 80 is automatically redirected to port 443.
SSH	TCP	ANY: Ephemeral	CTS-MAN: 22	Accesses the administrative CLI interface of CTS-MAN.
SNMP	UDP	ANY: Ephemeral	CTS-MAN: 161	Receives SNMP queries from a management station.
	UDP	CTS-MAN: Ephemeral	SNMP: 162	Sends SNMP traps to a management station.
CAPF	TCP	CTS-MAN: Ephemeral	CUCM: 3804	Obtains a Locally Significant Certificate (LSC) from the CUCM Certificate Authority Proxy Function (CAPF) service.
CTL	TCP	CTS-MAN: Ephemeral	CUCM: 2444	Downloads the Certificate Trust List (CTL) from the CUCM CTL Provider service.
JTAPI	TCP	CTS-MAN: Ephemeral	CUCM: 2748	Uses JTAPI to register with CUCM CTI Manager service to receive device event status of CTS endpoints.

continues

Table A-4   *Cisco TelePresence Manager (1.5 (0)) for IBM Domino Protocols (continued)*

Protocol	TCP or UDP	Source Device:Port	Destination Device:Port	Description
LDAP	TCP	CTS-MAN: Ephemeral	Domino: 389,636	Discovers the Domino mailbox name of each CTS endpoint and for authentication of users logging into CTS-MAN. If Domino uses LDAP over Secure Sockets Layer (LDAP/SSL), port 636 is used. Otherwise, port 389 is used. SSL is recommended.
IIOP	TCP	CTS-MAN: Ephemeral	Domino: 80,443	Negotiate an IIOP session to the Domino mailbox of each CTS endpoint to process meeting requests. If Domino is set up to support SSL, port 443 is used. Otherwise, port 80 is used. SSL is recommended.
	UDP	CTS-MAN: Ephemeral	Domino: 63148	Queries and synchronizes the Domino mailboxes it is subscribed to.

Cisco TelePresence Multipoint Switch Protocols

Table A-5 lists the protocols used by the Cisco TelePresence Multipoint Switch (CTMS) in a Cisco TelePresence deployment. The primary purpose of the CTMS is to support TelePresence meetings consisting of three or more endpoints. Note that the list of protocols in Table A-5 is specific to the latest shipping version of the CTMS software as of the time this appendix was written—software release 1.5(0). Previous software revisions might have slight differences in the protocols supported.

Table A-5   *Cisco TelePresence Multipoint Switch (Release 1.5 (0)) Protocols*

Protocol	TCP or UDP	Source Device:Port	Destination Device:Port	Description
CDP	—	—	—	Advertises its existence to the upstream Cisco Catalyst Ethernet Switch to which it is attached. CDP is a Layer 2 management protocol and, hence, does not use TCP or UDP.

Table A-5 *Cisco TelePresence Multipoint Switch (Release 1.5 (0)) Protocols*

Protocol	TCP or UDP	Source Device:Port	Destination Device:Port	Description
DHCP	UDP	0.0.0.0: 68 CTMS: 68	Broadcast: 67	Requests an IP address from the DHCP server. It is recommended to use static IP addressing instead of DHCP.
	UDP	0.0.0.0: 67 DHCP: 67	Broadcast: 68	Sent by the DHCP server in response to a request for an IP address.
ICMP	—	ANY: N/A	ANY: —	Determines whether a device is reachable (that is, ICMP echo request/response), and ICMP unreachables might sometimes be sent by a device to indicate that a device or port is no longer reachable. ICMP time-exceeded might be sent by a device to indicate that the Time To Live (TTL) of a packet was exceeded.
NTP	UDP	CTMS: 123	NTP: 123	Synchronizes the hardware clock on the CTMS with an NTP server.
DNS	UDP	CTMS: Ephemeral	DNS: 53	Resolves hostnames to IP addresses.
HTTP	TCP	CTMS: Ephemeral	CTS-MAN: 80	Uses XML/SOAP to coordinate meeting schedule and system operational status with CTS-MAN.
	TCP	ANY: Ephemeral	CTMS: 80,443	Accesses the administrative web interface of CTMS. Port 80 is automatically redirected to port 443.
	TCP	CTS: Ephemeral	CTMS: 9501	Uses XML between each CTS and the CTMS for in-meeting controls such as Site/Segment Switching and Meeting Lock/Unlock.
SSH	TCP	ANY: Ephemeral	CTMS: 22	Accesses the administrative CLI interface of CTMS.
SNMP	UDP	ANY: Ephemeral	CTMS: 161	Receives SNMP queries from a management station.
	UDP	CTMS: Ephemeral	SNMP: 162	Sends SNMP traps to a management station.

continues

Table A-5   *Cisco TelePresence Multipoint Switch (Release 1.5 (0)) Protocols (continued)*

Protocol	TCP or UDP	Source Device:Port	Destination Device:Port	Description
SIP	UDP	CTMS: Ephemeral	CUCM: 5060	Used for call signaling with CUCM. Can be UDP port 5060 or TCP port 5060. Unlike the CTS endpoints that always initiate the SIP TCP socket to CUCM, for CTMS either side can initiate the connection.
		CUCM: Ephemeral	CTMS: 5060	
	TCP	CTMS: Ephemeral	CUCM: 5060	
		CUCM: Ephemeral	CTMS: 5060	
RTP	UDP	CTMS: 16384–32768	ANY: ANY	Sends and receives audio and video media.

Cisco IOS IP Service Level Agreement (IPSLA) Protocols

A Cisco IOS IP Service Level Agreement (IPSLA) is commonly used prior to the installation of Cisco TelePresence to measure and assess the network path. Table A-6 provides the ports most commonly used by IPSLA Agent and IPSLA Responder routers. Because IPSLA runs on Cisco IOS Software, there might be a myriad of other ports used for communications by those routers. Table A-6 lists only the specific ports relevant for the IPSLA UDP Jitter probe operation used to conduct Cisco TelePresence Network Path Assessment (NPA) testing. The term *Agent* refers to the router who generates the IPSLA test packets, and *Responder* refers to the router that replies to those requests. *Both* means that either the Agent or the Responder can generate such a packet.

Table A-6   *Cisco IPSLA Protocols*

Protocol	TCP or UDP	Source Device:Port	Destination Device:Port	Description
CDP	—	—	—	Advertises its existence to the upstream Cisco Catalyst Ethernet Switch to which it is attached. CDP is a Layer 2 management protocol and, hence, does not use TCP or UDP.

Table A-6 *Cisco IPSLA Protocols*

Protocol	TCP or UDP	Source Device:Port	Destination Device:Port	Description
ICMP	—	ANY: —	ANY: —	Determines whether a device is reachable (that is, ICMP echo request/response), and ICMP unreachables might sometimes be sent by a device to indicate that a device or port is no longer reachable. ICMP time-exceeded might be sent by a device to indicate that the Time To Live (TTL) of a packet was exceeded.
NTP	UDP	Both: 123	NTP: 123	Synchronizes the hardware clock on the Cisco IOS IPSLA router with an NTP server.
DNS	UDP	Both: Ephemeral	DNS: 53	Resolves hostnames to IP addresses.
SSH	TCP	ANY: Ephemeral	Both: 22	Accesses the administrative CLI interface of the Cisco IOS IPSLA router.
SNMP	UDP	ANY: Ephemeral	Both: 161	Receives SNMP queries from a management station.
	UDP	Both: Ephemeral	ANY: 162	Sends SNMP traps to a management station.
IPSLA	UDP	Agent: Ephemeral	Responder: 1967	Signal a new IPSLA operation between the Agent and the Responder.
RTP	UDP	Agent: Ephemeral	Responder: 16384 – 32768 (configurable)	Sends and receives audio and video media from the Agent to the Responder. The Responder then returns these packets back to the Agent. The specific destination UDP ports can be defined in the IPSLA Agent configuration.

Index

G - H

M

O

Q

R

U - V

W

X - Y - Z

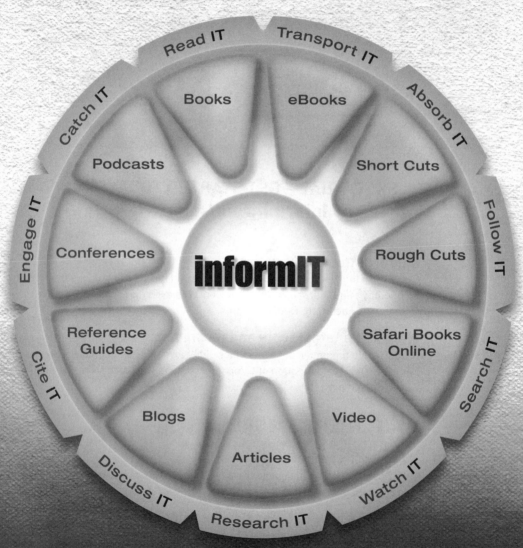

cisco

ciscopress.com: Your Cisco Certification and Networking Learning Resource

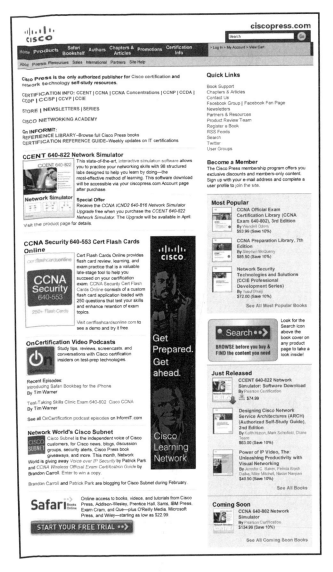

Subscribe to the monthly Cisco Press newsletter to be the first to learn about new releases and special promotions.

Visit **ciscopress.com/newsletters.**

While you are visiting, check out the offerings available at your finger tips.

– Free Podcasts from experts:
  - OnNetworking
  - OnCertification
  - OnSecurity

Podcasts

View them at **ciscopress.com/podcasts.**

– Read the latest author **articles** and **sample chapters** at ciscopress.com/articles.

– Bookmark the Certification Reference Guide available through our partner site at **informit.com/certguide.**

Connect with Cisco Press authors and editors via Facebook and Twitter, visit **informit.com/socialconnect.**

FREE Online Edition

Your purchase of **Cisco TelePresence Fundamentals** includes access to a free online edition for 45 days through the Safari Books Online subscription service. Nearly every Cisco Press book is available online through Safari Books Online, along with more than 5,000 other technical books and videos from publishers such as Addison-Wesley Professional, Exam Cram, IBM Press, O'Reilly, Prentice Hall, Que, and Sams.

SAFARI BOOKS ONLINE allows you to search for a specific answer, cut and paste code, download chapters, and stay current with emerging technologies.

Activate your FREE Online Edition at www.informit.com/safarifree

> **STEP 1:** Enter the coupon code: NSORIWH.

> **STEP 2:** New Safari users, complete the brief registration form.
> Safari subscribers, just log in.

If you have difficulty registering on Safari or accessing the online edition, please e-mail customer-service@safaribooksonline.com